Psychological Development in the Elementary Years

EDUCATIONAL PSYCHOLOGY

Allen J. Edwards, Series Editor
Department of Psychology
Southwest Missouri State University
Springfield, Missouri

Published

Judith Worell (ed.). Psychological Development in the Elementary Years

Wayne Otto and Sandra White (eds.). Reading Expository Material

John B. Biggs and Kevin F. Collis. Evaluating the Quality of Learning: The Solo Taxonomy (Structure of the Observed Learning Outcome)

Gilbert R. Austin and Herbert Garber (eds.). The Rise and Fall of National Test Scores

Lynne Feagans and Dale C. Farran (eds.). The Language of Children Reared in Poverty: Implications for Evaluation and Intervention

Patricia A. Schmuck, W. W. Charters, Jr., and Richard O. Carlson (eds.). Educational Policy and Management: Sex Differentials

Phillip S. Strain and Mary Margaret Kerr. Mainstreaming of Children in Schools: Research and Programmatic Issues

Maureen L-Pope and Terence R. Keen. Personal Construct Psychology and Education

Ronald W. Henderson (ed.). Parent–Child Interaction: Theory, Research, and Prospects

W. Ray Rhine (ed.). Making Schools More Effective: New Directions from Follow Through

Herbert J. Klausmeier and Thomas S. Sipple. Learning and Teaching Concepts: A Strategy for Testing Applications of Theory

James H. McMillan (ed.). The Social Psychology of School Learning

M. C. Wittrock (ed.). The Brain and Psychology

Marvin J. Fine (ed.). Handbook on Parent Education

Dale G. Range, James R. Layton, and Darrell L. Roubinek (eds.). Aspects of Early Childhood Education: Theory to Research to Practice

The list of titles in this series continues on the last page of this volume.

Psychological Development in the Elementary Years

EDITED BY

JUDITH WORELL

Department of Educational and Counseling Psychology
University of Kentucky
Lexington, Kentucky

ACADEMIC PRESS   **1982**
A Subsidiary of Harcourt Brace Jovanovich, Publishers
New York   London
Paris San Diego San Francisco São Paulo Sydney Tokyo Toronto

ACADEMIC PRESS, INC.
111 Fifth Avenue, New York, New York 10003

United Kingdom Edition published by
ACADEMIC PRESS, INC. (LONDON) LTD.
24/28 Oval Road, London NW1 7DX

Library of Congress Cataloging in Publication Data
Main entry under title:

Psychological development in the elementary years.

    (Educational psychology)
    Includes bibliographical references and index.
    1. Child development. 2. Learning, Psychology of.
I. Worell, Judith, Date. II. Series. [DNLM:
1. Child development. WS 105 P9735]
LB1131.P78   155.4'24   81-17655
ISBN 0-12-764050-9   AACR2

PRINTED IN THE UNITED STATES OF AMERICA

82 83 84 85   9 8 7 6 5 4 3 2 1

Contents

List of contributors

Numbers in parentheses indicate the pages on which the authors' contributions begin.

RICHARD BOYD (411), Department of Studies in Behavioral Disabilities, University of Wisconsin–Madison, Madison, Wisconsin 53706

GENE H. BRODY (321), Department of Child and Family Development, College of Home Economics, University of Georgia, Athens, Georgia 30602

WILLIAM I. GARDNER (411), Department of Studies in Behavioral Disabilities, University of Wisconsin–Madison, Madison, Wisconsin 53706

JOAN E. GRUSEC (151), Department of Psychology, University of Toronto, Toronto, Ontario, Canada M5S 1A1

RONALD W. HENDERSON (359), Committee on Education, University of California, Santa Cruz, Santa Cruz, California 95064

BETTY J. HOUSE (187), Department of Psychology, University of Connecticut, Storrs, Connecticut 06268

DEBORAH G. KEMLER (233), Department of Psychology, Swarthmore College, Swarthmore, Pennsylvania 19081

ROSEMARY MILLS (151), Department of Psychology, University of Toronto, Toronto, Ontario, Canada M5S 1A1

WENDY CONKLIN ROEDELL[1] (97), Child Development Research Group, University of Washington, Seattle, Washington 91895

RONALD G. SLABY (97), Laboratory of Human Development, Harvard University, Cambridge, Massachusetts 02138

DANIEL SOLOMON (269), The Child Development Project, PMI, Inc., San Ramon, California 94583

ZOLINDA STONEMAN (321), Department of Child and Family Development, College of Home Economics, University of Georgia, Athens, Georgia 30322

BONNIE TYLER (53), Institute for Child Study, University of Maryland, College Park, Maryland 20742

JUDITH WORELL (3), Department of Educational and Counseling Psychology, University of Kentucky, Lexington, Kentucky 40506

[1]*Present address:* Educational Service District No. 121, Seattle, Washington 98148.

Preface

... a theory of development must be linked to a theory of knowledge and to a theory of instruction—Bruner (1966, p. 21)

This book is the second in a series of reviews relating current theory and research on psychological development to educational practice. The first volume (Hom & Robinson, 1977) concentrated on development in the preschool years and applications to early education. The present volume focuses on the period from school entrance until early adolescence, ranging approximately from age 5 through 12. The research reviews that comprise this book are intended for advanced undergraduate or graduate students, so that prior background in educational psychology and developmental theory is assumed. The range and level of topics covered in this volume will be of most interest to graduate students in psychology, educational psychology, human development, instruction, or curriculum design. Colleges of education that offer advanced courses on development for continuing education or for potential college instructors will also find these reviews of interest.

In considering the age range selected, it is recognized that development and learning do not respect artificial age barriers and are, in many respects, continuous processes. However, the significance of developmental trends in middle childhood is tied directly to expectations for children to adjust to the school environment and to cope with relatively novel, complex, and multistimulus social and cognitive demands. A companion requirement for the socializing agents represented by the schools is to channel these diverse and individual human beings into some moderately convergent patterns of learning and behavior. The linkage between the psychological characteristics of the developing child and the educational demands of the instructional community lies in determining their points of interface and accommodating their differences. It is the theme of this book that psychological development and instructional practices are intimately related in a reciprocal fashion, with each set of processes providing an important influence for the other. Theories of development, learning, and instruction can best be understood and translated into practice when their areas of overlap and divergence are brought clearly into focus. It is no accident, therefore, that the reader will find a planned emphasis in each chapter on some form of learning theory. Although each author was free to select the theoretical orientations that best suited his or her style, it will be clear to the discerning reader that the authors converge in their focus on teachable behaviors, attitudes, and skills. In those chapters in which age progressions are discussed, age is used not as an independent variable but as a marker for describing observable developmental change.

The selection of chapter topics was guided by two considerations: first, that the developmental processes under consideration were relevant and specific to the early school years; and second, that the behaviors under consideration were open to educational change. Each of the selected chapters covers an aspect of children's development that I consider to be amenable to modification by socializing agents. Each chapter, therefore, is explicit in suggesting how the research on developmental trends can be translated into strategies for behavioral change. In keeping with a broad social learning focus, each chapter contains at least three emphases: a consideration of developmental trends as revealed in recent research; a discussion of relevant determining variables; and a discussion of implications for educational intervention. Finally, the chapters attempt to restrict their reviews to research published in the past decade, with the intent of emphasizing the "new look" in each topical area. It can be expected, therefore, that the book may become obsolete within the next decade as newer theories and empirical findings take precedence and lead us into new insights.

I would like to extend my appreciation to those individuals who contributed their efforts and expertise to the development and publication of this book. First, I wish to express my gratitude to the nine authors whose excellent reviews form the basis of the volume. Each author provided an individual format and conceptualization, and followed through with uncomplaining revisions following some occasional heavy-handed editing. Next a special thanks is due Suzanne Henry Martorano, with whom I spent many enjoyable hours discussing the field of developmental psychology and the pros and cons of including a variety of topics and authors in the volume. For helpful assistance and suggestions on the sex-role chapter, my thanks are due to Nikki Garret-Fulks and Kathy Miller.

PART ONE / Social interaction processes

1 / Psychological sex roles: significance and change

JUDITH WORELL

In most societies, gender assignment at birth is a primary determinant of an individual's participation in many aspects of the organized culture. The label of female or male provides a framework for stereotyped sociocultural expectancies about how peers and adults should react to the child and the roles that each child will enact in his or her personal environment. Although social norms for male and female roles in the United States have been changing at a fast pace during the 1970s, current research on both children's and adults' attitudes suggests that stereotyped conceptions of appropriate sex-role behaviors have not disappeared. The evidence suggests that gender-related distinctions exist in many situations that involve academic, interpersonal, occupational, and family considerations. To the extent that girls and boys evoke differential expectations from peers and adults and are responded to in gender-distinctive ways, we can see the persistence of sociocultural sex roles in practice.

The cultural expectations for gender differences in behavior are reflected in the play interests and sex-role conceptions of even very young children (Blakemore, LaRue, & Olejnik, 1979; Kuhn, Nash, & Brucken, 1978; Myers, Weinraub, & Shetler, 1979). By the time girls and boys arrive at kindergarten and first grade, they have adopted for themselves a well-structured conception of how each gender ought and ought not to

3

behave (Edelbrock & Sugawara, 1978; Garrett, Ein, & Tremaine, 1977; Katz, 1979a; Tryon, 1980; Urberg, 1979; Williams, Bennett, & Best, 1975). In free-choice situations, they tend to divide themselves into female or male majority groups, and they fill their leisure time with activities that are discriminately gender-differentiated (Damon, 1977; Fagot, 1974; Waldrop & Halverson, 1975). During the elementary school years, it appears that the children themselves live out the sex-role prescriptions of the larger society.

In contrast to the cleavage in companionship and activities, however, there is general consensus among researchers and reviewers that prior to adolescence, girls and boys are considerably more alike than they are different on most cognitive, affective, and behavioral dimensions (Gullahorn, 1979; Maccoby, 1980; Maccoby & Jacklin, 1974; Sherman, 1978; Waber, 1979; Weitz, 1977; Williams, 1977; Wittig & Peterson, 1979). Accumulated research on "sex differences" reveals few, if any, categorical distinctions aside from obvious anatomical structures such as external genitalia. The behavioral differences that do appear between groups of prepubertal girls and boys are mainly ones of degree: frequency, intensity, and timing. The marked overlap and apparent "teachability" of most of the behaviors and capabilities of boys and girls have directed attention to the development of psychological sex roles. Rather than focus on sex differences, this chapter will concentrate on the learned attitudes, cognitions, and behaviors that reflect self and other's expectations about what is appropriate and desirable for males and females in American society.

Theory and research on sex-role development in the middle elementary years have had three major concerns:

1. What are the commonly held personal and cultural expectations for present and future sex-role behavior of boys and girls in American culture and how do these expectations change over time?
2. How can we account for gender-related trends in cognitive, affective, and behavioral domains?
3. What are the possibilities (and desirability) of externally induced changes in children's sex-role orientations?

The first question relies primarily on data obtained through natural and structured observations and introduces issues of construct definitions, construct validity, and methods of measurement. The second question relates to theoretical issues and explores alternative socialization paradigms. Finally, the third question, although data based, raises issues of personal values as well as ethical and ideological concerns.

This chapter will examine these three questions in the context of recent literature. Emphasis will be placed on studies published within the past 10 years, to avoid overlap with other excellent reviews (Maccoby & Jacklin, 1974; Mischel, 1970). The introductory sections will discuss recent conceptions of sex-role behavior and some issues in its measurement. The middle sections will cover developmental patterns in sex-role behavior prior to school entrance and in the middle elementary years. A third section will review educational influences on sex-role functioning: schools, teachers, and the media. The final section will consider recent attempts to modify traditional sex-typed behavior within educational settings and will discuss the value implications of these efforts. A guiding theme throughout the chapter will be the significance of these sex-role orientations for individual satisfaction and productivity, not only during middle childhood but throughout the life span.

CONCEPTIONS OF SEX ROLES

Within a rapidly changing field of sex-role research, there is considerable variation in terminology and methods of measurement. Conceptions of sex roles differ across investigators and theories, and measurement strategies are frequently dissimilar across experimental paradigms. The following section will cover major concepts of *gender, sex roles, sex-typing,* and *androgyny* and will discuss their use in current research. It should be noted that not all researchers use these constructs in the same manner.

Gender

Gender is used here to denote categorical assignment of persons into two groups, one judged to be male and the other female. Although initial gender assignment for each child is made on the basis of external genitalia, several other criteria may be brought into the decision, including hormonal and chromosomal indicators of gender (Luria & Rose, 1979; Money & Ehrhardt, 1972). It is interesting that preschool children, many of whom are unaware of genital criteria, are quite expert at making a gender decision about others, using mainly clothing and hair styles to determine the categorization (Levin, Balistrieri, & Schukit, 1972; Thompson, 1975; Thompson & Bentler, 1971). When discriminative cues are unavailable or ambiguous, both children and adults become uncomfortable and seek gender clarification (Marcus & Overton, 1978; Seavy, Katz, & Zalk, 1975).

Psychological research has used gender in two major ways: first, as an independent variable for predicting categorical differences between groups of females and males on some criteria (Maccoby, 1966; Maccoby & Jacklin, 1974); and second, as a stimulus variable that provides information for individuals to regulate and monitor their future behavior. When gender is used as an independent variable, the outcomes are frequently regarded as the result of the sexual dimorphism and as the separate and legitimate properties of each gender group. The stimulus function of gender may influence reactions to oneself as well as to others, and is reflected in differential gender-related expectancies, attributions, and stereotyped responses in many situations (Bem, 1979; Condry & Condry, 1976; Deaux, 1976; Johnson, 1978; Unger, 1979; Worell, 1981). Although each of these approaches may have utility for certain purposes, it is difficult to design situations in which gender categorization is independent of its sociocultural meanings. Within developmental and educational contexts, it appears more useful to examine the interaction between gender and its psychological stimulus value.

Several major theories have emphasized gender as a major determinant or organizer in the development of sex-typing in children. Since there are a number of detailed reviews of psychological theory related to the development of sex-typed behaviors, these theories will be outlined only briefly here (Emmerich, 1973; Frieze, Parsons, Johnson, Ruble, & Zellman, 1978; Maccoby & Jacklin, 1974; Mussen, 1969; Weitz, 1977; Worell, 1981). Psychoanalytic theory assumes that identification with the same-gender parent, combined with resolution of oedipal attraction to the cross-gender parent, are prerequisites for normal sex-typing (Freud, 1965). Within this context, the availability and nurturance of the like-gender parent becomes a critical determinant of "normal" psychosexual development. Early social learning theorists, borrowing from identification theory, also assigned a primary role to the nurturance of the same-gender parent, but interpreted the process in learning theory terminology that emphasized stimulus and reinforcement control (Sears, Rau, & Alpert, 1965). The development of dependency needs was thought to motivate matched-response imitation of the same-gender parent and to result in gender-"appropriate" sex-typing by the age of 5 or 6 years.

In contrast to an emphasis on parental gender, cognitive-developmental theory proposed that the child's self-categorization as a boy or girl (*gender identity*) is the basic organizer of sex-typed development. The positive value attached to gender categorization motivates the child to acquire and retain gender-relevant information. The child then uses this information to construct schemata of the self and others and actively chooses to match his or her behavior with others most like the self (Kohlberg, 1966; Lewis & Weinraub, 1979). Acordingly, socialization practices by parents may play a very minor role. In cognitive–developmental theory, age-related sequential progression of gender-related concepts (*gender constancy*) is but one representation of the underlying cognitive structures that culminate in concrete operational thought (Kohlberg, 1966).

More recently, cognitive social learning theorists have emphasized the stimulus function of gender and mediation by gender labels in providing information about the appropriateness of an activity for either self or others and the probable personal and social consequences of engaging in such behavior (Bussey & Perry, 1976; Mischel, 1970; Perry & Bussey, 1979). Cognitive social learning views have focused on the relevant antecedents and consequences of modeled behavior for the imitation of sex-typed patterns, with gender of parental models as only one of many gender-related antecedents. The theoretical distinction between learning and performance suggests that children may gain information from observing both female and male models but selectively display same-sex behaviors in externally monitored contexts. Flexibility of sex-typing becomes possible through variations in models, reinforcers, and novel situations, as well as through the child's gradual formulation of personal sex-role standards that become increasingly self-monitored (Bandura, 1977; Mischel, 1966, 1970).

Many of the studies reviewed here were designed to examine hypotheses related to one of these theoretical approaches. The influence of the child's assigned gender on self-directed and observational learning continues to intrigue developmentalists and has direct relevance for educational applications. As gender-related expectancies and dispositions are activated into observable interpersonal behaviors, they tend to create differing social and physical environments for males and females. The reciprocal interactions between the child's self-selected behavior patterns and the socialization practices of the developmental environment provide fertile ground for the transmission and persistence of psychological sex roles.

Sex roles

Sex roles refers to sociocultural expectations for behaviors and activities that are considered to be appropriate and desirable for either males or females (Bem, 1974; Katz, 1979a; Laws, 1979; Worell, 1978). Although each society and subculture may provide particular requirements for appropriate sex-role behavior, there is considerable agreement across cultures on many of these gender-related expectations. In a majority of societies, males are expected to show more behaviors characterized as aggressive, autonomous, and dominant; females are expected to demonstrate more nurturance, compliance, and passivity. Furthermore, activities and tasks tend to be divided, so that females are more frequently assigned to home and child care, whereas males are expected to take on more active positions within the larger community (Barry, Bacon, & Child, 1957; Block, 1973; D'Andrade, 1966; Whiting & Edwards, 1973). *Sex-role stereotypes* refers to categorical judgments about the characteristics and activities of an individual on the basis of membership in a gender group (Unger, 1979).

Unlike gender, however, which is firmly rooted in human biology, sex-role behaviors are less clearly predetermined and thus contain the potential for individual variability and change. Although questions concerning the biological underpinnings of some gender-related behaviors remain unanswered, particularly in reference to aggression and spatial abilities, these issues will not be addressed here. Rather, this chapter will concentrate on those aspects of sex-role functioning that appear to have particular relevance for developmental and educational decisions.

Current conceptions of sex roles in American research are diverse and complex, encompassing a broad range of cognitive, affective, and behavioral functioning. Previous approaches to categorizing the various components of sex roles have resulted in a number of similar, tripartite taxonomies. One of the more widely used of these is Lynn's (1969) division of sex roles into preference, adoption, and identity. The preference measures tap what the child likes or would like to do or to become; the adoption measures assess observable behaviors; and the identity measures represent internalized orientations that are presumably unavailable to individual awareness and must be elicited indirectly.

In examining the recent research literature, however, it becomes evident that little agreement exists on how each of these three components is to be operationalized. Furthermore, there are few published studies on how the three components relate to each other. One recent study on the widely used IT Scale for Children (ITSC) (Brown, 1957; Sher & Lansky, 1968), which is a projective toy-activity preference measure, found no significant correlations between preschool children's scores on the ITSC and either free-play observations of activity–toy preferences or choice of same-gender playmates (Smith, Goldman, & Keller, 1979). These authors caution against the use of any specific preference measure as a global assessment of sex roles and suggest a set of multiple measures even for individual preference ratings. They also suggest, in agreement with Fling and Manosevitz (1972), that preference measures may be influenced by situational factors and what the child believes to be the correct responses in that situation. Thus, expressed sex-typed preference may frequently assess knowledge of cultural stereotypes and situational expectations rather than personal desirability. Support for this hypothesis is found in several studies that obtained differences in verbal sex-role preference scores depending on the gender of the examiner (Edelbrock & Sugawara, 1978; Williams *et al.*, 1975).

Given the current difficulties in developing a taxonomy of sex-role functioning that represents "true" underlying factors, the following division of sex roles into cognitive, evaluative, and behavioral categories makes no pretense at representing homogeneous clusters of behavior. The diversity of content within each category reflects the breadth of measurable items, both sociocultural and psychological, that have been included in varying conceptions of sex-role functioning. The broad range of possible behavioral involvements by any one individual in various aspects of sex-role functioning precludes a simple dichotomous classification into masculine or feminine typologies. The diversity of content subsumed under sex-role development also poses a challenge to any single cohesive theory to encompass the range of available data. Although sex-role content items may vary according to the age or developmental level of the individual (Katz, 1979b), developmental considerations become too complex to integrate into these categories.

Cognitive components. Research on early sex-role development has documented the impressive acquisition by young children of gender-related information: labels for self and others; classification of objects, tasks, and behaviors that are gender-dichotomized both within the child's real world and in the larger culture (stereotypes); and many rules for behavior that include what males and females should and should not do in particular situations and at varying age levels. By the time of entry into first grade, children are already developing gender-related life plans and goals (e.g., I want to be an engineer), expectations about achievement and employment opportunities (e.g., Girls are nurses and teachers), causal attributions for their successes and failures (e.g., I failed because I didn't try hard), as well as standards for evaluating their own and others' gender-typed behavior (e.g., Boys should be braver than girls).

It is assumed here that certain cognitive skills are involved in the acquisition and utilization of gender-related information, including those related to modeling and information processing such as attention, coding, retention, and retrieval (Bandura, 1977; Bem, 1979). Therefore, some aspects of cognitive acquisition and utilization should be modified as children gain increasing intellectual competence and educational exposure. At any age, these cognitive components may function as relevant antecedents or mediators of overt behavior, but they do not necessarily determine its form (e.g., Children may "know" the rules but choose to behave differently). It seems clear, however, that cognitive variables do not form a unitary factor in sex-role development. Cognitive components may operate independently or in relationship to other variables, depending on the context, the developmental level of the child, and individual experience.

Evaluative components. Here we include the affective and evaluative responses of children to gender-related information, as well as to their own and others' behavior when it does or does not match this information. Research in this category includes self-reported gender-related preferences, attitudes, interests, values, and ideals. Since these evaluative reactions are given to a variety of content items, differing assessments may fail to correlate. Less frequently assessed, but probably of equal importance, are the personal expectancies for self- and other-reinforcement for meeting or falling short of sex-role standards. Children's responses of pride, shame, or anxiety regarding their adherence to sex-role norms or ideals provide important sources of motivation for conformity to group expectations. Some of these evaluative components may act as antecedents to control the performance of subsequent sex-typed behavior, or they may function as self-reinforcing consequences. As indicated earlier, the behavioral indicators of evaluative and cognitive components may be difficult to distinguish, especially in situational contexts in which children are making decisions between what they believe and what they prefer and stating their choices.

Behavioral components. Aside from what children tell us they know, believe, and prefer, what do they actually do in their natural environments? Here researchers have observed sex-role indicators in children's play and leisure activities, interpersonal interactions, clothing choices, language patterns, achievement behavior, task selection at home and school, and peer choices. It seems apparent from the diversity of these behaviors that a single descriptor for *sex-role adoption* would be difficult to determine. Any of these behaviors may be elicited by some cognitive or evaluative components of sex roles and, in turn, may function to modify other cognitions and evaluations.

Summary. What can we conclude from a cataloging procedure of sex-role activities? For present purposes, it conforms to the proposition that sex role conceptions are complex and multivariate, reflecting many aspects of human interpersonal functioning. In any situation, observable sex-typed behavior is likely to be a function of what children know and believe to be true about their world and how they anticipate they will perform (cognitive), how they expect these performances to be evaluated by self and others, and what the functional outcomes will be in that context (evaluative). Thus, it seems important to distinguish between acquisition and performance of these gender-related behaviors, and to discriminate between what children are able to do and what they are willing to do (Kelly & Worell, 1977; Mischel, 1970). The following sections will consider how a multivariate conception of sex roles coordinates with more recent views of sex-typing and androgyny.

Sex-typing

Prior to 1970, developmental psychologists generally assumed that the coordination of sex roles with gender was an indication of satisfactory psychosexual development. Girls and boys were judged to be appropriately sex-typed as feminine or masculine if their interests and play activities matched the culturally dichotomous stereotypes: dolls and dishes for girls, for example, and trucks and trains for boys (Brown, 1957; Kagan, 1964; Mussen, 1969; Rabban, 1950). Behavioral choices that diverged from traditional sex-role prescriptions were considered deviant and changeworthy; boys who preferred flowers to fielding balls were "effeminate," and girls who chose baseball over babies were "tomboys" (cf. Rosenberg, Sutten-Smith, & Morgan, 1961). If these cross-sex-typed activities persisted well into the elementary years, there was concern about the child and frequently efforts were initiated to suppress overt manifestations of cross-sex-typed behavior.

With increased interest in the women's movement and concern about equality between males and females, bipolar conceptions of sex-typing were brought into question. Constantinople's incisive review (1973) of current measures of adult sex-typing pointed to the logical and assessment problems inherent in dividing psychological masculinity and femininity into two mutually exclusive domains. In particular, it appeared that two critical assumptions about masculinity and femininity remained unvalidated: that these are bipolar, mutually exclusive sets of traits, and that they are unitary rather than multidimensional. More recently, both theory and scale development relevant to sex-typed functioning have questioned these two assumptions and have proposed some alternative views.

In the following sections, two of these contrasting views will be considered further: (*a*) that masculine and feminine sex-typed traits are separate, orthogonal dimensions that can be assessed independently; and (*b*) that sex-role orientations are more complex than is suggested by a simple, dichotomous division into masculine and feminine traits. A third position that interfaces with each of these revised conceptions of sex-role functioning concerns the evaluation of developmental deviance. Rather than viewing cross-gender behaviors as necessarily undesirable, recent formulations propose that more equalized combinations of masculine and feminine sex-role attributes within the same individual may have positive adjustment value (Bem, 1974, 1975, 1976; Block, 1973; Kaplan, 1976; Katz, 1979b; Spence, Helmreich, & Stapp, 1975).

Psychological androgyny

Several recent measures of adult and child sex-role orientations are constructed around the premise that psychological masculinity and femininity are independent, orthogonal dimensions (Bem, 1974; Hall & Halberstadt, 1980; Katz, 1979a; Simms, Davis, Foushee, Holahan, Spence, & Helmreich, 1978; Spence *et al.*, 1975). It follows that masculine and feminine traits, attitudes, and interests can coexist within healthy individuals. Persons are considered to be sex-typed to the extent that they select or self-endorse relatively more of one set of stereotyped characteristics than the other. Within this framework, *androgyny* is defined as a relatively equal preference for both masculine and feminine characteristics. Construct validations studies with several new sextyping scales show positive but low intercorrelations between masculinity and femininity, suggesting their conceptual independence (Bem, 1974; Berzins, Welling, & Wetter, 1978; Simms *et al.*, 1978; Spence & Helmreich, 1978). Furthermore, these studies report that a substantial proportion (about 30%) of individuals place themselves within the androgynous range, depending on variations in measurement, scoring, and sampling. These data lend support to both an orthogonal model of certain sex-typed interpersonal traits and a new sex-role population to be further explored.

Conceptions of sex-role orientations that are gender-free, such as androgyny, have been integrated into several recent theories as the ideal end state of life-span sex-role development (Block, 1973; Katz, 1979a; Rebecca, Hefner, & Oleshanksy, 1976; Ullian, 1976). From a life-span perspective, childhood sex-typing is seen as a transitional stage in a continuous progression of sex-role adjustments. Androgyny represents the most mature of these levels by successfully integrating both masculine and feminine role behaviors. Empirical evidence for these formulations is sparse, but several studies do suggest that individuals tend to modify certain sex-role orientations according to their present life situations (Abrahams, Feldman, & Nash, 1978; Eiseman, 1978). As a result of the androgyny research with adults, investigators have begun to examine the incidence and correlates of non-sex-typed functioning in children (Eisenberg-Berg, Boothby, & Matson, 1979; Katz, 1979b; Lott, 1978). The relationship between androgyny and children's adjustment will be discussed in a later section. Foremost among the barriers in applying androgyny conceptions to the study of children's behavior has been the absence of appropriate measurement instruments. Recent attempts to explore alternatives to traditional measurement of children's sex-role functioning have produced a number of innovative approaches and have raised some unresolved issues.

ISSUES IN THE MEASUREMENT OF SEX ROLES

Measurement of sex-typing in children

Traditional measures of children's sex-typing have accepted a bipolar distribution of responses and have generally neglected to provide opportunities for nonstereotyped responding (e.g., Brown, 1957; La Voie & Andrews, 1976; Thompson, 1975; Williams *et al.*, 1975). Thus, children are required to select toys and activities that are either strongly dichotomous (e.g., trucks versus dolls), or are gender-restricted (e.g., Who is the boss, mommy *or* daddy?) The supporting rationale for these approaches was frequently based on theories that propose a normalcy–deviancy model of sex-role development (e.g., Freud, 1965; Kohlberg, 1966, 1969), which assumes that one set of choices is developmentally healthier and more appropriate than the other. One outcome of these dichotomized measurement procedures has been an exaggeration of stereotyped population characteristics and an underemphasis on areas of overlap and concordance in the behavior of boys and girls.

In addition to these artificial restrictions on response outcomes, traditional measurement procedures have frequently failed to separate gender from sex-role criteria in selecting test items (Worell, 1978, 1981). Gender discrimination of items requires demonstration that response differences are obtained between categories of boys and girls (e.g., More boys play with trucks than girls) (Connor & Serbin, 1977). Sex-role differentiation of items entails social judgments by persons of both genders that particular activities or attributes are more appropriate or typical for either girls or boys (Girls and boys may be rated on competitiveness, for example) (Bem, 1974). In either procedure, it is important that measurement outcomes can be dimensional; both boys and girls can be ordered from most to least on some characteristic. In this way, we can examine the independent contributions of gender and sex roles and their separate interactions with other response variables.

Innovations in measurement

In response to the androgyny literature, researchers are exploring new measurement strategies. In particular, they have begun to include opportunities for children to indicate neutral or egalitarian choices, have developed multiple measures of sex-typed functioning, and have examined situational influences on sex-typed responses. Some of the more encouraging examples of measurement include the following:

1. Children are given the opportunity to select both males *and* females as appropriate for an activity (Brush, Gold, & Sprotzer, 1979; Edelbrock & Sugawara, 1978; Falkenberg, Rahm, & Waern, 1977; Flerx, Fidler, & Rogers, 1976; Garrett *et al.*, 1977; Katz, 1979a; Urberg, 1979).
2. Children may select both masculine and feminine traits as descriptive of themselves (Hall & Halberstadt, 1980; Katz, 1979b; Simms *et al.*, 1978).
3. Neutral concepts or play activities as well as sex-typed ones are included and the percentage of positive response to each are compared (Dickstein & Seymour, 1979; Masters & Wilkinson, 1976; Simms *et al.*, 1978; Smith *et al.*, 1979).
4. Responses to both positive and negative sex-typed traits are obtained (Edelbrock & Sugawara, 1978; Williams *et al.*, 1975).
5. Sex-typed responses are compared on a variety of response modalities, tasks, and settings and with respect to self, peers, parents, and adults (Flerx *et al.*, 1976; Katz, 1979a; Simms *et al.*, 1978; Smith *et al.*, 1979; Urberg, 1979).
6. The biasing effects of examiner gender are considered (Edelbrock & Sugawara, 1978; Williams *et al.*, 1975), as well as interactions with same-gender peers (Eisenberg-Berg *et al.*, 1979) on sex-typed responses.

The outcomes of recent attention to measurement parameters may modify some current conceptions of children's sex-role behavior. For example, variations in examiner gender changed the sex-typing results in several studies. Edelbrock and Sugawara (1978) found significantly increased sex-typing of toy choices in the presence of a cross-sex examiner and a concomitant avoidance of cross-sex choices. Williams *et al.*

(1975) found an age progression from 4 through 8 years of age in stereotyped trait attributions for a male, but not for a female, examiner. Age differences in trait attributions disappeared for both boys and girls in the presence of a female examiner. In both studies, the Male E was eliciting increased stereotyping effects, which may have several interpretations. Children may expect males to adhere more stringently to cultural stereotypes or they may expect increased disapproval from males for failure to provide stereotyped responses. The sensitivity of sex-typed choices and attributions to examiner gender, as well as to other situational variables, points to the potent affective components of sex-role content and the difficulty in discriminating between what children know, prefer, and openly display.

Each of these measurement issues involves a legitimate research area itself and deserves more attention than can be devoted to it in this chapter. The recency of the publications suggests that measurement concerns are of great interest to current researchers and will continue to be a focus of effort.

Katz (1979a) has suggested that the concept of androgyny is too restrictive to encompass the range of children's sex-role orientations and has replaced it with a broadened concept of *sex-role flexibility*. According to Katz, the child with flexible sex-role orientations chooses non-stereotyped over traditional behaviors in many settings. The flexible child (*a*) is willing to engage in same- as well as cross-sex-typed activities; (*b*) is tolerant of peers and adults who participate in same- or cross-sex-typed activities; (*c*) plays with peers of both genders; (*d*) selects media that are free of sex-role stereotyping or chooses both male and female stereotypes equally; (*e*) endorses androgynous personality traits; (*f*) perceives that adults can participate in both male- and female-typed activities; (*g*) anticipates future social roles and occupations in non-stereotyped terms; and (*h*) assigns positive and negative values equally to female and male activities. Katz (1979c) is currently developing more complete assessment strategies to probe the variety of sex-role orientations that appear to characterize the behavior of developing children. Implicit in Katz' approach to assessment is the recognition of multiple sources of influence for learning sex-role conceptions, including peers, parents, various media, and schools. Given the "barrage of sex-role stereotypes" to which children are constantly exposed by many differing sources, it can be expected that for any individual child, the degree of stereotyping or flexibility will vary across tasks, situations, and developmental time.

The rejection of a unitary conception of sex-role measurement is also seen in the work of Spence and her associates (Simms *et al.*, 1978;

Spence, 1979; Spence & Helmreich, 1978, 1979). These authors maintain that the concept of psychological androgyny, as measured by relatively equal endorsement of stereotyped personality traits, is empirically unrelated to several other measures of sex-typed functioning, including attitudes toward the roles of women, assumption of gender-related tasks in the home, or selection of play activities. The measurement implications of these data support the Katz model of flexibility in intra-individual sex-role functioning as well as the multivariate model presented earlier in this chapter.

Summary

Within our present state of knowledge, each of these innovative approaches to measurement adds new dimensions to our understanding of children's sex-typed responding. In particular, it is clear that both measurement characteristics and situational cues can alter the obtained sex-typed responses. Additionally, it appears that alternative measures are tapping differing and frequently uncorrelated aspects of sex-role functioning in children. In view of the current fluidity of instrumentation for measuring children's sex-role orientations, the researcher can no longer discuss such abstract terms as *sex-role identity* or *sex-role preference* without specific references to measurement strategies. In the following section, it should be recognized that the reported age-related trends in sex-role development are based on wide variations in instrumentation and conceptualization.

ACQUISITION OF CHILDREN'S SEX ROLES

Developmental trends will be viewed from three broad perspectives: age-correlated changes in sex-typed behaviors, mediating variables in sex-role development, and individual differences in adherence to cultural sex-role standards.

Age-correlated trends

Indicators of sex-typed choices in cognitive, evaluative, and behavioral domains appear as early as 2 and 3 years of age. Three-year-old children can identify themselves and others by gender, tend to select sex-typed toys and play activities, list common household activities in sex-typed terms, and assign many child and adult personality traits according to gender (Blakemore *et al.*, 1979; Etaugh, Collins, & Gerson,

1975; Fagot, 1974, 1978; Kuhn *et al.*, 1978; Thompson, 1975; Urberg, 1979). By the age of 7 or 8 years, most children show increased conformity to a wide range of cultural stereotypes. In addition to earlier trends in sex-typed activities, they evidence heightened awareness of adult occupational roles, strong preferences for same-sex-typed media, and considerable resistance to cross-sex play and peer interactions (Garrett *et al.*, 1977; Katz, 1979b; Looft, 1971; Scheresky, 1976; Williams *et al.*, 1975; Wolf, 1973).

Evidence on the period from second through eighth grade shows considerable variability, depending on the content areas assessed, the measurement instruments, and the population characteristics, for example, socioeconomic status (SES). Although there is some evidence that preadolescence marks a period of relaxation in rigid stereotyping (Emmerich, 1979; Falkenberg *et al.*, 1977), research support is scanty. Emmerich (1979) hypothesizes a U-shaped course of development in sex-role preferences. Early rigid classifications become more flexible in preadolescence as children consider alternative possibilities. In later adolescence, an increased rigidification occurs as young people begin to confront the realities of the social structure. The utility of this hypothesis rests on further research support. With the fluid status of attitudes and opportunities in current society, it may be difficult to clarify the separate contributions to sex-role development of age status and historical time (Baltes, 1979; Baltes, Reese, & Lipsitt, 1980). At the present time, there appears to be more evidence for continuity, rather than relaxation, of sex-role behaviors and attitudes during the elementary years.

Significant differences between boys and girls appear across all age ranges, however, in degree and content of sex-typing. Recent research confirms many previous findings that boys learn sex-typed content at an earlier age, persist in more stereotyped activities and attitudes through adolescence, and demonstrate more resistance to cross-gender activities. In contrast, girls develop sex-typed play and activity preferences at a later age than boys, are more flexible and less traditional in their attitudes, and are more open to cross-gender behavior (Blakemore *et al.*, 1979; Brush *et al.*, 1979; Edelbrock & Sugawara, 1978; Emmerich, 1979; Etaugh & Riley, 1979; Flerx *et al.*, 1976; Garrett *et al.*, 1977; Hyde & Phillis, 1979; Maccoby & Jacklin, 1974; Urberg, 1979; Wolf, 1973). At least three hypotheses regarding the more stringent sex-typing in boys and greater flexibility in girls have been proposed:

1. Males are more physically and socially salient and their interpersonal roles have higher power and prestige.
2. Male activities have greater interest and creative value for both girls and boys.

3. Males experience stricter socialization practices, which encourage increased attention to sex-typed cues and avoidance of cross-gender behavior.

Probably, each of these hypotheses has some validity for some children on some measures and in certain situations. Of particular interest also is the recency of the studies reviewed, which were all completed during the period from 1972 to 1980. This is a historical time during which the women's movement has presumably had some significant impact on social attitudes toward appropriate sex roles. It appears clear that for the majority of preadolescent children, these liberated attitudes have not filtered down to a functional level that effectively modifies their traditional behavior. The following examples of selected research demonstrate the continuities in sex-typed behavior during the preadolescent years on multiple sex-role criteria, leisure and play activities, personality and trait attributions, and occupational choice.

The Katz flexibility model of sex-role development (1979a, b, c) proposes a life-span progression in which both the content of sex roles and the sources of influence that shape these role behaviors will differ for males and females across three major developmental stages. For purposes of this review, only the first level of preadolescent development will be considered. From birth until about the age of 12 years, the major task for the developing child is to gain knowledge of gender identity of self and other, and to acquire information and skills about what the culture regards as appropriate behaviors for males and females. Developmental trends toward traditional sex-typing are influenced early by parents and later by increasing input from peers, schools, and media. Characteristics of cognitive development also encourage high stereotyping and gender categorizations, and sex-role flexibility is expected to be low for both boys and girls.

In support of her model, Katz (1979b) has generated some recent data using multiple measures of children's sex-role orientations. Children in the sample included 156 kindergarten and 220 third-grade boys and girls. The fourteen sections of the assessment covered self-reported sex-role functioning in cognitive, affective, and behavioral domains, as well as perceived influences of peers, parents, and various media. Items were scored on a 4-point continuum from 0 (most traditional) to 4 (most flexible), with a score of 2 indicating neutrality or equality of choices. For the total group, sex-role flexibility was decidedly traditional, with an overall mean of 77 (the possible range of scores was 0–240). Differences between age groups was small but significant, with third graders showing increased evidence of traditionality as compared to kindergarteners.

Katz hypothesizes that this finding does not reflect increased knowledge of sex-role stereotypes, since her measures tapped behavioral choices, but may be attributable to the increased influence of stereotyped messages from peers and media during this age period. In addition to age trends, the data revealed greater flexibility in girls as compared to boys on all but three subscales, and girls' flexibility scores decreased less from kindergarten to third grade than did those of boys.

Differences in flexibility scores across individual subscales support a multidimensional view of sex-role development. Children were generally more traditional when assessed on adult roles, future role expectancies, and media choices. Greater flexibility was evidenced on current measures, such as tolerance of peer behavior and stereotyped personality traits. The strength of current influences on sex-role orientations was supported by a multiple regression analysis; peer and television influences contributed a combined 60% of the variance, whereas parent influence was nonsignificant. The apparent absence of parent impact on sex-role choices supports the view that multiple modeling and reinforcement influences are functional and dominant during this age period. These results suggest that it may be possible (*a*) to change some sex-role functioning without affecting other content; and (*b*) to make effective use of peer and media resources in implementing educational interventions.

Centering on children's play and leisure activities as a measure of persistence in sex-typed behavior, Lever (1976) used multiple assessments with 181 fifth-grade children from two schools. Four measures of leisure behavior were used to obtain both total play preference scores and distribution of activities according to location, space, content, and peer participation. These included observations of playground activity during school hours, semistructured interviews, written questionnaires, and diary records of playtime activities. Lever concluded that children's activities at this age level are reliably divided by gender-related preferences and that the very nature of these activities contributes to the encouragement of further sex-typing. Major findings included the following:

1. Boys play outdoors more than girls.
2. Boys play in larger groups; girls play in smaller groups (less than four), even when outdoors.
3. Boys play more frequently in age-heterogeneous groups, ranging from 9 to 16 years of age.
4. Girls play in male games (such as softball) more than boys play in female games (such as jumprope).

5. Boys play in more competitive games with explicit rules and a known goal (such as basketball or racing).
6. Boys' games last longer and involve more procedural disputes.

Lever points out several characteristics of these gender-differentiated play activities that encourage males and females to develop different skills, including large-muscle activity, independence from home, experience in mediating disputes in heterogeneous groups, and persistence in achieving difficult goals. Since 52% of all reported activities involved real, rather than vicarious, play, Lever suggests that leisure time play is an important area for parents and educators who are concerned about modifications in sex-typed behavior.

In addition to sex-typed trends in leisure activities, children appear to hold stereotyped conceptions of academic and intellectual skills that become increasingly more inclusive and consolidated. Nash (1975) tested 105 sixth graders and 102 ninth graders on two measures of sex-role stereotyping that tapped views of men and women in general, as well as real and ideal self. Items were considered stereotypic if they were assigned more frequently to either males or females by both girls and boys of a given grade level. A wide range of personality traits received stereotyped ratings and 10 were considered to have implications for intellectual achievement. For sixth graders these were "enjoys art and literature" (feminine typed), and "active, feels superior, thinks men are superior to women, skilled in business" (masculine typed). In addition, ninth graders stereotyped on "likes math and science, can make decisions easily, independent, not at all easily influenced" (masculine) and "minds very much when things are not clear" (feminine). Ninth-grade children increased both the total number of stereotyped items and those that appeared to influence academic performance. The correlation of these stereotypes to visual–spatial performance will be considered in the next· section. Nash concluded that sociocultural stereotypes· increase from sixth to ninth grade, and especially for many male-stereotyped traits that may be related to continued interest and persistence in academic performance. Since several aspects of achievement motivation in the elementary years are predictive of later adolescent and adult achievement behavior (Crandall & Battle, 1970), these early stereotypes may lay the groundwork for future patterns of academic and intellectual performance. It appears that for most elementary and junior high students, intellectual success is still linked with masculinity (Nash, 1979).

Finally, as children move toward adolescence, occupational considerations should take on greater salience. Although many parents and teachers tend to discount the importance of career orientation prior to high school, these early conceptions of future life roles and goals may be

influential in shaping future choices. The findings related to occupational stereotyping differ depending on the questions that are asked.
Especially discriminating are questions about whether or not males and
females *could* occupy various adult roles, what people *really* occupy
these positions, what are each child's personal *aspirations,* and finally
what each child believes and expects she or he will actually be doing in
adulthood.

The evidence on sex-typed conceptions of occupations suggests that
children are still quite traditional in preadolescence. Kindergartners
through sixth graders seem to show little age-correlated variation in their
knowledge of adult stereotyped roles, and both boys and girls tend to
choose occupations in which their gender is dominant. Girls are far
more limited in their occupational aspirations than boys, with
elementary-age boys selecting preferences for two to four times as many
occupations as girls (Iglitzin, 1977; Lerner, Bensen, & Vincent, 1976;
Looft, 1971; Scheresky, 1976; Schlossberg & Goodman, 1972; Siegel,
1977). Although these children may agree that cross-gender occupational attainment is possible and girls are more open to equal opportunities than are boys (Garrett *et al.,* 1977; Greenberg, 1977), their personal choices remain traditional. Both boys and girls select occupations
that reflect current societal patterns, with girls restricted primarily to
teaching, nursing, secretarial work, and homemaking. A recent review
of studies on adolescent aspirations (Marini & Greenberg, 1978) concluded that high school girls and boys are still choosing careers that
closely match the 1976 U.S. Department of Labor statistics for sex segregation in the occupational structure. It seems that young people are not
going to be significantly changed in their sex-typed perceptions until
they can match these perceptions with a different reality.

Summary

Tracing the acquisition of sex-typed orientations across the primary
and elementary years, it appears that children (*a*) increase their knowledge, activities, and preferences for traditional roles from preschool to
school age; (*b*) do not change substantially in most of these role orientations throughout the elementary years; (*c*) are more sex-typed in some
areas than in others; (*d*) are stereotyped in intellectual and occupational
conceptions that may influence later academic and career choice; and
(*e*) are consistently differentiated by gender, with greater flexibility and
less stereotyping in girls. The following section considers some selected
variables that are thought to mediate and transmit these stereotyped
trends in children's sex-role development.

Mediating variables in sex-role acquisition

Apart from specific parental socialization practices, which will not be reviewed here, three cognitive and social learning variables are thought to influence the acquisition of sex-typed behaviors: gender identity or constancy, gender labels, and imitation of like-gender models. Each of these variables will be reviewed and discussed in terms of its implications for the acquisition and stabilization of sex-typed behavior in early and middle childhood.

Gender identity and gender constancy. These two concepts have been used respectively to denote self-categorization as a boy or girl, and the cross-situational resistance of this classification to modifications in appearance, activities, or personal desires (Kohlberg, 1966; Money & Ehrhardt, 1972). According to Money and Ehrhardt, gender identity becomes consolidated and difficult to reverse at about the age of 3 years. Kohlberg maintains that gender constancy is completed at about the age of 5 years, and is then irreversible. According to Kohlberg, gender categorization becomes the critical organizer of all sex-role values and attitudes. The child is motivated by "the need to preserve a stable and positive self-image [p. 88]," and increases same-sex activities to achieve consistency with gender. Several recent studies on gender constancy support the hypothesis that this cognitive skill increases with age, but suggest that it is not mastered by many children until about the age of 8 years. However, the relationship between gender constancy and endorsement of sex-typed activities is less clear. Two studies are relevant here.

Slaby and Frey (1975) defined gender constancy in terms of three types of information: gender identity (e.g., Are you a boy or a girl?), gender stability over time (e.g., When you were a little baby, were you a boy or a girl?), and gender consistency (e.g., If you wore girls' [boys'] clothes, would you be a boy or a girl?). Gender constancy, reported as a composite score, showed low to moderate correlations with age from 26 to 67 months, suggesting a developmental progression. Prediction to a hypothesized sex-typing variable, attention to same-sex models portrayed on a videotaped sequence, was confirmed only for boys. Both boys and girls spent more time looking at male than female models. Boys higher in gender constancy scores attended to the male model significantly longer than boys with low gender constancy, and boys also spent more time attending to the male model than did girls. Although these results appear supportive of Kohlberg's hypothesis of advancement in gender constancy as an organizing factor in self-selected sex-role learning, the absence of positive findings for girls is discomforting.

A second interesting study on gender constancy by Marcus and Overton (1978) used constancy measures that included both live and pictorial stimuli for self and a same-sex peer, as well as a four-question interview assessment of sex-typed preferences. Gender constancy increased with age from kindergarten to second grade, but only for the pictorial stimuli. Contrary to cognitive–developmental theory, measures of gender constancy had no relation at all to sex-role preference as assessed by open-ended questions on activities, media and peer choices, and aspirations. The authors concluded that Kohlberg's hypothesis about the relation of gender constancy to the development of sex-typing was not supported.

In both studies, no differences were found in age of acquisition of gender constancy concepts between boys and girls, a finding that is supported in similar research (Emmerich, Goldman, Kirsh, & Sharabany, 1977; Thompson, 1975). In addition, Emmerich *et al.* found intellectual differences in age of attainment of some gender constancy concepts, suggesting that a general intellectual development factor underlies this discrimination task. These findings conflict with the extensive literature that indicates that boys acquire many sex-typed concepts and behaviors at an earlier age than girls and that they persist in more stereotyped behaviors throughout the school years. Marcus and Overton (1978) suggest that gender constancy is cognitively based, while sex-typed preferences are influenced by societal expectations. The failure of gender constancy tasks to discriminate the preference patterns of young boys and girls suggests that it is related more to cognitive–intellectual than to sex-role development. However, cognitive components other than specific concrete operational skills may influence the development of some sex-typed behaviors. The previous discussion of sex roles suggested that cognitive mediators such as language, expectancies, and attributions may be potent determinants of sex-role attitudes and behavior. Gender labels represent one of these cognitively based mediators.

Gender labeling. Activities labeled "for boys" or "for girls," whether or not accompanied by the attributions of "good boy" and "good girl," have been shown to influence the toy and play preferences of even very young children (Blakemore *et al.*, 1979; Thompson, 1975). Cross-gender activities become increasingly avoided, especially by boys, when they are gender-labeled. Gender labeling may be viewed as either an organizing factor that motivates the child to increase sex-typing by matching his or her behavior with the label (Kagan, 1964; Kohlberg, 1966) or as a social learning variable that provides cues for the discrimination, retention, and selective utilization of gender-related behaviors (Masters, Ford, Arend, Grotevant, & Clark, 1979).

Several studies have demonstrated that in young children, no direct relationship exists between gender labeling as a cognitive skill and toy or activity preferences, but that this relationship appears at later age levels. Blakemore *et al.* (1979) presented groups of 2-, 4-, and 6-year-olds with 24 sets of pictured toys that had previously been rated by adults as clearly stereotyped for either girls or boys. For boys, gender-related choices were strong at all ages and there was no increase across age groups. In contrast, 2-year-old girls chose both sets of toys equally, and increased in preference for same-sex toys only at the later ages. More significantly for the labeling hypothesis was the finding that not one of the 2-year-old boys who selected boys' toys was able to sort these toys into piles labeled "for girls" or "for boys" at better than a chance level. The authors suggest that cognition and sex-role development do not show a straightforward relation, and that socialization factors other than gender-labeling were probably responsible for toy preferences in young boys.

In a second study, the same investigators reported that 3-year-old girls selected sex-typed toy preferences only after these activities were gender-labeled. Once more, cognitive information and overt behavior did not present a close match. In this second study, girls may have matched their choices to adult gender labels in order to (*a*) demonstrate knowledge and competence; (*b*) please a strange adult; or (*c*) avoid anticipated disapproval. The design of this study does not allow us to select among these possibilities.

Masters *et al.* (1979) provided relevant data on gender-labeling in conjunction with a study on children's imitative behavior. The experiment used two types of toys, balloons and xylophones that had previously been rated as neutral in terms of male or female sex-typing. Groups of 4- and 5-year-old children were then provided with labeling of these toys as either for boys or for girls, and were left alone for 5 minutes in the playroom with all the toys. Toy preference was measured by means of the number of observed 6-second intervals in which the child either touched or played with the toys. In a free play situation with no observations of a model's choices, there was a significant effect of gender-labeling on children's toy preferences. Children spent about 75% of their play time with toys labeled for same sex, and only 25% of their time with toys labeled for cross sex. No differences between boys and girls in this situation were reported. The importance of this portion of the findings lies in the elicitation of sex-typed behavioral preferences associated with the gender-labeling of formerly neutral activities. The complex findings on gender-labeling and modeling effects when play activities are either matched or cross-matched for the gender of the model will be considered in the following section.

The tendency of girls and boys to avoid activities that are cross-gender-labeled continues through elementary and high school. Several studies have examined this phenomenon in laboratory settings with neutral tasks, finding differences in skilled performance when tasks are labeled for same gender (Montemayor, 1974), and on expectancies for success and task persistence when children are told that girls or boys "generally do better at this task" (Stein, Pohly, & Mueller, 1971). As children mature toward adolescence, however, it is important to determine how their gender-labeling discriminates between present and future stereotyping of academic and occupational domains. In particular, the perception by boys and girls of peer and adult stereotypes of mathematics may funnel their efforts toward or away from this area. Boswell (1979) assessed 562 children from grades 3 through 6 on a measure of toy and activity preference, a measure of attitudes toward math, and actual math achievement in school. Children generally view math in like-gender terms in elementary school (girls believe girls are better and boys believe boys are better in math) but view it as a male-typed skill in adulthood. Boys continue to enjoy math through grade 6, but girls' preference for math significantly declines in the sixth grade! For girls, but not for boys, the degree of math stereotyping in adults was negatively correlated with math achievement. Current interest in gender-labeling of mathematics and other masculine-typed intellectual skills as an antecedent to further skill development and career choice has focused on intervention strategies to counteract this stereotyping process (Fox, Tobin, & Brody, 1979; Nash, 1979; Sherman, 1978). A widely accepted hypothesis about the increasing differentiation between boys' and girls' achievement in math and spatial skills during early and later adolescence places a major source of responsibility on the culturally determined masculine stereotyping of these activities.

The studies on gender-labeling provide evidence that the stimulus function of gender plays a significant role in directing the activities of even very young children. The strength of children's motivation to select or avoid gender-labeled behavior suggests that children may increasingly become agents or producers of their own sex-role development. If children create their own environments partly by means of their stimulus value to others as well as by their self-selected activities, then substantial changes in individual sex-role behaviors may require modifications in both the individual child as well as in the effective environment (Worell, 1981). The influence of gender-labeling on self-directed activity thus has direct implications for educational practice. Wherever activities, ideas, media presentations, courses of study, and future life–career goals are discriminated by gender labels, we may expect to find a significant portion of developing children who fashion their behavior accordingly. Many of the current efforts to combat sex-role stereotyping in the schools are aimed, in part, at the labeling procedures that inform boys and girls about what is or is not considered appropriate for their lives. Apart from gender labels, however, the influence of gender in observational learning continues to intrigue developmentalists and has relevance for both theoretical and practical applications.

Gender effects in observational learning. Most theoretical models propose imitation of same-gender models as one important antecedent of sex-typed behavior. In a comprehensive review of the literature on the effects of model gender on observational learning, Maccoby and Jacklin (1974) concluded that "there is little consistent tendency for children of preschool or grade school age to select same-sex models [p. 295]." These authors also concluded that the degree of sex-typing in children is unrelated to that of the same-sex parent, thereby refuting social learning formulations. A more recent review of 80 studies arrived at a similar conclusion (Barkley, Ullman, Otto, & Brecht, 1977).

Although these reviews appear to reject gender components of modeling as relevant antecedents to sex-typing, several current research studies suggest that is worthwhile to examine more complex interactions. In addition to gender-related task labels (Master *et al.*, 1979), support has been found for the influence of the following variables on imitation of like or cross-gender models: sex-role appropriateness of task to the observed gender of model (Barkley *et al.*, 1977; Wolf, 1973), frequencies of observed performances of an activity in relation to gender of model (Perry & Bussey, 1979), direct reinforcement for imitation of modeled behavior (Grusec & Brinker, 1972), vicarious reinforcement and expectancies for shared reinforcement with the model (Bussey & Perry, 1976), and sex-typed characteristics of the observing child (Perry & Perry, 1975). In the latter study, masculine-typed children, regardless of gender, spontaneously verbalized and subsequently recalled more of the male than females models' behavior. In contrast, feminine-typed children recalled both models' behavior equally and verbalized less. The complex determinants of observational learning are still being unravelled; these recent studies point to the effects of multiple stimulus and consequence variables as well as cognitive mediating factors on the imitation of gender-related behaviors. Two studies are summarized here to support the interactive effects of socialization variables and gender of model on imitation of sex-typed behavior.

Masters *et al.* (1979, cited earlier) found no direct effects on imitation of gender models who played with carefully selected neutral toys. Toy preference was influenced only by gender labels; same-gender labels significantly increased and cross-gender labels significantly decreased toy play, regardless of the gender of the model. These authors suggest that single models performing neutral activities do not provide sufficient information from which children can infer and generalize to sex-appropriate activities.

Support for these findings was provided by Perry and Bussey (1979), who proposed that children learn what behaviors are appropriate for each gender by watching the behavior of multiple models in many situations and by noticing the relative frequencies of behaviors performed by females and males. These authors invoke the social learning theory distinction between learning and performance, assuming that children learn the behavior of both females and males but perform only those behaviors that they anticipate will have positive response consequences. In two well-designed experiments, 8- and 9-year-old children viewed varying proportions of female and male models performing two-choice preference tasks between similar but neutral items. Examples of these choices include an apple or a banana and a toy cow or horse. Children were then asked to indicate their own preferences, as well as to recall whether men or women models had liked each of the toys more or chose them equally. Results supported the hypotheses that sex-typed preferences for activities derives from observation of many models of the same gender performing an activity. From these observations, the child abstracts a definition of appropriate behavior for members of his or her gender. The children's equal recall of female and male model choices suggests that children were observing and coding both sets of behaviors but were selectively performing those with higher observed gender frequency. The authors suggest that these results assign less importance to imitation of the same-gender parent and more to observation of a variety of socializing agents.

The educational implications of modeling theory and research are multiple. If children are imitating persons and activities on the basis of observed frequencies, gender-related cognitive mediators, and direct or vicarious response contigencies, each of these variables requires modification in educational environments. Each variable can be approached separately or model–mediation–consequence sequences can be arranged. For gender-related frequencies alone, it is possible to concentrate on visual media, classroom examples and task assignments, and community models as exemplars. The problems in transfer arise, of course, when children compare their classroom experiences with observed frequencies and contingencies in the external world. Programs in schools that encourage sex-role equality in education will need to consider how to promote transfer and generalization to outside environments.

Individual patterns of sex-typing

If all behaviors were dichotomously gender-classified, the conception and measurement of androgyny would not have been possible. Within every group of boys and girls, large overlaps are found on any sex-typed activity. Numerous observational studies have supported the contention that many children are not traditionally sex-typed on many activities. This means that, depending on the observed activity, these children may show cross-gender preferences, may select both male and female preferences equally, or may select neutral, non-gender-related choices. The question of most interest to androgyny researchers is the implications of non-sex-typed responding for the psychological well-being of the child. The early returns on the personal and social outcomes of androgynous or cross-gender orientations for children are mixed.

Several studies have looked at children's play, focusing on those children who showed nonconcordance with situational sex-typed expectations. Lott (1978) compared two groups of kindergarten children who were "matched" or "nonmatched" with group expectation scores for gender-related play and social behavior. The nonmatched children were selected by above-median scores on the ranked differences between their social activity behavior and 10 behaviors with high sex-typed expectations as rated by parents and teachers. In comparison to matched (sex-typed) children, nonmatched children had significantly higher scores on the Creative Uses Test (Wallach & Kogan, 1965), indicating a tendency to use divergent thinking. No differences were found between boys and girls on this measure. In free-play situations, there was a significant tendency for nonmatched boys, but not girls, to play less often in same-sex situations. Lott concludes that children who do not behave in ways that are considered gender-appropriate by adults may be at a relative advantage by experiencing a wider range of situations and acquiring a larger repertoire of response alternatives. This formulation, which is backed by preliminary data, is supportive of Bem's (1974) hypothesis concerning the adjustment advantages of flexible sex-role orientations in adults. Follow-up data is needed here.

The social impact of individual variations in sex-typed behavior has been studied in a series of observational studies by Fagot (1977, 1978). Her findings suggest that children who display nontraditional social behaviors may receive negative feedback from others. In one study (1978), 67 preschool children were rated in free play on 33 social and activity behaviors, and 15 teacher and peer categories of response were also recorded. Behaviors that were gender-preferred were used to classify children into one of four quadrants on the basis of a median split: masculine, feminine, androgynous, and low–low. The 15 teacher and peer reactions were classified into negative and positive responses. Children in the androgynous category received less total peer reaction than children in the sex-typed categories, and more negative peer feedback than children in all three quadrants. Teacher response was significantly lower only for the low–low category of children. With a small sample of cross-gender children (one girl and two boys), the two boys were found to play alone more frequently and they received less positive peer response than other boys in the class.

The impact of clearly observable cross-gender play activities appears to be negative for both boys and girls, and increasingly so for boys as they move into elementary school. Fagot (1977) reported results of analyses conducted on data from observations of peer and teacher responses to the play activities of over 200 preschool children. In general, boys received significantly more peer and, on some measures, teacher criticism when they engaged in feminine-typed activities such as kitchen play and dress-up. Girls received more negative peer criticism when playing in the sandbox or when hammering. A subgroup of "gender-reversed" children was identified; they were significantly above the mean for cross-gender play and below the mean for same-gender play. Although teacher response did not differentiate these children from their peers, peer response to boys with gender-reversed play patterns was clearly negative. These boys ($N = 7$) received less positive and more negative feedback from their peers, and played alone almost three times as often as other children in the group. The author concludes that even at this age, children who adopt traditional gender-related play and social behaviors are more socially acceptable to their peers. Conversely, children who adopt nontraditional patterns of behavior pay a price in peer isolation and rejection. Longitudinal data is needed here to trace these outcomes to later school adjustment.

The evidence for an interaction between age of child and negative response to boys engaging in cross-gender behavior was found in an analogue study using paragraph descriptors of various sex-typed combinations of girls and boys (Braunstein, 1976). Teachers at two grade levels, first and second, and fifth and sixth, reported more negative reactions to cross-gender behavior in a 10-year-old hypothetical boy than did teachers for a 7-year-old boy. Remedial treatment was more frequently recommended for the 10-year-old. Although analogue studies may be subject to criticism (Kazdin, 1978), these findings are supported by the work of specialists who study and treat "gender-disturbances" in children. Boys who display open preferences for "feminine" play such as dress-up and dolls in middle elementary years are more likely to be referred for psychological treatment than girls who prefer baseball and tree climbing (Bradley, Doering, Zucker, & Finegan, 1979; Rekers, 1977). The ethical and ideological implications of these differential reactions to cross-gender play in boys and girls is beyond the scope of this chapter. The interested reader is referred to recent dialogue on professional responsibilities involving intervention with gender-reversed children.

Studies using self or teacher ratings on personality traits present mixed results. Using 89 third through sixth graders, Hall and Halberstadt (1980) examined several correlates of masculine, feminine, and androgyny scores on a children's form of the Personality Attributes Questionnaire (CPAQ) (Spence *et al.*, 1975). For both boys and girls, low to moderate correlations were reported with the Piers-Harris self-concept scale on CPAQ masculinity, and androgynous children were significantly higher on self-concept for appearance and intellectual status. On teacher ratings, a marginally significant trend was found for sex-typed children to be rated higher on social maturity and leadership. The authors interpret this finding as evidence that teachers prefer the socially conventional child. In a camping situation, counselors rated CPAQ masculine children as more assertive and less dependent. The authors comment that androgyny was not as advantageous to these children as might be expected on the basis of the theory. It appeared that either sex-typed or masculine response patterns in both girls and boys produced the most positive ratings from others.

Further support for the advantages of masculine-typed responding in girls was found in two additional studies conducted in academic settings. Nash (1975) found low but significant correlations between sex-role stereotyping and preferences, and a measure of visual–spatial aptitude. For ninth-grade boys and girls, masculine actual and ideal self-ratings were associated with higher spatial performance. For both sixth- and ninth-grade girls and boys, preference for being a boy was predictive of higher scores on spatial ability. These findings correspond with earlier studies on masculine preference and spatial ability (Ferguson & Maccoby, 1966), suggesting that some of the advantages in boys' spatial skills in high school may be a function of sex-role orientation.

Sola and Phye (1979) used multiple regression analyses on masculinity, femininity, and *t* scores (androgyny) on the Bem Sex Role Inventory (Bem, 1975). Second semester sophomore and junior high school girls ($N = 376$) with high masculine self-ratings were evaluated by their teachers as being less dependent, more responsible, and having greater insight than girls who rated high on the feminine scale. Perhaps as students move toward achieving emancipation from the academic system, teacher ratings of cross-gender behaviors, at least in girls, become more positive.

Conclusions. The small sample of studies on androgynous orientations in children presents a mixed outcome. One problem has been the relative absence of research that looks at both masculine and feminine scores as equal contributors to personal functioning, and the preponderance of studies that have focused on "cross-gender" behavior. The result of this inequity is a skewed pool of current information regarding the effects of more flexible sex-role functioning on the psychological well-being of young people. Cross-gender behavior is frequently unacceptable in social contexts, particularly for boys' play activities and increasingly for girls' intellectual interests. As girls mature, masculine-typed orientations may have some advantages in both intellectual and social domains, but the evidence is sparse and has not included observations in natural interpersonal contexts.

It seems clear to this writer that when nontraditional sex-role behavior is displayed in social situations, it is likely to violate the expectations and standards of significant others such as peers and teachers. If nontraditional sex-role behaviors are to be encouraged in children, it appears that a supportive environment should be arranged that stimulates and nourishes, rather than punishes, these atypical response patterns. The implications for educational settings suggest that implementation of programs to modify traditional sex-typing will have to target all the human factors that impinge on the developing child: self-reactions, peers, teachers, parents, and possibly the community at large.

SEX ROLES IN EDUCATIONAL SETTINGS

Responsibility for developing and shaping the sex-role orientations of children is clearly not the sole domain of the schools. Children arrive at school with well-formulated conceptions of male and female sex-role requirements, and they are exposed to many other cultural agents that function to maintain these stereotypes: parents, television, peers, films, and the social structure around them. However, considerable literature has recently been published suggesting that schools are contributing their share of socialization practices that maintain and affirm these stereotypes. Studies on gender-related behaviors of school-age children present some clear evidences of school-related sex-typing. Among the factors that encourage the persistence of sex-role inequalities in schools are curriculum and allocation of resources, textbooks and media, and personnel practices involving teachers, administrators, and counselors. Each of these topics represents a growing body of literature that can only be summarized here. The interested reader is referred to more detailed treatments of this research area (Anderson, 1972; Frazier & Sadker, 1973; Guttentag & Bray, 1976; Hansen & Rapoza, 1978; Harway & Astin, 1977; Mednick, Tangri, & Hoffman, 1975; Nilsen, Bosmajian, Gershuny, & Stanley, 1977; Pottker & Fishel, 1977; Sexton, 1976; Sherman, 1978; Stockard, Schmuck, Kempner, Williams, Edson, & Smith, 1980; Wittig & Peterson, 1979). The focus of concern in this section is on those characteristics of students and of the elementary school environment that presently support sex-role stereotyping and that are potentially open to change.

Sex roles and school achievement

There are at least two ways to view the effects of sex-role socialization on children's school achievement. The most common of these approaches is to document the cognitive and behavioral differences that are found between groups of girls and boys, that is, differences apparently due to gender. Detailed inventories of these gender-related differences are available in many reference sources and will be only briefly considered here (cf. Frieze, 1975; Frieze, Fisher, Hanusa, McHugh, & Valle, 1978; Hoyenga & Hoyenga, 1978; Maccoby, 1966; Maccoby & Jacklin, 1974; Sherman, 1978; Stein & Bailey, 1973; Wittig & Peterson, 1979). A second way to view these between-group variances in achievement behaviors is to examine their interaction with sex-role variables. Documentation of sex-role contributions to achievement behavior is more difficult to obtain and involves multiple factors that are generally more complex to assess than gender. When sex-role variations are considered, it becomes possible to examine within-group individual differences. For example, although boys excel in spatial abilities after the onset of puberty, many girls exceed some boys on these skills. What are the variables that contribute to individual competencies on mathematics and spatial tasks?

A consideration of both gender and sex-role views is essential if boys and girls are to reach their fullest potential in school, career, and community settings. Inequitable academic experiences that segregate or penalize by gender are particularly important as we consider strategies for revising educational structures and procedures. Examples in this category include institutional staffing patterns, differential assignment of boys and girls to athletic and prevocational activities, and unequal allocation of financial resources to these areas. Likewise, attention to sex-role variables in achievement helps us to focus on those aspects of the educational environment that are detrimental to the development of competence, self-esteem, and behavioral flexibility in either girls or boys. Sex-role variables are reflected in biased textbook portrayals of male and female activities, as well as in differential teacher responses to boys and girls based upon cultural stereotypes. Sex-role contributions to achievement are particularly important in understanding within-group differences. We are interested in the development of competence and proficiency in all children, regardless of whether they are boys or girls.

Gender-related behaviors in school. Gender differences in achievement-related behaviors appear in both cognitive and affective domains. During the preadolescent elementary years, girls more frequently receive higher grades, score higher on tests of verbal fluency and comprehension of prose, and report that they enjoy school and find it meaningful. In contrast, boys experience higher frequencies of reading problems, grade retention, and clinical referrals for problem (usually disruptive) behavior. After puberty, as indicated earlier, boys show increasing competence in visual–spatial skills, score higher than girls on tests of mathematics achievement, and more frequently enroll in advanced math and science courses. The increasing deficits in girls' interest and achievement in quantitative areas have become a matter of concern equal to that expressed about the earlier reading deficits in boys. Although total high school dropout rates are higher for boys as a group, the escalated enrollment by boys in quantitative courses of study enhances their opportunities for future employment in higher paying occupational fields (Stockard *et al.*, 1980).

Across all age ranges from preschool to college, differences appear between boys and girls in cognitive processing concerning their intellectual and achievement efforts. Several reviews have documented that

1. Girls tend toward lowered expectancies for success, regardless of task content, and boys are prone to overestimate their probabilities for successful outcomes (Crandall, 1969; Maccoby & Jacklin, 1974; Parsons, Ruble, Hodges, & Small, 1976; Stein & Bailey, 1973.

2. Girls and boys tend to attribute their good and poor performance to different factors. For the most part, boys attribute their successes, but not their failures, to a stable factor of ability, while girls are more likely to attribute their successes to an unstable factor of

effort and their failures to lack of ability (Dweck, 1975; Dweck, Davidson, Nelson, & Enna, 1978; Etaugh & Ropp, 1976; Kaczala, Futterman, Meece, & Parsons, 1979; Nicholls, 1975).

The relationship between expectancies and attributions for success and failure and task persistence and achievement are reviewed and discussed in Chapters 7 and 9. The net effect of these gender-related causal attributions may have differing long-term implications for boys and girls. The child who frequently uses the female-typed attributional pattern will be prone toward less persistence and impaired performance following failure, and less pride and self-competency following success (Dweck *et al.*, 1978). The impact of self-detrimental attributions becomes increasingly evident as advanced curriculum and career choices must be confronted. Kaczala *et al.* (1979) reported that ninth graders rated math as more difficult than did seventh graders, but boys regarded both current and future math courses as easier that did the girls and had higher expectancies for success. Facing an increasingly difficult task (math and science courses) with lower expectations and ineffectual achievement attributions, girls will be far less likely to elect math and science as their preferred alternatives. Additional influences of sex-role factors on mathematics achievement will be discussed in the following section.

Sex-role variables in school achievement. The reported differences between female and male achievement patterns may have maturational as well as socialization antecedents. The focus here will be on those variables that appear to have sociocultural significance for gender-related performance patterns. In reviewing the evidence on sex role as a mediator of intellectual functioning, Nash (1979) points out that most cognitive–intellectual domains are culturally sex-typed. Among the mediating factors that appear relevant to gender-related performance, the following have current research support:

1. Task labeling as masculine or feminine—Support was given earlier in this chapter for the inhibitory effects of cross-gender labeling on performance in a variety of tasks. Since there are few intellectual domains that are sex-typed neutral, it is inevitable that many girls and boys will be influenced by this factor. The early reading problems of many boys have been attributed, in part, to the feminine sex-typing not only of this activity but of the entire elementary school environment (Austin, Clark, & Fitchett, 1971; Dwyer, 1973; Lee & Gropper, 1972; Sexton, 1969). The increasing disenchantment with mathematics by girls is clearly mediated by stereotyping it as a male domain. Fennema and Sherman (1977) report that

definition of math as a male discipline inhibits both female math achievement and selection of math courses in high school. As students mature, gender-labeling of cognitive domains becomes more complex and may be related to a number of other mediating variables, including personal values, expectancies, attitudes, peer support or rejection, fears of failure, and career goals (Fox *et al.*, 1979; Nash, 1979).

2. The attainment value of the task for the individual—Females as a group report higher attainment values for verbal, as compared to athletic or mathematic skills and are more likely to persist in areas in which achievement has personal value (Stein & Bailey, 1973). As early as seventh grade, girls view math as less useful to their future lives than do boys (Fennema & Sherman, 1977).

3. Expectancies for success and failure on particular gender-labeled tasks—Dweck *et al.* (1978) have shown that expectancies for failure can mediate subsequent effort and task persistence, and have called this phenonemon "learned helplessness" (see Chapter 9). For girls and mathematics, this may be a potent factor in their increasingly lower achievement scores.

4. Self-defined sex-role characteristics or preferences—Girls' self-description as masculine-typed appears to predict achievement on gender-related tasks. Nash (1975) reported that 14-year-old girls who preferred to be boys did not demonstrate the expected deficits in spatial skills.

5. Prior experiences with the skills and behavioral domains related to the task—Connor and Serbin (1977) found that frequency of preschool boys' activity with masculine-typed play showed positive correlations with two measures of visual–spatial ability, and Fennema and Sherman (1977) reported no differences in mathematics achievement between adolescent boys and girls when the number of previous math courses was controlled. Girls and boys who remove themselves from an activity or cognitive domain may never develop the skills necessary for later excellence.

6. Expectations and response patterns of significant others—High school girls report fear of peer rejection for taking masculine-typed courses such as math (Fennema & Sherman, 1977). Evidence will be presented in a later section. (Dweck *et al.*, 1978) to support the influence of gender-related teacher responses on task performance.

7. Personal sex-role standards—Perception of particular response patterns such as competitiveness or assertion may inhibit achievement strivings in certain contexts. The "fear of success" literature

suggests that conflicting goals that are perceived as mutually exclusive (e.g., to be smart and to be feminine) may result in achievement avoidance for some females as they approach adolescence.

Nash (1979) maintains that sex-role variables mediate cognitive
functioning only for those individuals who view them as salient or central to self-definitions. The diversity of sex-role factors that contribute to
individual performance variance suggests that simple intervention procedures will be insufficient to effect significant change across all behaviors. Two school-related influences on sex-role development are
considered next: instructional materials and teacher behavior.

Instructional materials

At every level from preschool to college, textbook and other instructional materials have been evaluated as sex-typed and discriminatory.
Three major trends emerge from recent reviews of educational materials
that are in common use in public school settings:

1. There is a marked imbalance in the frequencies with which texts
   discuss, portray verbally, and display visually males and females
   in social and historical roles.
2. The social roles that are portrayed are restricted to sex-typed activities and stereotyped personality traits.
3. The language that children read in their primers and texts is biased
   in the direction of androcentrism, with numerous generic concepts
   and descriptors that appear in exclusionary male language for-
   mats.

Some examples of these stereotyped practices follow.

First, frequencies of males and females appearing in textbooks is
heavily imbalanced in favor of males. Weitzman and Rizzo (1974)
analyzed the illustrations in the most widely used texts over a period of 5
years in science, math, reading, spelling, and social studies. Of the more
than 8000 pictures analyzed, 5500 (69%) were of males. Furthermore,
the percentage of females declined by grade, so that by sixth grade there
were four pictures of males to every one of females. Central characters in
stories were more frequently boys than girls; in one reading series, 102
stories were about boys and only 35 were about girls. Science and history books reduced the appearance of adult females to as low as 1%.
Studies of high school texts confirm the continued ignoring of women in
the history of "mankind"; Arlow and Froschl (1976, as cited in Foxley,
1979) surveyed 36 textbooks, finding that women and their contributions

to history were given an average of one page total in texts of 500–800 pages. Similar studies have confirmed these imbalances in male–female portrayals (Nilsen, 1977b; Saario, Jacklin, & Tittle, 1973).

Second, the restrictive social and occupational roles presented by textbook characters present role models that are frequently caricatures of societal stereotypes. Men appear in more than 150 occupational roles, whereas almost all women are mothers. When women do appear in working positions, they are restricted to four occupations: teacher, secretary, salesperson, and nurse (Weitzman & Rizzo, 1974). Activities of boys and girls are also stereotyped, with boys portrayed as adventurous, active, curious, and skillful. Girls, in contrast, engage in homemaking activities, groom themselves to appear attractive, and ask the boys for help on difficult tasks. Girls are more frequently described as incompetent, fearful, and emotional, and they fall apart in emergencies (Trecker, 1973; *Women in Words and Images*, 1972).

Finally, it is still common to find androcentric or exclusionary language in textbook materials throughout the school curriculum. Indeed, some current university texts in educational psychology still refer to all students as he, all teachers as she, and devote as little as half a page to sex-role development (Sadker & Sadker, 1978). Johnson (1977) reviewed current research on the interpretations given to generic language forms (e.g., mankind, manpower, brotherhood), and concluded that generic male terms are interpreted as exclusionary. Citing studies from preschool through college, Johnson reported that when generic exclusionary terms are used, both male and female subjects are more likely to interpret the antecedent as a male rather than as a female. She concluded that generic terms reduce the visibility of females in written and spoken language and should be replaced by inclusionary terms or reference to both males and females when appropriate. Nilsen (1977a) points out, however, that many of our traditional academic words are masculine typed and may be more difficult to modify. For example, *penmanship, sportsmanship, bachelor's degree, fellowship, mastery, master's degree,* and *freshman* may be so ingrained in the academic community that inclusionary terms will be strongly resisted. Finally, if children cannot trust their books to reflect the outside world with accuracy, surely they can depend on the dictionary? In two studies of popularly used dictionaries, Nilsen (1977b) and Gershuny (1977) report sex-role stereotypes that are similar to those appearing in children's texts in terms of male–female ratios, social roles, and more positive qualities assigned to male behavior.

In summarizing the data on textbook influences in educational stereotyping, it seems clear that schools are not only helping to maintain the status quo but are supporting conceptions of male and female roles that do not accurately reflect contemporary American society. Several researchers into textbook stereotyping point out that children are learning two kinds of lessons from their texts. In addition to the intended academic content, there is a "hidden curriculum" or "latent content" that is teaching them about how to be a boy or girl, woman or man. It seems appropriate and timely, therefore, to target the revision of all text materials in schools at every level as a first step toward intervention and change.

Teacher behavior

Children spend about 90% of their school hours in the presence of a teacher. To what extent can we hold teachers responsible for supporting the sex-role socialization system? Evidence on teacher behavior is mixed; as awareness of sex-role issues permeates society, teachers are becoming increasingly sensitive to their stereotyped attitudes. Therefore, earlier reports of gender differences in teacher feedback may not accurately reflect current teaching practices. On the other hand, some very recent research suggests strongly that teachers do react differentially to girls and boys in both success and failure conditions and that these reactions feed back to the children some important sex-role messages.

In what ways might teacher behavior reinforce sex-role stereotypes and sex-typed behaviors? Several studies have found that assessed sex-role stereotypes were unrelated to what teachers actually did in the classrooms (Weber, Freidin, & McKinnon, 1978; Woolever, 1976). Therefore, it is essential to obtain observational data on specific teacher responses to specific child behaviors in particular achievement settings. The three contexts in which differential treatment of boys and girls in elementary school settings have been found include (a) reinforcement of sex-typed behavior by means of differing task assignments or attention to children when they are engaged in sex-typed activities; (b) frequency of student–teacher interaction across all types of activities, and the ratio of positive or negative qualities of this interaction; and (c) specific types of feedback to girls and boys separately under particular performance conditions.

The first context is the most overt and definable, and therefore the easiest to identify and modify. In 28 classrooms with almost 800 girls and boys, Mulawka (1972) found that teachers assigned girls and boys to sex-typed tasks and more frequently displayed and discussed males in leadership and higher wage-earning roles. Serbin, O'Leary, Kent, and Tonick (1973) found that preschool teachers more frequently reinforced girls for proximal behavior, thus encouraging dependency on adults. In contrast, teachers gave boys equal attention when they were either proximal or distal and gave boys additional attention for independent work.

The second context in which teachers differentiate between boys and girls may be less amenable to change, because it is more pervasive and possibly more conditioned by the gender-related behaviors of the children themselves. Regardless of whether the teacher is a woman or a man, boys receive more positive and more negative attention from teachers (Brophy & Good, 1974; Good, Sikes, & Brophy, 1973). Thus, the behavior of boys is more salient in the classroom, and they are encouraged in both prosocial and disruptive behavior patterns. The negative feedback is directed more heavily toward disruptive and off-task behaviors, which Dweck *et al.* (1978) contend teaches boys to ignore negative feedback from teachers in all contexts—academic as well as social. Since teachers tend to perceive girls as more obedient and passive, and boys as more assertive and active, it is difficult to determine whether teachers are responding reciprocally to different student behavior patterns or are initiating novel patterns of reinforcement. Teachers reward girls with better grades than they assign to boys (McCandless, Roberts, & Starnes, 1972), but they also ignore girls more frequently. Girls ask for either positive or negative attention less frequently than do boys (Good *et al.*, 1973), and these reciprocal teacher—student response systems may reinforce each other in a spiral fashion.

Transsituational teacher–student interaction patterns tell us less about encouragement of sex-typed behaviors, however, than studies in which individual differences in student responses are considered. In an observational study using 16 seventh- and eighth-grade classrooms taught by equal numbers of women or men, Good *et al.* (1973) found that teachers' assessment of children's achievement capabilities was an important determinant of gender-related response feedback. Boys who were ranked high by their teachers in expected level of classroom achievement exceeded all other students in proportion of positive teacher feedback, positive teacher-initiated contact, and intense positive affect. Boys who were judged low in expected achievement received the most negative feedback, especially for off-task and disruptive behavior, and the least positive initiation; girls fell midway between these groups. Girls who ranked low in expected achievement received high rates of teacher criticism and they seldom initiated contact with their teachers. These findings suggest that teachers may be differentially supporting boys' and girls' achievement, with highly promising boys receiving the most encouragement. Since this study was done in a secondary school in order to obtain both male and female teachers (who incidentally did not differentiate significantly according to gender of student), we do not know whether these interaction patterns occur also in the earlier grades. At the junior high level, however, it seems that teachers are discriminating most between the high- and low-achieving boys, which may be telling the girls that their achievement levels are unimportant.

In an interesting analogue study, Frey and Slaby (1979) confirmed that "teachers"—in this case, parents instructed to tutor a confederate child—may fail to support high levels of achievement in girls. Confederate children were trained to appear as either high achievers or moderate achievers according to the percentage of correct responses they gave on a set of math and verbal concept problems. High-achieving girls received less positive feedback from their "tutors" than either high-achieving boys or moderately achieving girls. Furthermore, these tutors were least likely to tell a high-achieving girl that she was competent and most likely to indicate to her that the task was an easy one; in contrast, high-achieving boys were most often told they were competent and least often told that their work was easy. Although these findings were obtained in a nonschool setting, they support the previous school-related results that adults who act in the role of teacher appear to deprecate and underreward the achievements of girls and to elevate those of boys.

Finally, we will consider some recent research that examined differential patterns of evaluative feedback to boys and girls and the effects of these patterns on subsequent attributions for task failure. Dweck *et al.* (1978) conducted two studies designed to determine teacher contributions to the "learned helplessness" syndrome. The authors hypothesized that children who attribute failure to uncontrollable factors such as lack of ability will come to view their failures as insurmountable and will show decreased effort and persistence following subsequent failures (see again Chapters 7 and 9 for further explanations of attribution theory in relation to children's achievement). Girls, more than boys, display these achievement patterns despite that fact that they receive higher grades in elementary school and less negative classroom feedback. How might teachers contribute to ineffectual and self-defeating achievement behavior in some children?

In the first study, teacher evaluative feedback to girls and boys within naturally occurring fourth- and fifth-grade classroom interactions was coded in terms of positive or negative, intellectual or conduct, competence or neatness, and effort or ability attributions following success and failure. Although absolute amounts of positive feedback did not differ for boys and girls, boys received significantly more teacher praise for intellectual competence (90%), whereas almost 20% of positive feedback to girls was for intellectually irrelevant aspects, such as neatness. For negative feedback, only 54% of the work-related criticism to boys was for intellectual inadequacy, whereas 89.9% of work-related criticism to girls was addressed to inadequate intellectual performance. Finally, of the 38 teacher attributions for failure observed, all were motivational (effort)—34 to boys and only 4 to girls across all classrooms. The authors conclude that the patterns of observed teacher evaluations for girls are exactly those hypothesized to produce learned helplessness.

A second controlled laboratory study (Dweck *et al.*, 1978) assessed the effects of these differential teacher behaviors on children's attributions for failure. Here, *both* girls and boys who received failure feedback that was specific to their competence (typical observed classroom girl pattern) were more likely to view subsequent failure on a new task as indicative of their low ability than children who received failure feedback that was frequently solution-irrelevant (typical boy classroom pattern). From the outcomes of both studies, the experimenters concluded that teachers are directly contributing to self-defeating achievement patterns in girls by (*a*) giving them infrequent but highly specific negative feedback directed to intellectual failure; and (*b*) providing them few effort attributions following failure. As a result, girls will be more likely than boys to attribute their failure to ability and to show decreasing persistence and interest in intellectual pursuits. Additionally, the more diffuse positive evaluations given to girls may convince them that teacher approval is not contingent on intellectual competence, further weakening their achievement efforts. In contrast, boys may be encouraged to ignore negative teacher evaluation as irrelevant to their intellectual competence and to attribute their failures to lack of effort, an easily modifiable condition.

Conclusions. The studies that look at the more subtle aspects of teacher–student interactions have been discovering explicit instructional conditions that encourage the maintenance and persistence of gender-related achievement patterns in school. The evidence suggests that teachers are discriminating between high-achieving girls and boys and are encouraging boys, but not girls, to ignore external criticism and to increase their efforts following failure. It seems clear that boys and girls are experiencing different learning environments in the elementary and early high school years—environments that differentially encourage future intellectual achievement and persistence. Although male and female teachers differ in many instructional styles, there is little evidence that they provide significantly different learning environments for girls and boys across high and low levels of achievement. Increasing the proportion of male teachers in the elementary schools may provide a desirable model of male involvement to both girls and boys, but sex-typed achievement and career patterns of girls and boys are not apt to be significantly impacted by this type of intervention. If sex-role patterns of intellectual and occupational attainment are to change, a concerted effort in the direction of modifying specific teacher–student interaction seems essential, regardless of the gender of the teacher.

INTERVENTIONS IN EDUCATIONAL SETTINGS

From the tangled network of influences on children's sex-role development, we can identify two major sources for change: natural and planned. The impetus for natural change comes from contemporary political, social, and economic movements that predispose individuals within the larger culture to modify their lifestyle activities and value systems. Among these natural change sources, the most salient are the force of the women's movement, the changing composition of American families, and legal remedies for economic and status inequalities such as the 1972 Title IX amendment to the Civil Rights Act of 1964. As a result of these broad pressures for cultural change, major resocialization is taking place within individuals and institutions that may generally alter many of the sex-typed characteristics we have been discussing (Hoffman, 1977; Worell, 1979). As children are exposed to increasing examples of educational and occupational equity and to revised role models in their families, in the media, and in the world of work, attitudes and aspirations may be reshaped to correspond to a new reality. Perhaps by virtue of their position within the larger social system, schools will reflect and enact the contemporary themes that encourage gradual transition toward flexible and androgynous interpersonal roles.

The more impatient and proactive approach to implementing change has been to design planned intervention programs that focus on specific strategies directed toward specific targets in particular settings. In planned intervention programs, the goals have generally been to (*a*) correct situational inequities so that all students have equal access to educational resources and activities; (*b*) revise curricula, textbooks, media, test materials, and counseling practices that restrict flexible role definitions, and develop new curricular programs that emphasize flexible roles and life-span career development; (*c*) modify the attitudes and values of students, teachers, school counselors, and parents toward more acceptance of flexible sex roles in family, school, and occupations; and (*d*) directly train new behaviors in students and teachers that encourage sex-role flexibility (Worell & Stilwell, 1981).

What is the evidence that planned programs of intervention can result in effective outcomes that are resistant to extinction over time and across situations? Since 1974 the Women's Educational Equity Act has been funding large and small projects that are implementing one or more of the goals outlined above. In addition, researchers in many settings have been conducting independent studies with similar goals. Some programs are multifaceted and include all four goals in a major effort to modify many aspects of the educational environment—for example, the *Nonsexist Intervention Program* (Guttentag & Bray, 1976), *Project Born Free* (Hansen, 1978a), and *Promoting Equal Status Behavior* (Lockheed & Harris, 1978). Other studies have targeted more limited goals in attempting to modify specific aspects of the learning environment—for example, de-stereotyping of textbooks and the media (Flerx *et al.*, 1976; Schau, 1978), modifying counselor and teacher attitudes (ACES Commission on Sex Equality Concerns, 1978; Smith, 1978), and encouraging teacher cueing and reinforcement of nonstereotyped behaviors (Serbin, Connor, & Citron, 1978; Serbin, Tonick, & Sternglanz, 1977). Each of these direct intervention programs has reported success in changing sex-typed responses on some behavioral and attitudinal measures with some teachers and counselors and with children in certain age and gender groups.

Since the efforts to modify social and educational sex-role stereotyping are very recent, the variables that contribute to effective intervention are largely unknown. In viewing both the successes and failures of these programs, however, it seems clear that all three domains of sex-role functioning require attention—affective, cognitive, and behavioral. Studies that target only teacher or student attitudes find that classroom behavior and student responses may remain unchanged (Weber *et al.*, 1978). Cognitive interventions may require consideration of gender, developmental level, and present value structure of the child. For example, Flerx *et al.* (1976) found that following exposure to nonstereotyped stories, 4- and 5-year-old boys still maintained that boys are smarter than girls, and Guttentag and Bray (1976) report that ninth-grade boys became *more* stereotyped in occupational choice following exposure to a 6-week training program. Likewise, behavioral interventions that target only teacher cueing and reinforcement patterns may influence situational responses of children that disappear when current contingencies are removed (Serbin *et al.*, 1978). Although many interpretations of these findings are possible, Serbin and Connor (1979) conclude that stimulus discrimination of environmental cues and reinforcers maintains many early sex-typed behaviors that are then mediated by cognitive factors when such external contingencies are removed.

Each of the above examples supports a three-pronged approach that integrates affective, cognitive, and behavioral components. Furthermore, it is suggested that intervention toward nonstereotyped orientations should be planned early and should be organized differentially across developmental levels. Hansen (1978b), for example, has proposed a Career Development Curriculum that begins at kindergarten level and proceeds through senior high school, providing a sequence of developmental experiences for infusion into the regular curriculum. Several other curriculum and training proposals have been developed that teachers and counselors can adopt for implementation and research evaluation (cf. Harway & Astin, 1977; National Project on Women in Education, 1978). The mandate for change, however, requires sensitivity to the powerful emotional and evaluative reactions to sex-role conceptions by students, school personnel, parents, and the larger community in which they operate. Questions of value orientation need to be addressed both before and during these intervention programs to monitor personal and institutional investment in stereotyped sex-role postures. Within each of us, the deeply ingrained sex-role messages are not easily dislodged.

REFERENCES

Abrahams, B., Feldman, S. S., & Nash, S. C. Sex-role self-concept and sex-role attitudes: Enduring personality characteristics or adaptations to changing life situations? *Developmental Psychology*, 1978, *14*, 393–400.

Association for Counselor Educators and Supervisors (ACES), Commission on Sex Equality Concerns. *For women and for men: Sex equality in counselor education and supervision*. Washington, D.C., American Personnel and Guidance Association, 1978.

Austin, D., Clark, V., & Fitchett, G. *Reading rights for boys: Sex roles in language experiences*. New York: Appleton, 1971.

Baltes, P. On the potential limits of child development: Life-span developmental perspectives. *Society for Research in Child Development Newsletter*, Summer, 1979, 1–4.

Baltes, P. B., Reese, H. W., & Lipsitt, L. P. Life-span developmental psychology. In M. R. Rosenzweig & L. W. Porter (Eds.), *Annual Review of Psychology*, Palo Alto, Calif.: Annual Reviews, Inc., 1980, *31*, 65–110.

Bandura, A. *Social learning theory*. Englewood Cliffs, N.J.: Prentice-Hall, 1977.

Barkley, R. A., Ullman, D. G., Otto, L., & Brecht, J. M. The effects of sex typing and sex appropriateness of modeled behavior on children's imitation. *Child Development*, 1977, *48*, 721–725.

Barry, H., Bacon, M. K., & Child, I. L. A cross-cultural survey of some sex differences in socialization. *Journal of Abnormal and Social Psychology*, 1957, *55*, 327–332.

Bem, S. L. The measurement of psychological androgyny. *Journal of Consulting and Clinical Psychology*, 1974, *47*, 155–162.

Bem, S. L. Sex-role adaptability: One consequence of psychological androgyny. *Journal of Personality and Social Psychology*, 1975, *31*, 634–643.

Bem, S. L. Probing the promise of androgyny. In A. G. Kaplan & J. P. Bean (Eds.), *Beyond sex-role stereotypes: Readings toward a psychology of androgyny.* Boston: Little, Brown, 1976. Pp. 47–62.

Bem, S. L. Theory and measurement of androgyny: A reply to the Pedhauzer-Tetenbaum and Locksley-Colten critiques. *Journal of Personality and Social Psychology,* 1979, *37,* 1047–1054.

Berzins, J. I., Welling, M. A., & Wetter, R. E. A new measure of psychological androgyny based on the Personality Research Form. *Journal of Consulting and Clinical Psychology,* 1978, *46,* 126–138.

Blakemore, J. E. O., LaRue, A. A., & Olejnik, A. B. Sex-appropriate toy preferences and the ability to conceptualize toys as sex-role related. *Developmental Psychology,* 1979, *15,* 339–340.

Block, J. H. Conceptions of sex roles: Some cross-cultural and longitudinal perspectives. *American Psychologist,* 1973, *28,* 512–526.

Boswell, S. L. *Sex roles, attitudes and achievement in mathematics: A study of elementary school children and Ph.D.'s.* Paper presented at the biennial meeting of the Society for Research in Child Development, San Francisco, 1979.

Bradley, S. J., Doering, R. W., Zucker, K. J., & Finegan, J. K. *Assessment of the gender-disturbed child: A comparison to sibling and psychiatric controls.* Paper presented at the Symposium on the Sexuality of the Child, University of Quebec, Montreal, 1979.

Braunstein, M. *The teacher's part in sex-role reinforcement.* Unpublished doctoral dissertation, Yeshiva University, 1976.

Brophy, J. E., & Good, T. L. *Teacher-student relationships: Causes and consequences.* New York: Holt, 1974.

Brown, D. G. Masculinity–femininity development in children. *Journal of Consulting Psychology,* 1957, *21,* 197–202.

Brush, L. R., Gold, A. R., & Sprotzer, E. R. *The importance of a "same" category in research on sex-role stereotypes.* Paper presented at the biennial meeting of the Society for Research in Child Development, San Francisco, 1979.

Bussey, K., & Perry, D. G. Shared reinforcement contingencies with a model: A social learning analysis of similarity effects in imitation research. *Journal of Personality and Social Psychology,* 1976, *34,* 1168–1176.

Condry, J., & Condry, S. Sex differences: A study of the eye of the beholder. *Child Development,* 1976, *47,* 812–819.

Connor, J. M., & Serbin, L. A. Behaviorally-based masculine and feminine activity preference scales for preschoolers: Correlates and other classroom behaviors. *Child Development,* 1977, *48,* 1411–1416.

Constantinople, A. Masculinity–femininity: An exception to a famous dictum? *Psychological Bulletin,* 1973, *80,* 389–407.

Crandall, V. C. Sex differences in expectancy of intellectual and academic reinforcement. In C. P. Smith (Ed.), *Achievement-related motives in children.* New York: Russell-Sage Foundation, 1969.

Crandall, V. C., & Battle, E. S. The antecedents and adult correlates of academic and intellectual achievement effort. In J. P. Hill (Ed.), *Minnesota Symposia on Child Psychology* (Vol. 4). Minneapolis: Univ. of Minnesota Press, 1970.

Damon, W. *The social world of the child.* San Francisco: Jossey-Bass, 1977.

D'Andrade, R. G. Sex differences and cultural institutions. In E. E. Maccoby (Ed.), *The development of sex differences.* Stanford, Calif.: Stanford Univ. Press, 1966.

Deaux, K. *The behavior of women and men.* Monterey, Calif.: Brooks/Cole, 1976.

Dickstein, E. B., & Seymour, M. W. *The effect of the addition of neutral items on IT scale scores.* Paper presented at the biennial meeting of the Society for Research in Child Development, San Francisco, 1979.

Dweck, C. S. The role of expectations and attributions in the alleviation of learned helplessness. *Journal of Personality and Social Psychology,* 1975, *31,* 674–685.

Dweck, C. S., Davidson, W., Nelson, S., & Enna, B. Sex differences in learned helplessness: II. The contingencies of evaluative feedback in the classroom. III. An experimental analysis. *Developmental Psychology,* 1978, *14,* 268–276.

Dwyer, C. A. Sex differences in reading: An evaluation and critique. *Review of Educational Research,* 1973, *43,* 455–467.

Edelbrock, C., & Sugawara, A. I. Acquisition of sex-typed preferences in preschool-aged children. *Developmental Psychology,* 1978, *14,* 614–623.

Eiseman, M. F. *Interrelationships among psychological androgyny, moral judgement, and ego development in an adult population.* Unpublished doctoral dissertation, University of Kentucky, 1978.

Eisenberg-Berg, N., Boothby, R., & Matson, T. Correlates of preschool girls' feminine and masculine toys preferences. *Developmental Psychology,* 1979, *15,* 354–355.

Emmerich, W. Socialization and sex-role development. In P. B. Baltes & K. W. Schaie (Eds.), *Life span developmental psychology: Personality and socialization.* New York: Academic Press, 1973.

Emmerich, W. *Developmental trends in sex-stereotyped values.* Paper presented at the biennial meeting of the Society for Research in Child Development, San Francisco, March 1979.

Emmerich, W., Goldman, K. S., Kirsh, B., & Sharabany, R. Evidence for a transitional phase in the development of gender constancy. *Child Development,* 1977, *18,* 930–936.

Etaugh, C., Collins, G., & Gerson, A. Reinforcement of sex-typed behaviors of two-year-old children in a nursery school setting. *Developmental Psychology,* 1975, *11,* 255.

Etaugh, C., & Riley, S. Knowledge of sex stereotypes in preschool children. *Psychological Reports,* 1979, *44,* 1279–1283.

Etaugh, C., & Ropp, J. Children's self-evaluation of performance as a function of sex, age, feedback, and sex-typed task label. *Journal of Psychology,* 1976, *94,* 115–122.

Fagot, B. I. Sex differences in toddler's behaviors in the preschool child. *Developmental Psychology,* 1974, *10,* 554–558.

Fagot, B. I. Consequences of moderate cross-gender behavior in preschool children. *Child Development,* 1977, *48,* 902–907.

Fagot, B. I. *The consequences of same-sex, cross-sex, and androgynous presences in early childhood.* Paper presented to the Western Psychological Association, San Francisco, 1978.

Falkenberg, S., Rahm, T., & Waern, Y. Sex role concepts in eight- and twelve-year-olds. *Scandinavian Journal of Psychology,* 1977, *18,* 31–37.

Fennema, E., & Sherman, J. Sex-related differences in mathematics achievement, spacial visualization and affective factors. *American Educational Research Journal,* 1977, *14,* 51–71.

Ferguson, L. R., & Maccoby, E. E. Interpersonal correlates of differential abilities. *Child Development,* 1966, *37,* 549–571.

Flerx, V. C., Fidler, D. S., & Rogers, R. W. Sex role stereotypes: Developmental aspects and early intervention. *Child Development,* 1976, *47,* 998–1007.

Fling, S., & Manosevitz, M. Sex typing in nursery school children's play interests. *Developmental Psychology,* 1972, *7,* 146–152.

Fox, L. H., Tobin, D., & Brody, L. Sex-role socialization and achievement in mathematics. In M. A. Wittig & A. C. Peterson (Eds.), *Sex-related differences in cognitive functioning: Developmental issues.* New York: Academic Press, 1979.

Foxley, C. H. *Nonsexist counseling: Helping women and men redefine their roles*. Dubuque, Iowa: Kendall Hunt, 1979.

Frazier, N., & Sadker, N. *Sexism in school and society*. New York: Harper, 1973.

Freud, S. *New introductory lectures on psychoanalysis*. New York: Norton, 1965.

Frey, K. S., & Slaby, R. G. *Differential teaching methods used with girls and boys of moderate and high achievement levels*. Paper presented at the Society for Research in Child Development, San Francisco, 1979.

Frieze, I. H. Women's expectations for and causal attributions of success and failure. In M. T. S. Mednick, S. S. Tangri, & L. W. Hoffman (Eds.), *Women and achievement: Social and motivational analyses*. New York: Wiley, 1975.

Frieze, I. H., Fisher, J., Hanusa, M., McHugh, M., & Valle, V. Attributions of the causes of success and failure as internal and external barriers to achievement in women. In J. A. Sherman & F. L. Denmark (Eds.), *The psychology of women: Future directions for research*. New York: Psychological Dimensions, 1978. Pp. 519–552.

Frieze, I. H., Parsons, J. E., Johnson, P. B., Ruble, D. N., & Zellman, G. L. *Women and sex roles: A social psychological perspective*. New York: Norton, 1978.

Garrett, C. S., Ein, P. L., & Tremaine, L. The development of gender stereotyping of adult occupation in elementary school children. *Child Development*, 1977, *48*, 507–512.

Gershuny, H. L. Sexism in dictionaries and texts. Omissions and commissions. In A. P. Nilsen, H. H. Bosmajian, H. L. Gershuny, & J. P. Stanley (Eds.), *Sexism and language*. Urbana, Ill.: National Council of Teachers of English, 1977.

Good, T. L., Sikes, J. N., & Brody, J. E. Effects of teacher sex and student sex on classroom interaction. *Journal of Educational Psychology*, 1973, *65*, 74–87.

Greenberg, S. Attitudes toward increased social, economic, and political participation by women as reported by elementary and secondary students. In J. Pottker & A. Fishel (Eds.), *Sex bias in the schools: Research evidence*. Rutherford, N.J.: Fairleigh Dickenson Univ. Press, 1977. Pp. 200–206.

Grusec, J. E., & Brinker, D. B., Jr. Reinforcement for imitation as a social learning determinant with implications for sex-role development. *Journal of Personality and Social Psychology*, 1972, *21*, 149–158.

Gullahorn, J. E. Sex-related factors in cognition and brain lateralization. In J. E. Gullahorn (Ed.), *Psychology and women in transition*. New York: Wiley, 1979.

Guttentag, M., & Bray, M. *Undoing sex role stereotypes*. New York: McGraw-Hill, 1976.

Hall, J. A., & Halberstadt, A. G. Masculinity and feminity in children: Development of the children's personal attributes questionnaire. *Developmental Psychology*, 1980, *16*, 270–280.

Hansen, L. S. *Born free: Change process evaluation of a psychoeducational intervention to reduce career sex role stereotyping for women and men*. Paper presented at the annual convention of the American Educational Research Association, Toronto, 1978. (a)

Hansen, L. S. Promoting female growth through a career development curriculum. In S. L. Hansen & R. S. Rapoza (Eds.), *Career development and counseling of women*. Springfield, Ill.: Charles C Thomas, 1978. (b)

Hansen, S. L., & Rapoza, R. S. *Career development and counseling of women*. Springfield, Ill.: Charles C Thomas, 1978.

Harway, M., & Astin, H. S. *Sex discrimination in career counseling and education*. New York: Praeger, 1977.

Hoffman, L. W. Changes in family roles, socialization, and sex differences. *American Psychologist*, 1977, *32*, 644–657.

Hoyenga, K. B., & Hoyenga, K. T. *The question of sex differences: Psychological, cultural and biological issues*. Boston: Little, Brown, 1978.

Hyde, J. S., & Phillis, D. E. Androgyny across the life span. *Developmental Psychology,* 1979, *3,* 334–336.

Iglitzin, L. Sex-typing and politicization in children's attitudes. In J. Pottker & A. Fishel (Eds.), *Sex bias in the schools: Research evidence.* Rutherford, N.J.: Fairleigh Dickenson Univ. Press, 1977. Pp. 178–199.

Johnson, C. S. *Sexism in language: The case for including everybody.* Paper presented at the annual convention of the International Reading Association, 1977.

Johnson, P. B. Doing psychological research. In J. E. Parsons, P. B. Johnson, D. N. Ruble, & G. Zellman (Eds.), *Women and sex roles: A social psychological perspective.* New York: Norton, 1978.

Kaczala, C., Futterman, R., Meece, J., & Parsons, J. E. *Developmental shifts in expectancies and attributions for performance in mathematics.* Paper presented at the annual meeting of the American Educational Research Association, San Francisco, 1979.

Kagan, J. Acquisition and significance of sex-typing and sex-role identity. In M. L. Hoffman & L. W. Hoffman (Eds.), *Review of child development research.* New York: Russell Sage Foundation, 1964.

Kaplan, A. G. Androgyny as a model of mental health for women: From theory to therapy. In A. G. Kaplan & J. P. Bean (Eds.), *Beyond sex-role stereotypes: Readings toward a psychology of androgyny.* Boston: Little, Brown, 1976.

Katz, P. A. *Determinants of sex-role flexibility in children.* Paper presented at the Society for Research in Child Development, San Francisco, March 1979. (a)

Katz, P. A. The development of female identity. *Sex Roles,* 1979, *5,* 155–178. (b)

Katz, P. A. *Correlates of sex-role flexibility in children.* Progress Report, NIMH Grant No. 29417, May 1979. (c)

Kazdin, A. E. Evaluating the generality of findings in analogue therapy research. *Journal of Consulting and Clinical Psychology,* 1978, *46,* 673–686.

Kelly, J. A., & Worell, J. New formulations of sex-roles and androgyny: A critical review. *Journal of Consulting and Clinical Psychology,* 1977, *45,* 1101–1115.

Kohlberg, L. A cognitive–developmental analysis of children's sex-role concepts and attitudes. In E. E. Maccoby (Ed.), *The development of sex differences.* Palo Alto, Calif.: Stanford Univ. Press, 1966. Pp. 83–173.

Kohlberg, L. Stage and sequence: The cognitive–developmental approach to socialization. In D. A. Goslin (Ed.), *Handbook of socialization theory and research.* Chicago: Rand McNally, 1969. Pp. 347–480.

Kuhn, D., Nash, S. C., & Brucken, L. Sex role concepts of two- and three-year-olds. *Child Development,* 1978, *49,* 445–451.

La Voie, J. C., & Andrews, R. Facial attractiveness, physique, and sex-role identity in young children, *Developmental Psychology,* 1976, *12,* 550–551.

Laws, J. L. *The second X: Sex roles and social roles.* New York: Elsevier, 1979.

Lee, P. C., & Gropper, N. B. Sex-role culture and educational practice. *Harvard Educational Review,* 1972, *44,* 369–410.

Lerner, R. M., Bensen, P., & Vincent, S. Development of societal and personal vocational role perception in males and females. *Journal of Genetic Psychology,* 1976, *129,* 167–168.

Lever, J. Sex differences in the games children play. *Social Problems,* 1976, *23,* 478–487.

Levin, S. M., Balistrieri, J., & Schukit, M. The development of sexual discrimination in children. *Journal of Child Psychology and Psychiatry,* 1972, *13,* 47–53.

Lewis, M., & Weinraub, M. Origins of early sex-role development. *Sex Roles,* 1979, *5,* 135–154.

Lockheed, M. E., & Harris, A. M. *The effects of equal status cross-sex contact on students' sex-stereotyped attitudes and behavior.* Paper presented at the annual meeting of the American Educational Research Association, Toronto, 1978.

Looft, W. R. Sex differences in the expression of vocational aspirations by elementary school children. *Developmental Psychology,* 1971, *5,* 366.

Lott, B. Behavioral concordance with sex role ideology related to play areas, creativity, and parental sex typing of children. *Journal of Personality and Social Psychology,* 1978, *36,* 1087–1100.

Luria, Z., & Rose, M. *Psychology of human sexuality.* New York: Wiley, 1979.

Lynn, D. B. *Parental and sex role identification.* Berkeley, Calif.: McCutchen, 1969.

McCandless, B. R., Roberts, A., & Starnes, T. Teachers' marks, achievement test scores, and aptitude relations with respect to social class, race, and sex. *Journal of Educational Psychology,* 1972, *63,* 153–159.

Maccoby, E. E. *The development of sex differences.* Stanford, Calif.: Stanford Univ. Press, 1966.

Maccoby, E. E. *Social development: Psychological growth and the parent–child relationship.* New York: Harcourt, 1980.

Maccoby, E. E., & Jacklin, C. N. *The psychology of sex differences.* Stanford, Calif.: Stanford Univ. Press, 1974.

Marcus, D. E., & Overton, W. F. The development of cognitive gender constancy and sex-role preferences. *Child Development,* 1978, *49,* 434–444.

Marini, M. M., & Greenberger, E. Sex differences in occupational aspirations and expectations. *Sociology of Work and Occupations,* 1978, *5,* 147–478.

Masters, J. C., Ford, M. E., Arend, R., Grotevant, H. D., & Clark, L. V. Modeling and labeling as integrated determinants of children's sex-typed imitative behavior. *Child Development,* 1979, *50,* 364–371.

Masters, J. C., & Wilkinson, A. Consensual and discriminative stereotypes of sex-typed judgements by parents and children. *Child Development,* 1976, *47,* 208–217.

Mednick, M. T., Tangri, S. S., & Hoffman, L. W. *Women and achievement: Social and motivational analyses.* New York: Wiley, 1975.

Mischel, W. A social learning view of sex differences in behavior. In E. E. Maccoby (Ed.), *The development of sex differences.* Stanford, Calif.: Stanford Univ. Press, 1966.

Mischel, W. Sex typing and socialization. In P. H. Mussen (Ed.), *Carmichael's handbook of child psychology* (Vol. 2, 3rd ed.). New York: Wiley, 1970.

Money, J., & Ehrhardt, A. A. *Man and woman, boy and girl.* Baltimore: Johns Hopkins Press, 1972.

Montemayor, R. Children's performance in a game and their attraction to it as a function of sex-typed labels. *Child Development,* 1974, *45,* 152–156.

Mulawka, E. J. *Sex role typing in the elementary school classroom as reinforcement of sex role stereotypes learned at home.* Unpublished doctoral dissertation, Wayne State University, 1972.

Mussen, P. H. Early sex-role development. In D. A. Goslin (Ed.), *Handbook of socialization theory and research.* Chicago: Rand McNally, 1969.

Myers, B. J., Weinraub, M., & Shetler, S. *Preschoolers' knowledge of sex role stereotypes: A developmental study.* Paper presented at the American Psychological Association, New York, 1979.

Nash, S. C. The relationship among sex-role stereotyping, sex-role preference, and sex difference in spatial visualization. *Sex Roles,* 1975, *1,* 15–32.

Nash, S. C. Sex roles as a mediator of intellectual functioning. In M. A. Wittig & A. C. Peterson (Eds.), *Sex-related differences in cognitive functioning: Developmental issues.* New York: Academic Press, 1979.

National Project on Women in Education. *Taking sexism out of education.* Washington, D.C.: U.S. Department of Health, Education and Welfare, 1978.

Nicholls, J. G. Causal attributions and other achievement-related cognitions: Effects of task outcomes, attainment values, and sex. *Journal of Personality and Social Psychology,* 1975, *31,* 379–389.

Nilsen, A. P. Linguistic sexism as a social issue. In A. P. Nilsen, H. H. Bosmajian, H. L. Gershuny, & J. P. Stanley, *Sexism and language.* Urbana, Ill.: National Council of Teachers of English, 1977. (a)

Nilsen, A. P. Sexism in children's books and elementary teaching materials. In A. P. Nilsen, H. H. Bosmajian, H. L. Gershuny, & J. P. Stanley. *Sexism and language.* Urbana, Ill.: National Council of Teachers of English, 1977. (b)

Nilsen, A. P., Bosmajian, H. H., Gershuny, H. L., & Stanley, J. P. *Sexism and language.* Urbana, Ill.: National Council of Teachers of English, 1977.

Parsons, J. E., Ruble, D. N., Hodges, K. L., & Small, A. Cognitive–developmental factors in emerging sex differences in achievement-related expectancies. *Journal of Social Issues,* 1976, *32,* 47–61.

Perry, D. G., & Bussey, K. The social learning theory of sex differences: Imitation is alive and well. *Journal of Personality and Social Psychology,* 1979, *37,* 1699–1712.

Perry, D. G., & Perry, L. C. Observational learning in children: Effects of sex of model and subject's sex role behavior. *Journal of Personality and Social Psychology,* 1975, *31,* 1083–1088.

Pottker, J., & Fishel, A. *Sex bias in the schools: Research evidence.* Rutherford, N.J.: Fairleigh Dickenson Univ. Press, 1977.

Rabban, M. Sex-role identification in young children in two diverse social groups. *Genetic Psychology Monographs,* 1950, *42,* 81–158.

Rebecca, M., Hefner, R., & Oleshansky, B. A model of sex-role transcendence. In A. G. Kaplan & J. B. Bean (Eds.), *Beyond sex-role stereotypes: Readings toward a psychology of androgyny.* Boston: Little, Brown, 1976.

Rekers, G. A. Assessment and treatment of childhood gender problems. In B. B. Lahey & A. E. Kazdin (Eds.), *Advances in child clinical psychology* (Vol. 1). New York: Plenum, 1977.

Rosenberg, B. G., Sutten-Smith, B., & Morgan, E. The use of opposite sex scales as a measure of psychosexual deviancy. *Journal of Consulting Psychology,* 1961, *25,* 221–225.

Saario, T. N., Jacklin, C. N., & Tittle, C. K. Sex-role stereotyping in the public schools. *Harvard Educational Review,* 1973, *43,* 44–54.

Sadker, M. P., & Sadker, D. M. *Beyond pictures and pronouns: Sexism in teacher education textbooks.* Washington, D.C.: U.S. Department of Health, Education and Welfare, 1978.

Schau, C. G. *Evaluating the use of sex-role reversed stories for changing children's stereotypes.* Paper presented at the annual meeting of the American Educational Research Association, Toronto, 1978.

Scheresky, R. The gender factor in six- to ten-year-old children's views of occupational roles. *Psychological Reports,* 1976, *38,* 1207–1210.

Schlossberg, N. K., & Goodman, J. A woman's place: Children's sex stereotyping of occupation. *Vocational Guidance Quarterly,* 1972, *20,* 266–270.

Sears, R. R., Rau, L., & Alpert, R. *Identification and child rearing.* Stanford, Calif.: Stanford Univ. Press, 1965.

Seavy, C. A., Katz, P. A., & Zalk, S. R. Baby X: The effect of gender labels on adult responses to infants. *Sex Roles,* 1975, *1,* 103–110.

Serbin, L. A., & Connor, J. M. *Environmental control of sex-related behaviors in the preschool.* Paper presented at the biennial meeting of the Society for Research in Child Development, San Francisco, 1979.

Serbin, L. A., Connor, J. M., & Citron, C. C. Environmental control of independent and dependent behaviors in preschool girls and boys: A model for early independence training. *Sex Roles*, 1978, *4*, 867–875.

Serbin, L. A., O'Leary, K. D., Kent, R. N., & Tonick, I. J. A comparison of the teacher response to preacademic and problem behavior of boys and girls. *Child Development*, 1973, *44*, 796–804.

Serbin, L. A., Tonick, I. J., & Sternglanz, S. H. Shaping cooperative cross-sex play. *Child Development*, 1977, *48*, 924–929.

Sexton, P. *The feminized male: Classrooms, white collars, and the decline of manliness.* New York: Vintage, 1969.

Sexton, P. *Women in education.* Bloomington, Ind.: Phi Delta Kappa Educational Foundation, 1976.

Sher, M. A., & Lansky, L. M. The IT scale for children: Effects of variations in the sex-specificity of the IT figure. *Merrill-Palmer Quarterly*, 1968, *14*, 323–330.

Sherman, J. A. *Sex-related cognitive differences: An essay on theory and evidence.* Springfield, Ill.: Charles C Thomas, 1978.

Siegel, C. L. F. Sex differences in the occupational choices of second graders. In J. Pottker & A. Fishel (Eds.), *Sex bias in the schools: Research evidence.* Rutherford, N.J.: Fairleigh Dickenson Univ. Press, 1977. Pp. 173–177.

Simms, R. E., Davis, M. H., Foushee, H. C., Holahan, C. K., Spence, J. T., & Helmreich, R. L. *Psychological masculinity and femininity in children and its relationship to trait stereotypes.* Paper presented at the annual meeting of the Southwestern Psychological Association, New Orleans, 1978.

Slaby, R. G., & Frey, K. S. Development of gender constancy and attention to same-sex models. *Child Development*, 1975, *46*, 849–856.

Smith, J. E., Goldman, J. A., & Keller, D. *Sex-role preferences: What are we measuring?* Paper presented at the Society for Research in Child Development, San Francisco, March 1979.

Smith, W. S. *Evaluation of modules on sex-role stereotyping integrated into preservice elementary teacher education.* Paper presented at the annual meeting of the American Educational Research Association, Toronto, March 1978.

Sola, J. L., & Phye, G. D. *Development of sex-role orientation in adolescent females and its relationship to teacher ratings.* Unpublished paper, Iowa State University, 1979.

Spence, J. T. Traits, roles, and the concept of androgyny. In J. E. Gullahorn (Ed.), *Psychology and women in transition.* New York: Wiley, 1979.

Spence, J. T., & Helmreich, R. L. *Masculinity and femininity: Their psychological dimensions, correlates and antecedents.* Austin: Univ. of Texas Press, 1978.

Spence, J. T., & Helmreich, R. L. On assessing androgyny. *Sex Roles*, 1979, *5*, 721–738.

Spence, J. T., Helmreich, R., & Stapp, J. Ratings of self and peers on sex-role attributes and their relation to self-esteem and conceptions of masculinity and femininity. *Journal of Personality and Social Psychology*, 1975, *32*, 29–39.

Stein, A. H., & Bailey, M. M. The socialization of achievement orientation in females. *Psychological Bulletin*, 1973, *80*, 345–366.

Stein, A. H., Pohly, S. R., & Mueller, E. The influence of masculine, feminine, and neutral tasks on children's achievement behavior, expectancies of success and attainment values. *Child Development*, 1971, *42*, 195–207.

Stockard, J., Schmuck, P. A., Kempner, K., Williams, P., Edson, S. K., & Smith, M. A. *Sex equity in education.* New York: Academic Press, 1980.

Thompson, S. K., Gender labels and early sex role development. *Child Development*, 1975, *46*, 339–347.

Thompson, S. K., & Bentler, P. M. The priority of cues in sex discrimination by children and adults. *Developmental Psychology*, 1971, *5*, 181–185.

Trecker, J. L. Sex stereotyping in the elementary school curriculum. *Phi Delta Kappan*, 1973, *55*, 110–112.

Tryon, B. W. Beliefs about male and female competence held by kindergarteners and second graders. *Sex Roles*, 1980, *6*, 85–98.

Ullian, D. Z. The development of conceptions of masculinity and femininity. In B. Lloyd & J. Archer (Eds.), *Exploring sex differences*. London: Academic Press, 1976.

Unger, R. K. *Female and male: Psychological perspectives*. New York: Harper, 1979.

Urberg, K. A. *The development of androgynous sex-role concepts in young children*. Paper presented at the biennial meeting of the Society for Research in Child Development, San Francisco, 1979.

Waber, D. P. The meaning of sex-related variations in maturation rate. In J. E. Gullahorn (Ed.), *Psychology and women in transition*. New York: Wiley, 1979.

Waldrop, M. R., & Halverson, C. F. Intensive and extensive peer behavior: Longitudinal and cross-sectional analysis. *Child Development*, 1975, *46*, 19–26.

Wallach, M. A., & Kogan, N. *Modes of thinking in young children*. New York: Holt, 1965.

Weber, M. B., Freidin, M., & McKinnon, E. *The relationship between teachers' sex-role attitude and stereotypic reinforcement of student behavior*. Paper presented at the American Educational Research Association meeting, Toronto, 1978.

Weitz, S. *Sex roles: Biological, psychological and social foundations*. New York: Oxford Univ. Press, 1977.

Weitzman, L. J., & Rizzo, D. Images of males and females in elementary school textbooks in five subject areas. In *Biased textbooks*. Washington, D.C.: Resource Center on Sex Roles in Education, National Foundation for the Improvement of Education, 1974.

Whiting, B., & Edwards, C. P. A cross-cultural analysis of sex differences in the behavior of children aged three through eleven. *Journal of Social Psychology*, 1973, *91*, 171–188.

Williams, J. E., Bennett, S. M., & Best, D. L. Awareness and expression of sex stereotypes in young children. *Developmental Psychology*, 1975, *11*, 635–642.

Williams, J. H. *Psychology of women: Behavior in a biosocial context*. New York: Norton, 1977.

Wittig, M. A., & Peterson, A. C. (Eds.) *Sex-related differences in cognitive functioning: Developmental issues*. New York: Academic Press, 1979.

Wolf, T. M. Effects of live adult modeled sex-inappropriate play behavior in a naturalistic setting. *Developmental Psychology*, 1973, *9*, 120–123.

Women in words and images: Dick and Jane as victims: Sex stereotyping in children's readers. Princeton, N.J.: NOW, 1972.

Woolever, R. M. *Expanding elementary pupils' occupational and social role perceptions: An examination of teacher attitudes and behavior and pupil attitude change*. Unpublished doctoral dissertation, University of Washington, 1976.

Worell, J. Sex roles and psychological well-being: Perspectives on methodology. *Journal of Consulting and Clinical Psychology*, 1978, *46*, 777–791.

Worell, J. *Changing sex roles*. Invited address presented at a meeting of the Southeastern Psychological Association, New Orleans, March 1979. (ERIC Document Reproduction Service No. ED 170 066)

Worell, J. Gender and sex role contributions to life-span development. In R. Lerner (Ed.), *Individuals as contributors to their development: A lifespan perspective*. New York: Academic Press, 1981.

Worell, J., & Stilwell, W. E. *Psychology for teachers and students*. New York: McGraw-Hill, 1981.

2 / Peer relations

BONNIE TYLER

The purpose of this chapter is to review theory and research data relevant to the development of peer relations in children, giving special consideration to those aspects of peer behavior that are amenable to educational intervention. We know that, in the long run, successful peer relations not only enhance the quality and enjoyment of life but are basic to survival for both the individual and society. Thus, it is important that we understand how successful peer relations develop and how the conditions that facilitate their growth are created, particularly in the school setting.

The term *peers* is used here to designate children of approximately the same age and general level of development. *Peer relations* refers to social behaviors or acts carried out among peers, varying in intensity from superficial relations that may develop in a classroom to the more intense relations of the neighborhood gang. The terms *interpersonal relations, peer contacts,* and *peer interaction* are used synonymously with peer relations. The more sustained, intense, positive relations in which peers spontaneously seek the company of one another without situational factors or authorities demanding the contact are called *friendships.*

Interpersonal skill refers here to behaviors that are used effectively by a child to initiate and maintain interaction with peers. Interpersonal competence, social skills, and peer group skills are used interchangeably with this term. Interpersonal skill may be demonstrated in either socially

53

PSYCHOLOGICAL DEVELOPMENT
IN THE ELEMENTARY YEARS

acceptable or unacceptable behavior. For example, a child may reveal high-level interpersonal skills as a member of a group interacting positively in the classroom or as a member of a gang committing antisocial acts on the street. Positive behavior intended to benefit another child or group of children, without the actor anticipating an external reward, is labelled *prosocial behavior*. This includes such behaviors as generosity, sharing, sympathy, and helping. It is generally assumed that as children get older their motives become less external, with self-rewards—feelings of self-esteem, satisfaction, pride—determining much of their behavior. Underlying the acquisition of interpersonal skills is the development of a core of "social knowledge," which consists of a basic understanding of the nature of relations between people and some awareness of the types of interactions that allow these relations to succeed or cause them to fail. Clearly, social knowledge is considerably more complex than an accumulation of factual information about people.

In presenting the material on peer relations, the following topics will be discussed: (*a*) the current status of the field of peer relations; (*b*) theoretical bases for the development of peer relations; (*c*) development and peer experiences; (*d*) personal characteristics and peer acceptance; and (*e*) educational interventions and peer behavior.

CURRENT STATUS OF THE FIELD OF PEER RELATIONS

The empirical study of peer relations has experienced a slow start, particularly in the developmental period addressed in this book—middle childhood. At the turn of the century, Charles Cooley (1909) theorized that by the age of 12 the peer group has displaced the family as the prime influence on the child; he gave special attention to the ways in which group experiences affected the child's development. This emphasis, however, was unique to Cooley, for little interest was shown in understanding the role of peers until the 1930s when the number of investigations in this area reached a peak, with five times more references to children's behavior in groups from 1930 to 1939 than in the previous decade (Hare, Borgatta, & Bales, 1955). This increase was not maintained during the 1940s, when emphasis shifted to research on adult social behavior. About this time, methodology in the study of group behavior became more systematic, as direct observation procedures were utilized, and more reliable methods for recording data were devised. The Lewin, Lippitt, and White (1938) study, investigating the effects on young boys of different types of adult leadership, became a classic in research on small group behavior, primarily because it adapted experimental method to natural social situations. It was during this period that Moreno's sociometric technique became a well-accepted method of measuring acceptance in a group.

More recently, the study of peer relations has been influenced by shifts in areas of emphasis in child development. Probably the greatest influence has been the current focus on cognitive development, accompanied by an interest in the study of children's social cognition. Within this area special attention has been directed toward implications for the development of peer relations (Shantz, 1975), including the study of children's conceptions of others, children's ability to take another's perspective, and children's conceptions of friendship.

A second shift in emphasis has been toward the attribution of greater significance to the early years of life. This movement has directed attention to the beginnings of social development and the acquisition of social behavior in very young children (Lewis & Rosenblum, 1975). A third area, the fairly recent impetus to explain moral development in children, has prompted researchers to examine the role of social experiences in the formation of moral concepts and in the determination of moral judgments.

The consensus among many behavioral scientists engaged in these current areas of study is that interaction with peers from an early age is critical in the total development of the child. Some writers maintain that peer relations may be more important to the child's social development than associations with adults (Lewis & Rosenblum, 1975). Hartup's investigations have led to a similar conclusion, namely, that peer relations help the child acquire social and communication skills in a way that child–adult relations "either cannot or will not produce" (Hartup, 1977).

In explaining the uniqueness of children's peer relations, Piaget (1932/1965) contended that since peers are on an equal footing, their reciprocity results in a mutual understanding that is not present in children's interactions with adults. That is, children interact with adults according to rules that are impressed on them—rules that may be arbitrary, and in some instances even incomprehensible. On the other hand, when children interact, they work out procedures together, rather than imposing them on one another. Thus they understand what the other is thinking, having jointly arrived at the perspectives that they share (Piaget, 1932/ 1965). Other writers have carried this distinction even further, suggesting that child–child and child–adult relations are "not simply different, they may be the sources of two types of social understanding, with each serving a distinctive developmental function [Youniss & Volpe, 1978, p. 21]."

This differential reaction of children to adults and to peers is present even in infants. Several studies have shown that whereas infants respond negatively to an adult stranger, they respond positively to a child stranger (Greenberg, Hillman, & Grice, 1973; Lewis & Brooks, 1974). Maccoby and Masters (1970) conclude that the bonds children establish with peers are different from those earlier established between mother and child. For example, asking for help, attention, and nurturance does not decline with age but changes in nature, so that by preschool age, the child is not only asking for, but also giving help, attention, and nurturance to others. These data consistently indicate a special quality in the reciprocal interaction patterns that develop among peers. However, they do not go beyond these to define the critical factors that account for their development.

Cross-cultural observations reported by Whiting and Whiting (1975) suggest that peer interactions may be more important than parent–child interactions in teaching socialized aggression, a critical ingredient in competitive games and competitive verbal interchanges, such as arguing. Their data show that peers teach one another effective control of aggressive tendencies, so that even angry outbursts are controlled enough to prevent serious injury. In addition to control over negative social behaviors, their observations showed peers also reinforcing prosocial behaviors such as sharing and helping.

In contrast to this emphasis on the uniqueness of peer contacts and the critical role children play in reinforcing their peers' behavior, Konner stresses the importance of nonpeer (different age) children as facilitators of social interaction (in Lewis & Rosenblum, 1975). Looking back into history, he presents data showing that play groups among human hunter–gatherers, apes, and monkeys have been made up of juveniles of all ages. Konner concludes, "In man . . . and in the species most closely related to man, relationships between and among peers are of small importance compared with relationships among non-peer juveniles [Lewis & Rosenblum, 1975, p. 99]." Konner suggests that we may be harming youngsters by consistently putting them with children their own age. In his opinion, behavioral observations have exaggerated the importance of peers in the child's development.

In summary, much of our knowledge about the social world of children has, in the past, come from descriptions of the effects of peers as one of the primary agents of socialization in the life of a child. We now have research that goes beyond this descriptive approach to include several new ways of looking at peer relations. For example, consideration is now given to the ways in which the child contributes to his or her social development, in contrast to traditional socialization theory, which describes the socialized child as a product of the impact of significant persons and social institutions. By including the child's contribution, attention is directed toward the reciprocity between the child and persons in the environment, which means that the child's influence on

others' behavior is now considered. There has also been some movement away from describing peer behavior as the result of specific situations or specific conditions, implying that one causes the other. Rather,
more investigators are studying the dynamics of the development of peer
relations, with emphasis on developmental processes rather than on
static developmental stages. The goal is to explain what happens when a
child relates to a peer—what occurs, how it occurs, and the outcome of
the interaction. This approach has recently led to several systematic
attempts to explain the development of friendships in children (Asher &
Gottman, 1981; Damon, 1977; Youniss & Volpe, 1978).

Finally, while there has been considerable theorizing about peer interaction in the past, until recently few principles had been developed
that allowed for an integration of information about children's peer relations. Now theorists have begun to develop more systematic
frameworks for conceptualizing the processes involved in the child's
acquisition of skills in interpersonal relations. As mentioned earlier,
there has been a surge of interest in theories of the development of social
cognition in children and the implications of these theories for interpersonal relations (Damon, 1978). Another systematic approach utilizes a
drive reduction model for designing empirical studies of the role of
reward in developing positive attitudes toward other persons (Lott &
Lott, 1974). Several of these systems will be discussed in the next section, which is devoted to theory.

The direction in which we are moving in the study of peer relations
parallels, to some extent, current emphases in the field of child development. These changes point toward the building of a more dynamic
explanation of the role of peer relations in the child's development,
which should result in the production of more useful information about
how children learn to relate to one another.

THEORETICAL BASES FOR THE DEVELOPMENT
OF PEER RELATIONS

Currently there is incomplete agreement in the field of child development as to the importance of theory in explaining the process by
which children become knowledgeable about the nature of interpersonal
relations. Hartup (1970) contends that since the general principles of
behavior development provide a sufficient basis for understanding interaction, there is no need for a theory designed specifically to explain
the development of a child's interpersonal relations. In contrast, other
theorists maintain that the nature of relationships between children is
sufficiently different from adult–child relationships that this pattern of

interacting demands its own unique theory. A clear-cut solution to this conflict is not available at the moment. Differences will begin to be resolved when we can demonstrate which theories are effective, or ineffective, in explaining the dynamics of children's interpersonal relations.

The two major systems to be discussed here are cognitive–developmental theory and social learning theory. Writers chosen to represent the cognitive–developmental point of view are Piaget, Damon, Shantz, Selman, Flavell, Youniss, and Volpe. Included in the social learning area are Bandura, with his emphasis on modeling, and Lott and Lott, with their emphasis on reinforcement.

Cognitive–developmental theory

Piaget's observations of social behavior provide one basis for predicting children's responsiveness to peers on the basis of developmental stages (Piaget, 1932/1965). According to Piaget, the children we are addressing in this book are moving out of the egocentric stage, with individual needs lessening and social needs intensifying. Prior to this, however, egocentrism in the young child has served as a cognitive limitation inhibiting the development of peer relations. Even when part of a group, the child behaves idiosyncratically because of the difficulty experienced in taking another child's point of view. When peer contacts do occur, they begin to serve as effective means for breaking down egocentric thought, since the child is exposed to other points of view in the interaction (Kohlberg, 1976; Piaget, 1932/1965).

It should be noted here that several writers have questioned Piaget's conception of the preschool child as extremely egocentric, since studies find considerable social understanding in children of this age (Donaldson, 1978; Maratsos, 1973; Shatz & Gelman, 1973). Donaldson (1978) attempts to reconcile Piaget's findings with these data. For example, she suggests that children's difficulty with the "mountains" task is not for the reason Piaget indicates; rather, the "egocentric" children quite possibly do not understand what they are supposed to do. Donaldson (1978) concludes, "For all human beings, the taking of another point of view requires a certain effort, and the difficulty is bound to vary from one situation to another. . . . But the gap between children and adults is not so great in this respect as has recently been widely believed [pp. 55–56]."

In the next developmental stage defined by Piaget—the concrete operational period—the child is capable of cooperating and of coordinating different points of view. At the same time, during this period of middle childhood the peer group is developing a more solidly structured system of values and standards and a greater awareness of social norms. By the age of 7 years the child is extremely responsive to peer influences, and private beliefs are readily sacrificed for the group norms. As the child moves toward preadolescence, however, the need to conform begins to diminish, and reciprocal interactions become stronger. Now the child can accept feedback, as well as provide it, and can adjust to the rules of the peer group and society.

Piaget assumed a correlation between stages of social and cognitive development. However, studies to assess this parallel growth are limited, since most of the research within a Piagetian framework has focused on the child's growth in logical and physical thought. In one exception, Rardin and Moan (1971) tested Piaget's proposal of parallelism, namely, that peer relations develop parallel to the development of physical concepts. They also hypothesized that the quality of peer relations would effect the child's progress in cognitive development. Studying kindergarten through third-grade children, the quality of peer relations was judged by popularity rankings; cognitive development was assessed by two measures of physical concept development—conservation and classification; and social development ratings were a combination of three friendship measures and a "names not known" measure. The first proposal was well substantiated by their data—both cognitive and social skills developed in a similar manner from kindergarten through third grade. However, the quality of peer relations, as measured by popularity ranking, was not directly related to cognitive development, although it was closely related to social development.

Damon (1977), another cognitive–developmental theorist, agrees with Piaget's thesis that children's social knowledge develops in a predictable, age-related manner, paralleling cognitive development. However, he describes the process of learning to interact as a matter of reorganizing principles of social knowledge, rather than as a matter of developing structure, as Piaget conceptualized the process. According to Damon, these organizing principles are in operation at each developmental stage, although they become more complex and have different social referents as the child gets older.

This emphasis on children reorganizing principles in the process of learning to relate to peers is in contrast to the more traditional approach of describing developmental change in quantitative terms, for example, greater empathy, more friendships, fewer rejections. This more-or-less explanation is inadequate for Damon, who sees social development as involving qualitative changes unique to each child, rather than just "more of the same" (1977).

Uncertainty about the relationship between the development of cognitive and social operations has prompted extensive discussion of the relation between social knowing and cognitive knowing. Whereas

Piaget, for one, did not make a distinction between social and physical knowledge, most investigators do. For example, in a book entitled *The Development of Social Understanding* (Glick & Clarke-Stewart, 1978), all of the contributors make a distinction between cognitive knowing and the social domain of knowing. Glick maintains that having made the distinction between knowing objects and knowing people, it is difficult to apply Piaget's cognitive–developmental scheme to the social world, "since it remains a distinct possibility that people do not behave as objects do [Glick & Clarke-Stewart, 1978, p. 2]." Other writers suggest that because we are people, we have "built-in" ways of knowing about people, but not about things. However, the advantages for the individual of knowing about people as opposed to objects may be overshadowed by the more complicated realm of social knowledge. For example, social events are not only less stable than physical events, but situational factors play a more important, but not always predictable, role in social behavior. These complexities are confounded by the fact that as children relate to peers they must take into account feedback information, both from themselves about others and from the others being known.

Beyond the realm of social and cognitive knowledge, there is also uncertainty as to the interchangeability of principles of cognitive development and social development. It would seem to follow that if cognitive development is a prerequisite for social development, then cognitive principles should be related to social principles. These relationships have yet to be established.

Recently writers have extended the cognitive–developmental framework beyond the confines of logical reasoning to include social cognition. Although social cognition usually refers to thinking about social relations, social institutions, or social events, most of the research on children's social cognition has defined some measure of cognitive ability basic to the process of knowing and understanding others; for example, the ability to take the perspective of another (role taking), or to form a conception of others (person perception). This "perspective taking," or role taking, is defined as the ability to understand the point of view of the other in relation to that of the self. According to Kelly (1955), children can interact constructively with others because they develop concepts of them. To the extent that their concepts are not accurate, their interpersonal relations will suffer. This thesis that children come to understand their social world by becoming familiar with the characteristics of the people with whom they come in contact is fully developed in Mischel's book, *Understanding Other Persons* (1974).

Writing extensively in the area of social cognition, Shantz (1975) has defined social cognition as "the child's intuitive or logical representation of others, that is, how he characterizes others and makes inferences about their covert, inner psychological experiences [p. 258]." According to Shantz, the goal in studying social cognition is to understand how children learn to conceptualize other people and develop the ability to understand others' feelings, thinking, motives, and viewpoints. This knowledge is important not only because of the need to understand the social aspect of a child's development, but also because the success of children's social behavior is effected by the extent of their understanding of other people. Piaget (1932/1965, 1967) gave further emphasis to the relation between role-taking ability and social behavior by contending that peer interaction is a requisite for the development of role-taking skills, and vice versa.

In spite of this strong interest in social cognition, there has been no single, general theory advanced to explain its development. From Shantz's (1975) review of the work on social cognition, she concludes that the two most "promising" theories are those of Selman (1971) and Flavell (1974). Selman has developed a stage model theory in which role taking provides the structural basis for the child's learning about interpersonal relations (Selman, 1971; Selman & Byrne, 1974). From studies of friendships, developmental levels in conceptions of friendship are assigned based on childrens' progression through stages of understanding the point of view of others in relation to their own point of view. For example, children before the age of 6 years are described as unable to distinguish between their perceptions of social situations and others' perceptions. At this stage, children may know that a peer can have a different viewpoint but cannot say what it is; consequently they usually assume they are all thinking alike. During middle childhood, children can accurately infer what the other is thinking and feeling, as well as understand that they can be subjects for others' thoughts. Around the age of 12 years, well-developed role-taking ability allows adolescents to generalize beyond themselves and peers to the social system.

Selman (1971) has tested his stage theory of role taking and friendship development using a clinical interview and children's verbal responses to a story and dilemma situation. His data reveal developmental levels in children's conceptions of friendship and provide significant support for the thesis that children's friendship knowledge is a reflection of an underlying role-taking ability.

Although Flavell (1974) has been interested in the child's developing ability to be aware of others' thoughts, feelings, motives, and perceptions, his approach to explaining the development of social cognition in children goes beyond the description of role-taking stages to the analysis of a single act of role taking. Using an information-processing approach, his data show that each role-taking act involves four events: (*a*) an awareness of self and other; (*b*) needs presented by the situation; (*c*) inference about the other; and (*d*) application of what was inferred about the other subsequently resulting in appropriate behavior. For example, as a consequence of the child's inference, he or she may change approaches to a game or accommodate behavior to a peer about whom an inference has been made. Flavell notes that we have much more information about the developmental stages children go through in inferring others' thoughts than we have about how they manage to do so—that is, the process involved in making inferences. Flavell's model is based on empirical data obtained from children responding in game situations, telling stories from pictures, or planning game strategies by thinking out loud.

Youniss and Volpe (1978) do not accept the cognitive–developmental thesis that the major criterion for successful social development is the ability to take the other's point of view. Rather, they focus on peers working together to construct each other's perspective, so that when they take another's point of view, they both have shared in developing it. "Consequently, children's social development may best be described as a gradual transforming into principles and social practice the mutuality experienced by the child early in the peer relation and not as a fundamental structural–developmental transformation in children's role taking ability [1978, p. 2]."

In this "relational" theory, *relation* is defined as a continuous mutuality between the thought of self and other, implying that each child has insight into what social interaction means personally and to others. Youniss and Volpe (1978) maintain that individuals could not interact without this sharing of meaning, or mutuality. The process of interpersonal development is described as follows: A child is motivated to discover some order in social events in which he or she is involved, and the source for this order is in interpersonal experiences. However, interactions themselves do not provide this order; it must be found in the "procedures" of interaction. For example, one procedure occurs when authority is imposed on a child by someone who has control; another procedure occurs when neither the child nor the other person has power and the exchange is reciprocal. Interactions with both authorities and peers contribute to the process of acquiring knowledge about relating, which they call "socialization of thought" (Youniss & Volpe, 1978).

The empirical data Youniss and Volpe (1978) present to support relational theory are from analyses of clinical interviews with 130 children between the ages of 6 and 14. Questions are structured to elicit information about the ways children understand friendship relations ("How does someone show they are a friend?") and children's perceptions about the important characteristics of relations ("Describe a friend"). Their data support the developmental trends reported by other investigators, namely, the younger the child, the more often friendship relations are defined by fixed rules ("Friends should share") and friendship interactions are confined to physical activity (playing together). As children get older, a friendship relation is more likely to be described as having psychological components, with an ongoing, integrated system of rules, and friends taking the responsibility to initiate interaction. These developmental stages are described by Youniss and Volpe (1978): "First, children of about six to seven years of age understand the rules by which peers interact as friends in a practical way. . . . Children of age nine to ten years have carried these rules a step further. They have integrated them into a concept of relation [p. 11]." Thus Youniss and Volpe do not see the child's major social developmental task to be the acquisition of the ability to take the other's point of view. Rather, they contend that social perspectives, from the beginning, are dependent upon the mutuality of peer experiences.

In summary, cognitive–developmental theories suggest that social knowledge grows and changes as other cognitive operations do—as a function of maturational changes and environmental events. Although social development evidently proceeds through a sequence of stages, the nature of this pattern and the process accounting for its development have not been well established. However, information from cognitive–developmental theorists as to the nature of age changes in children has made a significant contribution to the understanding of the development of interpersonal skills and peer relations.

Social learning theory

This theory allows for little built-in "programming" to influence social development, as there is in cognitive–developmental theory. Social learning theorists assume that most human behavior is learned as a result of environmental events—human, societal, or situational. Thus young children are socialized to behave in ways appropriate to the situation and to adopt attitudes, values, and beliefs that may last throughout a lifetime. According to Bandura (1977), three regulative functions control children's social behavior: stimulus control, reinforcement control, and cognitive control. Stimulus control results from individuals responding to stimuli because of their association with positive or negative consequences. The most common stimulus cue is others' behavior, and since children tend to behave as other children do, it is a critical factor in understanding peer relations. Reinforcement control refers to the variety of reinforcements that acquire the power to regulate behavior, including symbolic rewards, social reinforcers, vicarious reinforcement, and self-reinforcement. In addition, several reinforcement parameters—for example, continuous reinforcement versus intermittent reinforcement—have been demonstrated to be important in determining reinforcement consequences. Cognitive control accounts for the effectiveness of reinforcement, since behavior is cognitively related to the reinforcer, thus giving significance to the child's perception of an event as possibly the most important determiner of his or her behavior. Bandura emphasized that the interactions of all three functions—stimulus, reinforcement, and cognitive control—must be considered when explaining behavior from a social learning point of view.

Two concepts basic to social learning theory are particulary critical in understanding the development of peer relations. These two concepts, modeling and reinforcement, will be considered here.

Modeling. According to social learning theory, behavior can be acquired in two ways: through direct experience and through observing others' behavior. It is assumed that everything learned directly can also be learned vicariously by observing others' behavior and the consequences of their behavior (Bandura, 1974). Thus, modeling, or imitation, using the terms interchangeably, is one of the primary concepts utilized in a social learning framework to explain the acquisition of behavior, and peer modeling is a basic process in children's socialization.

According to Bandura, when imitating peers brings about rewarding results for a child, the cues from peer models are strong determinants of behavior. On the other hand, when a child sees peer models punished for their behavior, the child will tend to select other models or other behaviors to imitate. Thus, when the teacher leaves the classroom and the children who misbehave get attention, it is rewarding to join them. However, if the children see their peers punished for their misbehavior when the teacher returns, the modeled behavior is inhibited. This principle has been demonstrated in a study by Bandura (1965), in which children observed physically and verbally aggressive models who were either punished, rewarded, or neither punished nor rewarded for their aggression. The children who saw a model punished were less aggressive than children who saw a model rewarded or saw a model receive no consequences. Other studies on aggression have demonstrated that aggressive behavior may be learned through modeling whether the model is presented live, on film, or in verbal reports (Bandura, Ross, & Ross, 1961, 1963).

As in the study just described, much of the empirical data on modeling involves using an adult as a model, frequently modeling prosocial behavior. In a typical modeling study, children observe an adult engaged in prosocial acts and are then given the opportunity to imitate that behavior. The findings have consistently shown an increase in children's generosity following the modeling of prosocial behavior. In one study, children who imitated a model's donations of candy were also more generous than control subjects in sharing pennies with other children in the study (Elliot & Vasta, 1970). This altruistic behavior was demonstrated to continue for several months after the children had observed the modeling of prosocial behavior (Rice & Grusec, 1975; Rushton, 1975).

In some research the effects of *peer* modeling have been investigated. In studying third and fourth graders' resistance to temptation, Rosenkoetter (1973) found that children who observed a peer model yield to temptation were likely to do the same. This finding is corroborated in a review of the moral development literature (Hoffman, 1970), in which the author concludes that peer models clearly have a disinhibitory but not an inhibitory effect on other children's behavior. In other words, children are most likely to imitate the misbehavior of peer models (Rosenkoetter, 1973; Ross, 1971; Stein, 1967). In studying preferences for peer models, Hartup and Coates (1967) found that children's past relations with peers affected their choice of models. Specifically, children who had had positive peer relations imitated the peers who had been rewarding to them, and children who had infrequently been reinforced by peers imitated peers with whom they had had no contact.

In summary, systematic investigations of modeling have been concentrated in the areas of prosocial behavior and moral development, with the desired behavior modeled more often by an adult than by a child. The implications of the findings of these studies for peer relations are not known, although one would expect that some of the effects of modeling prosocial behavior could be generalized to children's interactions with peers. A further question can be raised concerning the effectiveness of adult modeling in contrast to peer modeling, which one might expect to vary as situational factors vary, for example, status of adult and peer and type of behavior being modeled. But the area of major importance, and an area that until recently has been overlooked, is the role of modeling in the development of social behavior in children. Investigations in this area are needed, with both adults and peers modeling effective interpersonal behavior.

Reinforcement theory. Within social learning theory, there are several approaches to explaining interpersonal relations that employ reinforcement principles. The model to be discussed here, developed by Lott and Lott (1974), stems from a behavioral orientation dealing with the role of reward in the formation of positive interpersonal attitudes. Although there are numerous studies of the determinants of interpersonal attraction that conclude, "you like the people who reward you," these authors see this as an inadequate explanation for liking behavior. Rather, their approach has been to analyze the meaningfulness of reward and related variables, including the individual's past experiences, needs, and values. In addition, they have studied the applicability of general learning theory principles for making predictions regarding the development of positive attitudes toward others. They suggest that if general learning principles can be used to derive the antecedents of liking, and also to explain its development, then liking is no different from any other behavioral phenomenon, and the outcomes of liking should be predictable.

The basic hypothesis regarding the antecedents of personal attraction, as stated by Lott and Lott, is that "receipt of reward in a person's presence is a primary antecedent for the development of positive attitudes toward that person [1974, p. 188]." Through extensive research they have systematically investigated the antecedents of liking within a general learning framework, defining interpersonal attraction as an anticipatory response. These authors assume that the conditions that influence anticipatory responses in general will also influence an individual's acquiring a liking for another person, with the liked person identified as a secondary reinforcer. The validity of such a role has been empirically demonstrated (Lott & Lott, 1960).

While Lott and Lott have not specifically applied their model to the development of interpersonal attraction in children, the principles they have derived can appropriately be applied to children's social behavior. These principles can be stated as follows:

1. Children will like a peer who directly rewards them (The more you do for me, the more I like you).
2. Children will indirectly be influenced to like a peer by the nature (good–bad) of his or her characteristics (I like a peer better if he or she is a good person).
3. Children will like peers who positively evaluate them better than peers who give negative evaluations (The higher the opinion you have of me, the better I like you).
4. Children who first react negatively to peers and subsequently react positively are liked more by peers than children who are consistently positive (I like you more if you've changed from disliking me to liking me).
5. Children like peers who have social and personality characteristics similar to their own (I like peers best who are like me).

6. Children like peers whose attitudes are similar to their own (I like peers who think as I do).
7. Being rewarded by the teacher influences children to like peers more (Good feelings about myself help me like peers better).
8. Successfully achieving the goals of the group results in children preferring peers in their own group rather than peers outside the group (Sharing success with peers increases liking for these peers).

Lott and Lott present significant empirical data in support of these principles. In addition, they have empirically demonstrated a relation between the development of attraction and reward (Lott & Lott, 1960), between attraction and frequency of reward (James & Lott, 1964), between variable reward conditions and immediacy of reward (Lott, Aponte, Lott, & McGinley, 1969), and between variable reward conditions and desirability of the rewarding stimuli (Lott, Bright, Weinstein, & Lott, 1970). The unique feature of Lott and Lott's model is their utilization of general learning theory as a source of hypotheses regarding antecedents of positive interpersonal attitudes, as well as a base for predicting outcomes of liking. Their perception of the significance of the role of reward is described as follows: "It seems to us that while only a small number of investigators unabashedly make systematic use of reinforcement-related principles to generate stable hypotheses regarding interpersonal attraction, a great many investigators actually manipulate conditions of reward in their investigations and utilize the concept of reward to explain their empirical results [Lott & Lott, 1974, pp. 188–198]."

In summary, social learning theory discounts the influence of internal factors in children's social development, attributing the major part of their learning to environmental forces. According to this theory, children acquire interpersonal skills by means of both direct and observational learning. In explaining the development of peer relations, then, reinforcement is seen as a significant model for direct learning, and modeling assumes importance in observational learning.

DEVELOPMENT AND PEER EXPERIENCES

As discussed earlier, the contribution of peer interaction to a child's development begins early, since there seems to be no time when children are not responsive to peers. The ultimate indication of positive peer power is provided by infants responding with "concentration, concern, and some negative affect" to strange adults, yet with "great interest and positive affect" to strange peers (Lewis & Rosenblum, 1975). We do not know, of course, which comes first: attainment of a developmental stage that allows the child to benefit from peer interaction or experience with peers that triggers developmental change in the child. Rather than attempt to solve this riddle, we will assume an interaction effect and investigate the developmental benefits the child derives from peer interaction.

As the individual moves through middle childhood, certain areas of development are especially vulnerable to peer influence. Three of these, aggression, morality, and conformity, will be discussed here.

Aggression

Developmentally, aggression follows an age-related pattern. Immediately after early childhood, aggressive behavior declines for most children, followed by an increase in person-directed, retaliatory, and hostile out-bursts during the elementary school years. As the child moves through middle childhood, aggression tends to become more verbal than physical. Beyond the cues provided by the developmental stage of the child, most writers agree that the specific occurrence of aggressive behavior is difficult to predict. In his book dealing with the analysis of aggression, Bandura (1973) describes in detail the complex ways in which a child's expectancies can bring about antisocial aggression at one time and prosocial behavior at another.

In attempting to account for the acquisition of aggressive behavior, Patterson and Cobb (1971) have demonstrated that peers are one of the primary sources of direct reinforcement of aggression. At the same time, control over aggressive impulses can often be more effectively taught through peer contacts than through adult contacts. Much of the evidence to support this differential effect comes from animal research. For example, studies of nonhuman primates show that adequate socialization among juveniles requires rough and tumble play that is both aggressive and playful (Hamburg & Van Lawick-Goodall, 1974). Such play experiences are common to the young in all primate species, including humans, where peers play the role of teacher in establishing the rules of give and take. So although adults may spend a great deal of time attempting to control aggression in children, it may be that peers are more effective in defining the appropriate limits of aggressive behavior and in providing training in its control.

Although there is an absence of evidence to support a direct relation between aggressive behavior and acceptance or rejection by peers, the data do indicate that inappropriate aggression is characteristic of children not accepted by peers, and "friendly" aggression is more common with popular children than nonpopular children (Hartup, 1970). Hartup discusses the effects of the absence of peer interaction on the development of aggression: "Children who show . . . unusual modes of aggressive behavior, or children who are unusually timid in the presence of aggressive attack, may be lacking exposure to certain kinds of contacts with peers. . . . Peer contacts that never allow for aggressive display . . . may be precursors of malfunctioning in the aggression system [Hartup, 1976, p. 207]."

Another influence in the development of aggression that indirectly involves peers is television. Although we will not examine the effects on the child of TV violence, we will discuss briefly some of the data relating to its effects on aggressive behavior among peers. Liebert and Baron (1972) showed either a TV sports sequence (neutral) or a violence sequence (from *The Untouchables*) to 5- to 6- and 8- to 9-year-old boys and girls. Following this exposure, the children were given an opportunity to hurt a child they thought was in the next room. The children who had seen the violence film hurt the other child for a longer period of time than did those who had viewed the neutral film. Similarly, preschoolers and first graders who viewed violent cartoons in a classroom setting became more aggressive against peers both on the playground and in the school (Ellis & Sekyra, 1972; Stein & Friedrich, 1972; Stever, Applefield, & Smith, 1971).

Examining the long-range effects of television violence, a longitudinal study was completed with data from 400 children at the age of 9 years and again at the age 19 (Lefkowitz, Eron, Walder, & Huesmann, 1972). Based on several measures of aggression, including peer ratings, findings showed a significant relationship between exposure to TV at age 9 and aggressive behavior at age 19, for boys. This cumulative, adverse effect was evident across the entire range of boys, not only those who were already very aggressive at age 9. These data suggest that although peers may be a primary source of reinforcement as well as control in the development of aggression in children, television violence is also a contributor to the development of aggressive behavior toward peers.

Morality

A second area in the child's development in which peers play a major role is the learning of morality. Moral development and behavior have been the subject of much theorizing and research in the last two decades (Hoffman, 1970; Kohlberg, 1969, 1976). In a recent book addressing topics related to moral development (Lickona, 1976), Saltzstein describes a relation between social development and moral development that changes as a function of age. He suggests that at Kohlberg's Stage 2 in moral development, peers will respond to one another in terms of material reciprocity (I'll give you this, if you'll give me that), and at Stage 3 in terms of emotional reciprocity (I'll try to please you because I like you and want you to like me). At Stage 4, however, adults again take on greater importance than peers, since the child is now feeling dutiful toward traditional authority. As the child approaches adolescence, peers assume more significance. Saltzstein's account of the relation between social development, peer interaction, and moral development is primarily descriptive, with little empirical data to support his contentions. Although there are data to support a parallel progression in moral and cognitive developmental stages, there is little evidence to support such a relation between moral and social development. However, it would seem to follow that the move from an objective moral stage (concern with absolute rules) in early childhood to a more subjective orientation in later childhood would be facilitated to a large extent by the child's involvement in group decisions and peer give-and-take. This movement is strongly supported by the nonauthoritarian climate of the peer group in contrast to the less reciprocal interactions characteristic of the adult–child relation.

In a study in which the social behavior of preadolescents was investigated, Keasey (1971) found that children who belonged to more clubs and social groups achieved higher stages of moral reasoning, as measured by Kohlberg's moral judgment interview. Going beyond his analysis of frequency of social participation, Keasey studied the relation between quality of peer interaction and the development of moral reasoning (1971). Using self-reports of leadership, teacher ratings of leadership and popularity, peer reports of leadership, and friendship choices by peers as criteria for quality of peer interaction, the data showed that among preadolescents each of these factors was positively related to level of moral development, again using Kohlberg's moral judgment interview. Further studies of the effects of peer group participation show that children have been helped to make more mature judgments following participation in group discussions about moral conflicts (Jensen & Hughston, 1971; Kohlberg, 1976).

Conformity

A third developmental area in which children are significantly influenced by peers is in conforming behavior. Although conformity has traditionally been defined as yielding to group pressure, implying a somewhat undesirable action, it recently has been conceptualized more positively as "modeling behavior practiced in groups" (Worell & Stilwell, 1981). According to the latter definition, children might conform by choosing to behave in a way consistent with their reference group; by the former definition, a child would be more likely to change an attitude, or behavior, because of group pressure. Regardless of definition, the motive behind conformity behavior is often seen as extrinsic in nature— fear of retaliation, hope for reward, or deference to an authority in the group. Even though children may expect peer approval to depend on saying a particular thing or making a particular choice, there will be significant differences in how often a child says or does these things because the importance of peer approval will be different to each child. Thus, some children may value peer approval more than parental approval, or vice versa, whereas for other children approval from anybody may have minimal value.

Most of the research data on conformity indicate that a child's responsiveness to the influence of peers clearly follows a curvilinear relation to age, with conforming behavior reaching a peak during middle childhood and decreasing as the child approaches adolescence (Hartup, 1970). Data reported by Costanzo and Shaw (1966) did not confirm this curvilinear relationship. Rather, they found that conformity is not characteristic of 7–9-year-old children, but reaches a maximum in early adolescence (ages 11–13) and decreases after that (ages 15–21).

Although conformity behavior is presumed to occur frequently in the area of moral judgments, there is little empirical research investigating peer influences on moral behavior, as noted earlier. There are some studies of peer influence in the area of perceptual judgments. Landsbaum and Willis (1971) tested the hypothesis that conformity behavior characterizes early adolescence but diminishes in later adolescence. They point out that although there is general agreement among developmentalists that children in early adolescence are rigidly conforming, there are few studies to support this conclusion. Boys and girls aged 13–14 years and 18–21 years were compared on their readiness to be influenced by a partner in making judgments about length of lines. Their data show the younger group to be significantly more vulnerable to the influence of peers than the older adolescents. Using a similar task, Saltzstein, Diamond, and Belenky (1972) studied seventh graders' conformity to erroneous peer judgments of the lengths of lines and its relation to the children's stage of moral development. Using Kohlberg's stages of moral reasoning, they found that Stage 3 moral reasoning children (age 7–8) conformed to the erroneous judgments more than children in lower Stages 1 and 2 (before age 7) or higher Stages 4 and 5 (age 11–12). The older children were the least conforming. In a later study involving children aged 5–14 years, Saltzstein and Osgood (1975) report that the younger children felt little need to conform to group requests, whereas the older children felt a personal loyalty and commitment to conform. In explaining these inconsistent findings, Saltzstein (1976) suggests that this type of research does not take into account all of the complexities of the relationship between moral development and conformity. Nevertheless, he concludes, "in general, the moral development of the child should determine the kind and amount of the child's susceptibility to peer and adult influence [Lickona, 1976, p. 264]." Thus, the emphasis here is on the child's moral stage as the primary "determiner" of the extent of conformity to the peer group, rather than on peers as the determiner.

Other writers have suggested the need to take into account variables other than age or developmental level. For example, in analyzing their conformity data by sex of subject, Iscoe, Williams, and Harvey (1963) found a tendency toward a decrease in conformity after age 12 for females but not for males. In a later study (1964), these authors found significant differences related to race, with conformity for black children decreasing after age 9 but for white children after age 12. Other factors that have been shown to effect the relationship between conforming behavior and level of moral development include ambiguity of the task being performed and accuracy of the subjects' judgment (Hoving, Hamm, & Galvin, 1969).

As noted earlier, yielding to peer pressure is frequently perceived as negative, especially by parents, and perhaps as developmentally "unsound." It may be just as appropriate, however, to consider conformity behavior in most instances as a constructive step toward learning interpersonal skills, with the peer group serving as a supportive force in reinforcing compliance to, and punishing deviation from, group norms. It is in this context that Worell and Stilwell's (1981) concept of conformity as "modeling behavior practiced in groups" is especially meaningful.

In summary, the data reported here suggest that peer experiences are a primary influence in the child's mastery of aggression, morality, and conformity; they are, no doubt, influential in other areas of development as well. Since we do not know precisely the consequences of a peer deficient childhood, a next step is to determine the extent to which successful peer relations are critical to later adjustment.

Peer acceptance and adjustment

According to Hartup, "Access to agemates, acceptance by them, and constructive interaction with them are among the necessities of child development [1976, p. 215]." The implication here is that an absence of positive peer relations is a primary contributor to inadequate development. Unfortunately, the majority of studies related to this question are of cross-sectional design; consequently, the long-term developmental effects of poor peer relations have not been traced. For example, one early study reported that the rate of social isolation in childhood was higher in adult mentally ill patients than in normal adults (Kohn & Clausen, 1955). Similarly, Stengel (1971) found that early social isolation was a basic ingredient in factors related to a high suicide rate in adults. In neither of these studies, however, was the developmental course of the isolation investigated.

In one longitudinal study designed to discover factors significant to later mental adjustment, Cowen, Pederson, Babijian, Izzo, and Tost (1973) reported that peer ratings made during the third grade were the best predictors of mental health status in young adults. In this study, the children whom peers had described negatively were disproportionately represented in a communitywide psychiatric register 11 years later. Roff (1961) also reported a positive relation between the quality of a child's behavior with peers and social adjustment in adulthood. In a later study of 40,000 urban children, Roff, Sells, and Golden (1972) found that children who were less liked by peers were more likely to be involved in delinquent behavior when observed 4 years later. This relation was true for middle and upper class children, but not for lower class children. Bronson's analysis (1966) of data from the Berkeley Growth Study, covering four periods from ages 5 to 16, revealed that boys who were socially reserved displayed more hostile than friendly behavior to peers, showed higher anxiety and discomfort, and were less active than those who were involved with peers. Low peer interaction for girls related to vulnerability, low activity, caution, and passivity.

Clearly the data in this area are limited, and restricted to correlational studies, thus not allowing us to infer a cause and effect relation between later maladjustment and isolation from peers or nonacceptance in a peer group, However, available evidence suggests that acceptance by peers may be related to general adjustment in adolescence and adulthood. There are many other factors influencing adjustment that have not been considered in these studies—home relationships, family crises, and academic failure, for example—all of which may contribute to social isolation and later adjustment problems.

PERSONAL CHARACTERISTICS AND PEER ACCEPTANCE

In addition to understanding the influence peers exert on the child in specific developmental areas, it is also necessary to consider how personal characteristics of the child influence acceptance or rejection by peers. Two excellent chapters on peer relations contain material relevant to this topic, one by Campbell (1964), and a later chapter by Hartup (1970). Rather than repeat this material, findings of the studies these authors have reviewed will be summarized and more recent research findings will be presented in greater detail.

A variety of personal characteristics have been studied, some of which seem obviously predictive of peer acceptance (e.g., friendliness, sociability) and some clearly predictive of peer rejection (e.g., social indifference, withdrawal, rebelliousness, hostility) (Campbell, 1964). Other variables studied are less clearly related to any specific peer behavior (e.g., birth order, name of child). It should be noted that here again most of the research data in this area are correlational, thus allowing only for a statement of relationship. Even then, unwarranted inferences must be avoided. For example, although the data may indicate a significant correlation between friendliness and peer acceptance, one cannot infer that the nonfriendly child will necessarily be rejected by peers. Nor can conclusions be drawn as to the developmental sequence (i.e., which came first, friendliness or acceptance?).

In this section, we will discuss the effect on peer acceptance of the following factors: self-esteem, adjustment, intelligence, sex, social class, race, dependency, cooperation, and physical and mental disabilities.

Self-esteem

Research findings do not consistently confirm a positive relation between self-esteem and peer acceptance, as might be expected. Several earlier studies conclude that a child's self-image does influence the way peers perceive him or her (Campbell, 1964), and one study (Reese, 1961) reports a curvilinear relation (i.e., moderately high self-concept children are more accepted by peers than either low or very high self-concept children).

The child's skill at coping with peer rejection is related to self-esteem. In studying children's perception of interpersonal failure, Dweck and Goetz (1977) found that children tend to respond in one of two ways: some blame temporary conditions, such as lack of effort or misunderstanding that could be corrected, and others blame their own failure or lack of ability. When blaming themselves, children are less likely to initiate interaction again. Kohn's hypothesis (1971) that children are instrumental in determining their peers' approach to them means that when children communicate to peers how they feel about themselves, their attitude is reflected in the peers' response to them. Kohn's prediction that the child will get back what he or she "puts out" is supported by data from 6-year-old subjects—peers responded hostilely to the hostile children and in a friendly manner to friendly children.

Adjustment

Numerous early studies reported a positive relation between general emotional adjustment in children and peer acceptance, with popularity the most frequently used measure of acceptance (Trent, 1954). A later study by Ullmann (1957) showed that maladjustive behavior (e.g., dropping out of school) was more likely to occur among children without friends. A summary of the findings in Hartup's review (1970) shows that socially rejected children are not as friendly or outgoing as accepted children, they need more emotional support from adults, they are more anxious, and their aggressive behavior is frequently inappropriate.

It should be noted here that frequency of interaction with peers cannot be taken as an indication of popularity. In fact, some data suggest that there is little relation between frequency of interaction and acceptance by peers (Gottman, 1977). In other words, some children who are well liked may interact minimally, and other children who are disliked may interact frequently with peers.

Intelligence

There have been many correlational studies hypothesizing a relation between intelligence and peer acceptance. In most of the findings, correlations have been positive and usually significant (Hartup, 1970). In Campbell's (1964) review, it was concluded that creativity, as well as intelligence, led to acceptance by peers. In a related area, academic performance has been shown to be positively correlated with peer acceptance, with low-achieving children having fewer friends (Gronlund, 1959). Similarly, Sells and Roff (1967) reported a significant correlation between school marks and peer acceptance for children in the fourth to seventh grades. In attempting to explain the relation between academic achievement and peer acceptance, Isen, Horn, and Rosenhan (1973) hypothesize that children feel good after success experiences and as a result are more concerned with other children. In their study of children's generosity following experiences of success or failure at a game, the children who succeeded were more generous than those who failed, at least when the experimenter was not present. When contributions were made in the experimenter's presence, the groups were equal.

Sex

A large body of research data indicates that, from preschool to adolescence, sex of peer is a primary element in friendship choices and in peer group formations (Campbell, 1964; Hartup, 1970). Although children consistently prefer like-sex peers to opposite-sex peers, this sex cleavage is least strong in early childhood, becomes stronger in middle childhood, and reaches a peak in preadolescence. Data reported by Asher (1973) and Singleton (1974) corroborate this strong preference for same-sex friends. In a recent study of gender attitudes in children (Zalk & Katz, 1978), children in the second and fifth grades were shown slides of children interacting in a school setting and asked which of the two children in the slide should be credited with, or blamed for, the behavior portrayed. One prediction was that peer identity would be the strongest motivator and both boys and girls would favor their own sex. The results showed that boys chose more boys in both positive and negative situations, whereas girls chose more boys in negative situations and their own sex in positive situations. Thus the prediction was supported except for the boys' choice of boys for the negative situation.

In investigating whether sex-appropriate behavior results in greater peer acceptance, Marshall (1961) found this to be the case for boys but not for girls. Although we might speculate that expectancies for sex-appropriate behavior are changing as a function of today's less rigid sex-role stereotypes, there are no recent studies in this area to support such a notion. However, there are data in a related area. In contrast to earlier studies that have shown girls' preferences for their own sex role to be relatively weak (Broverman, Vogel, Broverman, Clarkson, & Rosenkrantz, 1972; Ward, 1972), a recent study (Silvern, 1977) finds that fourth and sixth grade boys and girls judge their own sex role as more desirable than the opposite sex role, with girls' opinions of feminine traits perceived as stronger and more desirable than boys' judgments of their traits of masculinity.

In an attempt to overcome the social distance between boys and girls, DeVries and Edwards (1972) organized a seventh-grade math class so that one group was rewarded for individual achievement and another for team achievement. In choosing friends at the end of 4 weeks, the number of cross-sex choices in the team group was considerably larger than in the "no team" group. It seems clear that as more school classes become gender-integrated as a function of Title IX regulations and greater awareness of inappropriate sex restrictions, more peer groups will spontaneously become heterosexual.

Apart from preferences in choice of peers, there are significant sex differences in other areas of interaction. Noting the lack of information on how relationships get started, McGrew (1972) investigated "initiation" skills and entry behaviors, that is, children's initiation of peer interaction and their entry into new peer situations in the nursery school. McGrew reported no sex differences in children's initiation behaviors, but found clear-cut sex differences in their entry behaviors. In contrast to girls, boys were more fearful, laughed less, walked less, and looked at other children less. However, after the fifth day in the new situation, these differences disappeared. Sex differences were also observed in children's responses to newcomers in that girls were more attentive and nurturant than boys toward a new child. There are no data to indicate whether these sex differences persist as the child moves into elementary school.

Race

Data on the relation between race and peer acceptance do not present a consistent picture—peer acceptance among majority group children and racial minorities is quite variable. Some studies show cleavage to be stronger in the majority group; in other studies it is stronger in the minority group. Racial cleavage among blacks and whites is found not only in racially mixed groups but also in subcultures that are well integrated or highly segregated. Within mixed-race peer groups, children of minority groups are significantly less popular than children of majority groups (Hartup, 1970). When third-grade children were asked to rate each of their classmates as a work partner and play partner, both black and white subjects rated members of their own race higher (Singleton, 1974). In a study of friendships among fourth and fifth grade children (Asher, 1973), each child was asked to name five best friends. With a school population of about 40% blacks, children made fewer cross-race selections than would have occurred by chance. In a similar study (Shaw, 1973), in which children were asked whom they preferred to be with, both blacks and whites overselected from their own race. Of the 80% white children and 20% black in this study, roughly 33% of the black children's choices were white, and 6% of the white children's choices were black. Similar results have been reported in other recent research (Bartel, Bartel, & Grill, 1973; Gerard, Jackson, & Conolley, 1975).

In contrast, Singleton and Asher's (1977) results give a positive picture of interracial relations in several third grade classrooms. Although both race and sex were found to be significant in determining sociometric ratings by peers, race accounted for a very small percentage (1%) of the variance. The authors attribute this almost complete absence of race effect to the fact that these third-grade children had been together since kindergarten in racially integrated classrooms.

The data from most of these studies indicate that even though children are more likely to choose friends among their own race, there are a substantial number of cross-race friendships.

Dependency

There is little research on the relationship between dependency behavior in children and acceptance by peers; consequently, data from studies of both elementary and preschool children will be included. First, it is important to point out a distinction that children make in their perception of dependency in peers. On the one hand, seeking help and approval from adults is seen as an acceptable kind of dependency, whereas seeking affection or attention in a negative fashion is seen as immature dependency, leading to nonacceptance by peers. This distinction is supported in studies of preschoolers that show that emotional dependence on adults and excessive time spent interacting with them not only makes children less popular with peers (Maccoby & Masters, 1970; Moore & Updegraff, 1964), but also interferes with their movement into the peer culture. In studies of elementary school children in which the relation between popularity–likability and mature–immature dependency was analyzed, the results were similar to those with preschool children (Campbell & Yarrow, 1958; Wiggins & Winder, 1961; Winder & Rau, 1962). So although the data are limited in this area, they do suggest that children are highly discriminating in their perception of dependency behavior in peers; the differentiation they make may lead to acceptance or rejection of their peers.

Cooperation

There is a positive relation between peer acceptance and a child's willingness to comply with group rules and cooperate with peers in a group situation (Hartup, 1970). In addition, it has been demonstrated that peers are more likely to cooperate voluntarily with an individual child who asks for something than with a child who aggressively seeks it (Spivak & Shure, 1974). Ladd and Oden (1977) demonstrated that the child who was cooperative and helpful to peers had more best friends and was more valued as a playmate and work companion than the uncooperative child. In attempting to produce this positive behavior, Oden and Asher (1977) found that coaching children in social skills, including cooperation, resulted in increased overall acceptance by peers. Similarly, cooperative behavior increased when children in group situations were reinforced for cooperating, working together, or sharing a reward (Altman, 1971; Kagan & Madsen, 1971). When children are involved in group reward, they become friendlier, more cooperative, and less antagonistic toward each other (Bryan, 1975; Krumboltz & Krumboltz, 1972). Children also have been shown to like each other better after playing a game together, with everybody winning prizes (Blau & Rafferty, 1970; Lott & Lott, 1960).

Studying children from the fourth to eleventh grades, Emmerich (1974) found that cooperation was highly valued in the fourth and fifth grades, but declined in importance after that. Brighter children in the fourth and fifth grades highly valued cooperation in peers; this valuing reached its peak later in less bright children during the sixth and seventh grades. The author cautions that there is a critical point in development where lowered cooperation may indicate autonomy rather than un-cooperativeness. Finally, Ceresnie (1974) investigated cooperative behavior as it relates to role-taking ability and found no relation between the two.

Physical and mental disabilities

There is consensus in the research literature that physical attractiveness has a significant influence on children's acceptance of peers, beginning at an early age. Dion and Berscheid (1974) found that among 4- to 6-year-olds the unattractive child was relatively less popular than the attractive child. In addition, unattractive children, particularly males, were more frequently rated as exhibiting antisocial behavior than were attractive children. In selecting peers with whom they would like to be friends, physical appearance had a significant influence on children's choices (Kleck, Richardson, & Ronald, 1974). In spite of the critical role that attractiveness plays in peer acceptance, there seems to be considerable ambiguity as to what constitutes an acceptable definition of attractiveness. After reviewing the literature on physical attractiveness, Berscheid and Walster (1974) conclude that there is no agreement on a definition of *beauty*. Yet Cross and Cross (1971) found no significant differences among choices made by different age groups (ages 7, 12, 17, and adult) as to "most beautiful face."

Children with specific physical problems are even more likely to encounter rejection by peers. This is true for children with minor physical difficulties, such as lack of coordination or slowness in running, as well as for physically disabled children. Ten- and 11-year-old children from a variety of social classes, regions, and ethnic groups ranked figures of disabled children low in desirability, with high agreement on the type of disability considered most undesirable (Richardson, Goodman, Hastorf, & Dornbusch, 1961). Siperstein and Gottlieb (1977) examined the effects of physical appearance and academic performance on attitudes of fourth- and fifth-grade students toward handicapped children. Competent and nonstigmatized children were rated more favorably than incompetent and physically stigmatized children. These findings are supported by a review of several studies on children's attitudes toward their handicapped peers (Wylie, 1976) that concluded: (*a*) children become aware of physical handicaps at about 4 years of age; (*b*) nonhandicapped children tend to have a negative attitude toward the handicapped; (*c*) younger children have less negative attitudes than older children; and (*d*) contact with handicapped children does not necessarily reduce negative attitudes toward them.

Similar negative attitudes are expressed toward mentally retarded peers. Gottlieb and Gottlieb (1977) questioned junior high students about their attitudes toward mentally retarded and crippled children and rated their responses for same- and opposite-sex stereotypes. Their results indicated that stereotypic attitudes toward the crippled child were more favorable than attitudes toward the mentally retarded child. The sex of the child rating, or being rated, did not affect attitude scores. With the implementation of Public Law 94–142, and the resulting mainstreaming in the schools, the number of studies on attitudes toward children with learning disabilities has increased significantly. Although the majority of these investigations have been concerned with assessing and/or changing teachers' attitudes, some have studied attitudes of peers toward children with learning disabilities. Bruininks (1978) found that learning-disabled students in elementary school mainstreaming programs were significantly less socially accepted than their classmates in regular classrooms. In addition, the learning-disabled students were less accurate than their classmates in assessing their own personal status in the group. In another study in which learning-disabled children were shown to be less popular than their peers, a major factor in their social rejection was their verbal communication habits (Bryan & Bryan, 1978). Bryan (1976) did a follow-up study of 25 learning-disabled elementary school children who had been rated on peer popularity a year earlier. Compared to the normal group, the learning-disabled children received a higher number of rejection ratings and a lower number of acceptance ratings, leading the author to conclude that children's friendship and rejection ratings are reliable over time.

Several approaches to improving children's attitudes toward handicapped peers have been studied. Siperstein, Gottlieb, & Bak (1977) analyzed the effects of group discussion on sixth graders' attitudes toward normal and handicapped peers. They found that children's individual attitudes toward academically incompetent, abnormal-appearing children became more negative after group discussions. However, the discussions did not affect attitudes toward the normal children. In an effort to improve the social status of retarded children among their nonretarded classmates, educable mentally retarded children mainstreamed into third, fourth, and fifth grade classrooms worked on highly structured tasks in small cooperative groups, along with nonretarded classmates. Two to 4 weeks after completion of the 8-week treatment, social acceptance of the retarded children by their nonretarded peers was significantly better than that of the control group children (Ballard, Corman, Gottlieb, & Kaufman, 1977). After studying the attitudes of preschool- and school-age children toward handicapped children, Cohen (1977) concludes that changing attitudes toward these children must involve personnel training, use of special curricula, and parent education. Clearly the data on the effects of physical and mental handicaps on peer acceptance indicate that children in the American culture place a very high premium on physical attractiveness and mental capacity. These conditions become translated into stringent criteria for developing friendships and for achieving popularity with the peer group.

In summary, although significant correlations between personal characteristics in children and acceptance by peers have been demonstrated, extreme caution must be used in attaching undue importance to them. Knowing that such relationships exist provides little information as to their origin or developmental pattern. For example, we do not know if the child acquires self-esteem and then gains acceptance by peers, or vice versa. Furthermore, the extent to which situational factors influence these relationships has often been ignored. Finally, with regard to correlational studies, it seems fruitless to spend time exploring variables that have limited implications for the child in gaining acceptance from peers. For example, it has been demonstrated that children with more desirable names are liked better by peers (McDavid & Harari, 1966). Although this is interesting information, its utility is limited, particularly as it relates to educational intervention. A more meaningful approach would direct our efforts toward defining the social skills that lead to greater peer acceptance and more effective peer relations, with an awareness that the contribution of social skills must be studied in the context of the many other factors that influence peer behavior.

EDUCATIONAL INTERVENTIONS AND PEER BEHAVIOR

The acquisition of social skills by young children is frequently assigned low priority by parents and teachers. Although adults typically define for the child what they consider to be unacceptable behavior toward peers, they give minimal attention to providing direction in the development of competent interpersonal behavior. Obviously, many people assume that social behavior evolves automatically, just as it is often assumed that appropriate play behavior comes about just by "doing what comes naturally." In contrast, time and effort are devoted to children's cognitive growth, with considerable concern expressed over the consequences of low achievement. Low peer acceptance seldom receives the same attention. Shantz (1975) discusses this imbalance in the field of education: "Public education has emphasized children's understanding of their physical environment far more than their social environment.... Given the implication that it has for fostering prosocial behavior . . . it seems particularly important that our formal education system give more attention in the curriculum to facilitating greater breadth and depth of social comprehension [p. 315]."

It is clear that merely providing the opportunity for peer interaction is not a sufficient basis to insure its occurring. Rather, adequate instruction, both explicit and implicit, must be present before social skills can be learned. Children who do not acquire the motivation or skills for interacting with peers will either actively avoid socializing or learn maladaptive patterns of social behavior.

If we assume that through intervention we can facilitate the development of skills in relating to peers, the following questions need to be addressed: What specific techniques for the teaching of social skills have evolved from the theories discussed earlier? To what extent have these techniques been utilized in the school setting?

Although a considerable number of teaching approaches are related to the two theoretical positions discussed earlier, those most applicable to the acquisition of social skills will be discussed here. These include modeling, coaching, peer tutoring, and reinforcement techniques from social learning theory, and training in empathic behavior from cognitive–developmental theory. In discussing how these techniques have been used in the classroom, research with preschool children is included, since data from elementary school children are limited.

Modeling social skills

Most of the recent research on modeling effects has involved the modeling of altruistic or prosocial behavior, often using adults as models. A few studies have explored other areas of behavior, some utilizing peer models. For example, the results of a study in the area of cognition showed that peer models can facilitate children's cognitive development (Botvin & Murray, 1975). In this study, children aged 6 through 9 made significant gains in conservation of number, amount, mass, and weight by observing the performance of peer conservers on mass and weight problems and by arguing with peer conservers about the solutions to these problems. The authors conclude that social participation, demonstrated in the social conflict situation, is equally as effective as passive observation of peers, and that a child can be as effective a model as an adult. In another peer modeling study in the area of problem behavior (Csapo, 1972), highly disruptive, emotionally disturbed children were told to model the behavior of six "exemplary" peers. Following the modeling, the disruptive behavior decreased significantly.

In the few studies available on the effects of modeling social skills, competent social behavior has most frequently been modeled on film or television. These studies show that the effects of modeling positive social interaction tend to persist when modeled on film (Evers & Schwarz, 1973; O'Connor, 1972). Films which portray specific techniques for initiating peer interaction have been most effective. In the classroom, an accompanying narrative by the teacher is useful for explicitly describing what the model does and says in approaching a peer or in joining an ongoing group. The narrative can also emphasize the consequences of the model's behavior.

Since the advent of television there has been a plethora of studies describing the effects on children of watching violence on TV shows. According to Stein and Friedrich (1975), the majority of these studies find that after viewing violent models on television the frequency of children's aggressive behavior increases. These same authors found that from brief exposure to television models children can also learn positive responses, such as understanding feelings, sharing, and helping. Using tapes of *Mr. Rogers' Neighborhood*, they found that children were able to generalize from television material to their own peer relations. The ideas were learned most effectively if adults helped the children practice the behaviors (Stein & Friedrich, 1975).

The degree to which teachers model social behavior in their teaching styles influences their students' social behavior. Teacher modeling of feelings of trust in students in interactions in the classroom leads to greater interpersonal trust among the students. Similarly, the teacher collaborating with students—for example, participating in group projects or discussion groups—serves as a model for increased interaction among students. Similarly, when the teacher models flexibility, the students are more flexible in their interactions with peers (Schmuck & Schmuck, 1975).

It has been shown that when teachers ignore misbehavior and attend to positive behavior, children often imitate the teacher—they stop responding to peers' negative behaviors and complement each other's constructive behavior (Scott, Burton, & Yarrow, 1967). Modeling is particularly effective when the modeling behavior being observed is reinforced—for example, when children observe the teacher reinforcing peers for cooperating. Altman (1971) demonstrated that children can learn social skills just by watching peers work and play together cooperatively.

Coaching social skills

Promising results, particularly in terms of maintenance of change, have resulted from coaching in social skills (Lamb, 1978; Eisler & Frederikson, 1980). This technique is especially appropriate for use in the classroom. In a study by Oden and Asher (1977), socially isolated third- and fourth-grade students were coached on the importance of participating, cooperating, communicating, and supporting their peers. They were also given practice in these skills through games. Following this coaching, the children were more accepted by peers; a year later their acceptance was even greater. These results are particularly significant considering that the training involved only six instructional and play sessions over a 4-week period.

For such a training program to be effective, children must first be given information about how to cooperate and be helpful to one another and then be placed in situations that demand that they cooperate (e.g., group projects, equipment that requires several children to operate, brainstorming creative solutions to problems). Group incentives facilitate group effort and almost guarantee that group members will cooperate and help one another. In these types of situations, teachers can give attention to children who cooperate and ignore negative social behavior. This approach has been used in studies in which group members were coached to ignore specific peer behaviors and attend to other behaviors of their peers. Wahler (1967) reported that when aggressive behavior was ignored and cooperative behavior given attention by peers, cooperative behaviors increased and aggressive behaviors decreased significantly. Similarly, when children in a sixth-grade classroom were trained to ignore a child's disruptive behavior, the frequency of disruptive behavior decreased significantly (Solomon & Wahler, 1973).

Coaching as a mode of intervention in training social skills emphasizes *telling* the child what to do, in contrast to showing, as in modeling. It is assumed that if children are taught a general approach or strategy for interacting with peers, they will be able to choose the appropriate behavior in different peer situations on the basis of the general concept they have learned.

Peer tutoring of social skills

Children are unusually receptive to the influence of their peers; they also help one another in ways that adults cannot help them. Teachers have taken advantage of this potential by pairing students for tutoring in academic subjects, with both the tutor and the tutee gaining from the interchange (Feldman, Devin-Sheehan, & Allen, 1976). Aside from the cognitive gains resulting from this interaction, it is possible that peer tutoring can be utilized for teaching interpersonal skills (Strain, 1981). Unfortunately, there are few data available on peer tutoring of social skills. Although studies on the effectiveness of peer tutoring show significant gains in cognitive achievement (Bloom, 1976; Jenkins, Mayhall, Peschka, & Jenkins, 1974), these studies have not revealed concomitant gains in social achievement. In giving attention to the social aspects, Thelen (1969) has emphasized the "human relations" character of peer tutoring and the potential for the development of caring relationships in these interactions. In addition, he describes feelings of camaraderie that develop between tutors and tutees. According to Thelen, these feelings are often accompanied by a change in the climate of the classroom from anxiety and competitiveness to concern for each other. In the absence of further evidence, we can only speculate that the peer tutoring situation presents the potential for a variety of positive "side effects" of a social nature—more frequent peer interaction, less competitiveness, and greater incidence of students regularly helping each other.

The effects of involvement in prosocial behavior are somewhat related to the effects of peer tutoring. For example, in a study of prosocial behavior involving peer helping relations (Damico & Watson, 1974), students defined techniques they used to offer help and to receive help from peers. Results showed that even though there was wide variability among the elementary school children in their ability to work with peers, being involved in peer helping relations had positive effects on peer acceptance, as well as on school attitude and self-esteem.

As for the planning of peer tutoring, it has been shown that tutors trained in a well-planned tutoring program are more effective than untrained tutors, not only in producing greater cognitive gains, but also in developing positive interpersonal relations with their tutees (Harrison, 1971; Neidermeyer & Ellis, 1971). Several authors stress the importance of the correct use of appropriate tutoring material for producing positive results, the majority favoring materials prescribed for highly structured programs (Hassinger & Via, 1969; McCleary, 1971; Neidermeyer & Ellis, 1971). Since most structured academic tutoring programs also include specific teaching techniques that are adaptable to any subject matter, it would seem feasible to apply these techniques to a program for tutoring in the subject matter of interpersonal relations. Although publishers have produced volumes of material for individualization of instruction, including programmed packages for tutor and tutee, none of these programs has included material on peer relations. The applicability of the peer tutoring method to teaching social skills has great potential.

Reinforcement and social skills

Teachers have a tremendous amount of control over the extent and nature of the patterns of peer interaction that develop in the classroom. For example, teachers tend to reinforce those students who are attractive to their peers, who respond positively to others, and who meet the standards of the school (Schmuck & Schmuck, 1975). In a reciprocal fashion, a positive, reinforcing peer group produces greater responsiveness in the teacher, and students are most positive to teachers who build them up in their peer group.

Significant gains in the sociometric status of rejected students have been produced through planned and systematic reinforcement by the teacher (Flanders & Havumaki, 1960; Retish, 1973). Several studies have demonstrated the effectiveness of making attention from an adult contingent upon the child becoming involved in peer interaction (Keogh, Miller, & LeBlanc, 1973; Oden & Asher, 1977; Pinkston, Reese, LeBlanc & Baer, 1973).

The effect of different types of reinforcement on peer relations may vary in as many ways as the characteristics of peer groups vary. Gottman, Gonso, & Rasmussen (1975) found nonverbal reinforcement to be related to friendship in a lower income school, with verbal reinforcement related to friendship in a middle income school. These findings indicate the need to plan different modes of intervention to improve peer relations in different school situations. A teacher's awareness of discrepancies in children's valuing of different types of reinforcement will determine, at least in part, the nature of his or her response to group members.

Training in empathy

It has been hypothesized by several theorists that the ability to "take the role of the other" is basic to successfully relating to peers (Gottmann *et al.*, 1975; Rubin, 1973). Similarly, Feshbach's research findings (1975, 1976) suggest that the ability to empathize has a positive effect on children's social adjustment. In a current research program described by Feshbach (1978), children in the upper elementary grades are being trained to develop empathic skills. As conceptualized by Feshbach, these skills include (*a*) a discriminative skill, which is the ability to discriminate affective states of others; (*b*) social comprehension, or the ability to assume the role of another person; and (*c*) emotional responsiveness, or the ability to experience the negative or positive emotion being expressed in order to be capable of sharing that emotion. The goal of this research is to modify aggressive behavior in children by "enhancing" their empathic skills. The findings of a pilot study (Feshbach, 1978) indicate that participation in empathy training leads to reduced aggression and more positive social behaviors. Other research data support this outcome (Spivak & Shure, 1974; Staub, 1971).

Assuming that this relation between empathy and interpersonal skills is valid, it would follow that training in empathy, or role-taking skills, would have a facilitative effect in helping children gain greater peer acceptance. Contrary to Piaget's notions that limit children's capabilities for seeing another's viewpoint, there are data to indicate that preschool children spend a great deal of their free playtime in sharing, helping, and comforting behavior (Yarrow & Waxler, 1976). These findings suggest that even very young children would be amenable to empathy training.

In teaching children to respond empathically to peers, several steps are involved. To begin with, children must be able not only to see that their peers have needs, but also to perceive accurately what those needs are. The latter step involves being able to accept that a peer's needs may be different from your own. To train for perceiving needs, the teacher may initially stress similarities in people, since it is easier for children to empathize with peers whom they see as similar to themselves (Hoffman, 1976), or as having the same experiences, problems, and feelings they have (Kagan & Madsen, 1971). Teachers can encourage students to describe their feelings to one another and label them; they thus become aware of the extent to which the same emotions are shared. In addition, children can be taught to identify feelings through cues communicated by body language, as well as through actual behavior. For many children, this may be their first organized feedback from a peer, as well as their first verbalized reaction to a peer. In some classrooms, children empathize with feelings of their peers by involvement in role-playing situations where the more aggressive children take the role of victim and the submissive children the role of aggressor. The children can then describe the feelings experienced in each of these roles. In addition, the teacher can anticipate, on the basis of past classroom experiences, the types of group conflicts that are likely to occur, and use "what if..." situations. A class discussion of feelings experienced in each of these roles moves the group toward a more cooperative attitude and capitalizes on the power of the peer group to influence the behavior of the disruptive student. At the same time, the more submissive children will have practiced, through role playing, assertive behavior, and will have been reinforced by the group. Although there are no research data available on these procedures, in the writer's opinion these techniques can be effective in improving empathic skills in the classroom.

Finally, in learning to empathize, the child comes to understand that not only can a peer frequently be helped, but also that he or she can be the helper who has a positive effect on the peer. At the same time, the teacher should be aware that a decision on the child's part not to help may be due to not knowing how to help or feeling too incompetent even to offer. As the child gets older, the ability to accept differences in feelings and to see the other's point of view improves, even though peer interaction becomes more complex (Borke, 1971; Rubin & Schneider, 1973).

Conclusion

Assuming that attention and recognition from peers and the need to conform to group standards are major influences on children's behavior in the classroom, it is essential that the teacher use this power constructively. For example, if students are allowed to be involved in planning the work of the classroom—curriculum, schedules, examinations—the group will be likely to establish a standard of active participation and high productivity. When the teacher encourages involvement in classroom affairs—establishing rules, defining punishments—taking responsibility becomes the norm, and the group then operates to support this norm. This shared expectation for participation in the functioning of the classroom provides a powerful incentive for "cooperative," constructive conformity.

Although some teachers prefer to give their primary attention to the teacher–student learning process, they need to be aware that almost everything that goes on in the classroom involves, to some extent, student–student as well as student–teacher interaction. To be most effective, teachers need to capitalize on the strength of these interpersonal relations, since they substantially influence the learning situation.

REFERENCES

Altman, K. Effects of cooperative response acquisition on social behavior during free play. *Journal of Experimental Child Psychology,* 1971, *12,* 387–395.

Asher, S. R. *The influence of race and sex on children's sociometric choices across the school year.* Unpublished manuscript, University of Illinois, 1973.

Asher, S., & Gottman, J. *The development of children's friendships.* New York: Cambridge Univ. Press, 1981.

Ballard, M., Corman, L., Gottlieb, J., & Kaufman, M. Improving the social status of mainstreamed/retarded children. *Journal of Educational Psychology,* 1977, *69,* 605–611.

Bandura, A. Influence of models' reinforcement contingencies on the acquisition of imitative responses. *Journal of Personality and Social Psychology,* 1965, *1,* 588–595.

Bandura, A. *Aggression: A social learning analysis.* Englewood Cliffs, N.J.: Prentice-Hall, 1973.

Bandura, A. Behavior theory and the models of man. *American Psychologist,* 1974, *29,* 859–869.

Bandura, A. *Social learning theory.* Englewood Cliffs, N.J.: Prentice-Hall, 1977.

Bandura, A., Ross, D., & Ross, S. Transmission of aggression through imitation of aggressive models. *Journal of Abnormal and Social Psychology,* 1961, *63,* 575–582.

Bandura, A., Ross, D., & Ross, S. Imitation of film mediated aggressive models. *Journal of Abnormal and Social Psychology,* 1963, *66,* 3–11.

Bartel, H., Bartel, N., & Grill, J. A sociometric view of some integrated, open classrooms. *Journal of Social Issues,* 1973, *29*(4), 154–173.

Berscheid, E., & Walster, E. Physical attractiveness. *Advanced Experimental Social Psychology,* 1974, *7,* 157–215.

Blau, B., & Rafferty, J. Changes in friendship status as a function of reinforcement. *Child Development,* 1970, *41,* 115–121.

Bloom, S. *Peer and cross-age tutoring in the schools.* Washington, D.C.: U.S. Department of Health, Education and Welfare, National Institute of Education, 1976.

Borke, H. Interpersonal perception of young children. Egocentrism or empathy? *Developmental Psychology,* 1971, *5,* 262–269.

Botvin, G., & Murray, F. The efficacy of peer modeling and social conflict in the acquisition of conservation. *Child Development,* 1975, *46,* 796–799.

Bronson, W. C. Central orientations: A study of behavior organization from childhood to adolescence. *Child Development,* 1966, *37,* 125–155.

Broverman, I., Vogel, S., Broverman, D., Clarkson, F., & Rosenkrantz, P. Sex-role stereotypes: A current appraisal. *Journal of Social Issues,* 1972, *28,* 59–78.

Bruininks, V. Actual and perceived peer status of learning disabled students in mainstreaming programs. *Journal of Special Education,* 1978, *12,* 51–58.

Bryan, J. H. Children's cooperative and helping behavior. In M. Hetherington (Ed.), *Review of child development research* (Vol. 5). Chicago: Univ. of Chicago Press, 1975.

Bryan, T. Peer popularity of learning disabled children: A replication. *Journal of Learning Disabilities,* 1976, *9,* 307–311.

Bryan, T., & Bryan, J. Social interactions of learning disabled children. *Learning Disability Quarterly,* 1978, *1,* 33–38.

Campbell, J. Peer relations in childhood. In M. Hoffman & L. Hoffman (Eds.), *Review of child development research* (Vol. 1). New York: Russell Sage Foundation, 1964.

Campbell, J. D., & Yarrow, M. R. Personal and situational variables in adaptation to change. *Journal of Social Issues,* 1958, *14,* 29–46.

Ceresnie, S. *Communication and cooperation in dyads of children of varying levels of egocentrism.* Unpublished master's thesis, Wayne State University, 1974.

Cohen, C., Improving attitudes toward the handicapped. *Educational Forum,* 1977, *42,* 9–20.

Cooley, C. H. *Social organization.* New York: Scribner's, 1909.

Costanzo, P., & Shaw, M. Conformity as a function of age level. *Child Development,* 1966, *37,* 967–975.

Cowen, E. L., Pederson, A., Babijian, H., Izzo, L. D., & Tost, M. A. Long-term follow-up of early detected vulnerable children. *Journal of Consulting and Clinical Psychology*, 1973, *41*, 438–446.

Cross, J. F., & Cross, J. Age, sex, race, and perception of facial beauty. *Developmental Psychology*, 1971, *5*, 433–439.

Csapo, M. Peer models reverse the "one bad apple spoils the barrel" theory. *Teaching Exceptional Children*, 1972, *5*, 20–24.

Damico, S., & Watson, K. *Peer helping relationships: An ecological study of an elementary classroom.* Paper presented at the annual meeting of the American Educational Research Association, Chicago, April 1974.

Damon, W. *The social world of the child.* San Francisco: Jossey-Bass, 1977.

Damon, W. (Ed.) *New directions for child development: Social cognition.* San Francisco: Jossey-Bass, 1978.

DeVries, D. L., & Edwards, K. J. *Student teams and instructional games: Their effects on cross-race and cross-sex interactions.* Baltimore: Center for Social Organization of Schools, John Hopkins Univ., 1972.

Dion, K., & Berscheid, E. Physical attractiveness and peer acceptance among children. *Sociometry*, 1974, *37*, 1–12.

Donaldson, M. *Children's minds.* New York: Norton, 1978.

Dweck, C. S., & Goetz, T. E. Attributions and learned helplessness. In J. H. Harvey, W. Ickes, & R. F. Kidd (Eds.), *New directions in attribution research* (Vol. 2). Hillsdale, N.J.: Erlbaum, 1977.

Eisler, R., & Frederiksen, L. *Perfecting social skills: A guide to interpersonal behavior development.* New York: Plenum, 1980.

Elliot, R., & Vasta, R. The modeling of sharing: Effects associated with vicarious reinforcement, symbolization, age, and generalization. *Journal of Experimental Child Psychology*, 1970, *10*, 8–15.

Ellis, G., & Sekyra, F. The effect of aggressive cartoons on the behavior of first-grade children. *Journal of Psychology*, 1972, *81*, 37–43.

Emmerich, W. Developmental trends in evaluation of single traits. *Child Development*, 1974, *45*, 172–183.

Evers, W. L., & Schwarz, J. C. Modifying social withdrawal in preschoolers: The effects of filmed modeling and teacher praise. *Journal of Abnormal Child Psychology*, 1973, *1*, 248–256.

Feldman, R., Devin-Sheehan, L., & Allen, V. Children tutoring children: A critical review of research. In V. L. Allen (Ed.), *Children as teachers.* New York: Academic Press, 1976.

Feshbach, N. D. Empathy in children: Some theoretical and empirical considerations. *The Counseling Psychologist*, 1975, *5*(2), 25–30.

Feshbach, N. D. *Empathy and the regulation of aggression in children.* Paper presented at the XXI International Congress of Psychology, July 1976, p. 55.

Feshbach, N. D. *Empathy training: A field study in effective education.* Invited address, American Educational Research Association, Toronto, Canada, March 1978.

Flanders, N., & Havumaki, S. The effect of teacher–pupil contacts involving praise on the sociometric choices of students. *Journal of Educational Psychology*, 1960, *51*, 65–68.

Flavell, J. The development of inferences about others. In T. Mischel (Ed.), *Understanding other persons.* Oxford: Blackwell, 1974.

Gerard, H., Jackson, T., & Conolley, F. Social contact in the desegregated classroom. In H. B. Gerard & N. Miller (Eds.), *School desegregation.* New York: Plenum, 1975.

Glick, J., & Clarke-Stewart, K. A. *The development of social understanding.* New York: Gardner Press, 1978.

Gottlieb, J., & Gottlieb, B. Stereotypic attitudes and behavioral intentions toward handicapped children. *American Journal of Mental Deficiency*, 1977, *82*, 65–71.

Gottman, J. M. Toward a definition of social isolation in children. *Child Development,* 1977, *48,* 513–517.

Gottman, J., Gonso, J., & Rasmussen, B. Social interaction, social competence and friendship in children. *Child Development,* 1975, *46,* 709–718.

Greenberg, D. J., Hillman, D., & Grice, D. Infant and stranger variables related to stranger anxiety in the first year of life. *Developmental Psychology,* 1973, *9,* 207–212.

Gronlund, N. E. *Sociometry in the classroom.* New York: Harper, 1959.

Hamburg, D. A., & Van Lawick-Goodall, J. Factors facilitating development of aggressive behavior in chimpanzees and humans. In J. deWit & W. Hartup (Eds.), *Origins and determinants of aggressive behaviors.* The Hague: Mouton, 1974.

Hare, A. P., Borgatta, E. F., Bales, R. F. (Eds.). *Small groups.* New York: Knopf, 1955.

Harrison, G. V. *Structured tutoring.* Provo, Utah: Division of Communication Services, Brigham Young Univ., 1971.

Hartup, W. Peer interaction and social organization. In P. Mussen (Ed.), *Carmichael's manual of child psychology* (Vol. 2). New York: Wiley, 1970.

Hartup, W. Peer interaction and the behavioral development of the individual child. In E. Schopler & R. Reichler (Eds.), *Psychopathology and child development.* New York: Plenum, 1976.

Hartup, W. Peer interaction and the processes of socialization. In M. Guralnick (Ed.), *Early intervention and the integration of handicapped and non-handicapped children.* Baltimore: Univ. Park Press, 1977.

Hartup, W., & Coates, B. Imitation of a peer as a function of reinforcement from the peer group and rewardingness of the model. *Child Development,* 1967, *38,* 1003–1016.

Hassinger, J., & Via, M. How much does a tutor learn through teaching reading? *Journal of Secondary Education,* 1969, *44,* 42–46.

Hoffman, M. L. Moral development. In P. H. Mussen (Ed.), *Carmichael's manual of child psychology* (Vol. 2). New York: Wiley, 1970.

Hoffman, M. L. Empathy, role taking, guilt, and development of altruistic motives. In T. Lickona (Ed.), *Moral development and behavior.* New York: Holt, 1976.

Hoving, K., Hamm, N., & Galvin, P. Social influence as a function of stimulus ambiguity at three age levels. *Developmental Psychology,* 1969, *1,* 631–636.

Iscoe, I., Williams, M., & Harvey, J. Modification of children's judgments by a simulated group technique: A normative developmental study. *Child Development,* 1963, *34,* 963–978.

Iscoe, I., Williams, M., & Harvey, J. Age, intelligence, and sex as variables in the conformity behavior of Negro and white children. *Child Development,* 1964, *35,* 451–460.

Isen, A., Horn, N., & Rosenhan, D. Effects of success and failure on children's generosity. *Journal of Personality and Social Psychology,* 1973, *27,* 239–247.

James, G., & Lott, A. J. Reward frequency and the formation of positive attitudes toward group members. *Journal of Social Psychology,* 1964, *62,* 111–115.

Jenkins, J., Mayhall, W., Peschka, C., & Jenkins, L. Comparing small group and tutorial instruction in resource rooms. *Exceptional Children,* 1974, *40,* 245–250.

Jensen, L., & Hughston, J. Effects of training children to make moral judgments that are independent of sanctions. *Developmental Psychology,* 1971, *5,* 367.

Kagan, J., & Madsen, M. C. Cooperation and competition of Mexican, Mexican-American, and Anglo-American children of two ages under four instructional sets. *Developmental Psychology,* 1971, *5,* 32–38.

Keasey, C. B. Social participation as a factor in the moral development of preadolescents. *Developmental Psychology,* 1971, *5,* 216–220.

Kelly, G. A. *A theory of personality: The psychology of personal constructs.* New York: Norton, 1955.

Keogh, W. J., Miller, R. M., & LeBlanc, J. M. *The effects of antecedent stimuli upon a preschool child's peer interaction.* Paper presented to the Society for Research in Child Development, Philadelphia, April, 1973.

Kleck, R., Richardson, S., & Ronald, L. Physical appearance cues and interpersonal attraction in children. *Child Development,* 1974, *45,* 305–310.

Kohlberg, L. Stage and sequence: The cognitive–developmental approach to socialization. In D. A. Goslin (Ed.), *Handbook of socialization theory and research.* Chicago: Rand McNally, 1969.

Kohlberg, L. Moral stages and moralization: The cognitive–developmental approach. In T. Lickona (Ed.), *Moral development and moral behavior.* New York: Holt, 1976.

Kohn, M. The child as a determinant of his peers' approach to him. In B. Thompson, R. Divesta, & J. Horrocks (Eds.), *Social development and personality.* New York: Wiley, 1971.

Kohn, M., & Clausen, J. Social isolation and schizophrenia. *American Sociological Review,* 1955, *20,* 265–273.

Krumboltz, J. D., & Krumboltz, H. B. *Changing children's behavior.* Englewood Cliffs, N.J.: Prentice-Hall, 1972.

Ladd, G. W., & Oden, S. L. *The relationship between children's ideas about helpfulness and peer acceptance.* Paper presented to the Society for Research in Child Development, New Orleans, April, 1977.

Lamb, M. (Ed.), *Social and personality development.* New York: Holt, 1978.

Landsbaum, J., & Willis, R. Conformity in early and late adolescence. *Developmental Psychology,* 1971, *4,* 334–337.

Lefkowitz, M., Eron, L., Walder, L., & Huesmann, L. Television violence and child aggression: A follow-up study. In G. A. Comstock & E. A. Rubinstein (Eds.), *Television and social behavior. Vol. 3: Television and adolescent aggressiveness.* Washington, D.C.: U.S. Government Printing Office, 1972. Pp. 35–135.

Lewin, K., Lippitt, R., White, R. K. Patterns of aggressive behavior in experimentally created "social climates." *Journal of Social Psychology,* 1938, *10,* 271–299.

Lewis, M., & Brooks, J. Self, others and fear: Infants' reactions to people. In M. Lewis & L. Rosenblum (Eds.), *The origins of fear.* New York: Wiley, 1974.

Lewis, M., & Rosenblum, L. A. (Eds.). *Friendship and peer relations.* New York: Wiley, 1975.

Lickona, T. (Ed.). *Moral development and behavior.* New York: Holt, 1976.

Liebert, R., & Baron, R. Some immediate effects of televised violence on children's behavior. *Developmental Psychology,* 1972, *6,* 469–475.

Lott, A. J., Aponte, J. F., Lott, B. E., & McGinley, W. H. The effect of delayed reward on the development of positive attitudes toward persons. *Journal of Experimental Social Psychology,* 1969, *5,* 101–113.

Lott, A. J., Bright, M. A., Weinstein, P., & Lott, B. E. Liking for persons as a function of incentive and drive during acquisition. *Journal of Personality and Social Psychology,* 1970, *14,* 66–77.

Lott, A. J., & Lott, B. E. The role of reward in the formation of positive interpersonal attitudes. In T. L. Huston (Ed.), *Foundations of interpersonal attraction.* New York: Academic Press, 1974.

Lott, B. E., & Lott, A. J. The formation of positive attitudes toward group members. *Journal of Abnormal and Social Psychology,* 1960, *61,* 297–300.

McCleary, E. K. Report of results of tutorial reading project. *Reading Teacher,* 1971, *24,* 556–560.

Maccoby, E. E., & Masters, J. C. Attachment and dependency. In P. H. Mussen (Ed.), *Carmichael's manual of child psychology* (Vol. 2). New York: Wiley, 1970.

McDavid, J. W., & Harari, H. Stereotyping of names and popularity in grade school children. *Child Development,* 1966, *37,* 454–459.

McGrew, W. C. *An ethological study of children's behavior.* New York: Academic Press, 1972.

Maratsos, M. Nonegocentric communication abilities in preschool children. *Child Development,* 1973, *44,* 697–700.

Marshall, H. R. Relations between home experiences and children's use of language in play interactions with peers. *Psychological Monographs,* 1961, *7.*

Mischel, T. (Ed.). *Understanding other persons.* Oxford: Blackwell, 1974.

Moore, S. G., & Updegraff, R. Sociometric status of preschool children related to age, sex, nurturance-giving and dependency. *Child Development,* 1964, *35,* 519–524.

Neidermeyer, F., & Ellis, P. Remedial reading instruction by trained pupil tutors. *Elementary School Journal,* 1971, *71*(7), 400–405.

O'Connor, R. D. Relative efficacy of modeling, shaping, and the combined procedures for modification of social withdrawal. *Journal of Abnormal Psychology,* 1972, *79,* 327–334.

Oden, S., & Asher, S. R. Coaching children in social skills for friendship making. *Child Development,* 1977, *48,* 495–506.

Patterson, G. R., & Cobb, J. A. A dyadic analysis of "aggressive" behavior. In J. Hill (Ed.), *Minnesota Symposia on Child Psychology* (Vol. 5). Minneapolis, University of Minnesota Press, 1971.

Piaget, J. *The language and thought of the child.* New York: Harcourt, 1926.

Piaget, J. *The moral judgment of the child.* New York: Free Press, 1965. (Original translation, London: Kegan Paul, 1932.)

Piaget, J. *Six psychological studies.* New York: Random House, 1967.

Pinkston, E., Reese, N., LeBlanc, J., & Baer, D. Independent control of a preschool child's aggression and peer interaction by contingent teacher attention. *Journal of Applied Behavior Analysis,* 1973, *6,* 115–124.

Rardin, D. R., & Moan, C. E. Peer interaction and cognitive development. *Child Development.* 1971, *42,* 1685–1699.

Reese, H. Relationship between self-acceptance and sociometric choice. *Journal of Abnormal and Social Psychology,* 1961, *62,* 472–474.

Retish, P. M. Changing the status of poorly esteemed students through teacher reinforcement. *Journal of Applied Behavioral Science,* 1973, *9,* 44–50.

Rice, M., & Grusec, J. Saying and doing: Effects of observer performance. *Journal of Personality and Social Psychology,* 1975, *32,* 584–593.

Richardson, S. A., Goodman, N., Hastorf, A. H., & Dornbusch, S. A. Cultural uniformity in reaction to physical disabilities. *American Sociological Review,* 1961, *26,* 241–47.

Roff, M. Childhood social interactions and young adult bad conduct. *Journal of Abnormal and Social Psychology,* 1961, *63,* 333–337.

Roff, M., Sells, S. B., & Golden, M. M. *Social adjustment and personality development in children.* Minneapolis: Univ. of Minnesota Press, 1972.

Rosenkoetter, L. Resistance to temptation: Inhibitory and disinhibitory effects of models. *Developmental Psychology,* 1973, *8*(1), 80–84.

Ross, S. A. A test of generality of the effects of deviant preschool models. *Developmental Psychology,* 1971, *4,* 262–267.

Rubin, K. H., & Schneider, F. W. The relation between moral judgment, egocentrism, and altruistic behavior. *Child Development,* 1973, *44,* 661–665.

Rushton, J. Generosity in children: Immediate and long term effects of modeling, preaching, and moral judgment, *Journal of Personality and Social Psychology,* 1975, *31,* 459–466.

Saltzstein, H. Social influence and moral development: A perspective on the role of parents and peers. In T. Lickona (Ed.), *Moral development and behavior.* New York: Holt, 1976.

Saltzstein, H., Diamond, R., & Belenky, M. Moral judgment level and conformity behavior. *Developmental Psychology,* 1972, *7,* 327–336.

Saltzstein, H., & Osgood, S. The development of children's reasoning about group interdependence and obligation. *Journal of Psychology,* 1975, *90,* 147–155.

Schmuck, R., & Schmuck, P. *Group processes in the classroom.* Dubuque, Iowa: W. C. Brown, 1975.

Scott, P. M., Burton, R. V., & Yarrow, M. R. Social reinforcement under natural conditons. *Child Development,* 1967, *38,* 53–63.

Sells, S. B., & Roff, M. *Peer acceptance–rejection and personality development.* Final Report, Project No. OE 5–0417, U.S. Department of Health, Education and Welfare, 1967.

Selman, R. L. Taking another's perspective: Role taking development in early childhood, *Child Development,* 1971, *42,* 1721–1734.

Selman, R. L. Social–cognitive understanding: A guide to educational and clinical practice. In T. Lickona (Ed.), *Moral development and behavior.* New York: Holt, 1976.

Selman, R. L., & Byrne, D. F. A structural developmental analysis of levels of role taking in middle childhood. *Child Development,* 1974, *45,* 803–806.

Shantz, C. The development of social cognition. In E. M. Hetherington (Ed.), *Review of child development research* (Vol. 5). Chicago: Univ. of Chicago Press, 1975.

Shatz, M., & Gelman. R. The development of communication skills: Modifications in the speech of young children as a function of listener. *Monographs of the Society for Research in Child Development,* 1973, *38*(5, Serial No. 152).

Shaw, M. E. Changes in sociometric choices following forced integration of an elementary school. *Journal of Social Issues,* 1973, *29-* 143–157.

Silvern, L. Children's sex-role preferences: Stronger among girls than boys. *Sex Roles,* 1977, *3,* 159–171.

Singleton, L. *The effects of sex and race in children's sociometric choices for play and work.* Urbana, Ill. Univ. of Illinois, 1974. (ERIC Document Reproduction Service No. ED 100 520)

Singleton, L., & Asher S. Peer preferences and social interaction among third-grade children in an integrated school district. *Journal of Educational Psychology,* 1977, *69,* 330–336.

Siperstein, G., & Gottlieb, J. Physical stigma and academic performance as factors affecting children's first impressions of handicapped peers. *American Journal of Mental Deficiency,* 1977, *81,* 455–462.

Siperstein, G., Gotlieb, J., & Bak, J. Effects of group discussion on children's attitudes toward handicapped peers. *Journal of Educational Research,* 1977, *70,* 131–134.

Solomon, R. W., & Wahler, R. G. Peer reinforcement of classroom problem behavior. *Journal of Applied Behavior Analysis,* 1973, *6,* 49–56.

Spivak, G., & Shure, M. B. *Social adjustment in young children.* San Francisco: Jossey-Bass, 1974.

Staub, E. The use of role playing and induction in children's learning of helping and sharing behavior. *Child Development,* 1971, *42,* 805–816.

Stein, A. Imitation of resistance to temptation. *Child Development,* 1967, *38,* 157–169.

Stein, A., & Friedrich, L. Television content and young children's behavior. In J. P. Murray, E. A. Rubenstein, & G. A. Comstock (Eds.). *Television and social behavior, Volume 2, Television and Social Learning.* Washington, D.C.: U.S. Government Printing Office, 1972, 202–317.

Stein, A., & Friedrich, L. Impact of television on children and youth. In E. M. Hetherington (Ed.), *Review of child development research* (Vol. 5). Chicago: Univ. of Chicago Press, 1975.

Stengel, E. *Suicide and attempted suicide.* Middlesex: Penguin, 1971.

Stever, F., Applefield, J., & Smith, B. Televised aggression and the interpersonal aggression of preschool children. *Journal of Experimental Child Psychology,* 1971, *11,* 442–447.

Strain, P. *The utilization of classroom peers as behavior change agents.* New York: Plenum, 1980.

Thelen, H. Tutoring by students. *School Review,* 1969, *77,* 229–244.

Trent, R. D. Some individual and group differences in voting for self. *Journal of Social Psychology,* 1954, *39,* 61–65.

Ullmann, C. A. Teachers, peers and tests as predictors of adjustment. *Journal of Educational Psychology,* 1957, *48,* 257–267.

Wahler, R. G. Child–child interactions in free field settings: Some experimental analyses. *Journal of Experimental Child Psychology,* 1967, *5,* 278–293.

Ward, W. Sex-role preference and parental imitation within groups of middle-class whites and lower-class blacks. *Psychological Reports,* 1972, *30,* 651–654.

Whiting, B., & Whiting, J. *Children of six cultures.* Cambridge, Mass.: Harvard Univ. Press, 1975.

Wiggins, J. S., & Winder, C. L. The peer nominations inventory: An empirically derived sociometric measure of adjustment in preadolescent boys. *Psychological Reports,* 1961, *9*(Monograph Supplement No. 5), 643–677.

Winder, C. L., & Rau, L. Parental attitudes associated with social deviance in preadolescent boys. *Journal of Abnormal and Social Psychology,* 1962, *64,* 418–424.

Worell, J., & Stilwell, W. E. *Psychology for teachers and students.* New York: McGraw-Hill, 1981.

Wylie, R. Attitudes of children toward their handicapped peers. *Childhood Education,* 1976, *52,* 171–173.

Yarrow, M. R., & Waxler, C. Z., with Barrett, D., Darby, J., King, R., Picket, M., & Smith, J. Dimensions and correlates of prosocial behavior in young children. *Child Development,* 1976, *47,* 118–125.

Young, L. L., & Cooper, D. H. Some factors associated with popularity. *Journal of Educational Psychology,* 1944, *35,* 513–535.

Youniss, J. Another perspective on social cognition. In A. Pick (Ed.), *10th Annual Minnesota Symposium on Child Psychology.* Minneapolis: Univ. of Minnesota Press, 1975.

Youniss, J., & Volpe, J. A relational analysis of children's friendship. In W. Damon (Ed.), *New directions for child development: Social cognition.* San Francisco: Jossey-Bass, 1978.

Zalk, S., & Katz, P. Gender attitudes in children. *Sex Roles,* 1978, *4,* 349–357.

3 / The development and regulation of aggression in young children

RONALD G. SLABY
WENDY CONKLIN ROEDELL

A major theme connecting the rather diverse collection of research findings on children's aggression is that many of the factors that foster aggression are potentially alterable. Thus, most studies designed to investigate the development of aggression contain at least an implicit suggestion of how children's aggression may be regulated. Recognizing that parents, teachers, and other adults who provide care for young children find it important not only to understand the factors that stimulate children's aggression but also to assume a responsible role in its regulation, we will focus our discussion on the research findings that address two primary questions: (*a*) How does aggression develop? and (*b*) What can be done to regulate children's aggression?

Factors that influence the development and regulation of aggression during the preschool and elementary school years have been identified within each of the major socialization systems in which children typically participate—including family interaction, television viewing, peer group interaction, teacher interaction, and particular programmed environmental settings. Yet, the interrelationship among these distinct sources of influence on the aggressive behavior of individual children is not well understood. What is clear is that during the years from age 2 to 12, children typically develop large and relatively stable individual differences in their patterns of aggressive behavior, suggesting that these

97

PSYCHOLOGICAL DEVELOPMENT
IN THE ELEMENTARY YEARS

distinct socialization systems may ultimately have a coordinated effect on the development and maintenance of children's aggression. Thus, we will begin our discussion by identifying some general patterns of aggression that children display in a variety of social settings. Following this analysis of broad patterns, we will discuss the development and regulation of children's aggression, as influenced by (*a*) family; (*b*) television; (*c*) peer groups; and (*d*) situational factors.

Although several previous reviews of the research on the development and control of aggressive behavior are available (e.g., Bandura, 1973; Berkowitz, 1973a; Feshbach, 1970), this review will emphasize those conclusions, deriving from research findings, that may aid the child development practitioner in understanding and dealing with children's aggression in a variety of social settings. We have presented elsewhere a teacher's guide to specific sets of procedures found to be effective in regulating a variety of social behaviors, including aggression, typically displayed by children in the preschool and elementary school classroom (Roedell, Slaby, & Robinson, 1977).

Previous attempts to define aggression in precise, yet broadly applicable terms have raised a number of important methodological, practical, and theoretical issues (e.g., Bandura, 1973). For purposes of this review, we will simply use the term *aggression* to refer to those actions that involve actual or intended physical or psychological injury to another individual. The aggression most commonly displayed by preschool and elementary school children includes such physical acts as hitting, kicking, and destroying another's property, as well as such verbal acts as shouting insults, calling names, and making threats.

It should be noted that this definition specifically excludes assertive behavior, such as standing up for one's rights in a nonhostile manner. It also excludes fantasy or symbolic aggression, such as simple play acting or expressing hostility that is not directed toward other individuals. Furthermore, our discussion of aggression specifically disregards the assumption that aggressive behavior automatically results from a biological or motivational drive. The notion, currently popular among some clinicians, that children's aggressive behavior necessarily signifies the "acting out" of aggressive urges universally residing within individuals is regarded as speculative and inconsistent with current research evidence (e.g., Berkowitz, 1972). Discussion of the role of both biological factors (e.g., Johnson, 1972; Maccoby & Jacklin, 1980; Tieger, 1980) and cross-cultural factors (e.g., Lambert, 1974; Whiting & Whiting, 1975) in the development of human aggression is beyond the scope of this chapter. Instead, we will discuss the numerous social, cognitive, and situational factors that have been found to play a major role within the North

American culture in the development and regulation of children's aggression.

GENERAL PATTERNS OF AGGRESSION

Age-related patterns of aggression

Attempts to formulate broad normative conclusions concerning the overall amount of aggression typically displayed by children at various ages have been largely precluded by the fact that levels of aggression vary extensively as a function of the particular sample of children, the measures of aggression, and the social and environmental settings under investigation. However, several studies, taken together, provide a partial view of age-related changes in children's aggression. Specifically, these studies reveal that as children develop, their expression of aggression changes markedly in its form, its function, and its instigating circumstances.

In a classic study, Florence Goodenough (1931) collected daily parental records of aggressive outbursts shown by children between 1 and 8 years of age. She found that with increasing age, children showed (*a*) a decrease in the proportion of undirected and diffuse aggressive outbursts, such as temper tantrums; (*b*) an increase in the proportion of retaliatory aggressive responses directed toward securing revenge for immediate injury; (*c*) an increase in the use of language in aggressive outbursts; (*d*) an increase in physical aggression to the age of 3 years, followed by a decline in favor of more verbal forms of aggression; and (*e*) an increase in the frequency and duration of the aftereffects of aggression, such as sulking, whining, and brooding. Furthermore, the immediate instigating circumstances most likely to elicit aggression were found to shift with the age of the child. One-year-old children showed aggression primarily in response to either mild physical discomfort or a desire for attention; 2- and 3-year-old children were instigated primarily by authority conflicts with adults over "habit training" procedures; and 4- to 8-year-old children were instigated primarily by social conflicts with playmates.

Other researchers have found that whereas the aggression of preschool children is typically carried out for instrumental purposes related to quarrels over possessions, the aggression of elementary school children generally represents a mixture of both object-oriented and person-oriented harm-doing (Dawe, 1934; Hartup, 1974). The finding that as children get older, a greater proportion of their aggression is directed toward injuring another individual is consistent with the hypothesis that this type of aggression requires relatively sophisticated judgments about the motives of the provocateur (Hartup & de Wit, 1974).

As children advance in their social–cognitive functioning, they can be expected to make more highly differentiated judgments about the motivations underlying aggressive actions directed at themselves, and about the relative justifiability of retaliating with aggression. In one study, first-, third-, and sixth-grade boys were asked to indicate how aggressively they would respond to an aggressive act that was characterized in a story as being either intentional or accidental (Shantz & Voydanoff, 1973). Whereas the first-grade boys generally failed to alter their retaliatory response in accordance with the intent behind the provocation, older boys reduced their level of retaliation when the provocation was accidental. Similarly, an age-level difference was found in a study comparing second- and eighth-grade children's evaluations of an aggressive act presented in different stories as involving varying levels of responsibility by the aggressor (Ferguson & Rule, 1980). Whereas second-grade children generally failed to vary their evaluations in accordance with different levels of aggressor responsibility, eighth-grade children made several distinctions. They viewed an aggressive action as more reprehensible when a harmful outcome was intended than when a harmful outcome was foreseeable but unintended. They also judged foreseeable aggression as more reprehensible than either accidental or justified aggression. It should be pointed out that children as young as preschool age are capable of altering their evaluative response to aggression based on the aggressor's intentions, particularly if they are provided with unambiguous information about the intention underlying the aggressive act (Rotenberg, 1980; Rule, Nesdale, & McAra, 1974). However, in naturalistic settings, children are often faced with provocations for which the aggressor's intentions must be inferred from subtle cues and sophisticated knowledge of human motivation. Particularly in these circumstances, children's level of social–cognitive functioning would be expected to be an important factor in determining how they would respond to provocation.

Stability in patterns of aggression

The aggressive behavior displayed by children at various ages typically changes in form, function, and instigating circumstances. These developmental shifts have presented difficulties for longitudinal assessments of children's individual stability in aggression. Nevertheless, longitudinal studies have consistently found a substantial degree of stability in children's aggression regardless of whether assessment techniques consisted of direct observation of aggressive behavior or ratings of aggression made by either teachers, peers, or clinicians. In a review of 16 longitudinal assessments of aggression in males, Olweus (1979b) found that marked individual differences in boys' habitual levels of aggression emerged early in life—at least by 3 years of age. These relative levels of aggression remained quite stable over intervals as long as 21 years (Kagan & Moss, 1962). In fact, the longitudinal stability of measured aggressiveness for boys is roughly equivalent to the stability of IQ scores (Olweus, 1979b). Interestingly, the relative predictability across a given interval of time was negatively correlated with the age of the boys at the time of the first assessment, suggesting that the aggressive behavior of younger boys may be relatively less well established and more amenable to change than that of older boys.

Girls also have been found to show a considerable degree of individual stability in their patterns of aggression throughout childhood, but stability beyond adolescence has not been clearly demonstrated. For example, in one longitudinal study, girls' aggression, as rated by peers at the age of 8 years, was found to be highly correlated with their peer ratings of aggression at the age of 19 years (Eron, Walder, Huesmann, & Lefkowitz, 1974). However, in another study, it was found that although clinical ratings of girls' aggression were stable between childhood and early adolescence, adult women's rated levels of aggression were not predictably related to their levels of aggression during adolescence (Kagan & Moss, 1962).

The findings of extensive individual stability in children's patterns of aggression raise some important issues concerning both the interrelationships among distinct socialization systems and the differences in the short-term and long-term effectiveness of various regulatory procedures within each system. One interpretation of long-term stability in children's aggression suggests that individual differences in children's temperament, or behavior style, may differentially predispose them to behave aggressively. Differences in temperament among infants have been shown to remain relatively constant throughout childhood (Thomas, Chess, Birch, Hertzig, & Korn, 1963; Thomas & Chess, 1977). Activity level, one of the most stable aspects of an infant's temperament, generally remains quite stable throughout the preschool and elementary school years, and children's aggression has frequently been found to be correlated with their level of activity (e.g., Billman & McDevitt, 1980; Buss, Block, & Block, 1980; Matthews & Angulo, 1980). For example, children whose temperaments were rated by mothers and by teachers to include high activity or intensity levels were observed to show more aggressive behavior in the preschool classroom than children rated to have low activity or intensity levels (Billman & McDevitt, 1980). An excitable child whose actions are typically carried out with force and vigor may be more likely to produce responses that are labeled aggressive.

Even predispositions contributing to aggression, however, are strongly influenced by the responses from members of the child's social environment. Thus, long-term stability in aggression further suggests that a child's various "social worlds" (e.g., family, peers) ultimately provide relatively concordant, overlapping, or mutually supportive socialization influences (Hartup, 1979). In addition, the individual child may ultimately internalize relatively enduring and generalizable mediators of aggression—such as cognitive standards concerning aggression (e.g., Feshbach, 1974), and habitual patterns of response (e.g., Eron *et al.*, 1974). It is likely that both a concordant pattern of socialization influences and an individual set of internalized mediators are established relatively early in a child's development, in interaction with the child's unique temperament characteristics. As the child develops, these patterns are likely to become increasingly resistant to change.

Several factors related to children's social–cognitive functioning have been found to be predictive of aggression—measured not only at the same time, but also years later in young adulthood. In an exemplary longitudinal study (Eron *et al.*, 1974), measures of social–cognitive functioning and peer-rated measures of aggression were obtained for 8-year-old children. Ten years later when they were 18, aggression was again assessed. One childhood factor that was predictive of aggression in young adults was children's degree of identification with their parents, as indicated by the similarity between the parents' and the child's independent ratings of their own styles of expressing common behavior (e.g., walking fast or slow, talking fast or slow). Children who were closely identified with their parents at the age of 8 years tended to be less aggressive 10 years later. Although the significance of this factor is open to a variety of interpretations, children's identification with their parents may broadly reflect their level of acceptance of direct and indirect parental socialization influences, including parents' attempts to control children's aggression. Children's propensity to confess misbehavior to their parents was a second factor found to be predictive of low levels of aggression 10 years later. Confession has traditionally been regarded as an indication that a child has internalized parental or societal values concerning right and wrong. Finally, children's high IQ scores were found to be predictive of low levels of aggression 10 years later. Taken together, these findings are consistent with the position that the enduring and generalizable nature of children's aggression may be largely mediated by internalized aspects of children's social–cognitive functioning. It remains to be determined to what extent various sources of socialization may influence the formation of social–cognitive mediators related to aggression.

Sex-differential patterns of aggression

A reliable finding throughout the literature on aggression is that boys typically exhibit higher levels of both verbal and physical aggression than do girls (Maccoby & Jacklin, 1974). This sex difference is found as early as the age of 2 years, when extensive social play begins, and it extends at least throughout adolescence. It is interesting to note, however, that despite vast differences in reported violent assaults by adult men and women, sex differences in aggression are not consistently found in experimental studies with adults (Frodi, Macaulay, & Thome, 1977). Although adult men and women differ in their self-reports of aggression and general hostility in a way that conforms with the sex-role stereotype, they have not been found to behave differently in laboratory studies in which aggression is presented as a justified or even prosocial behavior. In addition to raising a cautionary note against overgeneralizing from non-naturalistic measures of aggression, these findings highlight the potential influence on aggressive behavior of the individual's perception of the sex-role appropriateness of aggression in various situations.

In an attempt to account for sex differences in both the level of aggression typically displayed and the degree of long-term stability of aggression, Kagan and Moss (1962) present an explanation of differential sex-role socialization for boys and girls. They contend that although girls may be allowed to engage in a limited degree of aggression, competitiveness, and "tomboyish" behavior during the preschool and elementary school years, they face strong socialization pressure during the adolescent years to suppress these tendencies in favor of traditionally feminine behavior, such as nurturance, dependency, and approval seeking. For boys, on the other hand, aggression may be consistently tolerated, or even explicitly encouraged and rewarded by socializing adults, since aggression is generally viewed as an integral component of traditional masculine behavior.

More recent explanations of the socialization influences on the development of sex-differential behavior patterns have emphasized children's own "self-socialization" role in formulating social rules and standards that guide them in their display of relatively enduring and generalizable response patterns (Maccoby & Jacklin, 1974). There is ample opportunity for children to learn from a variety of sources that aggression is widely regarded as a masculine activity. Thus, boys and girls may develop sex-role-related cognitive standards for seeking, interpreting, and responding to aggressive stimulation. Recent evidence from longitudinal research regarding such internal cognitive standards is consistent with the position that boys and girls may play a major role in defining their own socialization experiences related to aggression. In one study, it was found that children's aggressive behavior at the age of 5 years was independently related to both their television violence viewing and their sex-role preferences, as measured 2 years earlier (Eron, 1980). For boys, aggression was related to a high preference for traditionally masculine activities, and for girls, aggression was related to a low preference for traditionally feminine activities.

In a second longitudinal study with older children, the factors of television violence viewing and sex-role preference were similarly found to be independent and stable predictors of aggression for boys, although not for girls (Eron *et al.*, 1974). Specifically, the preferences shown by 8-year-old boys for watching violent television and for avoiding traditionally feminine activities were found to be predictive of their peer-rated aggression, measured both at that time and 10 years later. The authors suggest that for boys, the watching of television violence is likely to have both an immediate effect and a long-term cumulative effect on building aggressive habits. The overall pattern of the data further suggested that by the time the boys had reached the age of 19 years, their aggressive behavior patterns were strongly established and no longer as responsive to the conditions that influenced the development of this behavior 10 years earlier.

Television violence may have a more enduring effect on boys than on girls due to a variety of sex-role-related factors, including the following:

1. Boys are more likely than girls to choose to watch violent programs (Lyle & Hoffman, 1972).
2. Boys are more likely than girls to regard violent programs as being realistic (Eron *et al.*, 1974).
3. The television characters who perform violence are much more likely to be male than female (Slaby & Quarfoth, 1980).
4. Male television characters are more likely than female television characters to perform violence in a way that leads to "success" in accomplishing the desired end (Gerbner, Gross, Jackson-Beeck, Jeffries-Fox, & Signorielli, 1978).

5. Female television characters are more likely to be the victims than the perpetrators of violence (Gerbner *et al.*, 1978).

Thus, television provides children with a variety of sex-role-related standards regarding aggression.

Social class patterns of aggression

Children from lower socioeconomic families typically show higher levels of aggression than children from middle or upper class backgrounds (Feshbach, 1970). The specific factor or combination of factors that might account for this rather global finding has not been clearly identified. Nevertheless, a wide variety of potential explanations could be put forth, including those that focus on patterns of family interaction, television viewing, or peer interaction. For example, lower class children have been found to be more likely than middle class children (*a*) to receive physical punishment from their parents (Sears, Maccoby, & Levin, 1957); (*b*) to watch greater amounts of television violence (Lyle, 1972); and (*c*) to become members of delinquent gangs (Short, 1966). As we will demonstrate in the following sections of this review, research evidence has reliably linked each of these factors with high levels of aggression in children. Thus, the general finding of socioeconomic class differences in children's aggression may serve as a point of departure for researchers to investigate the interrelationship among the diverse systems of influence in a child's life—systems such as the family, the television, and the peer group. Considering that violence is particularly prevalent among poor inner-city residents of all ages, research on the particular combinations of factors that govern aggression within lower class urban settings is sorely needed—not only to broaden our understanding of aggression, but most importantly to address this pressing social problem in a responsible way.

FAMILY INFLUENCES ON AGGRESSION

Development of aggression in the family

The family provides the first, and potentially most intense, socialization experiences in the life of the child. Although family members often provide each other with emotional support and warm intimacy, the rights and responsibilities that they feel toward one another can result in the frequent use of "justified violence." Family members often believe that they have a right to compel each other to behave in certain ways, and that resistance to such attempts at coercion can justifiably be countered with various forms of aggression (Straus, Gelles, & Steinmetz, 1979). For example, a mother who spanks her child for running into the street may have "the child's own good" as a basic motivation for her aggressive behavior.

Observations of family interactions reveal that a great deal of coercive behavior occurs on a daily basis in most families. However, families with highly aggressive children are likely to show unusually high levels of coercive behavior and unusually low levels of approval in interacting with each other (Patterson, 1976a, 1979). In one study of children referred to a clinic because of their highly aggressive behavior outside of the home, it was found that each of these children's family members exhibited more physical aggression in their daily interactions than the family members of nonaggressive children (Goldberg & Wilensky, 1976).

Besides living in an aggressive family context, aggressive children typically receive high levels of both physical and nonphysical punishment from their parents. Aggressive children in one study were found to receive three times as much punishment as nonproblem children, and these children received more punishment even when they were behaving appropriately (Patterson, 1976a). Indeed, it appears that one of the most reliable predictors of children's level of aggression is the heavy use by parents of harsh, punitive discipline and physical punishment.

Parental punitiveness has been found to be positively correlated with children's aggression in over 25 studies (see Martin, 1975). Furthermore, the generalizability of this finding is strengthened by the wide range of samples and methodologies for which it holds. For example, this relationship holds across differences in the following factors: (*a*) age level of the children (preschool, preadolescent, adolescent); (*b*) sex of the children; (*c*) clinical history of the children (delinquent, nondelinquent); (*d*) socioeconomic class of the family (lower class, middle class); (*e*) sex of the parent providing the data (mother, both mother and father); (*f*) method of assessing the effect (interview, direct observation, peer ratings, ratings from case notes); (*g*) measures of aggression; (*h*) targets of aggression (parents, siblings, peers at school, teachers, society in general); and (*i*) level of severity of the punishment. Although findings are not always statistically significant for all measures, for both parents, or for both sexes, they nevertheless provide broad-based support for the contention that parental punitiveness and children's aggression are reliably linked.

Unfortunately, the explanation for this link is neither clear nor simple. The studies that report a correlation between parents' punitiveness and children's aggression are limited insofar as they specify neither the direction of the effect nor the causal mechanism that links these two factors. One plausible explanation is that highly aggressive children may cause their parents to escalate the amount and severity of their disciplinary behavior (Bell, 1968). On the other hand, a variety of alternative explanations focus on the parents' punitive behavior as the primary cause of their children's aggression, including the following possibilities (Becker, 1964):

1. Punitive parents may directly encourage and reinforce their children to aggress against individuals outside of the family.
2. Harsh punishment itself may serve as a frustrating instigation to aggression for children.
3. The punitive parent may serve as a model of aggressive behavior, demonstrating for children how to behave aggressively while implicitly sanctioning the use of aggression in response to interpersonal conflict.

An argument could be made for each of these individual explanations of why parents who use punitive discipline tend to have children who are highly aggressive. Yet these explanations are neither exhaustive nor mutually exclusive. Each potential causal explanation offers a particular perspective from which to view the role of parental punitiveness in the development of children's aggression. However, singular and unidirectional causal explanations that are based on a global assessment of parents' general style of administering discipline do not provide a complete picture of the socialization process.

Rather, it appears that parental punitiveness is one important aspect of a general pattern of intercorrelated parental behaviors that influence the child's aggression. This pattern includes such additional factors as parental permissiveness for aggression, negativism or lack of warmth, low use of reasoning, and inconsistent application of discipline. For example, in an interview study, preschool children's aggressiveness, as reported by their mothers, was found to be related to their mother's: (*a*) use of physical punishment; (*b*) permissiveness for aggression; and (*c*) lack of warmth (Sears *et al.*, 1957). The most aggressive children had mothers who were generally permissive, but who used severe punishment when they did punish. Mothers also reported that when the parents used physical punishment in an attempt to control their children's aggression, the children's overall levels of aggression tended to increase.

A remarkably similar pattern of results was found in a recent study of the early parental rearing conditions that predict the aggression of adolescent boys, as rated by their peers (Olweus, 1979a). Parental retrospective reports of the rearing conditions during their son's childhood revealed four factors that contributed in an additive way to the development of the adolescent boy's aggression: (*a*) mother's and father's use of physical punishment, threats, and violent outbursts; (*b*) mother's permissiveness for aggression; (*c*) mother's negativism; and (*d*) boy's temperament, as indicated by his general activity level and his calm or hot temper in early years.

For children who show deviantly high levels of aggression, similar patterns of punitive parental behaviors have been identified. In a study of highly aggressive 9-year-old boys observed over a period of 5 years, it was found that their parents were generally very likely to use physical punishment on their children, threaten them frequently, reject them often, and engage in a high degree of intense conflict with one another (McCord, McCord, & Howard, 1961). A closer analysis of the pattern of parent behaviors revealed that aggressive boys typically lived in a family in which both parents were highly permissive, and one parent was punitive whereas the other was not. This pattern of parental behaviors occurred infrequently in a control group of families with nonaggressive boys. In a study designed to specify which pattern of parental variables would differentiate highly aggressive from nonaggressive boys 9 to 12 years of age, a more thorough account of the typical family pattern emerged (Martin & Hetherington, 1971). Highly aggressive boys characteristically had a family in which both parents used highly punitive discipline, both parents showed inconsistency in their application of punishment, the mother (but not the father) showed low acceptance of the boy, and both parents perceived the boy to be highly aggressive toward father, mother, and peers alike.

Children who show unusually high levels of aggression in the preschool or elementary school years are typically regarded as "problem children" by parents or school authorities. In the preadolescent and adolescent years, unusually aggressive children often face the additional problem of delinquency charges by legal authorities. Studies of adolescent boys have revealed that the pattern of childrearing techniques reported by parents of delinquents differs markedly from that of nondelinquents, as does the pattern of sociological factors, such as whether the family is located in a high-delinquency neighborhood (Glueck & Glueck, 1950). But even when a variety of sociological factors are controlled, the childrearing behavior pattern of parents of delinquent and nondelinquent boys has been found to differ significantly.

For example, Bandura and Walters (1959) have identified major differences in parental behaviors in a detailed study specifically designed to assess why boys from comparatively "good" homes became delinquent for reasons of antisocial aggression. The sample of aggressive and nonaggressive boys was confined to adolescents who were of average intelligence or above; who came from homes not broken by separation, divorce, or death of a parent; whose parents were steadily employed; and who did not live in a high-delinquency neighborhood. From extensive interviews with the mothers and fathers about the childrearing techniques they had used during their sons' earlier years, distinctive patterns emerged. Compared to parents in the control group, one or both parents of the aggressive delinquent boys actively encouraged and sometimes even required their sons to use aggression outside the home. This encouragement of aggression took several different forms, including:

1. **Threatening punishment for not fighting**
   MOTHER [p. 111]: *So I told him one night, the next time he came crying, he was going to get a spanking.*
   FATHER (as reported by mother) [p. 107]: *You're going to whip these boys or else I'm going to whip you.*
2. **Giving direct advice to fight**
   MOTHER [p. 116]: *I told him, "Go out and fight it out yourself."*
   FATHER [p. 115]: *I told him many times that if someone wanted to fight with him and started the old idea of the chip on the shoulder, "Don't hit the chip, hit the jaw, and get it over with."*
3. **Labeling not fighting as unmasculine or immature**
   MOTHER [p. 115]: *I've told him to look after himself and don't let anybody shove him around or anything like that, but not to look for trouble. I don't want him to be a sissy.*
   FATHER [p. 108]: *I don't want him to be a baby and have somebody push him around.*
4. **Permitting fights to continue**
   MOTHER [p. 112] *The fight? I'd stop it if they got too vicious. As long as they're fighting with their hands and have nothing in them—if it's fair— I'd just let it go. You know, not till they hurt each other, but I wouldn't let them hit with sticks and things.*
   FATHER [same father as previously cited from p. 115]: *I'd let it* [the fight] *go until one won. See who was the best man.*

Parents of delinquent aggressive boys differed from parents of nondelinquent boys not only by more often encouraging their sons to use physical aggression in dealing with social problems outside the home (rather than using nonaggressive assertion), but also by more often using punitive techniques to discipline their sons (rather than using nonpunitive techniques such as reasoning). Although all parents reported little current use of physical punishment with their teenage boys, the disciplinary practices they reported using during the boys' earlier years differed markedly for the two groups of parents. In particular, fathers of delinquent aggressive boys were more prone to resort to physical punishment to discipline their sons than were fathers of nondelinquent boys, and mothers of the aggressive boys showed some tendency in the same direction. The pattern of behaviors associated with these parents' use of physical punishment suggests that this form of punitive discipline may have been employed, not so much as a specific technique of training, but rather as an expression of a generalized rejecting attitude. Thus, mothers who frequently used physical punishment with their boys tended also to reject them, to ridicule them, and to show hostility toward them. In addition, these mothers showed a great deal of hostility and little warmth toward their husbands. Fathers who often used physical punishment also showed a lack of warmth toward their sons, and they actively discouraged the formation of a close emotional relationship between father and son.

Considering that parents' use of physical punishment is one of the most reliable predictors of children's aggression (Martin, 1975), both the prevalence of its use in American society and its role in child abuse deserves to be mentioned in a discussion of children's aggression. Various surveys have indicated that between 80% and 93% of parents in American families use physical punishment as a form of child discipline, although some use it only rarely and only with young children (Stark & McEvoy, 1970; Steinmetz & Straus, 1974); and 36% of all secondary schools report physically punishing students for disciplinary reasons during a typical month (Boesel, 1978). In light of this widespread use of physical punishment, it is perhaps not surprising that one common form of child abuse consists of an excessive or extreme use of physical punishment that injures the child and violates community standards for treatment of children. Yet, the difficulty of specifying precisely when the line of community standards has been crossed, together with the difficulty of detecting domestic crimes, makes it likely that extremely aggressive forms of physical punishment within the family are often tolerated or overlooked by community authorities.

One of the most popular notions related to child abuse is that the abused child often grows up to be an abusive parent, such that in some families "violence breeds violence across generations." An adequate test of this notion would require cross-generation longitudinal data on abusing and nonabusing families, and such data have not been collected. Limited support for this notion comes from a number of studies in which parents who physically abuse their children are more likely than nonabusive parents to report that they themselves were severely physically punished in childhood and/or that they had parents who physically assaulted one another (e.g., Straus *et al.*, 1979). On the other hand, this explanation is not exhaustive, since some parents who abuse their children report having had no such history of physical abuse during childhood (e.g., Flynn, 1970). It should be noted that findings such as these are clearly limited insofar as they derive from retrospective accounts of childhood experiences, reported by adults who may be motivated to provide an "acceptable" rationale for their deviant behavior.

More direct support for the "violence breeds violence" hypothesis comes from the consistent finding that physically abused children have been observed to show very high levels of aggression outside of the home, in addition to showing a variety of serious emotional problems (e.g., Kinard, 1979). For example, in a recent study, toddlers 1–3 years of age were observed while interacting with peers and caregivers in a daycare setting (George & Main, 1979). Toddlers who were physically abused at home were compared to a control group of toddlers from nonabusive families that were nevertheless experiencing stress. The abused children showed much more physical aggression toward their peers and engaged in much higher levels of verbal and physical harassment of their caregivers. Furthermore, they were the only children in the day care center to threaten the caregivers and to attack them physically. It was noted that the behavior pattern of the abused children resembled that of their parents to a striking degree. Both the abusive parents and their children showed periodic outbursts of aggression, and both attempted to avoid social interaction whenever possible. Nevertheless, it remains to be demonstrated conclusively that abusive treatment by parents is causally related to their children's aggressive behavior, and that aggressive young children are more likely than nonaggressive children to grow up to become abusive parents.

Although it may be tempting to place the blame for children's aggression on parents who use punitive or abusive childrearing techniques, it is important not to overlook the child's contribution to the system of parent–child interaction. In the case of child abuse, it is rare for all children in a family to be abused. Usually a particular child in the family is singled out for abusive treatment, and there are even reports of the same child being abused in a series of foster homes (Parke & Collmer, 1975). Clearly a child who is selectively and repeatedly abused in relatively independent settings must show particular characteristics or behavior patterns that make him or her a likely target for abuse. As the abuse continues, the child's tendency to exhibit problem behaviors may increase, thereby attracting further abuse and perpetuating an escalating cycle of problem behavior and abusive treatment.

Children's aggression is one such behavior that presents management problems for parents. Thus, the fact that highly aggressive children may have experienced high levels of physical punishment from their parents may be due, in part, to the difficulties inherent in disciplining aggressive children (Martin, 1975). The opportunity for a child's particular brand of misbehavior to play a major role in eliciting particular types of discipline is illustrated in a recent study of mothers' disciplinary choices (Grusec & Kuczynski, 1980). Reports by mothers of elementary-school-age children indicated that the type of discipline they were likely to use depended more on the particular form of misbehavior shown by the child than on the individual mother's general style of discipline. Mothers commonly chose to deal with children's physical aggression by using one of various power-assertive techniques (e.g., forcing compliance, withdrawing privileges, threatening, or punishing physically), followed by a matter-of-fact statement of the rules or consequences related to this form of misbehavior. Parents presumably choose to use a particular disciplinary technique based on their belief that this technique will effectively stop and correct the misbehavior to which it is applied. However, research evidence indicates that although power-assertive techniques are sometimes effective in stopping aggression temporarily, more frequently they are counterproductive because they can stimulate further aggression in the future, particularly when used inconsistently (Parke, 1972).

Research investigator Gerald Patterson has described how this counterproductive effect operates within families. He views the family as a system of interacting members who develop particular patterns of behavior in the process of learning to respond to each other. Through detailed home observations of the sequences of behavior that frequently occur within both aggressive and nonaggressive families, Patterson and his colleagues have identified a particular coercive pattern that serves to elicit, maintain, and even increase aggression among all family members (e.g., Patterson, 1976a, 1979; Patterson & Cobb, 1971; Patterson, Cobb, & Ray, 1973). A coercive pattern of interaction occurs when one family member presents an aversive behavior (e.g., teasing, whining, yelling, hitting), and another family member attempts to alter it by presenting a second aversive behavior. The coercive interchange often continues, escalates in intensity, and draws in other family members until one member backs down and withdraws his or her aversive behavior, thereby breaking the cycle of aversive interchange for the moment. However, since the others have been "negatively reinforced" or rewarded by successfully stopping the aversive behavior of one family member, they will be even more likely to use highly aversive behaviors and to direct them at the submitting family member again in the future.

Through this process of coercive interaction within families, children can quickly learn to become both initiators and victims of aggression, while inadvertently training their parents to become highly punitive and even abusive. For example, a coercive interchange might have its beginnings in the usual sibling squabbles experienced in most families: younger sister teases brother; brother hits sister; sister stops teasing. In this case, the initial aversive stimulus was the teasing, and the hitting was rewarded by the cessation of teasing. Hitting was immediately successful in stopping the sibling's teasing, and under these conditions hitting will quickly become a habitual response. However, most parents are unlikely to sit by and allow one sibling to hit another, particularly if this is a recurring behavior. Mother may step in, yell at the boy, and hit him as punishment for his aggressive behavior. If this punishment produces momentary peace and quiet in the family, the mother has been rewarded by the cessation of quarreling, and the boy has inadvertently helped to train his mother to use physical aggression against him. Patterson and Cobb (1971) suggest that as a result of this process of coercive interaction, "there are many grown women with no past history of Hitting, who are shaped by interactions with infants and children to initiate physical assaults [p. 124]."

Although coercive interactions occur in most families, they are particularly likely to be found in those families that are referred to clinics due to their problems with an aggressive child. These aggressive children have been found to be nearly twice as likely as nonaggressive children to respond to punishment from parents by either continuing or increasing their aversive behavior (Patterson, 1976a). One reason for their persistence in misbehaving may be that the parents tend to be inconsistent in their responses to misbehavior, initially punishing it in the hopes of stopping it, but later rewarding the continued misbehavior by giving in. When a behavior is rewarded intermittently, it becomes extremely resistant to attempts to eliminate it. In many problem families, Patterson has observed that in a contest of wills, the mother frequently plays the role of loser or victim by eventually retreating when the child's rate and intensity of aversive behavior becomes sufficiently high (Patterson, 1980).

Unless the parents are adept in the use of child management skills, all family members may eventually adopt aversive behaviors as a method of coping with each other, and the entire family system may become disrupted. Indeed, the coercive pattern of family interaction has often been found to be accompanied by a wide variety of disruptions in family interaction, including: (*a*) avoidance of interaction among family members; (*b*) cessation of family recreational activities; (*c*) disruption in communication and problem-solving abilities; (*d*) loss of self-esteem, particularly for mothers; and (*e*) development of marital conflicts. For the aggressive child who lives in such a family, the consequences reach well beyond the family setting. The aggressive child typically must face such consequences as (*a*) acquiring the label of "deviant"; (*b*) developing a negative evaluation of self and others; (*c*) being rejected by peers; (*d*) becoming less responsive to positive social reinforcement; and (*e*) failing to develop social skills (Patterson, 1979). Clearly in families that support the development of high levels of aggression in their children, each family member will face serious and distressing consequences.

Regulation of aggression in the family

Not surprisingly, research indicates that the childrearing techniques used to raise relatively nonaggressive children are generally the opposite of techniques used to raise aggressive children. Parental warmth, consistency of discipline, high expectations for good behavior, and infrequent exposure to aggressive models have all been related to low levels of aggression in children (e.g., Baumrind, 1967; Eron, Walder, & Lefkowitz, 1971; Feshbach, 1970; McCord *et al.*, 1961; Sears *et al.*, 1957). The study by McCord and his associates is illustrative. In an investigation into the childrearing antecedents of delinquency, 174 boys and their families were observed over a 5-year period. Some of the boys were judged by authorities to be potentially delinquent, and others were judged to be normal, nondelinquent boys. Information about the boys' backgrounds was collected from social agencies, schools, observations of staff members, psychiatrists, physicians, and psychologists. The resulting case histories of the boys were then coded, providing the primary data for the study. As a first step, the boys were divided into three groups: (*a*) aggressive boys, who were frequently involved in fights, destruction, and general violence; (*b*) assertive boys, who sometimes participated in fights but generally responded moderately to aggression; and (*c*) nonaggressive boys, who were rarely if ever involved in any aggressive behavior and whose general pattern of social interaction was peaceful and friendly. It is important to note that the boys labeled "assertive" by McCord would be more accurately labeled "moderately aggressive" under our definitions. When the backgrounds of these groups of boys were compared, a number of differences in their parents' childrearing techniques were identified. The results offer strong support for the view that nonaggressive children grow up in family environments different from those experienced by aggressive children. Table 3.1 summarizes the findings.

In interviews with parents of aggressive and nonaggressive boys, Bandura and Walters (1959) also identified childrearing techniques that were frequently used by the parents of nonaggressive boys. First, parents of nonaggressive boys directly encouraged their sons to understand the perspectives of other people rather than to act aggressively toward them. They encouraged their sons to maintain their standards and principles by asserting themselves in socially acceptable ways, and to view the use of hostile aggression as a sign of weakness:

> MOTHER [p. 114]: *We've always taught Dan that it takes a bigger man to keep from getting into a fight than it does to pick a fight, that anybody can fight.*
>
> MOTHER [p. 114]: *That's what I try to explain to Keith. "Try to think how the other person feels. How would you feel if you were having to take the same treatment that you're giving?" This gets him to think about it.*
>
> MOTHER [p. 113]: *Well, I usually tell him that the best way to meet a problem like that (being given a rough time) is to either avoid the boy or to try to see to it that the boy doesn't dislike him, so that the problem doesn't come up.*

In addition, parents of nonaggressive boys used the technique of reasoning to a greater extent, and in qualitatively different ways, than parents of the delinquent aggressive boys. Whereas parents of aggressive boys were more likely to use reasoning to point out that their son's behavior would bring external punishments as a consequence, parents of nonaggressive boys tended to use reasoning to emphasize the injury or suffering their son's behavior might bring to the parents themselves, and to help their son label and thereby modify his feelings. Furthermore, the use of reasoning by parents was found to be part of a larger pattern of parental behaviors including parental warmth, nurturance, acceptance, and nonpunitiveness.

Parents' use of reasoning as a disciplinary technique generally has been found to be associated with the development of a moral orientation based on internal beliefs of right and wrong, coupled with concern for others and a desire to make reparation when involved in wrongdoing. In particular, reasoning that emphasizes the consequences for others of the child's actions is particularly effective in promoting this sort of moral orientation, which may help prevent antisocial behavior (Hoffman, 1970; Hoffman & Saltzstein, 1967). Explanations that emphasize the consequences for others may even be effective with toddlers under 3 years of

Table 3.1
Backgrounds of Aggressive, Moderately Aggressive, and Nonaggressive Boys[a]

Environmental conditions	Aggressive boys	Moderately aggressive boys[b]	Nonaggressive boys
Parents' emotional relationship with the boy	Rejecting Punitive Frequent use of threats	Affectionate Moderately punitive[c] Infrequent use of threats	Affectionate Nonpunitive Little use of threats
Instillation of direct controls	Overcontrolled or subnormally controlled by mothers Low demands on the child Lack of supervision	Normally or subnormally controlled by mothers Low demands Moderately little supervision of the child[c] Moderately inconsistent in discipline[c]	High demands Firm supervision of the child Consistent in discipline
Parental model	Socially deviant	Moderately deviant[c]	Socially conformist
Parental relationship to each other	A high degree of general conflict Lack of mutual esteem Dissatisfaction with role in life Unaffectionate	High degree of general conflict Moderately low mutual esteem[c] Moderately dissatisfied with role[c] Affectionate	Low degree of general conflict High mutual esteem Satisfied with role Affectionate

[a] Adapted with permission from McCord, McCord, & Howard, *Journal of Abnormal & Social Psychology*, 1961, 62, p. 90.
[b] To be consistent with current usage, the label *moderately aggressive* was substituted for the authors' label of *assertive*.
[c] To specify the appropriate level of this factor, the term *moderately* has been substituted for the authors' label of *relatively*.

age. Toddlers whose mothers used this form of reasoning in their home have been found to be more likely to attempt to help other children in distress and to make amends to other children who have been hurt by their actions (Zahn-Waxler, Radke-Yarrow, & King, 1979). Other-directed reasoning was particularly influential when the message was embellished with the full range of maternal feelings, judgmental reactions, and convictions of right and wrong. Parents who actually demonstrate their own concern for others, as well as explaining their concern to their children, are likely to help their children develop both a strong concern for the welfare of others and an associated tendency to refrain from behaving aggressively toward others.

Some families, for whatever reason, find themselves coping with a child whose aggressive behaviors continually disrupt ongoing family interaction. Such a child may not respond well to reasoning or to attempts to provide general positive reinforcement, particularly if reasoning follows misbehavior, thereby serving as reinforcing attention. In such families, intervention in the form of a family treatment program may be needed in order to diminish the level of aggression within the family. In one successful family treatment program designed by Patterson (e.g., 1976a), parents begin by reading one of two books that outline in practical terms the techniques to be used. The books are: *Families: Applications of Social Learning to Family Life* (Patterson, 1975); and *Living with Children: New Methods for Parents and Teachers* (Patterson, 1976b). In the process of reading the book parents learn to define, track, and record a variety of antisocial and prosocial child behaviors. Next, parents participate in parent training groups in which modeling and role-playing techniques are used to teach them the specific procedures for dealing with the behaviors of concern. Finally, parents learn to negotiate contracts with their children that specify contingencies for both prosocial and problem behaviors, and to respond contingently to different behaviors of their children in accordance with the contract. As a result of this process, parents learn to give positive reinforcement to desired behaviors and to ignore or withdraw reinforcement from the aggressive behaviors exhibited by their children. In addition, they learn to use nonaggressive forms of punishment, such as withdrawing privileges or sending children to a separate room for a very brief period of isolation, known as "time-out."

Thus, the family treatment program provides parents with nonviolent, yet effective techniques for dealing with their child's aggressive behaviors. The program helps parents to become more consistent, less punitive, and more effective in their disciplinary practices. Rather than limiting the treatment to individual family members, the entire family is treated as a system for which aversive control techniques are replaced by contingent exchanges of positive behaviors. Such family treatment programs have been shown to be successful not only in altering parents' perceptions of their child's aggressiveness, but also in reducing the independently observed aggressive behaviors displayed by both parents and children in the home (e.g., Walter & Gilmore, 1973).

TELEVISION INFLUENCES ON AGGRESSION

Television effects on the development of aggression

Considering the extent of television use, its content, and its demonstrated effects on viewers, television must now be viewed as a major source of socialization, together with that of family, peers, and environmental factors. Children in the preschool and elementary school years typically watch television for an average of over 27 hours per week (*Nielsen Television Index*, 1981). Since this amount of television watching includes weekends, school holidays, and summer vacations, children can be said to spend more time watching television than they spend engaging in any other single waking activity, including attending school, interacting with family members, or playing with peers (Lyle, 1972). Furthermore, much of the television programming that children typically watch presents violence as a common form of social interaction. For example, about 75% of prime time dramatic fiction programs sampled from 1967 through 1975 were found to contain some violence (Gerbner *et al.*, 1978). About 88% of Saturday morning children's programs were found to contain at least some violence, and over one-third of these programs were considered to be "saturated" with violence (Barcus, 1971). It should be noted, however, that individual children differ dramatically in both their overall use of television and their selective exposure to violent programming (Slaby & Quarfoth, 1980). An individual child's particular experiences with television presentations of violence on the one hand, and presentations of prosocial activities on the other hand, can have a significant influence on the development and regulation of the child's aggressive behavior.

The large body of research evidence on television's influence on children has been reviewed rather thoroughly in a number of recent publications (e.g., Comstock, Chaffee, Katzman, McCombs, & Roberts, 1978; Liebert & Schwartzberg, 1977; Murray & Kippax, 1979; Slaby & Quarfoth, 1980; Stein & Friedrich, 1975). Each review points out that the central task of assessing the influence of television on children has been approached from a wide variety of methodological perspectives, including the use of laboratory experiments, correlational field studies, content analyses, surveys, diary records, and naturalistic observations. Considering the diversity of the methods used, there is an impressive convergence of the research evidence documenting the general conclusion that television can indeed influence children's aggressive behavior. This discussion will focus on the research evidence indicating that the observation of television violence can (a) increase children's aggressive behavior; and (b) increase children's passive acceptance of real-life aggression.

In his testimony before the United States Congress in 1972, Surgeon General Steinfeld stated that "Certainly, my interpretation is that there is a causal relationship between television violence and subsequent antisocial behavior, and that the evidence is strong enough that it requires some action on the part of responsible authorities, the TV industry, the government, the citizens [U.S. Congress, 1972, p. 28]." Support for this conclusion has been documented across a wide variety of types of viewers, televised materials, and viewing circumstances. For example, an increased probability of viewer aggression has been demonstrated for each of the following variations:

1. Children or adults (Berkowitz, 1971; Liebert & Baron, 1972)
2. Viewers with or without documented histories of unusually aggressive behavior (Hartmann, 1969; Parke, Berkowitz, Leyens, West, & Sebastian, 1977; Stein & Friedrich, 1972; Steuer, Applefield, & Smith, 1971; Wolf & Baron, 1971)
3. Viewers who have or have not experienced frustration prior to viewing violence (Hartmann, 1969; Liebert & Baron, 1972)
4. Cartoon violence, fantasy violence, or realistically portrayed violence (Bandura, 1965; Bandura, Ross, & Ross, 1961, 1963; Ellis & Sekyra, 1972; Steuer, et al., 1971)
5. Violent programs presented just as they are televised or specially constructed and edited for research purposes (Bandura, 1965; Stein & Friedrich, 1972)
6. Violence presented on a television set, a movie screen, or by live models (Bandura, 1965; Bandura et al., 1963; Parke et al., 1977; Stein & Friedrich, 1972)
7. Naturalistic viewing circumstances or controlled laboratory circumstances (Bandura, 1965; Steuer et al., 1971)
8. Single or repeated exposure to violent programs (Bandura et al., 1963; Parke et al., 1977)
9. Situations permitting viewer aggressive responses to be similar to or different from those portrayed (Bandura, 1965; Liebert & Baron, 1972; Stein & Friedrich, 1972)
10. Viewer aggressive responses measured immediately following or

with a long-term delay of up to 10 years following exposure to violence (Lefkowitz, Eron, Walder, & Huesmann, 1972; Liebert & Baron, 1972)

Although these and other findings provide broad support for the existence of a general causal relationship, exposure to television violence must be regarded as only one of many factors that can influence—but not solely determine—the aggressive behavior of an individual child. The claim of a causal relationship is based on the demonstrated overall statistical likelihood that "if large groups of children watch a great deal of televised violence they will be more prone to behave aggressively than similar groups of children who do not watch such TV violence [Rubinstein, 1978, p. 688]." Less is known about the observed fluctuations and variations in individual children's susceptibility to the influence of television violence.

The conclusion that television violence can cause an increase in children's aggressive behavior stands in direct opposition to the popularly held and often publicized "catharsis" notion. According to this notion, the observation of television violence constitutes a vicarious experience of aggression that serves to drain the aggressive energy from the viewer, and thereby results in a *reduction* in the viewer's subsequent expression of aggression. Although some researchers still consider the catharsis hypothesis to be viable in limited circumstances (e.g., Feshbach & Singer, 1971), the overwhelming weight of the research evidence directly contradicts the catharsis prediction. In fact, the Surgeon General's Scientific Advisory Committee made one of its few unequivocal statements when it concluded that there was "no evidence that would support a catharsis interpretation [Rubinstein, 1978, p. 687]."

A second effect of viewing television violence is that children tend to become passively accepting of real-life aggression, showing increased behavioral and emotional indifference toward the aggression of others. In a series of laboratory studies, the behavioral responses of elementary school children who had just watched a violent program were compared to the responses of similar children who had just watched a nonviolent program (Drabman & Thomas, 1974, 1975; Thomas & Drabman, 1975). Following television viewing, each individual child was assigned the responsibility of "baby-sitting" for younger children who were playing in an adjacent room. The experimenter told the child to call an adult "if anything goes wrong," thereby requiring the child to determine when something had gone wrong. While the baby-sitting child watched, the younger children first began to argue and then to fistfight with one another. It was found that those "baby-sitters" who had previously watched a violent television program were far slower and were less likely than those who had seen a neutral program to respond to the aggressive behavior of their charges either by intervening themselves or by calling upon an adult to stop the fight.

This behavioral indifference to real-life aggression has been hypothesized to occur because repeated exposure to televised violence may progressively blunt children's emotional responses to the aggression of others (Thomas, Horton, Lippincott, & Drabman, 1977). Several recent studies provide some support for the "emotional desensitization" hypothesis. For example, children have been found to show greater emotional responses, as measured by skin conductance, to violent cartoons and films than to similar programs that contain no violence (Osborn & Endsley, 1971). Children's level of emotional response to televised violence has been found to be negatively correlated with a viewing history of high levels of exposure to either television in general (Cline, Croft, & Courrier, 1973) or television violence in particular (Thomas *et al.*, 1977). Furthermore, children who were previously shown a violent television program segment (from the police series *S.W.A.T.*) were found to show less emotional arousal to a subsequent videotape depicting the real-life aggression of two children fighting than did children who had previously watched an exciting but nonviolent sports program (about a championship volleyball game) (Thomas *et al.*, 1977). What is needed is research designed to assess the extent to which children's overt behavioral responses can be predicted from their internal emotional and cognitive responses to television violence.

In summary, two major effects of watching television violence are an increase in children's aggressive behavior and an increase in children's passive acceptance of real-life aggression. The relationship between these two responses has not been investigated, but it would be possible for both effects to occur simultaneously. It has been noted that for a child to develop both increased aggressiveness and increased passive acceptance of aggression is no more incompatible than for a child to simultaneously develop meanness and callousness (Comstock, 1977). It may be that television's stylized presentation of violence as a commonplace, effective, acceptable, and often rewarded form of social action serves the primary role of reducing a child's inhibitions against the use of aggression in real life—thereby potentially leading to both an increased use of aggression by the child and an increased indifference toward others' use of aggression.

Regulation of television effects on aggression

Since most television viewing occurs in the home, the family can play a major role in altering television's effects on children—both by directly regulating children's "television diet" and by helping children interpret and evaluate what they view. Most parents, however, put very few restrictions on either the amount or the content of young children's viewing choices (Bower, 1973; Lyle, 1972; Lyle & Hoffman, 1972). Within the family, television often has the status of a "children's medium" for which the young have become the acknowledged resident experts (Comstock, 1978). Also, the growing tendency for families to own two or more television sets (as is currently the case in 51% of U.S. households) is likely to result in increased separate viewing by children and adults, which would further reduce parents' involvement in the selection and interpretation of what children view (Bower, 1973; *Nielsen Television Index*, 1981).

Television's particular influence on aggression derives from children's specific viewing of violent programs, rather than from their total amount of television viewing. In fact, children's total amount of viewing has sometimes been found to be negatively correlated with aggression (e.g., Lefkowitz *et al.*, 1972). Thus, one suggestion for altering the effects of television on young children's aggression is to reduce the amount of violent programming they watch. Such a reduction might also be expected to stimulate a number of related alternative behaviors, such as self-control and tolerance for frustration (Stein & Friedrich, 1975). Although a great deal of research evidence indirectly supports this suggestion, it should be noted that there have been no specific experimental investigations designed to assess directly the effects of reducing children's viewing of violent programs.

A second reasonable, but as yet empirically unsupported suggestion for regulating young children's aggressive behavior is to increase children's exposure to prosocial television programs. Viewing programs that stress themes of positive and socially valued interaction among people has been shown to result in increases in a wide range of children's prosocial behaviors, including helping, sharing, cooperating, showing nurturance, verbalizing feelings, showing empathy, and playing imaginatively (e.g., Murray & Kippax, 1979; Rushton, 1979; Slaby & Quarfoth, 1980; Stein & Friedrich, 1975). Since aggressive and prosocial behaviors frequently represent alternative choices for interpersonal interaction, it might be expected that aggressive and prosocial television programs would have somewhat opposite effects on these behaviors. In one of the few studies assessing these potential effects, prosocial television programming was found to have no effect on children's aggression in a preschool classroom when children's normal home viewing experiences were supplemented with a daily viewing session of either aggressive, neutral, or prosocial programming for a 4-week period (Friedrich &

Stein, 1973). Research is needed on the effects of children's viewing of television diets that are designed to be *selective* with regard to prosocial and aggressive programming.

Beyond regulating children's television diet, parents and teachers can directly influence children's understanding and expression of aggression by participating in the evaluation and interpretation of televised violence. One effective method is for adults to coview television with children and make specific comments on the program content. Variations of this procedure are commonly practiced in the home, but rarely in a systematic way. Family members frequently talk to each other while watching television, and many of their comments are related to the program content (Lyle, 1972; Lyle & Hoffman, 1972). Several laboratory studies have assessed the influence on children's aggressive behavior of having the individual children coview a violent television program with an adult who systematically makes either approving, neutral, or disapproving comments about the observed violence (DeRath, 1963; Grusec, 1973; Hicks, 1968). The findings of each of these studies indicate that negative adult evaluations of violence can successfully reduce the subsequent aggressive behavior of children, particularly but not solely in the presence of the adult coviewer. Although these children has presumably learned the aggressive material presented on the program, they were also responding to the adult's implicit standards related to the inappropriateness of behaving in that way in the real world.

Adults can also increase children's comprehension of televised material through various forms of interaction related to coviewing. In both the home and the school classroom, it has been repeatedly demonstrated that the participation of adults in the viewing process can enhance children's understanding of the program material (e.g., Ball & Bogatz, 1970, 1973; Bogatz & Ball, 1971; Collins, Sobol, & Westby, 1981; Salomon, 1977; Singer & Singer, 1976). However, it is not clear which aspects of coviewing play a key role. For example, coviewing adults may enhance children's learning from television by guiding their attention to the relevant aspects of the presentation, by helping them structure and remember the material, by providing opportunities for verbal labeling, rehearsing, and role playing, or by providing general encouragement, arousal, and motivation. Coviewing adults may also guide children in forming their own evaluations and critical judgments about the violent and prosocial acts they view on television.

The potential importance of adult participation in helping young children interpret violent programming is highlighted by various sources of evidence that children's own particular *interpretation* of violent events may be directly related to their subsequent performance of aggression.

One source of evidence indicates that children's emotional responses to televised violence may be predictive of their subsequent aggressive behavior. Violent episodes depicted in children's programming are frequently accompanied by bursts of adult "laugh track" laughter, presumably cueing children to regard these violent acts as funny. Thus, it is not particularly surprising that some children also regard serious portrayals of violence with no accompanying laugh track as funny. What makes this observation significant are the findings from a study in which children were observed while viewing violent scenes involving a federal agent shooting one man to death and fistfighting with another (portrayed in the adult detective series *The Untouchables* (Ekman, Liebert, Friesen, Harrison, Zlatchin, Malmstrom, & Baron, 1972). Happy facial expressions made by the 5- and 6-year-old boys while viewing these violent scenes were found to be strong predictors of their subsequent aggressive behavior directed toward another child. Also, sad facial expressions during the shooting scene were *negatively* correlated with subsequent aggression for boys. Girls' facial expressions during the viewing of violence were not clearly related to subsequent aggression.

A second source of evidence indicates that young children's failure to make interpretive links between separate scenes that are related to an aggressive act can influence children's subsequent aggression (Collins, 1973). In one study, children were shown a television program in which an aggressive act was portrayed in one scene, but in an earlier scene the aggression was shown to have hostile motivation, and in a later scene the aggression was shown to have harmful consequences. Thus, for children who understood the links between scenes, the aggression would be interpreted as an undesirable act to emulate. Subsequent aggression scores suggested that third-grade children had failed to link the aggressive act with its motivation and its consequences when the three scenes were separated by short commercial messages, as frequently occurs in normal television viewing. These children subsequently showed more aggressive choices in written responses to interpersonal conflict than did similar children who had viewed the three scenes without interruption. Older children were apparently able to make the interpretative links regardless of whether or not the scenes were temporally separated. Thus, young children appear to be particularly vulnerable to the eliciting effects of television violence due in part to their failure to understand all aspects of the violent acts they see on television. It has been demonstrated that an adult coviewer can play an important role in helping young children to understand the implicit motives guiding an act of violence simply by making explanatory comments at key points during the program (Collins, Sobol, & Westby, 1981).

In conclusion, the evidence strongly suggests that adults can play an important role in regulating children's aggression by helping them to become more selective and more critical television viewers. Currently, Dorothy and Jerome Singer at the Yale University Television Research Center are developing curricula designed to teach parents to limit and to monitor their children's television viewing and to encourage the development of critical viewing skills while sharing the viewing experience with their children. Also, Eron and Huesmann are developing procedures designed to determine the best intervention strategies for ameliorating the relation between violence viewing and subsequent aggressive behavior in children (Eron, 1980). Such direct assessments of the effects of workable programs for altering children's television diet over an extended period would be of great practical relevance. In addition, since a *total* restriction on observed television violence does not seem practical, necessarily desirable, or even possible for the vast majority of children in our culture, adults should be encouraged to participate with children, at least intermittently, in sessions of co-observation and interpretation of the program content that the children do observe. Young children, in particular, stand to benefit from the opportunity to discuss with adults the relationship of television violence to the real-world of social interaction, since they have relatively little real-world experience to provide a basis for comparing and interpreting the amount and nature of television portrayals of violence. There is currently no direct evidence that adult participation can alter children's emotional response to violence or their understanding that aggressive acts may have undesirable motivations and consequences. Nevertheless, the evidence that adults can directly influence children's comprehension of a wide variety of program materials and can influence their behavioral responses to televised aggression is promising.

PEER GROUP AND TEACHER INFLUENCES ON AGGRESSION

Development of aggression in peer groups

We have seen that children's tendency to be aggressive outside the home is influenced by their parents' childrearing techniques and by the media. However, the behavior of peers and supervising adults in group settings such as classrooms and playgrounds can also have a decided effect on the occurrence of aggression. Aggression in peer group settings is influenced by (*a*) reinforcement and modeling among peers; (*b*) children's previous experiences with aggression in particular settings; and (*c*) behaviors and attitudes of supervising adults. These factors will be discussed in turn.

Aggression can be a successful method for obtaining a desired response from peers. When children observe others being rewarded for their aggressive acts, they are motivated to try aggression themselves. The snowballing effects of reinforcement and modeling in group settings have been clearly demonstrated in a study of preschool children's aggressive interactions observed in the fall and again in the spring of a school year (Patterson, Littman, & Bricker, 1967). In the two preschools involved in the study, an average of 80% of children's aggressive behaviors were directly rewarded by particular actions of the victims, such as giving up toys to their attackers, crying, or withdrawing from the scene. These actions by the victims served to reinforce the aggressor, demonstrably increasing the likelihood that he or she would use a similar aggressive technique on the same victim in the near future. When an aggressor's behavior was not rewarded by the victim, the aggressor was likely to change both the type of aggression and the choice of victim. At the beginning of the school year, many of the children were passive victims who seldom initiated an aggressive encounter. Upon observing the success of the aggression of their peers, however, some of the victims began to counterattack. Those initially passive children whose counterattacks were generally successful in terminating the aggression of their attacker became increasingly aggressive as the year progressed. By the end of the year these children began to initiate their own aggressive attacks, resulting in a dramatic increase in their level of aggression. The combination of observing the successful aggression of their peers and being rewarded for their own attempts at aggression had apparently taught these initially passive children to use aggressive behavior as a major social interaction tool. On the other hand, some initially passive children were generally unsuccessful in their counterattacks, and their level of aggression did not increase over the course of the year. These children had apparently learned that aggression did not pay off for them.

The aggressive behavior so successful for some children in preschool carries on through the elementary school and secondary school years. In studies of adolescent bullies in Sweden, it was found that certain boys tended to victimize certain other boys with some degree of regularity, and with the approval and reinforcement of the peer group (Olweus, 1978). The victims tended to be weaker and less self-confident than the bullies. Yet, no clear-cut reason for victimization was found beyond the fact that victimized boys had been successfully attacked in the past and so seemed to provide a stimulus for further attack—much the same as the previous finding that preschoolers who had been successfully victimized were likely to be selected as victims in the future (Patterson *et al.*, 1967).

Individuals who have a history of using aggression frequently and with consistent success may not be deterred easily. For example, highly aggressive boys tend to respond to punishment with increased aggression, presumably because their counterattacks have sometimes been successful in getting the punishment to be withdrawn (Patterson, 1979). When a peer performs an aversive action for which the intent is not obvious, highly aggressive boys are more likely than nonaggressive boys to attribute a hostile intention to the peer, to mistrust the peer, and to expect continued hostile actions from the peer (Dodge, 1980). Even an expectation of peer retaliation can have a differential influence on children with different histories of aggression. In one study, habitually low-aggressive third-grade boys inhibited their aggressive behavior when they expected retaliation from the victim, while high-aggressive boys increased their level of aggression when retaliation was expected (Peterson, 1971). The expectation of retaliation seems to be taken as a challenge by children whose aggression has presumably permitted them to "win" many such challenges in the past.

Children's experiences with success or failure in aggression against their peers may, in the long run, shape their internal self-reward system as well as their behavior. For some individuals, successful aggressive interactions are a source of personal pride and feelings of self-satisfaction (Bandura, 1973). For example, aggressive juvenile delinquents often boost their self-esteem through some form of violent behavior (Bandura & Walters, 1959).

For individuals who have internalized the rewards provided by peers or adults for aggression, evidence of successful violence, such as pain cues provided by the victim, may become a cue for self-praise. In one laboratory study, it was found that highly aggressive boys of elementary school age were particularly likely to increase the intensity of aversive auditory stimulation to a peer when they believed that the victim was in pain but was refusing to admit it (Perry & Perry, 1974). In a second study, high- and low-aggressive fifth-grade boys were initially annoyed by a peer and then given the opportunity to administer aversive auditory stimulation to him (Perry & Bussey, 1977). Feedback from the victim was manipulated so that half the boys in each group believed they had seriously hurt the peer, while the other half believed the noise had had little effect. The boys were then instructed to reward themselves according to what they felt they deserved for what they had done to the other boy. When faced with high pain-cue feedback, the low-aggressive boys severely curtailed their self-reinforcement, while high-aggressive boys maintained their initial level of self-reinforcement. Taken together, these findings suggest that highly aggressive boys may have failed to internalize culturally accepted standards against harming other individuals. In fact, they may have even internalized standards that foster self-praise for injurious behavior.

Besides provoking a response from other children, an aggressive act often draws some sort of attention from nearby adults. The response of adults can have a profound effect on the rate of recurrence of aggression. For example, when teachers reprimand a child for aggression, they are at the same time providing the child with potentially reinforcing attention. It has been demonstrated in several studies that many forms of teacher attention to aggressive behavior result in an increase in that behavior (e.g., Pinkston, Reese, LeBlanc, & Baer, 1973; Slaby & Crowley, 1977). The advice given by experts to parents and teachers often fails to acknowledge that scolding or reasoning generally has a reinforcing effect when it is administered at the time of the aggressive act (Combs & Slaby, 1977).

One popular recommendation is to encourage an aggressive child to redirect his or her aggression to some inanimate object. A child who wishes to hit other children might be encouraged to hit a pillow or doll instead (e.g., Dodson, 1970). Teachers may be advised to set up a punching bag or an inflatable rubber clown to help children "drain off" the aggressive energy that supposedly accumulates. There has been no empirical support for this technique. On the contrary, the available evidence indicates that encouraging any form of aggression generally *increases* the likelihood that aggression will also be used against other children (Bandura, 1973; Berkowitz, 1973a; Feshbach, 1970). In one study, elementary school boys were encouraged to punch a rubber clown, and some of the boys received rewards for their punches (Walters & Brown, 1963). Two days later, the boys' interactions were observed during both a competitive game and a free-play period. The boys who received intermittant rewards for punching the clown showed many more aggressive behaviors directed toward other children, including kicking, kneeing, elbowing, punching, and pushing, than did boys who had not been rewarded for hitting the doll.

Not only does scolding, reasoning, and encouraging aggression toward inanimate objects often stimulate children's interpersonal aggression, but even noninterference by an adult who observes aggressive acts may be interpreted by children as tacit approval (Berkowitz, 1973a). For example, preschool boys who played together while an adult sat passively and watched were found to behave more aggressively in a second play session than boys who had not been observed by the passive adult (Siegel & Kohn, 1959). The passive attention from the adult served to encourage aggression. Clearly, many of the typical responses that adults use in an attempt to reduce children's aggression can actually have the reverse effect of stimulating aggression in a classroom.

Regulation of aggression in peer groups

Teachers often lay the blame for a child's aggressive behavior on the home environment, the child's temperament, or other factors over which they have little or no control. However, since a child's tendency to show aggressive behavior is strongly influenced by characteristics of the setting in which the behavior occurs, teachers can have a major effect on children's aggressive behavior by controlling the social setting in the classroom. There are many techniques teachers can use to reduce the probability that aggression will occur in their classrooms, including (*a*) removing rewards for aggression and providing rewards for coopera- tive behavior; (*b*) explaining the methods and relative advantages of nonaggressive conflict resolution; and (*c*) teaching social skills. In a later section of the chapter we will discuss additional ways that adults can re- duce aggression by controlling the more general situational factors that influence aggressive behavior.

As we have discussed, children learn that aggression is a successful social response when their aggressive behavior is rewarded by adult attention or by peers who cry and give up their toys. The converse of this principle is that aggression will diminish if children do not receive reinforcement for aggressive behavior, but instead are rewarded for ap- propriate prosocial responses. In one nursery school class, a dramatic reduction in aggression occurred when teachers were simply instructed to ignore aggression and attend to children only when they were en- gaged in cooperative behavior (Brown & Elliot, 1965). Teachers noted that the most aggressive boys became more cooperative than they had ever thought possible. Teachers also noted that they did not ignore aggression entirely. When intervention seemed to be called for, they simply separated the children and then walked away without giving undue attention to the behavior.

It is very difficult for teachers to ignore aggressive behavior entirely. Moreover, simply paying no attention to aggression may not be the most effective technique, since many of the rewards for aggression are pro- vided by peers (Patterson *et al.*, 1967) and children tend to interpret adult nonintervention as approval (Siegel & Kohn, 1959). On the other hand, it has been demonstrated that giving attention by rebuking or lecturing a child for an aggressive act usually increases the likelihood that the same act will occur again (Risley & Baer, 1973). Clearly needed are teacher interventions that are effective in reducing the aggression without providing the reinforcement of teacher attention.

One technique that has proven successful in reducing aggression is for the teacher to step between the children involved in the incident, ignoring the aggressor but paying attention to the victim (Allen, Turner, & Everett, 1970; Pinkston *et al.*, 1973). Attention to the victim might include comforting a hurt child, giving the victim something interesting to do, or suggesting to the victim assertive, nonaggressive ways of dealing with the aggressor. For example, the teacher can suggest that the victim use specific assertive phrases, such as "No hitting!" or "I'm playing with this now." There are several advantages to this technique. First, the aggressor receives no reward for the aggressive act, either from teacher attention or from victim submission. Second, the victim receives practice in coping assertively with conflict. Third, other children in the group observe that aggression is not a successful method of social interaction, that teachers will support nonviolent assertiveness, and that an appropriate response to a victim is a sympathetic one. These observations are likely to reduce aggression throughout the classroom and to increase both assertiveness and sympathetic behavior. The behavior of an adult who has developed a nurturant relationship with children in a classroom can have a powerful modeling effect on the observing children (Yarrow, Scott, & Waxler, 1973).

In some cases, aggressive behavior may be so persistent that merely ignoring the behavior and attending to the victim will not be sufficient to reduce it. In these cases, it has been effective in many programs to use a "time-out" procedure contingent on the aggressive behavior (e.g., Green, Budd, Johnson, Lang, Pinkston, & Rudd, 1976; Porterfield, Herbert-Jackson, & Risley, 1976; Risley & Baer, 1973; Tams & Eyberg, 1976). The purpose of time-out is to remove the child from all reinforcing stimuli for a designated short period of time (e.g., 1–10 minutes) *immediately* following a specific inappropriate behavior. With some children it may be effective to tell them they can rejoin the group when they are "ready" to behave appropriately. At home, time-out might consist of sending the child to his or her room, to a specially designated room (such as the bathroom), or to a chair in a "quiet corner." At school, time-out might simply involve sitting on a chair away from the group, or going to a special place as a back-up if the chair is ineffective. When using a time-out procedure, it is critical that all adults involved be consistent in the application of time-out for specified behaviors. It is also important that adults not become so involved in watching for behaviors to be punished that they forget to "catch the child being good." Time-out for misbehavior will be most effective when paired with a great deal of adult attention and praise for cooperative helpful interactions.

When attending to children's social interactions, adults often overlook children's verbal responses. Several studies have shown that adult attention to either aggressive or cooperative speech can have an effect on both future verbalizations and actual physical behaviors related to the verbalizations (Slaby, 1974; Slaby & Crowley, 1977). In one study, preschool teachers were instructed to attend to children's verbal cooperative statements, while ignoring both aggressive language and aggressive physical behavior. When teachers heard a cooperative statement, they were asked to say the child's name and then repeat the child's phrase, saying "I heard you say . . . ." (Slaby & Crowley, 1977). After 2 weeks of applying these contingencies to verbal behavior, the amount of both verbal and physical cooperation in children's free-play behavior was observed to have increased, while both verbal and physical aggression decreased. These results are striking considering that teachers were successful in attending to an average of only 14% of all cooperative verbal statements observed to occur during the 2-week period. The findings also indicate that cooperative behavior may be incompatible with aggression. As cooperation increases, aggression may decrease. One approach to dealing with aggression, then, is for adults to take every opportunity to encourage and attend to cooperative behavior in both its verbal and nonverbal forms.

Children's social behavior is affected by their own level of cognitive understanding, in addition to reinforcements provided externally. The ability to understand the point of view of others is a particularly influential social–cognitive skill that develops with age. Younger children, for instance, are more likely than older children to respond with aggressive retaliation even to an accidental affront. They do not seem to be able to take into account the intentions of their opponent (Shantz & Voydanoff, 1973). Adults can help to correct this situation, however. In one study, third-grade children were prevented from winning a prize by a clumsy peer, and then they were given a chance to help or hurt that child when he was performing a similar task (Mallick & McCandless, 1966). Children were less inclined to choose a response that would hurt their frustrator when the experimenter explained that the frustrator's actions had been accidental. By providing a reasonable, positive interpretation of the frustrating situation, the adult was able to reduce the children's level of aggression.

Whereas the use of reasoning and discussion can be effective in reducing aggression, it is important that the adult use this technique only at "neutral" times. Reasoning with a child who has just committed an aggressive act only serves to reinforce aggression by providing adult attention (Combs & Slaby, 1977). Furthermore, even at neutral times, reasoning may be relatively ineffective if it is confined to lecturing children on the evils of aggression. A more effective method of reasoning is to discuss alternative ways of resolving conflict and the relative advantages of using nonaggressive solutions to social problems. For example, teachers in one study made use of neutral occasions to explain to aggressive preschool children about the harm that results from aggression, the ineffectiveness of aggression as a problem-solving technique, and the benefits of using prosocial techniques (Zahavi & Asher, 1978). Following this instruction, the amount of aggressive behavior was observed to decrease during free play and the amount of prosocial behavior increased.

One broad approach that goes beyond the simple use of reasoning is to regulate aggression by teaching social skills. This approach involves teaching children the skills necessary for understanding social conflict, generating and evaluating alternative solutions, and performing nonaggressive solutions effectively (see Combs & Slaby, 1977). The social-skills-training approach is based on the assumption that an individual's problems in social settings often derive from a behavioral skills deficit, rather than from an excess of a personality trait (Asher, 1978). For example, it may be more useful to assume that a shy child may have a lack of skill in initiating social interaction, rather than an excess of anxiety. An aggressive child might be assumed to lack skill in responding prosocially, rather than possessing an excess of hostility. The more socially skilled child might be regarded as having the freedom that accompanies a broad behavioral repertoire and an ability to use an appropriate response effectively. A reduction in children's aggression has been found to be a by-product of programs designed to teach such social skills as empathizing, solving social problems, showing self-control, and responding assertively.

Based on the assumption that empathy fosters behavior incompatible with aggression, Feshbach (1978) developed a social skills training program designed to develop empathy in elementary school children. Training is designed to enhance such skills as identifying others' emotional states, understanding situations from others' point of view, and experiencing in oneself the emotions felt by other individuals. Activities in the program include having children identify emotions of people seen in photographs and videotapes, role playing different emotions, playing games of perspective taking, listening to stories and retelling them from different points of view, and playing several different roles in a short skit. The activities are accompanied by a variety of discussions focusing on emotions. Pilot investigation of this program has demonstrated some success in reducing aggression among children who participate in these empathy training sessions. Nevertheless, research attempts to relate empathy and aggression have had inconclusive results (e.g., Feshbach & Feshbach, 1969; Iannotti, 1978).

Another successful technique for reducing aggression is to involve children in activities designed to enhance their social problem-solving skills. In a classic study, preschool children actively participated in discussions evaluating alternative ways to resolve interpersonal conflict (Chittenden, 1942). For each conflict situation, the teacher used two dolls to act out a variety of solutions. In a typical incident, both of the dolls wanted to play with the same wagon. In the aggressive solution, the dolls fought, broke the wagon, and felt unhappy. In a cooperative solution, the dolls took turns and had a good time playing together. Children were involved in telling the dolls what to do after watching several alternatives played out. Results showed a reduction in aggression during free play in the preschool setting and an increase in cooperative behavior.

A similar technique was used for therapy with a 6-year-old boy who was highly aggressive (McNamara, 1970). Together with three nonaggressive peers, the boy met several times a week with a therapist who showed pictures representing conflict situations intended to provoke aggression. Children were asked what they would do. If an aggressive response was proposed, the therapist asked if they could think of any alternatives, and he rewarded suggestions of prosocial solutions. Later, the children acted out various prosocial responses to conflicts. This procedure was successful in reducing the boy's aggression in the classroom.

Spivack and Shure (1974) have developed a comprehensive program designed to help children learn to generate and evaluate their own alternative solutions to interpersonal conflicts. The 10-week series of lessons includes stories, picture stimuli, and puppet dramas that encourage children to label and discuss their feelings, to identify emotion in others using behavior as a guide, and to practice trying out and evaluating different problem-solving techniques. These investigators report a decrease in the aggressive solutions offered during dramatized situations and an increase in general behavioral adjustment as rated by teachers for children who have participated in the full program.

Other training programs have been directed more specifically toward teaching children how to make particular kinds of responses to different social conflicts. One valuable social skill children need to learn is how to be assertive. Children who learn how to stand up for their rights in a nonhostile way, and how to make known their own needs and wants without resorting to aggression will have the behavioral repertoire needed to resolve interpersonal conflict without becoming either an aggressor or a victim of aggression. Nonassertive submission to a peer's aggressive demands has been shown to reinforce the aggressor and increase the likelihood that the attack will be repeated (Patterson *et al.,* 1967). A program developed by Arezzo (1977) uses role playing, discussion, direct guidance, and contingent teacher attention to teach preschool and elementary school children specific assertive responses. In structured practice situations, the child and teacher alternately use a doll to play the roles of child, peer, or teacher, while the other responds in the reciprocal role. For example, children practice ignoring insults by turning their head away when the doll makes nasty remarks, and only respond when the doll says something appropriate, such as *I'd like to play. Will you play with me?* They learn to say *I'm playing with this now,* when a peer tries to grab a toy, and to say *No hitting,* when a peer strikes. Children also practice asking nicely for objects instead of grabbing, asking other children to play in a friendly voice, or saying *No* to requests in a nice way, sometimes adding phrases such as *You can have it when I'm done.* Teachers follow-up the structured practice situations by cueing or specifically guiding children in responding assertively in ongoing interactions in the classroom and by offering support when they do. Teachers also intervene in a potential conflict before aggression occurs, guiding children in using assertive phrases and actions to solve their problem.

An important innovation introduced by this program lies in directly teaching young children how to respond to specific situations that are likely to elicit aggression, rather than providing general instruction in prosocial behavior or broad-based problem-solving techniques. A similar approach has been used with older boys, 12–14 years of age (Gittelman, 1965). Individual aggressive boys were asked to describe situations that had provoked them to be aggressive, and to practice alternative responses to such situations. Their responses were rated by the therapist and by other members of the therapy group. The boys started with mild situations and gradually increased the intensity. As a result, the boys learned to control aggressive responses in specifically provoking situations.

SITUATIONAL FACTORS THAT INFLUENCE AGGRESSION

Situational influences on the development of aggression

The physical and programmatic setting for children's behavior has a considerable influence on whether aggressive acts will occur and continue to occur. The same children, for example, may show different levels of aggression at home and at school (Bernal, Delfini, North, & Kreutzer, 1976; Johnson, Bolstad, & Lobitz, 1976; Patterson & Cobb, 1971; Sears, Rau, & Alpert, 1965). Even superficially similar settings may elicit differing amounts of aggression. In one study, an average of 181 instances of aggression were observed during recess on the playground at one elementary school, while an average of only 61 instances were observed during a similar recess period at a different school (Johnston & Drovetz, 1976). Patterson and his colleagues (1967) found large differences in the rate of aggression between the two preschools in their observational study of aggressive interactions, and they attributed this difference to the program activities characteristic of each school. Of course, some of these observed differences may have been caused by children's different childrearing experiences, or by the reactions of adults and peers to aggressive behavior. However, some portion of observed differences in aggression is attributable to differences in the basic physical aspects of the environment, to the availability of play equipment, and to the types of activities and toys provided.

For example, research indicates that the degree of crowding experienced by a group of children may influence the rate of aggression, although results are not entirely consistent (Gump, 1975). It makes sense that crowded conditions may result in generally accelerated aggressive behavior, particularly for young children who are more likely to retaliate against accidental pushing and shoving (Shantz & Voydanoff, 1973).

There are two methods of assessing the effects of crowding on behavior. Changing the *spatial density* conditions of a group involves placing the same size group of children in spaces of differing sizes. Changing the *social density* of a group involves changes in the numbers of children interacting in the same size space. In one study, the influence of spatial density was assessed by observing the interactions of elementary school boys on large and small playgrounds (Ginsburg, 1975). On the small playground, children engaged in more frequent but shorter fights, and the fights generally involved more children than those occurring on the large playground. However, on the large playground, fights were more likely to last for longer periods of time, since other children were less likely to intervene. In contrast, in another study *less* aggression was found when a group of 4- and 5-year-old children were confined to a small indoor room than when they were situated in a larger room (Loo, 1972). This apparently inconsistent finding may have resulted from the inclusion of play fighting in the definition of aggression. Several other studies have found that play chasing and play fighting are generally reduced under crowded conditions that inhibit large motor activity (Smith, 1974a, b).

In a study of social density involving groups of three sizes interacting in a hospital playroom, significantly more aggression was observed as group size increased (Hutt & Vaizey, 1966). When both social and spatial density conditions were varied in an English nursery school, the highest level of hitting was observed when the largest group was concentrated in the smallest space (McGrew, 1972). On the other hand, no effect of spatial or social density on aggression was found in a cross-cultural observational study of five different preschools in the United States and the Netherlands (Fagot, 1977). In fact, in the schools with the highest density, in the Netherlands, the only effect was that the Dutch children more often interacted positively and less often played alone than in other schools. The author argues that the effects found in other studies might be the result of either making arbitrary changes in natural social groupings or changing the availability of play materials. It is also possible that the differing cultural contexts of the schools observed in this study outweighed any effects of differing densities.

The effect of changes in the amount of play equipment on aggression has also been examined in several studies. In one study at an elementary school, aggression increased when the amount of play equipment available at recess time was reduced (Johnson, 1935). A similar effect has been found when the amount of indoor play equipment was varied in a preschool classroom (Smith, 1974a, b). In the preschool studies, aggressive encounters most frequently occurred around arguments over the possession of toys or use of apparatus, and these conflicts increased when the number of toys was reduced. However, in addition to increased aggression, there were also increases in sharing under conditions of less equipment and in the size of groups playing together with similar toys. Aggression also increased when one or two new and desirable toys were added, particularly when they were toys that could only be played with by one or two children at a time.

It has been noted that alterations in social density are often confounded with changes in the amount of play equipment per child (Smith, 1974b). For example, in studies in which the number of children is reduced but the amount of equipment remains the same, a finding of reduced aggression might be explained by the relative increase in amount of play equipment per child (e.g., McGrew, 1972). In summary, it appears that crowding large numbers of children in a small space can have the effect of increasing aggression, particularly if there is insufficient play equipment to keep all the children occupied. The effect of crowding on aggression does not always occur, however, and it is presumably affected by such variables as the guidance and response of teachers, the amount of play equipment, and the particular types of toys and activities available.

Several studies have shown that objects in the immediate environment that have previously been associated with aggression have the potential to instigate aggression (Berkowitz, 1973b; Berkowitz & LePage, 1967). For example, aggressive cues, such as the presence of a gun, can elicit increased aggression from adults (Berkowitz, 1973b). Pacifists have long deplored the highly lucrative sales of guns and toy soldiers designed for children's play. Research evidence forms a solid basis to support their concern. In one study, a group of preschool children were observed during several free-play sessions with various kinds of toys (Turner & Goldsmith, 1976). During some sessions, novel aggressive toy guns were made available, and in other sessions, novel nonaggressive toy airplanes were available. In two replications of the study, children behaved more aggressively toward others during sessions with the toy guns than during sessions with their usual toys or with the new toy airplanes. Aggression in this study was scored only when it was unrelated to the theme of the children's play.

In another study a similar effect of aggressive toys and games was found for children of elementary school age (Feshbach, 1956). Children were brought together in groups of five for sessions during which a group leader played records, read a story, and allowed free play. In some of the play sessions, the songs, stories, and play materials revolved around aggressive themes, such as cowboys and Indians, soldiers, or pirates. In other sessions the materials revolved around nonaggressive themes, such as trains, circuses, farms, and stores. During sessions involving aggressive themes children were observed to engage in more inappropriate interpersonal aggression unrelated to the theme of their play than during nonaggressive sessions.

In addition to having an immediate influence on children's behavior, the experience of playing with aggressive toys may also influence children's general response tendencies in frustrating situations. Elementary-school-age children in one study participated in groups of four in a series of sessions involving either aggressive or cooperative activities (Davitz, 1952). Groups participating in aggressive games were encouraged and praised by the experimenter for showing aggression. The aggressive activities included trying to stand on a particular spot despite challenges, attempting to remove a cloth from the arm of another player without losing one's own cloth, and trying to break the ping-pong ball of another player without losing one's own ball. Other groups of children engaged in constructive games in which cooperation and constructive activities were encouraged and praised. Constructive activities included drawing murals and completing jigsaw puzzles. Following participation in either aggressive or constructive activities, children were placed in the frustrating situation of having a film interrupted and snack taken away, and then they were observed in a free-play session. Results indicated that the children who had previously participated in aggressive activities behaved more aggressively and less constructively during the free-play session than did the children who had participated in constructive activities. It seems that participation in activities that encourage aggressive behavior had supported the children's tendency to resort to aggression when frustrated.

In light of this evidence, it is surprising that many educators continue to encourage play with aggressive themes. Teachers of creative dramatics are often advised to have children act out classic folk tales that contain much violent and aggressive material. For example, the folk tale "The Three Billy Goats Gruff" is recommended as "an excellent first story for little children to create into a play. . . . It provides for a good energy release in a make-believe fight . . . [Siks, 1958, p. 170]." Participating in dramatization of such stories is tantamount to rehearsing aggressive behavior, and it may well increase the likelihood that the child–actors will use aggressive behaviors during their everyday interactions as well. The effects of aggressive story material were observed in one preschool classroom by the second author of this chapter. Children were videotaped while they were lined up waiting to present their puppet in a play of an African folktale. Each time an aggressive incident occurred in the plot, a rash of scuffling, hitting, and arguing broke out among the waiting players. Whenever the plot shifted from the aggressive event, the incidental aggression among the actors also subsided.

Another aspect of program activities that can have a decided effect on the level of children's aggression is the degree to which the activities are competitive. Direct competition can set the stage for aggressive interaction (Christy, Gelfand, & Hartmann, 1971; Feshbach, 1970; Perry & Perry, 1976). In one study, pairs of kindergarten and first-grade boys played a tower-building game in which the winner was promised a prize (Rocha & Rogers, 1976). Competition was varied by controlling the number of blocks available. High levels of competition and high levels of promised reward increased the aggressive behavior displayed by the boys during the game. In some cases, boys abandoned their own constructive action in attempts to knock down their opponent's tower.

Inherent in a competitive situation may be the feeling that a child's performance is being evaluated in comparison to that of his or her peers. Situations in which unequal social comparisons are made can have influence on aggressive behavior even in the absence of competition. In one study, preschool children were divided into groups of three and given differing numbers of chips redeemable for prizes (Santrock, Smith, & Bourbeau, 1976). One designated child in each group received either less, more, or the same number of chips as the other two children in the group. Subsequent observations during a structured free-play period indicated that the boys (but not the girls) who had received fewer chips during the first phase of the experiment showed more physical aggression during the play period than the boys in the other groups. The authors suggest that children evaluate their performance according to the amount of reinforcement they receive relative to that given to other children. An experience of negative social comparison may stimulate aggression performed in attempts to regain social equality.

Just as individual competition may increase individual aggression within a group, competition between groups may result in increased aggression. Sherif and his colleagues (Sherif, Harvey, White, Hood, & Sherif, 1961) invited two groups of 12-year-old boys to a summer camp. In the first phase of the experiment, they developed cohesiveness within the two groups by introducing activities that required joint problem solving. The second phase of the study involved producing intergroup tension by setting up typical camp competition between the two groups. A tournament was announced, prizes offered, and competition encouraged. The result was an increase in incidents of raids on the opposing group, name-calling, taunting, and physical fighting that was at times so intense that it had to be broken up by the staff. These fights provided a vivid example of aggression as a by-product of competition. In the third phase of the study, the intergroup tension was dispersed through the introduction of "superordinate goals" that required the efforts of both groups for solution.

Situational influences on the regulation of aggression

Since the incidence of aggression is strongly influenced by characteristics of the setting in which the behavior occurs, adults can have a major effect on controlling aggression by creating nonaggressive physical and programmatic environments for children. Providing ample space for children to carry on their activities, for example, can eliminate the accidental pushing and shoving that often leads to retaliatory aggression (Gump, 1975). Children are less likely to engage in aggressive actions when they are provided with sufficient materials to keep them busily involved in constructive activities without having to compete for desired resources (Smith, 1974a, b). The types of play materials made available can induce children to interact cooperatively rather than aggressively. Certainly toys that encourage play with aggressive themes, such as guns and toy soldiers, can be removed from the play environment (Feshbach, 1956; Turner & Goldsmith, 1976).

Adults can also minimize competition and subsequent aggression by organizing activities that require cooperation for successful completion. Children who have prior experience in performing cooperative activities are likely to respond to frustrating situations by behaving cooperatively rather than aggressively (Davitz, 1952). Such activities can include working together on group projects such as murals, games with a team goal, and group stories. Competition can be further reduced by administering rewards contingent upon the performance of the group, rather than the individual. The administration of group rewards has consistently been found to be effective in producing cooperative behavior while reducing competition and antagonism (Bryan, 1975; Nelson & Madsen, 1969).

Activities that promote friendship and goodwill within a group of children can produce a climate that fosters cooperation rather than aggression. Children tend to like each other better when they have participated together in enjoyable activities or when they have been rewarded for a joint effort (Blau & Rafferty, 1970; Heber & Heber, 1957; Lott & Lott, 1960). When a group of children is faced with the challenge of a group goal that can only be reached through cooperative effort, even sworn enemies can be led to work together and diminish their conflict. In the study by Sherif and his colleagues (1961), the aggression that had erupted as a result of the competition between the two groups of 12-year-old boys was eliminated through the introduction by camp counselors of several such superordinate goals. For example, when the truck bringing food for a general campout became stuck, boys from both groups worked together to drag the truck along. When something happened to the flow of drinking water from the tank at the camp, all the boys joined in the effort to solve the problem. By the time they had participated in several of these joint efforts, the original animosity had disappeared and boys from the two previously warring groups became fast friends. It is interesting to note that merely bringing the two groups of boys together for joint activities, such as eating dinner, did not succeed in reducing antagonism. In fact, this procedure led to several antagonistic encounters, including a food fight. It was only when the superordinate goal structured the course of their interactions that cooperation replaced aggression.

CONCLUDING NOTE

In this review we have emphasized children's socialization experiences within their separate "social worlds"—largely because little is currently known about the ways in which children's experience with aggression in one social setting may influence their responses in other settings. Similarly, we have emphasized the external and variable sources of influence on children—largely because relatively little is known about the ways in which children internalize stable and generalizable dispositions toward aggression. Finally, we have emphasized children's socialization experiences at distinct age levels—largely because little is known about the processes by which children's aggression develops. Thus, our current view of children's aggression may be characterized as rather segmented, external, and static. A more complete picture of the development and regulation of aggression will be provided by further investigation of the convergent socialization influences on the development of the social–cognitive processes underlying children's aggressive behavior.

ACKNOWLEDGMENTS

The authors wish to thank Diana Arezzo for providing suggestions on an early draft and Kim Storey for reviewing a final draft of this chapter.

REFERENCES

Allen, K. E., Turner, K. D., & Everett, P. M. A behavior modification classroom for head start children with problem behaviors. *Exceptional Children*, 1970, *37*, 119–127.

Arezzo, D. *Verbal assertive training, role playing, and role reversal techniques in social skills development.* Paper presented under the author's former name, Diana Arezzo Slaby, at the Eleventh Annual Conference of the Association for the Advancement of Behavior Therapy, Atlanta, Georgia, December 1977.

Asher, S. R. Children's peer relations. In M. E. Lamb (Ed.), *Social and personality development.* New York: Holt, 1978. Pp. 91–113.

Ball, S., & Bogatz, G. A. *The first year of Sesame Street: An evaluation.* Princeton, N.J.: Educational Testing Service, 1970.

Ball, S., & Bogatz, G. A. *Reading with television: An evaluation of The Electric Company.* Princeton, N.J.: Educational Testing Service, 1973.

Bandura, A. Influence of models' reinforcement contingencies on the acquisition of imitative responses. *Journal of Personality and Social Psychology*, 1965, *1*, 589–595.

Bandura, A. *Aggression: A social learning analysis.* Englewood Cliffs, N.J.: Prentice-Hall, 1973.

Bandura, A., Ross, D., & Ross, S. A. Transmission of aggression through imitation of aggressive models. *Journal of Abnormal and Social Psychology*, 1961, *63*, 575–582.

Bandura, A., Ross, D., & Ross, S. A. Imitation of film-mediated aggressive models. *Journal of Abnormal and Social Psychology*, 1963, *66*, 3–11.

Bandura, A., & Walters, R. H. *Adolescent aggression.* New York: Ronald Press, 1959.

Barcus, F. E. *Saturday children's television: A report of TV programming and advertising on Boston-commercial television.* Boston: Action for Children's Television, 1971. (ERIC Document Files No. 055 461)

Baumrind, D. Child care practices anteceding three patterns of preschool behavior. *Genetic Psychology Monographs,* 1967, *75,* 43–88.

Becker, W. C. Consequences of different kinds of parental discipline. In M. L. Hoffman & L. W. Hoffman (Eds.), *Review of child development research* (Vol. *1*). New York: Russell Sage Foundation, 1964. Pp. 169–208.

Bell, R. Q., A reinterpretation of the direction of effects of socialization. *Psychological Review,* 1968, *75,* 81–98.

Berkowitz, L. The contagion of violence: An S–R mediational analysis of some effects of observed aggression. In W. J. Arnold & M. M. Page (Eds.), *Nebraska Symposium on Motivation* (Vol. *19*). Lincoln: Univ. of Nebraska Press, 1971. Pp. 96–135.

Berkowitz, L. *Two cultures of violence: Some opposing views of aggression in therapy.* Presidential Address to Division 8, Personality and Social Psychology, American Psychological Association, Honolulu, Hawaii, September 1972.

Berkowitz, L. Control of aggression. In B. M. Caldwell & H. N. Ricciuti (Eds.), *Review of child development research* (Vol. *3*). Chicago: Univ. of Chicago Press, 1973. Pp. 95–140. (a)

Berkowitz, L. Words and symbols as stimuli to aggressive behavior. In J. F. Knutson (Ed.), *The control of aggression.* Chicago: Aldine, 1973. Pp. 113–143. (b)

Berkowitz, L., & LePage, A. Weapons as aggression-eliciting stimuli. *Journal of Personality and Social Psychology,* 1967, *7,* 202–207.

Bernal, M. E., Delfini, L. F., North, J. A., & Kreutzer, S. L. Comparison of boys' behaviors in homes and classrooms. In E. J. Mash, L. A. Hamerlynck, & L. C. Handy (Eds.), *Behavior modification and families.* New York: Brunner/Mazel, 1976. Pp. 204–227.

Billman, J., & McDevitt, S. C. Convergence of parent and observer ratings of temperament with observations of peer interaction in nursery school. *Child Development,* 1980, *51,* 395–400.

Blau, B., & Rafferty, J. Changes in friendship status as a function of reinforcement. *Child Development,* 1970, *41,* 115–121.

Boesel, D. *Violent schools—Safe schools.* Washington, D.C.: National Institute of Education, 1978.

Bogatz, G. A., & Ball, S. J. *The second year of Sesame Street: A continuing evaluation.* Princeton, N.J.: Educational Testing Service, 1971.

Bower, R. T. *Television and the public.* New York: Holt, 1973.

Brown, P., & Elliot, R. Control of aggression in a nursery school class. *Journal of Experimental Child Psychology,* 1965, *2,* 103–107.

Bryan, J. H. Children's cooperation and helping behavior. In E. M. Hetherington (Ed.), *Review of child development research* (Vol. *5*). Chicago: Univ. of Chicago Press, 1975. Pp. 127–182.

Buss, D. M., Block, J. H., & Block, J. Preschool activity level: Personality correlates and developmental implications. *Child Development,* 1980, *51,* 401–408.

Chittenden, G. E. An experimental study in measuring and modifying assertive behavior in young children. *Monographs of the Society for Research in Child Development,* 1942, *7*(1, Serial No. 31).

Christy, P. R., Gelfand, D. M., & Hartmann, D. P. Effects of competition-induced frustration on two classes of modeled behavior. *Developmental Psychology,* 1971, *5,* 104–111.

Cline, V. B., Croft, R. G., & Courrier, S. Desensitization of children to television violence. *Journal of Personality and Social Psychology,* 1973, *27,* 360–365.

Collins, W. A. Effect of temporal separation between motivation, aggression, and consequences: A developmental study. *Developmental Psychology,* 1973, *8,* 215–221.

Collins, W. A., Sobol, B. L., & Westby, S. Effects of adult commentary on children's comprehension and inferences about a televised aggressive portrayal. *Child Development,* 1981, *52,* 158–163.

Combs, M. L., & Slaby, D. A. Social skills training with children. In B. Lahey & A. Kazdin (Eds.), *Advances in clinical child psychology* (Vol. 1). New York: Plenum, 1977. Pp. 161–201.

Comstock, G. Types of portrayal and aggressive behavior. *Journal of Communication,* 1977, 27(3), 189–198.

Comstock, G. The impact of television on American institutions. *Journal of Communication,* 1978, 28(2), 12–28.

Comstock, G., Chaffee, S., Katzman, N., McCombs, M., & Roberts, D. *Television and human behavior.* New York: Columbia Univ. Press, 1978.

Davitz, J. The effects of previous training on post-frustration behavior. *Journal of Abnormal and Social Psychology,* 1952, 47, 309–315.

Dawe, H. C. An analysis of two hundred quarrels of preschool children. *Child Development,* 1934, 5, 139–157.

DeRath, G. W. *The effects of verbal instructions on imitative aggression.* Unpublished doctoral dissertation, Michigan State University, 1963.

Dodge, K. A. Social cognition and children's aggressive behavior. *Child Development,* 1980, 51, 162–170.

Dodson, F. *How to parent.* New York: Signet, 1970.

Drabman, R. S., & Thomas, M. H. Does media violence increase children's tolerations of real-life aggression? *Developmental Psychology,* 1974, 10, 418–421.

Drabman, R. S., & Thomas, M. H. Does TV violence breed indifference? *Journal of Communication,* 1975, 25(4), 86–89.

Ekman, P., Liebert, R. M., Friesen, W. V., Harrison, R., Zlatchin, C., Malmstrom, E. J., & Baron, R. A. Facial expressions of emotion while watching televised violence as predictors of subsequent aggression. In G. A. Comstock, E. A. Rubinstein, & J. P. Murray (Eds.), *Television and social behavior.* Vol. 5: *Television's effects: Further explorations.* Washington, D.C.: U.S. Government Printing Office, 1972. Pp. 22–58.

Ellis, G. T., & Sekyra, F. The effect of aggressive cartoons on the behavior of first grade children. *Journal of Psychology,* 1972, 81, 37–43.

Eron, L. D. Prescription for reduction of aggression. *American Psychologist,* 1980, 35, 244–252.

Eron, L. D., Walder, L. O., Huesmann, L. R., & Lefkowitz, M. M. The convergence of laboratory and field studies of the development of aggression. In J. de Wit & W. W. Hartup (Eds.), *Determinants and origins of aggressive behavior.* The Hague: Mouton, 1974. Pp. 347–380.

Eron, L. D., Walder, L. O., & Lefkowitz, M. M. *Learning of aggression in children.* Boston: Little, Brown, 1971.

Fagot, B. I. Variations in density: Effect on task and social behaviors of preschool children. *Developmental Psychology,* 1977, 13, 166–167.

Ferguson, T. J., & Rule, B. G. Effects of inferential set, outcome severity, and basis of responsibility on children's evaluations of aggressive acts. *Developmental Psychology,* 1980, 16, 141–146.

Feshbach, N. D. *Empathy training: A field study in affective education.* Paper presented at the Annual Meeting of the American Educational Research Association, Toronto, Canada, March 1978.

Feshbach, N. D., & Feshbach, S. The relationship between empathy and aggression in two age groups. *Developmental Psychology,* 1969, 1, 102–107.

Feshbach, S. The catharsis hypothesis and some consequences of interaction with aggressive and neutral play objects. *Journal of Personality,* 1956, 24, 449–462.

Feshbach, S. Aggression. In P. H. Mussen (Ed.), *Carmichael's manual of child psychology* (Vol. 2). New York: Wiley, 1970. Pp. 159–259.

Feshbach, S. The development and regulation of aggression: Some research gaps and a proposed cognitive approach. In J. de Wit & W. W. Hartup (Eds.), *Determinants and origins of aggressive behavior.* The Hague: Mouton, 1974. Pp. 167–192.

Feshbach, S., & Singer, R. D. *Television and aggression: An experimental field study.* San Francisco: Jossey-Bass, 1971.

Flynn, W. R. Frontier justice: A contribution to the theory of child battery. *American Journal of Psychiatry,* 1970, *127,* 375–379.

Friedrich, L. K., & Stein, A. H. Aggressive and prosocial television programs and the natural behavior of preschool children. *Monographs of the Society for Research in Child Development,* 1973, *38*(4, Serial No. 151).

Frodi, A., Macaulay, J., & Thome, P. R. Are women always less aggressive than men? A review of the experimental literature. *Psychological Bulletin,* 1977, *84,* 634–661.

George, C., & Main, M. Social interactions of young abused children: Approach, avoidance, and aggression. *Child Development,* 1979, *50,* 306–318.

Gerbner, G., Gross, L., Jackson-Beeck, M., Jeffries-Fox, S., & Signorielli, N. Cultural indicators: Violence profile no. 9. *Journal of Communication,* 1978, *28*(3), 176–207.

Ginsburg, H. J. *Variations of aggressive interaction among male elementary school children as a function of spatial density.* Paper presented at the Biennial Meeting of the Society for Research in Child Development, Denver, Colorado, April 1975.

Gittelman, M. Behavior rehearsal as a technique in child treatment. *Journal of Child Psychology and Psychiatry,* 1965, *6,* 251–255.

Glueck, S., & Glueck, E. *Unraveling juvenile delinquency.* Cambridge, Mass.: Harvard Univ. Press, 1950.

Goldberg, L., & Wilensky, H. Aggression in children in an urban clinic. *Journal of Personality Assessment,* 1976, *40,* 73–80.

Goodenough, F. L. *Anger in young children.* Minneapolis: Univ. of Minnesota Press, 1931.

Green, D. R., Budd, K., Johnson, M., Lang, S., Pinkston, E., & Rudd, S. Training parents to modify problem child behaviors. In E. J. Mash, L. C. Handy, & L. A. Hamerlynck (Eds.), *Behavior modification approaches to parenting.* New York: Brunner/Mazel, 1976. Pp. 3–18.

Grusec, J. E. Effects of co-observer evaluations on imitation: A developmental study. *Developmental Psychology,* 1973, *8,* 141.

Grusec, J. E., & Kuczynski, L. Direction of effects in socialization: A comparison of the parent's versus the child's behavior as determinants of disciplinary techniques. *Developmental Psychology,* 1980, *16,* 1–9.

Gump, P. V. Ecological psychology and children. In E. M. Hetherington (Ed.), *Review of child development research* (Vol. 5). Chicago: Univ. of Chicago Press, 1975. Pp. 75–126.

Hartmann, D. P. Influence of symbolically modelled instrumental aggression and pain cues on aggressive behavior. *Journal of Personality and Social Psychology,* 1969, *11,* 280–288.

Hartup, W. W. Aggression in childhood: Developmental perspectives. *American Psychologist,* 1974, *29,* 336–341.

Hartup, W. W. The social worlds of childhood. *American Psychologist,* 1979, *34,* 944–950.

Hartup, W. W., & de Wit, J. The development of aggression: Problems and perspectives. In J. de Wit & W. W. Hartup (Eds.), *Determinants and origins of aggressive behavior.* The Hague: Mouton, 1974. Pp. 595–620.

Heber, R. F., & Heber, M. E. The effect of group failure and success on social status. *Journal of Educational Psychology,* 1957, *48,* 129–134.

Hicks, D. L. Effects of co-observer's sanctions and adult presence on imitative aggression. *Child Development,* 1968, *39,* 303–309.

Hoffman, M. L. Moral development. In P. H. Mussen (Ed.), *Carmichael's manual of child psychology* (Vol. 2). New York: Wiley, 1970. Pp. 261–359.

Hoffman, M. L., & Saltzstein, H. D. Parent disciplines and the child's moral development. *Journal of Personality and Social Psychology,* 1967, *5,* 45–57.

Hutt, C., & Vaizey, M. J. Differential effects of group density on social behavior. *Nature,* 1966, *209,* 1371–1372.

Iannotti, R. J. Effect of role-taking experiences on role taking, empathy, altruism, and aggression. *Developmental Psychology,* 1978, *14,* 119–124.

Johnson, M. W. The effect on behavior of variations in amount of play equipment. *Child Development,* 1935, *6,* 56–68.

Johnson, R. N. *Aggression in man and animals.* Philadelphia: Saunders, 1972.

Johnson, S. M., Bolstad, O. D., & Lobitz, G. K. Generalization and contrast phenomena in behavior modification with children. In E. J. Mash, L. A. Hamerlynck, & L. C. Handy (Eds.), *Behavior modification and families.* New York: Brunner/Mazel, 1976. Pp. 160–188.

Johnston, K. D., & Drovetz, M. L. Levels of aggression in a traditional and a pluralistic school. *Educational Research,* 1976, *18,* 146–151.

Kagan, J., & Moss, H. A. *Birth to maturity.* New York: Wiley, 1962.

Kinard, E. M. The psychological consequences of abuse for the child. *Journal of Social Issues,* 1979, *35*(2), 82–100.

Lambert, W. W. Promise and problems of cross-cultural exploration of children's aggressive strategies. In J. de Wit & W. W. Hartup (Eds.), *Determinants and origins of aggressive behavior.* The Hague: Mouton, 1974. Pp. 437–460.

Lefkowitz, M. M., Eron, L. D., Walder, L. O., & Huesmann, L. R. Television violence and child aggression: A followup study. In G. A. Comstock & E. A. Rubinstein (Eds.), *Television and social behavior.* Vol. 3: *Television and adolescent aggressiveness.* Washington, D.C.: U.S. Government Printing Office, 1972. Pp. 35–135.

Liebert, R. M., & Baron, R. A. Short-term effects of televised aggression on children's aggressive behavior. In J. P. Murray, E. A. Rubinstein, & G. A. Comstock (Eds.), *Television and social behavior.* Vol. 2: *Television and social learning.* Washington, D.C.: U.S. Government Printing Office, 1972. Pp. 181–201.

Liebert, R. M., & Schwartzberg, N. S. Effects of mass media. *Annual Review of Psychology,* 1977, *28,* 141–173.

Loo, C. M. Effects of spatial density on social behavior of children. *Journal of Applied Social Psychology,* 1972, *2,* 372.

Lott, B. E., & Lott, A. J. The formation of positive attitudes towards group members. *Journal of Abnormal and Social Psychology,* 1960, *61,* 297–300.

Lyle, J. Television in daily life: Patterns of use. In E. A. Rubinstein, G. A. Comstock, & J. P. Murray (Eds.), *Television and social behavior.* Vol. 4: *Television in day-to-day life: Patterns of use.* Washington, D.C.: U.S. Government Printing Office, 1972. Pp. 1–32.

Lyle, J., & Hoffman, H. Children's use of television and other media. In E. A. Rubinstein, G. A. Comstock, & J. P. Murray (Eds.), *Television and social behavior.* Vol. 4: *Television in day-to-day life: Patterns of use.* Washington, D.C.: U.S. Government Printing Office, 1972. Pp. 129–256.

Maccoby, E. E., & Jacklin, C. N. *The psychology of sex differences.* Stanford, Calif.: Stanford Univ. Press, 1974.

Maccoby, E. E., & Jacklin, C. N. Sex differences in aggression: A rejoinder and reprise. *Child Development,* 1980, *51,* 964–980.

McCord, W., McCord, J., & Howard, A. Familial correlates of aggression in nondelinquent male children. *Journal of Abnormal and Social Psychology,* 1961, *62,* 79–93.

McGrew, W. C. Aspects of social development in nursery school children, with emphasis on introduction to the group. In N. B. Hones (Eds.), *Ethological studies of child behavior.* New York: Cambridge Univ. Press, 1972. Pp. 129–156.

McNamara, J. R. The broad based application of social learning theory to treat aggression in a preschool child. *Journal of Clinical Psychology,* 1970, *26,* 245–247.

Mallick, S. K., & McCandless, B. R. A study of the catharsis of aggression. *Journal of Personality and Social Psychology,* 1966, *4,* 591–596.

Martin, B. Parent–child relations. In F. D. Horowitz (Ed.), *Review of child development research* (Vol. 4). Chicago: Univ. of Chicago Press, 1975. Pp. 463–540.

Martin, B., & Hetherington, E. M. *Family interaction and aggression, withdrawal, and nondeviancy in children.* Progress Report, National Institute of Mental Health Project No. MH 12474. Univ. of Wisconsin, 1971.

Matthews, K. A., & Angulo, J. Measurement of the Type A behavior pattern in children: Assessment of children's competitiveness, impatience-anger, and aggression. *Child Development,* 1980, *51,* 466–475.

Murray, J. P., & Kippax, S. From the early window to the late night show: International trends in the study of television's impact on children and adults. In L. Berkowitz (Ed.), *Advances in experimental social psychology* (Vol. 12). New York: Academic Press, 1979. Pp. 253–320.

Nelson, L., & Madsen, M. C. Cooperation and competition in four-year-olds as a function of reward contingencies and subculture. *Developmental Psychology,* 1969, *1,* 340–344.

Nielsen television index. National audience demographics reports, November, 1980. Northbrook, Ill.: A. C. Nielsen Co., 1981.

Olweus, D. *Aggression in the schools.* New York: Wiley, 1978.

Olweus, D. Familial and temperamental determinants of aggressive behavior in adolescent boys: A causal analysis. *Developmental Psychology,* 1979, *16,* 644–660. (a)

Olweus, D. Stability of aggressive reaction patterns in males: A review. *Psychological Bulletin,* 1979, *86,* 852–875. (b)

Osborn, D. K., & Endsley, R. C. Emotional reactions of young children to TV violence. *Child Development,* 1971, *42,* 321–331.

Parke, R. D. Some effects of punishment on children's behavior. In W. W. Hartup (Ed.), *The young child* (Vol. 2). Washington, D.C.: National Association for the Education of Young Children, 1972. Pp. 264–283.

Parke, R. D., Berkowitz, L., Leyens, J. P., West, S. G., & Sebastian, R. J. Some effects of violent and nonviolent movies on the behavior of juvenile delinquents. In L. Berkowitz (Ed.), *Advances in experimental social psychology* (Vol. 10). New York: Academic Press, 1977. Pp. 135–172.

Parke, R. D., & Collmer, C. W. Child abuse: An interdisciplinary analysis. In E. M. Hetherington (Ed.), *Review of child development research* (Vol. 5). Chicago: Univ. of Chicago Press, 1975. Pp. 509–590.

Patterson, G. R. *Families: Applications of social learning to family life.* (Rev. ed.). Champaign, Ill.: Research Press, 1975.

Patterson, G. R. The aggressive child: Victim and architect of a coercive system. In E. J. Mash, L. A. Hamerlynck, & L. C. Handy (Eds.), *Behavior modification and families.* New York: Brunner/Mazel, 1976. Pp. 267–316. (a)

Patterson, G. R. *Living with children: New methods for parents and teachers* (Rev. ed.). Champaign, Ill.: Research Press, 1976. (b)

Patterson, G. R. A performance theory for coercive family interaction. In R. B. Cairns (Ed.), *The analysis of social interactions: Methods, issues and illustrations.* Hillsdale, N.J.: Erlbaum, 1979. Pp. 119–162.

Patterson, G. R. Mothers: The unacknowledged victims. *Monographs of the Society for Research in Child Development,* 1980, *45*(5, Serial No. 186).

Patterson, G. R., & Cobb, J. A. A dyadic analysis of "aggressive" behavior. In J. P. Hill (Ed.), *Minnesota Symposia on Child Psychology* (Vol. 5). Minneapolis: Univ. of Minnesota Press, 1971. Pp. 72–129.

Patterson, G. R., Cobb, J. A., & Ray, R. S. A social engineering technology for retraining the families of aggressive boys. In H. E. Adams & I. P. Unikel (Eds.), *Issues and trends in behavior therapy.* Springfield, Ill.: Charles C Thomas, 1973. Pp. 139–210.

Patterson, G. R., Littman, R. A., & Bricker, W. Assertive behavior in children: A step toward a theory of aggression. *Monographs of the Society for Research in Child Development,* 1967, *32*(5, Serial No. 113).

Perry, D. G., & Bussey, K. Self-reinforcement in high- and low-aggressive boys following acts of aggression. *Child Development,* 1977, *48,* 653–657.

Perry, D. G., & Perry, L. C. Denial of suffering in the victim as a stimulus to violence in aggressive boys. *Child Development,* 1974, *45,* 55–62.

Perry, D. G., & Perry, L. C. A note on the effects of prior anger arousal and winning or losing a competition on aggressive behavior in boys. *Journal of Child Psychology and Psychiatry,* 1976, *17,* 145–149.

Peterson, R. Aggression as a function of retaliation and aggression level of target and aggressor. *Developmental Psychology,* 1971, *5,* 161–166.

Pinkston, E. M., Reese, N. M., LeBlanc, J. J., & Baer, D. M. Independent control of a preschool child's aggression and peer interaction by contingent teacher attention. *Journal of Applied Behavior Analysis, 1973, 6,* 115–124.

Porterfield, J. K., Herbert-Jackson, E., & Risley, T. R. Contingent observation: An effective and acceptable procedure for reducing disruptive behavior. *Journal of Applied Behavior Analysis, 1976, 9,* 55–64.

Risley, T. R., & Baer, D. M. Operant behavior modification: The deliberate development of behavior. In B. M. Caldwell & H. M. Ricciuti (Eds.), *Review of child development research* (Vol. 3). Chicago: Univ. of Chicago Press, 1973. Pp. 283–329.

Rocha, R. F., & Rogers, R. W. Ares and Babbitt in the classroom: Effects of competition and reward on children's aggression. *Journal of Personality and Social Psychology,* 1976, *33,* 588–593.

Roedell, W. C., Slaby, R. G., & Robinson, H. B. *Social development in young children.* Monterey, Calif.: Brooks/Cole, 1977.

Rotenberg, K. J. Children's use of intentionality in judgments of character and disposition. *Child Development,* 1980, *51,* 282–284.

Rubinstein, E. A. Television and the young viewer. *American Scientist,* 1978, *66,* 685–693.

Rule, B. G., Nesdale, A. R., & McAra, M. J. Children's reactions to information about the intentions underlying an aggressive act. *Child Development,* 1974, *45,* 794–798.

Rushton, J. P. Effects of prosocial television and film material on the behavior of viewers. In L. Berkowitz (Ed.), *Advances in experimental social psychology* (Vol. 12). New York: Academic Press, 1979. Pp. 321–351.

Salomon, G. Effects of encouraging Israeli mothers to co-observe "Sesame Street" with their five-year-olds. *Child Development,* 1977, *48,* 1146–1151.

Santrock, J. W., Smith, P. C., & Bourbeau, P. E. Effects of social comparison on aggression and regression in groups of young children. *Child Development,* 1976, *47,* 831–837.

Sears, R. R., Maccoby, E. E., & Levin, H. *Patterns of child rearing.* Evanston, Ill.: Row, Peterson, 1957.

Sears, R. R., Rau, L., & Alpert, R. *Identification and child-rearing.* Stanford, Calif.: Stanford Univ. Press, 1965.

Shantz, D. W., & Voydanoff, D. A. Situational effects on retaliatory aggression at three age levels. *Child Development,* 1973, *44,* 149–153.

Sherif, M., Harvey, O. J., White, B. J., Hood, W. R., & Sherif, C. W. *Intergroup conflict and cooperation: The Robber's Cave experiment*. Norman, Okla.: Univ. of Oklahoma Press, 1961.

Short, J. F. Juvenile delinquency: The sociocultural context. In L. W. Hoffman & M. L. Hoffman (Eds.), *Review of child development research* (Vol. 2). New York: Russell Sage Foundation, 1966. Pp. 423–468.

Siegel, A., & Kohn, L. Permissiveness, permission and aggression: The effect of adult presence or absence on children's play. *Child Development*, 1959, *30*, 131–141.

Siks, G. B. *Creative dramatics: An art for children*. New York: Harper, 1958.

Singer, J. L., & Singer, D. G. Can TV stimulate imaginative play? *Journal of Communication*, 1976, *26*(3), 74–80.

Slaby, R. G. Verbal regulation of aggression and altruism. In J. de Wit & W. W. Hartup (Eds.), *Determinants and origins of aggressive behavior*. The Hague: Mouton, 1974. Pp. 209–216.

Slaby, R. G., & Crowley, C. G. Modification of cooperation and aggression through teacher attention to children's speech. *Journal of Experimental Child Psychology*, 1977, *23*, 442–458.

Slaby, R. G., & Quarfoth, G. R. Effects of television on the developing child. In B. W. Camp (Ed.), *Advances in behavioral pediatrics* (Vol. 1). Greenwich, Conn.: JAI Press, 1980. Pp. 225–266.

Smith, P. K. Aggression in a preschool playgroup: Effects of varying physical resources. In J. de Wit, & W. W. Hartup (Eds.), *Determinants and origins of aggressive behavior*. The Hague: Mouton, 1974. Pp. 97–106. (a)

Smith, P. K. Social and situational determinants of fear in the playgroup. In M. Lewis & L. Rosenblum (Eds.), *The origin of fear: The origins of behavior* (Vol. 2). New York: Wiley, 1974. Pp. 107–129. (b)

Spivack, G., & Shure, M. B. *Social adjustment of young children*. San Francisco: Jossey-Bass, 1974.

Stark, R., & McEvoy, J. Middle class violence. *Psychology Today*, 1970, *4*, 52–65.

Stein, A. H., & Friedrich, L. K. Television content and young children's behavior. In J. P. Murray, E. A. Rubinstein, & G. A. Comstock (Eds.), *Television and social behavior*. Vol. 2: *Television and social learning*. Washington, D.C.: U.S. Government Printing Office, 1972. Pp. 202–317.

Stein, A. H., & Friedrich, L. K. Impact of television on children and youth. In E. M. Hetherington (Ed.), *Review of child development research* (Vol. 5). Chicago: Univ. of Chicago Press, 1975. Pp. 183–256.

Steinmetz, S. K., & Straus, M. A. *Violence in the family*. New York: Harper, 1974.

Steuer, F. G., Applefield, J. M., & Smith, R. Televised aggression and the interpersonal aggression of preschool children. *Journal of Experimental Child Psychology*, 1971, *11*, 442–447.

Straus, M. A., Gelles, R. J., & Steinmetz, S. K. *Behind closed doors: Violence in the American family*. Garden City, N.Y.: Doubleday/Anchor, 1979.

Tams, V., & Eyberg, S. A group treatment program for parents. In E. J. Mash, L. C. Handy, & L. A. Hamerlynck (Eds.), *Behavior modification approaches to parenting*. New York: Brunner/Mazel, 1976. Pp. 101–123.

Thomas, A., & Chess, S. *Temperament and development*. New York: Brunner/Mazel, 1977.

Thomas, A., Chess, S., Birch, H. G., Hertzig, M., & Korn, S. *Behavioral individuality in early childhood*. New York: New York Univ. Press, 1963.

Thomas, M. H., & Drabman, R. S. Toleration of real-life aggression as a function of exposure to televised violence and age of subject. *Merrill-Palmer Quarterly*, 1975, *21*, 227–232.

Thomas, M. H., Horton, R. W., Lippincott, E. C., & Drabman, R. S. Densitization to portrayals of real-life aggression as a function of exposure to television violence. *Journal of Personality and Social Psychology*, 1977, *35*, 450–458.

Tieger, T. On the biological basis of sex differences in aggression. *Child Development*, 1980, *51*, 943–963.

Turner, C. W., & Goldsmith, D. Effects of toy guns and airplanes on children's antisocial free play behavior. *Journal of Experimental Child Psychology*, 1976, *21*, 303–315.

United States Congress, Senate Committee on Commerce. Hearings before the Subcommittee on Communications. *Surgeon General's report by the scientific advisory committee on television and social behavior*. 92nd Congress, 2nd session. Washington, D.C.: U.S. Government Printing Office, March 21–24, 1972.

Walter, H., & Gilmore, S. Placebo versus social learning effects in parent training procedures designed to alter the behavior of aggressive boys. *Behavior Therapy*, 1973, *4*, 361–377.

Walters, R. H., & Brown, M. Studies of reinforcement of aggression: III. Transfer of responses to an interpersonal situation. *Child Development*, 1963, *34*, 562–571.

Whiting, B. B., & Whiting, J. W. M. *Children of six cultures*. Cambridge, Mass.: Harvard Univ. Press, 1975.

Wolf, B. M., & Baron, R. A. Is laboratory aggression related to aggression in naturalistic social stiuations: The influence of an aggressive model on the behavior of college student and prisoner observers. *Psychonomic Science*, 1971, *24*, 193–194.

Yarrow, M. R., Scott, P. M., & Waxler, C. Z. Learning consideration for others. *Developmental Psychology*, 1973, *8*, 240–260.

Zahavi, S., & Asher, S. R. The effect of verbal instructions on preschool children's aggressive behavior. *Journal of School Psychology*, 1978, *16*, 146–153.

Zahn-Waxler, C., Radke-Yarrow, M., & King, R. A. Child rearing and children's prosocial initiations toward victims of distress. *Child Development*, 1979, *50*, 319–330.

4 / The acquisition of self-control

JOAN E. GRUSEC
ROSEMARY MILLS

Full-fledged membership in human society requires a remarkably long apprenticeship. A wealth of knowledge, both formal and informal, must be transmitted to children before the rights and responsibilities of independent functioning are bestowed on them. One of the major teaching jobs for both parents and teachers is to instill in children society's values, attitudes, and beliefs about morality. And the ultimate goal of this job is to make these attitudes and beliefs so firmly entrenched that they become the child's own. Thus morality must be internalized: Children must be capable of regulating their own behavior. They must learn to resist temptation, delay gratification, control aggression, and show concern for the needs and welfare of others, and they must learn to do these things independently of external surveillance. Only when morality is adhered to for its own sake and not through fear of punishment or hope of reward—only when self-control is truly achieved—can socialization be said to have been successfully accomplished.

It has been suggested (Hoffman, 1970a) that the concept of internalization is a middle class one, necessary where property rights are important and where people are given major responsibilities with minimal external surveillance. Internalization may, in reality, be an impossible goal: Perfect self-control may be unattainable by all but the most saintly.

PSYCHOLOGICAL DEVELOPMENT
IN THE ELEMENTARY YEARS

As parents and teachers, however, we do strive for at least some degree of self-control on the part of those placed in our charge. This chapter will deal, then, with those techniques of training for self-control that have been the object of attention by researchers in recent years.

Beliefs about the basic nature of human functioning and therefore about the ease of socialization differ. Perhaps the most popular has been of the developing child as a system of impulsive and self-centered behaviors that must be suppressed in order for that child to take its place in society. More recently, some investigators have suggested that human nature is innately moral, that children will achieve a high level of morality with minimal guidance and encouragement (e.g., Kohlberg, 1964), or that the human species is genetically endowed with a predisposition to conform to group norms or to show concern for others because these activities further the survival of the species (e.g., Stayton, Hogan, & Ainsworth, 1971). By far, however, most research on the development of self-control has been based on the premise that children must be actively taught to engage in behaviors that involve the denial of immediate gratification for the sake of longer-term goals or the greater good of society. That is the premise that will underlie what follows.

Children who are truly self-controlled (or at least somewhat self-controlled) must know what are the values and beliefs of society and must want to behave in accord with them. Second, they must know how to behave morally. Children must know it is wrong to injure others, demand immediate pleasure, and show no concern for others, and they must be motivated not to do these things. As well, they must learn the skills that enable them to behave in a moral way. The student who stays home to study for an examination rather than going to a movie with friends has accomplished two goals. He or she has learned that a brief night of pleasure is not worth academic failure and is motivated to work to obtain a good education. Secondly, our student has acquired the ability to take immediate goals—a movie and the company of friends—and make them less psychologically attractive than the delayed goal of academic success.

This chaper will be divided into two major segments. In the first segment we shall attempt to show how children learn the values of society and are motivated to conform to them through the use of reward, punishment, reasoning, and verbal exhortation, as well as through the example set by others. In the second segment we shall consider the techniques children can be taught to help them lessen temptation and satisfy their desire to behave in accord with the demands of society.

TEACHING SELF-CONTROL THROUGH CONSEQUENCES, VERBAL MEANS (REASONING, MANIPULATION OF ATTRIBUTION), AND EXAMPLE

By far the greatest research attention paid to the development of self-control has focused on the role of discipline. Parents and teachers place heavy reliance on the encouragement or reinforcement of desirable behaviors and the discouragement or punishment of undesirable behaviors. They also supplement these techniques with more verbal ones—providing reasons for why certain things should be done, exhorting, and preaching. In addition to these methods of socialization, the example of behavior (either intentional or unintentional) that others set has an important impact on children's morality. Good examples facilitate good behavior, bad examples facilitate bad behavior.

Response consequences

Punishment is by far the most maligned technique of socialization. Repeatedly claims have been made that it is ineffective in suppressing behavior (e.g., Skinner, 1971) or that it is effective but results in all kinds of undesirable side effects (e.g., Masserman, 1943). In spite of the bad publicity, however, socializing agents continue to rely heavily on the administration of negative consequences for undesirable behavior. In a study carried out in our own laboratory, for example, 95% of the middle class mothers of a group of 4- and 7-year-old boys and girls whom we interviewed reported that they would use punishment in the form of verbal censure, withdrawal of privileges, or spanking and hitting when they were disciplining their children (Grusec & Kuczynski, 1980).

There is ample evidence that moderate intensities of punishment are effective in suppressing the specific behavior that they follow (see Walters & Grusec, 1977, for a review of the relevant research). Nor are the side effects of punishment as devastating as they have been claimed to be. Moderate punishment applied so that the relationship between the behavior and the punishment is clear, and so that it does not attack a child's self-esteem or sense of security, does not produce neurotic behavior in the punished child, nor does it lead to inappropriate suppression of related but desirable behaviors. Children who are punished do not avoid the person who punished them if that person is a source of pleasurable outcomes as well (Walters & Grusec, 1977).

It is important to remember, however, that the disciplinary interaction between adult and child provides a model or prototype for the child's future attempts at persuading others to conform to his or her desires. And it is here that one major shortcoming of the punitive approach becomes apparent. Parents or teachers who extract compliance by exerting their superior power—be it physical, psychological, or material—teach children that the way to induce compliance in others is to rely on one's own greater strength. There are a number of studies that demonstrate that children imitate the disciplinary techniques of adults. Gelfand, Hartmann, Lamb, Smith, Mahan, and Paul (1974), for example, found that children trained to play a game by being fined for incorrect responses used a similar training technique when they were later asked to teach another child to play the game. Mischel and Grusec (1966) forced preschoolers to wait before they could play an attractive game, and they criticized them and deprived them of rewards when they played poorly. Even though the children had personally experienced the (mild) aversiveness of these events, they nevertheless treated another individual in the same unpleasant way when they were assigned the task of teaching her the game. The most striking evidence that disciplinary styles are transmitted across generations comes from clinical studies of child-abusing parents. A number of studies have delineated the various characteristics of parents who maim and even kill their children. The finding that consistently emerges, however, is that parents who abuse their children were themselves abused or neglected, physically or emotionally, as children (Spinetta & Rigler, 1972).

Is there, then, an alternative approach to punishment? One frequently advocated alternative is to reward acceptable behaviors and ignore unacceptable ones. Although there is ample evidence that behavior followed by positive reinforcement will increase in its frequency of occurrence, this provides no guarantee that bad behaviors will decrease in their occurrence. If some aspect of the undesirable behavior is inherently satisfying (and giving in to temptation surely does meet that criterion) then the behavior will continue even when it is not maintained by the attention or consequences it receives from the external environment. Particularly in the development of self-control or morality (so long as one adheres to the position that it is easier to be impulsive than to be self-controlled), active measures to suppress immorality must be taken. One solution to the difficulty would be to reinforce behaviors incompatible with that which is not desired. Children who talk in class, for example, could be reinforced for not talking in class. Often, however, it is not so easy to find incompatible behaviors or to find a reinforcer so powerful that it can completely overcome the satisfaction of deviant behavior.

Recall that the major goal of socialization is the internalization of moral values and behavior. Herein lies an important problem posed by both reinforcement and punishment as disciplinary techniques. When a behavior is no longer followed by punishment, it will reappear. Similarly, when a behavior is no longer followed by reinforcement, it will disappear. With only the tools of reinforcement and punishment, socializing agents would never be able to accomplish their job. They would always need to be around to administer rewards and punishments, so that the good behavior of children would never become independent of their surveillance. It is for this reason that developmental psychologists have turned to other disciplinary techniques as better candidates for successful internalization of morality.

Reasoning

Hoffman (1970a) has suggested that socializing agents who reason with their children and who use, in particular, "other-oriented induction," that is, who make children aware of the consequences of their behavior for others, will be especially successful in the development of self-control. Other-oriented induction works, he believes, because it arouses children's empathic capacities, making them aware of the needs and feelings of others. At the same time, knowledge that one has harmed others by behaving immorally is inescapable, unlike the threat of punishment. In that way it is more likely to motivate good behavior even in the absence of surveillance. Punishment (power assertion), in the form of verbal rebuke, withdrawal of privileges, spanking, and so on, should not only be ineffective but counterproductive, both because it is inescapable and because it arouses anger and hostility in the child and, therefore, refusal to conform. A third form of discipline— withdrawal of love (social isolation, personal rejection)—Hoffman assumes to be neutral in its effects on response suppression. Although it does not arouse hostility, it does dull the child's empathic capacities.

In an analysis of 11 studies of childrearing practices that had been reported in the psychological literature, Hoffman found substantial support for his hypotheses. Generally, maternal use of other-oriented induction was positively related to an internal moral orientation, guilt, resistance to temptation, and confession and acceptance of blame—all indices of moral development. There was no correlation between the use of withdrawal of love and moral development, and a negative relationship between power assertion and moral development. Other studies addressed to the more positive side of morality—altruism—have generally yielded similar findings. Hoffman and Saltzstein (1967) found that parents of seventh-grade girls who reported that they used induction had daughters who were rated by their peers as being considerate. For boys, however, consideration of others was unrelated to induction: In fact, it was positively related to parental use of power assertion. On the other hand, Dlugokinski and Firestone (1974) reported that 10- and 13-year-old boys and girls who said that their mothers frequently used inductive discipline were seen by their classmates as more considerate, attached more importance to helping others, and donated more money to charity.

Although not entirely consistent, the correlational data do provide support for the idea that other-oriented induction, and not power assertion, facilitates moral development. There have been no experiments, however, in which the effects of other-oriented induction and power assertion have been adequately compared. Thus, the difficulty of asserting that induction *causes* moral development remains. It may be that parents who reason also do other things that are directly responsible for moral growth. Or children who are well-behaved may enable their parents to rely on mild discipline, such as reasoning, rather than on more extreme forms of discipline, such as power assertion.

The situation is made more complex by the fact that there is evidence from a great many studies that punishment *does* suppress responding. A formulation that dictates that power assertion be always harmful cannot account for these findings. Hoffman himself (Hoffman, 1970b) has helped to resolve the paradox. He found that mothers who relied on other-oriented induction *also* tended to use power assertion when their children refused to comply. Baumrind (1973) found that mothers of children who were socially responsible, self-controlled, independent, achievement-oriented, and energetic used power assertion *and* reasoning to gain compliance more than did mothers of children who were not rated high on these characteristics. Zahn-Waxler, Radke-Yarrow, and King (1979) reported that mothers of preschoolers who were altruistic and who made reparations after they had transgressed reacted to their children's deviations with explanations about why they should not have done what they did. These explanations were described, however, as having a "strong affective loading"—presumably the explanations were not calm but had strongly implied disapproval and upset (punishment) associated with them. Also, we have found that mothers who use power assertion frequently tend to accompany this power assertion with some form of reasoning (Grusec & Kuczynski, 1980). One begins to suspect, then, that successful agents of socialization do not rely solely on reasoning, but that they back up their reasoning with the threat of consequences for misbehavior—*moderate* threats, but real ones.

If successful socialization involves a combination of punishment and some form of reasoning, there are any number of reasons why this combination would be necessary. First of all, children, particularly older ones, may be less hostile and reactive to the threat of punishment if they are given reasons for why they should behave well (Cheyne & Walters, 1970). Reasoning may also provide children with general rules to govern future behavior (e.g., *Always be careful with people's possessions because they get upset when they are damaged*), whereas punishment by itself provides information about one situation alone (*Don't be careless around mother's precious vase because she gets upset when it is almost broken*). Thus, the effects of reasoning would generalize to a variety of moral situations. Then again, although the threat of punishment may be needed to motivate behavior, its masking with verbal persuasion may provide a better model of how to influence others. Or finally, the content of adult reasoning may provide the material for self-instruction that helps the child to maintain self-control, a technique which will be described in a later section of this chapter.

The reader may note that none of these explanations requires that reasoning be of a particular nature. Although Hoffman stressed the importance of other-oriented reasoning, aimed at honing the child's empathic skills, our possible explanations do not require a specific content for the reasoning component. We shall, however, discuss the content of reasoning later on. For the moment, we turn to lengthier discussion of one final explanation for why punishment in combination with reasoning should be particularly suitable for fostering moral development. This explanation involves attribution theory (Kelley, 1967), an approach that is becoming increasingly important in research on self-control. The attribution formulation accounts for the importance of punishment's being combined with reasoning, as well as suggesting why other approaches to the development of self-control, such as mild rather than severe threat, manipulation of self-concept, and assignment of responsibility, may be effective.

The attributional approach

People seek reasons for their own behavior as well as for the behavior of others. In the simplest of situations, behavior can be attributed either to external, situational factors (*I was good because my mother wanted me to be*) or to internal, dispositional factors (*I was good because I am a good person*). When an external cause is not immediately apparent, behavior is highly likely to be attributed to internal causation. Accompanying this internal attribution will be a change in the value system. Thus, children who believe themselves to have behaved well for internal reasons will assume they value goodness, and their future behavior will be governed accordingly. Children who believe they were good for external reasons such as fear of punishment will not undergo any change in their value system.

Walters and Grusec (1977) saw this mechanism as a promising one for the internalization of self-control. We suggested that if children perceive that they have been coerced into conformity through fear of punishment or hope of reward, they will not be likely to bring their attitudes and values into line with their behavior and hence to continue to conform in the absence of surveillance. Children who are less conscious of coercion because, for example, reasoning has distracted them from external pressure, will be much more likely to undergo a change in values: They will perceive that they have conformed for internal reasons and therefore will continue to behave according to the wishes of society.

Dienstbier, Hillman, Lehnhoff, Hillman, and Valkenaar (1975) have offered a similar analysis. They suggest that the negative emotional states associated with punishment remain the same throughout a person's life, but that the causal attributions made about these states can change. If a child tells a lie, for example, and is punished, the temptation to lie in the future will be followed by anxiety that has its basis in this original punishment training situation. If the child attributes anxiety to the fact that good people do not tell lies, however—a bit of information that could be derived from adult reasoning—then the behavior of telling the truth should endure.

Further light has been shed on the mechanism underlying these processes by Perry, Perry, Bussey, English, and Arnold (1980). They have suggested that children who believe they possess desirable moral characteristics experience heightened self-criticism when they fail to live up to their image of themselves; therefore, they avoid self-criticism by behaving morally. Perry *et al.* found that children who were told they were compliant and self-controlled, but who subsequently yielded to a distracting temptation when they were supposed to be working, helped themselves to less reward than children who had not been provided with such a positive self-concept. Thus, it appeared that these children were behaving in a more self-critical manner.

Several studies have indicated that an attributional analysis of moral development is useful. Lepper (1973), for example, succeeded in keeping children from playing with a particular toy by threatening them either mildly or severely. Three weeks later the children were given the opportunity to cheat. Fewer children from the mild threat group cheated than from the severe threat group. Lepper suggested that children who had been mildly threatened were more likely to attribute their good behavior to internal causes, since there was really little obvious external justification for their conformity with the experimenter's request. Thus, they continued to behave in accord with a changed value system by cheating less. Lepper even found that children in the mild threat condition tended to rate themselves as more honest than those in the severe threat condition, a suggestion that their perceptions of themselves had been somewhat altered.

Character attribution. In most studies of attribution it has been assumed that subjects themselves are making inferences about their own behavior. It is also possible, however, for others to suggest reasons for an individual's behavior: This procedure also modifies subsequent behavior. Miller, Brickman, and Bolen (1975), for example, told children that they were the kind of people who are neat and clean. These children subsequently littered less than children who had not had such characteristics attributed to them, or who had been told they *ought* to be neat and clean. Similarly, Jensen and Moore (1977) told boys that a questionnaire they had filled out indicated that they were either competitive or cooperative, and found that when they played a game their behavior was affected accordingly. The attribution of a specific characteristic to someone, then, appears to produce a change in that person's value system, possibly because it changes the way they view themselves.

Telling children they are something that they are not, of course, should not be very effective. Suppose a teacher were to remark to a boy that he was well-behaved and cooperative immediately after he had assaulted another child and been rude to the principal. Such a statement would, at best, be perceived as bizarre. Attribution theory demands that a positive instance of moral behavior occur and that it occur in such a way that the external pressures are not apparent or salient. People can, in fact, be made to comply fairly easily and yet feel they have "freely" chosen to comply. Lepper did it by threatening children mildly. Other subtle techniques, such as saying, "You can do it if you want to... but you don't have to... it would certainly be a help, however," are also very effective. Reasoning, backed up by an implied threat of punishment, may be another way of obtaining compliance under conditions of apparent free choice.

Grusec, Kuczynski, Rushton, and Simutis (1978) carried out a study to test the hypothesis that attribution of character can modify moral behavior, but only when they are made after a child has complied apparently freely. Children were made to donate winnings from a game to poor children either by having them observe someone else do it—an ambiguous inducement—or by being instructed to do so—an unambiguous coercion. After the children had shared, their donation was attributed either to a personal disposition of goodness (*You must have shared because you're the kind of person who likes to help others*) or external pressure (*You must have shared because you thought I expected you to*). It was expected, of course, that these two attributions would differentially affect the subsequent sharing of children in the condition in which the cause of their original sharing was ambiguous, but that they would have no effect where it was unambiguous. Such, indeed, was the case. Children who shared because they had seen someone else share made more anonymous donations to poor children at a later time when their original sharing had been attributed to a personal disposition than when it had been attributed to external pressure. There was no difference between the two attribution conditions when children shared because they had been instructed to do so: They knew why they had donated and were therefore less likely to believe someone else's interpretation of their behavior.

In another study (Grusec & Redler, 1980) 7- and 8-year-old children were told that they could share some of their winnings with poor children if they wished to, but that they did not have to. The experimenter's presence, coupled with the occasional reminder to share if they wished to, was sufficient to persuade all children to donate half of their tokens to the poor children. Children who were then told, "I guess you're the kind of person who likes to help others whenever you can. Yes, you are a very nice and helpful person," not only subsequently made more anonymous donations but also shared more in another test of altruism than did children who did not have attributions made about their altruistic dispositions. After a second training session these children showed further evidence of generalized altruism. Three weeks after the end of the experiment they were asked by a stranger who came to their classroom to collect craft materials and make drawings for hospitalized children. Children in the attribution condition collected more items than those in the control condition.

It could be argued that the children in this study and the one by Grusec, Kuczynski, Rushton, and Simutis were really responding to the social reinforcement involved in being told that they were good and helpful people. In an attempt to assess this possibility some children in the Grusec and Redler study were told after they had donated, "It was good that you gave some of your tokens to the poor children. Yes, that was a nice and helpful thing to do." Although this statement facilitated subsequent donation of tokens to poor children, it had no effect on other tests of altruism. Apparently, praise of the person is required in order to produce generalized altruism, rather than praise or reinforcement for a specific act. (In another part of the study, however, 10-year-olds were equally affected by attribution and social reinforcement, an indication that older children may extrapolate from evaluations about their own acts to inferences about their own characteristics.)

Assignment of responsibility. Another technique that has received some attention as a facilitator of moral development is the assignment of responsibility (e.g., Parke, 1974). It has been suggested that children who are made responsible for the moral training of others will show positive changes in their own moral outlook. Toner, Moore, and Ashley (1978) instructed 6- and 7-year-old boys not to touch a set of toys. Some of the boys were videotaped as they successfully resisted temptation and told that the videotape would be shown to other children so as to help them resist temptation. Others were told they would be videotaped for the same purpose, but then the camera broke down and the session could not be completed. The boys who had actually served as teachers of morality subsequently showed greater self-control in a later test of resistance to temptation than did the boys who had not had such an opportunity. One explanation of this result is provided by attribution theory. If one supports a certain position publicly, in the absence of any obvious external pressure to do so, then one must believe in the position. Boys who were videotaped would be seen by other boys as having committed themselves to the position that resisting temptation is a good thing, and they would have to attribute this commitment to some internal disposition.

The study of moral development from an attributional viewpoint is just beginning. Although the procedures we have described are effective, their effects may eventually be accounted for by a somewhat different theoretical formulation. The ideas of attribution theory, however, lend themselves so well to the central issue of self-control—the maintenance of behavior independent of external control—that they seem eminently worthy of further pursuit.

The problem of reactance. It is virtually a truism that people do not like to be told or forced to do things. Earlier we suggested that one side effect of a punitive approach to discipline is that it arouses hostility and reactance—a determination *not* to conform. Such reactance has been observed in some studies of moral development after children have been exhorted to help others, although the effects do appear to dissipate with time (Grusec, Saas-Kortsaak, & Simutis, 1978; Staub, 1971). Attribution theory would suggest that attempts at manipulating behavior should be as subtle as possible. We are struck, nevertheless, with how certain forms of influence that do not appear all that subtle can produce conformity. Direct instruction can be very effective in producing self-control that carries over to later tests of self-control (Grusec, Kuczynski, Rushton, & Simutis, 1978; Israel & Brown, 1979), even though children are unaffected by character attributions under these conditions and so, presumably, recognize the external controls on their behavior. Mothers report that they very frequently force children to engage in appropriate behavior when they are attempting to encourage obedience (Grusec & Kuczynski, 1980). Although we are not equating general usage with effectiveness, it would appear at least that some mothers believe that ordering or forcing a child to behave well is a reasonable thing to do. Although reinforcement and punishment can be seen as coercive techniques, in the sense that they involve external pressure, some kinds of response consequences may be more coercive than others. Thus, Smith, Gelfand, Hartmann, and Partlow (1979) found that children who received social reward or punishment for helping or failure to help were more likely to attribute their helping to an inner desire to do so than were children who received material reward or punishment. It may be that a child's perception of what is directive or coercive differs from that of an adult. The nature of such differences remains to be described.

The content of verbal persuasion

Are some reasons better than others? Although no systematic attempt has been made to answer this question, certain regularities do appear in results reported in the research literature. Rationales that emphasize the effects or consequences of misbehavior for another appear to be particularly effective. Eisenberg-Berg and Geisheker (1979) found that 8- and 9-year-old children were more altruistic after they had heard exhortations about how happy the children they helped would be than when they heard normative statements saying it was a good thing to share. Kuczynski (1979) found that children resisted temptation to a greater extent after they were told the experimenter would be unhappy and have to do extra work if they deviated than if they were told that they themselves would be unhappy and have to do extra work if they deviated.

Reasons that include general rather than specific statements about a particular aspect of morality also appear to aid in the acquisition of a generalized value system that reveals itself in moral behaviors. When children were told they should share winnings from a game with poor children because it is a good thing to make other people happy by helping them in any way one can, they subsequently collected more craft materials for sick children than did children told to share because it is a good thing to make children happy by sharing (Grusec, Saas-Kortsaak, & Simutis, 1978). Recall our earlier description of the greater effectiveness of character attribution over social reinforcement in producing generalized altruism (Grusec & Redler, 1980). Since the attribution of a helpful disposition refers to a variety of possible behaviors in which the child could engage, whereas social reinforcement refers only to the act for which the reinforcement was given, character attributions may provide more material for generalization than social reinforcement.

Parke (1974) has pointed out that the kinds of rationales with which children are provided for their behavior should correspond to the level of moral reasoning they are capable of comprehending. Telling a 4-year-old not to play with a toy because it might break is more effective than telling the child not to play with a toy because it belongs to someone else. The first is a reason the 4-year-old can understand; the second is more abstract and therefore more difficult to comprehend. Parke found the two kinds of rationales, however, were equally effective for 7-year-olds. Similarly, rationales that involve a child's intentions when undertaking a deviant act become more effective with age, just as children, with increasing age, begin to think more and more in terms of intention rather than outcome when judging the morality of an act (LaVoie, 1974).

Finally, as we shall discuss later, children can control their own behavior by making statements to themselves. Some of these statements are more effective than others. To the extent, then, that adult reasoning provides the material on which these verbalizations are modeled, it would be useful for that reasoning to include content that is helpful in promoting self-control.

Example

One very potent determinant of children's moral behavior is the example set by those around them. We have already pointed out how an adult's style of discipline provides an example for the child's attempts at eliciting compliance from others. In this section we shall describe extensive research evidence that suggests that children imitate the moral behaviors of adults. (Although the studies do not involve imitation of peers, there is no reason to believe they would not also be sources of influence in this respect.)

A great many studies have shown that children will imitate adults who share or who help other people in distress (Bryan & Walbek, 1970; Grusec & Skubiski, 1970; Rushton, 1976). The situation with respect to more passive forms of moral behavior, such as resisting the temptation to play with an attractive but forbidden toy, has been more ambiguous. Although a number of investigators found that children imitate a model who yields to temptation, it appeared to be more difficult to demonstrate the imitation of a conforming or resisting model (Rosenkoetter, 1973; Ross, 1966; Stein, 1967; Wolf, 1973). Several recent studies, however, have found that children are as likely to imitate models who resist temptation as they are to imitate those who yield to it (Bussey & Perry, 1977; Grusec, Kuczynski, Rushton, & Simutis, 1979; Perry, Bussey, & Perry, 1975).

In one study (Grusec *et al.*, 1979) 4- and 5-year-old children were asked to sort a large collection of different-colored cards into neat, same-colored piles. While they did this they were left alone with Charlie, a talking table, who repeatedly tried to lure them away from their card sorting to play with him and the attractive toys he had. Children in one condition had observed a model who had also been tempted by Charlie but had told him she would like to play with him but could not because she had to work. In another condition children had observed a model who stated that Charlie's toys were more fun than sorting cards and who subsequently went over to play with them. In a control condition Charlie did not try to tempt the adult, so the child had no opportunity to witness someone either resisting or yielding to temptation. The results of this study are summarized in Figure 4.1. Children who saw a model resist temptation subsequently took longer to yield to Charlie's tempting, and yielded for a shorter time, than did those in the control condition, whereas children who saw the adult set an example of self-indulgence yielded more quickly and for a longer time than those in the control condition.

In a second study 5- to 8-year-olds were tempted to leave their work by an adult female who urged them to come and play with some toys she had. The results of this study can also be seen in Figure 4.1. This time only the children who heard the model give a rationale for why she would not deviate—that she was there to work, that she always tried to do what was right whenever she could, and that it would not be right for her to play—were affected in the latency with which they began to deviate. The resisting model affected duration of deviation only for girls. In this study children were not at all affected by the example of a model who yielded, even when she gave a rationale for yielding to temptation (namely, she had done enough work, that one must think of oneself on occasion, and that she deserved a little fun).

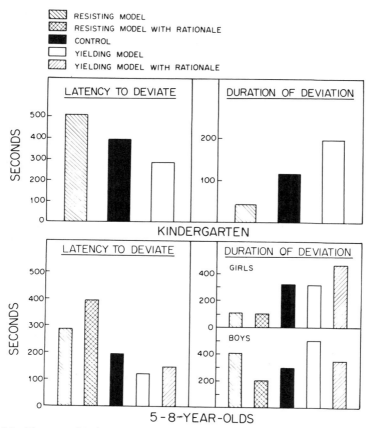

Figure 4.1. Measure of resistance to temptation in kindergarten and 5- to 8-year-old children.

It is difficult at this point to say precisely when children will be affected by adults who set good and bad examples and when they will not. We think it may have something to do with how salient the adult's behavior is. In the second Grusec *et al.* study, for example, the model who yielded may not have been doing anything unusual—she had worked hard, an adult suggested she take a break, and she did. The model who resisted was making an impressive show of self-control, and she may therefore have had a more profound impact on her young viewers. Boys required, however, that she also provide a reason for this self-control.

Whatever the specific set of relationships involved, it is evident that modeling is an important mechanism in the development of self-control. One limitation to this approach, however, may be the extent to which children learn general principles of moral behavior through the observation of others. Although there is evidence that the effects of modeling generalize to slightly different situations (e.g., sharing candy and sharing pennies, donation of candy solicited by two different adults in two different settings), generalization to more distant settings does not appear to be the rule (Elliott & Vasta, 1970; Midlarsky & Bryan, 1972). Grusec, Saas-Kortsaak, & Simutis (1978) reported that whereas the effects of moral exhortation—telling children that they would make others happy by helping them—generalized beyond the training situation, those of modeling did not. Thus, reasoning, exhortation, attribution of prosocial characteristics, and other verbal training techniques may have greater potential for encouraging a wide range of moral behaviors than an essentially nonverbal technique such as example. On the other hand, adults and teachers no doubt model a wide variety of moral (and immoral) behaviors. Even if there were not some point at which children would begin to extrapolate general principles of morality for themselves, they would still be exposed to a wide range of prosocial behavior. No doubt modeling is used in combination with verbal labeling, and the two techniques may complement each other. Finally, recall that one component of the self-control dimension involves knowing *how* to be prosocial—*how* to comfort others, for example, or *how* to resist temptation without angering others. Observing how others do this may be much more efficient than listening to a set of verbal instructions and having to translate these into action.

How children affect their teachers

To date we have made the process of socialization sound like a one-way street. Thus, socializing agents are cast in the mold of infinitely patient beings whose movements are guided by a conscious plan for the betterment of those with whose care they are charged. Children are seen as passive recipients of adult teachings. This is a view, in fact, that has guided much psychological theorizing, so it is not surprising that the data that have been collected reflect it. In recent years, however, developmental psychologists have come to realize that children are active and that their behavior affects how others react to them.

In the area of discipline the major proponent of this position has been Richard Bell (1968). Although most investigators have believed that particular discipline techniques are responsible for or cause particular moral orientations, Bell argues the opposite. He points out that children differ in such congenital temperamental characteristics as aggressiveness and person orientation and that, as a result of this, they respond differently to different discipline techniques. Parents therefore use the technique that works best with their child. Children who are not very compliant temperamentally and who, as a result, would be rated low in moral orientation would not respond to gentle techniques of discipline such as reasoning and social disapproval. Very quickly their parents would learn that they must resort to stronger forms of power assertion in order to force compliance in these children. Thus, one would find power assertion and low compliance associated because the child responded only to that form of discipline, not because the power assertion discouraged moral development.

Bell's position, taken to its extreme, is no doubt wrong. Adults clearly have more power and influence in the adult–child relationship than do children, they try to influence children's behavior more than children try to influence theirs, and they are more successful at it (Hoffman, 1975). But it is becoming increasingly evident that socializing agents are not impervious to the behavior of children. Sawin, Parke, Harrison, and Kreling (1975), for example, found that adult females administered more punishment to a child who behaved defiantly after a transgression than to a child who pleaded for less severe punishment. Children who apologized and promised to behave better were not punished at all—in fact, they were generally rewarded. Dion (1974) reported that women, but not men, are less punitive toward attractive boys when they make errors in a learning situation than they are toward attractive girls or toward unattractive children of either sex.

Another variable that appears to determine the kind of discipline technique employed by parents is the very nature of the child's misdemeanor (Grusec & Kuczynski, 1980). We asked 40 mothers of 4- and 7-year-old boys and girls to listen to the same set of tape recordings depicting 12 different situations in which a child behaved in an unacceptable way. In one situation, for example, the child repeatedly argued about turning off the television set, in another the youngster broke a vase (after repeated warnings) while bouncing a ball in the living room, and in another the child refused to share a chocolate bar with another child. The mothers were asked to imagine it was their child they were listening to in the tape recording and to say what they would do if this were happening to them.

If parents have a particular disciplinary style they rely on, then we should expect the same discipline technique to be used across a majority of situations. On the other hand, if the child's misdemeanor is affecting how mothers discipline them, a majority of mothers should use the same technique in the same situation, and a given mother should use many techniques overall. It was this latter outcome that we obtained. On the average, mothers reported using seven different disciplinary techniques across the 12 situations. If one looks at the relative contributions of mothers and situations to the variability in the data, the greater importance of the situation or misbehavior is evident: 26% of the variance was contributed by the interaction of misbehavior with technique, whereas only 5% was contributed by the interaction of mother with technique. And finally, 9 of the 12 situations elicited a consistent pattern of discipline. By far, the predominant response to a child who repeatedly refused to stop making a loud noise with a toy horn was to take away the horn. Children who fought with a peer and pushed the child off a tricycle were ordered to play properly. Children who were caught taking a dollar from their mother's purse were told it is wrong to steal. Children who ignored repeated requests to come to the dinner table were either punished verbally, ignored, or forced to come. Thus, there were a variety of disciplinary techniques employed—power assertion, which included loss of toys, verbal disapproval, and forced appropriate behavior; reasoning; and simply ignoring undesirable behavior—and the techniques all appeared to be specifically linked to specific misdemeanors.

It is unclear whether or not the "naturally occurring" disciplinary technique is the most effective. Nor is it evident what are the common characteristics of misbehaviors that elicit the same punishment. Nucci and Turiel (1978) have reported that nursery school teachers react to "moral transgressions" (e.g., aggression, failure to share) with reasoning and appeals to the feelings of others, whereas they react to violations of social convention (e.g., eating snacks in the wrong place) with commands, statements of sanction, and statements of rules. In the Grusec and Kuczynski study it appeared to us that mothers were using reasoning for those offenses that could be viewed as more serious than the rest, either because they involved the breaking of universal prohibitions or because they threatened the child's welfare. What *can* be safely concluded is that the disciplinary encounter between child and adult is a complex one, that it is determined by a whole variety of variables, and that a useful theory of socialization will have to take these complexities into account.

TEACHING SELF-CONTROL SKILLS DIRECTLY

Knowing what good and bad behaviors are and wanting to behave properly is not enough to ensure moral behavior and self-control. Children may internalize moral values, beliefs, and rules of conduct without showing any evidence of them in their actual behavior. For example, children who accept that it is wrong to steal may nevertheless do so simply because they do not know how to resist the temptation. Not stealing, waiting one's turn, giving comfort to another, or solving a conflict without resorting to violence all require not only the desire to conform to some moral value but also the skills to translate wishes into actions. The acquisition of these skills will now become the focus of this chapter.

We shall also discuss the role of expectations in the exercise of self-control skills. Putting moral values into action requires effort in addition to skill. Whether children imitate and maintain that effort depends a great deal on whether they expect their efforts to be successful. Expectations of success or failure affect the likelihood that children will practice self-control and this, in turn, influences their subsequent development of self-control skills.

Probably the most basic skill involved in self-control is apparent from the fact that people talk to themselves and that what they say, at least occasionally, has an influence on what they do. We have discussed the influence of adults' verbally communicated rules and rationales on children's behavior; now we turn to the way in which children develop the ability to use their *own* verbalizations to direct their *own* behavior.

Development of the verbal regulation of behavior

Both modeling and direct instruction contribute to the process of self-instruction, a proposition amply demonstrated by an extensive research literature on self-instructional training. One of the earliest studies was conducted by Meichenbaum and Goodman (1971) with a group of children between the ages of 7 and 9 years. The children were considered to be impulsive because they tended to act quickly without thinking, so Meichenbaum and Goodman set out to make them less impulsive by training them to control themselves through self-instruction. First of all, the children watched adults perform various perceptual and cognitive tasks while verbally directing themselves through each step. Following this, the children performed the same task themselves under adult verbal direction, and then again under their own verbal self-direction. In the final phases of training, they performed the tasks while whispering the self-instructions, and then without making any sounds or lip movements whatsoever. The children were successfully trained in this way to slow down and take more care in executing their work.

This study suggested that children can be helped in their intellectual performance through self-instructional training. A series of studies by Hartig and Kanfer (1973), Toner and Smith (1977), and Miller, Weinstein, and Karniol (1978) have explored the role of self-instructional training in the domain of moral behavior and have, moreover, shown how the effects of such training change as children grow older. Taken together, these studies suggest that the ability of preschoolers to resist temptation and to delay gratification is enhanced if they talk to themselves, and that the content of their talk is irrelevant unless it focuses directly on what is tempting them. Thus, saying, "I must not turn around and look at the toys," reciting, "Hickory-dickory-dock, the mouse went up the clock," and counting were all equally effective in increasing the ability to resist distraction or the temptation to select an immediately available but less attractive prize. Focusing directly on the tempting object (*The marshmallow is yummy*) was, however, not helpful in facilitating self-control. One can conclude that self-instruction works for preschoolers simply because the effort required in doing it distracts them from temptation, but that when it focuses their attention directly on the source of distraction, it then becomes detrimental.

Older children, on the other hand, were affected in these studies by the specific content of verbalizations. Often they were able to resist temptation even without the aid of verbalizations, suggesting that they may spontaneously generate their own self-instructions. For the verbalization to help, however, it had to be relevant to the temptation situation. It seems that older children find it easier to talk to themselves than do younger children. Thus, verbalization is not so distracting as it is with younger children and therefore irrelevant verbalizations are not particularly helpful in producing distraction from temptation. Nevertheless, self-instruction that is relevant can be helpful in aiding their self-control, for reasons that we shall explore in a short while.

Differential effects of verbalization as a function of children's age also have been demonstrated in a study by Sawin and Parke (1979). They found that second-grade boys were better able to resist the temptation to play with a forbidden toy when they said a prohibitive rule to themselves (*I'm not allowed to play with the crane*) or a redirective rule (*I am allowed to play with the tank*) than when they were given no self-instruction at all. Boys in grade 1 also touched the toy less often when they said the prohibitive rule, but, surprisingly, they touched it more often when they said the redirective rule. Why were self-instructions to redirect attention actually *detrimental* to the self-control of the younger boys? Since the redirective rule was simple and couched in language identical to the prohibitive one, these boys should not have failed to understand what it meant. Sawin and Parke suggested that they may have processed the information contained in the instruction rather superficially (just as younger children failed to process the content of verbalizations in the studies discussed just previously), extracting only the permissive tone. As a result, they failed to notice that only one toy was permissible. From past experience, children probably learn to pay closer attention to prohibitive rules than to other things they hear, in order to avoid the unpleasant consequences of failing to obey. As their cognitive capacity develops, however, information is processed with less effort, so that even less salient information will be interpreted correctly.

When relevant self-instructions facilitate behavior, how do they work? A study by Meacham (1978) suggests they may help by reminding children of the correct response. Children aged 3, 4, and 5 years were required to maneuver a tricycle in response to the commands of an adult (*Stop, Go, Up, Back*) presented at 3-second intervals in different sequences. The children were also instructed to repeat the verbal commands. An apparatus mounted alongside the front wheel of the tricycle recorded the rate and direction of its movement, and a microphone attached to the handlebar made a simultaneous record of the verbal activity of both the adult and the child. The children were quicker to act than they were to speak following the adult's commands, suggesting that their own speech had little or no effect on their initial motor responses. However, when they responded incorrectly to a command, they were more likely to correct the error before the 3-second interval was over if they had verbalized the command than if they had failed to do so.

These results suggest that verbalization, although not directly controlling behavior, may indirectly help to guide it. Meacham proposed that children were more likely to correct errors following self-instruction because the verbalization reminded them of the correct response, allowing them to compare their completed response with the actual goal and make a correction. Thus, self-instruction stimulates memory. In addition to memory, self-instructions also facilitate other cognitive processes that control behavior. We shall turn now to a discussion of how this happens.

Cognitive processes in self-control

Self-control involves a number of cognitive processes. For example, to resist temptation, children will find it helpful if they can do at least some of the following: keep their attention diverted from the source of the temptation, remember what it is they are trying to do, engage in fantasy about distracting activities, imagine the outcome of their efforts, and perceive an end to goals that extend over time. The acquisition of these processes is related to the development of representational thought. When children begin using mental images and words to represent objects and events, they acquire the capacity to think not only about what can be immediately perceived but also about things removed in space and time. It becomes possible for them to divorce themselves from the here and now, and therefore to exercise some control over what they think about and respond to.

In a study examining the effect of imaginative play on cognitive functioning, Saltz, Dixon, and Johnson (1977) provided some indirect evidence in support of the notion that the growth of representational thought promotes the growth of self-control. Children ranging from 3 to $4\frac{1}{2}$ years of age were trained in thematic fantasy play (acting out fairy tales), fantasy discussion (hearing and discussing fairy tales but not acting them out), or sociodramatic play (acting out realistic events). Children in a control condition spent the same sessions involved in activities like cutting and pasting that did not involve either fantasy or acting. Compared to the children in the sociodramatic and control conditions, those given fantasy experiences were subsequently better able to delay gratification and control their impulses, provided they were given instructions (to think about their favorite story or look at a picture book while they waited) that prompted them to use their representational skill. One explanation of these results is that fantasy activities free children from the control of external, concrete reality and therefore help to foster representational thought. When a strategy is provided to help them use this resource, self-control is facilitated.

Self-instructional plans. One of the most significant features of representational thought is the ability to think about the future: to think about goals and make plans to attain them. Because self-control involves this kind of purposeful behavior, children cannot control their own behavior until they acquire the ability to formulate and execute plans. It would be impossible, for example, for children to help another person or wait for a delayed reward without forming some intention of doing so and deciding upon some way of going about it. Thus, some of the things children say to themselves may consist of self-instructional plans that help them to exercise self-control.

There have been several studies of the role of self-instructional plans in facilitating self-control. Patterson and Mischel (1975) offered 4- and 5-year-olds a reward if they could complete a copying task during the experimenter's absence without allowing themselves to be distracted by an attractive, talking clown box. Some of the children were then provided with a set of plans to help them resist distraction. Two of the plans were statements to make when the clown box tried to entice them to play: *No, I can't, I'm working* and *I'm going to keep working.* The third plan was to imagine a brick wall between themselves and the clown box. The children given these simple plans spent more time working than those not given plans. All three plans were equally effective. Subsequent studies (Mischel & Patterson, 1976; Patterson & Mischel, 1976) compared the effects of a temptation-inhibiting plan (suppressing attention to the temptation: *I'm not going to look at Mr. Clown Box*), a task-facilitating plan (directing attention to the task: *I'm going to look at my work*), and a reward-oriented plan (directing attention to the rewarding conse-quences of completing the task: *I want to play with the fun toys and Mr. Clown Box later*). Children ranging from $3\frac{1}{2}$ to $5\frac{1}{2}$ years of age were left alone and required to fill all the holes in a pegboard by the time the experimenter returned in order to receive a reward. The temptation-inhibiting and reward-oriented plans enhanced the children's ability to resist distraction, whereas the task-facilitating plan did not. Recall the finding of Sawin and Parke (1979) that verbalizations redirecting atten-tion to permissible activities are ineffective for younger children. Thus, the preschool children given the task-facilitating plan by Mischel and Patterson may have responded more to its permissive tone than to its actual content, mistakenly understanding it as giving them general persmission to look at whatever they wished.

The role of attention, imagery, and time perception. Other studies clarify the role of attention, imagery, and time perception in facilitating self-control. In most of these studies a similar research paradigm has been used, in which preschoolers are given a choice between a more attractive reward available after a period of several minutes' delay or a less attrac-tive reward available immediately. They have then been left alone to wait, although they are able to obtain the less preferred reward at any time by pressing a button to summon the experimenter. The ability of children this young to tolerate frustration is impressive, and Mischel and his co-workers have been primarily responsible for describing those conditions particularly conducive to facilitating the delay of gratification. What children think or say to themselves while they are waiting is cru-cial to how well they resist the temptation to summon the experimenter. In assessing the effectiveness of various forms of mental activities, Mis-chel (1974) has distinguished between the motivational and informa-tional functions of reward objects. The presence of a reward arouses the desire to have it (the motivational function) and serves as a reminder of what must be done in order to obtain it (the informational function). Mischel and his co-workers found that children could not wait as long when left with the actual rewards in front of them as they could when no rewards, or only pictures of the rewards, were left facing them during the delay period. The symbolic representations, however, were more effective than pictures of other objects not involved in the delay choice (see Figure 4.2). Mischel concluded that children must keep a goal in mind, hence the superiority of relevant to irrelevant pictures. But to focus too strongly on the actual reward is frustrating and therefore detrimental to self-control. Images allow children to think in abstract rather than concrete terms, to remind themselves of the goal at hand without arousing an immediate desire for reward. Thus the best way for young children to resist temptation is to focus their attention on the informational rather than the motivational properties of rewards. Self-control is hindered if the focus of attention is on consuming the goal rather than achieving it.

Several other studies support Mischel's contention that what matters in self-control is not whether children pay attention to the temptation they are trying to resist, but *how* they think about it. Mischel and Baker (1975) had children choose between marshmallows and pretzels—the item they preferred was, of course, the one for which they were required to wait. When the children were told to think about marshmallows as puffy white clouds and pretzels as thin brown logs they could wait

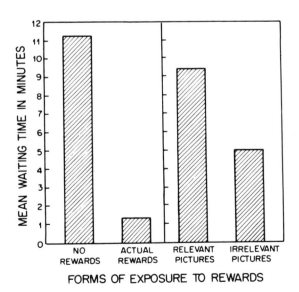

Figure 4.2. Forms of reward available for attention during the delay period and children's resistance to temptation (adapted from Mischel, 1974).

longer than when they were advised to focus on the chewy, soft taste of the marshmallows and the crunchy, salty taste of the pretzels. Patterson and Carter (1979) found that children who had to work during the delay period in order to get the preferred reward were helped to delay by looking at and thinking about the actual rewards. For children who did not have to work, of course, this procedure was detrimental. Presumably the children who worked thought of the delayed reward in terms of how to obtain it rather than in terms of actually having it. Again, they attended to achieving rather than consuming the goal. Finally, Miller and Karniol (1976) reported that children who were forced to wait, rather than having the option of summoning the experimenter, were less frustrated (as measured by their estimate of time elapsed) if rewards were present rather than absent. Again, we assume their thoughts were on how to achieve the goal, whereas for children who had a choice about waiting, the presence of rewards aroused too much interest in their consumption.

Another way to reduce the frustration involved in delay-of-gratification situations is to think about the increasing closeness of the goal as time passes. Six-year-olds who were provided with a sandglass timer so that they could actually see how much longer they had to wait were more successful than those who did not have a timer (Schack & Massari, 1973).

It is evident, then, that cognitive processes such as attention, fantasy, imagery, and time perception all help children to distance themselves from sources of temptation. The more children are able to control the focus of their thoughts, the better able they are to reduce the frustration involved in self-control situations. This ability, of course, increases with age. Thus Yates and Mischel (1979) have demonstrated that children formulate more effective attentional strategies as they grow older. Recall that viewing symbolic representations (pictures) of rewards makes waiting easier than viewing the actual rewards (Mischel, 1974). Thus, one strategy that would help children delay would be for them to direct their attention away from tempting forms of the delayed reward. Yates and Mischel, however, found that children under the age of 7 years preferred to look at real objects while they waited, rather than symbolically presented ones. In this study, the children could press buttons during the delay period to bring the actual rewards or pictures of the rewards (but not both simultaneously) into view. The children not only reported a preference for viewing the real objects rather than the symbolic representations, but also spent more time looking at the real objects. Even those children who were explicitly instructed to look at the stimuli they thought would most help them to wait failed to adopt the strategy of looking at the pictures rather than the objects themselves. Instead, these children viewed each about equally, an indication that they did not know which it would be best to look at.

Another strategy children might use to facilitate resistance to temptation would be to turn their attention away from the objects they were waiting for and toward other objects irrelevant to their goal. Yates and Mischel found that children up to the age of about 7 showed no inclination to view irrelevant more than relevant objects while they waited, even when they were instructed to choose the most helpful strategy. Above this age, however, children began to prefer looking at irrelevant objects. It is evident that as children develop they gradually formulate more effective strategies for controlling their own behavior.

The role of expectation in the acquisition of self-control skills

The better children are at giving themselves instructions, formulating plans, employing effective attentional strategies, and estimating time, the greater their accomplishment of self-control. In this sense, then, self-control can be regarded as a form of achievement, and, as in other achievement situations, attempts at self-control can result in either success or failure. Reactions to success and failure affect expectations about the outcomes of future efforts, and this in turn influences motivation to initiate and maintain further effort (Bandura, 1977). These considerations bring us to the final stage in teaching self-control skills—encouraging the motivation to initiate and maintain the effort it takes to use these skills. Regardless of how capable children are of controlling themselves, they are not likely to try—or to try very hard—if they believe their efforts will result in failure. When children expect to succeed, they are more inclined to expend effort than when they expect to fail. Children with a history of disruptive behavior in the classroom, for example, may not believe they could behave well even if they tried. When this kind of resignation occurs, children may well deny themselves opportunities to practice and improve their ability to control themselves.

Consideration of this aspect of self-control acquisition turns the discussion back to attribution theory, and to the kinds of reasons children give themselves to explain their performance. According to the attributional model of achievement motivation (Weiner, Frieze, Kukla, Reed, Rest, & Rosenbaum, 1972) the causes to which children attribute the outcomes of past performance influence subsequent performance by altering their expectations of future outcomes. Success and failure in achievement situations can be attributed to four main causes: ability, effort, luck, and task difficulty. Unstable causes (i.e., those subject to change, like effort and luck) have different effects on expectations than do stable causes like ability and task difficulty. Children who believe successes are due to stable causes and failure to unstable causes will try harder in the future, whereas those who attribute successes to unstable causes and failures to stable causes will be less motivated or believe themselves less likely to be successful in the future. LeSure (1978), for example, led some children to believe that their performance on an achievement task (matching ambiguous angles) would depend on ability or task difficulty and others to think it would depend on effort or luck. The children were then told, after they had completed the task, that they had either succeeded or failed. Subsequently they were given a choice between a small reward available immediately or a larger reward available after successful performance on a similar task. Children who thought that success was due to their ability or to the easiness of the task, or that failure was due to bad luck or minimal effort, made more delayed choices than those who attributed success to unstable causes or failure to stable causes.

We know of no studies designed to show that perceived causes of success and failure in self-control tasks affect subsequent self-control. It seems likely to us, however, that similar relationships would emerge in the area of self-control as in the area of achievement. Children who succeed in solving a problem through verbal means rather than physical aggression, for example, should be more likely to try again in the future if they attribute their initial success to ability or task ease rather than to luck or great effort.

The contribution of self-perception to causal beliefs. Knowledge of previous performance affects children's causal beliefs. Another major determinant of these beliefs is children's perceptions of how effective they are (Bandura, 1977; Weiner, 1979). Thus, Ames, Ames, and Garrison (1977) found that children with high social status, who presumably viewed themselves as socially competent, attributed negative social interactions to external factors, whereas those with low status, who presumably viewed themselves as socially incompetent, attributed negative encounters to themselves. Similarly, Ames (1978) found that children with high self-regard were more likely to attribute success in achievement situations to their own ability than were those with low self-regard. These findings suggest that children look for explanations of their behavior that are compatible with existing views of themselves. As a consequence, the reactions of those who are high and low in self-esteem to experiences of success and failure can be expected to differ significantly.

Dweck and Repucci (1973) found confirming evidence of this hypothesis in a study in which fifth-grade students were given a series of block designs to reproduce. When the designs became insoluble, some children persisted, whereas others gave up, even though both groups had been performing equally well. Those who tended to attribute their failures to a lack of effort rather than ability, and who saw themselves as responsible for the outcomes of their behavior, persisted in the face of failure on the block designs. Those who attributed failure to a lack of ability, and believed themselves to have no control over events, tended to give up when confronted with insoluble designs. Thus, children's beliefs about the causes of their behavior are based at least partly on their beliefs about their own capabilities. Moreover, these beliefs have significant effects on subsequent behavior.

Developmental considerations. Self-perceptions and causal beliefs cannot have an influence on the acquisition of self-control skills until children form stable self-perceptions and acquire explanations for their behavior. In a study of children 4–6 and 7–9 years of age, Ruble, Parsons, and Ross (1976) found that the older children were more likely than the younger ones to feel badly about their failures and to attribute them to low ability. This finding suggests that failure is less likely to have negative implications for the self-perceptions of younger children than for older children, and is less likely to affect their beliefs about the cause of their failure. Similarly, recall that Grusec and Redler (1979) found that attributions of prosocial behavior were effective in producing altruism in 7- and 8-year-old children. They were not effective, however, for 5-year-olds. It appears that children younger than 8 years of age do not think of themselves as possessing stable dispositional characteristics (Livesley & Bromley, 1973) and that self-concept does not, therefore, have an effect on their behavior.

It is not clear how self-perceptions and causal beliefs are acquired. However, studies in which attributions of character traits produced changes in children's behavior (e.g., Dweck, 1975; Grusec, Kuczynski, Rushton, & Simutis, 1978; Grusec & Redler, 1979; Jensen & Moore, 1977; Miller, Brickman, & Bolen, 1975) suggest that a major source of self-perceptions may be the reasons socializing agents provide for children's behaviors. When children who misbehave are told that they are bad, they may draw conclusions both about the kind of person they are judged to be and the reason for their behavior. On the other hand, when their transgressions are attributed to unstable causes such as lack of effort, they are more likely to maintain a positive self-image and positive expectations about their ability to behave better in the future. From this we conclude that teachers and parents can help children to perceive themselves as capable of self-control both by making them aware of the personal effectiveness they exercise when they succeed in controlling themselves and by stressing the unstable factors to which failures can be attributed.

CONCLUSIONS

The variety of techniques by which socializing agents can instill self-control in young children is great indeed. Psychologists are still investigating their importance, relative effectiveness, and the mechanisms through which they work. Nevertheless, we can say something about the behavior of teachers and parents who ought to be successful in getting children to conform to the desires and dictates of society. They provide full and adequate explanations for why conformity is desirable. They praise good behavior. They exercise control by invoking negative consequences (of a moderate kind) when necessary, and exhorting and instructing children to behave correctly. They provide an example of moral behavior themselves, and sensitize children to the feelings and needs of others. They promote in children a positive self-concept, encouraging them to see themselves as moral beings, capable of self-control. And, finally, they teach them effective attentional and self-instructional strategies.

Our review is by no means complete. Although we have pointed out that the relationship between adult and child is one of reciprocal interaction, the vast majority of studies in the research literature shed little light on the two-way nature of socialization; thus, the full implications of this reciprocity are missing. Peers no doubt play an important role in the acquisition of self-control, and Piaget has repeatedly stressed the importance of peer interactions on the development of children's reasoning about moral issues. Again, however, our chapter is a reflection of the relative paucity of research on the effect of peer groups on the growth of self-control. Finally, some misdemeanors may elicit more "natural" consequences than others (Dreikurs & Grey, 1968). A mother who attempts to get her child to move quickly in the morning may be more successful if she allows her child to experience the direct and logical consequences of being late for school than if she imposes some arbitrary punishment. Such a possibility remains open to investigation.

REFERENCES

Ames, C. Children's achievement attributions and self-reinforcement: Effects of self-concept and competitive reward structure. *Journal of Educational Psychology*, 1978, *70*, 345–355.

Ames, R., Ames, C., & Garrison, W. Children's causal ascriptions for positive and negative interpersonal outcomes. *Psychological Reports*, 1977, *41*, 595–602.

Bandura, A. Self-efficacy: Toward a unifying theory of behavioral change. *Psychological Review*, 1977, *84*, 191–215.

Baumrind, D. The development of instrumental competence through socialization. In A. D. Pick (Ed.), *Minnesota Symposium on Motivation* (Vol. 7). Minneapolis: Univ. of Minnesota Press, 1973.

Bell, R. Q. A reinterpretation of the direction of effects of socialization. *Psychological Review*, 1968, *75*, 81–95.

Bryan, J. H., & Walbek, N. Preaching and practicing generosity: Children's actions and reactions. *Child Development*, 1970, *41*, 329–353.

Bussey, K., & Perry, D. G. The imitation of resistance to deviation: Conclusive evidence for an elusive effect. *Developmental Psychology*, 1977, *13*, 438–443.

Cheyne, J. A., & Walters, R. H. Punishment and prohibition: Some origins of self-control. In T. M. Newcomb (Ed.), *New directions in psychology*. New York: Holt, 1970.

Dienstbier, R. A., Hillman, D., Lehnhoff, J., Hillman, J., & Valkenaar, M. C. An emotion-attribution approach to moral behavior: Interfacing cognitive and avoidance theories of moral development. *Psychological Review*, 1975, *82*, 299–315.

Dion, K. Children's physical attractiveness and sex as determinants of adult punitiveness. *Developmental Psychology*, 1974, *10*, 772–778.

Dlugokinski, E. L., & Firestone, I. J. Other centeredness and susceptibility to charitable appeals: Effects of perceived discipline. *Developmental Psychology*, 1974, *10*, 21–28.

Dreikurs, R., & Grey, L. *Logical consequences: A new approach to discipline*. New York: Hawthorn Books, 1968.

Dweck, C. S. The role of expectations and attributions in the alleviation of learned helplessness. *Journal of Personality and Social Psychology*, 1975, *31*, 674–685.

Dweck, C. S., & Repucci, N. D. Learned helplessness and reinforcement responsibility in children. *Journal of Personality and Social Psychology*, 1973, *25*, 109–116.

Eisenberg-Berg, N., & Geisheker, E. Content of preachings and power of the model/preacher: The effect on children's generosity. *Developmental Psychology*, 1979, *15*, 168–175.

Elliott, R., & Vasta, R. The modeling of sharing: Effects associated with vicarious reinforcement, symbolization, age, and generalization. *Journal of Experimental Child Psychology*, 1970, *10*, 8–15.

Gelfand, D. M., Hartmann, D. P., Lamb, A. K., Smith, C. L., Mahan, M. A., & Paul, S. C. The effects of adult models and described alternatives on children's choice of behavior management techniques. *Child Development*, 1974, *45*, 585–593.

Grusec, J. E., & Kuczynski, L. Direction of effect in socialization: A comparison of the parents vs. the child's behavior as determinants of disciplinary techniques. *Developmental Psychology*, 1980, *16*, 1–9.

Grusec, J. E., Kuczynski, L., Rushton, J. P., & Simutis, Z. M. Modeling, direct instruction, and attributions: Effects on altruism. *Developmental Psychology*, 1978, *14*, 51–57.

Grusec, J. E., Kuczynski, L., Rushton, J. P., & Simutis, Z. M. Learning resistance to temptation through observation. *Developmental Psychology*, 1979, *15*, 233–240.

Grusec, J. E., & Redler, E. Attribution, reinforcement, and altruism. *Developmental Psychology,* 1980, *16*, 525–534.

Grusec, J. E., Saas-Kortsaak, P., & Simutis, Z. M. The role of example and moral exhortation in the training of altruism. *Child Development,* 1978, *49*, 920–923.

Grusec, J. E., & Skubiski, L. Model nurturance, demand characteristics of the modeling experiment, and altruism. *Journal of Personality and Social Psychology,* 1970, *14*, 352–359.

Hartig, M., & Kanfer, F. H. The role of verbal self-instructions in children's resistance to temptation. *Journal of Personality and Social Psychology,* 1973, *25*, 259–267.

Hoffman, M. L. Moral development. In P. H. Mussen (Ed.), *Manual of child psychology.* New York: Wiley, 1970. (a)

Hoffman, M. L. Conscience, personality, and socialization techniques. *Human Development,* 1970, *13*, 90–126. (b)

Hoffman, M. L. Moral internalization, parental power, and the nature of parent–child interaction. *Developmental Psychology,* 1975, *11*, 228–239.

Hoffman, M. L., & Saltzstein, H. D. Parent discipline and the child's moral development. *Journal of Personality and Social Psychology,* 1967, *5*, 45–57.

Israel, A. C., & Brown, M. S. Effects of directiveness of instructions and surveillance on the production and persistence of children's donations. *Journal of Experimental Child Psychology,* 1979, *27*, 250–261.

Jensen, A. M., & Moore, S. G. The effect of attribute statements on cooperativeness and competitiveness in school-age boys. *Child Development,* 1977, *48*, 305–307.

Kelley, H. H. Attribution theory in social psychology. In D. Levine (Ed.), *Nebraska Symposium on Motivation* (Vol. 15). Lincoln: Univ. of Nebraska Press, 1967.

Kohlberg, L. Development of moral character and moral ideology. In M. L. Hoffman & L. W. Hoffman (Eds.), *Review of Child Development Research* (Vol. 1). New York: Russell Sage Foundation, 1964.

Kuczynski, L. *Reasoning with children: Motivational determinants of children's self-control.* Unpublished doctoral dissertation, University of Toronto, 1979.

LaVoie, J. C. Cognitive determinants of resistance to temptation in seven-, nine-, and eleven-year-old children of low and high maturity of moral judgment. *Developmental Psychology,* 1974, *10*, 393–403.

Lepper, M. R. Dissonance, self-perception, and honesty in children. *Journal of Personality and Social Psychology,* 1973, *25*, 65–74.

LeSure, G. E. Effects of causal belief for prior success or failure on preferences to delay gratification in task contingent versus task noncontingent conditions. *Journal of Personality,* 1978, *46*, 113–127.

Livesley, W. J., & Bromley, D. B. *Person perception in childhood and adolescence.* London: Wiley, 1973.

Masserman, J. H. *Behavior and neurosis.* Chicago: Univ. of Chicago Press, 1943.

Meacham, J. A. Verbal guidance through remembering the goals of actions. *Child Development,* 1978, *49*, 188–193.

Meichenbaum, D. H., & Goodman, J. Training impulsive children to talk to themselves: A means of developing self-control. *Journal of Abnormal Psychology,* 1971, *77*, 115–126.

Midlarsky, E., & Bryan, J. H. Affect expressions and children's imitative altruism. *Journal of Experimental Research in Personality,* 1972, *6*, 195–203.

Miller, D. T., & Karniol, R. The role of rewards in externally and self-imposed delay of gratification. *Journal of Personality and Social Psychology,* 1976, *33*, 594–600.

Miller, D. T., Weinstein, S. M., & Karniol, R. Effects of age and self-verbalization on children's ability to delay gratification. *Developmental Psychology,* 1978, *14*, 569–570.

Miller, R. L., Brickman, P., & Bolen, D. Attribution versus persuasion as a means for modifying behavior. *Journal of Personality and Social Psychology*, 1975, *31*, 430–441.

Mischel, W. Processes in delay of gratification. In L. Berkowitz (Ed.), *Advances in experimental social psychology* (Vol. 7). New York: Academic Press, 1974.

Mischel, W., & Baker, N. Cognitive appraisals and transformations in delay behavior. *Journal of Personality and Social Psychology*, 1975, *31*, 254–261.

Mischel, W., & Grusec, J. E. Determinants of the rehearsal and transmission of neutral and aversive behaviors. *Journal of Personality and Social Psychology*, 1966, *3*, 197–205.

Mischel, W., & Patterson, C. J. Substantive and structural elements of effective plans for self-control. *Journal of Personality and Social Psychology*, 1976, *34*, 942–950.

Nucci, L. P., & Turiel, E. Social interaction and the development of social concepts in preschool children. *Child Development*, 1978, *49*, 400–407.

Parke, R. D. Rules, roles, and resistance to deviation: Recent advances in punishment, discipline, and self-control. In A. Pick (Ed.), *Minnesota Symposium on Child Psychology* (Vol. 8). Minneapolis: Univ. of Minnesota Press, 1974.

Patterson, C. J., & Carter, D. B. Attentional determinants of children's self-control in waiting and working situations. *Child Development*, 1979, *50*, 272–275.

Patterson, C. J., & Mischel, W. Plans to resist distraction. *Developmental Psychology*, 1975, *11*, 369–378.

Patterson, C. J., & Mischel, W. Effects of temptation-inhibiting and task-facilitating plans on self-control. *Journal of Personality and Social Psychology*, 1976, *33*, 209–217.

Perry, D. G., Bussey, K., & Perry, L. C. Factors influencing the imitation of resistance to deviation. *Developmental Psychology*, 1975, *11*, 724–731.

Perry, D. G., Perry, L. C., Bussey, K., English, D., & Arnold, G. Processes of attribution and children's self-punishment following misbehavior. *Child Development*, 1980, *51*, 545–552.

Rosenkoetter, L. I. Resistance to temptation: Inhibitory and disinhibitory effects of models. *Developmental Psychology*, 1973, *8*, 80–84.

Ross, D. Relationship between dependency, intentional learning, and incidental learning in preschool children. *Journal of Personality and Social Psychology*, 1966, *4*, 374–381.

Ruble, D. N., Parsons, J. E., & Ross, J. Self-evaluative responses of children in an achievement setting. *Child Development*, 1976, *47*, 990–997.

Rushton, J. P. Socialization and the altruistic behavior of children. *Psychological Bulletin*, 1976, *83*, 898–913.

Saltz, E., Dixon, D., & Johnson, J. Training disadvantaged preschoolers on various fantasy activities: Effects on cognitive functioning and impulse control. *Child Development*, 1977, *48*, 367–380.

Sawin, D. B., & Parke, R. D. Development of self-verbalized control of resistance to deviation. *Developmental Psychology*, 1979, *15*, 120–127.

Sawin, D. B., Parke, R. D., Harrison, A. N., & Kreling, B. *The child's role in sparing the rod.* Paper presented at the meeting of the American Psychological Association, Chicago, 1975.

Schack, M. L., & Massari, D. J. Effects of temporal aids and frustration on delay of gratification. *Developmental Psychology*, 1973, *8*, 168–171.

Skinner, B. F. *Beyond freedom and dignity.* New York: Knopf, 1971.

Smith, C. L., Gelfand, D. M., Hartmann, D. P., & Partlow, M. E. Y. Children's causal attributions regarding help giving. *Child Development*, 1979, *50*, 203–210.

Spinetta, J. J., & Rigler, D. The child-abusing parent: A psychological review. *Psychological Bulletin*, 1972, *77*, 296–304.

Staub, E. The use of role playing and induction in children's learning of helping and sharing behavior. *Child Development*, 1971, *42*, 805–817.

Stayton, D. J., Hogan, R., & Ainsworth, M. D. Infant obedience and maternal behavior: The origins of socialization reconsidered. *Child Development*, 1971, *42*, 1057–1069.

Stein, A. H. Imitation of resistance to temptation. *Child Development*, 1967, *38*, 157–169.

Toner, I. J., Moore, L. P., & Ashley, P. K. The effect of serving as a model of self-control on subsequent resistance to deviation in children. *Journal of Experimental Child Psychology*, 1978, *26*, 85–91.

Toner, I. J., & Smith, R. A. Age and overt verbalization in delay-maintenance behavior in children. *Journal of Experimental Child Psychology*, 1977, *24*, 123–128.

Walters, G. C., & Grusec, J. E. *Punishment*. San Francisco: Freeman, 1977.

Weiner, B. A theory of motivation for some classroom experiences. *Journal of Educational Psychology*, 1979, *71*, 3–25.

Weiner, B., Frieze, I., Kukla, A., Reed, L., Rest, S., & Rosenbaum, R. M. Perceiving the causes of success and failure. In E. E. Jones, D. E. Kanouse, H. H. Kelley, R. E. Nisbett, S. Valins, & B. Weiner (Eds.), *Attribution: Perceiving the causes of behavior*. Morristown, N. J.: General Learning Press, 1972.

Wolf, T. M. Effects of televised modeled verbalizations and behavior on resistance to deviation. *Developmental Psychology*, 1973, *8*, 51–56.

Yates, B. T., & Mischel, W. Young children's preferred attentional strategies for delaying gratification. *Journal of Personality and Social Psychology*, 1979, *37*, 286–300.

Zahn-Waxler, C. Z., Radke-Yarrow, M. R., & King, R. A. Child rearing and children's prosocial initiations toward victims of distress. *Child Development*, 1979, *50*, 319–330.

PART TWO / Cognitive processes

5 / Learning processes: developmental trends

BETTY J. HOUSE

As children develop, they not only gain increased knowledge of the world, but also increased ability to acquire new knowledge. The purpose of this chapter is to examine some of the factors behind the growth of learning ability in grade school children. These factors have educational implications in two respects: First, it is useful to know what limitations on learning may exist at a given age; second, knowledge of the factors that influence learning rate may help in training learning skills.

The literature on learning in children is extensive. White (1962) and Offenbach (1966) collected bibliographies of over 1200 titles. For this reason, selectivity is essential. We will omit consideration of classical and instrumental conditioning, motor learning, and simple learning tasks, and concentrate on verbal learning and other processes most relevant to education. We will also concentrate on studies done in the past 10–15 years. This period has been especially rich in developmental theory and data relevant to learning skill.

Before considering the data let us take a brief overview of proposed solutions to the question of increasing learning ability with age. One possibility is that it is primarily maturational in nature, the result of neurological development. Although such an explanation is difficult to rule out, it is also difficult to demonstrate or test directly. Furthermore, the fact that learning speed can be manipulated by experimental oper-

PSYCHOLOGICAL DEVELOPMENT
IN THE ELEMENTARY YEARS

ations makes it seem plausible that factors other than maturation are involved.

In an alternative approach, increases in learning rate are related to previous learning. In general it is easier to learn new material if it is related to a body of knowledge in memory. The familarity of stimulus material is also a potent variable in experimental learning studies. Children, of course, know less than adults. They have also had less exposure to stimuli in general and to those encountered in the classroom in particular. It follows that they will be at a disadvantage academically. Previous learning also influences the degree of response complexity that can be achieved. Higher level responding often requires combination of simpler component responses. Thus, complex learning will be slow until the component subskills are well learned. Association theorists (e.g., Estes, 1970; Gagné, 1968, 1977), in particular, have stressed previous learning in accounting for developmental differences in learning skill. Chi (1976, 1978) is a more recent adherent to that view. Other theorists have emphasized another facet of previous learning, the acquisition of skills and procedures for acquiring new knowledge or learning to learn. Brown (1974), for example, hypothesized that the primary determinant of developmental differences in memory is the growth of mnemonic strategies. She predicted little developmental effect for tasks not requiring such strategies. The most recent development in theory is that metamemorial or metacognitive changes are of primary importance. This means that children become more knowledgeable about their own capabilities, about task demands, and about how to select the best strategies to meet them (Brown & DeLoache, 1978; Flavell, 1978, 1979). We will come back to these ideas in specific instances later in this chapter.

EARLIER LITERATURE

For those interested in studies done prior to 1970, there are several summary sources. Reese and Lipsitt (1970) provide a good general coverage. Keppel (1964) surveyed the literature of children's verbal learning for the preceding 14 years to determine whether there was a correspondence in the effective variables reported and in the relationships that had been identified with adult subjects. He concluded that there was little qualitative difference between children and adults in learning and retention of verbal material. The same laws appeared to hold. Goulet (1968) reconsidered the literature that Keppel had reviewed, pointed out some effects that should theoretically be affected by age, and suggested directions for developmental research. His predictions were based on the assumptions that children's language habits would be weaker and their tendency to mediate less than adults'.

Gagné (1965, 1968, 1977) has made the most systematic attempt to apply associative learning theory to developmental psychology. His cumulative learning theory stresses hierarchical organization. New learning is said to depend upon combining previously learned entities to form higher levels. Thus, complex principles are based on concepts that in turn require prior discrimination learning, and so on down to the lowest level, the stimulus–response (S–R) association. A theory of development based on cumulative learning was outlined by Gagné (1968). He spelled out details of his learning hierarchy and its application in the classroom in his book on the conditions of learning (Gagné, 1965). In a recent revision of his book (Gagné, 1977), the theory was updated with principles derived from information processing theory.

Estes (1970) related learning theory to mental development with emphasis on mental retardation. Like Gagné, Estes appealed to hierarchical stimulus and response organization and to transfer from previous learning to account for increased learning rate with age.

We may summarize the assumptions of the associative learning theory of development as follows. Children and adults learn in similar ways except for the influence of habit structures acquired previously. Adults have more complex structures than children and are therefore capable of learning more complex material. Also, adults are more likely to mediate responses by implicit symbolic processes intervening between stimulus and response.

CURRENT THEORETICAL TRENDS

The advent of the computer has had a profound influence on psychological theorizing. Many researchers abandoned the notion of S–R associations as the basic units in learning in favor of information processing models of learning analogous to computer programs. Information is assumed by these theorists to go through several stages, each with characteristic storage and operational properties. Learning as defined by information theory consists of the encoding and long-term storage of stimulus and response information. The mechanism by which stored information is translated into behavior is also different. Whereas S–R association theories assume that responses are elicited by stimuli (although complex events may intervene), information processing models postulate information retrieval and response organization mechanisms. Encoding, storage, retrieval, and response organization are regarded as theoretically distinct stages.

Information theory assigns a prominent role to strategic intervention in learning with emphasis on the encoding process. Although the term *encoding* was introduced fairly recently, it refers to a concept that has long been a matter of concern, namely, what is learned. The representation in memory of a stimulus or response event is not an exact copy. Those aspects that are entered into memory constitute the encoding of such an event. Encoding is usually selective in that only the most salient aspects are stored in memory while other details are lost. Encoding may also be elaborative, that is, additional information is stored along with the sensory information. A representation of a visual stimulus, for example, usually includes its identification as a meaningful object, a name, and other information derived from long-term memory. A verbal stimulus may elicit a visual image of the referent that becomes a part of the memory representation. Results of operations performed on stimulus material may also be encoded, such as the outcome of counting a set of objects. We will see in later sections that encoding differences have been found to be crucial in accounting for developmental learning effects.

Under the influence of information processing theories, recent developmental research has focused on children's proficiency at processing information. There are assumed to be several stages during which information may be lost before it is permanently stored. A developmental deficiency at any of these stages could be detrimental to learning. Before describing these studies, a brief description will be given of the major features assumed by most information processing models.

THE MEMORY SYSTEM

Many models have been proposed, some rather elaborate and detailed. For the purposes of this chapter, we will consider a simplified version consisting of components most agreed upon. The interested reader may find it instructive to read chapters by Bjork (1975), Craik and Jacoby (1975), and Shiffrin (1975), in which each theorist describes his own model and then discusses similarities and differences among the three. Although the models are superficially different, the authors concluded that similarities were more important than differences.

Information first enters into the *sensory register*. There is assumed to be one for each modality, but only visual and auditory modalities have been explored to any great extent. The sensory register is a memory store with a large capacity but very rapid decay. Sensory information remains in the register briefly in the same form as it was presented. Unless it is more durably encoded, it is lost in less than a second. Information in the sensory register has rapid access to long-term memory (LTM) for pattern recognition, identification, and possible recoding into another modality. For example, a visual pattern might be phonologically recoded as a word for further processing.

The next stage is *short-term memory* (STM), also called primary memory, immediate memory, and working memory. There are two theoretical functions of STM: storage and processing. Information from the sensory registers may reside temporarily in STM. As a repository, STM has limited capacity. It is often depicted as having a fixed number of slots, each of which can hold one item or chunk of information. Once the slots are filled, incoming information must displace information already in storage or be lost. Some theorists assume spontaneous decay from STM as well. Although the number of items that can be stored in STM at one time is limited, information can be increased by "chunking," or adding information to each item. For example, most adults can store from five to seven letters but they can also store about the same number of words, which increases manyfold the total number of letters that can be held in STM.

Also associated with STM is a *central processing unit*. Not all theorists regard the central processing unit as a part of STM, but it is not important to take a stand on this issue. The function of the central processor is to select from the sensory registers information to be entered into STM, to retrieve relevant information from LTM, to perform various operations and transformations on information in STM, and to transfer material from STM to LTM. The processing that occurs while information is in STM exerts strong control over what is stored in LTM (i.e., what is learned) and therefore will be a major concern in interpreting developmental effects in learning in later sections of this chapter.

Attention, one of the assumed functions of the central processor, has been a key concept in interpreting individual differences. It has been used in so many different senses that it does not seem possible to devise a definition that all would agree on. In broad terms, attention refers to the process or processes by which some stimulus input is selected or emphasized and the rest blocked or attenuated. From an information processing point of view, selection of input can occur at various stages. Selectivity occurs when information is transferred from the sensory register to STM; selectivity also occurs in STM when information is retained by rehearsal or displaced by incoming material. Both these processes, as well as others, have been regarded as attentional by various writers. In this chapter, we will use the term in its broad sense, while recognizing that it may in fact refer to several different mechanisms.

Long-term memory is a high-capacity, relatively permanent store containing all our knowledge of the world. Its structure is highly organized (Anderson & Bower, 1973). Almost nothing is known about whether children's long-term memories are organized in the same way as adults. Evidence is also scarce on the question of whether children's memories are less durable than adults. Thus, we will have little to say about developmental effects in LTM. However, we will show that children are less efficient than adults in retrieving information from LTM.

SENSORY REGISTERS AND TRANSFER TO SHORT-TERM MEMORY

The first direct evidence of a sensory memory store came from Sperling's (1960) classic study. College students were shown tachistoscopically a matrix of nine letters arranged in three rows. When they were asked to recall as many as possible from the total display (whole report), the mean score was 4.5 letters. This result could have meant that the subjects did not have time to perceive all the letters. As a check on that possibility, Sperling devised a partial report method with poststimulus cues; a high-medium-, or low-pitched tone instructed the subject to report the first, second, or third row of the matrix, respectively. When the tone came immediately after stimulus offset, subjects were able to report perfectly any row requested. Obviously, then, all the information in the matrix was available immediately after presentation. As poststimulus cues were presented at longer intervals after stimulus offset, performance decreased, reaching a level equivalent to the whole report method before one second.

Another phenomenon that reveals further properties of the visual sensory register is that of backward masking (Averbach & Coriell, 1961). If a tachistoscopically presented stimulus is followed in close succession by a second stimulus in the same area of the visual field, processing of the first may be interfered with. For example, if a letter is followed within .1 second by a circle surrounding the area where the letter appeared, subjects will report seeing the circle but not the letter. Subjectively, a masking stimulus may have an erasure effect as just described or the first and second stimuli may be combined into a complex stimulus such that the first cannot be distinguished.

Since the pioneering work of Sperling, Averbach, and Coriell, a great many studies have been done using their methods to explore stimulus processing prior to entry into STM. By varying the kinds of masking stimuli and the interstimulus interval, inferences can be made about the stage of processing of the target stimulus at a given time after presentation. The models that have arisen from these data are too complex to be discussed here (see Sperling, 1970; Turvey, 1973), but a few comments are in order. It has been shown that visual masking can occur at two levels, peripheral and central. Peripheral masking can occur with any sufficiently bright stimulus; central masking requires a masking stimulus with features in common with the target stimulus and presumably interferes at the processing stage of pattern recognition and/or identification. Theoretically, before sensory information enters STM, it is analyzed, compared with representations in LTM, and given a durable code. A masking stimulus arriving before durable recoding interrupts processing and prevents entry into STM.

Partial report and visual masking have been used as tools in investigating development of children's processing. A review of this literature may be found in a chapter by Day (1975). There is gradually increasing competence on these tasks from the age of 4 years (the youngest tested) to the age of 12. Children older than 12 years generally are about equivalent to adults. Because of the complexity of the processes involved, there is as yet no definitive answer as to the source of the developmental effect. Is the amount of information entering the processing system less in children? Is the visual memory trace more subject to decay? Or does the problem arise because children are less able to transfer information out of the visual memory system into STM? Although none of these possibilities can be ruled out, recent evidence points to the last as a major factor in accounting for children's low proficiency. They appear to be slower in encoding and transferring information. In this context, encoding means stimulus identification and often verbal recoding.

In an attempt to discover the locus of the developmental effect, Morrison, Holmes, and Haith (1974) examined partial report performance in 5-year-olds, 8-year-olds, and adults. The stimulus was a circular array of seven forms presented tachistoscopically and followed by an indicator pointing to the location of the form to be reported. When the indicator appeared 50 milliseconds after offset of the test stimulus, the three age groups were equivalent in performance. Morrison *et al.* took this to mean that initial registration of the stimulus was not impaired in younger subjects. When the indicator appeared at 300 milliseconds, however, the 5-year-olds performed more poorly than the other two groups, suggesting that information was decaying at a faster rate. However, other findings of the study led the authors to reject the decay theory in favor of an encoding theory. They concluded that the "basic hardware" of the visual memory system was present at the youngest age. Developmental changes were attributed to the appearance of organized strategies for encoding and rehearsal. Specifically, the older subjects began to identify and rehearse all the stimuli available in the register as soon as the display was terminated. The 5-year-olds apparently waited passively until the indicator appeared before attempting to encode the information. Thus, the older subjects were more likely to have a durably encoded representation in STM when the indicator appeared.

Two other studies also implicate speed of transferring information to STM as a source of developmental differences. When a single item is presented in a masking task, developmental effects are small. Blake (1974) and Liss and Haith (1970) reported no differences in reporting single items in age groups ranging from 4 years to adult. Blake compared ability to report forms presented in arrays of one, two, or four in a backward masking experiment. No age effects appeared for single items. When two items were presented, however, the 4-year-olds were significantly less accurate. The 8-year-olds and adults were equivalent at two items and both groups reported about twice as many items as in the single item condition. When four items were presented, the 8-year-olds and adults increased total recall still further, with adults reaching an asymptote of 2.5 forms and 8-year-olds of 2.3. Four-year-olds did not increase the number of forms reported from the two-item to the four-item display. These results showed that only a limited number of forms could be transferred to STM before the masking stimulus halted processing. The two older groups could transfer more than two on the average, but the 4-year-olds transferred fewer than two.

A study by Liss and Haith (1970) also implicated processing speed in accounting for differences due to age. In one condition, subjects were asked to report whether a single line was vertical or horizontal. In the other condition, a 3 × 3 matrix of lines was presented with one line in a different orientation from the others; the task was to report the location of the odd line. Since exposure was too brief to allow scanning of the display while it was visible, the task required scanning the visual memory. Five-year-olds, 10-year-olds, and adults did equally well with a single line, but 5-year-olds did less well than the older subjects under the matrix condition. A slower scan rate was inferred for the younger group.

Although existence of sensory registers for other sense modalities has been suggested, only the auditory register, called echoic memory, has been investigated to any great extent. Crowder (1976) has a good review of the area. Echoic memory is usually investigated by means of the suffix effect. Subjects are asked to repeat a sequence of numbers, letters, or other items presented auditorily and the sequence is followed by an irrelevant item that subjects are told to ignore. For example, the word *recall* is often used as a suffix. Performance is compared for sequences with and without a suffix. Recall is less when a suffix is present, especially for the final items in the sequence. The evidence suggests that the later digits are being held in a precategorical (i.e., unanalyzed) store. Subjects cannot prevent the suffix from entering the store and knocking out some of the material being retained there.

Engle (1977) has done one of the few studies on echoic memory with children. He used the suffix technique to test second and sixth grade children. The sixth graders were less adversely affected by the suffix than were the second graders. Engle inferred that the younger children were more dependent upon the precategorical store and that sixth graders had more quickly transferred items to STM. Thus, evidence from auditory memory agrees with that from visual memory studies.

To summarize developmental research on sensory memory, investigators found no strong evidence that the sensory registers are less capacious or durable in younger subjects, but the amount that can be transferred to STM in a brief period increases with age. Although the rigorous viewing or listening conditions characteristic of controlled laboratory tasks are not usually duplicated outside the laboratory, there is evidence that the skills are relevant to classroom behavior. Morrison, Giordani, and Nagy (1977) found that performance on visual memory tasks was correlated with reading ability. Schwantes (1979) also found a memory deficit for poor readers for material presented to the left visual field, indicating lack of an orderly left-to-right scanning pattern. If strategy differences are indeed responsible for developmental effects, as some have suggested, it might be possible to reduce deficits by training of efficient strategies. However, there is as yet no evidence that performance on visual memory tasks can be improved by training.

SHORT-TERM MEMORY

Storage capacity

Short-term memory is usually assumed to have a fixed number of slots, each of which holds one chunk of information (Miller, 1956). It is assumed that when all the slots are filled, no new information can enter without dislodging some of the old information. A traditional measure of STM capacity is the immediate memory span, the number of items that can be received and reported back immediately. In children, there is a gradual increase in the immediate memory span from about two digits at the age of 2½ years to about seven at age 16. Because digit span bears such a close and orderly relation to age, it is used as an item on most intelligence tests. Immediate memory span is relatively difficult to increase by practice and thus is often considered to reflect a structural feature of the memory system. However, some have suggested that adults are superior to children because they are better able to rehearse and/or organize the items. As stated earlier, information in STM can be increased by forming larger chunks. Thus, digit span could be increased by recoding digits as two- or three-place numbers rather than as single digits.

Belmont and Butterfield (1971) showed that normal teenagers used more efficient study strategies in a modified span test than did retarded teenagers. Stimulus presentation was self-paced, and pause patterns as well as subjective report indicated that the normal teenagers stopped after each group of three digits to rehearse the preceding digits. The retarded teenagers spent a fixed period of time on each digit and did not report cumulative rehearsal. Furthermore, when the retarded teenagers were trained to use the normal strategy, their recall performance improved and when the normal teenagers were prevented from using their usual strategy, there was a performance decrement. Belmont and Butterfield are among those theorists who suggest that the developmental growth of span may be due to acquisition of more efficient strategies rather than to an increase in capacity.

Several recent studies have addressed the question of the source of differences in memory span. Lyon (1977) tested the notion that individual differences in adult spans were due to differences in strategies. College students were tested for digit span and divided into a high-performance and a low-performance group. The two groups were compared at two presentation rates: 1 per second and 3 per second. Rehearsal was possible at the slower rate but not at the faster. Lyon reasoned that if individual differences were due to rehearsal efficiency, they would be eliminated at the faster rate. Although performance improved at the slower rate, the high-performance group was equally superior at both rates. In a second experiment, Lyon required both groups to group and chunk the digits in the same manner. Again, group differences were preserved. Thus, there was no evidence that rehearsal, grouping, or chunking strategies were responsible for individual differences. However, it is possible that the high performers were more skilled at using strategies than the low performers.

Huttenlocher and Burke (1976) performed a similar experiment with children. Children aged 4, 7, 9, and 11 years were tested with grouped or ungrouped digits. For the grouped digits, a 1-second pause was inserted between groups; within groups, the rate of presentation was one per half second. Ungrouped digits were presented at a uniform rate with total presentation time matched for the two conditions. The grouped condition produced better performance than the ungrouped condition, but not differentially over age groups. They also found that the primacy effect (better performance for initial digits) was about the same for all groups. Since the primacy effect is often regarded as a sign of rehearsal, there was no evidence of differential rehearsal among the groups. Huttenlocher and Burke rejected the hypothesis that differences in span could be attributed to rehearsal or organization. After considering the literature on memory span in adults, they offered a new hypothesis about the source of developmental differences, that growth of span may be due to an increase in speed with which children can identify each item and encode information about order. They summarized evidence that most experimental variables that affect span in adults are those that would be expected to affect the encoding stage, for example, familiarity, acoustic confusability, obscuring the symbols in visual presentation, word frequency, and second language versus native language.

Chi (1976) independently reached a similar conclusion based on a review of the literature. Chi (1977) showed that, in fact, 5-year-old children take about twice as long to name a familiar face than do adults and require a considerably longer exposure duration for recognition than do adults. Chi attempted to eliminate span differences between 5-year-olds and adults in two ways. First, she compared span for familiar and unfamiliar faces, reasoning that with unfamiliar faces the encoding advantage for adults would be removed. Although familiar faces produced longer spans for both groups than unfamiliar faces, group differences remained under both conditions. However, adults reported using verbal labels such as *curly hair* or *smiling*, so speed and skill of encoding were still possible factors. In the second experiment, Chi reduced exposure time for each item to 300 milliseconds for adults, but kept it at 600 milliseconds for children. Span differences were greatly reduced but not eliminated. Again, adults reported using special strategies to compensate for the more demanding viewing condition. Chi concluded that span differences need not be attributed to structural limitations of the nervous system.

To summarize the current status of this area, no one has succeeded in eliminating the span differences between children and adults by procedures designed to nullify effects of rehearsal, organization, or encoding speed. However, many researchers believe there are plausible alternatives to a structural limitation in the form of higher level strategies. Others believe the span difference represents a true capacity difference.

Indeed, Bachelder and Denny (1977) have developed a theory of intelligence based on the notion of innate, structural span differences. Whatever the ultimate resolution of this issue, the important point from an educational viewpoint is that teachers should recognize that children have a short-term memory deficit relative to adults. To compensate, teachers should take care not to present too much information at once and should repeat important points frequently. Short-term memory deficits may be a factor in poor reading comprehension. Comprehension of a sentence requires that the words of the sentence be present simultaneously in STM so that they can be integrated into a meaningful proposition. If a child has difficulty in decoding words, the early words of a sentence may be forgotten by the time the final words are decoded. Therefore, training such children to rehearse cumulatively from the beginning of the sentence as each word is decoded may help overcome the problem.

Selective attention

As stated earlier, the term *attention* has been used in a bewilderingly wide variety of contexts, and it is difficult to give a definition that would be appropriate for all usages. The term is used most often when there is evidence of stimulus selection. For example, if it is shown that a subject has learned about only part of the properties of the stimuli presented, selective attention is usually inferred. Theoretically, selection can occur either early in processing when information is transferred from the sensory registers or it can occur later in STM when information is allowed to be displaced before it is transferred to LTM. Most research does not allow inferences about how or when selection occurs. Therefore, in the following sections we will consider studies in which there is evidence of accentuation of some sources of information and attenuation of others without attempting to specify the exact mechanisms responsible.

Attention in learning. The importance of attentional factors in discrimination learning is well established. Zeaman and House (1963) showed that failure to attend to the relevant dimensions of a discrimination problem was responsible for learning failures among retarded children. Analysis of learning curves showed two distinct phases: first, a period of chance performance varying in length from a few trials to hundreds of trials and, second, a rapid rise to 100% correct. The interpretation was offered that during the first phase, subjects were not attending to the cues that predicted reward and nonreward. Once the relevant dimension was attended to, learning was rapid.

Another demonstration of attentional effects in discrimination learning lies in the easiness of an intradimensional problem as compared with the difficulty of an extradimensional shift problem. The basic design is to train subjects on original learning with one dimension relevant and another irrelevant and variable. Following criterion, half the group is shifted to a new problem with the same dimension relevant (intradimensional shift) and the other half is shifted to a new problem with the relevant dimension the same as the irrelevant dimension in the original problem (extradimensional shift). For example, the first problem might be that red is correct and green is incorrect, with circle and square paired randomly with the two colors and uncorrelated with reward. For a group trained in this manner, a new problem with blue correct and yellow incorrect will be quite easy, whereas a new problem with triangle correct and star incorrect, color varying randomly, will be difficult. The attentional explanation of this effect is that during original learning the subjects learn to pay attention to the colors of the stimuli but not to the forms. On entering the intradimensional shift problem, then, they are attending to the relevant dimension and quickly learn which cue is correct. When given the extradimensional shift, however, paying attention to color while ignoring form is detrimental to learning. They must shift attention before the problem can be solved. Other experiments investigating stimulus variables and transfer effects have yielded additional evidence about attention in discrimination learning. Since this research has been extensively reviewed elsewhere (Fisher & Zeaman, 1973; Zeaman, 1973; Zeaman & House, 1963, 1974, 1979), it will not be discussed further here. In particular, Zeaman and House (1974) consider developmental implications.

Another study showing the importance of direction of attention and also showing how apparent developmental differences in learning rate can be caused by attentional differences was done by Siegler (1976). He studied performance on a balance scale problem in subjects 5–18 years of age. The apparatus was a wooden balance scale with four pegs spaced equally on either side of the fulcrum. Weights with center holes could be placed on the pegs to provide test problems. For a test, a particular arrangement of weights was placed on the scale while the arms were supported by blocks. The subjects were asked, "If I take away the blocks, which side will drop?" Siegler devised a set of problems by which the rule being used by each subject to make predictions could be identified. At the lowest level, Rule I, prediction was determined by weight alone. These subjects always picked the side with more weights to drop or, if the weights were equal, subjects predicted no drop. As age increased, subjects took distance from the fulcrum into account with varying degrees of sophistication.

In Siegler's Experiment II, 5- and 8-year-olds who were at the Rule I level were given experience with demonstration trials of various combinations of weights and distances designed to increase their understanding of balance scales to the next higher level. Although both groups began at the same level of knowledge, the 8-year-olds learned more than the 5-year-olds. Siegler surmised that the 5-year-olds were not encoding the distance cues during the demonstration trials; in this context, encoding corresponds to what we have been calling attention, that is, stimulus selection. Corroboratory evidence was obtained from memory tests; children viewed a balance scale setting and attempted to reconstruct it from memory. Five-year-olds made many more distance errors than weight errors, whereas 8-year-olds were about equal on both dimensions. After a brief training period in which the 5-year-olds were taught to count the pegs so as to get a measure of distance, their reproduction scores for weight and distance were equalized. Further, after this training additional demonstration trials produced an increment in rule learning equal to that of the 8-year-olds. Mere exposure to stimulus information is ineffective unless attention is directed to relevant aspects.

In the Siegler experiment, it may seem that the training involved more than stimulus selection in that the children were required to count pegs in order to get a more accurate estimation of distance. No doubt children unable to count would be at a disadvantage even if attention were directed to the distance dimension. The counting operation, however, could be regarded as one extreme of a continuum of attentional behaviors. Typically, selection of relevant stimulation requires more than filtering information that happens to enter the sensory registers. Active information seeking or enhancement responses are integrally related to the selection process. Scanning the visual field with head and eye movements, tactual exploration of surfaces, and the like, in search of relevant stimulus information are common examples. At a slightly more complex level are manual responses that uncover stimulus for visual inspection or increase volume of auditory sources. Whether these overt responses should be called attentional or merely peripheral correlates of attention is a moot question. The efficiency of such responses increases with age (Day, 1974) and is, thus, a potential source of developmental differences in learning.

Direction of attention. The specification of those stimulus aspects being attended defines direction of attention. Developmental effects in direction of attention refer to differences in relative salience of various classes of stimulus aspects as a function of age. Since dimensional salience is strongly controlled by motivation and reinforcement history, it is difficult to separate maturational effects from those due to experience. However, there are certain strong and persistent dimensional preferences that vary with age. In discrimination learning, for example, preschool children have a strong tendency to attend to the positions of the stimuli. Examining the response patterns prior to learning criterion reveals a variety of position strategies—preference for a given position, win-stay, lose–shift strategies for position, alteration, and the like. Preschool children also tend to prefer color to form, but this tendency varies depending upon the particular colors and forms presented.

Another developmental trend in direction of attention is from absolute to relative properties of stimuli. Oddity learning is a case in point. In an oddity problem the child is presented a display with two or more cues identical and one different (e.g., red, red, blue). The stimuli change over trials so that sometimes blue is the correct, odd cue and sometimes the display has one red and two blue stimuli and red is correct. Under the usual procedures for such problems, almost no 3-year-old learns the solution. Performance increases linearly with age, so that by 7 or 8 years, failure is rare. Error patterns and other evidence show that the younger children are responding to the absolute cue values rather than to the relation of difference. If red is correct on one trial, they tend to choose it on the next trial even when the display has changed. Three- and 4-year-old children can learn oddity problems if the oddity relation is made more salient. For example, increasing the number of identical stimuli (e.g., nine identical stimuli, one odd) brings the oddity problem within the capability of preschool children (Gollin, Saravo, & Salten, 1967). House, Brown, and Scott (1974) reviewed the literature and summarized the evidence for regarding the developmental trend as an attentional effect.

Transposition problems also show a trend from absolute to relational solutions over the preschool to early school years. Consider a problem with a 4-inch square correct and a 1-inch square incorrect. This can be solved in two ways: An absolute solution is that the 4-inch square is correct; a relative solution is that the larger square is correct. To discover the basis of solution, the experimenter presents a new set, for example, a 4-inch square versus an 8-inch square. This is called a transposition test trial. If the child transposes, this response is made to the relative choice, namely, the larger 8-inch square. The absolute choice is the 4-inch square, which was correct during original learning. Reese (1968) reviewed the developmental literature and concluded that both absolute and relative cues were available at all ages but that the relative cues became more salient with age.

Another strong developmental trend is a growth of the tendency to attend to component aspects of stimuli when appropriate rather than to the compounds or stimuli regarded as wholes. Children's perception has been described as diffuse, undifferentiated, global, holistic (Werner, 1957). This somewhat vague notion has received support and clarification in recent studies. An attentional interpretation has been given by Zeaman and House (1974) with supporting evidence by Barnes (1978) and House (1979).

One area in which the notion of a shift from holistic responding to component selection has been invoked to account for certain developmental trends is discrimination transfer. Consider a problem with a black square and white circle as one setting, a black circle and white square as the other setting. The experimenter rewards a choice of black but not white regardless of form. Certain transfer effects suggest that preschool children learn such a problem holistically as *Black square is correct* and *Black circle is correct*. Older children respond selectively to the stimulus components that are common to the two settings and learn that *Black is correct*. Additional discussion of these effects may be found in Tighe (1973), Tighe, Glick, and Cole (1971), Tighe and Tighe (1978), and Zeaman and House (1974).

Another study that may help clarify the concept of holistic responding was done by Tighe and Nagy (reported in Tighe & Tighe, 1978). They trained children on a series of discrimination problems using geometric forms. Each problem consisted of a pair of forms identical except that one had rounded corners and the other had sharp corners. The rounded form was always correct for half the subjects and the angular form for the other half. Thus, if subjects attended to the angularity–curvature dimension, they could learn the rule and respond correctly on the first trial of each new problem. Tighe and Nagy found that percentages correct on the first trials of Problems 9 and 10 were 56%, 68%, 96%, and 96%, for kindergarten, second, fourth, and sixth grades, respectively. Thus, the younger children appeared to treat each form as a distinctive compound and solve each problem independently, whereas the older children isolated the common property of roundedness or angularity. In another study, second graders were trained under circumstances that emphasized the similarity of the positive stimuli of two successive problems. Under these conditions, percentages of correct choice went to 88% on first trials, whereas the scores of second graders not given this special treatment remained at 56%. These results show that the children were able to perceive the angularity–curvature components and that when the salience of this dimension was increased, they could selectively attend to component aspects.

Shepp and his colleagues have examined the growth of ability to selectively attend to components in a series of studies (Shepp, Burns, & McDonough, 1978). Shepp has related these findings to a distinction made by Garner (1974) between integral and separable dimensions. Combinations of integral dimensions tend to be perceived as unitary wholes. For adults, one example is hue and brightness. We regard different hue–brightness combinations as distinctive colors. In contrast, separable dimensions are seen as perceptually distinct components. An example is the size of an object and its color. Shepp interprets the shift from holistic to analytic responding in children as an indication that the number of separable dimensions increases with age. Dimensions that are separable for adults may be integral for children.

Garner showed that separable and integral dimensions follow different laws on several types of tasks. Using these same tasks, Shepp and his colleagues have compared children and adults to test the hypothesis that children are more likely to perceive dimensions as integral. The speeded classification task is one that reveals differences between types of dimensions. The subjects are asked to sort a set of stimuli into two piles as quickly as possible. For example, they may be asked to place all red cards in one pile and all blue ones in another. To test for integrality, the task is varied by having differences along other dimensions. The second dimension is either correlated with the target dimension or it is orthogonal. For example, a correlated dimensional task might be red circles and blue squares to be sorted into two piles; the orthogonal version would have red circles, red squares, blue circles, and blue squares to be sorted by color. One hallmark of integral dimensions is that sorting with a correlated second dimension is faster than with a single dimension varying, whereas sorting with an orthogonal second dimension is slower than with a single dimension. The example of hue and brightness may make this result more intuitive. It is easier to sort bright reds and dark blues than reds and blues of the same level of brightness. The reason is that with integral dimensions, a correlated dimension makes for more distinctive stimuli. When hue and brightness are orthogonal, however, the result is four distinct colors, which makes for a harder sorting task. When dimensions are separable, the irrelevant second dimension can be ignored or filtered out, so that it has no effect on sorting. As a result, sorting times for single dimensions are the same as for correlated and for orthogonal irrelevant dimensions.

Shepp and Swartz (1976) used the speeded sorting task to discover whether dimensions known to be separable for adults were integral for children. They tested abilities of first- and fourth-grade children to sort drawings of houses by type of door. Two sets of dimensions were tested, one set that was integral for adults and one that was separable.

Integral dimensions were hue and brightness of doors—dark or light, red or orange; separable dimensions were hue of door and shape of window—square or circle. When sorting was done with integral dimensions, both first and fourth graders showed results typical of adults; a correlated dimension speeded sorting, whereas an orthogonal dimension slowed it down. Data for the separable (for adults) dimensions were different for the two age groups. Fourth graders performed like adults, sorting at the same speed regardless of condition. The first graders, in contrast, were faster with a correlated dimension and slower with an orthogonal dimension. Thus, hue and shape of window appeared to be integral for the younger children. They were unable to focus attention on the relevant dimension and ignore the irrelevant one. In another study, Shepp and Eimas (reported in Shepp, 1978) used speeded classification with the letters *A* and *E* in large or small sizes. They found that for kindergarten children, form and size of letters acted as integral dimensions, but for second and fourth graders, the dimensions were separable.

Strutt, Anderson, and Well (1975) have also studied speeded classification in children aged 6, 9, and 12 years, and in adults. The dimensions used in the sorting task were forms (square or circle), orientation of a line through the form (either horizontal or vertical), and position of a star (above or below the form). These were combined in different decks to provide zero, one, or two irrelevant dimensions. With two irrelevant dimensions, for example, all eight combinations of the three dimensions would appear in the deck, but the subjects would be instructed to sort by one specific dimension such as form. The detrimental effect of orthogonal, irrelevant dimensions decreased with age. The 6-year-olds were very much slower at sorting with one irrelevant dimension than with none, and they were even slower with two irrelevant dimensions. The 9- and 12-year-olds were significantly affected but to a lesser extent. The adults showed no significant effect. Thus, these results corroborate those of Shepp and others.

Before leaving the topic of speeded classification, a brief theoretical note is in order. We have presented this research in the context of direction of attention and have regarded it as evidence that compounds are more salient than components for younger children and hence more likely to be attended. The view of Shepp and his colleagues is somewhat different (Burns, Shepp, McDonough, & Weiner-Ehrlich, 1978; Shepp *et al.*, 1978). They argue that the effects are perceptual phenomena rather than attentional and that when dimensions are integral, selective attention is not an option. The differential consequences of these two views lie in the effects of training. If the effects are perceptual in nature, they should be strongly resistant to training. If they are due to attentional preference, however, they may be altered by appropriate training. There is little evidence on this point. Although two studies have shown that relative salience of color–form compounds and components are affected by differential reinforcement (Barnes, 1978; House, 1979), other dimensions have not been tested. In still another interpretation of the results of speeded classification tasks, Strutt *et al.* (1975) inferred inability to focus attention or distractibility in younger children. This means either inability to look at one component at a time (failure to focus) or a tendency to shift attention from the relevant to the irrelevant cues (distractibility). The contributions of perception, direction of attention, focusing ability, and distractibility are difficult to disentangle in this research. Whatever the reason, we can say that children in the early grades may be more adversely affected by irrelevant stimulus variation. For example, a child who has learned to read with black letters on a white background may perform poorly when white letters are written on a blackboard.

A different kind of test for integrality of dimensions is called restricted classification; subjects are shown three stimuli and asked which two go best together. The triads are selected to throw light on bases for judgments of similarity, whether dimensional or holistic. For example, in one type of triad, two of the stimuli are identical on one dimension but quite different on another; the third member of the triad is not the same on either dimension as the other two but is close in overall similarity to one. For example, one might present two circles, A and B, of exactly the same size but different in brightness (light gray versus dark gray); the third circle, C, might be slightly larger and slightly darker than B. In overall similarity, C is more like B than is A. When dimensions are separable, subjects choose A and B as the two that go together because they are identical on one dimension; when dimensions are integral, the two that are most alike in overall similarity are chosen (e.g., B and C in the example described earlier). Using this technique, Smith and Kemler (1977) found that kindergarten children treated size and brightness as integral dimensions, whereas fourth graders treated them as separable. Second grade children were mixed in their approach to the problem.

Shepp *et al.* (1978) tested other dimensions using a restricted classification task similar to that used by Smith and Kemler. Children of 4, 9, and 11 years of age were subjects. The dimensions tested were size and brightness of squares and size of circle and angle of radius. For triads of the kind described earlier, the dimensional choices were 13%, 48%, and 79% for 4-, 9-, and 11-year-olds, respectively. For the circles, corresponding percentages of dimensional choices were 15, 50, and 67. Other types of triads yielded similar conclusions that the younger children were less likely to respond dimensionally.

Results from restricted classification tests are consistent with those from speeded classification and seem more amenable to interpretation as an effect of perceptual differences or differences in direction of attention than of distractibility.

Breadth, focusing, and adjustability of attention. Some researchers have said that young children have narrow attention, are overselective, and learn less about the stimuli presented to them than do older children. Others have said that the problem is one of too broad attention, inability to focus and to screen out irrelevant information. There is evidence to support both these seemingly contradictory views. The resolution appears to be that older children are better able to adjust attention to task demands. When relevant stimulus input is rich and broad attention is needed, older children learn more about what is presented. When there is a high proportion of irrelevant information and narrow attention is desirable, older children are better able to focus, that is, to attend just to the relevant information.

It was shown in earlier sections that the amount of information that can be transferred to STM from the sensory registers increases with age and that short-term memory span also increases. Both these effects have been interpreted as growth in breadth of attention. Other evidence of increased breadth with age comes from incidental learning tasks. In such tasks, subjects are instructed to learn about one aspect of stimuli and are later tested on other aspects. In one study, Hagen (1967) tested first, third, fifth, and seventh graders on a task requiring memory of the positions of picture cards displayed in a row. The cards had pictures of animals and household objects. The children were told to remember the positions of the animals but were given no instructions about the objects. Later they were tested not only for animal positions but for knowledge about which object was paired with each animal. All age groups learned approximately the same amount about the object–animal pairings (incidental task) but memory for animal positions (central task) increased with age. The results were interpreted as evidence for greater breadth of attention in the older children. The reasoning behind this interpretation was that although the older children apparently allotted more attention to the central task than did the younger children, this was not done at the expense of the incidental task.

Multiple component testing is another method that has been used to measure breadth of attention. Children are asked to learn about stimuli with several relevant dimensions and then tested for each component dimension separately. Hale and Morgan (1973) tested 4-, 8-, and 12-year-old children for memory of order of stimuli having both color and form relevant. They were first trained to criterion with color and form serving as redundant relevant cues. They were then tested for memory of the order of the colors and the forms separately. The three groups were approximately equal on form tests but the 8- and 12-year-olds learned more about colors. Greater breadth of attention was inferred for the older children on the grounds that apparent greater attention to color was not accompanied by a decrease in attention to form.

Another experimental technique for measuring breadth of attention is to require performance of two tasks simultaneously. Usually one task is designated the target task and the experimenter looks for a decrement in performance when a second task is required. Manis, Keating, and Morrison (1980) presented a letter-matching task as the target. Pairs of letters were presented in succession and the subjects were asked to indicate as quickly as possible whether the second letter presented was the same as or different from the first. The distractor task was a response to an auditory signal presented on some of the trials. Subjects were told to press a button as soon as they could after hearing the auditory signal but without interrupting their responses to the letter stimuli. To the extent that subjects had to interrupt their processing of the letters to register the occurrence of the auditory signal, reaction times would be increased. Second-grade children were more adversely affected by the distractor task than sixth graders who were, in turn, worse than adults. Manis *et al.* were able also to pinpoint the locus of the distracting effect in the later stages of the letter processing. When the auditory signal was given after a warning signal but before the first letter appeared, there was little distracting effect for any age group. The developmental effect increased as the distractor appeared later and later in the trial. The greatest effect occurred while the first letter was being rehearsed and compared with the second letter. Manis *et al.* inferred greater attentional capacity in older subjects. In this context attention has a broader meaning than selection of stimulus input in that subjects were required to divide attention between mental events and external stimuli. An analysis of this concept of attention may be found in Kahneman (1973).

Turning now to studies of focusing of attention, we find that similar techniques are used. A target task and a distractor are presented. However, in focusing studies, subjects are instructed to ignore the distractor, unlike the breadth tasks in which attention must be divided between the two tasks. A good example of a focusing task is selective listening in which subjects listen to two voices speaking simultaneously and are asked to report the words spoken by one of the voices and ignore the other. Younger children are less able to attend to the relevant voice. They make more intrusive errors by reporting words spoken by the wrong voice or by reporting a combination of two words spoken at once (Maccoby & Konrad, 1966, 1967).

Doyle (1973) carried out a study to discover the locus of the focusing deficit in younger children. According to some theories of attention (e.g., Broadbent, 1958), voices can be filtered out before semantic processing on the basis of gross qualitative differences. If so, words spoken by a voice identified as incorrect by pitch or other physical characteristic would not be further processed and the words and their meanings would not enter the STM system. Doyle tested children 8, 11, and 14 years of age for memory of a list of words recorded by a male speaker. The children were asked to repeat each word immediately after hearing it and were later given recognition memory tests. The control group heard only the male voice. For the distraction group, a female voice spoke a different list of words simultaneously but subjects were instructed to repeat and try to remember just the male voice. Results replicated previous findings of more intrusions of the wrong voice when repeating words in the younger children. Distraction had a greater disrupting effect on recognition of target words in the younger children. The 14-year-olds recognized about as many target words regardless of the presence or absence of an irrelevant voice but the 8- and 11-year-old children recalled fewer target words when the distractor was present. To test for the locus of the focusing effect, Doyle tested memory for the distractor words. All age groups recalled about the same number of distractor words, showing that blocking out did not occur before the words were identified. Doyle inferred an inability to inhibit intrusions from the distracting material during the selection task in the younger children.

Smith, Kemler, and Aronfreed (1975) investigated the effect of distinctiveness of the source of irrelevant information. They reasoned that the more easily analyzable and distinguishable the distractor, the more easily it could be screened out. The central task was a visual monitoring one in which subjects had to indicate whether the posture of each stick figure in a sequence was different from the preceding posture. One type of distractor was auditory; the other two were visual but one was clearly separate, consisting of a border around the stick figure, whereas the other visual distractor was the color of the stick figure itself. Each distractor consisted of two possible stimuli that changed from trial to trial in a manner uncorrelated with the changes in the postures of the stick figures. Second-grade students provided data that confirmed the hypothesis; they were much less affected by the auditory distractor than by the visual and less by the border distractor than by the color of the figure. Fifth-grade students performed equally well under all distractor conditions. Evidence from kindergarten children suggested that they were attempting to divide attention between the distractor and the relevant stimuli instead of attending to the relevant stimuli alone.

Most studies of the ability to focus attention suggest that it does not develop before early school years and that growth continues until adolescence. However, a study by Howard and Goldin (1979) showed that much younger children can focus under some circumstances. Kindergarten children were given the task of remembering a doll's clothing. The doll had interchangeable accessories consisting of four different hats, belts, neckpieces, and flowers. The children were told that the doll was a spy who wore particular items as secret identification. Either one, two, or four accessories were worn by the doll and either one, two, or four were designated as secret identification. The children were told which of the accessories were relevant either before the doll was shown to them or after it was removed. For example, the child might be told that the belt was the secret identification but not told the specific belt. When irrelevant accessories were worn by the doll, the children had better recall when told which were relevant before viewing the doll, which was indicative of selective attention. The Howard and Goldin results are consonant with data from discrimination learning studies (e.g., Eimas, 1970). A possible reason for the finding of selectivity at a younger age than other studies is that selection was partly under the control of peripheral responses. That is, the children could move their eyes to the clothing items identified as relevant and look less at the other items. These data suggest that elementary school children should have little trouble in attending to relevant features of visual displays, provided that they are told what to look at. Teachers can improve performance of children by identifying the important aspects of pictures, diagrams, and written material.

Summary. The studies considered in this section have shown substantial changes in attentional ability during early school years. Attention becomes more abstract and more analytic in direction. This means that children become more sensitive to relations among stimuli. They also become more able to attend to components of stimuli independently of context. For that reason older children have a greater ability than younger children to detect common elements among disparate objects, for example, to see that a ball, a cherry, and an orange have the common property of roundness.

In addition to changes in what children are likely to attend to, there are increases with age in breadth of attention for material having high levels of relevant information and increases in ability to filter out irrelevant information when required for competent performance.

Can attention be trained? Certainly direction of attention can be altered rather easily by instructions or differential reinforcement (Barnes, 1978; House, 1979; Tighe & Tighe, 1978; Zeaman & House, 1974). With respect to breadth, focusing, and adjustability of attention, the picture is less clear, but it appears that these abilities cannot easily be improved. Therefore, educators should take care not to place too great demands on attention capacity of young children.

Short-term memory dynamics

Mnemonic strategies and learning. Adult humans can influence their learning efficiency and memory by means of operations performed on the contents of STM. Although psychologists have recognized this ability for a long time, it has not been the object of concentrated study until recently. Earlier learning researchers attempted to bypass complex human processing in order to develop species-independent laws of learning. Today, an active research area is the effect of cognitive processing on learning and memory. Emphasis on effects of memory strategies has been especially strong in developmental research. Several theorists (e.g., Brown & DeLoache, 1978; Flavell, Friedricks, & Hoyt, 1970) have argued that the major change in learning and memory as children grow older is an increase in the use of deliberate memorial strategies.

Mnemonic strategies can be roughly divided into two types. One kind, sometimes called maintenance rehearsal, consists of simple repetition of material that has been presented. Its primary functions are to keep items in STM until they are needed and/or to preserve the order of items. A good example from everyday life is repetition of a phone number between the time of looking it up and making the call.

The second type of memory strategy is often called elaborative. It refers to a variety of techniques for improving long-term memory and retrieval. It involves an interaction between STM and related material from LTM such that the to-be-remembered material is transformed or enriched and made more meaningful and memorable.

Maintenance rehearsal in children. This type of rehearsal is a familiar strategy to most adults and is used spontaneously when appropriate. Preschool children do not usually rehearse spontaneously but acquire the strategy during early school years.

Flavell and his colleagues (1970) investigated rehearsal in order to discover the nature of the mediational deficiency said to characterize young children. Flavell distinguished between two possible meanings of the term *mediational deficiency:* production deficiency (or failure to make the appropriate mediating responses) and mediational deficiency (or failure of an appropriate mediating response to affect performance). Several studies have revealed evidence of production deficiencies. In one study (Flavell, Beach, & Chinsky, 1966), the experimenter displayed an array of seven easily nameable pictures, touched three of them, and asked the subject to touch the same pictures in order after a 15-second delay. Lip movements were unobtrusively observed during the interval and children were also questioned about rehearsal. Only 10% of kindergarten children rehearsed, as compared with 80% of second graders and 100% of fifth graders. In another study, evidence of mediational deficiency was sought. Keeney, Cannizzo, and Flavell (1967) tested first graders in the manner previously described. Those who did not rehearse spontaneously were trained to whisper the words during the interval. When they did so, their performance scores increased to the level of the spontaneous rehearsers. Thus, mediational deficiency was not observed. These studies and others reported by Flavell *et al.* (1970) revealed several types of production deficiencies in young school children. There were also cases of production inefficiencies in which rehearsal was attempted but errors occurred causing a decrement in performance. However, mediational deficiencies were not observed in any of these studies; when appropriate and correct mediators were produced, performance improved to the level of spontaneous producers of the same age.

Many investigations of rehearsal deficiency have been done with a serial position recall task devised by Atkinson, Hansen, and Bernbach (1964). Picture cards are displayed in a row; each card is shown briefly to the subject and then turned face down. Cards are displayed in temporal sequence from left to right. The experimenter then shows a probe card that is a duplicate of one of the face-down cards and asks the subject to point to the matching picture. Over trials the same cards are generally used but in different orders. This method provides orderly data for subjects from 4 years of age to adulthood and for that reason has been very popular for studying developmental differences in learning strategies.

As one would expect, performance on the serial position recall task improves with age. However, the developmental effect is relatively small on the final items, as opposed to the earlier items. This finding suggests a rehearsal deficit in the younger children, since rehearsal is necessary to maintain the earlier items in memory, whereas the more recent items are still in STM at the time of the probe test.

Hagen and Kail (1973) tested the rehearsal hypothesis more directly. They compared 7- and 11-year-olds under two conditions—one designed to encourage rehearsal and one designed to prevent it. The experimenter delayed 15 seconds after the final card was shown before presenting the probe. For the rehearsal condition, subjects were told to think about the pictures. For the nonrehearsal condition, they were required to count aloud during the interval. The 7-year-old children performed about the same under both conditions. The 11-year-olds, however, did better under the rehearsal condition than when required to count. The implication of the finding is that the older children used the delay period for rehearsal and the younger ones did not.

McCarver (1972) found similar results. Kindergarten, first-grade, fourth-grade, and college students were compared when an opportunity to use an effective learning strategy was present or absent. The strategy group was told that it is better to learn picture sequences by pairs. Temporal and spatial cues were also provided to set off the pairs. The control group had no special instructions or cues. Again, kindergarten and first-grade students did not profit from instruction and special cues, whereas fourth-grade and college students did considerably better under the strategy condition.

The two studies previously described could have been affected by mediational deficiencies rather than production deficiencies. Research by Allik and Siegel (1976) and Conrad (1971) provided stronger evidence of production deficit. Allik and Siegel tested children from nursery school, kindergarten, and first, third, and fifth grades on two types of serial tasks. In one condition, all the pictures in the set had a one-syllable name, for example, *drum, leaf, cow*; in the other condition all pictures had two-syllable names, for example, *monkey, zipper, table*. Allik and Siegel reasoned that cumulative rehearsal would be easier with one-syllable words. Third and fifth graders found the two-syllable lists more difficult than the one-syllable lists, but younger children did equally well on both types. Conrad (1971) tested children from 3 to 9 years of age on serial recall with two different kinds of picture card sets. One set had names that were all very similar, for example, *cat, hat, mat*. The other had names that were unlike, for example, *girl, bus, train*. Conrad hypothesized that rehearsal of like-sounding names would produce interference. In order to avoid interpretational difficulties associated with unequal overall performance levels, Conrad first equated the age groups for performance on the list with like-sounding names by adjusting the number of cards to be recalled. After achieving a 50%

correct baseline for each group on like-sounding names, the unlike names were presented. Children from 3 to 5 years of age did equally well on both lists. Children between 5 and 6 years did slightly better (60%) on unlike names, and children between 8 and 11 years scored an average of 75%. Results from these two studies confirm that failure to rehearse occurs in younger children and, thus, tend to corroborate the interpretations of McCarver (1972) and Hagen and Kail (1973) of production rather than mediational deficiencies.

The studies previously described suggest that if young children were trained to rehearse, performance on the serial order task would improve. Recent research confirms this prediction but shows that maintenance of the rehearsal strategy may be a problem. Kingsley and Hagen (1969) trained 5-year-olds to rehearse cumulatively and found improved performance. They also corrected rehearsal errors throughout the experiment. When Hagen, Hargrave, and Ross (1973) repeated the experiment, they found that rehearsal was not maintained after prompting and correction were discontinued. A similar finding was reported by Keeney *et al.* (1967). First graders trained to rehearse did not continue to do so unless specifically reminded. However, later work has shown that strategy maintenance occurs if sufficient training is given (Borkowski & Cavanaugh, 1979). Also, Asarnow and Meichenbaum (1979) found that a more elaborate training procedure was effective. They compared the Keeney *et al.* training procedure with their own technique, termed a self-instructional method. This involved, among other features, impressing on the children the reasons for rehearsal and its value in increasing performance. Asarnow and Meichenbaum found that kindergarten children who did rehearse a little bit spontaneously, but not consistently, maintained rehearsal following either the Keeney *et al.* procedure or the self-instructional method. However, kindergarten children who showed no signs of rehearsing required the more intensive self-instructional method for strategy maintenance.

Imagery, elaboration, and other mnemonic devices. Mnemonics, the art of memory improvement, was developed 25 centuries ago. Yet it is only recently that psychologists have attempted to gain a scientific understanding of the various techniques and how they work. There is little doubt that substantial gains in memory can be achieved by such devices. Professional mnemonists amaze their audiences by memorizing long lists of words in one hearing. However, the techniques are simple ones that could be mastered by any normal adult. The method of loci, used by Greek and Roman orators to keep track of the points to be made in their speeches, is a case in point. To learn an ordered list of 20 nouns in one trial, choose a well-known route, either outdoors or indoors, and pick out 20 distinct locations. These must be memorized first. Then, as each of the 20 nouns is presented, form an image in which the referent of the noun interacts with its location. For example, if the first location is the front door and the first noun is *letter,* picture a letter being pushed under the door. To retrieve the list, simply recall each location and the associated image will provide the word. The method can be extended to even larger numbers of words with practice. The same list of memorized locations can be used to learn new lists of words, although some interference may be experienced if it is attempted too soon. This and other methods used by professional mnemonists have been shown to be very effective even for non-memory-experts (Bower & Reitman, 1972; McCarty, 1980).

A key feature of most mnemonic systems is an image relating the elements to be associated. Paivio was the first in modern times to stress the importance of visual imagery, and his work has been extremely influential (Paivio, 1971). It is beyond the scope of this chapter to consider the theoretical arguments with regard to the nature of images and reasons for their effectiveness in memory tasks. Analyses of the problem may be found in Paivio (1971), Pylyshyn (1973), Reese (1977), and in a symposium edited by Reese (1970). It should be pointed out, however, that imagery per se is not always effective. When the task is to associate two elements, it is not sufficient to form images of two independent elements. A compound image must be formed with the two elements interacting (Wollen, Weber, & Lowry, 1972).

One question that has received a great deal of experimental attention in the developmental literature is whether it is better to provide an image by showing a picture or to ask subjects to generate their own images. In a typical study, Clarkson, Haggith, Tierney, and Kobasigawa (1973) tested the ability of fourth- and sixth-grade children to learn a list of picture pairs by one of three methods. One group was shown a picture of two objects separated, for example, a fish and a telephone; another group saw a picture of the pair interacting, for example, a fish talking on a telephone; the third group saw the pictures separated and were asked to close their eyes and picture the two things doing something together. On the test trial, children were shown one member of each pair and asked to name the other. Both interacting conditions were better than the noninteracting control. In this study, performance was better when children generated their own images than when the experimenter supplied one pictorially. However, other studies have found little difference (Reese, 1977).

Another experimental question that has been well researched is whether presenting sentences relating two elements has as much effect on memory as pictorial interactions or imagery instructions. Such a sentence might be *The rock hit the bottle,* termed verbal elaboration by Rohwer (1973). Reese (1977) surveyed some 40 studies in which visual imagery and verbal elaboration were compared over age ranges from kindergarten to college. Results were quite variable, but visual elaboration was better than verbal more often than not. Some data suggest a developmental effect with verbal more effective than visual elaboration for kindergarten and first-grade children, but the replicability of this effect is in doubt (Rohwer, 1973).

The evidence is clear that children from kindergarten on up, as well as adults, benefit from imagery and elaborative mediation. What about spontaneous usage in children and adults? It has been shown that college students typically use mediational strategies when given laboratory learning tasks. Bugelski (1962) asked 100 students to learn a set of nonsense syllable pairs and then asked them to describe their learning methods. All 100 students had used some form of mediation. A typical method was to transform syllables into words suggested by the syllables such as *general nurse* for *gey-nur.* Adams and Montague (1967) studied acquisition of word pairs by college students and found that 67% used mediation of various types including mediation by sentences. For example, for the words *inshore, victor,* one student used the phrase *troops landing on a shore* to help memory. Adams and Montague also found that pairs for which mediators were generated were learned faster than nonmediated pairs.

Elementary school children are much less likely than college students to mediate spontaneously in paired associate learning. Pressley and Levin (1977) tested fifth-, seventh-, and ninth-grade students on a paired associate task and then questioned them as to method used. The percentages of children using repetitive rehearsal were 53, 26, and 6 for fifth, seventh, and ninth grades, respectively, whereas percentages using primarily visual imagery or verbal elaboration were 6, 15, and 22. The rest of the children used mixed strategies; they usually rehearsed, but used elaboration for some pairs that seemed to make sense together. The elaborators remembered over twice as many pairs as other subjects.

Although adults employ mediational devices when set a task of learning arbitrarily paired words or syllables, there is recent evidence that such mnemonic devices do not play a large role in everyday learning. Harris (1980) presented a detailed questionnaire to college students and to housewives about what memory aids were used and how frequently. The most frequently used methods were external such as marking a calendar, making a shopping list, writing a memo, and the like. Of the internal aids, the two most frequently used were retrieval methods—retracing ones movements to find a lost object and going through the alphabet to recall a name. Although most subjects used such methods at times, only 23% and 3%, respectively, used them more than once a week. Deliberate strategies to memorize material at the time of input were very infrequent. It appears that if voluntary strategic control over what goes into LTM is important in day-to-day learning, the strategies are not easy to recognize and describe. Possibly when material is intrinsically meaningful and related to what one already knows, deliberate mnemonic intervention is not required.

Summary. Adults engage in a variety of memorial strategies that improve performance in certain laboratory tasks and in classroom learning. Children are much less likely to do so. Maintenance or rote rehearsal does not usually occur spontaneously until around 8 years of age. Elaboration and imagery as deliberate mnemonic devices are rare in children below 12 years of age. Thus, increase in the use of such strategies may be a factor in the growth of learning ability, although it is not certain how important they are for everyday learning.

Children can be taught to use mnemonic strategies and performance is thereby improved. Thus, teachers may help students by showing them how to rehearse when appropriate, how to use imagery, and the like. Some examples of classroom application of these principles will be described in a later section of this chapter. Teachers should also be aware that children may need to be reminded to continue to use trained strategies, especially when new material is introduced.

LONG-TERM MEMORY STRUCTURE

The contents of LTM are highly organized. Some theorists (e.g., Tulving, 1972) have suggested that there are two kinds of LTM, episodic memory and semantic memory. Episodic memory contains records of specific events with definite times and places of occurrence. Semantic memory consists of an organized body of knowledge about the world. We usually have no recollection of when or where such knowledge was acquired. Laboratory studies have generally been concerned with episodic memory. Much less is known about semantic memory and its relation to episodic memory. Computer models attempting to simulate semantic memory organization (e.g., Anderson & Bower, 1973) have been only partly successful. Even less is known about organization of semantic memory in children. However, the available evidence does not suggest different structures in children and adults (Nelson & Kosslyn, 1975).

In the contents of semantic memory, children and adults differ a great deal, of course. Normal adults know more than children and this can affect learning speed in several ways. Speed of stimulus identification and entry into STM are affected by familiarity of stimuli. Learning is faster if new facts can be integrated into an existing body of knowledge. The importance of this factor was emphasized by Chi (1978), who showed that children chess experts had better memory for chess positions than did adult novices. Finally, adults have more information processing routines stored in LTM than do children.

Differences in the contents of semantic memory may account for a part of the difference in learning speed between children and adults. In general, there is little that teachers can do to erase this difference except to wait for the effects of time and experience to increase knowledge. Teachers can, however, attempt to build on what children already know when presenting new material.

RETRIEVAL FROM LONG-TERM MEMORY IN CHILDREN

Although retrieval is not a part of the acquisition process, it is important to consider when inferring age effects in learning. If older children appear to have learned more than younger children, one possibility is that the older children have better retrieval systems. Information may be *available* in LTM (i.e., stored) but not *accessible* at the time of recall (Tulving & Pearlstone, 1966). For example, normal adults know the names of the 50 states. Hence the knowledge is available. However, it is likely that if asked to name the states, most adults would not be able to recall all of them, that is, some states would not be accessible. A retrieval plan can increase the number of states recalled. For example, one might go through the alphabet trying to think of all states beginning with each letter, thereby recalling more names than would be possible with a random recall method. Externally provided retrieval cues can elicit further names. The phrase *famous for potatoes* would probably make *Idaho* accessible. These distinctions suggest three ways to account for poor recall: inadequate storage, poor retrieval strategy, or failure to benefit from retrieval cues. These possibilities have led researchers to ask how important retrieval factors are in accounting for performance differences between children and adults.

One of the earliest studies was done by Kobasigawa (1974) with children from grades 1, 3, and 6. The task was to recall a list of 24 nouns presented as pictures. Each set of three pictures was presented together with a card that could act as a retrieval cue. For example, a monkey, a camel, and a bear were presented with a picture of a zoo; pieces of furniture were presented with a picture of a room, and so on. One group was asked to recall as many pictures as possible (free recall). A second group had all the cue cards present but turned face down. As a test of voluntary use of retrieval aids, they were told that they could look at the cards if that would help them (voluntary cue). A third group was shown each cue card in turn and asked to name all the pictures that went with it (directive cue). When the directive cue was used, recall was very high for all groups, over 80% correct. When the use of cues was voluntary, 33% of first graders, 75% of third graders, and 92% of sixth graders used them. Unlike the directive cue condition, recall of spontaneous cue users was less for the lower grade levels. The difference was due to failure to name all the pictures that went with each card. When instructed to name all the pictures as in the directive cue condition, they were able to do so with considerable success. But a younger child who spontaneously exposed a cue tended to name just one picture and go on to the next cue card. Kobasigawa concluded that not only were younger children less likely to use a retrieval strategy but that cues were less effective for them.

Hall, Murphy, Humphreys, and Wilson (1979) noted that in previous studies, initial storage was not well controlled. Thus, results could have been due partly to unequal storage rather than to differences in retrieval efficiency. Hall *et al.* designed a study to test effectiveness of retrieval cues in second and fifth graders with storage controlled in a free-recall test. Storage was equated by giving a longer list to the fifth graders and by analyzing only eight target words in the middle of the list where recall was approximately equal for the two age groups. After listening to the list twice, children were asked to recall as many words as possible. When a 10-second pause in the recall phase occurred, different retrieval conditions were introduced. The no cue groups were simply asked to try to recall more words. They were not very successful, recalling only 3–5% of the remaining words. The other two groups at each age level were told that they would be given words that would help them remember. These retrieval aids were words chosen from association norms that were likely to elicit the target word as an associate. If the retrieval cue elicited the target word, the subject had only to recognize that the word was on the list. For one group (strong cue) the retrieval aid had a high probability of eliciting the target word (mean = 50%) and for the other group (moderate cue) the probability was lower (mean = 10%). For example, the strong cue for the target word *chair* was *table* and the moderate cue was *sit*. First, let us consider performance of the second-grade subjects. Recall that the theoretical model calls for the retrieval cue to elicit an association that the child edits. If it is recognized as a list word, it is reported; otherwise not. If this model is correct, the probability that the target word is recalled should equal the probability of being elicited as an associate. Second graders approximated the model quite closely. They recalled 52% of the words with the strong cues and 13% with the moderate cues. The fifth graders did considerably better—71% with strong cues and 33% with moderate cues. These findings were interpreted as showing a retrieval plan for the fifth graders but none for second graders. For the younger children, if the target word was elicited by free association, they were able to recognize and report it and were also able to reject incorrect associates. The fifth graders performed as though they had a plan. It appeared that if the first associate was not a target word, they continued to free associate, which increased the probability that the required word would be generated.

These and other studies (Kenniston & Flavell, 1979; Ritter, Kaprove, Fitch, & Flavell, 1973) show that a part of the deficit shown by children in learning studies could be due to incomplete retrieval of stored material. It seems likely that children could be taught retrieval strategies that would improve their test performance. As yet, this possibility has not been experimentally investigated. The importance of retrieval strategies has only recently been recognized. Future research may throw more light on their development and trainability.

DEVELOPMENT OF METAMEMORY

Recent memory research has taken a new direction by asking questions about children's knowledge of memory, or metamemory. Metamemory consists of knowledge of one's own memory capacity and skills as well as knowledge about the memory characteristics of various tasks. It has been suggested (Brown & DeLoache, 1978; Flavell, 1978) that a lack of such knowledge is important because it may lead to inefficient strategies. Deficiencies in metamemory could account for the production deficiencies described in an earlier section. A child may fail to rehearse, for example, because of failure to realize that forgetting will occur or that rehearsal will aid memory.

Research summarized by Flavell and Wellman (1977) shows that children are indeed less aware of their memory limitations. Elementary school children overestimate their immediate memory span, whereas adults are quite accurate. Younger children are less able to judge how well they know material than are older children. Children also show increasing knowledge with age of what makes material easy or hard to remember. Kreutzer, Leonard, and Flavell (1975) found that most 6- and

7-year-olds did not know that a paired-associate list consisting of opposites would be easier to learn than randomly paired words. Most 9–11-year-olds were aware of this. Similar age effects have been shown for effects of length of list and categorizability in free recall.

The educational relevance of metamemory deficits in young children is not clear as yet. Will teaching children about memory limitations and memory task properties improve their learning ability? Clearly, the answer is no unless the children have the appropriate strategies in their response repertoires. Even when that condition is met, metamemorial knowledge may not influence performance. Flavell and Wellman cited evidence that in young children metamemorial judgments may not be reflected in behavior. Thus, the importance of metamemory for educational practice is somewhat speculative at present. But Flavell (1979) has argued persuasively for the potential value of metamemorial and metacognitive research for education.

EDUCATIONAL IMPLICATIONS

Developmental limitations in processing efficiency

This survey of research has shown developmental effects at all stages of information processing. The major areas in which deficits were inferred were STM capacity, attention, knowledge base, and strategic control of learning and memory.

Some processing deficits appear to be fixed characteristics at given age levels, at least for practical purposes. That is, they cannot be substantially changed by any presently known methods. These include STM capacity, breadth of attention, and ability to focus attention. We may also include knowledge base in the list. Although children's knowledge is constantly increasing, the gap between the knowledge bases of older and younger children cannot be bridged by short-term training sessions. For these relatively fixed developmental deficits, the response of teachers must be to adapt teaching materials and methods to the limitations of the children. Other deficits, such as failure to rehearse, can be remedied by simple training procedures that can improve learning rate.

To compensate for capacity deficits, the rate of information flow should be adjusted. When presenting material orally, teachers should be aware that a child's capacity for assimilating information is less than an adult's. This means taking care not to present too many new items at once. Frequent repetition of key points is important. Asking questions about material just presented can help a teacher judge whether information is being presented at too great a rate.

The relative lack of knowledge of children makes it essential that a teacher find some common ground with young students. Teachers should find out what the children know about a given topic and relate new information to the existing knowledge base. Some concrete suggestions derived from associative learning theory may be found in Gagné (1977).

In addition to deficiencies in breadth of attention and focusing ability, children may have trouble identifying relevant and irrelevant information. For that reason, teachers should be careful to emphasize the relevant aspects of instructional material and eliminate irrelevant aspects as much as possible. The teacher should also be aware that stimuli placed in a different context may be perceived differently by young school children. A performance decrement might be expected when changing from small black letters on white paper to big white letters on a blackboard. Learning to count may be disrupted when going from counting apples to counting pennies.

The literature on strategy deficits shows a production deficiency in elementary school children but not a mediational deficiency. This means that teaching mnemonic techniques can improve performance, often dramatically. Teachers should know that children 8 years old or younger will likely not rehearse spontaneously but can be taught to do so. Imagery and elaboration techniques are not usually employed by children under 12 years of age, but these methods do have classroom application, as described in the next sections.

The research on retrieval mechanisms shows that children may know more than they are able to produce in classroom tests. That is, information in LTM may not be accessible. Little is known as yet about how retrieval strategies might be trained. Teachers may, however, discover more about what children actually know by giving hints that can act as retrieval cues. The experience of recalling apparently forgotten information by means of such hints may well encourage children to engage in more active memory searches.

Most of the work described in this chapter has been laboratory experimentation. The studies were designed to uncover general principles and their application to more complex classroom situations may not be obvious. However, there have been a few studies testing mnemonic methods in the classroom or in classroom-like situations. A brief description of some of these studies follows.

Imagery in classroom learning

We showed earlier that imagery instructions help children to learn paired associates. In another laboratory study, Paris, Mahoney, and Buckhalt (1974) found that imagery increased prose comprehension and semantic integration in retarded school children. Pairs of sentences such as *John is chasing the dog* and *The dog is in the school yard* were read to the subjects. The subjects were then given sentence recognition tests. Some test sentences were the same as ones that had been presented, and others were different. Of particular interest were sentences that had not been presented but did represent true inferences from the sentences. An example from the two sentences previously cited would be *John is in the school yard*. Paradoxically, subjects who understand the sentences best are more likely to make a mistake on such a sentence by falsely recognizing it as one that was presented. When Paris *et al.* instructed subjects to "make pictures of the sentences" in their heads, the ability to distinguish true inferences from false inferences increased, as did correct recognition of actual sentences.

Other researchers have found imagery instructions helpful in increasing reading comprehension. Lesgold, McCormick, and Golinkoff (1975) asked third- and fourth-grade children to draw stick figures illustrating a story as they read. Their recall was better than that of subjects who read the stories and answered questions. Pressley (1976) noted that the results of Lesgold *et al.* might have been due to greater attention to details rather than imagery. He provided a 20-minute imagery training session for 8-year-olds beginning with short sentences and gradually increasing length and giving examples of good imagery for each sentence. Following such training, children instructed to form images recalled about 25% more than children who merely read the stories. Pressley's conclusion, based on his work and a review of the literature, was that imagery can help reading comprehension provided that appropriate imagery training is given and that the reading and imagery are done successively rather than simultaneously. An imagery instruction technique found effective by Ross and Ross (1978) for retarded children was to tell the child to imagine turning on a TV set and watching the picture.

Imagery also forms the basis for a foreign language learning method developed by Raugh and Atkinson (1975; Atkinson & Raugh, 1975). They devised a keyword method for teaching definitions of foreign words. There are two steps to the process. First, the subject associates the foreign word to be learned with an English word (keyword) that sounds something like it. Second, the subject forms a mental image of the foreign and keyword referents interacting. For example, the Spanish word *carta* means *letter* and sounds something like the English *cart* (keyword). An appropriate image would be a letter lying in a shopping cart. The Spanish word reminds the subject of *cart* and the associated image provides the word meaning, *letter*. Raugh and Atkinson used the method successfully in teaching Spanish and Russian vocabulary to college students. Pressley and his colleagues have tested the method with grade school children. In one study, Pressley, Levin, Hall, Miller, and Berry (1980) taught Spanish vocabulary to sixth-grade students. Students using the keyword method learned the meanings of about twice as many Spanish words as control groups with the same amount of study time. Pressley and Levin (1978) showed that second graders as well as sixth graders could benefit from the keyword method, provided that interacting pictures were provided. Instructions to generate images were helpful to sixth graders but not to second-grade children.

The keyword method could be adapted for teaching the meanings of new English words. As a keyword, an English word already known could provide the link and an image could be formed that would supply the meaning of the new word. For example, *belligerent* starts with *bell*; imagine a bell ringing to start a boxing match.

Elaboration in classroom learning

Research cited earlier showed that paired associates are learned faster when paired in a sentence that relates them. It has also been shown that meanings of new words are learned better by elaborative methods than by simple definitions. Several studies have shown faster vocabulary acquisition by presenting new words in sentences or stories (Draper & Moeller, 1971; Taylor, Thurlow, & Turnure, 1977). Taylor, Thurlow, and Turnure developed a package of classroom materials for teaching vocabulary related to money, measurement, and time based on elaborative techniques. Thurlow and Turnure (1977) reported that the results of a field test of the program were promising.

One laboratory finding that seems particularly relevant to classroom practice is the value of questions in eliciting effective elaboration. Turnure, Buium, and Thurlow (1976) compared various methods for teaching paired associates to normal and retarded children with a mental age of 5. One group simply labeled the picture pairs that served as stimuli; another group was asked to make up sentences using the names of the pictures; a third group was provided with sentences. These groups replicated previous findings, with experimenter-supplied sentences producing the best performance. Children at this mental age level do not usually produce effective elaborations for themselves. Three other groups were asked questions with *what* or *why*. For example, for the items *soap* and *jacket*, the three forms of questions were as follows: *What is the soap doing in the jacket? Why is the soap in the jacket?* and *Why is the soap hiding in the jacket?* Subjects were required to make up possible answers to these questions. The three groups who were asked questions recalled almost twice as many associates as the best of the other three groups. These findings suggest that questions by a teacher that would relate new facts to previously learned material would be effective as a memory aid. However, such a technique should be used with caution in order to avoid eliciting wrong answers.

The development of study habits

Much learning in school is done by students alone reading a text. Learning from a text is a highly skilled activity that even many college students have not fully mastered. Recently investigators have begun to address the question of how these skills develop and how they may be improved (e.g., Brown & Campione, 1977). Not surprisingly, younger children have less effective study habits than older children, which suggests that training more effective strategies would be helpful to young children. However, it appears that young children's learning is not necessarily facilitated by inducing more mature study strategies.

Brown and Smiley (1978) investigated the effectiveness of training study strategies in students who failed to use them spontaneously. The task was to recall a story presented both aurally and visually. Half the subjects had an immediate-recall test after presentation and half had an additional 5 minutes to study the written story. An increase in recall after the 5-minute study session was the measure of study effectiveness. Eleventh-and twelfth-graders, as well as college students, recalled more of the important elements after a study period than did those who had an immediate-recall test. Students from fifth to eighth grade did not profit as much from the extra study. However, some students at each grade level spontaneously underlined or took notes as they studied and these students did show improved recall of important material. For those students who did not underline or take notes, an attempt was made to improve their performance by inducing a better study strategy. They were instructed to underline important points during the 5-minute study period. However, recall performance did not improve and an examination of the underlined texts revealed that students had not identified the important elements. They were as likely to underline unimportant points as important ones. The crucial factor in improved recall appeared to be the ability to separate relevant from irrelevant material.

A study by Brown and Campione (1977) also underscored the importance of matching study strategy to the cognitive abilities of children. They compared three strategies for multitrial, free-recall learning in two levels of mildly retarded children. The higher level had a mean mental age of about 8 and the lower level had a mean mental age of about 7. The task was to learn a set of pictures. On each trial, pictures were presented for study and then a recall trial was given. The most efficient strategy for normal adults is to study a subset of items on each trial that includes only items missed on the preceding trial. This method also proved to be most effective for the higher level retarded children. But the lower level retarded children did no better with missed items chosen for study than with randomly chosen items. They did, however, profit when items for study included just one missed item and the rest previously correct items. These children apparently needed the extra study time to maintain strength of recalled items.

These results suggest caution in attempting to impose on immature learners the study strategies that are effective for adults. This leaves open the question of how teachers are to know whether a particular strategy is appropriate. It is to be hoped that future research in this area will provide guidelines on this point.

CONCLUSIONS

One of the major themes running through the conclusions reached by the investigators surveyed in this chapter is the importance of cognitive strategies—strategies for selecting information from the environment, for maintaining information in STM, for transferring it to LTM, and for retrieving it from storage when needed. Several theorists proposed that developmental deficits in learning ability are primarily due to the absence of the strategies that enable adults to process information more efficiently rather than to fixed, structural limitations. Another prominent feature of this area of research is the interest in the training of information processing strategies in children and mentally retarded persons. The success of these efforts in several domains has led to an optimistic view by some about how much educators can do to increase intelligence. The reasoning is that if we can discover how bright people go about learning and solving problems, we can teach less bright people to use the same methods. In that way, children can be taught to be intelligent.

The notion that mental processes can be improved is not a new idea by any means. Throughout the history of educational theory there have always been advocates of mental training. Early writers such as Rousseau and Pestalozzi emphasized the importance of sensory or perceptual training, an approach that continues today in the Montessori method. In later work, the mind was portrayed as having faculties or powers such as reason, memory, and imagination that could be strengthened by exercising them. Still later, deficits in intelligence factors as inferred from intelligence and aptitude tests became objects of remedial attention. Mann (1979) has traced the history of these movements, showing that although theories have changed, the belief in trainability of mental processes has persisted. It is to be expected, therefore, that the research on cognitive and metacognitive strategy training will have an increasing influence on educational theory.

The test of whether a mental ability has been enhanced by training comes from transfer experiments. The question is whether the effects of training a particular ability in one situation will transfer to all tasks that require that ability. The evidence on this point is equivocal. Although transfer does occur from one task to another, the amount of transfer is closely tied to the degree of similarity of the two tasks. The most likely explanation, then, is that specific habit structures are activated by the elements that are common to the training and transfer tasks. Thus, transfer effects can be derived from associative learning principles and do not necessarily imply changes in mental ability (Gagné, 1977, pp. 148–149; Mann, 1979, pp. 366–381).

Current theories of how cognitive functioning can be improved are based on more sophisticated psychological analyses than were earlier theories. The notion that mere exercise strengthens mental ability has been discredited. The training of more effective strategies is currently stressed. Again, the question of transfer or generalization arises. To demonstrate a general improvement in cognitive ability, a strategy trained in a particular setting must transfer to other situations where such a strategy would be appropriate. Research findings in this area have been mixed (Borkowski & Cavanaugh, 1979; Brown & DeLoache, 1978). Frequently strategies trained with one task do not generalize to other tasks. Indeed, young children sometimes fail to maintain strategies on the same task. Note also the vagueness of the description, *situations where such a strategy would be appropriate.* How are children to judge whether a strategy will be effective in a new situation? Thus, it would appear that training cognitive strategies is not of itself a sufficient method for effecting improvement in general cognitive functioning.

The disappointing results cited earlier have led researchers in new directions. One is the study of transfer processes to discover how children can be induced to use trained strategies in wider domains (Borkowski & Cavanaugh, 1979). Another direction of investigation is the training of metamemory and metacognition so that children can be better able to analyze task demands and select the proper strategies (Brown & DeLoache, 1978; Flavell, 1979). Since these research efforts have begun only recently, there is little to report at present.

In summary, the results of psychological research have implications for improving performance in specific learning situations. However, we do not know as yet how to increase general learning ability in children or even whether it is possible to do so. It follows from our lack of knowledge in this area that educational programs should emphasize acquisition of basic knowledge and useful skills rather than cognitive modification.

REFERENCES

Adams, J. A., & Montague, W. E. Retroactive inhibition and natural language mediation. *Journal of Verbal Learning and Verbal Behavior*, 1967, 6, 528–535.

Allik, J. P., & Siegel, A. W. The use of the cumulative rehearsal strategy: A developmental study. *Journal of Experimental Child Psychology*, 1976, 21, 316–327.

Anderson, J. R., & Bower, G. H. *Human associative memory*. Washington, D.C.: Winston, 1973.

Asarnow, J. R., & Meichenbaum, D. Verbal rehearsal and serial recall: The mediational training of kindergarten children. *Child Development*, 1979, 50, 1173–1177.

Atkinson, R. C., Hansen, D. N., & Bernbach, H. A. Short-term memory with young children. *Psychonomic Science*, 1964, 1, 255–256.

Atkinson, R. C., & Raugh, M. R. An application of the mnemonic keyword method to the acquisition of a Russian vocabulary. *Journal of Experimental Psychology: Human Learning and Memory*, 1975, 1, 126–133.

Averbach, E., & Coriell, A. S. Short-term memory in vision. *Bell System Technical Journal*, 1961, 40, 309–328.

Bachelder, B. L., & Denny, M. R. A theory of intelligence: I. Span and the complexity of stimulus control. *Intelligence*, 1977, 1, 127–150.

Barnes, T. R. Transfer of compounds in the discriminative learning of retardates. *Journal of Experimental Child Psychology*. 1978, 25, 71–79.

Belmont, J. M., & Butterfield, E. C. Learning strategies as determinants of memory deficiencies. *Cognitive Psychology*, 1971, 2, 411–420.

Bjork, R. A. Short-term storage: The ordered output of a central processor. In F. Restle, R. M. Shiffrin, N. J. Castellan, H. R. Lindman, & D. B. Pisoni (Eds.), *Cognitive theory* (Vol. 1). Hillsdale, N.J.: Erlbaum, 1975. Pp. 151–171.

Blake, J. Developmental change in visual information processing under backward masking. *Journal of Experimental Child Psychology*, 1974, 17, 133–146.

Borkowski, J. G., & Cavanaugh, J. C. Maintenance and generalization of skills and strategies by the retarded. In N. R. Ellis (Ed.), *Handbook of mental deficiency, psychological theory and research* (2nd ed.). Hillsdale, N.J.: Erlbaum, 1979. Pp. 569–617.

Bower, G. H., & Reitman, J. S. Mnemonic elaboration in multi-list learning. *Journal of Verbal Learning and Verbal Behavior*, 1972, 11, 478–485.

Broadbent, D. E. *Perception and communication*. New York: Pergamon, 1958.

Brown, A. L. The role of strategic behavior in retardate memory. In N. R. Ellis (Ed.), *International review of research in mental retardation* (Vol. 7). New York: Academic Press, 1974. Pp. 55–111.

Brown, A. L., & Campione, J. C. Training strategic study time apportionment in educable retarded children. *Intelligence,* 1977, *1,* 94–107.

Brown, A. L., & DeLoache, J. S. Skills, plans, and self-regulation. In R. Siegler (Ed.), *Children's thinking: What develops?* Hillsdale, N.J.: Erlbaum, 1978. Pp. 3–35.

Brown, A. L., & Smiley, S. S. The development of strategies for studying texts. *Child Development,* 1978, *49,* 1076–1088.

Bugelski, B. R. Presentation time, total time, and mediation in paired-associate learning. *Journal of Experimental Psychology,* 1962, *63,* 409–412.

Burns, B., Shepp, B. E., McDonough, D., & Weiner-Ehrlich, W. The relation between stimulus analyzability and perceived dimensional structure. In G. H. Bower (Ed.), *Learning and motivation* (Vol. 12). New York: Academic Press, 1978. Pp. 77–115.

Chi, M. T. H. Short-term memory limitations in children: Capacity or processing deficits? *Memory and Cognition,* 1976, *4,* 559–572.

Chi, M. T. H. Age differences in memory span. *Journal of Experimental Child Psychology,* 1977, *23,* 266–281.

Chi, M. T. H. Knowledge structures and memory development. In R. S. Siegler (Ed.), *Children's thinking: What develops?* Hillsdale, N.J.: Erlbaum, 1978. Pp. 73–96.

Clarkson, T. A., Haggith, P. A., Tierney, M. C., & Kobasigawa, C. D. Relative effectiveness of imagery instructions and pictorial interactions on children's paired-associate learning. *Child Development,* 1973, *44,* 179–181.

Conrad, R. The chronology of the development of covert speech in children. *Developmental Psychology,* 1971, *5,* 398–405.

Craik, F. I. M., & Jacoby, L. L. A process view of short-term retention. In F. Restle, R. M. Shiffrin, N. J. Castellan, H. R. Lindman, & D. B. Pisoni (Eds.), *Cognitive theory* (Vol. 1). Hillsdale, N. J.: Erlbaum, 1975. Pp. 173–192.

Crowder, R. G. *Principles of learning and memory.* Hillsdale, N. J.: Erlbaum, 1976.

Day, M. C. Developmental trends in visual scanning. In H. W. Reese (Ed.), *Advances in child development and behavior* (Vol. 10). New York: Academic Press, 1974. Pp. 154–188.

Doyle, A. Listening to distraction: A developmental study of selective attention. *Journal of Experimental Child Psychology,* 1973, *15,* 100–115.

Draper, A. G., & Moeller, G. H. We think with words. *Phi Delta Kappan,* 1971, *52,* 482–484.

Eimas, P. D. Effects of memory aids on hypothesis behavior and focusing in young children and adults. *Journal of Experimental Child Psychology,* 1970, *10,* 319–336.

Engle, R. W. A developmental study of the prelinguistic auditory store. *Intelligence,* 1977, *1,* 358–368.

Estes, W. K. *Learning theory and mental development.* New York: Academic Press, 1970.

Fisher, M. A., & Zeaman, D. An attention–retention theory of retardate discrimination learning. In N. R. Ellis (Ed.), *International review of research in mental retardation* (Vol. 6). New York: Academic Press, 1973. Pp. 169–256.

Flavell, J. H. Developmental studies of mediated memory. In H. W. Reese & L. P. Lipsitt (Eds.), *Advances in child development and behavior* (Vol. 5). New York: Academic Press, 1970. Pp. 181–211.

Flavell, J. H. Comments. In R. S. Siegler (Ed.), *Children's thinking: What develops?* Hillsdale, N.J.: Erlbaum, 1978. Pp. 97–105.

Flavell, J. H. Metacognition and cognitive monitoring. *American Psychologist,* 1979, *34,* 906–911.

Flavell, J. H., Beach, D. R., & Chinsky, J. M. Spontaneous verbal rehearsal in a memory task as a function of age. *Child Development*, 1966, *37*, 283–299.

Flavell, J. H., Friedricks, A. G., & Hoyt, J. D. Developmental changes in memorization processes. *Cognitive Psychology*, 1970, *1*, 324–340.

Flavell, J. H., & Wellman, H. M. Metamemory. In R. V. Kail, Jr. & J. W. Hagen (Eds.), *Perspectives on the development of memory and cognition*. Hillsdale, N.J.: Erlbaum, 1977. Pp. 3–33.

Gagné, R. M. *The conditions of learning*. New York: Holt, 1965.

Gagné, R. M. Contributions of learning to human development. *Psychological Review*, 1968, *75*, 177–191.

Gagné, R. M. *The conditions of learning* (3rd ed.). New York: Holt, 1977.

Garner, W. R. *The processing of information and structure*. Potomac, Md.: Erlbaum, 1974.

Gollin, E. S., Saravo, A., & Salten, C. Perceptual distinctiveness and oddity-problem solving in children. *Journal of Experimental Psychology*, 1967, *5*, 586–596.

Goulet, L. R. Verbal learning in children: Implications for developmental research. *Psychological Bulletin*, 1968, *69*, 359–366.

Hagen, J. W. The effect of distraction on selective attention. *Child Development*, 1967, *38*, 685–694.

Hagen, J. W., Hargrave, S., & Ross, W. Prompting and rehearsal in short-term memory. *Child Development*, 1973, *44*, 201–204.

Hagen, J. W., & Kail, R. V., Jr. Facilitation and distraction in short-term memory. *Child Development*, 1973, *44*, 831–836.

Hale, G. A., & Morgan, J. S. Developmental trends in children's component selection. *Journal of Experimental Child Psychology*, 1973, *15*, 302–314.

Hall, J. W., Murphy, J., Humphreys, M. S., & Wilson, K. P. Children's cued recall: Developmental differences in retrieval operations. *Journal of Experimental Child Psychology*, 1979, *27*, 501–511.

Harris, J. E. Memory aids people use: Two interview studies. *Memory and Cognition*, 1980, *8*, 31–38.

House, B. J. Attention to components or compounds as a factor in discrimination transfer performance. *Journal of Experimental Child Psychology*, 1979, *27*, 321–331.

House, B. J., Brown, A. L., & Scott, M. S. Children's discrimination learning based on identity and difference. In H. W. Reese (Ed.), *Advances in child development and behavior* (Vol. 9). New York: Academic Press, 1974. Pp. 1–45.

Howard, D. V., & Goldin, S. E. Selective processing in encoding and memory: An analysis of resource allocation by kindergarten children. *Journal of Experimental Child Psychology*, 1979, *27*, 87–95.

Huttenlocher, J., & Burke, D. Why does memory span increase with age? *Cognitive Psychology*, 1976, *8*, 1–31.

Kahneman, D. *Attention and effort*. Englewood Cliffs, N.J.: Prentice-Hall, 1973.

Keeney, T. J., Cannizzo, S. R., & Flavell, J. H. Spontaneous and induced verbal rehearsal in a recall task. *Child Development*, 1967, *38*, 953–966.

Keniston, A. H., & Flavell, J. H. A developmental study of intelligent retrieval. *Child Development*, 1979, *50*, 1144–1152.

Keppel, G. Verbal learning in children. *Psychological Bulletin*, 1964, *61*, 63–80.

Kingsley, P. R., & Hagen, J. W. Induced versus spontaneous rehearsal in short-term memory in nursery school children. *Developmental Psychology*, 1969, *1*, 40–46.

Kobasigawa, A. Utilization of retrieval cues by children in recall. *Child Development*, 1974, *45*, 127–134.

Kreutzer, M. A., Leonard, C., & Flavell, J. H. An interview study of children's knowledge about memory. *Monographs of the Society for Research in Child Development,* 1975, *40*(1, Whole No. 159).

Lesgold, A. M., McCormick, C., & Golinkoff, R. M. Imagery training and children's learning from oral prose. *Journal of Educational Psychology,* 1975, *67,* 663–667.

Liss, P. H., & Haith, M. M. The speed of visual processing in children and adults: Effects of backward and forward masking. *Perception and Psychophysics,* 1970, *8,* 396–398.

Lyon, D. R. Individual differences in immediate serial recall: A matter of mnemonics? *Cognitive Psychology,* 1977, *9,* 403–411.

McCarty, D. L. Investigation of a visual imagery mnemonic device for acquiring face–name associations. *Journal of Experimental Psychology: Human Learning and Memory,* 1980, *6,* 145–155.

McCarver, R. B. A developmental study of the effect of organizational cues on short-term memory. *Child Development,* 1972, *43,* 1317–1328.

Maccoby, E. E., & Konrad, K. W. Age trends in selective listening. *Journal of Experimental Child Psychology,* 1966, *3,* 113–122.

Maccoby, E. E., & Konrad, K. W. The effect of preparatory set on selective listening: Developmental trends. *Monographs of the Society for Research in Child Development,* 1967, *32*(4, Whole No. 112).

Manis, F. R., Keating, D. P., & Morrison, F. J. Developmental differences in the allocation of processing capacity. *Journal of Experimental Child Psychology,* 1980, *29,* 156–169.

Mann, L. *On the trail of process.* New York: Grune & Stratton, 1979.

Miller, G. A. The magical number seven plus or minus two: Some limits on our capacity for processing information. *Psychological Review,* 1956, *63,* 81–97.

Morrison, F. J., Giordani, B., & Nagy, J. Reading disability: An information-processing analysis. *Science,* 1977, *196,* 77–79.

Morrison, F. J., Holmes, D. L., & Haith, M. M. A developmental study of the effect of familiarity on short-term visual memory. *Journal of Experimental Child Psychology,* 1974, *18,* 412–425.

Nelson, K. E., & Kosslyn, S. M. Semantic retrieval in children and adults. *Developmental Psychology,* 1975, *11,* 807–813.

Offenbach, S. I. *Bibliography of learning in children.* Unpublished manuscript, Purdue University, 1966.

Paivio, A. *Imagery and verbal processes.* New York: Holt, 1971.

Paris, S. G., Mahoney, G. J., & Buckhalt, J. A. Facilitation of semantic integration in sentence memory of retarded children. *American Journal of Mental Deficiency,* 1974, *78,* 714–720.

Pressley, G. M. Mental imagery helps eight-year-olds remember what they read. *Journal of Educational Psychology,* 1976, *68,* 355–359.

Pressley, M., & Levin, J. R. Developmental differences in subject's associative learning strategies and performance: Assessing a hypothesis. *Journal of Experimental Child Psychology,* 1977, *24,* 431–439.

Pressley, M., & Levin, J. R. Developmental constraints associated with children's use of the keyword methods of foreign language vocabulary learning. *Journal of Experimental Child Psychology,* 1978, *26,* 359–372.

Pressley, M., Levin, J. R., Hall, J. W., Miller, G. E., & Berry, J. K. The keyword method and foreign word acquisition. *Journal of Experimental Psychology: Human Learning and Memory,* 1980, *6,* 163–173.

Pylyshyn, Z. W. What the mind's eye tells the mind's brain: A critique of mental imagery. *Psychological Bulletin,* 1973, *80,* 1–24.

Raugh, M. R., & Atkinson, R. C. A mnemonic method for learning a second-language vocabulary. *Journal of Educational Psychology*, 1975, *67*, 1–16.

Reese, H. W. *The perception of stimulus relations*. New York: Academic Press, 1968.

Reese, H. W. Imagery and contextual meaning. In H. W. Reese (Chair), Imagery in children's learning: A symposium. *Psychological Bulletin*, 1970, *73*, 404–414.

Reese, H. W. Imagery and associative memory. In R. V. Kail, Jr. & J. W. Hagen (Eds.), *Perspectives on the development of memory and cognition*. Hillsdale, N.J.: Erlbaum, 1977. Pp. 113–175.

Reese, H. W., & Lipsitt, L. P. *Experimental child psychology*. New York: Academic Press, 1970.

Ritter, K., Kaprove, B. H., Fitch, J. P., & Flavell, J. H. The development of retrieval strategies in young children. *Cognitive Psychology*, 1973, *5*, 310–321.

Rohwer, W. D., Jr. Elaboration and learning in childhood and adolescence. In H. W. Reese (Ed.), *Advances in child development and behavior* (Vol. 8). New York: Academic Press, 1973. Pp. 2–54.

Ross, D. M., & Ross, S. A. Facilitative effect of mnemonic strategies on multiple-associative learning in EMR children. *American Journal of Mental Deficiency*, 1978, *82*, 460–466.

Schwantes, F. M. Cognitive scanning processes in children. *Child Development*, 1979, *50*, 1136–1143.

Shepp, B. E. From perceived similarity to dimensional structure: A new hypothesis about perceptual development. In E. Rosch & B. B. Lloyd (Eds.), *Cognition and categorization*. Hillsdale, N.J.: Erlbaum, 1978. Pp. 135–167.

Shepp, B. E., Burns, B., & McDonough, D. The relation of stimulus structure to perceptual and cognitive development: Further tests of a separability hypothesis. In J. Becker & F. Wilkening (Eds.), *The integration of information by children*. Hillsdale, N.J.: Erlbaum, 1978. Pp. 113–145.

Shepp, B. E., & Swartz, K. B. Selective attention and the processing of integral and nonintegral dimensions: A developmental study. *Journal of Experimental Child Psychology*, 1976, *22*, 73–85.

Shiffrin, R. M. Short-term store: The basis for a memory system. In F. Restle, R. M. Shiffrin, N. J. Castellan, H. R. Lindman, & D. B. Pisoni (Eds.), *Cognitive theory* (Vol. 1). Hillsdale, N.J.: Erlbaum, 1975. Pp. 193–218.

Siegler, R. S. Three aspects of cognitive development. *Cognitive Psychology*, 1976, *8*, 481–520.

Smith, L. B., & Kemler, D. G. Developmental trends in free classification: Evidence for a new conceptualization of perceptual development. *Journal of Experimental Child Psychology*, 1977, *24*, 279–298.

Smith, L. B., Kemler, D. G., & Aronfreed, J. Developmental trends in voluntary selective attention: Differential effects of source distinctiveness. *Journal of Experimental Child Psychology*, 1975, *20*, 352–362.

Sperling, G. The information available in brief visual presentations. *Psychological Monographs*, 1960, *74*(11, Whole No. 498).

Sperling, G. Short-term memory, long-term memory, and scanning in the processing of visual information. In F. A. Young & D. B. Lindsley (Eds.), *Early experience and visual information processing in perceptual and reading disorders*. Washington, D.C.: National Academy of Sciences, 1970. Pp. 198–215.

Strutt, G. F., Anderson, D. R., & Well, A. D. A developmental study of the effects of irrelevant information on speeded classification. *Journal of Experimental Child Psychology*, 1975, *20*, 127–135.

Taylor, A., Thurlow, M. L., & Turnure, J. Vocabulary development of educable retarded children. *Exceptional Children,* 1977, *43,* 444–450.

Thurlow, M. L., & Turnure, J. Children's knowledge of time and money: Effective instruction for the mentally retarded. *Education and Training of the Mentally Retarded,* 1977, *12,* 203–212.

Tighe, T. J. Subproblem analysis of discrimination learning. In G. H. Bower (Ed.), *The psychology of learning and motivation* (Vol. 7). New York: Academic Press, 1973. Pp. 183–226.

Tighe, T. J., Glick, J., & Cole, M. Subproblem analysis of discrimination-shift learning. *Psychonomic Science,* 1971, *24,* 159–160.

Tighe, T. J., & Tighe, L. S. A perceptual view of conceptual development. In R. D. Walk & H. L. Pick, Jr. (Eds.), *Perception and experience.* New York: Plenum, 1978. Pp. 387–416.

Tulving, E. Episodic and semantic memory. In E. Tulving & W. Donaldson (Eds.), *Organization of memory.* New York: Academic Press, 1972. Pp. 382–404.

Tulving, E., & Pearlstone, Z. Availability versus accessibility of information in memory for words. *Journal of Verbal Learning and Verbal Behavior,* 1966, *5,* 381–391.

Turnure, J. E., Buium, N., & Thurlow, M. L. The effectiveness of interrogatives for promoting verbal elaboration productivity in young children. *Child Development,* 1976, *47,* 851–855.

Turvey, M. T. On peripheral and central processes in vision: Inferences from an information-processing analysis of masking with patterned stimuli. *Psychological Review,* 1973, *80,* 1–52.

Werner, H. *Comparative psychology of mental development.* New York: International Univ. Press, 1957.

White, S. H. Bibliography: *Psychological studies of learning in children.* Unpublished manuscript, Harvard University, 1962.

Wollen, K. A., Weber, A., & Lowry, D. Bizarreness versus interaction of mental images as determinants of learning. *Cognitive Psychology,* 1972, *3,* 518–523.

Zeaman, D. One programmatic approach to retardation, In D. K. Routh (Ed.), *The experimental psychology of mental retardation.* Chicago: Aldine, 1973. Pp. 78–132.

Zeaman, D., & House, B. J. The role of attention in retardate discrimination learning. In N. R. Ellis (Ed.), *Handbook of mental deficiency: Psychological theory and research.* New York: McGraw-Hill, 1963. Pp. 159–223.

Zeaman, D., & House, B. J. Interpretations of developmental trends in discriminative transfer effects. In A. D. Pick (Ed.), *Minnesota Symposium on Child Development* (Vol. 8). Minneapolis, Minn.: Univ. of Minnesota Press, 1974. Pp. 144–186.

Zeaman, D., & House, B. J. A review of attention theory. In N. R. Ellis (Ed.), *Handbook of mental deficiency, psychological theory and research.* Hillsdale, N.J.: Erlbaum, 1979. Pp. 63–120.

6 / Cognitive development: foundations and directions[1]

DEBORAH G. KEMLER

The study of cognitive development—the area of psychological development concerned with the growth of knowledge and intellectual skills—addresses how the child's knowledge increases and changes with age as well as the developing processes by which the child acquires and uses knowledge. The products and skills of cognition are best understood in relation to one another. What we attend to, what we remember, and how we use new information to make decisions are strongly dependent on the knowledge we have when these cognitive processes come into play. Conversely, the knowledge we have is the consequence of the past exercise of cognitive processes. Since concepts and cognizing are so highly interlinked, to separate the study of what children know from the study of their cognitive functions would be an unprofitable exercise.

The elementary school years have long been recognized as a critical period for the development of cognition. This is particularly true for the early elementary school years, when, in Western culture, most children are between 5 and 7 years old. From the voluminous work done in this area, there is broad empirical support for a "5-to-7 shift" in cognition:

[1]Preparation of this chapter was supported by Grant No. P01 HD 10965 from the National Institute of Child Health and Human Development and Grant No. BNS 79–24035 from the National Science Foundation.

233

On a great many different laboratory tasks, the average 7-year-old performs quite differently from the average 5-year-old (White, 1970). Accordingly, all major developmental theorists posit some important underlying change in cognition occurring at about this time. For Piaget (e.g., Piaget & Inhelder, 1969) the shift signals the transition from one major cognitive stage to the next—from preoperational thought to concrete–operational thought. The child who has achieved concrete operations is capable of carrying out many more sophisticated logical mentations than the child who is preoperational. Bruner (1964; Bruner, Olver, & Greenfield, 1966) captures the 5–to–7 shift in different theoretical terms. The preschooler, he claims, is largely dependent on images or icons for representing information, a very "concrete" mode of representation that is limited in the mental operations it permits. With age the child progresses to a much more flexible and abstract mode, symbolic representation, of which language is a prime example. Having symbolic representation as the dominant mode, the child is now capable of contemplating possibilities beyond concrete reality. The Soviet theorists—most prominent among them Vygotsky (1962) and his successor, Luria (1959)—also emphasize the importance of language in the service of thought and action. They believe the shift reflects the increasing role of language as a means for self-control in the child. The younger child is dependent on external and impulsive control by others' language. In contrast, the older child's behavior is mediated by internal, meaningful language that permits self-guidance of action in a voluntary, thus potentially more effective, way. In a somewhat related fashion, some learning theorists mark the 5–to–7 shift as a change from direct, externalized stimulus–response modes of learning to language-mediated, internalized modes (cf. Kendler & Kendler, 1962).

The potential relevance of the field of cognitive development to the field of education requires no defense. Building the knowledge and the intellectual skills of the child is the central concern of education. The field of cognitive development provides a major scientific basis for the enterprise. Cognitive–developmental psychologists of the stature of Piaget (see Ginsburg & Opper, 1979) and Bruner (1960, 1966)—just two of many well-known figures—have closed the gap between the basic science of cognitive development and the applied concerns of the educator. Their work and views will not be discussed here, since they are highly available elsewhere. The focus of this chapter will be the newer looks in cognitive development and their relation to educational issues.

This new work is providing some encouraging news for the educator. One source of optimism is that basic research in the field is increasingly directed at addressing major concerns of elementary school educators.

Such an area of concern is the cognitive competencies of the child entering elementary school. The design of educational curricula for the first years of school can benefit from new insights into some of the cognitive strengths of the young child. Until recently, we knew much less about the skills and knowledge that 5-year-old children had than what they lacked. New research on preschool cognition has begun to redress the balance. Another weakness in the relevant psychological literature was the lack of explicit study of school-related skills and the performance of school-related tasks. Of late, some progress has been made in the investigation of how children learn to read, what they know about number concepts, and how they proceed to understand and remember textual material. The significance of this work for education is unquestionable and direct.

Educators can also take encouragement from the new understanding that is emerging on age differences in cognition. There is a growing consensus that many age differences in the performance of elementary school children are a function of strategies, skills, and specific knowledge—all modifiable—rather than differences in fixed and untrainable basic capacities. Such a view highlights the power of educational intervention and provides at least some preliminary suggestions for some important teachable strategies. In addition, cross-cultural research has established formal schooling as a major impetus to cognitive growth in more general and subtle ways than we might have imagined (Cole & Scribner, 1974; Luria, 1976).

Two of these new topics structure the body of this chapter. The presentation is divided into two major sections. The first section is responsive to the need of the elementary school educator to know the cognitive status of the child who is just entering the school environment. Thus, the focus is primarily on younger school children, and particularly on the recent work that highlights their cognitive strengths. The second section of the chapter more explicitly addresses developmental differences in cognition during the school years. It emphasizes analyses of these differences in terms of teachable skills. The new orientation of cognitive–developmental psychology toward the study of more school-related activities will be evident throughout both sections.

COGNITION IN THE EARLY ELEMENTARY SCHOOL YEARS

Until recently young elementary school children have been better known for what they could not do or think than for what they could. In many laboratory tasks, the failures of the child under 7 years of age relative to the older child are striking, and these comparative results have served in the past to frame our picture of early childhood cognition. The 5-year-old—we are told—*cannot* think logically, take another's point of view, behave in a goal-directed manner, or appreciate or entertain abstract thoughts. A most important new look in the current study of cognitive development is the characterization of cognition in the younger child in an explicit and positive way. The younger child is no longer viewed just as deficient relative to the older child. Now we are asking very specific questions about what young children *do* know and exactly how they succeed on certain tasks. As a result their story has become far more rich and interesting than the catalog of failures that typified earlier approaches.

From a purely methodological view, the value of the new search for competence should not be underestimated. The methodological point is that out of context the failure of a group of young children on a particular cognitive task is not informative, for failure to succeed on a given task is of itself quite ambiguous. Does the young child not succeed because he or she failed to understand the experimenter's instructions, or failed to be motivated to perform correctly? Was the child inattentive to the task? Did the requisite computations overload his or her memory? Or, did the child fail because he or she was lacking the particular cognitive skills or knowledge the investigator was trying to tap? Note that all these possibilities are plausible reasons for why the young child might fail the task, and they all enter into plausible accounts of why older children might perform better on the task. Finding the correct interpretation of failure requires varying the features of the task to find what combination or combinations of changes (including the availability of different kinds of training) lead to improvement in performance. Meaning emerges from *patterns* of successes and failures. Thus a by-product of the current search for cognitive competence in young children is that we are in a much better position to single out the interesting cases in which the children fail. Furthermore, we can focus on exactly what the young children are doing (the system underlying their performance) to produce the profile of successes and failures we observe.

This methodological point is as important to educators as it is to research psychologists. Pinpointing the locus of the child's difficulty is almost essential in any attempt to remediate the difficulty. Remediation might come through supplying performance aids (e.g., reducing memory load, if that is the problem) or it might come through specific practice on the isolated component that accounts for the failure. Alternatively, remediation might come from explicit verbal instruction directed at the source of difficulty, such as instructions to the child to use a different strategy. All these methods have been used with success in the psychological literature (e.g., Flavell, 1970; Siegler, 1976; Trabasso, 1975). Particular examples will be explored further within the discussion of specific studies. The point for the moment is that the educator, no less than the cognitive–developmental psychologist, must submit the failure of a child or group of children on a particular task to detailed analysis.

It is worth noting that the search for cognitive competence in the young child has directly increased with the ingenuity of the investigators in engaging the skills and knowledge of young children. Thus, alongside the "traditional" tasks that have long dominated the literature on cognitive development—standard discrimination learning problems, Piagetian conservation tasks—we now find the investigators giving particular attention in task design to both the head and the heart of the young child. This means that the investigator will sometimes turn to the systematic study of a cognitive activity already known to engage the young child outside the laboratory—as in the studies of Anderson, Alwitt, Lorch, & Levin (1979) of children's attention to the television program *Sesame Street*. Other times, it means modifying an existing paradigm to make it particularly suitable for young children. Often, it means abandoning the well-known tasks altogether and going after the basic process in question through entirely new tasks, assembled with the young child in mind. The reader will see how these strategies are used in the following sections (e.g., the invention of "magic" tasks to reveal preschoolers' knowledge of numerical concepts, Gelman, 1972; the invention of a detective game to elicit hypothesis testing in 5-year-olds, Kemler, 1978). The success of these new methods underscores the commonsense notion of classroom teachers that children will perform better when the task actively engages them.

The following examples of competence in young children were selected to illustrate several of the basic points made previously, as well as to suggest some general notions about the kinds of cognitive competencies these children have. As the examples unfold it will become clear that the current line of research is *not* leading us to abandon the notion of significant cognitive–developmental differences between younger and older children; rather, the search for cognitive competence in the young child is leading to more careful and specific statements of just what is developing.

Number concepts

Perhaps the best-known failure of young elementary school children existing in the literature on cognitive development is their inability to respond correctly on tests for conservation of quantity. According to

Piaget, failure to conserve is one of the hallmarks of preoperational intelligence; success in conservation indexes concrete operational thought. By this interpretation, the older child has cognitive capacities or, in Piaget's particular view, logical structures that support thinking about numerical equivalences, whereas the child under 7 years does not (Piaget, 1952). Here is a typical traditional example of the tendency to describe cognition in the young child in negative terms.

In the standard test for conservation of number, the child is shown two identical rows of elements (e.g., two rows of checkers arranged in one-to-one correspondence). One row is designated as the child's, the other as the experimenter's. After the child agrees that the two rows have the same number, the experimenter, in full view of the child, transforms one of them by moving the elements in the row to either lengthen or contract it without altering the actual number of elements. The child then is asked to compare the quantities again. The preschool child generally gives a nonconserving response, saying the two rows no longer have the same number—often believing the longer row has more. In contrast, the 7-year-old is usually a conserver, reporting that the two rows still have the same number, and often is able to justify verbally this response. Only the conserver, in Piaget's view, can be said to have a concept of number.

The replicability of the basic findings on conservation tests is remarkable. Even the most skeptical observer will be impressed by the robustness of the effect. But reliability is one thing; interpretation is another. Gelman (1972, 1978a), one of the leading proponents of the search for cognitive competence in preschoolers, has cogently argued from both her own data and those of others that although preschoolers fail to conserve, they have a considerable storehouse of number knowledge and number-related skills (see also Bryant, 1974; Mehler & Bever, 1967; Schaeffer, Eggleston, & Scott, 1974).

Gelman's case rests on both indirect and direct evidence. The indirect evidence derives from the large number of studies demonstrating the success of training procedures in producing conservation behavior in children who were nonconservers prior to training (Beilin, 1971). Gelman's training study (1969) is an excellent and early example. Four- to 6-year-olds who failed a conservation pretest were given positive feedback for attending selectively to quantity on a set of oddity trials. For example, the child was shown three linear arrays of elements on each trial and chose the two that were the same in number (rather than length or density). Incorrect choices were corrected and correct choices were approved. Following such training, 95% of the children were conservation successes on an immediate posttest for conservation

of number and the same percentage conserved on a delayed conservation test administered 2–3 weeks later. Perhaps even more remarkable,
the effects of training were generalized to other tests for conservation of
quantity, such as knowing that the amount of liquid does not change
when the liquid is poured from one container to a container different in
shape. According to Gelman (1969) the training succeeded because the
children were guided to attend selectively to quantity and to ignore
irrelevant properties of the array, such as length and density in the
number task. As she points out, the plausibility of this explanation rests
on the assumption that what had to be learned through training was that
number is relevant; what could not have been trained in so few trials and
with such minimal input information is the concept of number itself
(Gelman, 1969). Note that the nature of this argument suggests the
importance of training studies as a technique for unmasking partial cognitive competence in young children. If after minimal training, a child
succeeds on a test for capacity X when previously the child failed, one is
forced to conclude the child "had" at least some major components of
capacity X prior to training.

There is a rather extensive literature of successful training studies on
Piagetian tasks as well as conservation—for example, seriation, class
inclusion, transitive inference. Although not everyone would agree with
this statement (e.g., Inhelder & Sinclair, 1969), training successes are
starting to outnumber reported training failures in the literature. Thus,
on these grounds alone, the position that the older elementary school
child has qualitatively different concepts from the younger child is far
less secure than it seemed several years ago.

The direct evidence for young children's knowledge about number is
even more compelling. A particularly relevant example in light of the
conservation failure of the typical 5-year-old comes from a different,
highly original technique for eliciting knowledge of quantitative invariance. Here, the invention of a novel and particularly suitable task for
the child reveals a competence that the standard conservation task fails
to show. The issue is whether young children appropriately distinguish
between transformations of an array that are relevant to number (that
change number) and transformations that are irrelevant to number (that
leave number invariant).

Gelman (1972) conducted a series of "magic" studies to find out. In
the first phase of the procedure, children were simply shown two plates
containing different numbers of objects. One plate might have two toy
mice and the other three toy mice. One of these plates was designated
by the experimenter as the *winner* and the other as the *loser*. On each
trial the plates were covered and their position shuffled. The child then

had to find the winning plate, and, regardless of initial success (only guessing could be used), continued until the winner was found and correctly labeled as such. Incorrect designations of *winner* and *loser* were corrected in this phase. The purpose of the first phase was merely to establish an expectancy for number; the second phase tested knowledge of number invariance. During the second phase, the experimenter surreptitiously modified the winning plate. Sometimes number-relevant transformations were performed: a mouse was added or subtracted. Other times, only spatial arrangement of the elements or the identity of the elements (a toy soldier substituted for a mouse) was altered. Children's reactions to these transformations were probed: Had anything happened? If so, what? Did the game need to be fixed? If so, how?

Children as young as 3 years show some knowledge of number invariance in this magic procedure. They know, for example, that spatial displacements leave number intact; they even know that adding and subtracting are complementary operations and can be used to repair one another. Such knowledge, like many number-related skills, is more securely revealed in the context of small numbers of elements than when the numbers involved are larger. For example, the 3-year-olds had difficulty knowing that a plate of three mice could be turned into a winning plate of five mice by adding exactly two mice.

Gelman presents convincing evidence that what knowledge young children have of number invariance is dependent on counting operations (see particularly Gelman & Gallistel, 1978). Preschoolers reason about numbers they can and do count. Note that such a restriction does not hold for adults, who are satisfied that spatial displacement is irrelevant to the numerosity of a set whether or not they know exactly how many items are in the set. Adults also know that two sets are equal in number if the sets are in one-to-one correspondence, regardless of whether they know how many elements each set has (e.g., a full auditorium has as many persons as chairs, even if we have no idea of its actual capacity). Young children's ability to think better about small than about large numbers probably rests on their greater ability to accurately count small numbers.

One of the major unsolved questions in the development of number concepts is how the child comes to make the transition from the ability to think about specific, known numbers to the ability to think about number in a more abstract way. The child has made an important transition when at age 7 or so he or she can solve a Piagetian conservation task using only the one-to-one correspondence principle, rather than counting to establish equality after the transformation. It seems plausible that the abstraction process is facilitated by extensive firsthand experience that children get through frequent spontaneous counting. If so, counting is a procedure to be encouraged rather than discouraged when children encounter their first lessons about number.

Since young children rely so heavily on counting, it is critical to examine how they count, what principles guide their counting. Gelman and Gallistel (1978; also Gelman, 1978b), extensively analyze this problem. One of their most important conclusions is that preschool children have knowledge of the principles of counting before their performance is errorless. For example, they know that each item in a to-be-counted array must be given one and only one number tag even though, in practice, they sometimes slip in the application of the principles. Thus, the kindergarten child does not need to be informed about the basic principles of counting, though he or she may well need practice in executing an errorless count (and may need to be taught the appropriate number list to be utilized with large sets).

The structure of classes and concepts

Another domain in which the partial competence of the young child is an emerging theme is in the study of classification skills. Once again, the story is told by reexamining a well-established "deficiency." In this case, the deficiency—as described by such noted developmental theorists as Inhelder and Piaget (1958), Werner (1957), and Vygotsky (1962)—is the inability to apply systematic criteria to the categorization (or sorting) of sets of objects. For example, Vygotsky (1962) asserts that young children are unable to form "genuine concepts" in that they fail to consistently classify items on the basis of selected properties in the laboratory. They tend instead to group together items sharing "concrete, factual" bonds. Thus, having been instructed to put together the things that go together, kindergartners sort a red square with a red circle because the objects resemble one another in color and with a green square because they are similar in shape. The fifth-grade child uses "logical, abstract" criteria for grouping; for example, sorting all the squares together, regardless of color. Only the latter sorts, Vygotsky argues, are indicative of true conceptual thinking. In generalizing to natural everyday concepts, Vygotsky believes young children cannot comprehend the same meanings for words as older children and adults because they are incapable of using systematic, logical criteria for constructing classes.

Fodor (1972) counters that the very success of the young child in communicating with adults through language should make us suspicious of any argument, like Vygotsky's, that concludes with the inference that young children do not have the ability to form many of the same concepts as adults. Whether or not one accepts Fodor's contention, it is important to consider the gist of the argument because of its general applicability to the study of cognitive development. Too often, students of cognitive development become immersed in the results of a particular paradigm and fail to see that the conclusions their particular data lead them to are apparently contradicted by the spontaneous everyday behaviors that the same children engage in outside the laboratory. Such contradictions should alert the investigator to look more closely at the reason for failure in the experimental situation. Of course, it is possible—perhaps often the case—that the contradiction is more apparent than real, and the experimenter can show that the "spontaneous" behavior does not serve as solid evidence for the capacity in question. (The 1-year-old who successfully fetches the ball when mother says, "I would like to have the ball that is over there," is not necessarily in command of any more linguistic knowledge than the meaning of the word *ball*.) However, as Fodor argues, the investigator sometimes may have to reevaluate his or her own evidence or argument about the deficiency of the experimental subject. (Cole & Scribner, 1974, make the same point in the context of cross-cultural research.)

In the case of classificatory skills, the failure of the preschooler to sort consistently on the basis of a single property (or dimension) of the stimuli requires some rethinking in light of recent findings by Smith and Kemler (1977). They showed that kindergarten children classify objects consistently on the basis of overall similarity to one another rather than on the basis of common dimensional components. Given a set composed of a large white square (2 inches to a side), a small white square (1 inch to a side), and a medium-small light-gray square (1¼ inches to a side), the kindergartner selects the last two as "going together," the two that are globally similar. By contrast, the fifth grader selects the first two because they are identical in color. Importantly, the kindergartners are every bit as systematic in their use of overall similarity as the older children are in their use of common dimensional values. It appears that the kindergarten children treat the items as integral wholes (in fact, just as adults treat color patches that vary in saturation and brightness, Garner, 1974), relating them on overall resemblance. Second graders, Smith and Kemler (1977) found, show a classification pattern intermediate between kindergartners and fifth graders. Sometimes they classify using similarity and sometimes they use common dimensional values. So the overriding salience of component dimensional properties, consequent on the analysis of the stimulus wholes, develops gradually during the elementary school years (see also Shepp, 1978; Shepp & Swartz, 1976).

How do these findings bear on the nature of the child's everyday concepts, the issue that Vygotsky hoped to address with his classification studies? What they suggest is that the kindergarten youngster should be most facile with conceptual categories structured by overall resemblance rather than with categories defined by possession of a common critical attribute. Interestingly, Rosch (1973; Rosch & Mervis, 1975) has argued that many everyday concepts of adults have such a "family resemblance" or similarity structure. Membership in the category *dog* is determined for all of us by overall similarity of an instance to an ideal or "prototype" dog. Furthermore, although both the category *dog* and its superordinate category *animal* have this type of structure, the amount of overlap in similarity of members of the basic-level category *dog* is far greater than the amount of internal similarity within the superordinate category *animal*. Thus, one predicts that children should acquire basic-level concepts before superordinate-level concepts. In a classification task, they should group dogs together before they group animals together. This is just what Rosch, Mervis, Gray, Johnson, and Boyes-Braem (1976) found. In one study, kindergartners and first graders consistently grouped together items that belong to the same basic categories, though at least half of them failed to classify together items that belong to the same superordinate category. These results with "meaningful" objects and Smith and Kemler's results with "meaningless" objects suggest that young children can classify using the consistent criteria of overall similarity.

Smith and Kemler (1977) made another observation, one that has particular significance for education. Though the kindergarten children used overall similarity and not shared properties as their preferred basis for classifying, the other option was available to them. A simple request to sort the items another way produced a high proportion of classifications based on common properties. Thus, kindergartners are *capable* of classifying on the basis of selected properties, but that is not their first inclination. Consider what this means. Relating one item to another is an important intellectual tool. For example, it is what allows us to see that a new problem we encounter is analogous to one that we already know how to solve. It is also the basis on which we can construct useful generalizations. Yet rarely is it the case that overall similarity is an appropriate basis for such analogies or generalizations; much more often, it is a *particular* property shared by the multiple examples that serves to link them usefully (Baron, 1978).

What Smith and Kemler's investigation suggests is that children in the first years of elementary school are not preferentially tuned to the kinds of relations that will allow them to discover that different and diverse examples share a common property or that examples that are similar actually possess a critical difference. However, appreciation of property-based relations is often available to these children on a second consideration. Therefore, a very worthwhile teaching device is to call explicit attention to embedded commonalities and, even less directly, to encourage the youngsters to seek such commonalities. Unfortunately, little is known about how generally the child can transfer an "analytic" mode prompted in one situation to another. This is an issue in need of further study.

An interesting project by Baron and Treiman (1980) specifically relates the work done on classification to the acquisition of reading skills. Recently, several cognitive psychologists (Liberman, Shankweiler, Fischer, & Carter, 1974; Rozin & Gleitman, 1977; Savin, 1972) have pointed out that the process of decoding an alphabetic system (mapping visual symbols to sounds) requires the child to segment speech syllables into phonemes. Perhaps this segmentation process is the major obstacle in learning to read. Young children might treat speech syllables as wholes, related by overall similarity, rather than as strings of phonemes. Using the same paradigm as Smith and Kemler (1977), Baron and Treiman tested this hypothesis by comparing the classifications of 5-year-olds and adults for spoken syllables. On each trial, the subject heard three different syllables, two that shared a common phoneme (e.g., [bo] and [bɪ]) and another that was similar overall to one of the first two, but not identical to it in any phonemic component ([vɛ]). Baron and Treiman replicated the developmental trend from more frequent use of overall similarity to more frequent use of component identity relations in classification. More importantly, they also showed that individual differences in first graders' ability to classify by identical phonemic components are related to the children's reading skills. In fact, the ability to learn to classify on the basis of common phonemes correlates more highly with a measure of rule-based reading (which relies on a decoding operation) than with a measure of whole-word sight-reading (which does not). Thus, the proclivity to analyze appears to have more than a hypothetical relation to school-related tasks.

Scientific reasoning

According to Piaget (Inhelder & Piaget, 1958), it is not until adolescence that the child is fully capable of reasoning like a scientist. Recent evidence suggests, however, that some of the rudiments of scientific thinking are possessed even by kindergarten children. This evidence is of two kinds. The first is that 5-year-olds are systematic in their attempts to address scientific questions, that is, their scientific predictions are rule-governed. The second kind of evidence is that 5-year-olds respond rationally to feedback concerning the correctness or incorrectness of their rules. For example, under some conditions of feedback, they give up rules that fail to predict correctly and formulate new rules in their place. By far the most informative and detailed specification of the development of scientific thinking in elementary school is given by Siegler and his colleagues (Siegler, 1976, 1978; Siegler & Vago, 1978). They specifically studied how children address several of the "formal operational tasks" devised by Piaget. Some relevant information also comes from a study of children's hypothesis-testing strategies in discrimination learning tasks. This work will be discussed first because the nature of the problem put to the child is far simpler.

There is a vast literature concerning the ways children go about solving discrimination learning problems, and what changes occur with development (Spiker & Cantor, 1980; Tighe & Tighe, 1972; Zeaman & House, 1974). In a typical discrimination learning problem, the child is administered a series of two-alternative choice trials in which the child must eventually select consistently the correct item in the pair, given feedback on every trial from the experimenter. The choices on each trial are between two items that differ on a number of dimensions (e.g., color, size, form). Usually, the correct choice is determined by a rule, formulated by the experimenter, concerning one dimension of the items. The rule might be that the red item is always correct and the green item is always incorrect. In this example, color is the relevant dimension and size and form are irrelevant. Thus, an efficient way to solve the problem is to discover the dimension-based rule and attend exclusively to the relevant dimension, always selecting the object with the correct value on that dimension. This is not the only way to learn: one could also memorize by rote the specific objects that have been designated as correct on previous trials (e.g., the large red square, the small red square, the large red triangle, the small red triangle). The latter method does not require analyzing the objects into their component dimensions; the former method does. In light of the preceding discussion of stimulus analysis in the child, it should not be surprising to find young children more likely to do the former and older children the latter (Cole, 1973; Tighe, 1973; Tighe, Glick, & Cole, 1971), but even kindergartners sometimes learn the dimension-based rule (Tighe & Tighe, 1972; Zeaman & House, 1974).

Kemler (1978) devised a discrimination-learning problem designed to minimize the difficulties of stimulus analysis and to elicit rule learning in the kindergarten child. This was done by embedding the discrimination-learning problem in a kind of detective game. Her goal was to study the kinds of hypothesis-testing strategies that young children could use and the ways that rule-discovery strategies change over the course of development in the elementary school years. The "twin game" has all the formal features of a standard discrimination learning task: on each trial, two stimuli differing along several dimensions are presented, and the child must choose the correct one. Across trials, only one of the stimulus properties is consistently associated with the correct object; the appropriate solution depends on finding this relevant property. In the twin game, the properties are kinds of clothing (e.g., hats, belts, necklaces, hair ribbons). The game starts with a story. Two twins, Amy and Betty, switch their clothes to fool their friends but have a secret kind of clothing (told only to this teacher) that they do not switch and therefore can be used to tell them apart. On each trial, the child must find Amy (make a choice between the two items) and verbalize his or her best guess about "what the secret thing is" (state a hypothesized rule) after feedback on the correctness of the choice.

In the twin game, kindergarten children learned to find Amy by formulating rules (e.g., *Amy always wears the red hair ribbons*). Even more impressively, they were systematic and rational in many of the ways they changed their hypothesized rules within the learning trials. An example can help clarify the significant observations. Suppose a kindergarten child has verbalized a tentative rule on one trial (*Amy always wears the party hat*), and it is not the solution rule (actually Amy always wears the red hair ribbons). Since the child holds the wrong hypothesis, the next instance of Amy might disconfirm his or her current hypothesis (Amy is shown with the other hat). However, by chance, the next instance might still be consistent with his or her hypothesis. What happens in each of these events? When a new instance disconfirms a current hypothesis, the kindergartner switches to a new hypothesis. In other words, the child knows that the current hypothesis is disconfirmed and, in a rational manner, relinquishes the old hypothesis and finds a new one. Moreover, the new one, Kemler found, is almost always consistent with the information that the child has in view. Thus, if the new hypothesis concerns hair ribbons, and the last instance of Amy shows her with red hair ribbons, then the child will now hypothesize that Amy wears the red ribbons. The kindergartner is also generally rational on the other type of trial when the information confirms a tentative hypothesis. A majority of the time, the child will continue to hold a hypothesis until it is disconfirmed.

To the educator, these examples of rule testing in kindergartners may seem quite elementary, and so they are. But they are nonetheless significant. At least in simple rule-testing situations, like the twin game, kindergarten children are sensitive to how information "out there" bears on the accuracy of their current ideas or hypotheses or rules, and they change their ideas accordingly. They are responsive to feedback from the environment. Thus, they have the potential to learn new rules simply by making observations, at least if the rules are within their grasp.

Some further observations by Kemler (1978) suggest some limits on rule-testing strategies in the kindergartner, and thus point to an important source of developmental differences. What kindergartners did not do in the twin game was keep tract of what hypotheses they had tried and rejected earlier in the problem. Thus, when they were faced with a disconfirmation that required reformulating their hypotheses, they often returned to hypotheses they had rejected earlier. This is just the opposite of the rational course of action, and it considerably slows down the process of arriving at the solution rule. Interestingly, even some second graders in Kemler's studies showed remnants of this irrational behavior and were unable to benefit from the possibility of keeping track of their past hypotheses with a performance aid (an external crutch for memory). Fifth and sixth graders, by contrast, were quite efficient at remembering what hypotheses they had tried and rejected previously and using that information about their own rule-testing histories to efficiently discover the solution rule. (See also Gholson's work, for example, Gholson, Levine, & Phillips, 1972, for a discussion of important developments in hypothesis testing over the elementary school years.)

To summarize, even young elementary school children use rules and know when information confirms or disconfirms a rule they are contemplating. However, this does not mean they will efficiently discover the correct rule in a situation because they often tend to return to old hypotheses already disconfirmed. By the end of the elementary school years, this irrational strategy has disappeared and children learn efficiently from a series of hypothesis-testing trials. Teaching strategies can benefit from such observations. Providing children opportunities to observe discrepancies between their incorrect "rules" and reality can be an effective teaching device even for the younger child, but it needs to be supplemented by explicit guidance in resisting the return to rules that have already failed. Unfortunately, we are as yet ignorant about how best to accomplish this. Is it possible that resisting previously disconfirmed hypotheses is a general skill that can be trained in the young child?

Siegler's (1976, 1978) extensive investigations of scientific reasoning in children have been carried out in far more complicated, scientific-looking tasks than the one Kemler used. Moreover, Siegler has been concerned not only with how children change their rules as a function of feedback, but also with what kinds of rules children of different ages spontaneously formulate for these problems. One task used by Siegler is the balance scale problem. Children are shown a balance scale apparatus equipped with equally spaced pegs to each side of the fulcrum on which uniform metal weights can be placed. The child's task is to predict which side of the scale would go down if a lever holding the scale motionless were released. Siegler formulates several possible rules, ordered in sophistication, that the child might use. Rule 1 takes account only of the number of weights and totally ignores their distance from the fulcrum. Rule 2 takes into account distance, but only when the numbers of weights are the same. Rule 3 takes into account both numbers of weights and distance but does not specify how to resolve a conflict between them. Rule 4, the most sophisticated, correctly specifies the quantitative rule for combining weight and distance information.

Siegler's method for inferring what (if any) rule a child is using deserves our attention, not only because the method is clever but also because it has direct and general application to educational practice. Having analyzed what rules a child could use, Siegler sets up a series of specific problems for which the different rules would predict very different patterns of success and failure. Most elegantly, on some of these problems, a less sophisticated rule will lead to a higher probability of success than a more sophisticated rule. For example, a problem that shows four weights all placed two pegs distant from the fulcrum on one side and two weights both placed four pegs distant from the fulcrum on the other will be an occasion for guessing under Rule 3 (since weight and distance are in conflict), but will be answered correctly under Rules 1 and 2.

Equipped with such a diagnostic series of problems, Siegler has established that the predictions of most children between 5 and 17 years old, prior to any training, conform to one of the rules that he postulated. Not surprisingly, the older the child, the more sophisticated the child's spontaneous rule on average. Thus, kindergartners use the simplest, Rule 1; 8-year-olds use a mixture of Rules 1 and 2; 13-year-olds use Rule 3. These findings provided Siegler two very important questions about instruction. Does the child's ability to learn a new rule from instruction depend on the rule that the child is using prior to instruction? Does it also depend on the age of the child? Both questions were answered in the affirmative. Five- and 8-year-old children, all diagnosed as using Rule 1, were presented with feedback for their predictions in two kinds of problems. Some received distance-problem training, designed to give experience with the kinds of problems solvable by Rule 2. Others received conflict-problem training, experience with problems solvable by Rule 3. Five-year-olds benefited from distance-problem training but not from conflict-problem training. So effective instruction must take into account the beginning point of the learner. Eight-year-olds benefited from both training programs: Of an 8-year-old and a 5-year-old who start at the same point, the 8-year-old can learn more. Further work tells us why. Feedback in conflict-problem training supplies relevant information only if the child attends to both weight and distance in the examples. Rule-1 5-year-olds, unlike Rule-1 8-year-olds, spontaneously encode only weight. Indeed, the combination of training to encode both attributes plus conflict-problem training allows 5-year-olds to progress.

The implications of Siegler's research program for education are direct and numerous. To begin, his observations, like Kemler's, indicate that even at the beginning of elementary school, children apply rules to the solution of problems. Their predictions are guided by systematic hypotheses. Moreover, through observations that disconfirm their hypotheses, children can learn more sophisticated or more correct rules. But not just any opportunities for feedback will benefit the child. The instructor must be sensitive to whether or not the child encodes (attends to) the critical properties of the new information that is to be learned from. If the child does not, then specific training to pay attention to these properties of the situation must proceed the opportunity to learn from feedback. Thus, Siegler's work underlines the importance of establishing the level of competence of the individual child before proceeding to instruction. Happily, his work also suggests appropriate methods of assessing the child's competence. To discover the system that the child is using, first consider what alternative systems could be used in the situation. Then devise a series of diagnostic tasks on which particular patterns of responses would confirm and distinguish the alternative systems. The technique is potentially widely applicable. An example from Baron (1979) illustrates the method applied to reading. A child who primarily reads by matching whole words to whole visual patterns will do well on familiar words, regardless of whether the words are regular (e.g., *cat*) or irregular (e.g., *two*). That child will do poorly reading even simple pronounceable nonsense strings (e.g., *gat*). Alternatively, the child who reads by using spelling–sound correspondence rules will do well with both regular words and pronounceable nonsense strings and will do poorly on irregular words.

Conclusion

Frequently, the younger elementary school child is characterized as a concrete thinker (Bruner, 1964; Goldstein & Scheerer, 1941; Vygotsky, 1962; Werner, 1957), a description that has also been applied to unschooled adults in nontechnical cultures (cf. Cole & Scribner, 1974). Some of the findings that have been discussed can be assimilated to that view: (1) Young children reason better about numbers that they can estimate than about numbers they cannot; (2) they are not primarily disposed to analyze component properties of wholes; (3) kindergartners' efficiency in hypothesis testing is limited to local decision making; and (4) the rules that guide their scientific predictions are simple and usually wrong.

With the description of the 6-year-old as a concrete thinker, the beginning of formal schooling appears as a clash between the mind of the child and the properties of the educational system. The system values and inculcates abstract thinking. Moreover, instruction occurs outside of the context of concrete practical activities (Greenfield & Bruner, 1969; Luria, 1976; Scribner & Cole, 1973). Both the material and the method are ill-suited to the mind of the 6-year-old child.

A major consequence of surveying the cognitive strengths of young school children is to discredit such an analysis. Surely, there are limitations to the thinking of 6-year-old children, and, no doubt, both age and schooling are correlated with advances in abstract thought. Nevertheless, a global characterization of kindergartners as concrete thinkers is clearly undermined by the major findings presented in this section:

1. Even preschoolers have the rudiments of a concept of number, itself an abstract concept: They distinguish between number-relevant and number-irrelevant transformations, and their knowledge of counting principles is impressive.
2. Kindergartners systematically classify items on the basis of similarity relations and, if prompted, also show the ability to classify on the basis of abstract dimensional components.
3. Kindergartners are truly hypothesis testers: At least in the short term, they retain, reject, and reselect hypotheses in rational accordance with the information they perceive.
4. Kindergartners use rules to make scientific predictions and, with appropriate training, change their rules in the direction of greater sophistication.

Number knowledge, classification abilities, hypothesis-testing capacities, and rule usage all attest to some capacity for abstract thought in the child who is beginning formal schooling.

THE UTILIZATION OF STRATEGIES: IMPLICATIONS FOR DEVELOPMENTAL DIFFERENCES

The success with which recent investigations uncover some of the intellectual strengths of the young school child qualifies but certainly does not vitiate what any casual observer knows: There is a striking improvement in the performance of children on many mental tasks as they advance through the elementary school years. The major question the second half of this chapter addresses is how to conceptualize these differences in a way that is useful to the educator.

The ability to perform any task is, in principle, a function of three factors: strategies, factual knowledge, and capacity. Both strategies and factual knowledge are modifiable. They are nonfixed attributes of the performer, susceptible to training. Capacities are not modifiable by experience. Capacities can change over time, but only as a function of maturation (or injury). A distinction between fixed and nonfixed limitations of an information processing system has appeared in many guises in the literature on memory, learning, and intelligence (e.g., Atkinson & Shiffrin, 1968; Baron, 1978; Brown, 1974; Chi, 1978; Fisher & Zeaman, 1973; Flavell, 1977).

The relevant distinction can be clarified by reference to a specific task. The example is entirely hypothetical, but nevertheless plausible. Consider the ability of a school child to accurately add small integers (those that sum to 10) but no large integers. Such a limitation may be due simply to a lack of factual knowledge: knowledge of how the number series is extended beyond 10. The limitation may also be due to a combination of knowledge and strategic factors. The child may lack a strategy for adding numbers and may only have *memorized* the "addition facts" up to sums of 10. Alternatively, the child may have in his or her repertoire a strategy for adding—starting a count with the first addend in the problem and generating a series of additional number tags equal in length to the second addend (i.e., 6 + 3 as 6, 7, 8, 9). However, the child may only use the strategy in the context of everyday practical problems and not think to produce the strategy within a classroom or laboratory setting when the numbers do not refer to concrete things. Thus, in the classroom, the child would fall back on limited memorization of addition facts. In yet another alternative, the child actually may use the counting strategy to solve the classroom tasks but have difficulty executing it errorlessly. Such inefficiency or lack of skill in executing the strategy would be less likely to disrupt addition of small numbers than addition of large numbers. The inefficiency could simply be due to lack of practice with the strategy, but it could also result from capacity limitations. Perhaps because of limited space in working memory, the child cannot simultaneously keep track of where he or she is in the count sequence, retrieve the next count word, and know how many more tags have to be generated to complete the sum. Thus, the strategy may require more capacity than the child has. As a result, it may not be produced at all or it may be produced quite inefficiently.

It is certainly easier in principle than in practice to make these distinctions between knowledge, strategies, and capacity. In actual practice a deficiency may have the "look" of a capacity limitation, yet be equally analyzable as a deficit in knowledge or in strategy. Age differences in memory span, the maximum number of items an individual can repeat back in order immediately after hearing them once, would appear to directly index changing capacities in memory structures—the number of items the working-memory-store can accommodate at any time. In contrast, recent analyses stress that strategy differences (e.g., imposing structure on a list) and differences in specific knowledge (e.g., subjects' familiarity with the domain from which the to-be-remembered items are drawn) provide much, if not all, of the explanation for age differences in memory span (e.g., Chi, 1976). This implies that it is possible to erase age differences by training younger children to use the strategies older children use, by practicing them on the strategies so that they will execute the strategies as skillfully as older children do, and/or by giving them sufficient experience with the items so they will know as much as older children know about them. Another implication often easier to test is that if the task conditions minimize the need or the call for strategies only used by older children (Brown, 1975) and/or use materials equally familiar to the different age groups (Chi, 1978), then the age differences in their performance will disappear.

Another complication in distinguishing among knowledge, strategy, and capacity limitations is that they surely interact with one another (Baron, 1978). Executing certain strategies may depend on having particular knowledge (e.g., recoding the digit string 1963 as the year that John F. Kennedy was assassinated) or having sufficient capacity (e.g., being able to hold 1-9-6-3 in memory while simultaneously retrieving an event associated to the year 1963). Moreover, as the skill in executing strategies increases, the demand that the strategy makes on current capacity decreases. The relation works the other way around, too. The more capacity, the easier it is to acquire and to produce sophisticated strategies. The conclusion then, is that we can rarely pinpoint one or another type of limitation as *the* locus of a child's difficulty in a particular task.

These reservations aside, the current literature on cognition suggests that the educable or remediable limitations—strategies and specific knowledge—are extremely important sources of age differences in performance on school-related tasks. This section of the chapter will focus on the strategic component of performance as a source of developmental differences.

There is some ambiguity in the way the term *strategy* has been used in the psychological literature. Usually it refers to an intentional cognitive activity undertaken by the individual to meet a task goal. Sometimes, however, it refers more broadly to any cognitive activity, intentional or not, that serves to facilitate attainment of the goal. In the ensuing discussion, only the former will be referred to as a strategy; the latter will be called a *routine*.

The development of task-specific strategies

Any discussion of the importance of strategies in the development of cognition begins with the domain of memory development, and with a now classic paper by Flavell (1970). Flavell pointed out that developmental trends in laboratory memory tasks across the elementary school years can be accounted for largely in terms of developmental differences in the tendency to produce strategies directed at remembering. Furthermore, the lesser tendency of younger children to produce appropriate strategies is often not the result of an inability to execute the routines. In fact, if instructed to perform the routine the older children strategically produce, the younger children show a considerable increase in the amount they remember. The routine works to facilitate memory when it is induced in children who do not spontaneously use it. Flavell therefore characterized the absence of the strategy in young children as a *production deficiency*, a failure to initiate the routine, rather than as a *mediation deficiency*, a failure of the produced routine to have its beneficial effect.

Some examples will clarify the basis for the analysis. Flavell, Beach, and Chinsky (1966) presented a serial memory task to kindergarten, second-grade, and fifth-grade children. In front of the child was a set of seven pictures of objects that were familiar even to the kindergartners. On each trial, the experimenter pointed to three of these items one after the other. The child's task, after a delay interval of 15 seconds, was to point to the same three items in the same order. The investigator both measured the accuracy of performance and monitored the child's rehearsal activities during the delay interval. (An observer had been trained to lip-read.) Prior to any training, most of the fifth graders, about half of the second graders, and virtually no kindergartners showed use of verbal rehearsal; this age pattern was directly mirrored in the success of remembering. Thus, rehearsal as a spontaneous memory strategy increases with age and appears to be related to memory performance. The second significant finding comes from a follow-up study by Keeney, Cannizzo, and Flavell (1967): First graders who did not spontaneously rehearse could be taught to do so easily, and, when prompted to rehearse, their memory performance rose to the level of first-grade children who spontaneously produced the rehearsal strategy. Both the failure to produce the rehearsal strategy and the success of intervention in prompting rehearsal and increasing memory performance have been demonstrated also in older children at risk for special education (cf. Brown, 1974).

A parallel example can be found in the use of organizational strategies for memorizing lists of items. The importance of organizing strategies in adult memory is well known (e.g., Mandler, 1967; Tulving, 1968). Ordinarily, the laboratory paradigm for such demonstrations involves the presentation of a list of items (pictures or words) to be remembered. After the items are presented, the subject must try to recall as many as possible, in whatever order he or she wishes—a free-recall task. Often the items lend themselves to organization by membership in taxonomic categories (e.g., items of clothing, vehicles, food). This form of organization is consistently used by adults to guide their retrieval efforts.

Several investigators have studied the development of organizational strategies by externalizing the study activities of children who are trying to remember a set of items for free recall. Neimark, Slotnick, and Ulrich (1971) used such a procedure with college students and elementary school children spanning grades 1 through 6. The task was to remember as many items as possible from a set of 24 familiar pictures that were selected from four common taxonomic categories (e.g., animals: bear, camel, cow, dog, goat, horse; vehicles: bicycle, boat, bus, car, train, truck). Three minutes were given to study the pictures, which were all placed before the subject. Subjects were told they could "move (the pictures) around in a different order, pick them up, make notes, or do anything you like to help you learn them [p. 428]." After the 3 minutes of study the memory test was given. Each child completed three study-test trials, unless perfect recall was achieved earlier.

Neimark *et al.* rated the study activities of the children. A rating of 0 was given when the child showed no systematic arrangement of the pictures for study; 1 for partial rearrangement by category; 2 for complete categorical rearrangement, and 3 for a categorical organization that was elaborated further (e.g., forming subcategories within the larger categories). Children in grades 1 and 3 showed almost no deliberate organization during the study period. Even on the third study trial, third graders' average rating was .3. Thus, less than a third did any rearranging. Fourth, fifth, and sixth graders averaged ratings of .68, .85, and 1.10, indicating some strategic activity. One half of the sixth graders used at least a level 2 grouping. Still, the older elementary school children were considerably outdone by the college students, who earned a mean study rating over 2, frequently using the most elaborate grouping. Thus, an intentional strategy of organizing into taxonomic categories develops gradually over the school years, with memory concurrently improving. The correlation between number of items recalled and ratings of study strategies was .74 in Neimark *et al.*'s study.

Moely, Olson, Halwes, and Flavell (1969) showed that the organizational deficiency of younger children is reduced through training. In an explicit training condition, elementary school children were instructed in how to organize the pictures into categories during the study period and told to recall them according to these categories. Relative to peers who did not receive such instruction, kindergartners, first graders, and third graders who were instructed made considerably more use of the organizational routine and increased their recall scores accordingly. Third graders, but not the younger children, also benefited from a weaker instructional prompt: The experimenter merely named the categories and pointed to their members prior to the study period. In general the amount and directness of instruction that are needed to overcome a production deficiency decrease as the age of the child increases.

A final example of developmental differences in strategies is selected from a domain outside memory. The task is to judge whether pictures are identical or different in detail. Vurpillot (1968) observed the visual scanning strategies that children use in making such same–different comparisons. Her stimuli were sketches of houses, with potentially different objects portrayed in each of 6 windows of the house. On each trial, two stimuli, either the same or differing by 1, 3, or 5 windows, were presented side by side and remained in front of the child until he or she made a judgment. During stimulus presentation, a camera recorded the location of the child's visual fixations over time. Thus, it was possible to index the child's scanning strategies. The children who participated in the study ranged from age 3 through 9.

The ideal strategy in Vurpillot's task is to successively fixate homologous windows in the two houses, making paired comparisons until a difference is found, if any exist. Thus, for some pairs, the number of required visual fixations is greater than for different pairs, since one must scan exhaustively to ensure a correct *same* judgment. Also, the number of fixations required on the different trials decreases as the number of differences within the pair increases.

The scanning routines of the older children were closer to the ideal. Only children 6 years of age or older made more fixations to the same pairs than to the different pairs and more fixations to the pairs with fewer differences than to the pairs with more differences. Moreover, the strategy of making successive comparisons between paired windows was adopted not at all by the 3-year-olds, by only a third of the 5-

year-olds, and by a clear majority of the 6–9-year-olds. Finally, even the older children did not scan in the ideal manner. For example, the 9-year-olds failed sometimes to scan exhaustively on same pairs, making some errors in judgment. The pattern of developmental differences, like those in memory studies, can be described roughly as follows: (*a*) no detectable strategy in children under 6 years; (*b*) some crude strategies in children 6–8 years old; and (*c*) frequent and more efficient strategies in children over 8, with some clear evidence of still more improvement with age.

As a general description of the development of strategic behavior, this summary is undoubtedly more valid for its developmental pattern—no strategy, some strategy, more efficient and more frequent use of the strategy—than for the age norms. In fact, there is evidence of some strategic intervention by preschool children in selected tasks (Brown & DeLoache, 1978). One familiar example is their tendency to count in order to estimate number. The results from Gelman's magic tasks, as interpreted by Gelman and Gallistel (1978), suggest that children deliberately count in order to evaluate the cardinal number of a set and to prove the accuracy of their estimates to an observer. To demonstrate that a plate of mice is still the winner, despite spatial displacement, the 4-year-old executes a count. Thus, predicting whether the younger elementary school child will engage in strategic behavior requires knowing the characteristics of the task and the amount of experience the child has had with the relevant routine in the task. The same is true of older elementary school children who may lack strategies for some tasks that are only encountered in school (Brown & Smiley, 1978).

Egeland (1974), using a task related to Vurpillot's same–different paradigm, has presented suggestive evidence that scanning routines, like mnemonic routines, can be trained effectively in some children who do not spontaneously use them. He worked with second-grade children who had been classified as impulsive—that is, rapid and inaccurate—responders on a visual matching task. The Matching Familiar Figures test requires finding which one of several alternative items differs from a standard item. The difference is always one of detail. Egeland's training program, involving a number of exercises and materials designed to improve scanning routines, led to durable improvement in task performance. Evidence that the training worked specifically by improving scanning routines is only indirect because Egeland did not monitor visual scanning as Vurpillot had done. Still, the fact that the training in scanning resulted in greater improvement than simply instructing the children to slow down suggests that the effectiveness of the scanning training depended largely on training the routine itself.

Again, there is convergence between the results from different tasks: Some children who do not produce a routine or who produce an ineffi- cient one can be trained to produce an effective routine with consequent benefits for their task performance. In one sense this may seem to be just a statement that teaching works, which will come as no surprise to elementary school educators. More significantly, the finding is that training useful routines themselves is often successful and can be ac- complished sometimes with very little effort. Thus, if a child is deficient on a task, a reasonable suggestion is to evaluate what strategies the child is lacking and to train the child in the strategies themselves. Sometimes only a prompt will be necessary, although other times an extended training program will be needed. Almost certainly, training new and better routines will have more immediate and salutory consequences than simply having the child practice the task itself.

Transfer of training

When a child has been trained in a routine that another child uses spontaneously, is it appropriate to say that the training has successfully instilled the strategy? In other words, can strategies—as opposed to routines—be taught? The issue is whether providing the child the routine automatically results in the child using the routine in a deliberate and spontaneous manner. Unfortunately, the evidence suggests it does not.

Addressing the problem of transfer, Campione and Brown (1977) make an important distinction between maintenance and generalization of a strategy. Both refer to the individual's tendency to produce a routine when explicit training or prompting of the routine is removed. Mainte- nance occurs when such transfer is achieved within the same task envi- ronment in which training occurred. Generalization occurs when the transfer is achieved within a different task environment. Thus, generali- zation is a more demanding transfer condition than maintenance.

Even maintenance should not be taken for granted. Keeney *et al.* (1967) reported that fully one-half of the first graders trained success- fully to rehearse abandoned the rehearsal strategy when given the op- tion to do so on later trials within the same session. Though rehearsal had clearly benefited the memory performance of these children, the routine was not adopted as a strategy; it did not come under the chil- dren's voluntary control. Other studies have been able to demonstrate maintenance, but not generalization, when training in the routine is more extensive (Campione & Brown, 1977), or when feedback that the routine has improved performance is made very salient to the children

(Kennedy & Miller, 1976). For example, Brown, Campione, and Murphy (1974) administered 12 days of training on a rehearsal routine to 10 retarded adolescents. Six months later, eight of the subjects retained their memory advantage over an untrained control group on the original task, but failed to show an advantage on another task in which rehearsal was an equally appropriate strategy (Campione & Brown, 1977).

Is this transfer limitation confined to young or retarded children? Campione (1973; Campione & Beaton, 1972) investigated transfer of attention learned in one discrimination problem to a discrimination problem that had a different format. Kindergartners, second graders, and fifth graders first learned to attend to a particular dimension (color or form) in a successive discrimination task that involved assigning one of two responses to a series of stimuli presented one at a time. Lack of generalization resulted for all age groups when the children were transferred to a simultaneous discrimination problem that required the child to select between two stimuli: Subjects who had learned to attend to the appropriate dimension in the first problem solved the transfer problem no more quickly than those who had learned to attend to an inappropriate dimension. In the same studies, maintenance did occur for all age groups from one simultaneous discrimination task to another. Thus, even toward the end of the elementary school years, transfer of training can be quite narrow.

One factor that contributes to transfer is the tendency to notice common features in different contexts. As mentioned earlier, older children, given their greater proclivity for stimulus analysis, are more likely to attend to such commonalities than younger children. Thus, they should show a greater tendency to transfer than younger children. Tighe and Tighe (1978) examined the ability of kindergartners and second-, fourth-, and sixth-grade children to transfer learning across discrimination problems in which different stimulus objects appeared, but in which the same property of the objects (angularity of contour) was relevant. Ten such problems were presented in succession, with reminders of earlier solutions interspersed to ensure the potential for transfer. In these conditions, positive transfer on Problems 6–10 was evident in only 30% of the kindergarten children and 56% of the second graders, but in about 90% of the fourth and sixth graders. In this very simple transfer test, the kind of generalization that educators hope for occurred by the middle elementary school years. Still, only a simply learned response to a dimension was transferred, not a sophisticated skill. Moreover, many factors favored transfer in the Tighe and Tighe study. All the problems were administered in the same session by the same experimenter and all shared a common visual property (although the same could be said of

Campione's situation in which transfer failed). Thus, much doubt still remains about the degree of transfer that teachers can expect from task-specific training.

General strategies and metacognition

The failure to find broad and flexible transfer is potentially a serious problem for education. Only a small part of the educator's role is to ensure that children can perform particular tasks, like reading words. Even the task-specific goals of school instruction are formulated with a greater purpose, namely, to equip children with tools helpful for acquiring more knowledge and skills. As Baron (1980) points out, the importance of this broader view of educational aims becomes clearer now than ever before, because our rapidly expanding technology (in computers, for example) makes it virtually impossible to predict what tasks will have to be performed by the next generation of intelligent adults. One suspects that this argument will become timeless.

The question of transfer is only one of the problems. The usefulness of transfer is another. As Baron (1978) and Brown and DeLoache (1978) suggest, most of the psychological studies that have successfully trained routines have instilled special-purpose routines that are useful in very restricted situations. Rehearsal is certainly a routine of this type. More attention should be given to routines that have broader applicability— routines that are useful in many tasks that intelligent people do well and in many unforeseen tasks that they should do well.

Baron (1978) proposes three general-purpose strategies: relatedness search, stimulus analysis, and checking. Relatedness search is the strategy of trying to remember items that are related to a current item. Its usefulness for studying new material has been demonstrated convincingly in laboratory memory tasks (see Rohwer, 1973). Relatedness search also benefits retrieval of information. For example, in trying to remember the name that goes with a familiar face, it is useful to think of related information, like where the face has been seen before. In addition, relatedness search can improve transfer. When confronted with a new problem, one may attempt to think of related problems that one knows how to solve. The applicability of the strategy of relatedness search to transfer is probably its strongest claim to being a general-purpose strategy.

Stimulus analysis is a process encountered several times already. Early in elementary school, children are more likely to treat stimuli as integral wholes than to analyze them into their dimensional components. Yet, these children *can* analyze the stimuli (Kemler & Smith, 1979;

Smith & Kemler, 1977), so it is appropriate to think of stimulus analysis as a potential strategy for elementary school children. What qualifies stimulus analysis as a general-purpose strategy (Baron, 1978)? As with relatedness search, the justification is that stimulus analysis is useful in storing new information, in retrieving old information, and in promoting appropriate transfer. It is useful in finding relations that connect one item to another and thus aids storage of associations. It also helps retrieval by allowing one property to evoke the whole item. Tighe and Tighe's (1978) earlier mentioned developmental study is an excellent illustration of the significance of stimulus analysis for transfer.

Checking is the strategy of withholding an impulsive response and evaluating its accuracy before it is produced. Baron (1978) argues that failure to check may account for many deficits of young children in problem solving (even in conservation tasks). Vurpillot's (1968) findings on scanning problems are consistent with this view, and Egeland's (1974) training program can be considered to be a successful instance of facilitating checking. Checking, like the other proposed general strategies, is of particular importance for transfer. If relatedness search is used to elicit memories from a past-solved problem like a present one and if stimulus analysis helps to guide the memory search, checking is still essential to ensure that the transferred solution is really appropriate to the new situation. Related problems may not have related solutions.

Baron's proposals are convincing that general-purpose strategies do exist, and that their spontaneous use can account for not only many developmental differences but individual differences in performance at the same developmental level as well. Is there any reason to believe, however, that such general-purpose routines, if trained in one setting, will transfer to another? Why should the transfer of general routines by any more likely than the transfer of task-specific ones. One hopeful difference is that just because these strategies *are* general, the problem solver does not have to make the discrimination between what settings are appropriate for their use and what settings are not (Brown, Campione, & Barclay, 1979). Thus, transfer of general strategies does not require any subtle cognitive distinctions. However, the evidence does not suggest that transfer of specific strategies is hampered by this factor in particular.

It is useful to consider (*a*) the developmental trend toward increasingly effective strategic intervention; (*b*) the problem of eliciting transfer in younger children; and (*c*) the question of what strategies are general purpose as an interrelated set (cf. Campione & Brown, 1977). What general-purpose strategies do older children and more intelligent children have that lead them to behave more strategically in a variety of situations and cause them to transfer more easily (e.g., Brown *et al.*, 1979)? Brown (1974) has suggested that older children of normal intelligence have a strategy to use strategies, a general strategy par excellence. Brown and DeLoache (1978) have suggested more generally that older children are more likely to strategically control, monitor, and regulate their own cognitive routines. From this viewpoint younger children have many of the same basic routines in their repertoires as older children. What distinguishes younger and older children is the degree to which such routines are brought under conscious control and are available for self-selection and self-monitoring, so that they can be deployed flexibly and efficiently.

There is a good deal of evidence that conscious knowledge of one's own cognitive limits, cognitive states, and cognitive routines increases through the school years and is also related to differences in intelligence. These categories of knowledge have been called *metacognitive* because they constitute knowledge *about* cognition. Although most of the evidence for the growth of metacognition concerns the growth of metamemory, there is also research evidence concerning metalinguistic knowledge (Gleitman, Gleitman, & Shipley, 1972), metacomprehension (Markman, 1977), and meta-attention (Miller & Bigi, 1977).

Two examples of metamemory are the ability to estimate one's own memory span and the ability to monitor one's readiness to recall. Flavell, Friedrichs, and Hoyt (1970) were the first to put them into developmental perspective. In one task, children were shown series of familiar pictures, increasing in length from trial to trial, and asked on each trial: "Do you think you could remember N words (points to a strip of N pictures) if I said each of them just once and then covered them up [p. 326]?" The longest series presented was 10, well above the memory span of the average adult. Each child's predicted span was the length of the longest series that the child affirmed. These predictions were compared for accuracy with actual spans in the task. Many nursery schoolers and kindergartners knew no limits to their memory: Fully 60% of them predicted that they could recall the longest series. Even 25% of the second graders responded in this way. Of the children who estimated less than the maximum, there was still a considerable increase in accuracy of predictions with the grade level of the child. The fourth graders, the oldest group tested, were the best predictors, though they too showed room for improvement.

The recall readiness task was arranged by giving the children a supraspan series of items to study for as long as they wished, at which time they were to signal their readiness to recall it. The major question is whether children were prepared to recall at the time they signaled. Again, improvement with age was dramatic. Despite the fact that each child had three trials (with different pictures) on the task, preschoolers and kindergartners were accurate less than half the time they signaled; second and fourth graders were virtually always accurate. Inspection of the activities of the children during the study period showed that only the two older groups engaged in a significant amount of memory-monitoring behaviors during the interval—for example, anticipating the name of the next item in the series before showing it to themselves or rehearsing the entire series of items to check the state of their memory. Thus, metamemory improves with age. (See Flavell & Wellman, 1977, for an extensive review of metamemory research.) It is also deficient in educable retarded children (Campione & Brown, 1977).

What is the likely connection between development differences in metacognitive knowledge and the increasingly self-conscious regulation of cognitive routines by older children? In the Flavell *et al.* work (1970), the relation between the study strategies of the subjects and their ability to evaluate recall readiness is suggestive; so is the relation between young children's unrealistic estimates of their memory span and their oft-reported failure to do anything special to facilitate remembering (Appel, Cooper, McCarrell, Sims-Knight, Yussen, & Flavell, 1972). "Learners who are not aware of their own limitations, or strengths, or of their own strategic repertoire, can hardly be expected to apply appropriate strategies flexibly, and precisely in tune with task demands [Brown, 1980, p. 50]."

Can children be taught metacognitive strategies, general strategies of controlling their own basic cognitive routines? Such routines, if taught in one situation, might have the best possibility of transferring just because they *are* routines that involve the learner in cognitive introspection (Campione & Brown, 1977). Thus, they may be routines that have promising beginnings as strategies.

Checking is mentioned both by Baron (1978) as a general strategy and by Brown (1977) as a metacognitive strategy. Will training in self-checking generalize? There is preliminary evidence that it will. Suggestive is Egeland's (1974) finding that training impulsive second graders in visual scanning, a program that devoted much attention to checking, not only improved the accuracy of their performance on a visual matching task but also generalized 5 months later to a test of reading achievement.

More direct evidence comes from Brown *et al.* (1979), who assessed generalization of memory-monitoring training in a group of educable retarded children. The children were taught to monitor their recall readiness in a test for rote recall of picture names, like Flavell *et al.*'s (1970) problem. One year later, children not only maintained their advantage on the original task but showed transfer to a novel task that required estimating readiness for gist recall of a prose passage. Unfortunately, for neither Egeland's (1974) nor Brown *et al.*'s study is it possible to be certain that the successful generalization was due to the transfer of the checking strategy itself since in neither case was the routine monitored in the transfer situation. Still, the preliminary results are certainly encouraging. One suspects that the current interest in metacognitive skills among developmental psychologists will spawn more direct and relevant studies in the near future.

Conclusion

Recent advances in understanding the course of cognitive development during the elementary school years have been illuminated by the view that with age the child becomes an increasingly strategic participant in mental tasks. This trend is reflected in the greater likelihood that the older child will do *something* as a means to meet the goal of the task; it is also reflected in the greater likelihood that what the older child does is particularly well suited to the goal of the task. The relative absence of strategy production in younger children is not due solely to the lack of relevant routines in their repertoire. Minimal, external prompts may be enough to elicit production of routines and consequent improvement in task performance. Moreover, training routines in one task setting does not guarantee their generalization to another. What appears to be lacking in the younger children is self-control and self-regulation of cognitive routines. Both definite successes in the training of task-specific routines and more tentative successes in the training *and* generalization of general-purpose metacognitive routines are encouraging examples for educators.

Research on the increasingly strategic activities of elementary school children in our culture has been complemented by cross-cultural investigations of the effects of schooling in less technically advanced cultures. The results of cross-cultural studies (see Cole & Scribner, 1974; Luria, 1976) can be assimilated to the view that schooling itself plays a major role in facilitating the growth of the individual as a strategic performer in nonpractical contexts (e.g., Brown, 1977). Of course, that schooling already has such effects does not imply that schools could not better accomplish what they do. The research reviewed in this section suggests that an effort to teach and facilitate transfer of general-purpose strategies is an important goal and a realistic goal for educators. Happily, the psychological literature is becoming increasingly relevant to this effort.

SUMMARY

This chapter has selected two themes from the recent literature on cognitive development in the school years. One emphasizes the intellectual strengths of the child near the beginning of the elementary school experience. Both the methods used to detect those strengths and the conclusions that derive from their implementation have ramifications for educational practice. Often the young child (or by extension, the slow child) can be shown, by appropriate task analyses and consequent task modifications, to have more cognitive competence than is immediately apparent. Such was the case in an examination of their number concepts, their classification abilities, and their scientific thinking. Still, developmental differences are the rule rather than the exception on many laboratory and school-related tasks. The second theme of the chapter was that a significant factor underlying these differences is the greater tendency of the older child to behave strategically. On the positive side, the literature suggests that task-specific routines can be trained, sometimes remarkably easily, with consequent improvement in task performance for the child who does not use such strategies spontaneously. On the negative side, evidence for transfer of these trained routines is minimal. However, investigators are devoting increasing effort to delineating general-purpose strategies, particularly those that are metacognitive in nature, and preliminary evidence suggests that these strategies can be trained and do transfer. These are just the strategies that should continue to interest educators and psychologists alike. In general, there seems to be a growing convergence between the research efforts of cognitive developmental psychologists and the more practically motivated concerns of educators.

ACKNOWLEDGMENTS

The author expresses her appreciation to Jeanette Brack for her able editorial assistance.

REFERENCES

Anderson, D. R., Alwitt, L., Lorch, E. P., & Levin, S. R. Watching children watch television. In G. Hale & M. Lewis (Eds.), *Attention and cognitive development.* New York: Plenum, 1979.

Appel, L. F., Cooper, R. G., McCarrell, N., Sims-Knight, J., Yussen, S. R., & Flavell, J. H. The development of the distinction between perceiving and memorizing. *Child Development*, 1972, *43*, 1365–1381.

Atkinson, R. C., & Shiffrin, R. M. Human memory: A proposed system and its control processes. In K. W. Spence & J. T. Spence (Eds.), *The psychology of learning and motivation* (Vol. 2). New York: Academic Press, 1968.

Baron, J. Intelligence and general strategies. In G. Underwood (Ed.), *Strategies in information processing*. London: Academic Press, 1978.

Baron, J. Orthographic and word-specific mechanisms in children's reading of words. *Child Development*, 1979, *50*, 60–72.

Baron, J. *What kinds of intelligence components are fundamental?* Paper presented at NIE-LRDC Conference on Thinking and Learning Skills, Pittsburgh, 1980.

Baron, J., & Treiman, R. Use of orthography in reading and learning to read. In J. Kavanaugh & R. Venezky (Eds.), *Orthography, reading, and dyslexia*. Baltimore: Univ. Park Press, 1980.

Beilin, H. The training and acquisition of logical operations. In M. F. Rosskopf, L. P. Steffe, & S. Taback (Eds.), *Piagetian cognitive development research and mathematics education*. Washington: National Council of Teachers of Mathematics, 1971.

Brown, A. L. The role of strategic behavior in retardate memory. In N. R. Ellis (Ed.), *International review of research in mental retardation* (Vol. 1). New York: Academic Press, 1974.

Brown, A. L. The development of memory: Knowing, knowing about knowing, and knowing how to know. In H. W. Reese (Ed.), *Advances in child development and behavior* (Vol. 10). New York: Academic Press, 1975.

Brown, A. L. Development, schooling, and the acquisition of knowledge about knowledge. In R. C. Anderson, R. J. Spiro, & W. E. Montague (Eds.), *Schooling and the acquisition of knowledge*. Hillsdale, N.J.: Erlbaum, 1977.

Brown, A. L. *Learning and development: The problems of compatibility, access, and induction* (Tech. Rep. No. 165). Center for the Study of Reading, Univ. of Illinois at Urbana-Champaign, 1980.

Brown, A. L., Campione, J. C., & Barclay, C. R. Training self-checking routines for estimating test readiness: Generalization from list learning to prose recall. *Child Development*, 1979, *50*, 501–512.

Brown, A. L., Campione, J. C., & Murphy, M. D. Keeping track of changing variables: Long term retention of a trained rehearsal strategy by retarded adolescents. *American Journal of Mental Deficiency*, 1974, *78*, 446–453.

Brown, A. L., & DeLoache, J. S. Skills, plans and self-regulation. In R. S. Siegler (Ed.), *Children's thinking: What develops?* Hillsdale, N.J.: Erlbaum, 1978.

Brown, A. L., & Smiley, S. S. The development of strategies for studying texts. *Child Development*, 1978, *49*, 1076–1088.

Bruner, J. S. *The process of education*. Cambridge, Mass.: Harvard Univ. Press, 1960.

Bruner, J. S. The course of cognitive growth. *American Psychologist*, 1964, *19*, 1–15.

Bruner, J. S. *Toward a theory of instruction*. Cambridge, Mass.: Harvard Univ. Press, 1966.

Bruner, J. S., Olver, R. R., & Greenfield, P. M. *Studies in cognitive growth*. New York: Wiley, 1966.

Bryant, P. E. *Perception and understanding in young children*. New York: Basic Books, 1974.

Campione, J. C. The generality of transfer: Effects of age and similarity of training and transfer tasks. *Journal of Experimental Child Psychology*, 1973, *15*, 407–418.

Campione, J. C., & Beaton, V. L. Transfer of training: Some boundary conditions and initial theory. *Journal of Experimental Child Psychology*, 1972, *13*, 94–114.

Campione, J. C., & Brown, A. L. Memory and metamemory development in educable retarded children. In R. V. Kail & J. W. Hagen (Eds.), *Perspectives on the development of memory and cognition*. Hillsdale, N.J.: Erlbaum, 1977.

Chi, M. T. H. Short-term memory limitations in children: Capacity or processing deficits? *Memory and Cognition,* 1976, *4,* 559–572.

Chi, M. T. H. Knowledge structures and memory development. In R. S. Siegler (Ed.), *Children's thinking: What develops?* Hillsdale, N.J.: Erlbaum, 1978.

Cole, M. A developmental study of factors influencing discrimination transfer. *Journal of Experimental Child Psychology,* 1973, *16,* 126–147.

Cole, M., & Scribner, S. *Culture and thought: A psychological introduction.* New York: Wiley, 1974.

Egeland, B. Training impulsive children in the use of more efficient scanning techniques *Child Development,* 1974, *45,* 165–171.

Fisher, M. A., & Zeaman, D. An attention–retention theory of retardate discrimination learning. In N. R. Ellis (Ed.), *International review of research in mental retardation* (Vol. 6). New York: Academic Press, 1973.

Flavell, J. H. Developmental studies of mediated memory. In H. W. Reese & L. P. Lipsitt (Eds.), *Advances in child development and behavior* (Vol. 5). New York: Academic Press, 1970.

Flavell, J. H. *Cognitive development.* Englewood Cliffs, N.J.: Prentice-Hall, 1977.

Flavell, J. H., Beach, D. H., & Chinsky, J. M. Spontaneous verbal rehearsal in a memory task as a function of age. *Child Development,* 1966, *37,* 283–299.

Flavell, J. H., Friedrichs, A. G., & Hoyt, J. D. Developmental changes in memorization processes. *Cognitive Psychology,* 1970, *1,* 324–340.

Flavell, J. H., & Wellman, H. M. Metamemory. In R. V. Kail & J. W. Hagen (Eds.), *Perspectives on the development of memory and cognition.* Hillsdale, N.J.: Erlbaum, 1977.

Fodor, J. A. Some reflections on L. S. Vygotsky's *Thought and Language. Cognition,* 1972, *1,* 83–95.

Garner, W. R. *The processing of information and structure.* Potomac, Md.: Erlbaum, 1974.

Gelman, R. Conservation acquisition: A problem of learning to attend to relevant attributes. *Journal of Experimental Child Psychology,* 1969, *7,* 167–187.

Gelman, R. The nature and development of early number concepts. In H. W. Reese (Ed.), *Advances in child development and behavior* (Vol. 7). New York: Academic Press, 1972.

Gelman, R. Cognitive development. *Annual Review of Psychology,* 1978, *29,* 297–332. (a)

Gelman, R. Counting in the preschooler: What does and does not develop. In R. S. Siegler (Ed.), *Children's thinking: What develops?* Hillsdale, N.J.: Erlbaum, 1978. (b)

Gelman, R., & Gallistel, C. R. *The child's understanding of number.* Cambridge, Mass.: Harvard Univ. Press, 1978.

Gholson, B., Levine, M., & Phillips, S. Hypotheses, strategies, and stereotypes in discrimination learning. *Journal of Experimental Child Psychology,* 1972, *13,* 423–446.

Ginsburg, H., & Opper, S. *Piaget's theory of intellectual development* (2nd ed.). Englewood Cliffs, N.J.: Prentice-Hall, 1979.

Gleitman, L. R., Gleitman, H., & Shipley, E. F. The emergence of the child as grammarian. *Cognition,* 1972, *1,* 137–164.

Goldstein, K., & Scheerer, M. Abstract and concrete behavior: An experimental study with special tests. *Psychological Monographs,* 1941, *53*(2, Whole No. 239).

Greenfield, P. M., & Bruner, J. S. Culture and cognitive growth. In D. A. Goslin (Ed.), *Handbook of socialization theory and research.* Chicago: Rand McNally, 1969.

Inhelder, B., & Piaget, J. *The growth of logical thinking from childhood to adolescence.* New York: Basic Books, 1958.

Inhelder, B., & Sinclair, H. Learning cognitive structures. In P. H. Mussen, J. Langer, & M. Covington (Eds.), *Trends and issues in developmental psychology.* New York: Holt, 1969.

Keeney, T. J., Cannizzo, S. R., & Flavell, J. H. Spontaneous and induced verbal rehearsal in a recall task. *Child Development,* 1967, *38,* 953–966.

Kemler, D. G. Patterns of hypothesis testing in children's discriminative learning: A study of the development of problem-solving strategies. *Developmental Psychology,* 1978, *14,* 653–673.

Kemler, D. G., & Smith, L. B. Accessing similarity and dimensional relations: The effects of integrality and separability on the discovery of complex concepts. *Journal of Experimental Psychology: General,* 1979, *108,* 133–150.

Kendler, H. H., & Kendler, T. S. Vertical and horizontal process in problem-solving. *Psychological Review,* 1962, *69,* 1–16.

Kennedy, B. A., & Miller, D. J. Persistent use of verbal rehearsal as a function of information about its value. *Child Development,* 1976, *47,* 566–569.

Liberman, I. Y., Shankweiler, D., Fischer, F. W., & Carter, B. Explicit syllable and phoneme segmentation in the young child. *Journal of Experimental Child Psychology,* 1974, *18,* 201–212.

Luria, A. R. The directive function of speech in development and dissolution. *Word,* 1959, *15,* 341–352.

Luria, A. R. *Cognitive development: Its cultural and social functions.* Cambridge, Mass.: Harvard Univ. Press, 1976.

Mandler, G. Organization and memory. In K. W. Spence & J. T. Spence (Eds.), *The psychology of learning and motivation* (Vol. 1). New York: Academic Press, 1967.

Markman, E. M. Realizing that you don't understand: A preliminary investigation. *Child Development,* 1977, *48,* 986–992.

Mehler, J., & Bever, T. G. Cognitive capacity of very young children. *Science,* 1967, *158,* 141–142.

Miller, P. H., & Bigi, L. Children's understanding of how stimulus dimensions affect performance. *Child Development,* 1977, *48,* 1712–1715.

Moely, B. E., Olson, F. A., Halwes, T. G., & Flavell, J. H. Production deficiency in young children's clustered recall. *Developmental Psychology,* 1969, *1,* 26–34.

Neimark, E. D., Slotnick, N. S., & Ulrich, T. Development of memorization strategies. *Developmental Psychology,* 1971, *5,* 427–432.

Piaget, J. *The child's conception of number.* New York: Humanities Press, 1952.

Piaget, J., & Inhelder, B. *The psychology of the child.* New York: Basic Books, 1969.

Rohwer, W. D. Elaboration and learning in childhood and adolescence. In H. W. Reese (Ed.), *Advances in child development and behavior* (Vol. 8). New York: Academic Press, 1973.

Rosch, E. On the internal structure of perceptual and semantic categories. In T. E. Moore (Ed.), *Cognitive development and the acquisition of language.* New York: Academic Press, 1973.

Rosch, E., & Mervis, C. B. Family resemblances: Studies in the internal structure of categories. *Cognitive Psychology,* 1975, *7,* 573–605.

Rosch, E., Mervis, C. B., Gray, W. D., Johnson, D. M., & Boyes-Braem, P. Basic objects in natural categories. *Cognitive Psychology,* 1976, *8,* 282–339.

Rozin, P., & Gleitman, L. R. The structure and acquisition of reading. II: The reading process and the acquisition of the alphabetic principle. In A. S. Reber & D. L. Scarborough (Eds.), *Toward a psychology of reading: The proceedings of the CUNY conferences.* Hillsdale, N.J.: Erlbaum, 1977.

Savin, H. B. What the child knows about speech when he starts to learn to read. In J. F. Kavanaugh & I. G. Mattingly (Eds.), *Language by ear and by eye: The relationships between speech and reading.* Cambridge, Mass.: MIT Press, 1972.

Schaeffer, B., Eggleston, V. H., & Scott, J. L. Number development in young children. *Cognitive Psychology*, 1974, *6*, 357–379.

Scribner, S., & Cole, M. Cognitive consequences of formal and informal education. *Science*, 1973, *182*, 553–559.

Shepp, B. E. From perceived similarity to dimensional structure: A new hypothesis about perceptual development. In E. Rosch & B. B. Lloyd (Eds.), *Cognition and categorization.* Hillsdale, N.J.: Erlbaum, 1978.

Shepp, B. E., & Swartz, K. B. Selective attention and the processing of integral and nonintegral dimensions: A developmental study. *Journal of Experimental Child Psychology*, 1976, *22*, 73–85.

Siegler, R. S. Three aspects of cognitive development. *Cognitive Psychology*, 1976, *8*, 481–520.

Siegler, R. S. The origins of scientific reasoning. In R. S. Siegler (Ed.), *Children's thinking: What develops?* Hillsdale, N.J.: Erlbaum, 1978.

Siegler, R. S., & Vago, S. The development of a proportionality concept: Judging relative fullness. *Journal of Experimental Child Psychology*, 1978, *25*, 371–396.

Smith, L. B., & Kemler, D. G. Developmental trends in free classification: Evidence for a new conceptualization of perceptual development. *Journal of Experimental Child Psychology*, 1977, *24*, 279–298.

Spiker, C. C., & Cantor, J. H. Cognitive strategies in the discrimination learning of young children. In D. K. Routh (Ed.), *Learning, speech, and the complex effects of punishment.* New York: Plenum, 1980.

Tighe, T. J. Subproblem analysis of discrimination learning. In G. H. Bower (Ed.), *The psychology of learning and motivation* (Vol. 7). New York: Academic Press, 1973.

Tighe, T. J., Glick, J., & Cole, M. Subproblem analysis of discrimination-shift learning. *Psychonomic Science*, 1971, *24*, 159–160.

Tighe, T. J., & Tighe, L. S. Stimulus control in children's learning. In A. Pick (Ed.), *Minnesota Symposia on Child Psychology* (Vol. 6). Minneapolis: Univ. of Minnesota Press, 1972.

Tighe, T. J., & Tighe, L. S. A perceptual view of conceptual development. In R. D. Walk & H. L. Pick, Jr. (Eds.), *Perception and experience.* New York: Plenum, 1978.

Trabasso, T. Representation, memory, and reasoning: How do we make transitive inferences? In A. D. Pick (Ed.), *Minnesota Symposia on Child Psychology* (Vol. 9). Minneapolis: Univ. of Minnesota Press, 1975.

Tulving, E. Theoretical issues in free recall. In T. R. Dixon & D. L. Horton (Eds.), *Verbal behavior and general behavior theory.* Englewood Cliffs, N.J.: Prentice-Hall, 1968.

Vurpillot, E. The development of scanning strategies and their relation to visual differentiation. *Journal of Experimental Child Psychology*, 1968, *6*, 632–650.

Vygotsky, L. S. *Thought and language.* Cambridge, Mass.: MIT Press, 1962.

Werner, H. The conception of development from a comparative and organismic point of view. In D. Harris (Ed.), *The concept of development.* Minneapolis: Univ. of Minnesota Press, 1957.

White, S. H. Some general outlines of the matrix of developmental changes between five and seven years. *Bulletin of the Orton Society*, 1970, *20*, 41–57.

Zeaman, D., & House, B. J. Interpretation of developmental trends in discriminative transfer. In A. D. Pick (Ed.), *Minnesota Symposia on Child Psychology*, (Vol. 8). Minneapolis: Univ. of Minnesota Press, 1974.

7 / Theory and research on children's achievement

DANIEL SOLOMON

Anyone who has watched children working on puzzles, academic tasks, games involving skill, or intellectual problems will have noted that some of them work eagerly and wholeheartedly, appearing to enjoy responding to challenges and attempting to overcome difficulties, whereas others are much more tentative and hesitant, seeming to lack confidence in their own abilities and appearing worried about the prospect of possible failure. Because individual achievement is important in this culture (and most others) and many of society's rewards are tied to attained achievement levels, there has been much interest in attempting to understand and explain these and other variations in achievement orientations. Researchers have investigated achievement orientations, asking such questions as: How stable are they over time? To what degree do they generalize across achievement areas? How do they develop? How can they be changed or influenced? Why do children differ in them? What are their consequences? In this chapter, some of the approaches that have been taken toward answering these questions will be explored, and some of the research will be described. The emphasis will be on research and theory focusing specifically on elementary-school-age children, although some work that has involved older or younger subjects will be described in cases in which the content has general theoretical relevance or implications for children's achievement development.

269

THE CONCEPT OF ACHIEVEMENT

There are two major approaches to the study of achievement—that of Vaughn and Virginia Crandall and associates (Crandall & Battle, 1970; Crandall, Katkovsky, & Preston, 1960) and that of Atkinson and associates (Atkinson & Raynor, 1978). The Crandall approach is concerned with children's achievement, and focuses on achievement *behavior*. The Atkinson approach is concerned with achievement in general and emphasizes achievement *motivation*. In spite of these differences (and others that will be discussed later) there is similarity between the two approaches in their definitions of achievement. Both contain as a central element the notion of *competition with a standard of excellence*. It is by virtue of this central defining characteristic that achievement is usually conceptually distinguished from random, undirected exploratory behavior on the one hand and the young child's attempts to achieve mastery (at such things as walking, speech development, ability to manipulate objects, etc.) on the other. It is generally believed that young children and infants do not have the cognitive ability to monitor the outcomes of their behavior with respect to standards of excellence or even to conceive of such standards and of their own step-by-step improvement vis-à-vis those standards. Therefore, defining achievement in terms of a deliberate orientation of one's behavior toward the attainment of standards of excellence necessarily rules out achievement as a possibility for very young children. It has been suggested, however (e.g., by V. C. Crandall, 1972; Veroff, 1969), that the early attempts at mastery and exploration are the precursors of later achievement orientations in children. Children who find their early attempts at mastery and exploration to be rewarding and pleasurable would be expected to be the most likely later to develop positive achievement orientations (McClelland, Atkinson, Clark, & Lowell, 1953).

Several aspects of achievement have been identified and investigated. Two of these (achievement behavior and achievement motivation) have already been alluded to. Some of the aspects are presumed to be internal to the individual, while others are external (and therefore directly observable). One of the internal aspects is achievement motivation (Atkinson & Raynor, 1978; Heckhausen, 1967), which has been defined as an internal disposition to improve or maintain a high level of performance with respect to standards of excellence (this limits achievement to activities in which success or failure are possible). Achievement values constitute an additional internal aspect (see Strodtbeck, 1958; Williams, 1969). They refer to more general "principles that guide human conduct" (Rosen, 1959). Values are major tenets by which social or cultural groups implicitly or explicitly define themselves. Individuals take on these values to the degree that they identify with the particular group. In the context of the preceding definition of achievement, a group (or individual) with a value on achievement holds that continual improvement of one's performance, with respect to standards of excellence, is a desirable activity. Values, in this definition, are differentiated from motivation in that motivation refers to the degree to which the individual feels impelled or inclined to strive in achievement situations (irrespective of the value that the group places on this activity in general), whereas values refers to an individual's feeling about the general worthwhileness of achievement (irrespective of that person's specific inclinations to achieve). Although these undoubtedly often occur together, they need not necessarily do so. There are individuals, for example, who consider achievement striving a very worthwhile thing, yet find it too threatening or painful to devote much time or effort to such activity.

Other internal components or concomitants of achievement include individuals' beliefs, cognitions, and perceptions about the reasons for their participation in achievement-related activities (DeCharms, 1968), about the causes of their successes and failures with such activities (Bar-Tal, 1978; Crandall, Katkovsky, & Crandall, 1965; Solomon & Oberlander, 1974; Weiner, 1974), about the absolute and relative worth of their accomplishments (Katz, 1967; Pettigrew, 1967), and about the likelihood of their being successful in new achievement efforts (V. C. Crandall, 1969). Rosen (1956, 1959) described and studied an "achievement syndrome," which he believed could help explain differences in achievement among people from different ethnic groups. The achievement syndrome was defined as a pattern composed of positions on three value orientation dimensions: an activistic–passivistic orientation (concerning a belief that it is possible versus not possible to take action to improve one's status), an individualistic–collectivistic orientation (referring to the extent to which the individual is expected to subordinate personal needs to those of the group), and a present–future orientation (referring to the degree to which the emphasis is on immediate gratification versus planning and sacrificing in order to obtain future gains). The positions on these dimensions that would be expected to maximize achievement activity would be at the activistic, individualistic, and future-oriented poles (also see Strauss, 1962.).

The major aspects of achievement that are external (in the sense of being more directly observable, more clearly represented in an individual's overt behavior) are achievement behavior and achievement outcomes. *Achievement behavior* refers to the individual's active striving efforts in situations in which standards of excellence are applied; *achieve-*

ment outcomes refers to the individual's performance with respect to those standards of excellence. Among the indices of achievement behavior that have been employed in various studies are persistence (Battle, 1965; Feather, 1962) structured observations and ratings of striving and active involvement in achievement situations (Crandall, Katkovsky, & Preston, 1962; Solomon, 1969b), selection of tasks at different difficulty levels (Crandall & Rabson, 1960), and self-reports of achievement-related efforts (Crandall & Battle, 1970). Achievement outcomes investigated have covered a broad range, including task success and failure, achievement test performance; IQ test performance, and school grades.

The achievement domain thus encompasses a fairly broad set of general concepts and categories. Figure 7.1 presents these, with arrows representing presumed relationships among them. Some of these relationships have been investigated, and some have not, as yet. Of those that have been investigated, only a few can be considered to be well established. Figure 7.1 shows a series of hypothesized linkages, with the final categories, achievement behavior and outcomes, represented at the far right, the determinants of those outcomes moving to the left, with the most remote determinants (society and culture) at the far left. Thus it is suggested here that the achievement-related values of society and culture can be transmitted to the individual to the degree that they are represented in the stated values and the activities of the community, the home environment (which includes the specific behaviors of parents toward children, and parent–child interactions, as well as the examples set by parents) and the peer group. It is also suggested that achievement motivation is influenced primarily by the home environment and by the individual's disposition, that achievement-related beliefs, cognitions, and perceptions are influenced by home environment, peers, and ability and disposition, and that achievement values, achievement motivation, and achievement-related beliefs, cognitions, and perceptions have reciprocal influences on one another.

The possibility that achievement-related perceptions, cognitions, and motivations may be influenced by aspects of the achievement situation is also provided for in this model. It is assumed in this scheme that there is only one class of direct determinants of achievement outcomes—achievement behavior. The effects of all other antecedent factors must be mediated through achievement behavior in order to have any effect on achievement outcomes. Thus, for example, if a student has a high measured level of achievement motivation that has no effect on his or her classroom behavior or other school-related behavior, that motivation will be unable to show any effect on the student's school outcomes. Achievement behavior, however, is believed to have multiple determi-

Indirect or Long-Range Influences   Direct or Short-Range Influences

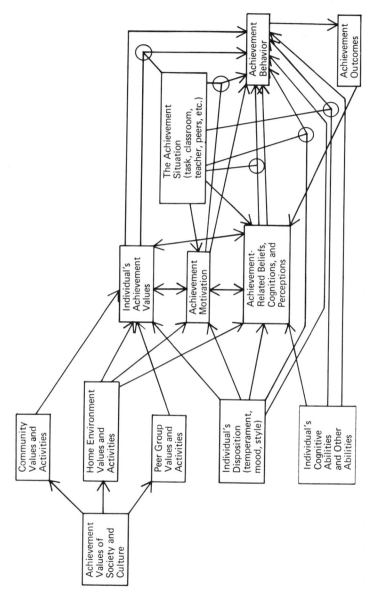

Figure 7.1. General scheme showing relationships among different aspects and determinants of achievement. Arrows indicate main effects. Circled intersections of arrows represent interaction effects.

nants. There are six factors that are suggested to be capable of exerting direct influences on achievement behavior—achievement values, achievement motivation, achievement-related beliefs, cognitions, and perceptions, dispositional factors (including mood, temperament, etc.), cognitive and other abilities, and the achievement situation (including specific achievement tasks, the classroom setting, teaching styles, group or classroom composition and atmosphere, etc.). In addition to these direct or "main" effects, each of the first five of these factors is also capable of showing joint or "interaction" effects with the sixth, the situational factor. Achievement behavior will be maximized in different situations for different types of children. Thus, for example, a self-confident, highly motivated child may perform best in situations that allow for self-definition and self-direction of activities, tasks, and goals, whereas a fearful and unmotivated child may do best in a situation in which there is a warm, supportive, and stimulating adult. Finally, it is suggested that achievement outcomes can have a reciprocal effect on achievement-related cognitions and perceptions, and thereby on the individual's motivations and values. Thus, achievement outcomes can exert an influence on a new phase of achievement behavior, which in turn shows effects on the achievement outcomes.

The remainder of this chapter will focus on the major theories that have been developed to account for children's achievement and the research findings that have been obtained in this area. The framework shown in Figure 7.1 may be useful in helping to place the theories and the results of specific studies into an overall context of hypothesized linkages.

DETERMINANTS OF ACHIEVEMENT AND ACHIEVEMENT BEHAVIOR IN THE IMMEDIATE SITUATION

As mentioned earlier, there are two major theories of achievement—those of Crandall and of Atkinson. In addition to the similarity of their definitions of achievement, the two theories are also similar in that they both represent variants of an "expectancy–value" model, that is, each conceptualizes achievement behavior as a combined function of the value placed on achieving by the individual and that individual's subjective probability or expectancy of being successful. The specific definitions and components of the expectancy and value elements of this general model differ between the theories, however. Each of these theories concentrates on direct or short-range influences on achievement. They do not ignore the more long-range effects (e.g., from socialization practices), but these have not been incorporated as basic elements of the predictive models.

The Crandall approach

The theory. The Crandall theory is the only one that explicitly deals with achievement in children. (Although some work in the Atkinson framework has looked at the development of achievement motivation of children—for example, Veroff, 1969; Winterbottom, 1958—the emphasis of this school has been on achievement motivation in general, not tied to any particular age group.) The Crandall theory is not basically a developmental theory, however. It looks at achievement behavior as something that is produced in a contemporaneous situation, and analyzes that behavior as a function of various forces (both internal and external to the individual) operating in the specific situation. The variables and constructs of the Crandall theory do not seem inherently limited to children. Rather, they are potentially applicable to the prediction of achievement behavior in people of any age. The development and major applications of the Crandall theory to date, however, have been in the context of research on achievement behavior in children.

In the first published account of the Crandall approach to children's achievement (Crandall, Katkovsky, & Preston, 1960), it was suggested that achievement behavior could be distinguished from other goal-directed behaviors by applying three criteria: the "inferred goal" of the behavior, the "unique characteristic" of the behavior, and the "nature of the situations" in which the behavior occurred. The authors suggested that the *goal* of achievement behavior was "the attainment of approval and the avoidance of disapproval" (with approval and disapproval coming either from others or from oneself). The unique defining attribute of achievement behavior was held to be *competence of performance*. The approval that is sought as the goal of achievement is given for performance that is judged to be competent. The judgment of competence in turn depends on the application of a *standard of excellence* against which the behavior can be compared. All of these aspects were included in the Crandall definition of achievement behavior: "Achievement behavior is behavior directed toward the attainment of approval or the avoidance of disapproval (the goal) for competence of performance (characteristic of the behavior) in situations where standards of excellence are applicable (nature of the situation) [p. 789]."

An important assumption in the Crandall theory is that achievement orientations are not general or global within individuals, but rather may be specific to given achievement areas. A child may be motivated to perform well in athletics but not in academic or artistic activities, for example. Thus, it would be appropriate to speak of an achievement orientation in a specific area, but not of a general achievement orientation. This differentiates the Crandall theory from "trait" approaches in psychology, which have tended to posit personality dispositions that generalize across situations. Crandall, Katkovsky, and Preston specify five achievement areas among which they felt achievement orientations could vary within individuals: intellectual achievement, physical skills achievement, artistic–creative achievement, mechanical skills achievement, and social skills achievement.

Several concepts, influenced by the "level of aspiration" paradigm of Lewin and his co-workers (Lewin, Dembo, Festinger, & Sears, 1944) and derived explicitly from several aspects of Rotter's (1954) social learning theory, were developed to help elucidate and define various components of a child's orientation toward achievement in different areas. These concepts were attainment value, achievement standards, and achievement expectancies.

Attainment value is defined as "the importance that an individual attaches to the attainment of approval and the avoidance of disapproval regarding the competence of his performance in a given achievement area [Crandall, Katkovsky, & Preston, 1960, p. 791]." It is assumed that a child comes to value achievement in a given area as a function of the prior reinforcements received for performance in that area, through a process of secondary reinforcement. It is predicted that children will be more likely to choose to work, and more likely to persist, in areas for which they have high attainment values than those for which they have low attainment values.

Achievement standards refer to a scale of excellence against which the competence or skill of an individual's performance may be judged. These are standards that are subjectively held by the individual and that may or may not correspond to the standards held by others. Several additional concepts are used to characterize achievement standards: The *height of standards* refers to the level of skill or performance that differentiates between the subjective experience of success and the subjective experience of failure. The *form of achievement standards* refers to the fineness of gradation of an individual's subjective scale of excellence of performance. Some individuals may make a crude dichotomous distinction between performance that surpasses a standard (succeeds) and that which falls short of a standard (fails) with no further differentiation of degrees of success and failure or degrees of consequent approval or disapproval. Others may perceive and respond to very slight differences on either side of the success–failure dividing point. The suggestion is made by Crandall, Katkovsky, and Preston (1960) that there may be developmental changes (perhaps corresponding to the development of cognitive abilities) with respect to this parameter, with young children more likely to make crude, all-or-none distinctions and older children, more finely differentiated ones. The *breadth of achievement standards* refers to the degree to which an individual's achievement standards generalize across achievement areas. Some children are satisfied only with high levels of proficiency in all areas; others are more easily satisfied in some areas than in others. *Stability of standards* refers to the degree to which individuals change their standards as a result of success and failure experiences and the reception of approval and disapproval. Some children may rigidly maintain standards across fluctuations in the fortunes of their achievement efforts; others may shift standards in response to subtle variations in the outcomes of their performance. One additional attribute of achievement standards is relevant to the intrinsic–extrinsic distinction, but has not been elaborated (or researched) beyond the statement in this initial (1960) formulation. This attribute is the *source of achievement standards.* Individuals who react to their own achievement efforts on the basis of subjectively held standards are said to hold autonomous achievement standards; those who depend on other people to determine how competent their performance is are said to hold reflective achievement standards. It is suggested that children with autonomous standards have incorporated the standards of significant others, whereas those with reflective standards have not.

The third major construct in the Crandall theory, in addition to those of attainment value and achievement standards, is *achievement expectancy.* This is defined as "the probability held by the individual that his achievement efforts will lead to goal attainment [Crandall, Katkovsky, & Preston, 1960, p. 795]." It was suggested that the expectancy or subjective probability of goal attainment should be an important predictor of achievement behavior, both alone and in combination with the other major achievement-related constructs. Thus, it is predicted that children with high expectancies of success are more likely to persist with a task, whereas those with low expectancies are more likely to abandon a task. It is further predicted that this effect will be maximized in achievement areas that are highly valued by the child. That is, given a high expectancy of success, a child will be likely to persist with a task longer if it relates to a highly valued achievement area rather than a lowly valued area; similarly, given a low expectancy of success (or high expectancy of failure), the child will be more likely to abandon the task if it is in a highly valued rather than a lowly valued area.

The predictive importance of achievement standards in this scheme (particularly the height of standards parameter) is that they define the "success" and "failure" that are the object of the expectancies. Thus, two children may have the same expectancy of achieving the same performance level (perhaps a grade of B in a course). But if one of the children define that level as a success and the other defines it as a failure, the predicted impact on achievement striving will be different. A high expectancy of achieving "success" in a valued area will lead to a higher level of achievement behavior, it is predicted, than the same expectancy of achieving "failure" in the same or an equally valued area, even if the *objective* performance level expected is the same in the two instances.

Since the initial formulation of the Crandall theory, some additions and elaborations have been developed, but the basic framework has not been altered. Battle (1965, 1966) subdivided attainment value into two subcategories—absolute attainment value (the value of attainment in a given area, independent of that in any other area), and relative attainment value (the value of attainment in a given area as compared with that in one or more other areas). The former was expected to be more useful in accounting for actual levels of achievement behavior in given areas; the latter in accounting for achievement behavior in one area compared with that in specific other areas. Battle also adopted from Rotter (1954) and from Crandall, Katkovsky, and Preston (1962) the concept of *minimal goal level,* referring to the lowest level of goal attainment that will produce a subjective feeling of satisfaction, and added the concept of *minimal goal certainty,* referring to the individual's subjective certainty of achieving the minimal goal. She predicted that the individual's degree of certainty of achieving at least a minimal goal would relate to the likelihood of striving and persisting toward reaching that goal.

Crandall and Battle (1970) found that it was useful to subdivide the intellectual achievement area into two subcategories: academic and general intellectual achievement. Academic intellectual achievement referred to school-related types of activities, whereas general intellectual achievement referred to efforts toward maintaining or increasing "knowledge or intellectual skills in activities that are not demanded by the individual's vocation, academic status, or other pragmatic demands of his life situation [p. 40]." The investigators then focused on predicting achievement *effort* in each of these areas.

Crandall and Battle also point out that, within this achievement theory, expectancy and value are assumed to be independent of each other, and thus can combine to achieve a more exact prediction of achievement behavior than can be produced by either considered alone. This is one major distinction between the Crandall and Atkinson approaches. In the latter (to be described in a later section of this chapter) incentive value is *defined* as the inverse of the subjective probability of success. The more difficult a task is perceived to be (i.e., the lower the subjective probability of success), the greater the value attached to accomplishing it successfully. Expectancy and value thus do not represent entirely separate variables in the Atkinson framework.

The concept of reinforcement (or approval–disapproval) is important—indeed central—to the Crandall theory (although Crandall & Battle, 1970, point out that the definition of achievement behavior refers to behavior *directed toward* the attainment of approval and avoidance of disapproval, independent of what reinforcements actually accrue as a result of the behavior). Therefore, the individual's beliefs and perceptions about the conditions producing reinforcement should also be important in predicting achievement behavior. Crandall, Katkovsky, and Crandall (1965) adapted Rotter's (1966) concept of "internal–external control of reinforcement" to the prediction of achievement behavior. (More recently, this concept has come to be known as locus of control— see Lefcourt, 1976; Solomon & Oberlander, 1974.) Locus of control refers to the individual's belief that reinforcements are a direct result of his or her own efforts rather than a result of chance, fate, or arbitrary actions of other people. If the individual does not believe that his or her efforts have any bearing on the reinforcements received, then there will be little reason to exert efforts toward receiving them. But if there is a perceived contingent connection between an individual's efforts and their outcomes, the person should be inclined, according to the prediction, to strive actively toward achieving them. This concept thus has a conditioning or mediating function within the Crandall framework. If a contingency between behavior and outcomes is not seen, none of the other variables (attainment value, achievement expectancy, etc.) can have an effect. It is thus seen as a necessary but not sufficient condition of achievement behavior. Crandall, Katkovsky, and Crandall (1965) expanded on Rotter's concept of locus of control by subdividing it into perceived control of positive and of negative reinforcements. It seemed possible that some individuals might see themselves as the cause of positive reinforcements, while seeing negative reinforcements as beyond their control, whereas for others the reverse might be true. It is important to note that this concept refers not to the sources controlling the *initiation* of activities, and not to the *expectation* of being successful or unsuccessful with them, but rather to the perception that the determinants of one's achievement outcomes (success and failure) are either within oneself or external to oneself.

Research based on the Crandall theory. Numerous studies have been conducted within the Crandall framework. In this section several of these will be described, some in detail and some briefly. The methodologies used in these studies have been varied: Some studies have been experimental, whereas others have been "naturalistic" and correlational; some have been contemporaneous, and others have been longitudinal; some have been exploratory and hypothesis-generating, and others have been hypothesis-testing. Most of the instruments used to measure the various concepts in the theory have been newly developed; some have represented children's versions of instruments originally designed for adults (e.g., the internal–external control scale), some have involved interviews, some have involved self-report questionnaires, and some have involved structured observation systems. Here we will concentrate on the research conducted within the Crandall framework that has explicitly tested its assumptions and hypotheses.

Two early studies provided evidence that expectancy and reinforcement value (a Rotter concept parallel to attainment value) were independent (unrelated), except under conditions in which the objective probabilities of reinforcement were ambiguous or intermediate (Crandall, Solomon, & Kellaway, 1955, 1958). The assumption that attainment of approval is the major goal of achievement behavior was tested in a study by Stein (1969). She created four reinforcement conditions in an experiment with fourth-grade children: a praise condition; a condition in which children were informed when they were correct, but not praised; a condition in which disapproval was given for incorrect responses, and an "alone" condition (with no experimenter present). The praise condition elicited better performance than the disapproval or the correct conditions (which, in turn, were better than the alone condition), leading the author to conclude that the assumption was supported, that "person-oriented" approval appeared to be more effective than mere information about correctness in determining achievement behavior. (As will be noted in the following section, however, there is some unclarity about whether the function of approval in the Crandall theory is affective or informational. In one publication—V. J. Crandall, 1963—it is implied that the function may be affective for girls and informational for boys.)

Several studies have provided evidence that achievement behavior tends not to generalize across areas, that achievement striving in one area tends to be unrelated or only moderately related to achievement striving in another area. In one study (V. C. Crandall, 1965), the amount of time and intensity of effort devoted by 6–9-year-old children to various freely chosen tasks representing different achievement areas was assessed and compared. Little correlation was found between tasks in different achievement areas. Similar results were obtained by Solomon (1969b) in a study that compared task persistence and apparent interest among several different achievement-related tasks (varying along dimensions of task requirements for verbal versus nonverbal responses and divergent versus convergent thinking).

Numerous studies have examined the relationships of the various motivational and cognitive variables included in the Crandall theory to indices of achievement behavior and/or achievement outcomes. Crandall, Katkovsky, and Preston (1962) obtained measures of intellectual attainment value, expectation of success in intellectual achievement situations, and minimal intellectual achievement standards from 40 children distributed among the first three elementary grades. To measure intellectual attainment value, each child was shown pictures of activities in four different achievement areas and asked to make paired comparisons rating which of each pair he or she would like to be able to do especially well. Expectancy of success was measured by showing the children a series of tasks of graduated difficulty (with the difficulty levels described to them) and then asking the children which of the tasks they thought they would be able to do. The same tasks were used to measure minimal achievement standards by asking the children, with respect to each task, whether they would be more satisfied or dissatisfied if that were to be the most difficult task they could succeed with; the minimal standard was set as the easiest task for which more satisfaction than dissatisfaction was reported. The children's belief in internal versus external control of reinforcement was also measured with a brief questionnaire. Dependent variables included amount of time spent in intellectual activities and intensity of striving in intellectual achievement activities (both rated by observers during free-play periods in a day camp), as well as intelligence test performance and achievement test performance.

Numerous significant relationships were found between these two sets of variables, although the patterns of relationship were quite different for boys and for girls. Intellectual attainment value related to both free-play achievement behavior variables for girls but not for boys; at the same time, internal locus of control, achievement standards, and expectancy of success were related to one or both of the achievement behavior variables for boys. Relationships with the achievement and IQ test scores showed a pattern of positive effects for boys' minimal standards, internal locus of control, and expectancy of success, and negative effects for girls' expectancy of success. Although this study gave evidence of the importance of the various motivational and cognitive variables of the Crandall theory, the sex differences were somewhat puzzling. The authors suggested that they might reflect a greater degree of "realism" on the part of boys in achievement situations, resulting from differences in socialization experiences.[1]

Other studies have found significant effects for most of the Crandall predictor variables. Thus Battle (1965, 1966) found academic performance among seventh- to ninth-grade students to be significantly related to absolute and relative attainment value, minimal goal level, minimal goal certainty, and expectancy of success, and found task persistence related to expectancy of success. Effects of expectancy of success on achievement behavior and outcomes have also been demonstrated by Crandall and McGhee (1968) and by V. C. Crandall, (1969). Effects of locus of control on both task persistence and academic achievement have been demonstrated in numerous instances (e.g., McGhee & Crandall, 1968; Solomon, Houlihan, Busse, & Parelius, 1971).

Some issues relating to the Crandall approach. .The Crandall theory's restriction of the goal of achievement to the attainment of approval has been criticized by Heckhausen (1967) for excluding the possibility that achievement striving might be intrinsically motivated, that is, be engaged in for its own sake. This criticism seems at least partially mistaken, however. The Crandall conception includes the attainment of approval (and avoidance of disapproval) from oneself as well as from others as goals of achievement behavior. Striving for the sake of one's own approval could be a reasonable definition of intrinsic motivation.

---

[1]Findings indicating sex differences in this area are more the rule than the exception. Thus V. C. Crandall (1969) summarized the results of several studies, encompassing diverse age levels, which indicated that girls tend to give lower estimates of their own intellectual and academic capabilities than do boys (in spite of objectively similar performance levels) and that girls' stated expectancies for future performance tend to be lower than past performance would indicate, whereas boys' expectancies tend to be higher. Among the possible explanations offered were differential reinforcement histories for the two sexes, differential sensitivity to positive and negative reinforcement, and cultural–social norms and sex-role expectations leading to verbal statements of modesty and self-deprecation, on the one hand, and self-confidence and optimism on the other. Stein and Bailey (1973) reviewed the research on achievement orientations in females and suggested that the sex differences in achievement orientations could be most appropriately considered to reflect not differential sensitivity to social approval (as V. J. Crandall had suggested, 1963) but rather differences in the types of tasks seen as achievement-related. It is argued that girls are more concerned about achievement with respect to social skills, whereas boys are more concerned about nonsocial skills, but that the achievement behavior and response patterns may be generally similar between the sexes in the types of tasks considered appropriate by each sex.

Aside from lumping together and treating as equivalent these two sources of approval and disapproval in the discussion of the goal of achievement behavior, little is said about the distinction between them in the Crandall theory. The distinction seems an important one, however, and perhaps warrants more elaborated development within this theory. It seems likely that individuals with primary orientations toward achieving one or the other of these goals (own approval or others' approval) might differ in the types of situations that they would prefer, in the antecedents of their orientations, and in numerous other achievement-related characteristics. There has been extensive theoretical and empirical work concerning intrinsic motivation in recent years (Day, Berlyne, & Hunt, 1971; Deci, 1975; J. McV. Hunt, 1965; Lepper & Greene, 1978); an explicit integration of this body of work with that produced by the Crandall approach could be very fruitful.

The Crandall theory is essentially a cognitive theory. Although reinforcement is a central concept within this theory, thus tying it in with learning theories, it has been influenced, via Rotter, by learning theories that combine cognitive variables with reinforcement in predicting behavior. But, as indicated earlier, the status of the reinforcement concept is made somewhat ambiguous, within the Crandall theory, by defining it to include approval and disapproval from oneself as well as from others. The various concepts and parameters in the theory essentially spell out the ways in which the individual interprets the meaning of a reinforcement. Thus, attainment value reflects how important it is to an individual to receive reinforcement in a given area, achievement standards allow an individual to determine whether his or her performance, as indexed by reinforcement, achieves personal goals, and achievement expectancies refer to the individual's subjective probability of achieving those goals. Reinforcement in this framework would seen to have a primarily informational role, rather than an affective one. Its function is to give the child information about whether or not the self-set achievement standard has been reached. There is some discussion of the possible sources of these standards and attainment values; it is suggested that they may be incorporated from parents through reinforcement processes, and that they may subsequently take on reinforcing qualities (secondary reinforcement) of their own. If this is so, it may be that external reinforcement may operate *affectively* in the early years (when the successful incorporation of achievement standards and values may derive from reinforcement given in the context of a close affective relationship with an adult), and *informationally* after achievement standards and values have been internalized.

The Atkinson approach

The theory and related research. The Atkinson theory is related to some of the same cognitive learning theory sources as the Crandall theory (e.g., Lewin *et al.*, 1944; Rotter, 1954; Tolman, 1955), in which behavior is seen as some function of the combination of expectancy (the individual's subjective probability that a behavior will lead to a specified outcome) and the value of the expected outcome to the individual. At the same time, the concept of psychogenic need or motive, as discussed by Murray (1938) and others, plays a very important role in the Atkinson approach to achievement. The coexistence of influence from these two streams sets up an interesting tension in the theory. The cognitive elements can allow for differences in perceptions of achievement situations and hence in achievement behavior across situations (e.g., an individual would be predicted to behave differently in a situation seen as having a high probability of goal attainment than one seen as having a low probability). The psychogenic motive, or achievement motive in the Atkinson theory, implies, on the other hand, a generalized internal orientation or disposition that seems more independent of situational fluctuations—it seems to imply that individuals with a high "need for achievement" will behave in ways consistent with that need in most situations.

The earliest statements of the theory concentrated on the internal, psychogenic motive (McClelland *et al.*, 1953). Additions and elaborations to the theory, which have proposed, among other things, ways in which the cognitive and motivational elements of the theory may be combined, have been produced periodically since then (Atkinson, 1958; Atkinson & Feather, 1966; Atkinson & Raynor, 1978).

The basic theory proposes a group of variables that, in combination, are hypothesized to determine the *resultant achievement-oriented tendency* of an individual in a particular situation. The achievement-oriented tendency, which is generally assumed to be reflected in the individual's task performance, is assumed to be a direct function of two components—*the tendency to achieve success* and the *tendency to avoid failure*. It is assumed that these two tendencies combine additively in situations in which performance can be evaluated against standards of excellence, and that the resultant tendency is composed of the tendency to achieve success minus the tendency to avoid failure.

Each of these component tendencies is produced by the combination of three factors—a motive, an expectancy, and an incentive value. Thus, the tendency to achieve success is seen as a multiplicative function of the motive to achieve success, the expectancy of success, and the incentive value of success. The motive is seen as a stable and general personality disposition that reflects the individual's degree of liking for success in general. Expectancy of success is the individual's subjective probability that his or her efforts will be successful in a particular situation. Incentive value is defined as the inverse of the expectancy of success. In other words, it is proposed that success is highly valued for tasks that are seen as difficult (having a low probability of success), and that it is lowly valued for tasks that are easy (having a high probability of success). The specific definition of incentive value is $1 - P_s$ (where P_s refers to expectancy—or subjective probability—of success). This suggested relationship between expectancy and incentive value was derived from Lewin *et al.* (1944) and, as stated earlier, constitutes one major difference from the Crandall theory (in which the two variables are seen as independent contributors to the prediction of achievement behavior). The implication of these assumptions (including the multiplicative combination of variables) is that the tendency to achieve success will be greatest for tasks seen as being of intermediate difficulty (since the product of .50 and .50 is larger than that of any other pair of proportions that add to 1.0), and that this effect will be greater as the generalized motive to achieve success is greater. Although a number of studies (done mostly with college students) have shown support for elements of the preceding formulation, task difficulty has usually been defined objectively, through experimental manipulation, rather than through questioning subjects about their perceived expectancies of success. This practice also contrasts with the Crandall approach, in which expectancy is usually assessed directly from subject's statements about their perceptions.

Parallel to the proposed determinants of the tendency to achieve success, the determinants of the tendency to avoid failure are suggested to be the motive to avoid failure, the expectancy of failure, and the incentive value of failure. The motive to avoid failure is seen as a capacity for reacting to failure with humiliation and shame; it is seen as separate and distinct from the motive to achieve success. It is assumed that the incentive value of failure and the expectancy of failure are negatively related, that is, failure is considered more shameful and embarrassing as tasks are perceived as easier, and less shameful as they are perceived as more difficult. Thus, similar to the prediction with respect to the tendency to achieve success, it is predicted that the tendency to avoid failure will be greatest at intermediate probabilities of failure, and that this effect will be greater as the motive to avoid failure is greater. The implications of these assumptions and predictions are that the tendency to achieve success (i.e., to approach achievement tasks) will be greatest when the subjective expectancy is .50, but that the tendency to avoid failure (i.e., to remove onself from the task) will also be greatest when the subjective expectancy is .50. The degree to which each of these tendencies is activated will depend on the relative strength of the two motives—the motive to achieve success and the motive to avoid failure. In general terms it is predicted, and has been found in quite a few studies, that individuals in whom the motive to achieve success is relatively greater than the motive to avoid failure will show most intense striving behavior in situations of intermediate success expectancies, whereas those whose predominant motive is to avoid failure will show more intense striving behavior with high- and low-probability tasks than with intermediate-probability ones.

An implication of this prediction was tested with children in a natural situation by Atkinson and O'Connor (described in Atkinson & Raynor, 1978, p. 34–35). In this study, which tested the effects of ability grouping among sixth-grade students, the need for achievement (motive to achieve success) was measured (as it is in most other studies) in terms of the achievement themes in stories told by the students in response to projective Thematic Apperception Test (TAT) pictures. In contrast, the motive to avoid failure was measured with a Test Anxiety Questionnaire (assuming, again in common with numerous other studies, that students who feel and express the most anxiety about testing situations are those for whom the prospect of failure is the most repulsive). It was assumed that the probabilities of success in academic tasks would be quite varied among different students in heterogeneous classes (with generally low expectancies for poor students, and generally high expectancies for good students). It was also assumed that success expectancies would be close to intermediate levels for most students in homogeneously grouped classes (since the ability levels of the students in the class would be similar). It was therefore predicted, in line with the preceding theory, that students whose predominant motive was to achieve success would show the best performance in ability-grouped classes, and that those whose predominant motive was to avoid failure would perform best in heterogeneous classes (for they would tend to avoid the intermediate-probability tasks of the grouped classes). It was found that the first group of students learned more and showed more interest in ability-grouped than in control (heterogeneous) classes, and that the second group showed less interest and satisfaction in the grouped than the control classes, but showed no differences in academic performance. Thus, the theory led to implications about responses of students with different personality characteristics to different educational arrangements that were, to a substantial degree, borne out.

Some additional implications and predictions of the Atkinson theory have been investigated in children by Smith (1969). Fourth- and fifth-grade boys' need for achievement was measured with a projective story-telling measure. A questionnaire measuring anxiety in testing situations was also given to the children, and considered to represent fear of failure. Several aspects of the children's achievement behavior were measured with a puzzle task in which they were to find and draw lines between sequential numbers that were arranged nonsequentially on a page. There were several such pages, each considered a separate "puzzle." The measure of performance was the number that was reached after working for 1 minute. Before doing each task, the children were asked to write down the number they would attempt to reach on that puzzle (their level of aspiration). Goal discrepancies were the level of aspiration scores minus performance on the previous trial.

To test the theoretical prediction that individuals whose motive to achieve success exceeded their motive to avoid failure would prefer tasks of intermediate difficulty, Smith divided the children into two groups: those with above-median need-for-achievement scores and below-median test-anxiety scores, and those with below-median need-for-achievement scores and above-median test-anxiety scores. The major dependent variable was the variance of the goal discrepancy scores. It was expected that the variance would be relatively small for those who consistently selected intermediate-difficulty puzzles, and relatively large for those who tended to select puzzles that were relatively difficult or relatively easy, but not intermediate. The expectation was generally confirmed, both for the fourth-grade and the fifth-grade boys. The goal discrepancy variances were higher, for each puzzle, for the group whose predominant motive was fear of failure than for the group whose predominant motive was need for achievement (motive to approach success). The differences were greater, however, for earlier than for later puzzles; as the boys progressed with the tasks, they were more able to predict their performance accurately and were thus presumably less influenced by motivational factors. It was also found that the goals for the need-for-achievement group tended to be set slightly above prior performance, as predicted by the theory, whereas discrepancies for the other group tended to be more extreme.

Several elaborations and extensions of the Atkinson theory have been proposed. Raynor (1969, 1978), observing that the effects of individual differences in achievement motivation seemed to be greatest with performance on tasks that had some relevance to long-range goals, developed an extension to the theory that focused on *future orientation*. The individual may view an immediate task as part of a contingent path (leading to a future goal) or as part of a noncontingent path (not leading to a future goal). Success with a task on a contingent path allows one to proceed to the next task on the path. The expectancy that one's activity will eventually lead to a future goal is seen as a multiplicative function of the expectancies of success for each of the steps (tasks) leading to the goal. Raynor also distinguishes between "open" and "closed" contingent paths. With open paths, one step has consequences that lead to new steps, as new possibilities or requirements become apparent. With a closed path there is a clear and fixed goal that does not change during the course of one's progress toward it. Because incentive value is defined, in the Atkinson theory, as the inverse of expectancy, the implication here is that the incentive value of closed-path goals will decrease as the goal is approached (as the subjective probability of goal attainment increases), whereas the incentive value of open-path goals will tend not to decrease because new steps are continually added, causing the expectancy of goal attainment (and hence its incentive value) to remain about the same. Raynor suggests that the open contingent path should be more appealing to a success-oriented person because the incentive value of success would remain at a high level. The Crandall theory would make a different prediction here. Since in that theory attainment value and expectancy are unrelated, attainment value would be unaffected by changes in expectancy, and achievement behavior with respect to a given goal would be enhanced as the expectancy increased.

The future orientation concepts discussed by Raynor have not been extensively explored in children. Differences between children, and across ages, might be expected in requisite cognitive abilities. Young children would probably be unable to conceive of current behavior in terms of far-distant goals. At least one study, however (described in Raynor, 1978), has demonstrated the relevance of the future orientation concepts among sixth- and eighth-grade black and Hispanic children in an inner-city school.

Horner (1968, 1978) proposed, as another addition to the Atkinson theory, the existence of a *motive to avoid success*. She suggests that people with this motive may become anxious in competitive situations, particularly those in which they have a moderate-to-high expectancy of success. She also suggests that the motive is especially important to women, who may see success as aggressive and therefore incompatible with socially accepted conceptions of femininity, and as possibly leading to social rejection and loss of self-esteem. It is assumed that the motive will be most strongly aroused in situations involving competition with other persons (as well as standards) and, in the case of women, when the competition is with males (especially "important" ones) and the tasks are considered masculine. Horner adapted the projective method for assessing need for achievement to the measurement of the motive to avoid success; stories told in response to verbal leads describing success situations were scored for negative affect, negative consequences, conflict, and avoidance. In one study, with college students, she found greater fear-of-success imagery among women than men, as predicted. She also found that women with high fear-of-success scores showed better task performance when working alone than when in competitive situations (which included some males), whereas those with low fear-of-success scores performed better in the competitive situations.

It is interesting to speculate about the possible connections between these findings and the V. C. Crandall compilation of findings (1969) showing girls' expectancies for success to be generally lower than boys', even after similar prior performance. However, there have been some failures to replicate the Horner findings. Reviews by Tresemer (1976), Zuckerman and Wheeler (1975), and Canavan-Gumpert, Garner, and Gumpert (1978) have discussed the Horner study and other related studies, and have raised questions about the reliability and validity of the motivation measure, the consistency of the sex differences in the motive, and the relationship of the motive to task behavior. Canavan-Gumpert *et al.* (1978) suggest that fear of success is important for both males and females and have developed a self-report (nonprojective) method for measuring it in children.

Some issues relating to the Atkinson approach. Although the Atkinson theory has generated a substantial amount of research, much of it producing results that were consistent with its hypotheses, the bulk of that research has been experimental and has used college students as subjects. Thus, the degree to which the theory and its findings can be generalized to children and to natural, "real life" situations is undetermined. The theory is conceived as a general theory and thus should be applicable to children and to various kinds of situations, but this has not yet been empirically demonstrated to any extensive degree.

The theory and related research have been criticized on several grounds. The reliability and validity of the projective measure of the achievement motive have been questioned (Entwisle, 1972). It has been suggested that the theory implicitly assumes that achievement is limited to competitive situations (Canavan-Gumpert *et al.*, 1978) and thus is unduly limiting. The theory has also been criticized on the grounds that although expectancy is defined as a subjective probability, in practice it is usually operationalized as manipulated task difficulty, without checking the subjective effect of that manipulation. It has been noted that much of the research done in the framework of this theory has been limited to male subjects and that, when females have been included, the theoretical predictions have been less well confirmed than with studies limited to males. The Horner (1978) extension was one attempt to incorporate particular achievement characteristics of females, but this extension, as noted earlier, is not without its own problems.

It also has been suggested that the concept of achievement motive implies a stable personality characteristic that is consistent across situations—so that a person with a strong achievement motive would be expected to feel a need to achieve in all or most situations in which a standard of excellence could be applied. The only situational variable in the theory is the subjective probability of success. The motive (of approach or of avoidance) is expected to be activated most strongly in situations of intermediate difficulty for the individual. This differentiates this theory from the Crandall theory, which assumes that an individual's prior experience may have created greater attainment values in one area than in another, no matter what the expectancies for performance outcomes are in the different areas.

Attribution theory and research

Although not strictly an "achievement" theory, attribution theory is concerned with individuals' perceptions of the causes of behavior. An important body of attribution theory and research has focused on perceptions that are relevant to achievement and achievement behavior. Much of this work has been produced by Weiner and his associates (Weiner, 1972, 1974, 1979; Weiner, Frieze, Kukla, Reed, Rest, & Rosenbaum, 1971). For a review of this area, see Bar-Tal (1978). It is assumed that a primary determinant of achievement behavior is the individual's perceptions and expectancies concerning the causes of success or failure. In this assumption, the approach is close to the concept of locus of control, as incorporated in the achievement theory and research of Crandall and Crandall. Where attribution theory differs is in the specification of the component dimensions and subcategories of the attributional perceptions and expectations. Although Weiner and associates suggest that a large number of different causes may be important in the attributions people make for their successes and failures, four specific causes have been the focus of most theoretical and research attention: ability, effort, task difficulty, and luck. These four causes have been further classified according to two dimensions: internality–externality and stability–instability. Thus, ability is seen as internal to the individual and relatively stable (not subject to situational fluctuation); effort is seen as internal and unstable (an individual may exert less effort on one task or in one situation than another); task difficulty is seen as external to the individual and stable (since the same task will be about equally difficult on different occasions); and luck is seen as external and unstable (unpredictable). Additional dimensions have also been proposed. Thus, Rosenbaum (1972) includes "intentionality" as an additional dimension. Weiner (1979) suggests "controllability" as a more accurate term for this dimension, referring to the degree to which an outcome is perceived as being under volitional control. Most work to date, however, has concentrated on the two dimensions of internality–externality and stability–instability.

Attribution theory proposes that there are both affective and cognitive reactions to success and failure, and that these reactions are determined by the attribution dimensions. The affective reactions include pride and shame, whereas the cognitive dimensions refer to expectancies for future performance. It is hypothesized that people feel most pride after success and most shame after failure if they attribute the outcome to internal causes (ability or effort). The cognitive reactions, on the other hand, are hypothesized to be most affected by the stability–instability dimension. If a cause is seen as stable (as in ability and task difficulty), the individual is likely to expect that future performance will be similar; if a cause is seen as unstable (as in effort and luck), the individual is more likely to expect that future performance may be different from present performance.

Research investigating these hypotheses has tended to confirm them. In addition, a number of studies have investigated the relationship of causal attributions to other achievement orientations and to achievement behavior. Several studies (summarized in Bar-Tal, 1978) have shown that individuals with high levels of achievement motivation tend to attribute their successes to ability and effort (internal causes) and their failures to lack of effort or to external causes, whereas those low in achievement motivation attribute success to external factors (i.e., not under their own control) and failure to lack of ability. In each case, it appears that outcomes that are unexpected or unusual are more likely to be attributed to the external causes. Thus, if those who are highly motivated generally expect to be successful, they attribute the unexpected failures to external causes (or to the internal–unstable lack of effort); similarly, those with low achievement motivation, who presumably expect failure, tend to attribute the unexpected successes to external factors. It is also suggested that individuals with high achievement motivation tend to see effort as more important as a cause of success or failure than those with low achievement motivation. The preference of high-achievement-motivated individuals for tasks of intermediate difficulty is seen as a result of a greater desire for feedback about their ability. Performance on tasks that are very easy or very difficult give information primarily about those tasks; performance on tasks of intermediate difficulty, on the other hand, give much more information about the ability of the task performer.

Some studies have tested the effect of causal attributions on achievement performance by attempting to alter those attributions. Dweck (1975), for example, identified a group of children who exhibited "learned helplessness" (a tendency to attribute failure to lack of ability and therefore to give up in response to failure). Verbal feedback was used in training sessions to teach the children to attribute their failures to lack of effort. This training was successful, both in changing the children's typical attributions and in causing improvements in their academic performance. Other studies have shown that similar training toward increased use of effort attributions produces greater task persistence in children (e.g., Chapin & Dyck, 1976). DeCharms (1972) has demonstrated successful results from similar training programs in which low-achieving children are taught to consider themselves the "origins" of their own behavior, rather than the "pawns" of external persons or forces.

Intrinsic motivation theory and research

The distinction between *intrinsic* and *extrinsic* motivation refers generally to the source of the individual's incentive for performing a task. If a task is undertaken in order to receive material or social rewards from others, the motivation for that task is extrinsic. If, on the other hand, the task is engaged in for the pleasure of the activity itself, the motivation is said to be intrinsic to the task. Both of these types of motivation can apply to a broad range of tasks, including achievement tasks (i.e., those involving competition with a standard of excellence, by the Atkinson and Crandall definitions). Although several different theoretical and research paradigms have been proposed for the study of intrinsic motivation (e.g., Day *et al.*, 1971; Deci, 1975; J. McV. Hunt, 1965), one that has been proposed by Lepper and Greene (1978) is essentially an attribution theory and thus is particularly relevant to the present discussion.

The Lepper and Greene approach, along with attribution theory in general, is an outgrowth of social psychological concerns with self-perception (e.g., Bem, 1972; Kelley, 1973). It is based on an assumption that the situation surrounding a task or activity provides the individual with information about his or her reasons for engaging in the activity. An individual who engages in an activity with little or no external pressure to do so is likely to infer that this participation was volitional or intrinsically motivated. If external pressures, on the other hand, are strong, clear, and "sufficient" to account for the behavior, that behavior is more likely to be seen as having been instigated or "caused" by those pressures. In the latter instance it is hypothesized that the individual will come to see the activity as relatively uninteresting and as being engaged in *only* for the sake of the external rewards or as a result of external pressures. An implication of this analysis is that the provision of external pressures or rewards for the performance of a task to an individual who had earlier engaged in the same task *without* external pressures or rewards (i.e., intrinsically) will cause a decrease in future intrinsic motivation for the task.

Several studies have reported results consistent with this hypothesis. Lepper, Greene, and Nisbett (1973) assessed intrinsic motivation for an art activity among a group of preschool children by unobtrusively timing their free-choice participation in the activity. Those who were judged as having shown intrinsic motivation for the activity were later asked to engage in it, under three different conditions—one in which they were told they could win an award for engaging in the activity, one in which they were given the award after engaging in the activity, but without having been told of it in advance, and one in which no reward was expected or received. Two weeks later, the initial free-choice activity was repeated and observed. It was found, as expected, that the children who had anticipated and received a reward for engaging in the activity later spent less time with it in the unrewarded situation than did those who had experienced the other two conditions, in which no reward had been expected or provided. The provision of rewards, according to the authors, had "undermined" the children's intrinsic interest in the activity.

Some other studies have indicated that for this effect to occur, the reward must be seen as having been contingent on the individual's behavior (Lepper & Greene, 1978). Furthermore, if a reward has a primarily informational function, as opposed to a primarily controlling function, it can enhance rather than diminish intrinsic motivation because the individual is using it as a means for judging performance rather than as a goal of the behavior (Deci & Porac, 1978). McGraw (1978) suggests that rewards should facilitate performance on tasks that are well structured and straightforward, but disrupt performance on tasks that require more thought and creativity in arriving at solutions. In addition, Kruglanski (1978) has summarized research evidence indicating that when tasks are oriented around the attainment of specific rewards, participants tend to do the minimum necessary to obtain the rewards, and tend to learn less incidental material than in situations not oriented around the provision of rewards. In the reward situation, attention is focused on the reward to the exclusion of other aspects of the task, whereas with intrinsic motivation, there is relatively more attention to the process.

The preceding results generally indicate negative effects of reward on intrinsic motivation for complex tasks among individuals with initially high levels of intrinsic task motivation. Implications for children with high levels of intrinsic motivation seem clear—rewards for performance of complex tasks should be used sparingly and should include informational components. But what are the implications for children with low levels of intrinsic task motivation? How can that motivation be developed? One consistent approach might be to begin with a fairly high level of reward containing clearly stressed informational components. After a persistent level of task participation has been achieved, the rewards (or at least the noninformational components) could gradually be reduced. If the child's performance level is maintained, and the child sees that the reward is insufficient to account for the task performance, the level of intrinsic motivation should increase.

Most of the studies in this area have looked at situational factors that cause increases or decreases in intrinsic motivation. A few have also looked at individual differences in intrinsic motivation, with the measurement consisting either of self-report questionnaires or of behavioral observations. In one study (Solomon & Houlihan, 1972), intrinsic motivation was operationally defined as the difference between children's persistence with tasks when an experimenter was present but uninvolved, and with parallel tasks when the experimenter was closely involved, attentive, and verbally praising.

Intrinsic motivation is seen by many as an important goal of education. Some recent educational movements (the "open school" movement, for example) have held that intrinsic motivation should be the prime determinant of children's educational participation, and that the development of a lifelong intrinsic orientation toward learning should be the major aim of teaching. The analysis of factors that enhance and that impede the development of intrinsic motivation could therefore have important implications for educational practices, particularly in settings and schools where these goals are held.

It seems possible, however, that an overly great emphasis on intrinsic motivation may be incompatible with striving for long-range goals. If individuals learn to strive only on tasks that they find immediately interesting and pleasurable, there may be little inclination to work on tasks that are steps toward the attainment of distant objectives but may, in themselves, be boring and tedious. The emphasis of intrinsic motivation seems to be on the immediate task rather than on distant goals or outcomes. An effort to make all school tasks immediately interesting may do a disservice to children if it impedes the development of orientations toward the attainment of future goals. Children may come to expect all tasks to be immediately interesting, and thus to avoid those that are not. The approach toward future goals that was developed by Raynor in the context of the Atkinson theory has proposed one way in which immediate and future tasks may be cognitively connected. Whether this approach is also applicable to intrinsic motivation is not clear, however. Intrinsic motivation seems, almost by definition, to be limited to immediate tasks, and not to apply to future goals. An educational approach that combines the two is conceivable, however. A teacher could identify long-range goals with logical connections to intrinsic task interests displayed by a child. If the child comes to see attainment of the long-range goal as a way to maintain and develop the intrinsic interest, the immediate motivation and long-range orientation could become mutually compatible.

The concepts of intrinsic and extrinsic motivation may also provide some additional insight into the differences between the Crandall and Atkinson theories of achievement, discussed earlier. The Crandall theory emphasizes the attainment of approval (internal *or* external) as a major goal. To the extent that the child is oriented toward external approval, it would seem to imply extrinsic motivation (particularly when the approval is not functioning as a source of information about task competence). The Atkinson theory posits an internal, general motive whose fulfillment or satisfaction is the major goal of achievement activity—implying an intrinsic orientation toward achievement. If task performance is seen as a means to an *intrinsic* end (self-judgment of competence), it is reasonable to hold that attainment value should be inversely related to subjective probability (or task difficulty). The more difficult a task one is able to perform successfully, the more competent one will have reason to feel. If, on the other hand, task performance is seen as a means to an *extrinsic* end (such as noninformational adult approval), it is reasonable to hold that attainment value should be unrelated to subjective probability (or task difficulty). If a reward is received, one will feel equally satisfied no matter how easy or difficult the task has been (assuming that receiving the reward is the only objective). If the reward is made contingent on both success and on the difficulty level of the task, elements of both extrinsic and intrinsic motivation would be present, and thus something intermediate between the two predictions might be expected. Generally then, it may be suggested that in intrinsic motivation, an important objective is self-appraisal, to which task difficulty is highly relevant; and that in extrinsic motivation, the major objective is reward attainment, for which task difficulty is irrelevant.

FACTORS INFLUENCING THE DEVELOPMENT OF
ACHIEVEMENT ORIENTATIONS AND DISPOSITIONS

The theories and research previously discussed have focused on the prediction of achievement behavior and outcomes in the immediate situation. A fair amount of work has also been done investigating longer range or more indirect determinants of achievement. Some of this work has incorporated concepts and frameworks from the theories described earlier, particularly those of Crandall and Crandall and of Atkinson. Other research on long-range determinants has derived from more general approaches to socialization and cognitive development, and still other research has been either theoretically eclectic or atheoretical. In this section, some of this research will be described; theoretical connections will be indicated where possible, but the emphasis here will be empirical.

Socialization practices

Factors in the child's social environment, particularly the home environment, that influence or promote the development of various of the variables central to the Crandall formulation have been investigated in several studies. Crandall, Preston, and Rabson (1960) found that the achievement behavior of 3-, 4-, and 5-year-old children (as rated by trained observers in nursery school free-play periods) was positively related to their mothers' tendencies to reward their approval seeking and their achievement efforts, but not to the amount of maternal affection displayed or to the amount of reward given by mothers for their children's help-seeking behavior. (The maternal variables were rated by trained observers in home interaction situations with their children.) The authors suggested that mothers' involvement in and reactions to specific achievement behaviors of their children appeared to promote the children's achievement behavior, whereas more indirect maternal reactions (such as overall affection and rewarding of general dependent behaviors) did not appear to promote it.

Crandall, Dewey, Katkovsky, and Preston (1964) interviewed fathers and mothers of second-, third-, and fourth-grade students and found significant effects relating several parent attitudes and self-reported behaviors of parents toward their children to measures of the children's reading and arithmetic achievement test performance. In this study also, the general parental behaviors showed less relationship with children's achievement than the more specific ones, with the exception of a subset of negative correlations between mothers' affection and nurturance and their daughters' achievement test scores. Parent attainment values tended not to be related to their children's achievement. Their evaluations of the child's work in general, their satisfaction with that work, and their achievement standards tended to be positively related to childrens' achievement (particularly for girls, and more strongly for mothers than fathers). In contrast, parental instigation of children's achievement activities, parental participation with the child in such activities, and negative reactions to the child's achievement activities tended to be negatively related to children's achievement levels. It was suggested that the negative relationships of instigation and participation to achievement may have indicated a parental reaction to child performance (with parents more likely to participate with children who are having school difficulties). The fact that relationships between parent behavior and child achievement were stronger and more numerous for girls than for boys was attributed to a possible greater susceptibility to adult influence by girls (compared with a more autonomous and independent approach to achievement by boys). This suggestion was also made by V. J. Crandall (1963) in reviewing other studies with similar sets of findings.

Although the Atkinson theory of achievement motivation has not focused specifically on achievement in children, some of the earlier writings (e.g., McClelland et al., 1953) included some retrospective data, and some speculation about parent socialization practices that might be expected to promote the development of achievement motivation in children. It was predicted by McClelland that achievement motivation would develop out of early affective experiences involving mastery attempts. Parental encouragement, training, and rewards would be important in providing these experiences. Some of these speculations were tested by Winterbottom (1958). She administered a questionnaire to mothers of elementary-school-age boys, asking about their practices with their children in earlier years. It was found that mothers of boys with high need-for-achievement scores reported that they had expected early self-reliant behavior from their sons, had given frequent and intense rewards for success, and had placed few restrictions on their sons' independence. When the same boys and their mothers were followed up by Feld (1967) after 6 years, it was found that early maternal independence training was less strongly related to sons' achievement motivation during adolescence than during childhood, and that maternal reactions to their sons' achievement efforts during adolescence were also only weakly related to the sons' achievement motivation.

In the study by Smith (1969), alluded to earlier, parents of fourth- and fifth-grade boys were given questionnaires similar in several respects to those used by Winterbottom, Feld, and others. Parents were asked at what ages they had made various demands for independence of their sons and how they typically reacted to their sons' achievement efforts (successes and failures). There were slight trends indicating that earliness of independence training and of caretaking expectations related to the development of achievement motivation. These parent variables did not relate to the children's test-anxiety scores. Factors representing child-rearing values were derived from items concerning the importance of various child behaviors and qualities, including values for independence, assertive achievement (involving competition), and responsible achievement (doing one's best, taking pride in doing things well, etc.). Parental value factor scores were unrelated to sons' achievement motivation, but a few individual value items were related to test anxiety (with high achievement values related to greater anxiety).

Parental reactions to successes and failures showed some moderate associations with the achievement-related motives. High need-for-achievement scores were related to verbal encouragement from mothers and infrequent anger from fathers in response to failure, and verbal rewards but infrequent hugging and kissing from mothers in response to successes. Test anxiety seemed to be highest for children whose parents expressed love and approval only in response to success (i.e., it was made contingent on the child's success). Thus, children high in achievement motivation received positive, but not overly demonstrative, parental reactions in response to both success *and* failure, whereas those high in test anxiety received such reactions only when they succeeded.

Somewhat different results were obtained by Teevan and McGhee (1972) in a study of maternal influences on the development of boys' fear of failure. They used a version of the Winterbottom questionnaire to assess early demands for mastery, and TAT slides as stimuli for stories from which fear-of-failure themes (or "hostile press,"—Birney, Burdick, & Teevan, 1969) were scored. Mothers of boys with high fear of failure expected earlier independence and achievement behaviors than mothers of boys with low fear of failure. There were also differences in the typical responses to their sons' failure (as self-reported) between these two groups of mothers. Those with high fear-of-failure sons typically responded neutrally to good performance and punished bad performance, whereas those with low fear-of-failure sons typically rewarded good performance and were neutral to bad performance. The authors suggest that early training expectations and demands may be similar for the development of achievement motivation and that of fear of failure, but that the pattern of reinforcement in response to the child's performance may determine the direction in which the motivational disposition develops. The early expectations may create the emphasis on achievement concerns; the reinforcement pattern may then help to determine whether the child will develop a positive or negative attitude toward achievement.

The Winterbottom (1958) study, and several of the others that most directly derive from it, have focused on the *timing* of parental independence and caretaking demands. The general prediction was that earlier independence training would lead to higher levels of achievement motivation. Veroff (1965) has proposed that there must be an interaction between the timing of demands and the child's perceptual and cognitive capacities to differentiate between different affects and different stimulating conditions. He suggests that the development of general motives should be maximized by giving mastery training at a time when the child has only a slight ability to differentiate between stimulating conditions. Because the child is not entirely clear about the differentiation between conditions, the motive that develops will tend to generalize across conditions. If training comes later, when the differentiation is clearer, motive development will tend to be tied to much more specific conditions. If, on the other hand, demands are too early, it is expected that strong negative motivational dispositions may develop. Timing must, of course, also take account of the physical capacities of the child with regard to the object of mastery (e.g., learning to walk, to talk).

Rosen and D'Andrade (1959) studied parental training from a contemporaneous perspective (with observations of parent–child interaction) rather than a retrospective perspective (with parent self-reports of earlier behaviors and practices). They proposed a distinction between "achievement training" (to do things well) and "independence training" (to do things by oneself), and predicted that the former should be more related to the development of achievement motivation. The researchers observed parents and their sons during the performance of several tasks, some of which were done by the sons alone (with parental advice and encouragement) and some of which required parental participation. The boys' need for achievement was measured with a projective procedure (with TAT pictures). The general finding was that achievement training was more important to the development of achievement motivation than was independence training. It was also found that the behavior of mothers and fathers was more differentiated in these situations for the high-achievement-motivation children than the low-achievement-motivation children. Fathers of those with high need-for-achievement scores tended to give their sons substantial degrees of self-reliance and autonomy, whereas the mothers showed more active participation, more emotional involvement (with expressions of both warmth and rejection), and more active concern with the child's success.

One of the more comprehensive studies of the socialization determinants of children's achievement orientations was conducted by Solomon *et al.* (1971) among fifth-grade black children in an inner-city Chicago neighborhood. This study investigated links between variables in several of the areas identified in Figure 7.1, including parent behavior, child personality, child achievement behavior, and child achievement outcomes. Parent behavior and parent–child interaction were measured while the child was working on a series of tasks in the home and the parents were giving advice and encouragement (similar to the procedure used by Rosen & D'Andrade, 1959). Child personality variables included the Crandall internal–external control measure (the Intellectual Achievement Responsibility Questionnaire, or IAR), projective assessments of hope for success and fear of failure, and another locus of control scale for children (Bialer, 1961). Children's achievement behavior was measured in two settings—in experimental tasks, individually, and in classroom settings, among classmates. Achievement behavior assessed in these settings included perseverance, attention, and apparent interest. Achievement outcomes included quality of performance on the individually administered tasks, grade average, and achievement test scores. IQ was also assessed, and considered another index of achievement.

A large number of parent behavior items were assessed and reduced to a smaller number of underlying "dimensions" through factor analysis. The father behavior factors were interpreted as representing general verbal participation, geniality, hostility, and interest in the situation and the tasks. The mother behavior factors appeared to reflect participation, encouragement of independent achievement efforts, warmth, and general interest. Items referring to the child's achievement behavior and achievement outcomes were also factor analyzed, resulting in the following six factors: general academic achievement, achievement behavior in classroom individual work situations, achievement behavior in classroom recitation situations, task perseverance, divergent task achievement behavior, and convergent task achievement behavior. (Divergent tasks are those with multiple possible appropriate responses; convergent tasks, those with only one.) The emergence of multiple achievement behavior factors (presented in detail in Solomon, 1969b) was considered evidence consistent with the Crandall assumption that achievement behavior tends not to generalize across achievement areas (although this finding went somewhat beyond the Crandall assumption, since it was a demonstration of behavioral diversity between tasks within a single achievement area rather than between areas).

Several of the parent behavior factors were significantly associated with child personality variables. For example, fathers' encouragement of independent achievement efforts related positively to boys' internal control (IAR) and hope for success. At the same time, a moderate amount of general interest shown by mothers related to maximal scores with respect to girls' hope for success and fear of failure.

Internal control was the only one of the child personality variables to relate clearly and strongly to achievement behavior or achievement outcomes. The measure of responsibility for positive outcomes (I+) showed strong positive associations with boys' general academic achievement and perseverance, and moderate positive associations with girls' academic achievement and divergent task performance. The total IAR score also related positively to boys' academic achievement. The measure of hope for success showed a moderate positive association with girls' general academic achievement, and an inverted-U-shaped relationship (with the moderate position optimal) with girls' perseverance.

The preceding sets of findings suggested that there were general relationships between parental behavior and child achievement that were being mediated by child personality. When direct relationships were examined between the parent behavior factors and the achievement factors, some were consistent with this assumption and some were not. Additional mediational possibilities were examined by looking at several more specific behavioral indices of the child's behavior in the home interaction situations. There was some suggestive evidence that fathers' overly intense participation in their sons' tasks evoked negative emotional responses in the boys, which in turn impacted negatively on their achievement behavior and achievement outcomes. Mothers who participated intensely seemed to have negative effects on boys' achievement (through an intermediate negative effect on locus of control), but positive effects on girls' achievement (through intermediate positive effects on girls' energy, interest, and positive emotion). It was suggested that some of these findings might represent the negative effects of parent intrusiveness or dominance. Some positive relationships also occurred. The strongest showed a link between fathers' encouragement of independent achievement efforts and girls' convergent task striving, and between mothers' warmth in the task situation and girls' general academic achievement.

Some of these results seemed most consistent with a modeling–identification view of the influence of parents on children, whereas others seemed more consistent with a reinforcement approach. The possibility that some of the relationships might be reflecting parental responses to child behavior was also raised. Parents might be inclined to participate in their children's tasks most when the children generally have difficulty with tasks; thus, negative relationships between parent participation and child achievement efforts and performance could indicate a parental reaction to poor performance rather than an inhibiting effect of parental participation on the child's performance. (A similar suggestion, relating to some similar findings, was made by Crandall *et al.*, 1964.)

Although some consistencies in results are apparent across these socialization studies, the results have not been clear or consistent enough for one to derive generalizations with a great degree of confidence. Furthermore, relatively few of the studies have included girls, and those that have have tended to find different patterns of relationships for girls and for boys. It may be useful, nevertheless, to summarize the similarities in findings that have emerged.

Several of the studies gave evidence that parental responses in specific achievement situations (including reward for approval seeking, achievement efforts and successes) related positively to children's achievement motivation, behavior, and outcomes. Earliness of training seems important to achievement motivation, but whether it is achievement training, independence training, or self-caretaking is not entirely clear. Fathers' provision of autonomy and encouragement of independence may be important. Finally, parent participation with children in their achievement efforts may be helpful to a point, but if it is too often or too intense, negative effects begin to emerge, reflecting either children's negative responses to parental domination or parental responses to children's poor achievement.

There is also some evidence that child personality and immediate behavioral reactions can play an intervening role in the relationship between parent behavior and child achievement.

The Winterbottom (1958), Feld (1967), and Smith (1969) studies, described earlier, were at least partly longitudinal in the sense that parents were asked to describe their earlier behaviors and expectations with their children, and variables derived from these recollections were related to current measures of the children's achievement and achievement motivation levels. Another way to do longitudinal studies, of course, is to obtain data from the same people over a long period of time. A large study of this type, described in two reports (Crandall & Battle, 1970; V. C. Crandall, undated), has examined long-term effects of parent socialization practices and children's early achievement tendencies and dispositions on adult academic effort, intellectual effort, and locus of control. The antecedent variables in this study included maternal behavior observed at regular intervals by a "home visitor" attached to the longitudinal project, and periodic ratings of the child's achievement behavior and relationships with parents and other adults.

Some of the results suggested that academic effort and orientation can develop out of a sensitivity to adult approval and influence. At the same time, it appeared that individuals whose parents had been relatively cool and aloof were more likely to develop their own inclinations, with less reliance or dependence on adult approval or disapproval. These and some similar parent behavior variables that here showed positive effects on independent achievement orientations when studied longitudinally have in other studies (in which the socialization and achievement variables were assessed contemporaneously) shown generally negative effects with children. The authors suggested that positive and affectionate relationships with parents during childhood may help give children the security and confidence to make achievement efforts and to feel that they control the contingencies, but that these same positive relationships may in the longer range unintentionally limit the child's fields of endeavors. Children with more critical and less affectionate home environments, on the other hand, may be impelled to try their hands in various areas, to become more dependent on their own judgments and their own evaluations, and thus eventually more likely to feel that they are in control of the outcomes of their own efforts.

Developmental stages

Several investigators have looked at the process or sequence of phases of the development of achievement orientations in children. Veroff (1969), in an approach closely related to the Atkinson framework, proposed a sequence of development across three stages, involving two distinct types of achievement motivation. He suggested that *autonomous achievement motivation* was the earliest stage of achievement motivation and developed out of earlier attempts at mastery. This stage or type of motivation involves the application of internal standards to one's goal-directed efforts. The self-evaluation necessary for it, according to Veroff, requires language ability and thus this stage probably does not begin before the child is $1\frac{1}{2}$ or 2 years old. The second stage is one of *social comparison achievement motivation,* and involves the comparison of one's own performance with that of others; the performance of others thus defines the achievement standards. It is suggested that this second stage begins during the early school years, when children first have many opportunities to compare their own efforts and performances with those of others. Its appearance, according to the theory, depends on the successful mastery of the prior, autonomous stage. The third stage involves the *integration* of autonomous and social comparison achievement motivation, and depends on the prior mastery of both prior types of motivation. In this stage, the individual is able to be guided by both types of motivations or by one primarily, if it is particularly relevant to the situation faced.

Veroff developed or adapted several methods to measure each of the three types of achievement motivation. For example, a task-repetition technique was used to assess autonomous achievement motivation, on the assumption that individuals with high levels of this motive would choose to repeat moderately difficult tasks (this combined the theoretical notions of Atkinson with a procedure of Crandall's). One of the methods used to assess social comparison achievement motivation was to ask a child to select a task to try that either "most" or "some" children of the same age can do, or "most" cannot do. Selection of the task that some could do was considered evidence of this type of motivation. For the measure of the integrated motive, Veroff used a projective assessment of stories told in response to ambiguous pictures, similar to the typical adult assessment of need for achievement. It was assumed that composing stories to these pictures required both individual autonomy concerns and sensitivity to the achievement activities and orientations of the different characters in the stories; hence both autonomous and social elements would be included. The validity of these assumptions was not directly assessed, however.

Veroff presented data that gave some support to the sequence of stages that he proposed. Each type of motivation was assessed with children of different ages. The fantasy measure was correlated with the autonomous achievement motivation measure at grade 1, with the normative level of aspiration measure of social comparison motivation at grades 3 and 4 (for boys only), and with both types at grades 5 and 6 (again, only for boys). These results occured only with boys, but seemed consistent with the notion that achievement motivation was expressed primarily autonomously for young children, through social comparison processes for slightly older children, and through both for still older children. When age trends were examined with each type of measure, the following results were obtained for children of both sexes: The choice of the "challenging" level of the normative social comparison task increased with age to grades 4 and 5. At the same time, the autonomous achievement motivation scores were highest between grades 2 and 4, with a decline in later grades. Finally, the fantasy measure (presumably reflecting the integrated motivation) showed regular increases through all the elementary grades included in the study (ending with grade 6). Studies examining some other implications of the theory are also described in the Veroff chapter.

Some other researchers have adopted the Veroff typology to examine developmental changes in achievement motivation. Feld, Ruhland, and

Gold (1979) assessed the different types of achievement motivation in first- and fourth-grade students. Each group of students was tested during one spring and the following fall and spring with several of the Veroff measures. The students also told fantasy stories, in response to verbal leads, which were scored for imagery relating to each of the three types of motivation. Although scores on the social comparison measures of motivation were clearly higher for the older group of students, as predicted by the Veroff theory, differences in the opposite direction for the measures of autonomous achievement motivation were not found. However, the ratio of social comparison to autonomous imagery, in the projective stories, did increase with age (and also showed some longitudinal changes across the three testing periods for each age group). For children in the lower grades, the autonomous motivation measure was more highly correlated with school performance than the social comparison measure; the reverse was somewhat true for children at the higher grades (but only for the projective measures).

The authors suggest that these results indicate that the development of achievement motivation is not so much a *transformation* from a primary reliance on autonomous standards to a primary reliance on social standards, as an *addition* of a concern for social standards to an existing concern for autonomous ones. Thus, in their view, the integration of the two types of motivation is a gradual and continuing process, beginning somewhat earlier than Veroff hypothesized.

NONINTERACTIONAL AND INTERACTIONAL ASSUMPTIONS IN THE STUDY OF ACHIEVEMENT

An issue cutting across much of the research and theory presented in the earlier sections of this chapter concerns the degree to which influences on achievement are expected to be simple and direct on the one hand, or the product of interactions between two or more predictive factors, on the other. Many research models focus on "main effects" and consider the effect of each predictor variable to be separate from and independent of the effects of others. Other models pay much more attention to the possibility that the effect of one variable may be conditioned or partially determined by the influence of one or more others.

The general scheme shown earlier (Figure 7.1) includes several joined arrows that represent the possibility of interactional effects combining the influences of situational factors with those of personal factors. Although interactions have been given more attention in recent years, the bulk of research on achievement (as well as in other areas of psychological and social–scientific investigation) has been noninteractional: The emphasis in any single study has been on person effects *or* situation effects, but not on the two combined. In this section, some of the major directions and findings of the noninteractional research will be briefly summarized, and some approaches that emphasize the investigation of interactive effects will be described.

Person effects

A "person" characteristic, in this context, is any enduring aspect of the individual that is brought into an achievement situation. Thus, such variables as social class, ethnic background, family size, and birth order could be included, along with such variables as achievement-related motives, beliefs, attitudes, and abilities. Variables of each of these types have been shown to be related to children's achievement outcomes, achievement behavior, and/or achievement dispositions. Measures of intelligence and prior performance in a given area are generally the strongest predictors of subsequent performance. Academic achievement, achievement motivation, and achievement behavior generally have been shown to be higher for middle class than lower class children, for white than for black children, for earlier born than later born children, and for those from small rather than large families (Banks, McQuater, & Hubbard, 1978; Baughman & Dahlstrom, 1968; Cicirelli, 1978; Deutsch, Katz, & Jensen, 1968; Solomon, 1969a). Numerous mechanisms have been proposed to account for these effects, but little concensus concerning them has been achieved. The sorts of motivational, attitudinal, and cognitive mechanisms contained in the theories previously discussed have functioned as intervening variables in some of these explanations. These variables themselves constitute person characteristics; their effects on achievement behavior and outcomes in children also have been investigated (in some of the studies discussed earlier, as well as in other studies).

Situation effects

Situational variables of relevance to achievement can include manipulated task characteristics in experiments, as well as various aspects of natural achievement settings and situations, such as teaching style and classroom atmosphere. A number of the experimental task variables that have been manipulated in various studies have been discussed earlier in the context of the several approaches (e.g., task difficulty in the Atkinson approach; approval–disapproval in the Crandall approach; manipulations of situational contingencies in research relating to attribution theory and locus of control).

A large number of educational research investigations have studied the effects of various situational characteristics of classrooms on academic achievement outcomes for students. Some of these have been experiments, in which students are taught in different experimental "treatments" to which they have been randomly assigned. Others have been "naturalistic" studies in which the normal process of classroom activities is observed and variables derived from the observations are related to the achievement outcomes. Some researchers have conducted educational experiments in which some of the treatments were developed on the basis of the results of naturalistic classroom studies (Gage, 1978).

Some of the classroom studies (e.g., McDonald & Elias, 1976) have converged on a concept of "direct instruction" as being generally maximally effective in promoting the academic achievement of elementary school children. Rosenshine (1976a, 1976b) has defined the concept of direct instruction as including (*a*) the amount of time spent on academic activities; (*b*) seat work with structured materials; (*c*) the use of narrow, direct, and focused questions; (*d*) immediate feedback to students; (*e*) closely monitored group work: (*f*) teacher control, dominance, and business-like behavior; (*g*) systematically organized sequences involving small steps; and (*h*) clear goals—all combined with teacher warmth, conviviality, and use of praise.

Person-by-situation interactions

An interaction effect is a joint, nonadditive effect on a dependent variable of two or more independent variables. If, for example, the effect of the competitiveness of an achievement task depended on the level of achievement motivation of the individual, such that those with high motivation performed best in the most competitive tasks and those with low motivation performed best in the least competitive tasks, an interaction would be present. Much current educational practice is based on the assumption that children who differ in knowledge, ability, cognitive skill, cognitive style, or personality may perform best with different educational programs (e.g., individualized instruction, diagnostic–prescriptive teaching, "alternative" programs); yet extensive research on this topic is relatively recent. In the past several years, however, interest in the investigation of person–situation interactions has greatly expanded, both in psychology (e.g., Ekehammer, 1974; Endler & Magnusson, 1976) and in education (e.g., Cronbach & Snow, 1977; D. E. Hunt, 1971, 1975).

Some aspects of both the Atkinson and the Crandall approaches to achievement involve elements that are, to a degree, consistent with the notion of person–situation interactions. Thus, in the Atkinson theory, task difficulty is a situational factor that is suggested to interact with resultant achievement motivation, so that the optimal task difficulty level for those whose primary aim is to achieve success is different from the optimal level for those whose primary aim is to avoid failure. (Task difficulty seems to be the only situational variable in the Atkinson theory; however.) In the Crandall theory, the achievement area represented by a task interacts with the individual's attainment values and expectancies for that area to influence achievement behavior. The effect of expectancy on behavior will be different in a valued area from that in a nonvalued area.

This focus on the distinction between achievement areas is an aspect of the Crandall assumption that achievement behavior tends not to generalize across areas. This assumption (also made by Mischel, 1968, 1973; and others) conflicts with some traditional notions in personality and "trait" theories that expect a greater degree of behavioral consistency across situations. An approach to this issue, in the context of achievement, has been made by Solomon (1977). Ninth-grade boys were given a series of descriptions of 12 different striving tasks and asked to rate their liking for each and their judgment of the degree of similarity between each pair of tasks. The standard deviation of each individual's preference scores, across tasks, was considered a measure of cross-task consistency. There was a good bit of variation on this measure, indicating that some boys did tend to generalize across tasks and some did not. There was also evidence that the perceptions of the similarity between tasks could be serving a mediating function: Those whose preferences were closer together tended to see the tasks as more similar, whereas those whose preferences were more spread tended to see the tasks as less similar. It might be expected that the achievement behavior of those who tended to generalize across tasks ("generalizers") would be primarily influenced by person factors, whereas the achievement behavior of those who tended not to generalize across tasks ("specifiers") would be relatively more strongly determined by situation factors. For the group as a whole, this would imply a person-by-situation interaction.

In this study, Solomon proposed the notion of task "preferences" as a primary motivational variable. This is similar to the Crandall concept of attainment value but is applied to a specific task rather than an achievement area. The notion of preferences seems well suited for one kind of an interactional approach. It is suggested that individuals will perform best in tasks that they prefer (or which they perceive as similar to those they prefer). This implies an interaction, for it suggests that certain individuals will perform optimally with some tasks, whereas others will do so with other tasks. A "preferential" model is one of three proposed by Salomon (1972) for interactional research in education. In this model, the attempt is made to "match" the skills and motives of the student with characteristics of the educational situation. The other two models proposed by Salomon are called "remedial" (in which the individual is taught prerequisite skills in which he is deficient) and "compensatory" (in which the student's deficiencies are bypassed either by providing substitutes for them or eliminating the need for them).

Most of the research on person-by-situation interactions (which in educational research has come to be known as aptitude–treatment interaction, or ATI) has involved small numbers of variables in experimental settings—often one or two person variables and one or two situation variables. Thus Grimes and Allinsmith (1961) reported that highly anxious (and compulsive) children made more progress in reading achievement with a structured (phonic) treatment than with an unstructured (whole word) treatment. In another study, Baron, Cowan, Ganz, and McDonald (1974) showed that the "form discrimination" of lower class black children was maximal for those with an internal locus of control in a "self-discovery of success" condition (involving intrinsic feedback), and was maximal for those with an external locus of control in an "unverifiable verbal praise" condition (involving extrinsic feedback). Some research on open and traditional education has found interactions indicating that open classes elicited more creativity from low-anxious children (Klein, 1975), more satisfaction for "internals" (Arlin, 1975; Judd, 1974), more learning for "persistent" boys (Reiss & Dyhdalo, 1975), better achievement for high-SES children (Epstein & McPartland, 1975), and better reading and math achievement for boys with low prior achievement (Bennett, 1976). Ward and Barcher (1975) found that high-IQ children performed better with respect to reading and creativity in traditional than in open classes. A program of research directed by D. E. Hunt (1971, 1975) has found interactions between students' "conceptual level" and "task structure." Those with a high conceptual level (including cognitive complexity and interpersonal maturity) perform best in situations with low structure (or they are unaffected by variations in structure); those with a low conceptual level perform best in situations with greater degrees of structure. The first group seems to benefit from situations that require their own intellectual performance; the latter group, from those without such requirements.

Cronbach and Snow (1977) produced an extensive review and critique of ATI research. They identified one general motivational variable that had shown fairly extensive evidence of interactive effects. They called this variable "constructive motivation," and summarized the evidence as indicating that constructively motivated students perform best in situations that are less directive, more spontaneous, and which require students to take more active roles.

Some of the interactive studies done since the time of the Cronbach and Snow review have become more complex and have included larger numbers of variables. Thus, Peterson (1977) reported a four-way interaction involving student ability, student anxiety, structuredness of instruction, and amount of class participation.

Solomon and Kendall (1979) attempted a complex, multivariate interactive study in a natural setting, and with a "natural state" approach. Repeated structured observations were made by trained observers of teacher and student behavior and classroom atmosphere in 50 fourth-grade classrooms during an academic year. Outcome variables included academic achievement, creativity, inquiry skill, satisfaction, writing skill, and some social attitudes. A number of child motivational variables (locus of control, achievement motivation, fear of failure, preference for structured settings) were also assessed. Each set of variables (classroom, outcome, personality) was reduced to a smaller number of dimensions through factor analysis. Cluster analysis was also used to develop a typology of classrooms and a typology of students. Each classroom cluster contained classrooms that had similar profiles in terms of the observed characteristics. Similarly, each child cluster contained children whose profiles of personality and prior achievement scores were similar. Analyses of variance were then computed to identify interactions between the classroom clusters and the child clusters. Interaction results were obtained indicating that students with low levels of motivation and prior achievement performed best in permissive, varied, warm, and expressive classes, whereas students with high levels of motivation and prior achievement did best in classes that combined teacher control and an orderly approach to tasks with the provision of opportunities for students to initiate varied activities. It was suggested that for the first group of children, the class situation was helping to provide the motivation that they lacked, whereas for the second group, additional motivation was not required and the children benefited by a setting that allowed them to progress with the development of relatively advanced academic skills and to be somewhat self-directing in the process. There was also some evidence that children who stated a preference for autonomy actually did better in some respects in more structured situations, and that those with a preference for greater structure obtained some benefits from experiencing autonomy. In these instances it seemed that the more effective situation for them was one that they would ordinarily tend to avoid, and that experience in a nonpreferred situation was possibly helping to temper unduly one-sided inclinations.

CURRENT STATUS OF RESEARCH ON CHILDREN'S ACHIEVEMENT

Each of the approaches to the study of children's achievement described in this chapter is still under active development. It is interesting, however, that few of the approaches are strictly developmental or concern themselves primarily with children. Most of the theories described are general theories; research done in their furtherance has sometimes included children as subjects and has therefore contributed to developmental knowledge even when that was not the primary intention. Further research and theoretical development that examines in detail the development of achievement orientations throughout childhood seems clearly needed. Longitudinal research of the kind reported by Crandall and Battle (1970) is extremely important in this regard, but is, of course, very difficult to arrange. Longitudinal research projects of shorter span (perhaps 3 or 4 years) would be easier to set up and could provide important contributions to knowledge in this area; it is to be hoped that more of these will be done.

Some of the research described here has reflected certain recent trends and methodological developments. One of these newer trends emphasizes examining children's behavior in the actual environments of daily life. Experiments are necessarily artificial, and it is often difficult to know the degree to which experimental findings can be generalized to natural settings. Some experiments have attempted to reproduce situational parameters identified in naturalistic studies, but even these can handle only a few variables at a time. The essential feature of a natural situation is its multivariate complexity. It therefore seems necessary for studies that aim to be faithful to the exigencies of actual situations to sample widely among the variables that are present and to use multivariate statistical methods, such as factor analysis, cluster analysis, causal modeling, multiple regression, and canonical correlation, to handle the natural groupings, mutual and reciprocal influences, and complex interactions that may occur in those situations. Although efforts have been made in this direction, much more remains to be done. An emphasis on natural situations also implies the necessity for the development of taxonomies of the situations that are relevant to children's achievement. Solomon (1969b) suggested that achievement tasks could be categorized according to their behavioral requirements, social requirements, and cognitive requirements; this represents one of many possible approaches to the development of a taxonomy of achievement tasks.

The development of research approaches that examine the interactions between child variables and situational variables requires much more detailed analysis and understanding of situational parameters than has yet been achieved. The importance of analyzing the situation in as much detail as the person has been emphasized by several social scientists (e.g., Fredericksen, 1972; Shulman, 1970; Snow, 1974). Although this suggestion has been applied both to experiments (as an argument for increasing their "ecological validity") and to natural-state studies, it seems particularly consistent with the latter, since they are exploring the natural situation to begin with. Thus, it can be argued that there should be substantial efforts to conduct multivariate studies in natural situations and to focus on exploring interactions between person characteristics and situational characteristics in those studies. A strategy that fluctuates between naturalistic and experimental studies (using experiments to conduct explicit causal tests of relationships identified in naturalistic studies) has been attempted (e.g., Gage, 1978), and seems worthy of further development.

Further development of comprehensive approaches to the study of children's achievement also would be useful. Figure 7.1 laid out a rough model of factors that are believed to impact on children's achievement. Yet there is no single study that has included variables from all the areas identified, and very few that cover more than two or three. Understanding of the determinants of children's achievement will depend on knowledge of the various linkages between the various areas and the specific factors. Although this can be partially accomplished in a piecemeal fashion by attempting to integrate different linkages identified in separate studies, it would appear to be more fruitful, ultimately, to include as many of these as possible within single studies (involving large samples) so that interactions among the various levels and areas can be explored. This, again, is not to say that this is the only way in which children's achievement should be studied. There is a need for small-scale studies as well, for they can explore minute particulars (e.g., specific sequences of interaction between teachers and students) that cannot be handled with the large samples necessary for large and comprehensive studies. But the smaller studies would be more meaningful and more useful if conducted within a context developed in a comprehensive approach. Reciprocal interplay between the two types of studies could be very beneficial.

Ultimately, accumulations of studies such as these could lead to the development of an inclusive, integrated theory that would encompass within it both long-range and short-range determinants of achievement behavior and outcomes. Developmental aspects, socialization aspects, environmental influences, perceptions, motives, goals, and expectancies all should have a place within this theory.

The investigations and approaches described in this chapter have, in several cases, accumulated an impressive amount of theory verification. There have as yet, however, been very few attempts to combine or integrate them, or to conduct studies to test contrasting predictions of the different theories. Such attempts could be quite valuable and could lay the groundwork for the development of a more inclusive and general theory than has yet been achieved.

REFERENCES

Arlin, M. The interaction of locus of control, classroom structure, and pupil satisfaction. *Psychology in the Schools,* 1975, *12,* 279–286.

Atkinson, J. W. (Ed.). *Motives in fantasy, action and society.* Princeton, N.J.: Van Nostrand-Reinhold, 1958.

Atkinson, J. W., & Feather, N. T. (Eds.). *A theory of achievement motivation.* New York: Wiley, 1966.

Atkinson, J. W., & Raynor, J. O. *Personality, motivation, and achievement.* New York: Wiley, 1978.

Banks, W. C., McQuater, G. V., & Hubbard, J. L. Toward a reconceptualization of the social–cognitive bases of achievement orientations in blacks. *Review of Educational Research,* 1978, *48,* 381–397.

Baron, R. M., Cowan, G., Ganz, R. L., & McDonald, M. Interaction of locus of control and type of performance feedback: Considerations of external validity. *Journal of Personality and Social Psychology,* 1974, *30,* 285–292.

Bar-Tal, D. Attributional analysis of achievement-related behavior. *Review of Educational Research,* 1978, *48,* 259–271.

Battle, E. S. Motivational determinants of academic task persistence. *Journal of Personality and Social Psychology,* 1965, *2,* 209–218.

Battle, E. S. Motivational determinants of academic competence. *Journal of Personality and Social Psychology,* 1966, *4,* 634–642.

Baughman, E., & Dahlstrom, W. G. *Negro and white children: A psychological study in the rural south.* New York: Academic Press, 1968.

Bem, D. J. Self-perception theory. In L. Berkowitz (Ed.), *Advances in experimental social psychology* (Vol. 6). New York: Academic Press, 1972. Pp. 2–62.

Bennett, N. *Teaching styles and pupil progress.* Cambridge, Mass.: Harvard Univ. Press, 1976.

Bialer, I. Conceptualization of success and failure in mentally retarded and normal children. *Journal of Personality,* 1961, *29,* 303–320.

Birney, R. C., Burdick, H., & Teevan, R. C. *Fear of failure.* New York: Van Nostrand-Reinhold, 1969.

Canavan-Gumpert, D., Garner, K., & Gumpert, P. *The success-fearing personality.* Lexington, Mass.: Lexington Books, 1978.

Chapin, M., & Dyck, D. G. Persistence of children's reading behavior as a function of N length and attribution retraining. *Journal of Abnormal Psychology,* 1976, *85,* 511–515.

Cicirelli, V. G. The relationship of sibling structure to intellectual abilities and achievement. *Review of Educational Research,* 1978, *48,* 365–379.

Crandall, V. C. *Parent's influences on children's achievement behavior* (Progress Report, USPHS Grant No. MH–02238). Yellow Springs, Ohio: Fels Institute, 1965.

Crandall, V. C. Sex differences in expectancy of intellectual and academic reinforcement. In. C. P. Smith (Ed.), *Achievement-related motives in children.* New York: Russell Sage Foundation, 1969. Pp. 11–45.

Crandall, V. C. The Fels study: Some contributions to personality development and achievement in childhood and adulthood. *Seminars in Psychiatry,* 1972, *4,* 383–397.

Crandall, V. C. *Differences in antecedents of internal–external control assessed in childhood and in young adulthood.* Yellow Springs, Ohio: Fels Institute, undated.

Crandall, V. C., & Battle, E. S. The antecedents and adult correlates of academic and intellectual achievement effort. In J. P. Hill (Ed.), *Minnesota Symposia on Child Psychology* (Vol. 4). Minneapolis: Univ. of Minnesota Press, 1970. Pp. 36–93.

Crandall, V. C., Katkovsky, W., & Crandall, V. J. Children's beliefs in their own control of reinforcements in intellectual–academic situations. *Child Development,* 1965, *36,* 91–109.

Crandall, V. C., & McGhee, P. E. Expectancy of reinforcement and academic competence. *Journal of Personality,* 1968, *36,* 635–648.

Crandall, V. J. Achievement. In H. Stevenson (Ed.), *Child psychology. Sixty-second yearbook of the National Society for the Study of Education.* Chicago: NSSE, 1963. Pp. 416–459.

Crandall, V. J., Dewey, R., Katkovsky, W., & Preston, A. Parents' attitudes and behaviors and grade school children's achievement development. *Journal of Genetic Psychology,* 1964, *104,* 53–66.

Crandall, V. J., Katkovsky, W., & Preston, A. A conceptual formulation for some research on children's achievement behavior. *Child Development,* 1960, *31,* 787–797.

Crandall, V. J., Katkovsky, W., & Preston, A. Motivational and ability determinants of young children's achievement behavior. *Child Development,* 1962, *33,* 643–661.

Crandall, V. J., Preston, A., & Rabson, A. Maternal reactions and the development of independence and achievement behavior in young children. *Child Development,* 1960, *31,* 243–251.

Crandall, V. J., & Rabson, A. Children's repetition choices in an intellectual achievement situation following success and failure. *Journal of Genetic Psychology,* 1960, *97,* 161–168.

Crandall, V. J., Solomon, D., & Kellaway, R. Expectancy statements and decision times as functions of objective probabilities and reinforcement values. *Journal of Personality,* 1955, *24,* 192–203.

Crandall, V. J., Solomon, D., & Kellaway, R. The value of anticipated events as a determinant of probability learning and extinction. *Journal of Genetic Psychology,* 1958, *58,* 3–10.

Cronbach, L. J., & Snow, R. E. *Aptitudes and instructional methods.* New York: Irvington, 1977.

Day, H. I., Berlyne, D. E., & Hunt, D. E. *Intrinsic motivation: A new direction in education.* Toronto: Ontario Institute for Studies in Education, 1971.

DeCharms, R. *Personal causation.* New York: Academic Press, 1968.

DeCharms, R. Personal causation training in the schools. *Journal of Applied Psychology,* 1972, *2,* 95–113.

Deci, E. L. *Intrinsic motivation.* New York: Plenum, 1975.

Deci, E. L., & Porac, J. Cognitive evaluation theory and the study of human motivation. In M. R. Lepper & D. Greene (Eds.), *The hidden costs of reward.* Hillsdale, N.J.: Erlbaum, 1978. Pp. 149–176.

Deutsch, M., Katz, I., & Jensen, A. R. (Eds.). *Social class, race, and psychological development.* New York: Holt, 1968.

Dweck, C. S. The role of expectations and attributions in the alleviation of learned helplessness. *Journal of Personality and Social Psychology,* 1975, *31,* 674–685.

Ekehammer, B. Interactionism in personality from a historical perspective. *Psychological Bulletin,* 1974, *81,* 1026–1048.

Endler, N. S., & Magnusson, D. (Eds.). *Interactional psychology and personality.* Washington, D.C.: Hemisphere, 1976.

Entwisle, D. R. To dispel fantasies about fantasy-based measures of achievement motivation. *Psychological Bulletin,* 1972, *77,* 377–391.

Epstein, J. L., & McPartland, J. M. *The effects of open school organization on student outcomes* (Report No. 194). Baltimore: Center for Social Organization of Schools, Johns Hopkins University, 1975.

Feather, N. T. The study of persistence. *Psychological Bulletin,* 1962, *59,* 94–115.

Feld, S. Longitudinal study of the origins of achievement strivings. *Journal of Personality and Social Psychology,* 1967, *7,* 408–414.

Feld, S., Ruhland, D., & Gold, M. Developmental changes in achievement motivation. *Merrill-Palmer Quarterly,* 1979, *25,* 44–60.

Fredericksen, N. Toward a taxonomy of situations. *American Psychologist,* 1972, *27,* 114–123.

Gage, N. L. *The scientific basis of the art of teaching.* New York: Teachers College Press, Columbia Univ., 1978.

Grimes, J. W., & Allinsmith, W. Compulsivity, anxiety, and school achievement. *Merrill-Palmer Quarterly,* 1961, *7,* 247–271.

Heckhausen, H. *The anatomy of achievement motivation.* New York: Academic Press, 1967.

Horner, M. *Sex differences in achievement motivation and performance in competitive and non-competitive situations.* Unpublished doctoral dissertation, University of Michigan, 1968.

Horner, M. The measurement and behavioral implications of fear of success in women. In J. W. Atkinson & J. O. Raynor (Eds.), *Personality, motivation and achievement.* Washington, D.C.: Hemisphere, 1978. Pp. 41–70.

Hunt, D. E. *Matching models in education.* Toronto: Ontario Institute for Studies in Education, 1971.

Hunt, D. E. Person–environment interaction: A challenge found wanting before it was tried. *Reviews of Educational Research,* 1975, *45,* 209–230.

Hunt, J. McV. Intrinsic motivation and its role in psychological development. In D. Levine (Ed.), *Nebraska Symposium on Motivation* (Vol. 13). Lincoln: Univ. of Nebraska Press, 1965. Pp. 189–282.

Judd, D. E. *The relationship of locus of control as a personality variable to student attitude in the open school environment.* Doctoral dissertation, University of Maryland, 1974.

Katz, I. The socialization of academic motivation in minority group children. In. D. Levine (Ed.), *Nebraska Symposium on Motivation* (Vol. 15). Lincoln: Univ. of Nebraska Press, 1967. Pp. 133–191.

Kelley, H. The processes of causal attribution. *American Psychologist,* 1973, *28,* 107–128.

Klein, P. S. Effects of open vs. structured teacher–student interaction on creativity of children with different levels of anxiety. *Psychology in the Schools,* 1975, *12,* 286–288.

Kruglanski, A. W. Endogenous attribution and intrinsic motivation. In M. R. Lepper & D. Greene (Eds.), *The hidden costs of reward: New perspectives on the psychology of human motivation.* Hillsdale, N.J.: Erlbaum, 1978.

Lefcourt, H. M. *Locus of control: Current trends in theory and research.* Hillsdale, N.J.: Erlbaum, 1976.

Lepper, M. R., & Greene, D. Overjustification research and beyond: Toward a means–ends analysis of intrinsic and extrinsic motivation. In M. R. Lepper & D. Greene (Eds.), *The hidden costs of reward: New perspectives on the psychology of human motivation.* Hillsdale, N.J.: Erlbaum, 1978. Pp. 109–148.

Lepper, M. R., Greene, D., & Nisbett, R. E. Undermining children's intrinsic interest with extrinsic reward: A test of the overjustification hypothesis. *Journal of Personality and Social Psychology,* 1973, *28,* 129–137.

Lewin, K., Dembo, T., Festinger, L., & Sears, P. S. Level of aspiration. In J. McV. Hunt (Ed.), *Personality and the behavior disorders* (Vol. 1). New York: Ronald Press, 1944. Pp. 333–378.

McClelland, D. C., Atkinson, J. W., Clark, R. A., & Lowell, E. L. *The achievement motive.* New York: Appleton, 1953.

McDonald, F. J., & Elias, P. *Beginning teacher evaluation study. Phase II: 1973–74.* Final report (duplicated). Princeton, N.J.: Educational Testing Service, 1976.

McGhee, P. E., & Crandall, V. C. Beliefs in internal–external control of reinforcements and academic performance. *Child Development,* 1968, *39,* 91–102.

McGraw, K. O. The detrimental effects of reward on performance: A literature review and a prediction model. In M. R. Lepper & D. Greene (Eds.), *The hidden costs of reward: New perspectives on the psychology of human motivation.* Hillsdale, N.J.: Erlbaum, 1978. Pp. 33–60.

Mischel, W. *Personality and assessment.* New York: Wiley, 1968.

Mischel, W. Toward a cognitive social learning reconceptualization of personality. *Psychological Review,* 1973, *80,* 252–283.

Murray, H. A. *Exploration in personality.* New York: Oxford Univ. Press, 1938.

Peterson, P. L. Interactive effects of student anxiety, achievement orientation, and teacher behavior on student achievement and attitude. *Journal of Educational Psychology,* 1977, *69,* 779–792.

Pettigrew, T. F. Social evaluation theory: Convergences and applications. In D. Levine (Ed.), *Nebraska Symposium on Motivation* (Vol. 15). Lincoln: Univ. of Nebraska Press, 1967. Pp. 241–311.

Raynor, J. O. Future orientation and motivation of immediate activity: An elaboration of the theory of achievement motivation. *Psychological Review,* 1969, *76,* 606–610.

Raynor, J. O. Future orientation in achievement motivation: A more general theory of achievement motivation. In J. W. Atkinson & J. O. Raynor (Eds.), *Personality, motivation, and achievement.* Washington, D.C.: Hemisphere, 1978. Pp. 71–115.

Reiss, S., & Dyhdalo, N. Persistence, achievement, and open-space environments. *Journal of Educational Psychology,* 1975, *67,* 506–513.

Rosen, B. C. The achievement syndrome: A psychocultural dimension of social stratification. *American Sociological Review,* 1956, *21,* 203–211.

Rosen, B. C. Race, ethnicity, and the achievement syndrome. *American Sociological Review,* 1959, *24,* 47–60.

Rosen, B. C., & D'Andrade, R. The psychosocial origins of achievement motivation. *Sociometry,* 1959, *22,* 185–218.

Rosenbaum, R. M. *A dimensional analysis of the perceived causes of success and failure.* Unpublished doctoral dissertation, University of California at Los Angeles, 1972.

Rosenshine, B. Classroom instruction. In N. L. Gage (Ed.), *The psychology of teaching methods, Part I. Seventy-fifth yearbook of the National Society for the Study of Education.* Chicago: NSSE, 1976. Pp. 335–371. (a)

Rosenshine, B. Recent research on teaching behaviors and student achievement. *Journal of Teacher Education,* 1976, *27,* 61–64. (b)

Rotter, J. B. *Social learning and clinical psychology.* Englewood Cliffs, N.J.: Prentice-Hall, 1954.

Rotter, J. B. Generalized expectancies for internal versus external control of reinforcement. *Psychological Monographs,* 1966, *80*(1, Whole No. 609).

Salomon, G. Heuristic models for the generation of aptitude–treatment-interaction hypotheses. *Review of Educational Research,* 1972, *42,* 327–343.

Shulman, L. S. Reconstruction of educational research. *Review of Educational Research,* 1970, *40,* 371–396.

Smith, C. P. The origin and expression of achievement-related motives in children. In C. P. Smith (Ed.), *Achievement-related motives in children.* New York: Russell Sage Foundation, 1969. Pp. 102–150.

Snow, R. E. Representative and quasi-representative designs for research on teaching. *Review of Educational Research,* 1974, *44,* 265–292.

Solomon, D. Psycho-social deprivation and achievement dispositions: Present knowledge and needed research. *Psychological Reports,* 1969, *24,* 227–237. (a)

Solomon, D. The generality of children's achievement-related behavior. *Journal of Genetic Psychology,* 1969, *114,* 109–125. (b)

Solomon, D. Perceptions of similarity between striving tasks and the generality of task preferences. *Motivation and Emotion,* 1977, *1,* 181–192.

Solomon, D., & Houlihan, K. Relationships of parental behavior to "disadvantaged" children's intrinsic–extrinsic motivation for task striving. *Journal of Genetic Psychology,* 1972, *120,* 257–274.

Solomon, D., Houlihan, K. A., Busse, T. V., & Parelius, R. J. Parent behavior and child academic achievement, achievement striving, and related personality characteristics. *Genetic Psychology Monographs,* 1971, *83,* 173–273.

Solomon, D., & Kendall, A. J. *Children in classrooms: An investigation of person–environment interaction.* New York: Praeger, 1979.

Solomon, D., & Oberlander, M. I. Locus of control in the classroom. In K. White & R. Coop (Eds.), *Psychological concepts in the classroom.* New York: Harper, 1974. Pp. 119–150.

Stein, A. H. The influence of social reinforcement on the achievement behavior of fourth-grade boys and girls. *Child Development,* 1969, *40,* 727–736.

Stein, A. H., & Bailey, M. M. The socialization of achievement orientation in females. *Psychological Bulletin,* 1973, *80,* 345–366.

Strauss, M. A. Deferred gratification, social class, and the achievement syndrome. *American Sociological Review,* 1962, *27,* 326–335.

Strodtbeck, F. L. Family interaction, values and achievement. In D. C. McClelland *et al.* (Eds.), *Talent and society.* Princeton, N.J.: Van Nostrand-Reinhold, 1958. Pp. 135–194.

Teevan, R. C., & McGhee, P. E. Childhood development of fear of failure motivation. *Journal of Personality and Social Psychology*, 1972, *21*, 345–348.

Tolman, E. C. Principles of performance. *Psychological Review*, 1955, *62*, 315–326.

Tresemer, D. The cumulative record of research on "fear of success." *Sex Roles*, 1976, *2*, 217–236.

Veroff, J. Theoretical background for studying the origins of human motivational dispositions. *Merrill-Palmer Quarterly*, 1965, *11*, 3–18.

Veroff, J. Social comparison and the development of achievement motivation. In C. P. Smith (Ed.), *Achievement-related motives in children*. New York: Russell Sage Foundation, 1969. Pp. 46–101.

Ward, W. D., & Barcher, P. R. Reading achievement and creativity as related to open classroom experience. *Journal of Educational Psychology*, 1975, *67*, 683–691.

Weiner, B. Attribution theory, achievement motivation, and the educational process. *Review of Educational Research*, 1972, *42*, 203–215.

Weiner, B. *Achievement motivation and attribution theory*. Morristown, N.J.: General Learning Press, 1974.

Weiner, B. A theory of motivation for some classroom experiences. *Journal of Educational Psychology*, 1979, *71*, 3–25.

Weiner, B., Frieze, I. H., Kukla, A., Reed, L., Rest, S., & Rosenbaum, R. M. *Perceiving the causes of success and failure*. Morristown, N.J.: General Learning Press, 1971.

Williams, R. M., Jr. Achievement and success as value orientations. In B. C. Rosen, H. J. Crockett, & C. Z. Nunn (Eds.), *Achievement in American Society*. Cambridge, Mass.: Schenkman, 1969. Pp. 13–17.

Winterbottom, M. The relation of need for achievement to learning experiences in independence and mastery. In J. W. Atkinson (Ed.), *Motives in fantasy, action and society*. Princeton, N.J.: Van Nostrand-Reinhold, 1958. Pp. 453–478.

Zuckerman, M., & Wheeler, L. To dispel fantasies about the fantasy-based measure of fear of success. *Psychological Bulletin*, 1975, *82*, 932–946.

PART THREE / Social influences

8 / Family influences on language and cognitive development

GENE H. BRODY
ZOLINDA STONEMAN

FAMILIES AS COMPETENT TEACHERS

For most of this century, the potential influence of the family on intellectual development has tended to be overlooked. This state of affairs is understandable when one recalls that when the nation entered the era of universal public education, the major responsibility for educating all children in society was transferred from the home and assigned to a social institution, the school. The task of promoting intellectual development under the system of universal education became the school's responsibility.

In the early 1960s, the primacy of the schools' role in promoting language and cognitive growth began to be challenged. During this period Dave (1963) and Wolfe (1964) identified a number of childrearing practices that they felt would stimulate cognitive growth in children. Their studies revealed a high correlation between home variables such as reading to children and achievement in school. This research, combined with the classic investigations by Hess and Shipman (1965), which also suggested that parental childrearing behavior could have an impact on cognition, began to make social scientists reevaluate the role that parents play in promoting cognitive growth.

The notion that cognitive and linguistic growth takes place primarily in the classroom is outdated. Children learn cognitive and language rules in a variety of contexts from an array of social agents. Cognitive

PSYCHOLOGICAL DEVELOPMENT
IN THE ELEMENTARY YEARS

and linguistic abilities can be thought of as rule-governed behaviors that children acquire through observing the behavior of live and symbolic models and through direct interactions with a diverse array of socialization agents that children are exposed to throughout development (Rosenthal & Zimmerman, 1978). Not only is a child exposed to parental behavior, but also to behavior displayed by extrafamilial adults, by siblings, by peers, and by models presented in symbolic forms such as television. Thus, cognitive and language growth is influenced by an ecological system that includes the child's family, peer group, and societal institutions such as schools.

We are suggesting that family socialization practices and teacher instruction are both concerned with socializing children. Although society ostensibly assigns the teacher specific responsibility for the cognitive domain and the parent specific responsibility for the social domain, there is obviously considerable overlap in function. In reality, teachers concern themselves with the development of social skills and self-control and parents have an enormous impact on cognition and language. From our vantage point, the terms *education* and *socialization* are interchangeable. This commonality between education and socialization makes the teacher a parent and the parent a teacher. Parents are, after all, the first and perhaps the most important teachers of their own children. Accordingly, this chapter seeks to document how families teach children cognitive and language skills. These skills were chosen for examination because they bear directly upon bringing about better continuity between the goals and socialization practices of schools and those of the home environments of children. To the extent that families fail to teach children a repertoire of cognitive and language skills, the child is at an initial disadvantage and the educational process becomes a game of "catch up."

In addition to reviewing the literature involving family members as teachers of cognitive and language skills, we will also review the impact of two phenomena that might influence the effectiveness of the family to serve as a competent teacher. Specifically, we will focus on how family television viewing and maternal employment impact on families as teachers of children.

FAMILY INFLUENCES ON LANGUAGE DEVELOPMENT

Roots of language competence

The ability of children to receive and process verbal information and to express their thoughts effectively underlies most elementary school curriculums. Reading, social studies, language arts, and even mathematics are founded upon basic communication competencies (Schumaker & Sherman, 1978). These important language skills are not learned primarily in schools, as most children have acquired the majority of the complex semantic and grammatical structures of their native language before entering first grade. The prime teacher of this sophisticated set of rule-based information is the family. Schools strive to elaborate this preexisting communication system, but, even for the school-age child, many of the opportunities for acquiring and generalizing language skills still occur outside of the classroom. For this reason, it is important to understand the processes by which young children abstract language information from their environment and to identify environmental factors that facilitate the development of communication competencies. Developmental research focusing on the family verbal environment of the language-learning child provides a wealth of information relating to these questions.

Although some parental language training may be deliberate, most occurs in spontaneous interactions that involve neither systematic planning nor conscious effort (Malouf & Dodd, 1972). Parents do not sit down with their children for set periods of time each day and "teach" them the rules and vocabulary of their native language. Instead, children must derive these rules from their ongoing interactions with family members. Brown (1968) describes family verbal interaction as a fluid learning environment in which the child abstracts important linguistic information from the family conversational flow. He offers the analogy of children's acquisition of conservation of liquid volume, which is discovered in the process of pouring liquids from container to container. Just as children do not learn conservation from observing static liquids, they do not learn speech from hearing unconnected words and sentences divorced from contextual meaning and social importance.

Brown (1958) has studied the labels that adults use to teach children about their world and has found striking consistency in adult naming practices. Although every referent has many potential labels, adults employ certain predictable rules when selecting which label they will use when addressing a child. The most potent determinant seems to be the utility of the name in relation to the child's world. Thus, the word *dog* is used instead of *animal* to label a picture in a book, but *fish* is used instead of *perch*, because the parent has decided that expressing the difference between a dog and other animals is functional for the young child, whereas expressing the difference between a perch and other fishes is not. Brown suggests that as parents talk to children they transmit their own cognitive structures, and thus, the initial vocabulary of the young child reflects not so much the cognitive preferences of the child as it does the naming practices of the child's parents.

The following sections will examine research findings concerning the family's role in teaching language to the young child. This review will focus on the language environment provided for the child by various family members (mothers, fathers, and siblings). Only brief mention will be made of the developmental research on child language acquisition, since thorough reviews on this topic are available elsewhere (e.g., Bloom, 1973; Brown, 1973).

In addition, theoretical arguments concerning the role that such factors as imitation, expansion, reinforcement, and cognition play in language development will not be covered due to space constraints. The reader is referred to Moerk (1977), Schumaker and Sherman (1978), Bloom, Hood, and Lightbown (1974) and Whitehurst and Vasta (1975) for research reviews in these areas.

Mothers' influence on language development

Until recently, it was assumed that the stream of maternal conversation was too rapid and dysfluent to serve as the child's primary source of linguistic information, leading to a widespread belief in the innateness of language acquisition structures (e.g., McNeil, 1966). Researchers have discovered, however, that mothers, as well as other adults, dramatically simplify their speech when addressing young children (e.g., Nelson, 1973; Phillips, 1973; Snow, 1972). This speech simplification originates in infancy and continues as the child becomes an increasingly competent language user. There is some evidence to suggest that the infant must reach a certain level of development before this process is fully active. Sherrod, Friedman, Crawley, Drake, and Devieux (1977) found that maternal utterances to 4- and 6-month-old infants were longer and more complex than those to 8-month-olds. The authors suggest that the older infants, but not the younger ones, emitted cues that informed the mothers about the level of speech complexity that would best match their receptive competencies. Sachs (1977) presents a cross-cultural description of maternal speech to infants that points to striking similarities across diverse cultures. Mothers use high vocal pitch, exaggerated intonational patterns, rhythmic and temporal patterning, and perceptually salient initial stop consonants when speaking to infants. Sachs argues that there is evidence that suggests that infants show a particular perceptual sensitivity to these features and that initial infant speech productions exhibit these same parameters.

Other research (Stoneman, 1978) relates Brown's (1968) conceptualization of a flowing conversational environment to mothers' language to their preverbal infants. Maternal question and answer sequences were found to provide a highly rhythmic teaching format, structuring the mother–infant interchange to allow for an interesting presentation of information. Unlike adult-oriented questions, the role of such maternal interrogatives seldom involves requesting unknown information from the infant. Rather, mothers used these structures to provide labels for environmental objects and events in the infant's perceptual field.

The literature on maternal speech to young children has consistently found that conversation topics are highly concrete, focusing on objects and events that are present in the immediate environment (Nelson, 1973; Snow, 1977). Messer (1978) studied the relationship between mothers' speech to infants and their ongoing play behaviors, and found that mothers synchronize their verbal references with their own manipulations of toy objects, as well as with those of their infants. By doing so, they sensitively interpret the ongoing stream of events to their infants, providing labels for objects and events. Stoneman (1979) investigated the effects of two settings, one a room containing numerous toys and other objects and the other an empty room, on the concreteness of maternal speech to 1- and 2-year-old children. She found that although environmental richness did effect the concreteness of conversational topics (speech was less concrete in the more deprived setting), the overwhelming tendency of mothers in *both* environments was to speak in highly concrete utterances. Thus, mother's speech seems to be tuned to those objects and events present in the child's awareness, providing labels for the child's immediate experiences. This would seem to be an excellent strategy for teaching language to the young child.

Holzman (1974) studied the explicit and implicit meanings of mothers' language to young children and found that utterances often had functional intents independent of their syntactic and semantic meanings. For instance, a mothers saying to her child, "Why don't you leave that alone?" is seeking a change in behavior, not an explanation; although syntactically and semantically the utterance is a question, its pragmatic function is that of a directive. Thus, through voice intonation, feedback, and direct behavioral intervention, mothers teach their children that utterances often have subtle, implicit meanings. Holzman suggests that some children (particularly from lower class environments) enter school without having learned that language can have implicit meanings, and thus do not know how to respond to such statements from teachers. This lack of understanding could easily be interpreted as defiance by someone who was unaware of the child's functional language deficit. Thus, the pragmatic characteristics of the mother–child language interaction can have important implications for the child's school performance.

Other researchers have focused primarily on the syntactic structure of maternal speech addressed to young children. Snow (1972) found that maternal speech to 2-year-old children was significantly simpler than that addressed to 10-year-olds, even when the children were not physically present. For 2-year-olds, mothers shortened their utterances and used fewer compound verbs, third-person pronouns, and subordinate clauses. Mothers of 2-year-olds also used more short phrases without verbs, repeated themselves more frequently, and paraphrased their speech more often. Broen (1972) also found significant differences between maternal speech directed toward younger (18–28 months) and older (over 45 months) children, as well as between speech directed to older children and adults. When speaking to the younger children, mothers spoke more slowly, used a more restricted vocabulary, spoke in shorter utterance strings, and had fewer dysfluencies. Phillips (1973) studied maternal speech to children at 8 months, 18 months, and 28 months of age, as well as to adults. Although she found no differences between speech to children at 8 and 18 months, she did find that mothers used fewer words and verbs and modifiers with the 8-month-old infants. She also found that these younger infants were exposed to fewer different vocabulary words than were the older children. Fraser and Roberts (1975) reported similar age-related findings for mothers' speech to children at 18 months, 30 months, 4 years, and 6 years of age. As children's age increased, mothers spoke more frequently, used longer, more complex utterances, and employed a richer vocabulary. These differences were particularly dramatic between speech addressed to the 18- and 30-month-olds.

Although some researchers have found child sex to be a nonsignificant factor when studying maternal speech simplification (e.g., Fraser & Roberts, 1975; Phillips, 1973), others have described significant sex effects. Cherry and Lewis (1976) found that mothers of 2-year-old girls talked more, asked more questions, repeated their daughters' utterances more frequently, and used longer utterances compared with mothers of boys, and that maternal speech to sons contained more directives. They interpreted these findings as indicating that mothers of girls use more conversation-maintaining devices and provide a richer language environment compared with mothers of boys. A recent study by Stoneman and Brody (1981) also found that mothers spoke more utterances to girls than they did to boys. Golinkoff and Ames (1977) examined the effects of child sex on a wide range of measures of mother's and father's speech to 19-month-old children and found only one marginally significant effect: Parents of girls repeated their daughter's utterances more frequently than did parents of boys. More research is needed on this question, since there is sufficient evidence to suggest that girls learn language more quickly than do boys (Koenigsknecht & Friedman, 1976). Since parents are the primary teachers of language, it is important to tease out those factors in parental speech that might allow girls to be verbally precocious.

Numerous authors have attempted to study the mother–child language system as a highly tuned feedback network. It has been posited that the simplified speech patterns employed when mothers speak to children provide linguistic input that is optimally effective in teaching language (Moerk, 1972). Mahoney (1975) and Moerk (1977) have likened this linguistic monitoring to Hunt's (1961) minimal discrepancy hypothesis, which suggests that the most facilitative learning environment involves supplying input that is slightly more complex than the current competency of the learner, thus pacing the acquisition of new information. If environmental input is too simplistic, or too complicated, learning does not occur. This idea assumes that a feedback system exists between adult and child, providing information to the adults that allows them to select the appropriate level of language complexity. Moerk (1972) studied 20 mother–child dyads interacting in their homes. The children, half girls and half boys, ranged in age from 21 to 60 months. A strong relationship was found between the age of the child and his or her mean utterance length, but child age was not found to be significantly related to the mean length of utterance (MLU) of the mother. Child MLU, however, did predict the MLU used by mothers, as did the modal and maximal child utterance length. In all 20 dyads, mothers used longer utterances than did the children. Maternal MLU, however, increased less over the child age range studied than did child MLU, resulting in a decrease in the difference between the two speakers as the child became older. Moerk interprets these findings as suggesting that mothers are aware of, and respond to, child utterance length as an indicator of language competence. T. G. Cross (1977) designed a large correlational study to determine which child language parameters most strongly predicted maternal speech adjustments. She audiorecorded language interactions of 16 mother–child (19–32 months) pairs specifically selected because the children exhibited rapid language acquisition. Like Moerk (1972), her findings suggested that maternal speech is more finely tuned to the child's linguistic and communications abilities than to age. She further found, however, that mothers were more sensitive to the child's receptive competencies than they were to MLU, child comprehensibility, or breadth of vocabulary. She suggested that rather than focusing on the length and complexity of the child's expressive speech, mothers monitor the child's comprehension of the verbal exchange and adjust the complexity of their language based on this feedback. She further suggests that most maternal speech repetitions, reductions, and elaborations are in direct response to cues given off by the child that signal misinterpretation or lack of comprehension.

Two ingenious studies by Bohannon and Marquis (1977) lend further support to the importance of child comprehension in maternal speech simplification. In the first study, they investigated a young child's differential comprehension of adult utterances with short and long mean lengths. They found that the group of utterances to which the child displayed comprehension responses (affirmative vocalizations, appropriate answers to questions, or continuation of conversational topics) were significantly shorter than those followed by no comprehension behaviors. They also found that the presence or absence of child comprehension cues influenced subsequent adult utterance length. Adults simplified their speech following noncomprehension feedback, although they did not dramatically increase their utterance length following child comprehension responses. The second study experimentally controlled child comprehension and noncomprehension feedback. Adults were asked to verbally interact with other adults, with imaginary children, and with actual children who had been prompted to emit either comprehension or noncomprehension responses to adult utterances. The sole presence of a child was found to be sufficient for adult speech simplification, even if the child consistently signaled comprehension of adult speech. A child's noncomprehension feedback, however, had an immediate effect on adult utterance lengths. Adult sentence lengths were only half as long in this condition as they were when the child displayed comprehension behaviors. These results indicate the presence of a powerful feedback system between the child and his or her linguistic environment, resulting in adult speech that is responsive to the child's level of receptive competency. J. Berko Gleason (1977) suggests that the range of child feedback cues is quite broad, including both global behaviors and very subtle, nonverbal responses. For instance, a child may respond to inappropriately complex adult speech by moving away or ceasing to pay attention. Other responses, however, may be much more subtle, such as shifting eye gaze, blinking, or nodding. At the present time, descriptive information concerning these nonverbal indicators of comprehension and noncomprehensions is very limited, and a more detailed understanding of the mother–child feedback system must await further research.

Fathers' influence on language development

The father has generally been neglected in the study of family influences on language and cognitive development. This apparent neglect of the father's role in these areas of development may be part of a prevailing attitude that the father has a low status in the American family. LeMasters (1970) presented four reasons that account for this attitude about the fathers' role in socialization:

1. Father's role is weaker than the mother's.
2. There is no biological basis for the father–child relationship, as there is for the mother–child relationship.
3. The father is not prepared for his parental role because he was not taught the skills and responsibilities of a father outside his role as provider.
4. The success of a father's parental role depends upon his success in the pair-bond with his spouse.

Fathers, then, tend to be stereotyped as slightly inept when it comes to caring for and socializing children. Ross Parke and his colleagues (Parke & O'Leary, 1976; Parke & Sarwin, 1976) sought to determine if fathers are indeed as inept in dealing with their offspring as many of our stereotypes would lead us to believe. Parke evaluated these notions in studies of parent–infant interaction. In observations of mother–father–infant triads, he found that fathers actually held and watched the infant more than the mother did. In addition, the father was as nurturant toward the infant as the mother was. Finally, in a study designed to examine whether fathers are as sensitive to infant cues during a feeding session as mothers are, Parke and Sarwin (1976) found no differences between the sensitivity of mothers and fathers. Fathers do not appear as inept in caretaking as some of our stereotypes suggest.

The role of fathers in children's development of language has received much less study than that of mothers. Friedlander, Jacobs, Davis, and Wetstone (1972) described in detail the language environments in the homes of two 12-month-old infants. Family verbal interactions were time-sampled for approximately 5 out of every 20 minutes of the child's waking day for one week, yielding about 3 hours of audiorecorded language interaction. Of conversation directed toward the infant in the first home, 65% came from the mother, 30% from the father, and 5% from guests. In the second home, mothers provided 59% of the child's verbal interactions, fathers provided 37%, and guests 4%. The ratio of verbalization time for both families among the child, mother, and father was 7:5:3. Thus, in both homes, mothers' speech accounted for most of their child's language environment. Although the fathers were out of the home part of the day (both were graduate students), they probably had more flexible life-styles than those experienced by many fathers. The authors point out that even though the largest portion of language stimulation came from the mothers, one of the two children was acquiring the Spanish language solely from her father's speech. Although he provided only 5% of the total language environment and 37% of all child-oriented speech, his input was obviously quite important. At 18 months, the child would follow simple instructions, answer questions, and form sentences in Spanish. The authors cite this dramatic paternal influence on language development as suggesting a need for a rethinking of the assumption that mothers are the primary teachers of language solely because of the quantity of their input.

Rebelsky and Hanks (1971) also provide evidence that fathers spend relatively little time interacting with their infants. They studied 10 infants and their families, beginning in the second week of life, by making 24-hour tape recordings for approximately every 2 weeks for a 3-month period. This yielded six 24-hour observation periods, audiorecorded from a microphone attached to the infants' clothing. The time of day, duration, and activity occurring each time the father vocalized to his infant were coded. The average number of father–child interactions per day was 2.7, totaling 37.7 seconds. The most interactive father spent only 10 minutes and 26 seconds per day vocalizing to his infant. Fathers interacted most frequently in the morning hours before work (41% of all vocalizations) and in the evenings (33% of vocalizations). The frequency of paternal vocalizations varied by the age and sex of the infant. Unlike mothers, who have been found to increase the quantity of their vocalizations during the first 3 months of the infant's life (Moss, 1967), most of the fathers in the Rebelsky and Hanks (1971) study spent less time vocalizing to older infants (8–12 weeks) than they did to younger ones (2–6 weeks). This decrease was more marked for fathers of female infants. Fifty-four percent of father vocalizations occurred during caretaking activities, and it was a decrease in these vocalizations that was responsible for the overall decrease in paternal verbalizations for older infants. Nelson (1973) reported that fathers spent an average of 29.8 hours per week with their children, but this amount of time spent in interaction was not correlated with any of her linguistic or cognitive indexes of the child's developmental progress. Like Friedlander *et al.* (1972), she speculates that it is the quality, and not the quantity, of paternal interaction that is the meaningful variable in father–child interactions.

Giattino and Hogan (1975) studied the speech of one selected father to his 3-year-old daughter. The father was selected because he took an active role in childrearing. During the 2-week period in which data was collected, the father spent approximately 25 hours per week with his child. Audiotaping of father–child interactions was done on evenings and weekends, with the father turning on the tape recorder for each session. No other persons were ever present when data was collected. In general, the authors found that the parameters of paternal speech were similar to those reported in the literature for mothers. He modified the length of his utterances in line with his daughter's speech (father's MLU = 5.2 words, child's MLU = 4.5 words) and used declarative, interrogative, and other sentence types with approximately the same frequency as has been reported elsewhere for mothers (Brown, 1973.)

Golinkoff and Ames (1977) present an investigation of paternal speech to language-learning children. They analyzed the speech of mothers, fathers, and their 19-month-old children interacting together in a free-play situation with an assortment of toys, as well as during two structured dyadic sessions in which each parent interacted alone with their child, teaching them to play with a specified toy. Overall, there were few differences between maternal and paternal speech, with both the qualitative and quantitative aspects of language being quite similar. The two differences that did emerge from their data occurred only in the free-play situation. In that setting, when all family members were together, mothers emitted twice as many utterances as fathers. Mothers also took significantly more conversational turns. Mean length of utterances, number of directives, frequency of questions and other sentence types, repetitions, reductions, and expansions did not differ between parents. When they examined questionnaires that mothers and fathers had completed independently, they found striking resemblances between parents in their perceptions of their child's language development. Research by Stoneman and Brody (1978) supports their findings regarding the similarity of mothers' and fathers' perceptions of their children's linguistic competencies and goes one step further by relating these parental perceptions to actual child language measures. Mothers and fathers of 54 preschool children were asked to independently complete the items of the Carrow Test for Auditory Comprehension of Language as they thought their child would respond to each test question. They were also asked to estimate the average number of words that their children put together in sentences when speaking spontaneously. Extremely high correlations were found between maternal and paternal responses to these measures, and both mother's and father's language estimates were found to be highly correlated with their children's linguistic competencies.

Stoneman and Brody (1981) examined how conversations among fathers, mothers, and their offspring change as a function of the number of family members interacting. The verbal interactions between 18 2-year-old children and their mothers and fathers were audiorecorded during two dyadic sessions (one with each of the parents alone with the child) and one triadic session (in which all three family members participated). Fathers were found to be competent language models for their children, but in triadic groupings they seemed to defer to mothers, talking less frequently and taking fewer conversational turns. No differences were detected on any child measures. Thus, although parents reduced their language output to accommodate an additional speaker in the conversation (the other parent), the children remained remarkably consistent across situations.

In summary, the literature on fathers' influences on the language development of their children suggests that although fathers spend significantly less time talking to their children than do mothers, they are quite aware of their children's level of language development and may have a much more influential role on language acquisition than would be expected by the quantity of time spent in child-oriented speech. Since the emphasis on including fathers in developmental research is quite new, much more still needs to be learned regarding the paternal role in linguistic development.

Siblings' influence on language development

Sibling relationships perform a number of functions. More than 80% of American children have one or more siblings, which simply means that most children spend a considerable amount of time in the presence of brothers or sisters. Interactions with a brother or sister function as one avenue for the socialization of children and on occasion siblings may act as parent substitutes. Given the occupational and social demands that are placed on parents in our society, it would come as no surprise if siblings turn to each other when sufficient attention or understanding is not shown by a harried or tired parent. Siblings also should be recognized as teachers who are capable of influencing the language and cognitive development of their brothers or sisters. Recently, researchers have begun to recognize that siblings are teachers and have shifted some attention to examining how siblings influence development. Unfortunately, other than studies of birth order and family size, there is only a limited body of knowledge in the area from which conclusions can be drawn regarding sibling influences.

There is early data (McCarthy, 1954) to suggest that sibling birth order plays an important role in language acquisition, with younger siblings showing slower rates of language development. Nelson (1973) found that young children with an older sibling were slightly less likely to develop vocabulary early than those without older siblings, as measured by the age at which the target child had acquired his or her first 50 words (an average age of 19.0 months for firstborns and 20.6 months for later born children). She also found a tendency for firstborn children to learn referential speech (object-oriented), whereas those with older siblings focused more on expressive (self-oriented) speech. When she examined the relationship between children's rates of language acquisition and amount of time spent with other children (primarily siblings), Nelson found a significant negative relationship with age and speed of speech acquisition. She interprets this finding as supporting the idea that other children are poor linguistic models for the language-learning child. There were no significant correlations between the number of other children seen per week and many language variables, so amount of exposure, and not number of child models, seems to be the important variable. Breland (1974) presents data to suggest that language decrements in younger siblings can still be detected in high school students taking the National Merit Scholarship Qualification Test.

Shatz and Gelman (1973) conducted three studies specifically focusing on the characteristics of child–child speech. In the first study, data was collected on the speech of 16 4-year-old-children, half of whom had younger siblings. In the first phase of the investigation, an "egocentrism" pretest was administered. Most children performed poorly on the pretest, not taking the listener's perspective into account in their behavior. In the second part of the study, the children were asked to explain how to play with a certain toy both to an adult and to a 2-year-old child. Children who had younger siblings were studied twice, once with their own sibling and once with an unrelated 2-year-old. During the third phase, a 15–20-minute tape recording of spontaneous parent–child conversation was obtained in a natural setting. The 4-year-old children were found to adjust their speech when addressing 2-year-olds, and the children who did not have younger siblings adjusted their speech as much as those who did. In those children with younger brothers and sisters, there were no differences in speech addressed to their own sibling and an unrelated younger child. The younger the listener, however, the shorter the utterances used by the child speaker (mean MLU of 3.7 words to children under 28 months and 4.9 words to those 28 months and older). Speech to younger children was also grammatically simpler and contained more attention-maintaining utterances (such as *hey* and *look*). No significant differences were found between speech addressed to adults in the experimental setting and that addressed spontaneously to mothers.

The second study conducted by Shatz and Gelman (1973) focused on child speech spontaneously addressed to younger children and to adults. Five 4-year-old children were audiorecorded in natural conversation with their mothers and with randomly assigned 2-year-old children. MLU's towards mothers averaged 7.0 words, whereas they averaged 4.6 words toward the younger children. Speech toward adults was also more complex. In the third study, Shatz and Gelman investigated the spontaneous speech of 4-year-old children addressed to same-age peers and adults. They found no significant differences between speech to adults and to peers, either in utterance length or linguistic complexity.

Cicirelli (1978), taking a systems orientation to studying the role of siblings in the family language environment, investigated the effects of an older sibling's presence on mother–child interaction. Eighty first-grade children, their mothers, and their third-grade siblings participated in the study. The results indicated that mothers gave more explanations and verbalized more frequently to young children with opposite-sex siblings when that sibling was absent rather than present. Siblings' interactions, however, did not differ according to their sex combination. Mother–child nonverbal interaction decreased with sibling presence, regardless of the sex of the children. No effects of family size were found on any of the measures studied. Although more research needs to be done on this question before definite conclusions can be drawn, it appears that the role of older siblings in the young child's language environment may be twofold: First, the speech of siblings themselves may be less attuned to the needs of young children than the speech of parents, thus diluting the impact of the language environment; second, mother's language behavior may be influenced by the presence of older siblings, decreasing both the quantity and quality of her verbal input to the language-learning child. If these conclusions are valid, they could explain the findings of McCarthy (1954), Nelson (1973), and others concerning the slower language development of children with older brothers and sisters.

FAMILY INFLUENCES ON COGNITIVE DEVELOPMENT

Roots of cognitive competence

How do children acquire concepts? We would probably all agree that children are not born with concepts, yet in a relatively short amount of time children acquire a mass of knowledge. Basically, concepts evolve through direct and vicarious contact with the environment. Children receive direct feedback from and observe the behavior of a multitude of influential socialization agents within their culture. This includes their parents, siblings, peers, other important extrafamilial adults (such as teachers), and the media. All of these socialization agents provide young children with feedback regarding the appropriateness of the concepts that are used in their presence. For example, when a young child labels a four-legged animal that meows as a *cat*, the child will probably be congratulated by the socialization agent sharing the experience. On the other hand, if the same child labels a four-legged animal that barks as a *cat*, the child will most likely receive some corrective feedback informing him or her that the correct label is *dog*. This process of reinforcing correct responses and providing corrective feedback for erroneous ones enables even very young children to discriminate among different categories of stimuli in their culture. The product of this process, whether it occurs in the home or on the playground, is the acquisition of a concept that allows the child to interact more efficiently with the environment (Bourne, 1970).

The second and most pervasive form of concept formation occurs through the observation of models within the child's milieu (Rosenthal & Zimmerman, 1978). Concept formation would be a tedious process if children only acquired concepts through direct feedback from socialization agents. Fortunately, children can abstract conceptual rules that guide the behavior of models and use these rules in turn to guide their own conceptual actions. To use the above example, a child could learn the concept *cat* by observing a multitude of models in his or her culture employ the label when they were confronted by an animal with a specific set of attributes. The concepts gleaned from models are not restricted to simple concepts; a vast array of abstract concepts have been shown to be amenable to modeled influences (Brody & Zimmerman, 1978). Thus, children acquire concepts through both social feedback processes and the observation of models within their culture.

Concepts, once they are abstracted, subsequently influence the child's acquisition and interpretation of future environmental information (Bandura, 1977). This means that concept learning influences future concept learning. In order to acquire higher mathematical concepts, a student first must acquire the more elementary mathematical concepts. However, it is important to note that not only does the formation of concepts influence the child's ability to understand and acquire new knowledge, but acquired concepts themselves are refined and sharpened by subsequent social experiences. For example, young children usually have a notion that the larger an object is, the more it weighs. As children directly and vicariously experience a wider array of objects, they learn that size alone is not the sole determinant of weight. What exists, then, is a reciprocal exchange between an individual's conceptual knowledge and the social environment. Concepts allow children to understand and interpret environmental events, and the environment in turn provides information that modifies the child's concepts. Just as this never-ending reciprocal process exists between a child's knowledge and environment, another reciprocal exchange occurs between a child's knowledge and behavior. Concepts direct a child's behavior and to a degree also influence the consequences that these behaviors receive. For example, a child who is taught to dislike a particular racial or ethnic group may behave aggressively toward them and receive negative reactions for these behaviors. This illustrates how a child's conceptual knowledge influences his or her behaviors and indirectly influences the environment, which dispenses the negative reactions toward the child. Thus, a reciprocal social influence system exists between concepts and the environment, concepts and behavior, and behavior and the environment (Bandura, 1977).

The following sections will examine research findings concerning the family's role in teaching concepts to the young child. This review will focus on the teaching strategies used by mothers, fathers, and siblings. Much less is known about how families teach cognitive skills and strategies than is known about how the family language environment influences language development. This deficiency in the extant literature will be apparent in the following sections.

Mothers' influence on cognitive development

Even though we have witnessed a dramatic change in the roles that women occupy in our society during the last 10 years or so, mothers still bear more responsibility for childrearing than do fathers. This fact is vividly depicted in a study for which time budgets were kept by working mothers and fathers in 12 countries (Szalai, Converse, Feldheim, Scheuch, & Stone, 1973). According to this study, when both parents work, parents in the United States averaged only 62 minutes each day with their children. Fathers spent an average of only 12 minutes per day with their children. In all 12 countries sampled, employed mothers spent more time with their children than employed fathers did. This data implies that even when both parents work, it is the mother who serves as the primary socialization agent in the home. In this section we will examine those studies that have investigated how mothers go about teaching their children congitive concepts.

Bing (1963) used a combination of self-report and observational methodologies with fifth-grade children in an attempt to determine childrearing antecedents of verbal ability. The childrens' responses to a retrospective questionnaire and interview suggested that mothers of "high verbal" children provided more verbal stimulation during the childrens' preschool years. In the observational situation, mothers of children with high verbal ability generally provided more assistance voluntarily, provided it sooner when requested by the child, and pressured the child more for improvement. Although this study does not directly investigate maternal teaching of a conceptual skill, it was one of the first that directly observed parent–child interactions and related them to the childs' cognitive competencies.

Every area of research has at least one paper that is considered a classic. A paper usually attains this status as much for its heuristic value or its ability to generate research as for the obtained results. The research reported by Hess and Shipman (1965) fills this bill. Hess and Shipman found marked differences in the ways in which middle class and lower class mothers instructed their children. Specifically, middle class mothers tended to be much more elaborate and complete in their verbal instruction to children than did lower class mothers. Compared with lower class mothers, middle class mothers relied less on physical feedback, preferred motivating the child to controlling through implied threat, gave more orientation to the task, reinforced correct responses more than errors, and used more specific language.

When the children's learning was examined following maternal instruction, it was found that the middle class children performed better than the other social class groups. The quality of the mother's teaching strategy was related to the level of the childs' cognitive functioning. In fact, maternal teaching behavior was as good a predictor of the childs' cognitive behavior as IQ measures.

It is interesting to note that not a single statistical test was reported in the Hess and Shipman (1965) paper. This is not a criticism; rather, it points out that at that time the scientific community was hungry for these types of data. Scientific support was needed to justify the large expenditures of money that were needed in the compensatory education movement.

Bee, Van Egeron, Streissguth, Nyman, and Leckie (1969) also examined social class differences in maternal teaching behavior. Seventy-six lower class mothers were compared to 38 middle class mothers in an unstructured "waiting room" setting and in a structured problem-solving situation with their child. In the waiting room, lower class mothers were more disapproving and controlling than middle class mothers. In the problem-solving situation, the teaching strategies of middle class mothers were characterized by the use of nonspecific suggestions and the infrequent use of nonverbal help and negative feedback to the child. Lower class mothers were more likely to intrude physically into the child's problem solving; they used relatively higher rates of negative feedback and more specific, concrete suggestions to their children than the middle class mothers. It should be noted, however, that the middle class sample consisted primarily of white university faculty and graduate students, whereas the lower class mothers were black. Moreover, the testing and interviewing were conducted in a university facility, in which it is conceivable that the faculty and graduate students may have felt more natural and relaxed than the lower class parents.

As part of the larger Hess–Shipman study, Brophy (1970) examined social class differences in mothers' specificity of verbal labels and attention-focusing techniques in a teaching situation. Middle class mothers were the only group to consistently spend much time orienting the child to the conceptual task, to help the child focus attention on·the salient aspects of the task, and to give preresponse instructions that included verbal labels. In contrast, the working class mothers tried to show the child what to do with a quick demonstration and then attempted to teach through corrective feedback.

Feshbach (1973) examined maternal reinforcement style or the use of positive and negative reinforcement on childrens' performance in a teaching situation. These series of studies contained two clever wrinkles that distinguished them from other studies in this area. First, after an initial mother–child teaching session the children were assigned to teach a similar task to younger children. Second, Feshbach examined the reinforcement styles of mothers not only in the United States, but in Israel and England as well. The results revealed that for the American sample middle class white children and their mothers used relatively more positive than negative reinforcement and lower class black children and their mothers used more negative than positive reinforcement. The cross-cultural comparisons indicated that middle class children and middle class mothers use more positive reinforcement while teaching than do lower class children and their mothers, regardless of whether the culture is American, English, or Israeli. On the basis of her data, Feshbach concluded that "reinforcement may be one factor—not the only factor or the most significant factor—but an important factor mediating socioethnic differences in cognitive performance and academic achievement [p. 107]."

The research reviewed thus far has concerned itself with social class differences in maternal teaching styles. Steward and Steward (1973, 1974) focused their research on ethnic rather than social class differences in maternal teaching styles. They videotaped and analyzed mother–child teaching interactions using an observational system that they refer to as the Parent Interaction Code. The components of the code include (a) alerting—gaining the child's attention; (b) format—providing an instruction to which the child may respond; (c) child's response to alert and format; (d) feedback—parent's response to the child's response. The completion of this sequence is termed a teaching loop. Ethnicity and not social class was the best predictor of maternal teaching styles and child behavior in both of Steward and Steward's studies. American mothers carefully focused their childrens' attention, provided an array of instructions, and used feedback in the form of information about the childs' performance. Chinese mothers used very specific teaching instructions and provided a high proportion of positive feedback. Mexican mothers presented the fewest number of teaching loops, exhibited slow pacing by taking more time to complete the loops, and used a large amount of negative feedback.

Finally, Laosa (1978) studied the relationship of maternal teaching behavior to educational level and occupational status among Mexican–American families. Mothers were observed teaching cognitive perceptual tasks to their own 5-year-old children. Mothers who had received more years of formal education used inquiry and praise more than mothers with less education. The lower the mother's formal education level, the more they used modeling. Maternal teaching strategies did not vary as a function of family occupational status, which is the most widely used index of social class. This data tends to suggest that studies that use only a rough index of social class fail to disclose what are the parameters within cultures and subcultures that discriminate different parenting styles.

Taken as a whole, studies of maternal teaching suggest that mothers who focus their children's attention, provide specific instructions, and use positive feedback for childrens' learning attempts make competent teachers. Unfortunately, most, if not all, the extant literature has concerned itself with social class differences in natural teaching strategies to the exclusion of pinpointing how maternal behavior and child competence interact to shape the learning situation.

Fathers' influence on cognitive development

Few studies have investigated how fathers teach their children. Whether this is due to the aforementioned attitudes about fathers or to the unavailability of fathers to participate in research is conjecture at this point. The answer probably involves an interaction of both explanations. Whatever the reason for this lack of research, we will review the sparse literature on fathers as teachers in this section. Ironically, the literature that makes the strongest case for fathers' contribution to cognitive development is the father absence literature, which will also be reviewed.

Although few studies exist that examine paternal teaching strategies, there are some studies that examine the relationship between father–child interactions and cognitive competence. Norma Radin's research (1972, 1973) probably best exemplifies this research tack. Her research strategy and staging of experiments were as follows. At the conclusion of an interview with the fathers, their 4-year-old children were given puzzles to work on. The fathers were simply instructed that they could help their children if they cared to. Surprisingly, paternal intervention during the puzzle task was negatively related to other cognitive measures. In other words, lack of paternal involvement when 4-year-old children were playing with puzzles was related to cognitive competence. The one father behavior that was positively related to cognitive competence was telling the child that he would not help them with the puzzles. Why would a father's attempts to help a child in a mastery situation be negatively related to cognitive performance on standardized measures of cognition competence? It could be that instead of allowing the child to benefit from errors by applying corrective feedback, fathers may simply decide to do the task for the child.

Is the type of paternal concern or nurturance always related to poor cognitive competence? The answer is no, especially for boys. Radin (1972, 1973) has shown paternal nurturance to be associated with intellectual ability in young boys but not in young girls. She has also found that paternal restrictiveness is associated with lower conceptual competencies. Evidently, the presence or absence of paternal nurturance does not have an impact on the cognitive development of daughters. Radin speculated that paternal nurturance in nonmastery situations facilitates the boy's identification with his father. In the course of the identification process the son is said to abstract the problem-solving strategies displayed by the father. The same process is said to operate for girls and their mothers, as they are said to prefer their mothers as their primary model (Radin, 1974).

We now will address how growing up in a home without a father influences cognitive development. Few research reports have examined whether the different causes of father absence impact on cognitive development in a similar manner. There are, however, four studies that have compared the different causes of absence. Crescimbeni (1965) administered the Metropolitan Achievement Test to boys and girls in the second through the sixth grade for 2 consecutive years. Half of the children in this sample were living with one parent, and half were living with both parents. Children in two-parent families performed better at both testings. Children from divorced homes and children whose fathers' had died scored lower than children from homes in which the father and mother were separated or children whose fathers had deserted the family.

J. W. Santrock (1972) compared the achievement test performance of 57 father-absent children with the performance of children whose parents were divorced, whose father was deceased, whose father had deserted, and whose mother and father were separated. Father absence due to divorce, desertion, or separation was related to lower third-grade achievement and lower school attendance than absence due to death.

Ferri (1976) tested the reading and arithmetic ability of 10,000 British children born in 1958. The children were tested when they were 7 and 11 years old. The results revealed that children living with both parents performed better on both reading and arithmetic at age 11. Thus, although father absence due to death, desertion, and separation all have an impact on cognitive development, the most consistent category of father absence that was related to lower cognitive functioning was divorce.

The effect of father absence has been found to be greatest when the onset of the absence occurred before age 5 (Blanchard & Biller, 1971; Landy, Rosenberg, & Sutton-Smith, 1969). Later in this section we will present some plausible explanations for father absence effects on cognitive development. For the moment, however, we will briefly speculate that the disruption that is associated with the father's leaving the household diverts energy away from the child. Instead of engaging in activities and interactions with the child, mothers channel their energy into coping with their new responsibilities and life-styles. It could be that these preschool children miss out on experiences that foster elementary conceptual skills that are important later to cognitive development.

If we reflect for a moment on the construct of father absence we realize that fathers can live in a household and be absent most of the time. Since children often go to bed early, there is a good chance that they may go to bed without spending any appreciable amount of time with their fathers. Blanchard and Biller (1971) sought to determine if the amount of time the father was present during the week had any influence on the scores of third-grade boys on the Stanford Achievement Test and school grades. Children in households in which the father was present less than 6 hours per week performed more poorly on both dependent measures than children in households in which the father was present 2 or more hours per day. This study suggests that the amount of time a child has access to a father does have an impact on cognitive development.

After reviewing the literature on father absence effects on cognitive development, the one question that comes to mind is, Why is this situation associated with relatively poor cognitive development? Two explanations seem very plausible. First, father absence may be a product of a home situation characterized by a high anxiety level. The anxiety and tension within the home may divert the mother's attention from her offspring and toward her own needs. Remember, those studies that examined father absence due to divorce found lower cognitive test performance than when the absence was due to other reasons. This explanation leads nicely into the second plausible reason for father absence effects; namely, that the disorganization that surrounds a father's leaving the home due to divorce may rob the child of parental attention. If parents have less energy to actively interact with their offspring, then they remove themselves as sources of information and feedback. Hetherington, Cox, and Cox (1975) reported that divorced mothers were less likely than mothers in intact homes to eat dinner with their children or read to them at bedtime. The quality as well as the quantity of interaction suffered. Divorced parents were less likely to engage their children in developmentally advanced activities and were less likely to employ reasoning strategies than were parents in intact homes.

Aside from the longitudinal data provided by Hetherington, Cox, and Cox (1978), there have been few analyses of the home environments of children from mother-headed divorced households. Previous research has concentrated on the consequences of divorce for children by comparing their performance with matched children from nuclear families. Although this approach has successfully identified differences between children from divorced and nuclear families, it has not directly investigated the home environments of children from divorced homes. MacKinnon, Brody, and Stoneman (in press) conducted a study that compared properties of intact and divorced households that have been found to relate directly to cognitive and social development. The home environments of the divorced and intact families were analyzed using the HOME (Home Observation for the Measurement of the Environment) Inventory Preschool Scale (Bradley & Caldwell, 1979). The results revealed that the home environments of children in divorced households were lacking in the quantity and quality of stimulation that has been found necessary to nurture different facets of development. These differences in the home environments persisted even when differences in family income were controlled through the use of a covariance analysis. Following these analyses, the divorced households were still found to contain less stimulation that related to cognitive development and academic performance. It is not surprising that children from divorced households have been found to experience difficulty in schools, if, as our data indicate, they are not obtaining the stimulation necessary for the development of preacademic skills.

Siblings' influence on cognitive development

Despite the presumed importance of sibling relations to social and cognitive development (see Sutton-Smith & Rosenberg, 1970; Zajonc & Markus, 1975), there has been an inordinately small number of studies that have observed sibling–sibling interactions. From a social systems perspective on socialization, this research void is noteworthy because sibling–sibling relations appear to differ qualitatively from parent–child interactions (Lamb, 1978a, 1978b) and provide younger siblings with the opportunity for interaction with older, more competent, children.

Lamb (1978a, 1978b) observed 24 infants and their preschool-aged siblings in a laboratory playroom in the presence of their parents. He found that both the infants and their older siblings preferred to interact with their parent rather than with one another. Young siblings appeared to monitor and model the behavior of their older siblings, whereas older siblings were more likely to offer toys and vocalize to their younger siblings. Lamb (1978b) observed the same siblings in the same laboratory context 6 months after the first observation. The younger and older siblings assumed similar roles as they had 6 months earlier. The infants monitored and imitated their older siblings, and the older siblings directed the attention of their younger siblings toward objects in the environment. Samuels (1980) also studied sibling interactions between infants and their older siblings and found results very similar to those cited earlier. Sibling presence was shown to increase infant locomotor and object exploration. Taken together, these studies suggest that daily exposure to an older preschool-age sibling facilitates locomotor exploration and mastery of the object environment.

Abramovitch and her colleagues (Abramovitch, Corter, & Lando, 1979; Abramovitch, Corter, & Pepler, 1980) explored the actual patterns of sibling interactions in their homes. The younger siblings averaged 20 months of age and the older siblings averaged 51 months. During the course of the naturalistic interactions, older siblings initiated agonistic and prosocial acts more often than their younger siblings. Younger siblings imitated their older siblings more often. These results parallel the aforementioned research and reveal consistent asymmetries in the behavior and roles assumed by infants and their preschool-aged siblings. Presumably, these asymmetries in role assumption have implications for development.

Bronfenbrenner (1979), among others (see Brim, 1960), has argued that development is facilitated through interactions with persons who occupy a variety of roles. In learning and practicing a role, the child learns not only his or her own role but also the complementary roles. Theoretically, role assumption affects both cognitive and behavioral competencies. At the cognitive level the child develops expectations regarding the appropriate roles for given social contexts and also expectations regarding how others are likely to behave toward him or her. The content of these expectations are of particular importance for the developing child. If, for example, a parent regularly places an older sibling in the role of caretaker or teacher, the sibling gradually develops the constituent behaviors that comprise the role so that his or her caretaking or teaching responsibilities can be accomplished.

Some recent reports suggest that assuming roles commonly associated with being an older sibling, such as teacher, caretaker, babysitter, or playmate, facilitates development. Zajonc (1976), in his confluence model of intellectual development, argues that firstborns excel on standardized measures of intelligence and achievement because they have had the opportunity to serve as teachers for their young siblings. Research on the effects of serving as a tutor provides additional support for this hypothesis, as it has been demonstrated that tutoring increases both the acquisition and organization of knowledge (see Bargh & Shul, 1980). Weist and Kruppe (1977) showed that children with younger siblings were able to comprehend the speech of unrelated children who were in the early phases of language development better than control children who had no younger siblings.

Few studies have directly investigated the teaching strategies of siblings. The studies that do exist indicate that older sisters are generally better teachers than older brothers (V. G. Cicirelli, 1972a, 1972b, 1976). Older sisters offer more explanations, cues, and provide more feedback than do older brothers. The aforementioned studies were all conducted in a laboratory setting with tasks that are novel to the ecology in which development takes place.

The authors of this chapter recently conducted two studies that were designed to directly assess the roles that children assume during interactions with siblings and peers (Brody, Stoneman, & MacKinnon, in press;

Stoneman, Brody, & MacKinnon, 1981). As predicted, older siblings assumed the teacher and manager roles when playing with their younger brothers and sisters, who, in turn, assumed learner and manager (the recipient of management) roles. Older siblings, however, displayed different roles when playing with their best friend (without siblings). They assumed playmate roles more often and manager roles less often. These role asymmetries displayed by the older siblings while participating in two distinct social systems would be advantageous to development. On the one hand, they practice roles associated with dominance, such as teacher, and on the other hand, they have the opportunity to practice roles associated with equalitarian relationships. Clearly, further research is needed to examine the generality of these role asymmetries in an array of contexts and to increase our understanding of their hypothesized contribution to cognitive development.

THE IMPACT OF CONTEMPORARY FACTORS ON FAMILY INTERACTIONAL SYSTEMS

While there is no doubt that the family has a tremendous impact on language and cognitive development, the effectiveness of the family in this task is often influenced by demographic and sociological factors. We often forget that families do not function independently from the larger society; indeed, they are very much influenced by external pressures that originate in the larger society. In this section we will focus on two very different factors that might influence the effectiveness of the family to serve as a competent teacher.

Television

One influence on the family as teacher, television viewing, is a phenomena that is often referred to during discussions of social behavior. We hope to point out that family television watching can also have an impact on language and cognitive development. Television has joined parents, siblings, peers, and schools as an important socialization agent in our society. In 1970, over 96% of American homes owned at least one television set (Lyle, 1972), and in the average home it was in operation for more than 6 hours per day (U. S. Office of Management and Budget, 1973). Because of the amount of time that television is watched by children and adults alike, policymakers and social scientists have focused much attention on the effect of television programs on the activities and social development of children. Recent concern about the influence of television on children has centered around the effects of children's television viewing on the acquisition and facilitation of prosocial and antisocial behaviors (e.g., Barker & Ball, 1969; Stein & Friedrick, 1971; Surgeon General's Scientific Advisory Committee on Television and Social Behaviors, 1972). These studies have clearly established that information presented in television programs is capable of influencing the development of a diverse array of social behaviors in young children. But how might television influence—or shall we say interfere with—the family's ability to serve as a competent teacher of cognitive skills? Unfortunately, there is no data that bears directly on this issue. There are, however, converging pieces of evidence that do allow us to speculate about the impact of television viewing by children and parents on family relations and the socialization process within the family.

In a commentary on contemporary family life, Bronfenbrenner (1975) argued that family life in the 1970s is drastically different from family life of preceding generations. The distinctive feature of today's family is a lack of involvement or sustained interaction between parents and children. Increased occupational and social demands on parents' time are alleged to be partially responsible for this, and the structuring of the physical environment within the home and the use of that environment by family members are also viewed as important contributors to the reduced level of interaction. Bronfenbrenner speculated that when parents and children are at home they spend much of their time absorbed in television viewing instead of with one another. This results in parents' having less association with and influence on their children, which allows for relatively greater influence on children by social agents outside the home.

The results of two early survey studies lend some credibility to the suggestion that television viewing changes the nature of family interactions. Hamilton and Lawless (1956) showed that television viewing was one of the only activities in which all family members participated during the course of a week. Although this research is a bit dated, it nevertheless lends some support to the argument that when families are at home, they tend to congregate about the television set. Maccoby's (1951) early survey work goes beyond these results by suggesting that when families and children watch television together, they stop interacting except for an occasional exchange during a commercial. Maccoby described the television viewing setting as follows: "The television atmosphere in most households is one of quiet absorption on the part of the family members who are present. The nature of the family social life could be described as 'parallel' rather than interactive, and the set does seem quite clearly to dominate family life when it is on [p. 428]."

A study by Brody, Stoneman, and Sanders (1980) sought to determine how television viewing influences family interactions by using an observational methodology. Twenty-seven middle class families were observed for 20 minutes in a familiar living room setting within a preschool facility. During half of this period a television program selected by the child in each family was shown. During the remaining time some toys that the child had selected were made available for the families to play with. Half of the families viewed television first and then played with the toys, whereas the order for the remaining families was reversed. The results revealed that children were oriented toward their parents less, talked less, and were less active, and that fathers were oriented toward their children and spouses less, talked less, and made fewer positive facial expressions during television viewing than during family play. Little behavioral difference, however, was found for mothers between the television-viewing and family play phases. The results for the fathers and children are consistent with Bronfenbrenner's (1975) commentary on family life, as well as with the results of Maccoby's (1951) self-report study. In the Brody *et al.* study, television was clearly a potent stimulus for the fathers and children and served to reduce the interactions of the family members with each other.

Given the number of hours that American families spend watching television, questions regarding a child's passive interaction with a television set rather than with a responsive parent become of great importance. How, for instance, do family interactions that characterized the television-viewing phase of the above study influence cognitive and language development? Families will only be competent teachers to the extent that either some direct or vicarious interactions occur. When both parents and children focus solely on the television, the opportunity for some type of information flow decreases. It was interesting to note, however, that mothers continued to interact with their children even while they were watching television. A recent study investigated the nature of mother–child interaction while viewing television at home (Stoneman & Brody, in press). Mother–child conversations were recorded during *Sesame Street* and a popular situation comedy. Mothers frequently took the role of teacher during both programs. During *Sesame Street*, however, mothers talked more about educationally relevant concepts such as size, color, and number, frequently labeling televised events, characters, and objects, as well as letters of the alphabet. Thus, the mothers focused their children's attention on important educational content and frequently asked their children questions to insure that they were actively processing the televised information. While viewing *Sesame Street,* children, engaged in more labeling of educationally relevant concepts than they did during the situation comedy, thus providing verbal rehearsal of the material to be learned.

During the situation comedy, mothers explained why television characters performed particular behaviors and assigned traits and emotions to characters more frequently than they did during *Sesame Street.* This finding makes sense in that the unfolding of the plot of a situation comedy provides more opportunity for discussing motives and reasons for certain behaviors than does the fast-moving, academically oriented format of *Sesame Street.* Likewise, the situation comedy affords more opportunity for developing the personalities of the characters in the program, allowing for the attribution of traits, such as honesty and courage, as well as the labeling of the character's emotional responses to certain plot events.

Thus, although numerous authors have expressed concern over television as a powerful socializing force, possibly competing with parents and schools as sources of social influence for children (Bronfenbrenner, 1975), the teaching potential of television can also be viewed as a positive educational force, opening up new areas of knowledge and exploration for children. The findings of the study by Stoneman and Brody (in press) suggest that the parent plays an important role in helping children maximally utilize television as a teacher.

Maternal employment

As of 1974, 42% of all mothers of school-age children held full-time jobs, as well as over 33% of the mothers of children under 6 years of age. Among families headed by women, 51% of all children under 18 had a mother in the labor force, compared with 38% of all children in two-parent families (U. S. Department of Labor, 1974). At every stage of their lives, women are more likely to be employed than in previous years, and because of numerous societal changes, it is likely that increasing numbers of women (including mothers) will continue to enter the labor force. Thus, it is important to understand the effects of maternal employment on child development and to consider possible ramifications for family–school relationships.

Because of the difficulty of doing research on the effects of maternal employment, much of the data that has been generated is confusing and methodologically weak (Hoffman, 1974). Many studies have failed to control for important covariants of maternal employment, such as parental education, social class, income level, family size, and child-care practices. Others have ignored child sex, age, birth order, and other important child characteristics. Conflicting findings often can be related to differential treatment of these variables (Hoffman, 1977). The multitude of retrospective studies yield only minimally useful information since the social connotations of being a working mother were very different when the individuals in these studies were younger. In our rapidly changing social climate, making generalizations across a 10–15-year time span is all but impossible, especially in areas of dramatic cultural change, such as the role of women in the family. With these cautions in mind, however, it is still possible to find several recurring themes in the research on the effects of maternal employment.

Most of the developmental research on maternal employment clusters into two major areas: (*a*) self-esteem and sex-role development; and (*b*) academic–intellectual achievement. Children (especially daughters) of employed women repeatedly have been found to view women as more competent and capable than do children of nonworking mothers. Vogel, Broverman, Broverman, Clarkson, and Rosenkrantz (1970), using a scale developed to assess sex-role perceptions, found that both male and female college students who had working mothers viewed man and women as more similar than did students with nonworking mothers. Additionally, daughters of employed mothers saw women as more competent than did daughters of nonworking mothers, and sons of employed mothers viewed men as being warmer and more expressive. Baruch (1972) gave college women journal articles to review, half of which had female names for authors and half male names. In contrast to an earlier study (Goldberg, 1967), which found that women tend to downgrade the value of articles attributed to female authors, Baruch found that only daughters of nonworking mothers were more critical of articles with female authors. Daughters of employed women were significantly less likely to view a manuscript negatively because it was written by a woman. There is evidence to suggest that daughters of working mothers have higher career aspirations (Almquist & Angrist, 1971; Ginzberg, 1971; Hoffman & Nye, 1974), are more independent and self-sufficient (Douvan, 1963; Hoffman, 1963), and are less accepting of traditional female role definitions (Douvan, 1963) than are daughters of nonworking mothers.

There is also some evidence to suggest that in lower class families children with working mothers score higher on intelligence tests (Rieber & Womack, 1968; Woods, 1972); this relationship in higher social class families is less clear (Hoffman, 1963). There is some suggestion that the IQs of girls, but not boys, are positively related to maternal employment

(Rees & Palmer, 1970). Jones, Lundsteen, and Michael (1967) found that the reading achievement of sixth-grade children who had working mothers was superior to that of children matched by SES, sex, age, and IQ who had nonworking mothers. They suggest that families that include professional women tend to spend more time reading to their children, set higher goals, and make more books and learning materials available than do families with nonworking mothers. Thus, although the quantity of time that professional women spend with their children is less than that spent by their nonworking counterparts, the quality of interaction may actually be richer. Unfortunately, the Jones *et al.* study did not match groups based on parental education, so clear interpretation of their results is not possible. There is some evidence that professionally employed women tend to have higher-achieving children than women employed in nonprofessional jobs (Frankel, 1964), but not all studies agree with this finding (e.g., Banducci, 1967). Nelson (1973) found maternal employment to be positively related to the rate at which young children acquire language. She posits that this increased acquisition rate may result from exposure to a larger number of adult language models. Her data, however, could yield to several alternative interpretations.

In summary, it appears that maternal employment does influence the development of children, particularly girls. Lessened parental sex-role differences in families in which both husband and wife are employed tend to create a family climate in which children also have fewer sex-related stereotypes. Daughters, particularly, tend to have higher career aspirations and more confidence in the capabilities of women when they are reared in a dual-career family. Intellectual and academic achievement tend to be slightly accelerated when mothers work, but these findings could be a product of parental educational level, parent–child interaction patterns, SES, or numerous other variables than maternal employment. There is a need for carefully designed research that could examine the selective contributions of these factors to child outcomes. Hoffman and Lippitt (1960) note that the distance between a family characteristic such as maternal employment and a child characteristic such as academic achievement is much too broad to be covered in a single cause–effect explanation. The many factors mediating these relationships, such as maternal employment satisfaction, family interaction patterns, parental role definitions, and child-care provisions, need to be systematically examined.

The increase in the number of working mothers has numerous implications for the educational system. One of the most obvious is the need for after-school activities. There are some indications that lack of supervision of children during nonschool hours sometimes accompanies maternal employment in lower class families. This lack of supervision has been associated with delinquency and poor social adjustment (Hoffman, 1974). After-school educational and athletic activities fill this time for many children, keeping them involved in constructive, supervised programs until parents return home from work. The benefits of such school activities are well worth the resources needed for their implementation.

School personnel must also become increasingly sensitive to sex-role stereotyping in textbooks and other curricular materials. Books depicting members of both sexes engaging in a wide variety of jobs should be selected. Additionally, materials that describe boys and men as being warm and sensitive individuals need to be provided, as well as materials that show men as gaining status through participation in household responsibilities and child care. In this way, both boys and girls can be prepared for their changing roles as fathers and mothers in dual-career families. There is also an increasing need for more expansive career education for girls and less-stereotyped career information for children of both sexes. These efforts need to begin in the early elementary grades (or even in preschool) and continue throughout the educational sequence.

Although the effects of maternal employment on daughters seem to be primarily positive, there is a slight amount of evidence to suggest that the effects on sons may be more varied (Hoffman, 1974). This suggests that teachers should be especially sensitive to the needs of boys in dual-career families. Just as fathers need to redefine the male role in the family when both parents work, sons are also in need of support as they respond to the changing societal roles of men and women. The schools can offer these boys a supportive environment in which to learn about the new expectations placed on them in a society in which both men and women share both career satisfactions and household–child-care responsibilities. It is important that the schools respond to the changing roles of men and women in order to facilitate the adjustment of children to rapidly changing role expectations.

CONCLUSIONS

It must be acknowledged that doing research on family influences is hard work. Unlike other areas of developmental research, research with families involves coordinating the schedules of at least two and often three persons. The actual staging of the research is always more complex since behavior has to be elicited from both children and adults simul-

352

taneously. Frankly, for those of you who have not attempted family research, it should be recognized that it is an expensive endeavor both for the researchers and for the subjects. With this knowledge in mind, we want to use some of our poetic license to comment on questions that future research should address.

First, the very nature of the term *family* most often implies a group of people. Yet most, if not all, the extant experiments and literature dealing with family influences on cognitive and language development have involved either one parent and child or sibling–sibling interactions. For a complete understanding of the ecology of family influences, future research needs to be directed at the outcomes of multiple sources of information on cognitive and language competencies.

Second, research has yet to identify those behaviors that family members use that are absolutely crucial to cognitive and language development. What are the processes that account for most of the variance in the impact of families on children? It seems likely that several behaviors or processes in combination are necessary to foster development.

Our third and final suggestion revolves around our belief that most of what children abstract from the family environment occurs during the flow of natural exchanges. In other words, families rarely set a child down with the intention of teaching a specific skill. It would be important to discover how children abstract complex rules from the ebb and flow of the family milieu. Research along these lines will allow us to discover the behaviors of parents and siblings that are specifically associated with cognitive and language development.

Both the family and the schools share the responsibility for facilitating developmental growth. It is important that both teachers and parents understand their unique contributions to cognitive and linguistic development and work together to achieve common goals. Such working together necessitates a high degree of mutual respect and understanding, for it is only when both the family and school function as equal partners that the best interests of children are served. It is our hope that the information presented in this chapter will help facilitate this family–school partnership.

REFERENCES

Abramovitch, R., Corter, C., & Lando, B. Sibling interaction in the home. *Child Development*, 1979, *50*, 997–1033.

Abramovitch, R., Corter, C., & Pepler, D. J. Observations of mixed-sex sibling dyads. *Child Development*, 1980, *51*, 1268–1271.

Almquist, E. M., & Angrist, S. S. Role model influences on college women's career aspirations. *Merrill Palmer Quarterly*, 1971, *17*, 263–279.

Banducci, R. The effect of mother's employment on the achievement, aspirations, and expectations of the child. *Personnel and Guidance Journal*, 1967, *46*, 263–267.

Bandura, A. *Social learning theory*. Englewood Cliffs, N. J.: Prentice-Hall, 1977.

Bargh, J. A., & Schul, Y. On the cognitive benefits of teaching. *Journal of Educational Psychology*, 1980, *72*, 593–604.

Barker, R., & Ball, S. *Mass media and violence: A report to the National Commission on Causes and Prevention of Violence*. Washington, D. C.: U. S. Government Printing Office, 1969.

Baruch, G. K. Maternal influences upon college women's attitudes toward women and work. *Developmental Psychology*, 1972, *6*, 32–37.

Bee, H., Van Egeron, L., Streissguth, A., Nyman, B., & Leckie, M. Social class differences in maternal teaching strategies and speech patterns. *Developmental Psychology*, 1969, *1*, 726–734.

Bing, E. Effect of childrearing practices on development of differential cognitive abilities. *Child Development*, 1963, *34*(3), 631–648.

Blanchard, R. W., & Biller, H. B. Father availability and academic performance among third-grade boys. *Developmental Psychology*, 1971, *4*, 301–305.

Bloom, L. *One word at a time: The use of single-word utterances before syntax*. The Hague: Mouton, 1973.

Bloom, L., Hood, L., & Lightbown, P. Imitation in language development: If, when, and why. *Cognitive Psychology*, 1974, *6*, 380–420.

Bohannon, J. N., & Marquis, A. L. Children's control of adult speech. *Child Development*, 1977, *48*, 1002–1008.

Bourne, L. Knowing and using concepts. *Psychological Review*, 1970, *77*, 546–556.

Bradley, R. H., & Caldwell, B. M. Home observation for measurement of the environment: A revision of the preschool scale. *American Journal of Mental Deficiency*, 1979, *84*(3), 235–244.

Breland, H. M. Birth order, family configuration, and verbal achievement. *Child Development*, 1974, *45*, 1011–1015.

Brim, O. G., Jr. Personality development as role-learning. In I. Iscoe & H. W. Stevenson (Eds.), *Personality development in children*. Austin: Univ. of Texas Press, 1960.

Broadcasters Yearbook, Washington, D.C.: Broadcasting Publications, 1971.

Brody, G. H., Stoneman, Z., & MacKinnon, C. *Role asymmetries between school-aged children, their siblings, and their best friends*. Child Development, in press.

Brody, G. H., Stoneman, Z., & Sanders, A. The effects of television viewing on family interactions. *Family Relations: Journal of Applied Family and Child Studies*, 1980, *29*, 216–220.

Brody, G. H., & Zimmerman, B. J. Concept formation: A social process. *Education and Urban Society*, 1978, *10*, 459–478.

Broen, P. A. The verbal environment of the language—learning child. *American Speech and Hearing Association Monograph*, 1972, *17*.

Bronfenbrenner, U. The origins of alienation. In U. Bronfenbrenner & M. Mahoney (Eds.), *Influences on human development*. Hinsdale, Illinois: Dryden Press, 1975.

Bronfenbrenner, U. *The ecology of human development*. Cambridge, Mass.: Harvard Univ. Press, 1979.

Brophy, J. E. Mothers as teachers of their own preschool children: The influence of socioeconomic status and task structure on teaching specificity. *Child Development*, 1970, *41*, 79–94.

Brown, R. How shall a thing be called? *Psychological Review*, 1958, *65*, 14–21.

Brown, R. The development of Wh questions in child speech. *Journal of Verbal Learning and Behavior*, 1968, *7*, 279–290.

Brown, R. *A first language.* Cambridge, Mass.: Harvard Univ. Press, 1973.

Cherry, L., & Lewis, M. Mothers and two-year-olds: A study of sex-differentiated aspects of verbal interaction. *Developmental Psychology*, 1976, *12*, 278–282.

Cicirelli, V. G. The effect of sibling relationship on concept learning of young children taught by child–teachers. *Child Development*, 1972, *43*, 282–287. (a)

Cicirelli, V. G. Family structure and interaction: Sibling effects on socialization. In M. McMillan & M. Sergio (Eds.), *Child psychiatry: Treatment and research.* New York: Brunner/Mazel, 1972. (b)

Cicirelli, V. G. Siblings helping siblings. In V. Allen (Ed.), *Children as teachers: Theory and research on tutoring.* New York: Academic Press, 1976.

Cicirelli, V. G. Effect of sibling presence on mother–child interaction. *Developmental Psychology*, 1978, *14*, 197–205.

Crescimbeni, J. Broken homes do not affect academic achievement. *Child and Family*, 1965, *4*(2), 24–28.

Cross, T. G. Mothers' speech adjustments: The contribution of selected child listener variables. In C. E. Snow & C. Ferguson (Eds.), *Talking to children.* New York: Cambridge Univ. Press. 1977.

Dave, R. *The identification and measurement of environmental process variables that are related to educational achievement.* Unpublished doctoral dissertation, University of Chicago, 1963.

Douvan, E. Employment and the adolescent. In F. I. Nye & L. W. Hoffman (Eds.), *The employed mother in America.* Chicago: Rand McNally, 1963.

Ferri, E. *Growing up in a one-parent family: A long-term study of child development.* London: National Foundation for Educational Research, 1976.

Feshbach, N. Cross-cultural studies of teaching styles in four-year-olds and their mothers. In Pick, A. (Ed.), *Minnesota Symposia on Child Psychology* (Vol. 7). Minneapolis: Univ. of Minnesota Press, 1973.

Frankel, E. Characteristics of working and non-working mothers among intellectually gifted high and low achievers. *Personnel and Guidance Journal*, 1964, *42*, 776–780.

Fraser, C., & Roberts, N. Mothers' speech to children of four different ages. *Journal of Psycholinguistic Research*, 1975, *4*, 9–16.

Friedlander, B. Z., Jacobs, A. C., Davis, B. B., & Wetstone, H. S. Time-sampling analysis of infants' natural language environments in the home. *Child Development*, 1972, *43*, 730–740.

Giattino, J., & Hogan, J. G. Analysis of a father's speech to his language-learning child. *Journal of Speech and Hearing Disorders*, 1975, *15*, 524–537.

Ginzberg, E. *Educated American women: Life styles and self-portraits.* New York: Columbia Univ. Press, 1971.

Gleason, J. Berko Talking to children: Some notes on feedback. In C. E. Snow & C. Ferguson (Eds.), *Talking to children.* New York: Cambridge Univ. Press, 1977.

Goldberg, P. *Misogyny and the college girl.* Paper presented at the meeting of the Eastern Psychological Association, Boston, April 1967.

Golinkoff, R. M., & Ames, G. J. *Do fathers use "motherese"?* Presented to the biannual meeting of the Society for Research in Child Development, New Orleans, 1977.

Hamilton, R., & Lawless, R. Television within the social matrix. *Public Opinion Quarterly*, 1956, *20*, 393–403.

Hess, R. D., & Shipman, V. Early experience and the socialization of cognitive modes in children. *Child Development*, 1965, *36*(4), 869–886.

Hetherington, E. M., Cox, M., & Cox, R. *Beyond father absence: Conceptualization of the effects of divorce.* Paper presented at the meeting of the Society for Research in Child Development, Denver, April 1975.

Hetherington, E. M., Cox, M., & Cox, R. The aftermath of divorce. In J. H. Stevens & M. M. Mathews (Eds.), *Mother-child, father-child relations.* Washington, D.C.: MAEYC, 1978.

Hoffman, L. W. Mother's enjoyment of work and effects on the child. In F. I. Nye & L. W. Hoffman (Eds.), *The employed mother in America.* Chicago: Rand McNally, 1963.

Hoffman, L. W. Effects of maternal employment on the child: A review of the research. *Developmental Psychology,* 1974, *10,* 204–228.

Hoffman, L. W. Changes in family roles, socialization, and sex differences. *American Psychologist,* 1977, *32,* 644–657.

Hoffman, L. W., & Lippitt, R. The measurement of family life variables. In P. Mussen (Ed.), *Handbook of research methods in child development.* New York: Wiley, 1960.

Hoffman, L. W., & Nye, F. I. *Working mothers.* San Francisco: Jossey-Bass, 1974.

Holzman, M. The verbal environment provided by mothers for their very young children. *Merrill-Palmer Quarterly,* 1974, *20,* 31–42.

Hunt, J. M. *Intelligence and experience.* New York: Ronald Press, 1961.

Jones, J. B., Lundsteen, S. W., & Michael, W. B. The relationship of the professional employment status of mothers to reading achievement of sixth-grade children. *California Journal of Educational Research,* 1967, *43,* 102–108.

Koenigsknecht, R. A., & Friedman, P. Syntax development in boys and girls. *Child Development,* 1976, *47,* 1109–1115.

Lamb, M. E. Interactions between 18-month-olds and their preschool-aged siblings. *Child Development,* 1978, *49,* 51–59. (a)

Lamb, M. E. The development of sibling relations in infancy: A short-term longitudinal study. *Child Development,* 1978, *49,* 1189–1196. (b)

Landy, F., Rosenberg, B. G., & Sutton-Smith, B. The effect of limited father absence on cognitive development. *Child Development,* 1969, *40,* 941–944.

Laosa, L. Maternal teaching strategies in Chicano families of varied educational and socioeconomic levels. *Child Development,* 1978, *49,* 1129–1135.

LeMasters, E. E. *Parents in modern America.* Homewood, Ill.: Dorsey Press, 1970.

Lyle, J. Television and daily life: Patterns of use (Overview). In E. Rubenstein, G. Comstock, & J. Murray (Eds.), *Television and social behavior* (*Vol. 4*). Washington, D. C.: U. S. Government Printing Office, 1972.

McCarthy, D. Language development in children. In L. Carmichael (Ed.), *Manual of child psychology.* New York: Wiley, 1954.

Maccoby, E. Television: Its impact on school children. *Public Opinion Quarterly,* 1951, *15,* 423–444.

MacKinnon, C., Brody, G. H., & Stoneman, Z. *The effects of divorce and maternal employment on the home environments of preschool children. Child Development,* in press.

McNeill, D. Developmental psychol-linguistics. In F. Smith & G. A. Miller (Eds.), *The genesis of language.* Cambridge, Mass.: MIT Press, 1966.

Mahoney, G. J. Ethological approach to delayed language acquisition. *American Journal of Mental Deficiency,* 1975, *80,* 139–148.

Malouf, R. E., & Dodd, D. H. Role of exposure, imitation, and expansion in the acquisition of an artificial grammatical rule. *Developmental Psychology,* 1972, *7,* 195–203.

Messer, D. J. The integration of mothers' referential speech with joint play. *Child Development,* 1978, *49,* 781–787.

Moerk, E. Principles of interaction in language learning. *Merrill-Palmer Quarterly,* 1972, *18,* 229–257.

Moerk, E. L. *Pragmatic and semantic aspects of early language development.* Baltimore: Univ. Park Press, 1977.

Moss, H. Sex, age, & state as determinants of mother–infant interaction. *Merrill-Palmer Quarterly,* 1967, *13,* 19–36.

Nelson, K. Structure and strategy in learning to talk. *Monographs of the Society for Research on Child Development,* 1973, *38*(1–2, Serial No. 149).

Parke, R. D., & O'Leary, S. E. Father–mother–infant interaction in the newborn period: Some findings, some observations, and some unresolved issues. In K. Riegel & J. Meacham (Eds.), *The developing individual in a changing world* (Vol. 2). The Hague: Mouton, 1976.

Parke, R. D., & Sarwin, D. B. The fathers' role in infancy: A reevaluation. *The Family Coordinator,* 1976, *25,* 365–372.

Phillips, J. R. Syntax and vocabulary of mother's speech to young children: Age and sex comparisons. *Child Development,* 1973, *44,* 182–185.

Radin, N. Father–child interaction and the intellectual functioning of four-year-old boys. *Developmental Psychology,* 1972, *6,* 353–361.

Radin, N. Observed paternal behaviors as antecedents of intellectual functioning in young boys. *Developmental Psychology,* 1973, *8,* 369–376.

Radin, N. Observed maternal behavior with four-year-old-boys and girls in lower-class families. *Child Development,* 1974, *45,* 1126–1131.

Rebelsky, F., & Hanks, C. Fathers' verbal interaction with infants in the first three months of life. *Child Development,* 1971, *42,* 63–68.

Rees, A. N., & Palmer, F. H. Factors related to change in mental test performance. *Developmental Psychology Monograph,* 1970, *3*(2, Pt. 2).

Rieber, M., & Womack, M. The intelligence of preschool children as related to ethnic and demographic variables. *Exceptional Children,* 1968, *34,* 609–614.

Rosenthal, T., & Zimmerman, B. *Social learning and cognitions.* New York: Academic Press, 1978.

Sachs, J. The adaptive significance of linguistic input to prelinguistic infants. In C. E. Snow & C. Ferguson (Eds.), *Talking to children.* New York: Cambridge Univ. Press, 1977.

Samuels, H. R. The effect of older sibling on infant locomotor exploration of a new environment. *Child Development,* 1980, *51,* 607–609.

Santrock, J. W. Relation of type and onset of father absence to cognitive development. *Child Development,* 1972, *43,* 455–469.

Schumaker, J. B., & Sherman, J. A. Parent as intervention agent. In R. L. Schiefelbusch (Ed.), *Language intervention strategies.* Baltimore: Univ. Park Press, 1978.

Shatz, M., & Gelman, R. The development of communication skills: Modifications in the speech of young children as a function of listener. *Monographs of the Society for Research on Child Development,* 1973, *38*(5, Serial No. 152).

Sherrod, K. B., Friedman, S., Crawley, S., Drake, D., & Devieux, J. Maternal language to prelinguistic infants: Syntactic aspects. *Child Development,* 1977, *48,* 1662–1665.

Snow, C. E. Mothers' speech to children learning language. *Child Development,* 1972, *43,* 549–565.

Snow, C. E. Mothers' speech research: from input to interaction. In C. E. Snow & C. Ferguson (Eds.), *Talking to children.* New York: Cambridge Univ. Press, 1977.

Stein, A., & Friedrick, L. Television content and young childrens' behavior. In *Social Behavior* (Vol. 2), Washington, D.C.: U.S. Government Printing Office, 1971.

Steward, M., & Steward, D. Effect of social distance on teaching strategies of Anglo-American and Mexican-American mothers. *Developmental Psychology,* 1974, *10,* 797–807.

Stoneman, Z. *An analysis of the role of questions in maternal speech to preverbal children.* Presented at the 24th Annual Meeting of the Southeastern Psychological Association, Atlanta, 1978.

Stoneman, Z. *The effects of setting richness on the concreteness of maternal speech to young children.* Presented at the 25th Annual Meeting of the Southeastern Psychological Association, New Orleans, 1979.

Stoneman, Z., & Brody, G. *Mothers' and fathers' perceptions of the language competencies of their preschool children.* Unpublished manuscript, 1978.

Stoneman, Z., & Brody, G. H. Two's company, three makes a difference: An examination of maternal and paternal speech to their young children. *Child Development,* 1981, *52,* 705–707.

Stoneman, Z., & Brody, G. H. *An in-home investigation of maternal teaching strategies during Sesame Street and a popular situation comedy. Journal of Applied Developmental Psychology,* in press.

Stoneman, Z., Brody, G. H., & MacKinnon, C. *Naturalistic observations of children's activities and roles while playing with their siblings and friends.* Unpublished manuscript, 1981.

Surgeon Generals' Scientific Advisory Committee on Television and Social Behavior. *Television and growing up: The impact of televised violence.* Washington, D.C.: Government Printing Office, 1972.

Sutton-Smith, B., & Rosenberg, B. G. *The sibling.* New York: Holt, 1970.

Szalai, A., Converse, P. E., Feldheim, P., Scheuch, E. K., & Stone, P. J. (Eds.). *The use of time: Daily activities of urban and suburban populations in twelve countries.* The Hague, Mouton, 1973.

U. S. Department of Labor, Bureau of Labor Statistics. Children of working mothers. *Monthly Labor Review,* 1974.

U. S. Office of Management and Budget. Washington, D. C.: U. S. Government Printing Office, 1973.

Vogel, S. R., Broverman, I. K., Broverman, D. M., Clarkson, F. E., & Rosenkrantz, P. S. Maternal employment and perception of sex roles among college students. *Developmental Psychology,* 1970, *3,* 384–391.

Weist, R. M., & Kruppe, B. Parent and sibling comprehension of children's speech. *Journal of Psycholinguistic Research,* 1977, *6,* 49–58.

Whitehurst, G. J., & Vasta, R. Is language acquired through imitation? *Journal of Psycholinguistic Research,* 1975, *4,* 37–57.

Wolfe, R. *The identification card measurement of environmental process variables related to intelligence.* Unpublished doctoral dissertation, University of Chicago, 1964.

Woods, M. B. The unsupervised child of the working mother. *Developmental Psychology,* 1972, *6,* 14–25.

Zajonc, R. B. Family configuration and intelligence. *Science,* 1976, *192,* 227–236.

Zajonc R., & Markus, G. Birth order and intellectual development. *Psychological Review,* 1975, *82,* 74–88.

9 / Personal and social causation in the school context

RONALD W. HENDERSON

Children enter their initial school experience displaying a wide variety of individual differences in their personal characteristics and capabilities. Although the initial range of differences is impressive, it is axiomatic that individual variations become more pronounced as children move through their elementary school experience. Most of the attention given to this phenomenon has focused on increases in the variance in academic achievement, and until recent work on mastery learning (Bloom, 1976), educators generally considered this situation to be the inevitable consequence of instruction.

Many educators consider intellectual ability to be the major contributor to the escalating variance in achievement that accompanies the progress of a cohort of children through the grades. From this perspective it is reasoned that children of high intellectual ability profit more readily from school instruction than their less capable peers, and their advantage is progressively amplified because, at any particular time, they have a larger repertoire of skills and information with which to respond to subsequent instruction.

The importance of intellectual differences cannot be discounted, but the expression of intellectual capability is often masked by a variety of behavioral and cultural factors, and teacher perceptions of ability and their consequent instructional behaviors may be heavily influenced by

359

PSYCHOLOGICAL DEVELOPMENT
IN THE ELEMENTARY YEARS

the personal characteristics of students. In any case, it seems clear that the effects of intellectual capability are mediated to a substantial degree by behavioral and personality differences among children. For example, children in school differ markedly in their willingness to initiate, attend to, expend effort on, and persist at academically relevant tasks. All of these behaviors are generally considered essential to academic success. Initial differences in these behaviors may be the consequence of forces outside the school, but once children are exposed to formal education, the development of academically adaptive behaviors becomes an important, albeit often unplanned, outcome of school experience. This influence is not a unidirectional one, flowing from school environment to behavioral dispositions of individuals, as older views of socialization suggested. The relationship is more likely to approximate the interdependent processes described by Bandura (1977).

This chapter reviews, and attempts to show interrelationships among, several bodies of literature that should help to carry explanations of variability in school behavior beyond simplistic, intellectual superiority views. Toward this end, the chapter opens with a discussion of two interrelated personality constructs, *locus of control* and *learned helplessness*. Although these constructs are often used to designate personality traits that are assumed to display great stability and cross-situational generalizability, they are used here in accordance with social learning interpretations. According to this view, behaviors associated with the locus of control and learned helplessness constructs may or may not be stable across time and situations, depending on the interactions of personal and environmental factors. Used in this way, the constructs of locus of control and learned helplessness are considered as designators of characteristic cognitive strategies, subject to both personal and social influence, that involve both individual attributions of cause and outcome expectancies. From this perspective, the attempt is to illustrate processes that may lead to individual differences in causal inferences, and to suggest how the outcomes of these learning processes may, in turn, have prolonged, cumulative influences on academic behavior. The assumption guiding this exploration is that children form causality hypotheses concerning the probable outcomes of a given behavior in a particular situation. Causality hypotheses are formed from children's experience and determine whether or not they will elect to participate in those behaviors that adults designate as appropriate or adaptive in relation to academic tasks. The ensuing discussion will amplify these generalizations.

In order to understand the processes contributing to causal inferences more fully, the topic of teacher expectancies is examined as a hypothesized determinant of the variations in school experiences. The educational implications of postulated interdependence between environmental and personal determinants of school behavior are discussed in the concluding segment of the chapter.

LOCUS OF CONTROL

Some children seem to learn very quickly, through their school experience, that no matter how hard they try, they are destined to do poorly compared to their classmates. They may conclude, among other things, that they lack the ability to do school work. Individual perceptions of the degree to which one has personal control over events may vary as a function of situational factors, but successful people seem more disposed to view the consequences of their actions as the result of personal effort and ability, whereas those who are less successful see the events that befall them as the result of good luck or misfortune. The situation is clearly more complex than these commonsense observations imply, but the general assertion is that an individual's perception of the likelihood of success due to effort has clear implications for the amount and kind of effort he or she is likely to put forth.

These observations are germaine to the locus of control personality construct. Locus of control, or the tendency to perceive the events that influence one's life either as the consequence of one's own actions or as the result of external forces beyond one's personal control (Rotter, 1966) is regarded by many psychologists as an important determinant of behavior. The layperson's understanding of how people act, or fail to act, in matters that might influence their own welfare has been subjected to clarification, elaboration, and incorporation through research. Clarification and eventual incorporation into theoretical systems are important to help us understand how perceptions of personal efficacy develop, what childrearing practices govern them, how these attribution modes are influenced by school experience, and how locus of control perceptions influence the development of academic skills and affective characteristics. At present the knowledge bearing on these questions is incomplete. The following discussion of the knowledge base is selective rather than comprehensive, with those studies that provide basic background or the clearest implications for education being discussed in fullest detail.

Empirical foundations

There is a history of experimental research behind the notion that the behavior of individuals is governed, in part, by their expectations that their behavior will be influential. Most of the early research was conducted with animals; much of the later work employed adults, primarily college students. Recently, research with school-age children has been accumulating rapidly. The total research output on the topic of locus of control has been described as phenomenal (Phares & Lamiell, 1977).

One forerunner of our understanding of the kinds of learning experiences that lead to differential perceptions of control involved subjecting food-deprived rats to an aversive stimulus in such a manner that one group had control over the termination of the aversive stimulus whereas the other group did not (Mowrer & Vieck, 1948, cited in Lefcourt, 1976). Shocks were presented just a few seconds after the rat took food presented to it. Those who could exercise some control over the situation showed less fear of the aversive stimulus than those who could not; the critical dependent variable was inhibition in eating proffered food. Since the rats were hungry, the behavior of those who feared to accept the food after exposure to an aversion stimulus over which they had no control was maladaptive.

Numerous additional laboratory studies of animals and humans support the conclusion that the manner in which individuals (humans, dogs, and rats) respond to aversive stimuli is governed by their perceptions of control or lack of control over these events (Lefcourt, 1976). But it is important to note that perceptions of control may not always be beneficial (Rotter, 1975). Lefcourt (1976) uses a well known "executive monkey" experiment (Brady, Porter, Conrad, & Mason, 1958) to illustrate this point. In this study pairs of monkeys were yoked in an apparatus so that when one received a shock the other did also. The critical difference in the treatment of the two monkeys was that one, designated as the *executive*, could avoid delivery of shocks by rapidly pressing a lever. The second monkey of the pair had no such control. After several days the animals were killed, and autopsies revealed that the executives had developed extensive gastrointestinal ulcers, whereas their partners had not. A refinement of this study, using rats rather than monkeys, produced an opposite set of findings (Weiss, 1971). Thus, it is not clear whether or not the burden of "decision making" under stressful conditions has deleterious effects.

The basic message to be heeded in acknowledging these mixed outcomes is that caution should be exercised in judging the general worth of a particular control orientation (Lefcourt, 1976). Most contemporary studies of locus of control carry the implicit assumption that perceptions of personal control have an adaptive value, whereas the belief that consequences are beyond one's control is maladaptive. Indeed, most evidence tends to support that point of view, but there are exceptions (Phares, 1976), and these may have particular relevance to the effects of schooling. It would be wrong to assume that internality has uniformly positive qualities and externality uniformly negative ones.

Theoretical foundations

Social learning theory. Social learning theory provided the general theoretical background for the internal–external control constructs proposed by Julian Rotter (1966). Rotter noted that people may perceive and react in varied ways to behavioral consequences. He proposed that one determinant of this reaction is the degree to which individuals perceive reinforcement as the consequence of their own action or as the product of outside forces independent of their own behavior. Seen in this way, the effect of reinforcement is not automatic. It depends on whether or not it is *perceived* as the consequence of one's own behavior. When events are interpreted as the product of luck, or fate, or when the complexity of forces in the individual's world makes reinforcement unpredictable, this perception is labeled as belief in *external control*. If events are seen as contingent on one's own behavior, or as the product of relatively stable personal characteristics, the belief is labeled as *internal control.*

As a result of their reinforcement histories, individuals develop *expectancies* that particular behaviors will or will not be reinforced in the future. Expectancies then generalize to situations perceived as similar (Rotter, 1966). The notion of internal–external control of reinforcement merely refers to a generalized expectancy based on the individual's perception of the relationship between his or her behavior and the occurrence of reward or punishment.

The internality–externality dimension is a continuum. The internal and external categories are not discrete and mutually exclusive (Phares, 1976), although the terms are sometimes used as though that were the case to designate individuals whose general orientation falls more toward one end of the continuum than the other. Furthermore, recent research with school children (Frieze & Snyder, 1980) indicates that even for a variety of tasks within the school setting, the causal belief structure of the child varies depending on the situation.

Attribution theory. Although initial interest in the effects of locus of control perceptions was guided largely by Rotter's version of social learning theory,[1] recent elaborations of the locus of control construct

---

[1]The version of social learning theory employed by Rotter was more limited than the recent formulations described by Bandura (1977) and Mischel (1973). The more recent formulations are sometimes referred to as cognitive social learning theory.

and of the concept of learned helplessness (discussed later in this chapter) have been stimulated by concepts borrowed from social psychology, especially as described in the naive psychology of Fritz Heider and his contributions to attribution theory.

In the opening discussion of locus of control we noted that many of the observations made about how people act as they do seem to be a matter of common sense. Even during the elementary school years children develop and apply a fairly sophisticated intuitive knowledge of psychological principles of social behavior (Mischel & Mischel, 1979). Heider was interested in people's beliefs about behavior, and he spent much of his career describing and systematizing the commonsense assumptions about interpersonal relationships among people. In the formulation derived from his analysis, Heider (1958) postulated that in their attributions of causes for outcomes, people distinguish between stable and unstable factors. The perception of the stability or variability of a cause has a major influence on the individual's expectation of success or failure. If the outcome of performance on a task is perceived as the result of stable factors, such as ability or task difficulty, failure on that task would lead to an expectancy of failure on future attempts at similar tasks. Consistency would be expected because ability is assumed to be a stable factor, and success expectancies would decline. On the other hand, if the cause is attributed to unstable factors, such as luck or effort, success expectancies would either remain stable or increase. Consistency would not be expected. The expression *Better luck next time* aptly captures the essence of this kind of expectancy.

Besides these perceptions of stable and unstable causes, Heider proposed that behavior also is determined by factors either within or outside the person. One within-the-person consideration is a personal power factor. In making attributions of causes for the performance outcomes of self or others, the relevant question may be, *Can I do it?* (or *Can he or she do it?*). This is Heider's *can* factor. In classroom settings, this factor is likely to be perceived as a stable characteristic. The norm-referenced goal structure of traditional classrooms does not generally emphasize the individual's progress against his or her own past performance. Rather, performance is implicitly or explicitly compared to the accomplishments of peers (Henderson & Henning, 1979), and under most circumstances that relative position is unlikely to change in any dramatic way. Even so, people recognize that certain skills improve over a developmental sequence, and if that perception dictates the attribution of cause, the *can* factor might be viewed as variable.

Heider used the term *try* to designate a second inside-the-person factor. Behavioral outcomes may be determined by the amount of effort the individual expends. Therefore, we would expect those who attribute successes to effort to be more willing to initiate a task, or to persist at it longer, compared to individuals who do not perceive effort as a crucial cause.

Outside-the-person factors to which causes might be attributed include all of the various environmental forces that influence success or failure. One may be successful because of good luck, or failure may result from misfortune. One may perform well because the task is easy, or do poorly because it is difficult. A child may get good grades because the teacher likes her, or be the recipient of poor marks for the opposite reason. A minority child may attribute his failing grades to prejudice on the part of the teacher. These perceived causes could be variable or stable, and it must be stressed that the person's perception rather than the fact is the critical variable. Clearly it would be possible for a child to develop a generalized expectancy of academic failure as a consequence of attributions to teacher bias as a stable cause.

Heider (1958) also hypothesized developmental changes in the kinds of attributional criteria used in attributing responsibility for outcomes. In general, younger children tend to attribute outcomes to external environmental forces, but as they mature outcomes are increasingly ascribed to their own internal characteristics. Research has provided support for this hypothesis (e.g., Harris, 1977).

Other investigations have demonstrated that locus of control orientations differ as a function of variables such as age, sex, social class, race, and ethnicity. The locus of control construct is also associated with such academically relevant variables as motivation and achievement.

Relationships to achievement

One aspect of locus of control research that seems potentially useful is that which examines the relationship between children's locus of control orientation and their academic achievement. With remarkable consistency, investigations have demonstrated that children who perceive themselves to be in control of the consequences of their behavior (internal locus of control) are superior in intellectual activities and school achievement compared to their peers who believe their fate to be determined primarily by chance or by other people (Crandall, Katkovsky, & Crandall, 1965; Crandall, Katkovsky, & Preston, 1962; Gordon, 1977; Nowicki & Strickland, 1973).

In the first of these studies (Crandall *et al.*, 1962) a number of measures (personality tests, an intelligence test, an achievement test, a measure of children's expectations and standards for academic success, and the Intellectual Achievement Responsibility Questionnaire, or IAR) were administered to children who attended a week-long day camp at the Fels Institute. The goal was to predict achievement behaviors occurring in a free-play situation. The children's activities in a playroom were observed and recorded with a time-sampling procedure to determine the amount of time spent in intellectual activities and the intensity of striving while engaged in these activities. Children were free to choose any materials or activities they wished from the wide range of play materials and books. The materials provided for intellectual activity or achievement behavior included jigsaw puzzles, form boards, quiz games, math and reading flash cards, informative books, and games requiring intellectual competition.

Of all the measures used, the IAR was most strongly correlated with both time spent in intellectual activities and intensity of achievement striving for the boys. For the girls, both time spent with intellectual achievement activities and the intensity of their striving on these activities were uncorrelated with the IAR. The intelligence and achievement measures were both positively correlated with the IAR for boys, but not for girls.

Crandall *et al.* (1965) later conducted a follow-up study of the relationships between achievement and IAR among third, fourth, and fifth graders. In this case report card grades and standardized achievement test scores of both boys and girls were positively associated with IAR scores. Furthermore, Chance (1965) replicated the original Fels Institute study and found that the IAR was significantly correlated with the Stanford–Binet Intelligence Scale and the California Achievement Tests, for both boys and girls.

The results mentioned thus far were based on the composite score yielded by the IAR, but half of the items of the IAR refer to failure situations and the other half to success experiences. Thus, the instrument yields a score pertaining to attributions of success (I+), a score for attributions of failure (I −), and a total score. Scores for attributions of failure and success have yielded different relationships to achievement measures for girls as compared to boys. For example Crandall *et al.* (1962) found that academic achievement in arithmetic and reading was positively related to I+ scores for boys, but not for girls.

A variety of measures developed by other investigators (e.g., Clifford, 1976; Nowicki & Strickland, 1973) have also proved capable of predicting academic performance. Although a general case can be made that achievement and locus of control are positively associated, inconsistencies in the findings leave the specifics of the relationship in doubt (Lefcourt, 1976). A number of researchers (Clifford, 1976; Dollinger &

Taub, 1977; Taub & Dollinger, 1975; Winetsky, 1978; Wolk & Du Cette, 1974) have attempted to clarify these inconsistencies and to explore the relationships of locus of control and achievement to additional person and environment variables.

Clarification studies

The Academic Achievement Accountability Questionnaire (AAA) (Clifford, 1976) was developed to assess some of the attributional variables suggested by Heider's work. Whereas the IAR assesses the degree to which outcomes are attributed to the self or to significant others, such as parents, teachers, or friends, the AAA was designed to assess the variable components of effort and luck while holding the stable components of ability and task difficulty constant. This is done by anchoring judgments to the respondent's own previous performance. The AAA is thus more restricted in its focus than the IAR. Clifford based her judgment of the potential utility of the measure on research that suggested that effort attributions may be more important than ability attributions as determinants of such characteristics as pride and shame, persistence, and self-reward.

One educationally relevant implication of locus of control research is that individuals who expect to exert a large degree of control over the rewards and punishments to which they are subject (internals) are likely to engage in more goal-oriented behaviors than individuals with an external orientation (externals) (Dollinger & Taub, 1977). Most of these findings relating to generalized expectancies have been derived from laboratory studies. Fairly consistent results over a wide age range and for a wide range of behavior suggest that the locus of control is a particularly useful predictor of intrinsically motivated behavior. It has been argued, for example, that internals may be more capable than their external peers of responding when a reason is provided for a desired behavior (Dollinger & Taub, 1977).

From his review of research on cognitive activity and locus of control, Lefcourt (1976) concluded that cognitive differences between internals and externals may account for differences in their response patterns to situations such as resistance to coercion. Several differences were identified. Compared to externals, internals were more perceptive and more likely to learn about their surroundings. They were also more curious than externals and more efficient information processers. The implication is that highly external individuals may be unable to examine and evaluate their decisions objectively (Lefcourt, 1976). Externals may be less aware of and less responsive to the environmental cues that convey information about the meaning of a particular behavior or the likelihood of success experiences in varied situations (Dollinger & Taub, 1977). Related findings have demonstrated that when college students were provided with information on the meaning of task behavior and on methods that would enhance success on the task, externals increased their internal control behavior, but the behavior of internals was not affected (Lefcourt & Wine, 1969). Lefcourt refers to such instructions as cue explication. In support of this general finding Wolk and Du Cette (1974) reported that externals attended more adequately to stimuli when those stimuli were made more salient through cue explication. The cue explication had no effect on internals, probably because they were already attending adequately.

Against this background, Dollinger and Taub (1977) set out to determine the relationship between locus of control and provision of cue explication in children. The study was partly motivated by an unexpected finding of an earlier study (Taub & Dollinger, 1975) in which external children's performance on a coding task increased in response to a statement giving a fictional purpose for the experiment, whereas the performance of internals was not similarly influenced. Dollinger and Taub (1977) measured motivation by performance on a boring coding task and by the subject's interest ratings and willingness to continue with the task. Subjects were middle class boys and girls from grades 4 through 6. The subjects were divided into thirds to represent three levels of locus of control, as measured by the IAR. Half of the subjects at each level were given a purpose, consisting of a message that their responses would help the physics department at the university develop a new instrument panel for the space program. The importance of the assigned task was emphasized.

The results of this investigation revealed that externals showed poorer performance and less interest in the task than internals when no purpose for the boring task was provided. When the purpose was provided, the performance of externals improved, whereas that of internals did not. Thus, previous findings relating to the salutory effects of cue explication in adults were extended to elementary-school-age children.

Dollinger and Taub also submit that their study lends support to Mischel's (1973) and Rotter's (1975) hypothesis that individual differences, such as those encompassed by the locus of control construct, may have a greater influence on performance in less structured, more ambiguous situations than under circumstances in which cues are salient and their meaning understood. This possibility has implications for the structuring of school experiences for poor and minority group children, who seem to be disproportionately represented among externals.

It is possible that the school situation may seem ambiguous to many such children because the cultural meanings of physical and behavioral cues in the classroom differ from the meanings acquired in the home environment. It also seems possible that children from homes in which the relevance of school is stressed are less in need of clear explication of the purposes of school tasks than are children from homes that do not share the school's value system. The stated purposes or justifications for school tasks may not be self-evident to many minority group and poor children and their parents (see Winetsky, 1978).

LEARNED HELPLESSNESS

Some individuals perceive themselves as incapable of overcoming failure. For them failure results in varying degrees of anxiety and deterioration of performance. Seligman (1975) proposed the term *learned helplessness* to describe this pattern of response, which he and his colleagues observed in a series of experiments (e.g., Seligman & Maier, 1967; Seligman, Maier, & Solomon, 1971) in which animals were exposed to an aversive stimulus from which escape was impossible. Subsequently, the subjects failed to employ instrumental escape–avoidance responses to aversive stimulation, and the impairment of these responses generalized to new settings. Seligman suggested that in situations in which organisms are unable to control aversive events, they learn that responding and reinforcement are independent of each other. This perception then influences behavior in other situations in which control of reinforcement would be possible if the subjects would *try* (to use Heider's term). In other words, organisms who have been subjected to such learning experiences come to perceive that there is no connection between their own behavior and the presentation or removal of aversive stimuli in a variety of settings.

The observation that led to the conceptualization of learned helplessness was not entirely original and Seligman and his associates. The concept of learned helplessness is very similar to Mowrer's (1960) notion of *hopelessness*, but Seligman and his associates were the first to study the phenomenon systematically. Whereas the early studies of learned helplessness were conducted with animal subjects, a number of studies of the effects of uncontrollable events with humans began to appear in the early 1970s (see Abramson, Seligman, & Teasdale, 1978). Since then, interest in this area has developed rapidly. The concept of learned helplessness has both a commonsense and a heuristic scientific appeal to educators and clinicians who see this formulation as a possible explanation for the debilitating behavior they witness among otherwise apparently capable individuals.

Learned helplessness has been manipulated in a number of different ways in studies in which human subjects have been exposed to aversive stimuli as a consequence of failure (experimenter manipulated) on problem-solving tasks (Wortman, Panciera, Shusterman, & Hibscher, 1976). Most of these studies have been conducted with college-age samples. After subjects have undergone helplessness training, their performance on subsequent problems of the same type deteriorates. In much of this research, failure outcomes have been linked to aversive stimuli such as shocks or loud noises, but the case for relevance to education is made more convincing in investigations in which the aversive event consists of feedback that leads subjects to believe they have failed to solve problems measuring important intellectual abilities (e.g., Roth & Kubal, 1975). The parallels to classroom situations in which some children seem destined to fail are obvious.

Relatively few studies of learned helplessness have been conducted with school-age children, but recently interest in this topic has escalated, now that learned helplessness has been linked to perceptions of reinforcement control, as conceptualized in locus of control studies within an attribution theory paradigm. As with locus of control orientations, learned helplessness exists along a continuum, and the terms *helpless* and *nonhelpless* are merely used as a convenience in referring to individuals whose responses tend to fall toward one pole or the other. The research indicates that children who are categorized as helpless, on the basis of teacher judgment or locus of control attributions, tend to attribute their failures to lack of ability rather than to the level of their own effort. Dweck and her associates (Diener & Dweck, 1978; Dweck, 1975; Dweck & Bush, 1976; Dweck & Reppucci, 1973) have found that even when they are as well motivated and as competent at a criterion task as their nonhelpless counterparts, helpless children evidence maladaptive reactions to failure. Following failure, children who have learned to feel helpless in the face of difficulties tend to attribute their failure to inability, and their performance on subsequent tasks is impaired. In contrast, nonhelpless children are likely to attribute lack of success to insufficient effort on their own part, and they display no deterioration in performance following the failure experience. In fact, the performance of children who attribute failure to lack of effort often shows improvement, apparently due to increased effort, following failure (Diener & Dweck, 1978).

Dweck's (1975) findings have clear educational implications. Since helpless children evidence little recognition of effort as a determinant of success or failure, they fail to see their own responsibility for outcomes. They are thus likely to see aversive situations as insurmountable, and following an unsuccessful effort they may fail to respond to subsequent tasks of the same sort by trying harder or by sticking to the task longer. Dweck has emphasized that an aversive event is not in itself the cause of the helplessness phenomenon; the critical difference between helpless and persevering children appears to lie in their perception of the relationship between their own behavior and the failure outcome. Dweck and Reppucci (1973) demonstrated that even when children expeience the same number and sequence of successes and failures, there are marked individual variations in response to failure experiences. An important dimension of these individual differences seems to be a function of whether or not the children perceive the situation to be within their personal control.

The findings of research on locus of control attributions and learned helplessness raise two questions for educators and for psychologists working in applied areas such as educational or clinical psychology: What kinds of socialization experiences lead to the development of these individual differences in causal attributions and response to failure, and how can the debilitating effects of learned helplessness be overcome?

ENVIRONMENTAL FACTORS

Home and community

Unfortunately, research bearing on the childrearing or home environmental variables that may be instrumental in the development of individual differences in mode of response to failure is scant. Furthermore, most of the evidence that has been produced in the search for antecedents is based on correlational analyses of locus of control scores and retrospective self-report responses to parent–child questionnaires (Phares & Lamiell, 1977). Collectively these studies have produced results that lack a common integrative theoretical framework to shed light on the social influence processes leading to the development of individual differences in locus of control attributions. Expectancy theory (Rotter, 1955) is too narrow for this purpose because, however useful it may be in identifying possible influences on the performance or nonperformance of behaviors that have already been acquired, it does not explain the mechanisms involved in the acquisition of new responses (Bandura & Walters, 1963).

In a general sense, it appears that children raised in circumstances in which they are able to exercise little control are likely to develop external locus of control perceptions (Lefcourt, 1976). A variety of different factors could influence such learning. The experience of being raised under conditions of poverty or discrimination could have such an influence, as could a variety of family constellation conditions. For example, Rotter (1966) has suggested that the experience of being raised without a father may lead children to develop the perception that their lives are drastically affected by fate. As a result, one might predict that children who had experienced such a loss would express more external perceptions of control than children from intact families. Parish and Copeland (1979) addressed this hypothesis in a study in which undergraduate university students responded to Rotter's internality–externality scale and to questions regarding family background. Presumably the results would bear on the relationship between a general class of childhood experiences and the internality–externality dimension. It turned out that males whose fathers had died did give significantly more external responses than those from intact families, but this was not true for males whose parents had divorced. Results for females did not follow the pattern found for males. The study shed little light on the reasons that sons of deceased fathers might see fate as a controlling factor in their lives, or why males whose parents had divorced might react differently. Neither is there an explanation for the reported sex differences. This study adds to a body of unexplained inconsistencies that make the interpretation of locus of control research problematic.

Several studies have examined the relationship between locus of control and a variety of self-reported childrearing variables (see Phares, 1976; Phares & Lamiell, 1977). Katkovsky, Crandall, and Good (1967) found a positive association between approving, nonrejecting, nurturant, and protective parental behavior and internal perceptions of control in children. Chance (1965) also found associations between mothers' scores on a measure of acceptance–rejection and their children's perceptions of internal or external control of achievement outcomes. Research in which children have reported on the practices of their parents suggests that children with internal perceptions of control experience less hostile control and rejection and more positive involvement than their external peers (Davis & Phares, 1969; Shore, 1967). It should be noted that these latter findings reflect children's perceptions and reports of parental practices, and the accuracy of their reports are unknown. It is interesting, however, that when Davis and Phares examined the reported practices of parents themselves, there were no direct relationships between childrearing variables such as control and rejection and the locus of control orientations of children.

There is no apparent reason to assume that either parental or child self-report captures reality better than the other, and there are very few studies of actual interactions to clarify the situation. Davis (1969, cited in Phares, 1976) attempted to overcome these limitations by assigning family groups that included either an externally or internally oriented son to situations in which each group performed certain assigned tasks together. There was no evidence that parents of externally oriented boys were more rejecting than parents of internals, or that parents of the boys with internal perceptions of control encouraged more participation or self-reliance. The findings of differences that did emerge suggested that the parents of externals were more dominating and controlling than parents of internals, and that inconsistent parental behavior was related to externality. The inconsistency seemed to stem from lack of family consensus concerning appropriate expectations and standards for child behavior. Phares (1976) suggests that inconsistency may make it difficult for children to learn the rules that govern the consequences of behavior, and such failure may lead individuals to believe they have no personal control over reinforcing and punishing outcomes. This interpretation is reasonable from a cognitive social learning perspective. It is quite clear that children abstract rules from the behavioral regularities observed in the behavior of socializing agents in the environment (Bandura, 1977; Rosenthal & Zimmerman, 1978).

In another study of actual interactions between parents and their internal or external sons (Loeb, 1975), fourth- and fifth-grade boys worked on a task in the presence of their parents. The parents were told that they could assist their child as much or as little as they wished. Parents of internal sons were less directive and intruded into the task less frequently than did parents of boys with external perceptions of control.

Some investigators have assumed that children from inner-city areas display generally high levels of externality because behavioral contingencies are clouded by environmental chaos. On the basis of this assumption Nowicki and Barnes (1971) assessed the locus of control orientations of groups of predominantly black seventh, eighth, and ninth graders who participated in a structured summer camp experience in which a high rate of social reinforcement was provided and in which specific efforts were made to emphasize the relationship between the campers' behavior and reinforcing consequences. Most of the youngsters spent $5\frac{1}{2}$ days at the camp, but some of them returned for an additional week at the end of camp. The campers did show an increase in internality over the 1-week experience, and those who returned for an additional session showed additional change toward a perception of internal control on a general locus of control instrument (the Nowicki–Strickland Locus of Control Scale). The results were interpreted to mean that the camping experience helped the youngsters to see the connection between their behavior and reinforcement outcomes. Unfortunately, there was no control group, so the changes in perceptions of control cannot be clearly attributed to the structured experiences employed in camp.

Schooling

A study by Kifer (1975) probed the relationship between home and school influences on the development of perceptions of personal control, and thus serves to open discussion of the question of how the debilitating effects of helplessness and similar perceptions of inability to control personal consequences might be overcome. The school is an important socialization institution, and although the development of academic competence is generally regarded as this agency's primary responsibility, the affective development of children is most certainly influenced in the process. Within the school environment children's successes and failures are based on comparisons with their peers. Kifer expected that success and failure experiences would lead to similar further experiences as children come to view themselves as successful or unsuccessful learners, and that these patterns of success or failure would influence the personality characteristics of students. Kifer also recognized the powerful influences of home environments, and therefore expected that the concerns and rewards for academic achievement expressed in the home would mediate the effects of school success on the personality characteristics of students. Personality measures, including the IAR, were administered to cross-sectional samples of second-, fourth-, sixth-, and eighth-grade students. In addition, children's perceptions of concern expressed and rewards provided at home for academic achievement were measured.

The findings suggested that personality characteristics such as self-esteem, self-concept of ability, and intellectual achievement responsibility are related to degrees of academic achievement. Although the cross-sectional design, in which subject selection served as a proxy for an experimental treatment, does not rule out plausible alternative explanations, the results do provide strong support for the possibility that success and failure histories produced in the school setting are antecedent to children's academic self-esteem and perceptions of personal control over outcomes. Kifer's data also provide support for well-documented contributions of the home environment to intellectual achievement (Bradley & Caldwell, 1976; Bradley, Caldwell, & Elardo, 1979; Davé, 1963; Henderson, 1972; Henderson & Merritt, 1968; Walburg & Marjoribanks, 1976) by demonstrating that the support and encouragement that children report is provided in their homes may also lead to more favorable self-concept and achievement attributions. However, Kifer found that home environment variables were more highly related to these personality measures in the early grades than in the later school years, whereas the personality variables were more highly related to success or failure in the upper grades. This finding suggests that the salutary influence of the home environment on feelings of academic self-worth and perceptions of control over achievement outcomes may gradually be eroded by the histories of success and failure children experience in the norm-referenced world of the classroom.

Success and failure experiences. Many investigators support the notion that histories of failure or success play a major role in the development of internality–externality and the more specific attributions of cause (e.g., effort versus ability, task difficulty, or luck) that influence future expectations and task-oriented behavior. The nature of schooling in the United States is such that certain children may be predestined to experience heavy and repeated doses of failure from the first grade on. A disproportionate number of poor and minority children whose outside-of-school socialization is not highly congruent with the curricular expectations of middle-class-oriented schools are likely to fall within this group. So too are children who suffer from a variety of handicapping behavioral and intellectual conditions, at least as defined in classroom settings.

There is little direct evidence concerning how the experience of repeated failure feedback in school may influence and have cumulative effects on the academic attitudes and performance of poor children or those from minority ethnic backgrounds. Recent attention, however, has been directed at examining the effects of failure, or implied failure, on children with exceptional needs. In this regard, Thomas (1979) has called attention to striking parallels between the features of the learned helplessness syndrome and the characteristics of children classified as learning disabled. Since the term *learning disabilities* refers to such a hodgepodge of symptoms, it is virtually impossible to identify common characteristics of the children to whom the label is applied (Lilly, 1979); but one very common element seems to be an overlay of frustration and defeat. Learning-disabled children are often portrayed as being convinced that they cannot learn, and much of the initial teaching effort with them is directed to motivating them to expend sufficient effort to achieve success (Thomas, 1979). Typically these children are easily frustrated, low in effort and persistence, and unwilling to attempt even those tasks that are within the range of their ability. Their learning histories are often dominated by failure, and it has been suggested that the more consistent the history of failure is, the more likely it is that failure will be attributed to lack of ability (Frieze & Weiner, 1971, cited in Thomas, 1979).

The proposition that the perception of helplessness may be learned from failure experiences, especially among children who experience heavy doses of failure, gains additional support from a study of nursery and elementary school children. Here mental age (MA) levels were completely crossed with IQ levels in an orthogonal design (Weisz, 1979). On a variety of measures of helplessness, retarded children were relatively more helpless than nonretarded children at the upper MA levels rather than at the lower MA levels. This finding is congruent with the view that retarded children may learn to perceive themselves as helpless over years of development, and the successive failure feedback these children experience is suggested as a likely cause. Data reported by Weisz (1981) indicate that black retarded children may be more susceptible to the effects of helplessness than their white counterparts, and that perceptions of helplessness in retarded children may supress their actual abilities.

Purposes, goal setting, and self-regulation. The provision of purposes for learning appears to be one important mediator of the relationship between locus of control motivation and performance. But there is also evidence to suggest that the effects of purpose may vary depending on whether learning objectives are set by a teacher or by the students themselves. Arlin and Whitley (1978) suggested that students may be more likely to accept personal responsibility for success or failure when they perceive a role in determining their own activities. They anticipated that the perceptions of academic control and self-management opportunities would have an interactive influence on each other. A bidirectional relationship was postulated, and Arlin and Whitley designed their study to determine whether or not one pattern of directionality is predominant over the other.

To address this problem they administered a short form of the IAR and an Attitude Toward Learning Processes questionnaire that purports to measure students' perceptions of opportunities for self-managed learning. Both instruments were administered at the beginning and end of the school year. Approximately half of the subjects were enrolled in traditional classrooms and half were from classrooms in which instruction was highly individualized. The pooled data for both groups were analyzed with a cross-lagged panel correlation technique. This analysis makes it possible to determine which of two variables, each of which is measured at two points in time, is *likely* to have causal priority over the other. This procedure cannot establish cause, but it gives a strong hint of cause. The results suggested that children's perceptions of opportunities for self-management of learning were prior to locus of control in academic situations.

Additional analysis suggested that students who have been encouraged to manage their own learning were more likely than their peers from traditional classrooms to develop willingness to accept personal responsibility for their academic successes and failures. The results also indicated that the causal priority of self-management over locus of control is more powerful for perceptions of responsibility for failure than for success. In their comments on these findings Arlin and Whitley suggest that it may be easier for students in either type of classroom situation to attribute responsibility for success to themselves, but the plausible rationalizations for failure may differ for the two types of classroom conditions examined. In situations in which activities are determined by the teacher, it may be relatively easy to attribute failure to the teacher or to bad luck, but more difficult for students who have determined their own goals and activities to attribute failure to external sources. The results are consistent with previous research that has demonstrated that a program in which students have an opportunity to manage important aspects of their own learning had a positive influence on student perception of responsibility for their own learning (Wang & Stiles, 1976).

Another aspect of student management of learning that may influence student attributions and performance is the opportunity for self-correction. In a study of the effects of the opportunity for students to determine the correctness of their own responses, Pascarella and Pflaum (1981) found differential outcomes in reading achievement for students whose attributions were to internal or external causes. Learning-disabled readers who were high in internal control benefited more from the opportunity to determine their own errors than from an approach in which the teacher determined the correctness of their responses. The opposite of this pattern was found for students who were high on external control, suggesting the need for careful matching between instructional variations and the preferred learning conditions of students.

Persistence. Clearly, the relationship between locus of control (LOC) and achievement in children is not a simple one. As the previous discussion has shown, the relationship of LOC to achievement seems to be mediated by complex interactions among variables such as purpose and the opportunity to participate in the setting of those purposes (Arlin & Whitley, 1978; Wang & Stiles, 1976). Strickland (1972) and Mischel, Zeiss, and Zeiss (1974) have provided evidence that delay of gratification forms an additional component of this relationship. Since other research has shown that task persistence is another factor associated with academic achievement (Feather, 1962), Gordon and his associates (Gordon, Jones, & Short, 1977) wondered if that relationship might underlie the effect of LOC on academic achievement. These investigators reasoned that extrinsic reinforcement is often very sparse in school. If internal children are able to delay gratification longer than external children, they also may be able to persist longer at academic tasks. Since both generalized and specific expectancies seem to influence task persistence (Altshuler & Kassinove, 1975), Gordon and his associates also wanted to examine the relationship between task persistence and both generalized and specific expectancies. In addition, they wanted to examine Rotter's (1975) assertion that as children get older, generalized expectations are replaced by specific expectations. This developmental trend is expected to result in a diminished relationship between LOC and achievement over time. Gordon *et al.*'s (1977) subjects were third and sixth graders. Generalized expectancies were measured with the Nowicki–Strickland Locus of Control Scale for children. Specific expectancies were manipulated by exposing half of each group (internals and externals) to a task administered under skill instructions and the other half to a task with chance instructions.

The main findings of the study supported the expected relationship between attributions of causality and task persistence in children. The results also confirmed the finding that children became more internal with age. Third-grade boys were more internal than third-grade girls, but there were no sex differences for sixth graders. Task persistence was affected by both sex and locus of control, with boys persisting longer than girls and internals longer than externals. There was no effect for chance and skill instructions. Age, sex, and LOC interacted in such a way that sixth-grade internal males were more persistent than their external male peers, while third-grade internal girls were more persistent than their external female peers.

On the basis of these results Gordon suggested that the relationship between task persistence and locus of control may constitute one component of the relationship between LOC and academic achievement.

Children's self-perceptions may be influenced by expectancies that are communicated to them by adults in a fairly simple fashion. Toner, Moore, and Emmons (1980) studied the effects of task relevant labeling on the self-control of kindergarten, first-, and second-grade girls. Girls who were labeled as patient exercised greater self-imposed delay of gratification than girls in a task-irrelevant labeling condition. Even though the label was embedded in a longer statement that served as part of a discussion between the subjects and the experimenter, an unfamiliar adult, it influenced their behavior. The results suggest that the use of positive labels by socialization agents telling children what they *can* do may have a significant effect on expectancies underlying other forms of self-control that are important in school. It also has been shown that children's persistence and self-efficacy attributions may be enhanced through the vicarious influence of models who demonstrate persistence and who make statements of self-confidence in the face of failure (Zimmerman & Ringle, 1981).

Relationship to self-esteem. Research has also demonstrated a positive association among locus of control, self-esteem, and academic achievement. Gordon (1977) attempted to assess the independent contributions of locus of control and self-esteem to academic achievement in a study with fourth graders. When either grades or a composite achievement test score was used to designate the achievement variable, partial correlations showed that the relationship between LOC and achievement was significant when the effects of self-esteem were removed. Similarly, the relationship between self-esteem and achievement was significant when the effects of LOC were removed. Math achievement was not significantly related to self-esteem when the effects of locus of control were partialled out. The general finding that locus of control and self-esteem were significantly related to achievement, independently of their relationship to each other, was later replicated with second graders. In the follow-up study, as in the initial one, sex was a significant variable. For boys, locus of control was significantly related to grades but not to achievement test scores. The situation was reversed for girls. Gordon suggests that grades are a more subjective measure than achievement test scores. Grades are also influenced by social and motivational variables, such as effort. The fact that the relationship between LOC and achievement has been found to be less consistent for girls than for boys may reflect conflicting role demands in socialization practices for girls.

Classroom goal structures. Support for the hypothesis that success and failure experiences influence the development of locus of control orientations was examined earlier. It seems unlikely, however, that the effects of success and failure operate independently of the social situation in which such experiences occur. Classrooms constitute the major social context in which social comparisons of performance are made routinely.

Those classrooms that employ a competitive goal structure are especially likely to encourage social comparisons (Ames, Ames, & Felker, 1977; Henderson & Hennig, 1979).

With this in mind, Ames and her associates at Purdue University set out to study how competitive and noncompetitive classroom settings influence children's beliefs about the causes of success and failure for themselves and others. In this investigation different reward conditions defined the cooperative or competitive nature of the social situations in which performance was set. Fifth- and sixth-grade boys were assigned first to one of two performance outcome conditions (success or failure) and then to competitive or noncompetitive reward structure conditions. The boys worked on achievement-related puzzles in a situation in which one member of the pair succeeded and the other failed at the task. Following the experimental treatment children were asked to respond to a questionnaire concerning the causal factors of ability, effort, task difficulty, and luck. They were then asked to judge their own performance and the performance of the other member of their pair.

The results of the study confirmed the expectation that the effects of success and failure experiences depend upon the nature of the social setting in which the attempted performance takes place. In this case children's attributions, their judgments of deservingness, and their satisfaction with the performance of self and other differed as a function of competitive and noncompetitive reward structures. Recall that for each pair of boys, one succeeded and the other failed. The children who failed were self-effacing. They saw themselves as less deserving than their more successful peers. Successful children, on the other hand, did not attribute less luck, deservingness, ability, or satisfaction to their partner as compared with themselves. Ames and her colleagues suggested that the successful children may have formed their attribution statements in a way that would not invite social criticism (cf. Feather & Simon, 1971). Social norms dictate that it is inappropriate to claim to be better than someone else. Similarly, social sanctions may inhibit statements that would be interpreted as overenthusiastic self-evaluations. The failing child, in contrast, did evidence some negative attributions of his own ability, but the effects of this self-effacing behavior could be tempered somewhat by attributing the success of the partner to better luck and an easier task.

The cooperative or competitive reward structure also influenced children's ratings of their own and their partner's ability, luck, deservingness, and satisfaction. The children who were successful under competitive conditions considered themselves to be more deserving of reward and more satisfied with their performance than their partners. Those whose success was experienced under noncompetitive conditions did not consider themselves more deserving or more satisfied.

When children were successful under competitive conditions, they tended to attribute their own outcomes to good luck, whereas failure was attributed to poor luck. Contrary to the investigator's expectations, children who failed did not make ego-defensive attributions. Instead, competition seemed to lead to self-derogation. Compared to children who failed in noncompetitive settings, those who failed under competitive conditions judged themselves to have less ability and to be less deserving of reward. They also experienced more negative affect than those who failed under noncompetitive circumstances. The researchers concluded that "failure appears to be critical factor causing negative self-evaluations, but competitive reward contingencies appear to accentuate the negativism in self-attributions and affective feelings [Ames *et al.*, 1977, p. 6]."

How does failure affect one's future achievement efforts? Certain children may respond to failure feedback by trying even harder on future tasks (Diener & Dweck, 1978), but Ames and her colleagues noted that if failure depresses children's beliefs in their own ability, and this is coupled with negative affect, as their research indicated, future achievement strivings may be discouraged. Repeated experiences of this sort could lead to what Ames calls a "low-achievement-motive syndrome," or what others have called learned helplessness. Ames and her associates suggest that "the consequences of failure are obviously negative, but the impact of failure in competitive conditions seems to be rather devastating to a child's self-perceptions [p. 7]."

The results of this study hold important implications for the understanding of conditions that influence achievement motivation in children. On the basis of data obtained on adults, it has been argued that achievement behavior may be motivated when effort attributions are associated with either positive or negative affect. The findings of Ames *et al.* (1977) are congruent with a quite different set of results reported by Nicholls (1975), suggesting that competitive goal structures highlight social comparisons and interfere with the relationship between effort attributions and subsequent achievement-motivated behavior. Ames *et al.* studied boys only and called attention to other evidence suggesting that competitive situations may be more damaging for girls than for boys. Under competitive circumstances girls may be even more self-critical of their families than boys, while at the same time taking less credit for success outcomes (Feather & Simon, 1971; Nicholls, 1975, cited in Ames *et al.*, 1977).

It should not be concluded that cooperative learning is automatically superior to the outcomes of instruction organized around competitive goal structures. Carole Ames (1981) found a much more complex pattern of outcomes in a study of the effects of competitive and cooperative goal structures on the attributions and affective reactions of sixth graders to success and failure. Success in a competitive situation led to self-aggrandizement, while failure resulted in a decline in feelings of satisfaction and in children's self-perceptions of their ability. Cooperative goal structures proved to provide an effective means of ameliorating the self-defeating thought processes that followed a poor performance under competitive circumstances, but when the efforts of a cooperative group failed, the attendant attributions were much like those associated with failure in a competitive situation. Thus, Ames concluded that although participation in a successful group may have a positive effect on self-concept of ability and on interpersonal perceptions, the consequences of cooperative structures that end in failure may be negative.

It seems clear from this research that the social context in which success and failure experiences occur affects how children judge the performance of themselves and others. In classrooms, the arrangement of reward contingencies that define competitive and noncompetitive contexts for behavior may have an important influence on children's views of their own efficacy and of the competence of their peers.

Planned interventions

Once established, whether through home or school experiences or through the interactive effects of both, can dysfunctional attributions of cause be changed, and does change in cognitive attributions lead to adaptive behavioral change? Several recent studies suggest that the answer to both questions is yes, although, with the exception of De-Charms' (1971) efforts to promote intrinsic motivation, the applicability of validated procedures to ongoing educational programs remains to be demonstrated.

Attribution therapy. The basis for efforts to change children's perceptions of cause and to reduce the debilitating effects of attributions to sources other than effort, as in the learned helplessness syndrome, is found in a variety of behavior change techniques that have proved successful with other problem behaviors. Both environmental control programs and cognitively oriented techniques emphasizing self-regulation have been shown to be effective facilitators of change (Bugenthal, Whalen, & Henker, 1977), but some investigators have raised the possibility that different approaches may vary in effectiveness with subjects differing in personal characteristics. Bugenthal *et al.* (1977) postulated that self-control and reinforcement methods may be differentially effective, depending on children's perceptions of causation.

Bugenthal and her colleagues expected therapies congruent with children's locus of control preceptions to be more effective than incongruent techniques. They postulated that those children who view outcomes as the result of external factors, such as luck or bias, would benefit most from procedures that systematize environmental contingencies in the classroom. On the other hand, children who perceive outcomes as the result of personal effort may benefit more from a program that focuses on self-regulation skills, thus improving on their personal control. These propositions were tested with hyperactive boys ranging from 7 through 12 years of age. Half of each treatment group was also receiving psychostimulant medication (Ritalin®) during training. The experimental interventions took place twice a week over an 8-week period, were conducted within regular classroom settings, and employed educational games and curriculum-relevant instructional games. The dependent measures consisted of the Conners Abbreviated Teacher Rating Scale for the assessment of hyperactive children and the qualitative scores on the Porteus Mazes, as a measure of general impulsiveness.

The teacher ratings did not reflect differences among the treatment groups, but an interesting pattern of interactions among subjects and treatments was revealed. As predicted, the self-regulation intervention was most effective for children who made high personal causation attributions and for children who were not on medication. In contrast, the social reinforcement procedures were most effective with children who scored low on personal causation and with those who were receiving the psychostimulant.

Although the expectation that a form of treatment congruent with the child's existing locus of control perceptions would be more effective than a noncongruent condition was supported, Bugenthal and her associates appropriately caution that these results should not be taken to mean that self-regulation instruction is inappropriate for children who attribute control to external factors. The development of self-control is essential to the durability and generalizability of desirable behavior. What Bugenthal *et al.* suggest is that, since external attributions precede internal attributions in a developmental sense, important matters of sequence and timing should be considered in choosing an appropriate intervention strategy. For example, with children who initially see environmental events as chaotic and unlawful, a program that systematizes the relationship between behavior and reinforcement consequences may be an appropriate precursor to training in self-management skills. Although this suggestion seems rational in view of the age-related sequence noted for the development of causal attributions, anyone who might consider implementing practices based on the implications of Bugenthal's research should be aware of the difficulty of providing the programmatic continuity needed to move children from one form of intervention to another in real school settings. As children move from classroom to classroom or school to school, under conditions in which programmatic coordination is a rare event, it may be quite difficult to ensure a shift in approaches at the appropriate time. In this connection it should be noted that at the time of a 6-month follow-up study, 6 of the 36 children (almost 19%) in Bugenthal's original study had transferred to other school districts (Bugenthal, Collins, Collins, & Chaney, 1978).

Psychostimulants and perceptions of control. The observation that psychostimulant medication and type of intervention have interactive effects raises important questions about the desirability of using medication to control behavior. The major controversy concerning the actual effectiveness of psychostimulant medication is beyond the scope of this chapter, but aside from the serious issues raised in that debate, Bugenthal *et al.* (1977) quite reasonably interpret their own and supportive findings to suggest that the use of medication for the purpose of behavioral control in the classroom may have powerful consequences for the attributional processes of children. They note that:

> It is quite plausible to speculate, for example, that many children taking medication are learning to attribute behavioral *improvement* to causes beyond personal control and to devalue their own potential contributions to problem solutions. These children may, in other words, come to believe that they need external help to solve their difficulties. When such external input (e.g., social reinforcement) is forthcoming, improvement is more likely to occur than when responsibility for change is given to the child (e.g., self-regulation) [p. 882].

Six months after the intervention previously described the original subjects were reassessed (Bugenthal *et al.*, 1978) to determine if the original interventions had any long-term effects. The medication–intervention interaction observed in the first study remained only as a nonsignificant trend. With initial scores on the attributional measure controlled statistically (used as the covariate), the analysis revealed that children who had experienced the self-regulation training scored higher on perceptions of personal control than those who had received social reinforcement training. Whereas in the first study teacher ratings for children in the two training conditions did not differ, the teacher rating measure of hyperactivity did reveal significant differences between the two interventions in the follow-up study. Surprisingly, the outcome ran counter to the investigators' prediction. The long-term effects of the social reinforcement approach on hyperactivity, as measured by the Conners Abbreviated Teacher Rating Scale, were superior to those of self-regulation instruction. This could mean that, for this small sample, social reinforcement procedures were more effective than self-regulation training in bringing hyperactivity under control. On the other hand, alternative plausible hypotheses should be considered. Bugenthal *et al.* (1978) point out that besides reflecting teacher perceptions of a child's impulsivity, the Conners Scale may be influenced by the child's social interaction with adults. If social reinforcement, controlled by adults, leads to more positive interactions with teachers, it would be reasonable to expect teachers to perceive the child's behavior more favorably. Teachers thus may perceive themselves as having control over the behavior of children whose hyperactivity has been treated with social reinforcement procedures. In contrast, the teacher may feel less of a sense of control over children who have learned to regulate their own behavior. Again, Bugenthal and her associates suggest that interventions might begin with social reinforcement procedures that might produce quick improvements in children's social interactions with adults, with a shift to self-control principles once social responsiveness had improved.

Attribution retraining versus success experience. Given reports of favorable results of a variety of cognitively oriented therapies (e.g., Davison, 1966; Ellis, 1962; Meichenbaum, 1975), Dweck (1975) designed a study to determine whether helpless children's perceptions of the relationship between their behavior and failure outcomes could be altered with a form of attribution therapy. Beyond merely changing the perceptions of these children, Dweck was interested in determining if alteration in the failure attributions of helpless children would result in the reduction of maladaptive responses to failure.

An attribution retraining program consisting of 25 daily sessions was carried out with children between the ages of 8 and 13. The effects of attribution retraining were compared to a success-only procedure recommended by many behavior modifiers. Dweck anticipated that the success-only intervention would improve the ability of helpless children to sustain their efforts despite failure, because the treatment was expected to raise their expectations of success. Attribution retraining was expected to produce even greater improvement because it should provide a new interpretation for failure. Children subjected to this instruction would attribute failure to insufficient effort rather than to uncontrollable factors. During the relatively long intervention (as attribution experiments go), both groups worked on mathematics problems appropriate to the current skill level of the individuals involved. Contrary to the investigator's expectation, consistent and sustained decreases in maladaptive reactions to failure were evidenced only by the attribution retraining group. Whereas these children were able to confront failure in a more adaptive manner, some of the children in the success-only condition displayed *increased sensitivity to failure* after an exclusive diet of success experiences. The effects of attribution retraining were also evident in responses to a scale design to assess effort versus ability attributions. After training, all of the subjects in the attribution retraining program showed increases in effort attributions, indicating that besides showing improved adaptation to failure in test situations, these children altered their attributions for failure with respect to mathematics in general.

The fact that subjects in the success-only condition continued to display deterioration of performance following the intervention was interpreted by Dweck (1975) to suggest that the success-only procedures that many behaviorists advocate may be shortsighted. In her words: "An instructional program for children who have difficulty dealing with failure would do well not to skirt the issue by trying to ensure success or by glossing over failure. Instead it should include procedures for dealing with this problem directly [p. 684]."

No direct measures of transfer to the regular classroom were taken, but teachers, who were unaware of which children had been involved in which treatment, reported that children who had experienced the attribution retraining had begun to display greater effort and a different attitude toward failure, as indicated by increased persistence with new tasks and by a willingness to seek help rather than withdrawing from a difficult task.

Helpless versus mastery-oriented responses to failure. In a subsequent study Diener and Dweck (1978) compared helpless and mastery-oriented children to determine how failure influences their performance on hypothesis-testing strategies. The majority of children classified as helpless indicated that they were unable to do the problems because they were not smart enough, whereas none of the mastery-oriented children gave this response when asked why they had trouble with the problems. The results tended to confirm that helpless children do not identify lack of effort as a cause for their failure, whereas mastery-oriented children do, and following failure, helpless children adopt ineffectual hypotheses to a greater degree than their mastery-oriented peers, even though the performance of the two groups did not differ prior to imposition of failure, unlike the helpless children, some mastery-oriented students improved in their use of hypothesis-testing strategies following failure feedback. The attributional statements made by help-less children to explain their failure reflected a perceived lack of ability, whereas the mastery-oriented students made few spontaneous attribu-tional statements of any sort. Perhaps the most important conclusion of the study was that mastery-oriented children did not search for a cause for their failure. Instead of making attributional statements they looked for a remedy, largely through self-monitoring and self-instruction. A large majority of the mastery-oriented students engaged in self-monitoring, as demonstrated by statements that indicated they were attending to the amount of effort or concentration they were exerting. Almost half of this group made such self-instructional statements as "I should slow down and try to figure this out," or "The harder it gets the harder I need to try [Diener & Dweck, 1978, p. 459]." Not only were the statements of helpless children characterized by attributions for their failure, but they also produced many solution-irrelevant statements.

Although most studies of helplessness have underscored the dif-ferences in types of attributions made by helpless and nonhelpless chil-dren, this research suggests that a crucial difference may lie in whether or not attributions are made at all, or how early in the failure experience they appear. Paper-and-pencil measures of attributions force children to choose between different types of attributions, but the Diener and Dweck study suggests that mastery-oriented children responded to fail-ure feedback as information relevant to the problem solution. Their posi-tive affect and optimistic prognostic statements (e.g., *I love a challenge*, and *I've almost got it now*) suggested that they did not interpret the failure feedback as failure, or as the basis for predicting future failure. Besides the attribution retraining advocated by Dweck (1975), these results suggest that it may be helpful to train helpless children to control task-irrelevant cognitions and to provide them with strategies for self-monitoring and self-instruction. These suggestions are predicated on the assumption that continued task involvement is more adaptive than withdrawal.

Attribution retraining and persistence.   The viewpoint that causal attribu-tions play an influential role in achievement behavior was tested in a pair of studies by Andrews and Debus (1978). They provided further sup-port for the rationale underlying Dweck's (1975) attribution retraining program. In a sample of male and female sixth graders in Australia, task persistence and resistance to extinction were positively related to effort attributions but inversely related to attributions of ability or task difficulty as the cause of failure. In the second study, boys who had displayed the lowest levels of effort attributions were assigned to a control group or to one of two different experimental procedures designed to train them to attribute success and failure experiences to effort. One attribution retraining group used social reinforcement procedures and the other employed tokens plus social reinforcement. The two treatments did not differ in effectiveness. Both procedures resulted in increased attributions of failure to effort, and task persistence also increased significantly. These results proved durable, with some attenuation, and they generalized to an experience with an unfamiliar tester 4 months later.

Since the intervention involved in this research required only a concentrated series of short trials, compared to the 25 daily training sessions used by Dweck (1975), Andrews and Debus argue that their procedures would be feasible for individualized instruction within a remedial context. They caution, however, that the application of experimental programs has yet to be investigated within the context of regular classroom programs.

Field application. These interventions have all been experimental in character, and even those efforts that have been carried out in classroom settings using curriculum-relevant tasks fall short of demonstrating feasibility for application in ongoing classroom situations. An exception to this pattern is found in a large-scale field study in which DeCharms (1971) trained 16 sixth-grade teachers to help children become "origins" rather than "pawns." A basic feature of the approach these teachers learned to apply could be interpreted as helping children to develop internal rather than external locus of control. DeCharms reported that the training increased achievement motivation, enhanced goal setting, reduced feelings of powerlessness, enhanced academic achievement skills, and reduced absences and tardiness.

TEACHER EXPECTANCIES

The concept of teacher expectancies usually refers to expectations for the future academic performance of students, although some researchers (e.g., Williams, 1976) distinguish between these *cognitive* expectancies and *normative* expectancies, which concern conformity to the behavioral norms of the classroom. The concept of teacher expectancies has become linked to the self-fulfilling prophecy hypothesis advanced by the sociologist, Robert Merton (1957). Merton suggested that if situations are perceived as real, real consequences in accordance with those perceptions will follow. Applied to teacher expectancies, this means that those children who are expected to do poor academic work will not be effective learners, whereas those who are seen as capable will be successful.

Few topics have generated so much research activity in so short a period of time or produced such equivocal results as the subject of teacher expectancies. Interpretations of existing findings have proved controversial because they have ideological, political, and educational implications parallel to those of the heredity versus environment debate. The fact that minority and poor children are overrepresented among poorly achieving students is well documented. What is still not established is *why*, and the teacher expectancy hypothesis offers one attractive potential explanation for those who reject genetic and/or socialization deficit explanations. Those who lean toward a revisionist view of the reasons for school failure among poor and minority children assert that successful progress through school does not depend on merit under present or historical circumstances. Rather, schools have operated in ways that serve to maintain the class structure of the United States (see Bowles & Gintis, 1976; Williams, 1976). Teacher expectancies, and the self-fulfilling prophecies associated with them, are thought by revisionists to constitute one of the processes by which the status quo is maintained.

Given the equivocal nature of the data on the effects of teacher expectancies, it is easy to slip into polemic debate concerning this issue. Sides are chosen largely on the basis of one's revisionist or meritocratic views. Nevertheless, the empirical findings are not in total disarray. There is little doubt that many teachers hold differential expectancies on the basis of student characteristics. What is debated is just which characteristics these expectancies are based on (e.g., socioeconomic markers or achievement behavior), and how, if at all, these expectations influence student progress. Relevant to this discussion there is a sizable literature on the nature of differential expectations held by teachers, the determinants of these expectancies, the relationship between differential expectations and differential treatment of students in classrooms, and the effects of expectancy-based teacher behaviors. These issues are examined in this section and the educational implications of existing information is explored.

Determinants of expectancies

A number of student characteristics have been suggested as determinants of teacher expectations. Brophy and Good (1974) documented differences in teacher expectancies toward children varying in personal characteristics such as sex, social class, race, and ethnicity. Subsequent work (Adams, 1978; Lockheed, 1977) has supported those observations. Physical attractiveness has also been found to covary with stereotyped teacher expectations (Adams, 1978). Even preschool teachers, who report strong nurturant feelings toward children, judged unattractive children to be less intelligent, to show poorer academic promise, and to be less well-behaved in the classroom than attractive children. Parallel findings have been reported for racial differences, with black children being judged less favorably on these characteristics than white children.

One investigation (Datta, Schaefer, & Davis, 1968) reported that when IQ was controlled statistically, blacks with high IQ's were described by their teachers in terms just as favorable as their high-IQ white peers, but low-IQ blacks were more likely that their white counterparts to be described as maladjusted, verbally aggressive, and lacking in task orientation. Of course, race, socioeconomic status (SES), and IQ share a substantial amount of variance, and Yee (1968) reported that SES was the single most important determinant of teacher attitudes toward students.

Since high correlations between teacher expectancies and student achievement have been reported, it is often suggested that expectations determine student achievement. On the other hand, some data (e.g., Dusek & O'Connell, 1973; Dusek, 1975; Williams, 1976) suggest that the causal relationship is just the reverse; that is, student achievement determines teacher expectancies.

Revisionists often cite standardized tests, which they assume to be culturally biased, as a source of information that may structure teacher expectations in a negative way. An investigation carried out in Ireland (Airasian, Madaus, Kellaghan, & Pedulla, 1977) indicated that very few second-grade teachers (less than 10%) altered their perceptions of students when standardized test information ran counter to their previously formed expectations. Those teachers who did revise their judgments of student performance tended to raise rather than lower their ratings. Since comparisons of Irish and American teachers have revealed that American teachers hold less positive attitudes toward standardized tests than their Irish counterparts, the researchers reasoned that the influence of standardized test data would be even smaller among American teachers.

Humphreys and Stubbs (1977) used cross-lagged correlation techniques to analyze longitudinal achievement and expectations data on a large sample of Canadian high school students. They concluded that teacher expectations seemed to have some influence on student expectations during the first 2 years of high school, but this relationship then diminished. To the degree that cross-lagged comparisons are indicative of causal sequences, the evidence suggested that academic performance causes teacher and student expectations, rather than the reverse sequence.

This position finds support in the work of Luce and Hoge (1978), who examined mechanisms postulated to mediate expectancy effects. The research was designed to examine the various links of Gardner and Bing's (1973) model, which posits that under some circumstances teacher expectancies → differential teacher behavior → differential pupil behaviors → differential levels of achievement. Teacher expectancies were measured by having fourth-grade teachers rank children on basic intellectual ability, motivation to do school work, reading achievement, and mathematics achievement. The outcomes of the correlational analysis are limited by the fact that the measures were collected in such a way that only the links among components of the model, and not their temporal sequence, could be examined. The findings indicated that teachers did not behave differentially on the basis of their perceptions of student ability or achievement. On the other hand, differential teacher behaviors were associated with motivation rankings. Interactions with students judged low in motivation to do school work were more procedural, more critical, and involved more behavioral warnings than were the interactions with students ranked higher in motivation.

A number of student behaviors were related to academic achievement. The fact that attentiveness was significantly related to academic achievement is especially interesting in view of the outcomes of a study by Klein (1971). In that experiment students systematically varied their behavior along the dimension of attending–nonattending. These variations had a marked influence on teacher behavior.

Among the other behaviors reported by Luce and Hoge to distinguish low-achieving from high-achieving pupils were higher levels of initiating and work-related behaviors on the part of high achievers. It must be mentioned, however, that when IQ was partialled out, most correlations between pupil behavior and achievement test scores were reduced to a nonsignificant level.

Willis and Brophy (1974) attempted to discover the origins of teacher attitudes of attachment, concern, indifference, or rejection as manifest toward individual students. They interviewed first-grade teachers before they had a chance to form impressions of their pupils. Later, after becoming acquainted with their classes, teachers were asked to nominate three students for each of the four attitude classifications. The teachers perceived major differences in the behavior of pupils assigned to the four categories. Pupils to whom attachment was expressed were successful and compliant. In their interactions they were rewarding to their teachers. Students about whom concern was expressed had difficulty with schoolwork, but they were compliant and, like attachment students, they reinforced teachers in their interactions with them. Teachers responded by providing them with a good deal of remedial help.

Those students to whom teachers felt indifferent failed to respond to teachers in a way their teachers found rewarding. Their negative responses led to a pattern in which teachers spent little time with them, even though they perceived these students' need for additional help. Rejected students not only failed to provide teachers with rewarding interpersonal contacts, but they also were credited with the creation of discipline problems and classroom disturbances. Teachers wanted to get rid of these students, and they attributed low ability traits to them that they did not actually possess as a group.

Altogether, the results of this study underscore the reciprocal nature of teacher–pupil interaction. These reciprocal relationships appear to constitute a critical influence on teacher attitudes and expectancies, independent of such personal characteristics as the sex or race of the students.

The investigations just described provide several kinds of evidence that teacher expectancies and attitudes may be more influenced by the observed behaviors of students themselves than by personal characteristics associated with group membership. Although it can be argued on the basis of evidence such as this that teacher expectancies may merely reflect previous experience with children displaying certain characteristics, it is instructive to note that teachers express stereotyped expectations based on labels assigned to children even when observable behavior is incongruent with the label assigned to them (Foster & Ysseldyke, 1976; Gillung & Rucker, 1977). For example, Foster and Ysseldyke (1976) had teachers identify behaviors they expected to be displayed by hypothetical children labeled as emotionally disturbed, learning disabled, mentally retarded, and normal. As anticipated, the teachers expressed more negative expectancies toward the children categorized with a deviance label than toward normal children. The teachers were then assigned to one of four groups. All groups viewed a videotape of a normal fourth-grade boy engaged in a variety of test-taking activities and in free play. Members of one group were told that the boy they were watching was normal. Another group was told he was mentally retarded. A third group was given to believe he was emotionally disturbed, and the last group was told he had a learning disability. After viewing the tape, negative expectancies were expressed toward the boy by those groups to whom he was described with a deviancy label, even though the deviancy label groups had observed behavior that was inconsistent with the label. These results are relevant to consideration of possible teacher expectancy influences on minority and poor children, because traditionally these children have been overrepresented among those to whom special category labels have been assigned.

Given that teachers may hold differential attitudes and stereotypic expectancies toward children differing in personal characteristics or academic behaviors, it is relevant to ask if these variations in expectations are associated with differential behavior toward students.

Teacher expectancies and instructional interaction

There is ample support for an affirmative answer to the question posed at the end of the last section (Cooper & Baron, 1977; Good, 1970; Good & Brophy, 1974; Good, Sikes, & Brophy, 1973; Laosa, 1978; Rist, 1970; Rubovits & Maehr, 1971). Good and Brophy (1974) put the case succinctly in the comment that "when investigators have looked for differential teacher behavior toward students differing in achievement, sex, or socioeconomic status, they have consistently found it [p. 340]."

The well-publicized Coleman Report (Coleman, Campbell, Hobson, McPartland, Mood, Weinfeld, & York, 1966) has led many people to believe that schools do not make a difference in pupil achievement anyway, so some may wonder if it matters whether teachers behave differentially toward students differing in personal and behavioral characteristics. Veldman and Brophy (1974) note that these conclusions were based on analyses in which schools rather than teachers were the unit of analysis. In a study of second- and third-grade teachers in Title I and non-Title-I schools, these investigators found that teachers did have a significant effect (both practical and statistical) on student learning. They also concluded that the teacher was relatively more important in the learning of disadvantaged than advantaged children. The specific process variables that distinguish effective from ineffective teaching are still being explored, but those teaching behaviors that vary on the basis of expectancies for academic progress are likely candidates for an effectiveness model.

In general, teachers' reinforcement practices are associated with expectations. For example, in one study (Cooper & Baron, 1977) first- and second-grade girls whose teachers expressed high expectations for their academic progress were praised more freely than average- or low-expectation students. Low-expectation students, in contrast, received more criticism than other students.

Socioeconomic status. Brophy and Good (1974) reviewed a number of studies demonstrating that teachers interact differently with students who vary in personal characteristics. Among the differences revealed in classroom interactions at the third-grade level (Gabbert, 1973; Hoehn, 1954) was that middle class and lower class students received equal amounts of attention from their teachers, but the *quality* of the contacts differed by social class. Contacts with lower class students were characterized as dominative, whereas middle class students received more supportive contacts. In one of these studies, SES effects dropped ·out when the analysis was controlled for achievement (Hoehn, 1954). The results were therefore interpreted to mean that teachers were responding to achievement rather than to SES. But, of course, a disproportionate number of the poor achievers were from lower SES origins. Rist (1970) followed ghetto children from kindergarten through second grade. He reported that children were assigned to ability groups from kindergarten on, and that initial placements were based largely on socioeconomic status information provided by social workers. These children were treated differentially from the beginning, with the higher status children receiving more frequent and positive interactions with teachers than lower status children. The differences that began in kindergarten intensified as the children moved on through the grades. Teachers were most concerned with instructing the children whom they regarded as fast learners, but with the lower status children teacher concern focused on control and discipline. These results are consistent with the findings of other studies of ability grouping described by Brophy and Good (1974).

Race and ethnicity. Similar studies have demonstrated the influence of children's race or ethnic group membership on instructional interaction patterns. Byers and Byers (1972) studied films of a white teacher interacting with a small group consisting of two black and two white children of nursery school age. The analysis suggested that white girls were more successful in gaining the teacher's attention, but the results did not necessarily imply overt discrimination. It appeared that the black girl who was most active in seeking the teacher's attention was unsuccessful because she and the teacher did not share expectations and gestural meanings. Obviously the small number of children involved in this study does not permit generalization, but the study does represent a useful beginning approach to the influence of cultural differences on interaction patterns.

Often it has been argued that differential teacher–pupil interaction patterns in which minority students receive less favorable treatment than their nonminority peers may be corrected by assigning same-race or same-ethnicity teachers to classrooms with large minority enrollments. Byalick and Bersoff's (1974) work suggests that same-ethnicity assignment alone is unlikely to produce the desired effects. These investigators observed teacher–pupil interactions in biracial elementary school classrooms (grades 1 through 6) headed by black and white teachers. The frequency with which reinforcement practices were used was virtually identical for both groups of teachers. Neither black nor white teachers made very frequent use of the reinforcement practices they professed to prefer. There were differences in the targets of reinforcement provided by white and black teachers. Surprisingly, black teachers provided more reinforcement to white children, and white teachers more frequently reinforced black children. Males of the opposite race were reinforced more frequently by their female teachers than any other group, while black girls taught by black teachers received the lowest rate of reinforcement. The finding that teachers most frequently reinforced children of the opposite race is congruent with some studies (e.g., Brown, Payne, Lankewich, & Cornell, 1970) but discrepant with work that has reported that black and white teachers distribute their approval evenly across black and white students. Given these mixed results, perhaps the most reasonable conclusion is that simple solutions, such as the assignment of teachers on the basis of their race or ethnicity, are likely to be unproductive. On the other hand, direct efforts to change teacher behavior may be effective. Good and Brophy (1974) demonstrated that a consultation strategy in which teachers are made aware of the differential attention they provide to various students was effective in increasing their supportive contacts with target children.

Ethnicity and language. There is also evidence that Mexican–American children receive less instructionally relevant interactions with their teachers than their Anglo–American peers (Jackson & Cosca, 1974). Jackson and Cosca's findings were contaminated by the fact that language and ethnicity covary. Luis Laosa (1977) attempted to untangle the influences of language and ethnicity in a complex observational study of teachers with Mexican–American and Anglo–American students. Laosa was seeking to determine if students from these two groups displayed different behavior patterns in the classroom, whether teachers behaved differently toward them, and whether differences in students' proficiency in English and Spanish comprehension influenced teacher–

student interactions. An initial analysis suggested that in kindergarten, Mexican–American children received fewer disapproving statements and more nonevaluative academic information than Anglo students. By third grade the reverse was true. At this level Mexican–American children received the least amount of academically relevant information and the highest frequency of disapprovals. Moreover, they received fewer cognitively stimulating statements from teachers. The most significant factor influencing teachers' disapproval was degree of bilingualism rather than ethnic group membership. For both Anglo and Mexican–American students whose language comprehension was better in English than in Spanish, disapproval decreased from kindergarten to second grade. For Mexican–Americans who displayed equal proficiency in both languages, or who were Spanish–dominant, the amount of disapproval increased. These findings are all the more interesting, given that the observations were taken in classrooms that were part of a bilingual program. The outcomes seemed to support and clarify the less specific results of an earlier study that revealed disparities in the ways teachers interacted with Mexican–American and Anglo–American students in fourth- through eighth-grade classrooms (Jackson & Cosca, 1974).

From these and numerous other studies with congruent results, it appears that the support and encouragement children receive in classrooms varies in amount and/or quality, although this is not always the case. Factors such as grade level may have a moderating influence. When differences do exist, the attention children receive is unequally distributed between academically relevant and supportive statements versus controlling, critical verbal statements by teachers. Students who are middle class, Anglo–American speakers of standard American English seem to receive a disproportionate amount of supportive, academically relevant interactions, whereas lower SES and minority children more often experience critical, blaming interactions that communicate relatively little academic information. Moreover, the value system into which teachers are socialized seems to be so pervasive that there is apparently little basis for the supposition that teachers of the same racial or ethnic background as the children they teach are any more positive in their interactions with minority children than are white teachers.

Do differential patterns of expectancies and interaction such as those described here actually lead to differences in pupil behavior, or is it the other way around? For the early school years the direction of effect is not clear, but there is some evidence that at the secondary school level the preponderant direction of causality does not begin with differential treatment of students. By this time it appears that teacher expectancies are largely determined by the achievement behaviors displayed by the students, at least where standardized tests constitute the criteria for achievement (Williams, 1976). It may well be that by the time students reach high school, teacher expections from earlier years have had ample time to work whatever influence they might, but here the insidious influence of teacher expectancies is present in the form of grades. Williams' (1976) analysis reveals that teachers adjust their own evaluations of student performance to agree with their previously formed performance expectations. In this process student conformity to classroom behavioral norms is given as much or more weight as actual academic performance. As Williams (1976) says, "Teacher prophecies do not affect so much what is learned, but affect instead the certification of this learning within the school [p. 234]."

CONCLUSIONS AND IMPLICATIONS

There are troublesome inconsistencies in certain aspects of the research pertaining to each of the domains examined in this chapter. The available research varies in quality and numerous questions remain unanswered. Practitioners and those who would teach and advise them would have to wait a very long time for the territory of any one of these domains to be fully mapped, and to specify the interdependent relationships among the processes of these areas of inquiry with any confidence will take a good deal longer. At present we are completely lacking investigations that would be capable of charting the reciprocal interactions among the person and the environmental variables that operate in classrooms. Even so, there are enough consistencies in the existing data to postulate certain relationships and to suggest plausible implications for educational practice. Systematic research must proceed, but it would be imprudent to postpone the examination of probable consequences of teacher expectancies until the unlikely time when conclusions can be drawn with complete confidence.

The evidence does show quite clearly that teachers entertain differential expectations for the achievement of children who vary in personal characteristics such as sex, age, race, ethnicity, and physical attractiveness, and that the amount and quality of instructional behavior interactions often differ along the same lines. The question of whether teacher expectancies are based on these personal characteristics per se or on achievement characteristics that happen to covary with these characteristics has not been answered with complete satisfaction. Some careful methodological work suggests that achievement is the determining factor. Even if that is the case, the results are the same. If, for example, a relatively high proportion of poor children enter school with achievement characteristics that elicit negative expectancies from their teachers, it makes little difference that the expectation was determined by achievement behavior rather than social class markers. The result is likely to be the same for the children involved.

Once formed, teachers' impressions of student ability seem remarkably resistant to change. This might be viewed as both good news and bad news. It is depressing to consider that stereotyped expectancies based on categorical labels or early impressions are resistant to change even when observable performance conflicts with expectations. On the other hand, it is encouraging to note that once impressions are formed, disconfirming data from standardized testing may result in very little change in those cases where the test data is more negative than the teacher's existing expectancy (Airasian *et al.*, 1977). Since these conclusions were derived from work in Ireland, where problems associated with heterogeneous populations are quite different from those in the United States, this hypothesis should be subjected to further testing.

Although some analyses suggest that achievement behavior is a major determinant of teacher expectancies, other work has demonstrated that differential teacher instructional behaviors may be more associated with judgments of students' motivation to do schoolwork than with estimates of ability or achievement in basic school subjects (Luce & Hoge, 1978). This finding, in combination with Klein's (1971) data showing that teachers are influenced markedly by attending–nonattending behavior of students, is particularly interesting with regard to what is known about how failure influences subsequent approaches to tasks by children with internal and external perceptions of causality. If helpless children respond to failure by declining to expend effort on subsequent trials, their own negative perceptions of their ability may be compounded by the use of more controlling, critical, externally determined influence on the part of the teacher.

Along similar lines, the work of Willis and Brophy (1974) suggests that teacher behavior toward children with similar achievement characteristics may vary as a function of student social behaviors, and especially by the degree to which interactions are experienced by teachers as rewarding. Under these circumstances, students whose behavior styles differ from the middle class norms of the classroom are likely to experience proportionally fewer supportive and content-relevant contacts from teachers. It would be no surprise if students from minority and poor family backgrounds were disproportionately represented among this group. The evidence suggests that discrimination of this sort is often unintentional, and that consultation that makes teachers aware of their differential interaction patterns might help some of them to overcome the tendency represented in the findings summarized here (Good & Brophy, 1974).

Socialization practices of parents appear to have an influence on the development of children's feelings of personal efficacy. Parents whose children develop predominantly internal perceptions of control apparently tend to be approving, nonrejecting, and nurturant. These characteristics are similar to those that have been identified in relationship to self-esteem, and the data indicate that there is, indeed, an overlap in the variances of self-judgments relating to self-esteem and locus of control. However, self-esteem and locus of control perceptions are also partially, and significantly, independent of each other. The socialization behavior of parents of internal children contrasts with the childrearing practices of parents whose children are prone to adopt more external attributions of causality. These parents tend to be dominating and controlling. They may also be inconsistent in the control procedures they use with their children. A lack of consensus among socialization agents makes it difficult for children to learn cognitive rules for action, and consequently they may anticipate little personal influence over situations.

Environmental process variables that have been shown to predict school achievement are also related to perceptions of control. Children who report high levels of parental support and encouragement for their academic effort are more likely to expect personal control of situations than children who report low levels of academic reinforcement and support at home. Kifer's (1975) work, however, suggests that school influences on personality factors such as achievement attributions become increasingly powerful in comparison to the influences of the home environment. His findings suggest that when children's efforts are met by failure at school, they develop expectancies of unsuccessful outcomes, and patterns of repeated failure develop. This research suggests the hypothesis, as yet not subjected to direct test, that the power of family support to mediate the effects of academic failure on locus of control perceptions diminishes as children advance by age and grade. Certain categories of children, such as those with special learning handicaps or those whose cultural backgrounds differ from that on which school norms and curricula are based, seem particularly vulnerable to self-perpetuating patterns of failure under the circumstances that structure most contemporary school practices.

The effects of failure on children's expectations and attribution of cause are meaningful only when considered in social context. It means little to be unsuccessful at a task that can be accomplished by only a few individuals. But to do poorly on tasks that are defined as normative social expectations is likely to impact on children's perceptions of their own ability. School tasks are widely regarded as normative social expectations, and under the competitive goal structures and the overt social comparisons that are implicit in norm-referenced assessment practices, failure is likely to be particularly salient. Children who experience failure in competitive settings are more likely than those who are unsuccessful in noncompetitive settings to experience negative affect and to engage in self-derogation. Thus, their future achievement strivings are likely to be discouraged. Competitive goal structures clearly highlight social comparisons and inhibit effort attributions.

Diminished effort is the natural consequence of attributions of outcome to inability. Children who learn to feel helpless in the face of difficulty attribute their difficulty to inability, which is detrimental to effort and persistence. Their responses are maladaptive and performance deteriorates. Nonhelpless children, in contrast, tend to attribute failure to insufficient effort and their response is likely to be to exert more effort (Dweck, 1975). In fact, the critical difference between responses to failure by helpless and nonhelpless, or mastery-oriented, children may be that children in the latter group do not ordinarily make spontaneous causal attributions at all. Rather than seeking causes, they may pursue solutions through self-monitoring and self-instruction (Diener & Dweck, 1978).

A number of procedures designed to facilitate the adoption of internal attributions of cause, especially effort attributions, have been tested with encouraging results. Since failure experiences seem to play a particularly important role in the development of attributions to inability and external causes and in the learning of helplessness, the most simple solution might appear to be to provide externally oriented and helpless children with a rich diet of success. The facts do not appear to bear out that assumption. Although failure may be instrumental in the learning of helplessness, the removal of failure does not appear to constitute a sufficient, or perhaps even constructive, condition to reverse the process. The finding that attribution retraining resulted in sustained decreases in maladaptive reactions to failure whereas a success-only experience was ineffective and, in fact, seemed to produce increased sensitivity to failure should be instructive for those who would attempt to help children develop feelings of efficacy within the context of schooling.

A variety of approaches, including attribution retraining, social reinforcement, and token systems in combination with social reinforcement, have demonstrated promise for effecting such changes. The research suggests that initial interventions may be more effective if they are congruent with the child's current mode of attribution (Bugenthal *et al.*, 1977), but in the long run the approaches with the greatest promise should be those that help the individual to set relevant and realistic purposes and goals and strategies for self-regulation and self-management. In this regard the use of psychostimulants to control hyperactive behavior may have a counterproductive effect on children's perceptions of their ability to control their own behavior.

Since teachers apparently have a tendency to regard children favorably if they respond readily to adult control, it may be necessary to demonstrate to educators the long-range advantage of self-directed learning and to provide the instruction necessary to help them teach children the requisite skills.

These suggestions are derived from the knowledge that the performance of externals seems to improve when clear purposes for tasks are communicated (Dollinger & Taub, 1977). Also, when children have a role in setting their own goals, they accept personal responsibility for success and failure to a greater degree than do peers whose goals are set for them by their teachers (Arlin & Whitley, 1978).

It should be cautioned that merely changing children's causal attributions of failure from external to internal, or from inability to effort, is not likely to produce sustained desirable results unless instruction is arranged to provide opportunities for successful outcomes from effort. In fact, to induce students to make effort attributions accompanied by effortful behavior is likely to have devastating results in the absence of opportunities for success. Hard work is a virtue of long standing in America, but Covington and Omelich (1979) have made a persuasive case that effort is a double-edged sword when it comes to school achievement. One of the few defenses a student facing academic difficulties may have available is to attempt to avoid the implication of inability by refusing to try. This assertion is supported by data (Covington & Omelich) showing that negative affect (shame) and attributions of inability were greater among college undergraduates following substantial effort than when they did little studying. These situations seem highly probable in cases in which students are presented with tasks for which they lack precursor skills. Failure may begin to set in early because traditional instruction so rarely provides for the careful identification and teaching of precursor skills and concepts required for the construction of behaviors that constitute instructional goals (Bandura, 1977; Bergan, 1980; Bergan & Parra, 1979; Bloom, 1976). Where such situations obtain, it is probably more adaptive for a child to attribute failure to external influences than to his or her own inability.

REFERENCES

Abramson, N. L., Seligman, M. E. P., & Teasdale, J. D. Learned helplessness in humans: Critique and reformulation. *Journal of Abnormal Psychology*, 1978, *87*, 49–74.

Adams, G. R. Racial membership and physical attractiveness effects on preschool teachers' expectations. *Child Study Journal*, 1978, *8*, 29–41.

Airasian, P. W., Madaus, G. F., Kellaghan, T., & Pedulla, J. J. Proportion and direction of teacher rating changes of pupils' progress attributable to standardized test information. *Journal of Educational Psychology*, 1977, *69*, 702–709.

Altshuler, R., & Kassinove, H. The effects of skill and chance instructional sets, schedule of reinforcement, and sex on children's temporal persistence. *Child Development*, 1975, *46*, 258–262.

Ames, C. Competition versus cooperative reward structures: The influence of individual and group peformance factors on achievement attributions and affect. *American Educational Research Journal*, 1981, *18*, 273–287.

Ames, C., Ames, R., & Felker, D. W. Effects of competitive reward structure and valence of outcome on children's achievement attributions. *Journal of Educational Psychology*, 1977, *69*, 1–8.

Andrews, G. R., & Debus, G. R. Persistence and causal perception of failure: Modifying cognitive attributions. *Journal of Educational Psychology*, 1978, *70*, 154–166.

Arlin, M., & Whitley, T. W. Perceptions of self-managed learning opportunities and academic locus of control: A causal interpretation. *Journal of Educational Psychology*, 1978, *70*, 988–992.

Bandura, A. *Social learning theory*. Englewood Cliffs, N.J.: Prentice-Hall, 1977.

Bandura, A., & Walters, R. H. *Social learning theory and personality development*. New York: Holt, 1963.

Bergan, J. R. The structural analysis of behavior: An alternative to the learning hierarchy model. *Review of Educational Research*, 1980, *50*, 625–647.

Bergan, J. R., & Parra, E. Variations in IQ testing and the letter-learning and achievement of Anglo and bilingual Mexican–American children. *Journal of Educational Psychology*, 1979, *71*, 819–826.

Bloom, B. S. *Human characteristics and school learning*. New York: McGraw-Hill, 1976.

Bowles, S., & Gintis, H. *Schooling in capitalist America: Educational reform and the contradictions of economic life*. New York: Basic Books, 1976.

Bradley, R., & Caldwell, B. M. The relation of infants' home environments to mental test performance at fifty-four months: A follow-up study. *Child Development*, 1976, *47*, 1172–1174.

Bradley, R. H., Caldwell, B. M., & Elardo, R. Home environment and cognitive development in the first two years: A cross-lagged panel analysis. *Developmental Psychology*, 1979, *15*, 246–250.

Brady, J. V., Porter, R. W., Conrad, D. G., & Mason, J. W. Avoidance behavior and the development of gastro-duodenal ulcers. *Journal of Experimental Analysis of Behavior*, 1958, *1*, 69–72.

Brophy, J. E., & Good, T. Teacher–student relationships: Causes and consequences. New York: Holt, 1974.

Brown, W. E., Payne, L. T., Lankewich, L., & Cornell, L. L. Praise, criticism, and race. *Elementary School Journal*, 1970, *70*, 373–377.

Bugenthal, D. B., Collins, S., Collins, L., & Chaney, L. A. Attributional and behavioral changes following two behavior management interventions with hyperactive boys: A follow-up study. *Child Development*, 1978, *49*, 247–250.

Bugenthal, D. B., Whalen, C. K., & Henker, B. Causal attributions of hyperactive children and motivational assumptions of two behavior change approaches: Evidence for an interactionist position. *Child Development,* 1977, *48,* 874–884.

Byalick, R., & Bersoff, D. N. Reinforcement practices of black and white teachers in integrated classrooms. *Journal of Educational Psychology,* 1974, *66,* 473–480.

Byers, P., & Byers, H. Non-verbal communication in the education of children. In C. Cazden, V. John, & D. Hymes (Eds.), *Functions of language in the classroom.* New York: Teachers College Press, 1972.

Chance, J. E. *Internal control of reinforcements and the school learning process.* Paper presented at the biennial meeting of the Society for Research in Child Development, Minneapolis, 1965.

Clifford, M. M. A revised measure of locus of control. *Child Study Journal,* 1976, *6,* 85–90.

Coleman, J. S., Campbell, E. Q., Hobson, C. J., McPartland, J., Mood, A. M., Weinfeld, F. D., & York, R. L. Equality of educational opportunity. Washington, D.C.: U.S. Department of Health, Education and Welfare, U.S. Government Printing Office, 1966.

Cooper, H. M., & Baron, R. M. Academic expectations and attributed responsibility as predictors of professional teachers' reinforcement of behavior. *Journal of Educational Psychology,* 1977, *69,* 409–418.

Covington, M. V., & Omelich, C. L. Effort: The double-edged sword in school achievement. *Journal of Educational Psychology,* 1979, *71,* 169–182.

Crandall, V. C., Katkovsky, W., & Crandall, V. J. Children's beliefs in their control of reinforcements in intellectual academic achievement behaviors. *Child Development,* 1965, *36,* 91–109.

Crandall, V. J., Katkovsky, W., & Preston, A. Motivational and ability determinants of young children's intellectual achievement situations. *Child Development,* 1962, *33,* 643–661.

Datta, L., Schaefer, E., & Davis, M. Sex and scholastic aptitude as variables in teachers' ratings of the adjustment and classroom behavior of Negro and other seventh-grade students. *Journal of Educational Psychology,* 1968, *79,* 94–101.

Davé, R. H. *The identification and measurement of environmental process variables that are related to academic achievement.* Unpublished doctoral dissertation, University of Chicago, 1963.

Davis, W. L. *Parental antecedents of children's locus of control.* Unpublished doctoral dissertation, Kansas State University, 1969.

Davis, W. L., & Phares, E. J. Parental antecedents of internal–external control of reinforcement. *Psychological Reports,* 1969, *24,* 427–436.

Davison, G. Differential relaxation and cognitive restructuring in therapy with a "paranoid schizophrenic" or "paranoid state." *Proceedings of the 74th Annual Convention of the American Psychological Association,* 1966, *1,* 177–178. (Summary)

DeCharms, R. From pawns to origins: Toward self-motivation. In G. S. Lesser (Ed.), *Psychology and educational practice.* Glenview, Ill.: Scott, Foresman, 1971.

Diener, C. I., & Dweck, C. S. An analysis of learned helplessness: Continuous changes in performance, strategy, and achievement cognitions following failure. *Journal of Personality and Social Psychology,* 1978, *36,* 451–462.

Dollinger, S. J., & Taub, S. I. The interaction of locus of control expectancies and providing purpose on children's motivation. *Journal of Research in Personality,* 1977, *11,* 118–127.

Dusek, J. B. Do teachers bias children's learning? *Review of Educational Research,* 1975, *45,* 661–684.

Dusek, J. B., & O'Connell, E. J. Teacher expectancy effects on the achievement test performance of elementary school children. *Journal of Educational Psychology,* 1973, *65,* 371–377.

Dweck, C. S. The role of expectations and attributions in the alleviation of learned helplessness. *Journal of Personality and Social Psychology*, 1975, *7*, 674–685.

Dweck, C. S., & Bush, E. S. Sex differences in learned helplessness. I: Differential debilitation with peer and adult evaluators. *Developmental Psychology*, 1976, *12*, 147–156.

Dweck, C. S., & Reppucci, N. D. Learned helplessness and reinforcement responsibility in children. *Journal of Personality and Social Psychology*, 1973, *25*, 109–116.

Ellis, A. *Reason and emotion in psychotherapy.* New York: Lyle-Stuart, 1962.

Feather, N. T. The study of persistence. *Psychological Bulletin*, 1962, *59*, 94–115.

Feather, N. T., & Simon, J. Attribution of responsibility and valence of outcome in relation to initial confidence and success and failure of self and other. *Journal of Personality and Social Psychology*, 1971, *18*, 173–188.

Foster, G., & Ysseldyke, J. Expectancy and halo effects as a result of artifically induced teacher bias. *Contemporary Educational Psychology*, 1976, *1*, 37–45.

Frieze, I., & Weiner, B. Cue utilization and attributional judgments for success and failure. *Journal of Personality*, 1971, *39*, 591–606.

Frieze, J. H., & Snyder, H. N. Children's beliefs about the causes of success and failure in school settings. *Journal of Educational Psychology*, 1980, *72*, 186–196.

Gabbert, B. *The influence of pupil socio-economic status on teacher behavior.* Unpublished doctoral dissertation, The University of Texas at Austin, 1973.

Gardner, J., & Bing, M. The elusiveness of Pygmalion and differences in teacher–pupil contacts. *Interchange*, 1973, *4*, 34–42.

Gillung, T. B., & Rucker, C. N. Labels and teacher expectations. *Exceptional Children*, 1977, *43*, 464–465.

Good, T. Which pupils do teachers call on? *Elementary School Journal*, 1970, *70*, 190–198.

Good, T. L., & Brophy, J. E. Changing teacher and student behavior: An empirical investigation. *Journal of Educational Psychology*, 1974, *66*, 390–405.

Good, T., Sikes, J., & Brophy, J. Effects of teacher sex, student sex and student achievement on classroom interaction. *Journal of Educational Psychology*, 1973, *65*, 74–87.

Gordon, D. A. Children's beliefs in internal–external control and self-esteem as related to academic achievement. *Journal of Personality Assessment*, 1977, *41*, 383–386.

Gordon, D. A., Jones, R. H., & Short, N. L. Task persistence and locus of control in elementary school children. *Child Development*, 1977, *48*, 1716–1719.

Harris, B. Developmental differences in attribution of responsibility. *Developmental Psychology*, 1977, *13*, 257–265.

Heider, F. *The psychology of interpersonal relations.* New York: Wiley, 1958.

Henderson, R. W. Environmental predictors of academic performance of disadvantaged Mexican–American children. *Journal of Clinical and Consulting Psychology*, 1972, *38*, 297.

Henderson, R. W., & Hennig, H. Relationships among cooperation–competition and locus of control in academic situations among children in traditional and open classrooms. *Contemporary Education Psychology*, 1979, *4*, 121–131.

Henderson, R. W., & Merritt, C. B. Environmental backgrounds of Mexican–American children with different potentials for school success. *Journal of Social Psychology*, 1968, *75*, 101–106.

Hoehn, A. A study of social status differentiation in the classroom behavior of 19 third grade teachers. *Journal of Social Psychology*, 1954, *39*, 269–292.

Humphreys, L. G., & Stubbs, J. A longitudinal analysis of teacher expectation, student expectation, and student achievement. *Journal of Educational Measurement*, 1977, *14*, 261–270.

Jackson, G., & Cosca, C. The inequality of educational opportunity in the Southwest: An observational study of ethnically mixed classrooms. *American Educational Research Journal*, 1974, *11*, 219–229.

Katkovsky, W., Crandall, V. C., & Good, S. Parental antecedents of children's beliefs in internal–external control of reinforcement in intellectual achievement situations. *Child Development*, 1967, *28*, 765–776.

Kifer, E. Relationships between academic achievement and personality characteristics: A quasi-longitudinal study. *American Educational Research Journal*, 1975, *12*, 191–210.

Klein, S. S. Student influences on teacher behavior. *American Educational Research Journal*, 1971, *8*, 403–422.

Laosa, L. M. Inequality in the classroom: Observational research on teacher–student interactions. *Aztlan International Journal of Chicano Studies Research*, 1977, *8*, 51–67.

Lefcourt, H. M. *Locus of control: Current trends in theory and research.* Hillsdale, N.J.: Erlbaum, 1976.

Lefcourt, H. M., & Wine, J. Internal versus external control of reinforcement and the development of attention in experimental situations. *Canadian Journal of Behavioral Science*, 1969, *1*, 167–181.

Lilly, M. S. (Ed.). *Children with exceptional needs.* New York: Holt, 1979.

Lockheed, M. E. Some causes and consequences of teacher expectations concerning pupil performance. *California Journal of Teacher Education*, 1977, *4*, 40–56.

Loeb, R. C. Concomitants of boys' locus of control examined in parent–child interaction. *Developmental Psychology*, 1975, *11*, 353–358.

Luce, S. R., & Hoge, R. D. Relations among teacher rankings, pupil–teacher interactions, and academic achievement: A test of the teacher expectancy hypothesis. *American Educational Research Journal*, 1978, *15*, 489–500.

Meichenbaum, D. Self-instructional methods. In F. H. Kanfer & A. P. Goldstein (Eds.), *Helping people change.* New York: Pergamon, 1975.

Merton, R. K. *Social theory and social behavior* (Rev. ed.). New York: Free Press, 1957.

Mischel, W. Toward a cognitive social learning reconceptualization of personality. *Psychological Review*, 1973, *80*, 252–283.

Mischel, W., & Mischel, H. N. *The development of children's knowledge of self-control.* Paper presented at the biennial meeting of the Society for Research in Child Development, San Francisco, March 18, 1979.

Mischel, W., Zeiss, R., & Zeiss, A. Internal–external control and persistence: Validation and implications of the Stanford Preschool Internal–External Scale. *Journal of Personality and Social Psychology*, 1974, *29*, 265–278.

Mowrer, O. H. *Learning theory and behavior.* New York: Wiley, 1960.

Mowrer, O. H., & Vieck, P. Experimental analogue of fear from a sense of helplessness. *Journal of Abnormal and Social Psychology*, 1948, *43*, 193–200.

Nicholls, J. Causal attributions and other achievement-related cognitions: Effects of task outcome, attainment value and sex. *Journal of Personality and Social Psychology*, 1975, *31*, 379–389.

Nowicki, S., & Barnes, J. *Effects of a structured camp experience on locus of control in children.* Paper presented at the annual meeting of the Southeastern Psychological Association, Miami Beach, May 1971.

Nowicki, S., & Strickland, B. R. A locus of control scale for children. *Journal of Consulting and Clinical Psychology*, 1973, *40*, 148–155.

Parish, T. S., & Copeland, T. F. *Locus of control and father loss.* Paper presented at the biennial meeting of the Society for Research in Child Development, San Francisco, March 16, 1979.

Pascarella, E. T., & Pflaum, S. W. The interaction of children's attribution and level of control over error correction in reading instruction. *Journal of Educational Psychology*, 1981, *73*, 533–540.

Phares, E. J. *Locus of control in personality.* Morristown, N. J.: General Learning Press, 1976.

Phares, E. J., & Lamiell, J. T. Personality. In M. R. Rosenzweig & L. W. Porter (Eds.), *Annual review of psychology* (Vol. 28). Palo Alto, Calif.: Annual Reviews, 1977. Pp. 113–140.

Rist, R. Student social class and teacher expectations: The self-fulfilling prophecy in ghetto education. *Harvard Educational Review*, 1970, *40*, 411–451.

Rosenthal, T. L., & Zimmerman, B. J. *Social learning and cognition*. New York: Academic Press, 1978.

Roth, S., & Kubal, L. The effects of noncontingent reinforcement on tasks of differing importance: Facilitation and learned helplessness effects. *Journal of Personality and Social Psychology*, 1975, *32*, 680–691.

Rotter, J. B. The role of the psychological situation in determining the direction of human behavior. In M. R. Jones (Ed.), *Nebraska Symposium on Motivation*. Lincoln. Univ. of Nebraska Press, 1955.

Rotter, J. B. Generalized expectancies for internal versus external control of reinforcement. *Psychological Monographs*, 1966, *80*(1, Whole No. 609).

Rotter, J. B. Some problems and misconceptions related to the construct of internal versus external control of reinforcement. *Journal of Consulting and Clinical Psychology*, 1975, *43*, 56–57.

Rubovits, P., & Maehr, M. Pygmalion analyzed: Toward an explanation of the Rosenthal–Jackson findings. *Journal of Personality and Social Psychology*, 1971, *19*, 197–203.

Seligman, M. E. P. *Helplessness*. San Francisco: Freeman, 1975.

Seligman, M. E. P., & Maier, S. Failure to escape traumatic shock. *Journal of Experimental Psychology*, 1967, *74*, 1–9.

Seligman, M. E. P., Maier, S. F., & Solomon, R. L. Unpredictable and uncontrollable aversive events. In F. R. Brush (Ed.), *Aversive conditioning and learning*. New York: Academic Press, 1971.

Shore, R. E. *Parental determinants of boys' internal–external control*. Unpublished doctoral dissertation, Syracuse University, 1967.

Strickland, B. R. The prediction of social action from a dimension of internal–external control. *Journal of social psychology*, 1965, *66*, 353–358.

Strickland, B. R. Delay of gratification as a function of race of the experimenter. *Journal of Social Psychology*, 1972, 108–112.

Taub, S. S., & Dollinger, S. J. Reward and purpose as incentives for children differing in locus of control experiences. *Journal of Personality*, 1975, *43*, 179–195.

Thomas, A. Learned helplessness and expectancy factors: Implications for research in learning disabilities. *Review of Educational Research*, 1979, *49*, 200–221.

Toner, I., Moore, L., & Emmons, B. A. The effect of being labeled on subsequent self-control in children. *Child Development*, 1980, *51*, 618–621.

Veldman, D. J., & Brophy, J. E. Measuring teacher effects on pupil achievement. *Journal of Educational Psychology*, 1974, *66*, 319–324.

Walberg, H. J., & Marjoribanks, K. Family environment and cognitive development: Twelve analytic models. *Review of Educational Research*, 1976, *46*, 527–551.

Wang, M. C., & Stiles, B. An investigation of children's concept of self-responsibility for school learning. *American Educational Research Journal*, 1976, *13*, 159–179.

Weiss, J. M. Effects of coping behavior in different warning signal conditions on stress pathology in rats. *Journal of Comparative and Physiological Psychology*, 1971, *77*, 1–13.

Weisz, J. R. Perceived control and learned helplessness among mentally retarded children: A developmental analysis. *Developmental Psychology*, 1979, *15*, 311–319.

Weisz, J. R. Learned helplessness in black and white children identified by their schools as retarded and nonretarded: Performance deterioration in response to failure. *Developmental Psychology*, 1981, *17*, 499–508.

Williams, T. Teacher prophecies and the inheritance of inequality. *Sociology of Education,* 1976, *49,* 223–236.

Willis, S., & Brophy, J. Origins of teachers' attitudes toward young children. *Journal of Educational Psychology,* 1974, *66,* 520–529.

Winetsky, C. Comparisons of the expectations of parents and teachers for the behavior of preschool children. *Child Development,* 1978, *49,* 1146–1154.

Wolk, S., & Du Cette, J. Intentional performance and incidental learning as a function of personality and task dimensions. *Journal of Personality and Social Psychology,* 1974, *29,* 90–101.

Wortman, C. B., Panciera, L., Shusterman, L., & Hibscher, J. Attributions of causality and reactions to uncontrollable outcomes. *Journal of Experimental Social Psychology,* 1976, *12,* 301–316.

Yee, A. Interpersonal attitudes of teachers and advantaged and disadvantaged pupils. *Journal of Human Resources,* 1968, *3,* 327–345.

Zimmerman, B. J., & Ringle, J. Effects of model persistence and statements of confidence on children's self-efficacy and problem solving. *Journal of Educational Psychology,* 1981, *73,* 485–493.

PART FOUR / Developmental problems

10 / Children with learning and behavior problems: a behavioral perspective

WILLIAM I. GARDNER
RICHARD BOYD

Childhood is a highly critical period in the psychological development of the individual. During the preschool and early school years, basic patterns of perceptual, motor, cognitive, language, self-concept, emotional, and social behaviors are acquired. Difficulties in development in any of these psychological areas, depending on the severity and pervasiveness, can have a devastating and long-lasting effect on the child's subsequent development.

In illustration, a child who fails to acquire basic skills for imitating the behaviors of others will experience extreme difficulty in acquiring speech and social skills. The child without an adequate speech repertoire will have difficulty interacting with others. This interpersonal difficulty impedes the development of other congitive, social, and emotional skills as well as more complex modes of interpersonal relationships. The retardation of these behavioral repertoires in turn disrupts the entire early psychological development of the child. The child has difficulty developing adequate ego, self-concept, and self-management characteristics. The older the child becomes, the greater the negative effects of the learning and behavior difficulties. These observations emphasize that, in most instances, a child in the elementary grades does not suddenly develop difficulties of learning and behaving. Rather, a child's difficulties represent the accumulative effects of a series of less obvious failures of development.

PSYCHOLOGICAL DEVELOPMENT
IN THE ELEMENTARY YEARS

CHANGING CONCEPTS AND PRACTICE

Diagnostic labels and educational practices

Many reports indicate that up to 20% or more of school-age children exhibit exceptional or out-of-the-ordinary learning and behavior characteristics that interfere significantly with their educational, personal, and social development (Dunn, 1973; Gardner, 1977; Meyen, 1978). The generic label *exceptional* has been devised to refer to a wide range of sensory, physical, learning, intellectual, and behavior characteristics of children that create instructional and management difficulties in the regular class school setting. Other more specific labels used by educational personnel to refer to children with exceptional learning and behavior difficulties include such negatively loaded terminology as *handicapped, disabled, atypical, disordered, impaired, maladjusted, delayed, disturbed, dysfunctional,* and *retarded* (Reynolds & Balow, 1972).

A "special" educational structure has been devised to handle various categories of these exceptional children. The disabilities, differences, or shortcomings involved in diagnosing and labeling these children traditionally have served as the major focus of such programs. In illustration, educational programs have been designed to deal with the mental *retardation,* the perceptual *handicap,* the emotional *disturbance,* the social *deviation,* or the learning *disabilities.* Children traditionally have been removed from the natural environment of the regular classroom, either on a part-time or full-time basis, because they have been unable to adapt appropriately to various requirements of the rather narrowly structured mainstream or regular education program provided. Special classes, remedial programs, resource rooms, schools, and residential centers have all been devised as a means of segregation and specialized education.

This three-step diagnostic and special education placement process may be summarized as follows:

1. A child, due to certain learning and behavior characteristics, does not adapt to the instructional arrangements or demonstrate the desired rate of instructional progress of the regular school program.
2. Diagnostic procedures of a medical nature (e.g., cerebral palsy, epilepsy, visual impairment), psychiatric nature (e.g., emotional disturbance), or psychometric nature (e.g., mentally retarded, learning disabled) are used to assign the child to a disability or difference category.

3. On the basis of this category diagnosis, the child is then assigned to alternative special instructional programs such as a special education program for the emotionally disturbed, a special class for the mentally retarded, or a diagnostic center for the learning disabled.

Limitations of category-based educational practices

The diagnostic labeling that underlies categorical special class placement provides nothing more than a summary or shorthand term for problematic learning and behavior characteristics of children. Although there are some common characteristics among children who are given similar categorical labels (e.g., emotional disturbance, learning disabled), the educationally related differences, which frequently are overlooked or underemphasized, far outnumber the similarities.

Grouping children under such umbrella terms as mental retardation, emotional disturbance, or learning disabilities on the basis of a few learning similarities (all deficit or undesirable excessive characteristics) creates the danger that the similarities along difficulty dimensions will be overemphasized and the more positive and educationally relevant individual differences will be minimized or ignored. For example, a group of children may be designated as *emotionally disturbed*. Once this label has been assigned, there is a tendency to assume that there are some essential psychological features and some specific educational strategies that should be used with all children so labeled. Furthermore, it may be assumed that these critical strategies differ in kind or degree from those educational strategies used with children provided such other diagnostic category labels as mentally retarded or learning disabled.

These viewpoints represent a variation of an aptitude–treatment interaction assumption (Gardner, 1977). That is, it is assumed that for each diagnostic category of children there is a corresponding best category of educational program that differs in specific and critical instructional aspects from that designed for children assigned to other diagnostic groupings. An interaction is assumed to exist between the general diagnostic category to which children are assigned (e.g., emotionally disturbed, mentally retarded, learning disabled) and the specific educational program (i.e., separate special education classes and related instructional procedures designed for each category) provided the children.

There is no evidence to support this assumption as it relates to major category groupings. There is no evidence that children labeled, for example, as emotionally disturbed learn any better, or worse, if placed in a learning disabilities program than if placed in a program for the emotionally disturbed. There are no instructional tactics used with the "learning disabled" child who presents, for example, a specific perceptual problem that differ from those provided the "emotionally disturbed" or the "mentally retarded" child with a similar perceptual problem. All may be provided the same instructional program, not because of their learning disabilities or emotional disturbance, but rather due to similar discrimination or related difficulties. Likewise, children with disruptive classroom behavior who attend different category-defined special classes would not be provided different behavior management programs based on different diagnostic categories.

Cooper (1970) gives a specific example of this position in his instructional program for remediation of letter and digit reversal in four children ranging in age from 8 to 16 years. One was "learning disabled," one "educable mentally retarded," one a third grader who attended a university learning center, and one was institutionalized in a state hospital. Although of different ages and diagnostic groupings, the same direct teaching procedures were used successfully with all children. Not only were reversal errors eliminated in a brief time, but the behavioral change also generalized for all children from trained letters and digits to untrained ones. These same procedures of corrective feedback and positive reinforcement for correct performance were used successfully by Stromer (1975, 1977) for similar academic deficiencies and by Lahey, Busemeyer, O'Hara, and Beggs (1977) to remediate the severe perceptual–motor (handwriting) difficulties of children identified as learning disabled.

As Hallahan and Kauffman (1976) emphasize:

> Everything else being equal, the ED hyperactive child with a figure–ground reversal problem, the LD hyperactive child with a figure–ground reversal problem, and the EMR hyperactive child with a figure–ground reversal problem will all be taught in the same manner. The behaviors exhibited, and not the diagnostic category in which the child has been placed, are the crucial variables on which the teaching strategy should hinge [p. 35].

This evidence would suggest, then, that the diagnostic categories used in current special education practices are not critical instructional variables. That is, these categories are unrelated or, at best, only minimally related to many of the variables critical to a specific child's learning and behaving. The diagnostic labels of *mental retardation, emotional disturbance,* or *learning disabilities,* as examples,

1. Do not explain why a child has difficulty learning or behaving appropriately.

2. Do not indicate the specifics of what the child can indeed learn or do.
3. Do not indicate the specific educationally relevant characteristics a child does exhibit.
4. Do not describe the conditions under which optimal learning or behaving will occur for an individual child.

Obviously, other types of information are needed to provide direction in designing successful instructional programs. As described later, this information would consist of more specific learner characteristics that are functionally related to various aspects of the educational environment.

In summary, there is considerable and increasing dissatisfaction over the merits of diagnostic practices used with children with learning and behavior difficulties that are based on the assumption of internal deviancy and the related practices of category-based special education placement. Bruininks and Rynders (1971), Gardner (1977), and Lilly (1979b) provide elaboration of these for the interested reader. The major areas of dissatisfaction include the following:

1. Special class placement results in stigmatizing the exceptional child, resulting in a loss of self-esteem and lowered acceptance by other children (Meyerowitz, 1967). It is not suggested, however, that mere placement in regular educational arrangements will ipso facto result in heightened self-esteem and peer acceptance. Recent studies, in fact, indicate that this does not happen (Bruininks, 1978; Bryan, 1978; Macmillan, Jones, & Aloia, 1974). Martin (1972) noted that attempts at providing an adequate education for handicapped children by integrating them into regular education programs:

   will not succeed without modification in the system . . . . our societal mechanisms for excluding handicapped children from schools, from transportation, from public parks, playgrounds, and buildings, from jobs, and from social contacts have worked all too well. This lack of familiarity and confidence in human relations with handicapped persons means that many teachers will need special assistance if they are to interact successfully to help handicapped children learn [p. 520].

2. Mildly handicapped children make as much or more academic progress in regular classrooms as they do in special classrooms (Bartel & Guskin, 1971; Calhoun & Elliott, 1977; Christoplos & Renz, 1969; Gottlieb, 1981; Jones, Gottlieb, Guskin, & Yoshida, 1978).
3. There are few if any reliable and educationally relevant differences between different categories of children nor com-

monalities within children comprising specific categories (Hallahan & Kauffman, 1976; Lilly, 1977a; Neisworth & Greer, 1975).
4. There is little point in investing further energy in improving
segregated special classes, since this arrangement poorly serves
the social and educational needs of children (Lilly, 1979b;
Sabatino, 1972).
5. Special class arrangements inappropriately place the responsibility for academic failure on children rather than upon schools and
teachers (Lilly, 1979b).
6. The very existence of special classes encourages the misplace-
ment of many children, particularly children from minority
groups (Franks, 1971; President's Committee on Mental Retardation, 1970; Rivers, Henderson, Jones, Lodner, & Williams, 1975).
7. Special class placement is inconsistent with the tenets of a demo-
cratic philosophy of education because it isolates exceptional from
normal children and vice versa (Abeson, Bolick, & Hass, 1975;
Kirp, Kuriloff, & Buss, 1975; Weintraub, Abeson, & Braddock,
1975).
8. Such diagnostic and related program placement practices may
contribute to and perhaps even create many of the problems
these practices were designed to alleviate. Gampel, Gottlieb, and
Harrison (1974) found that mildly retarded children in segregated
special classes in middle class suburban schools exhibit a higher
incidence of hostile and aggressive behavior and more restless-
ness than do comparable children who either had been reinte-
grated into regular classes or were never labeled nor removed from
the mainstream educational setting. These writers suggest that
these children were more apt to view their normal class peers as
more competent and thus were more apt to imitate their appropriate social behaviors. Bartel and Guskin (1971), Gardner (1971),
and Dunn (1968) all express similar views.
9. Once a child is labeled and segregated in one manner or another,
it is difficult to regain the original status of being "normal" like
everyone else (Gallagher, 1972; Reynolds & Balow, 1972; Rivers
et al., 1975). Gallagher (1972) suggested:

In a number of large city school systems far less than 10 percent of the children
placed in special education classes are ever returned to regular education. When
one considers that the referral error could well be that high, it is easy to conclude
that the bridge that should exist between special and regular education is, in fact,
not really there. The traffic all goes in one direction [p. 529].

10. The internal deviancy connotation of category labels may set into
action a self-fulfilling prophesy. The findings of Algozzine,

Mercer, and Countermine (1977), Chapman, Larsen, and Parker (1979), Foster and Salvia (1977), and similar studies support the notion that teachers do have different expectations for children labeled as handicapped and that these expectations influence their teaching styles. As emphasized by Gardner (1977), MacMillan *et al.* (1974), and Reschly and Lamprecht (1979), however, the effects of labeling on teacher behavior are complex ones that require continued research investigation.

11. When children with differences are labeled and segregated from the regular class, the children left in the mainstream have little opportunity to form desirable attitudes toward them. This effect is emphasized by Allport's theory that separateness among groups leads to exaggeration of differences (Allport, 1961). Hobbs (1975) noted:

> We strongly believe that normal children of all ages should have an opportunity to know handicapped children sufficiently well to appreciate them as people. If such experience were started early enough and continued under sensitive guidance, the handicapped would no longer be alienated and the lives of the non-handicapped would be enriched [p. 197].

12. There is little evidence to support the efficacy of grouping children for educational purposes on the basis of a limited number of "deviant" characteristics (Lilly, 1970, 1979b; Sabatino, 1972).

Mainstreaming and PL 94–142

The passage by the United States Congress of the Education for All Handicapped Children Act of 1975 (PL 94–142) mandates that each child with recurring learning and behavior difficulties be provided an individualized educational program in the least restrictive manner possible. This mandate has provided the major impetus for the current widespread practices of mainstreaming children with learning and behavior difficulties. Children with mild to moderate learning and behavior difficulties are being integrated into the regular classroom program as an alternative to the more traditional practice of self-contained special education programs (Abeson & Zettel, 1977).

These new requirements of mainstreaming and of development of individualized educational programs have created obvious difficulties for the general educator, as most teachers are trained to deal with the normally developing and easily managed child. Such placement without adequate teacher preparation also poses educational hazards for the child. As illustration, Chapman *et al.* (1979), in studying the nature and extent of teacher–child classroom interactions of mainstreamed children viewed as "learning disordered," found that these children received more teacher criticism in interactions concerning classroom procedures and more teacher criticism and warning regarding behavior than their "nondisabled" peers. In contrast, Bryan (1978) reported that educators who were specially trained to program for a child's learning and behavior difficulties provided more positive and fewer negative interactions than did the regular classroom teacher. (The interested reader should refer to Hauser, 1979, for a discussion of issues relating to mainstreaming.)

The remainder of this chapter is designed to assist the general educator in viewing the child with learning and behavior difficulties from a developmental perspective and in developing an awareness of concepts and related instructional practices that have been found useful in facilitating academic and personal–social development. A noncategorical behavioral approach that focuses on specific child features is followed in this presentation (Gardner, 1978; Lilly, 1979a). As described by Lahey and Johnson (1977), Lilly (1977b), and Lovitt (1977), the behavioral approach to instructional practices is defined by the following primary characteristics:

1. *Individualization and mastery learning.* The educational program is based on the individual child's strengths and limitations. The child learns each task to mastery prior to progressing to the next (Duffey & Fedner, 1978).
2. *Direct teaching.* The educational program is aimed directly at the behavioral deficits and excesses that require change, and not at inferred disorders believed to underlie the child's difficulties (Fuchs, 1979; Wehman, 1977).
3. *Emphasis on measurement.* Educational instruction is data-based. After instruction has begun, progress data that provide continual feedback are collected. Such data are used to determine whether the instructional intervention is successful and encourage modification of procedures when necessary (Norman, 1977).

DEVELOPMENTAL AND TRANSITIONAL NATURE
OF PROBLEMS

Children with learning and behavior difficulties have much in common with all children: They rarely exhibit any kinds of learning and behavior characteristics not seen in the typical child. For example, many children exhibit visual perceptual problems during their early exposure to reading instruction. Problems of form discrimination and of position in space, such as those involved in discriminating between stimuli that differ in up and down and right and left orientation, are prevalent. It is not unusual for *b* to be confused with *d*, 6 with 9, and *m* with *w*; for *p* to read as *q*, *41* to be seen as *14*, and *saw* to be read as *was*. But most children soon learn the appropriate visual discrimination and the associated letter–sound, that is, a grapheme–phoneme correspondence. However, a significant number of children, for a variety of reasons, continue to experience reversal and inversion problems as they move into middle-elementary-school age and thus have increasing difficulty with acquisition and use of language and math skills (Hallahan & Kauffman, 1976).

It is also true that most children at one time or another demonstrate various behavior problems. The kinds of problems exhibited in the middle childhood years run the gamut from severe acting-out behavior, difficulties with peer relationships, and negativism to virtual social isolation. Many of the problems that beset preschool children, such as sleeping, feeding, and toileting difficulties, have been resolved by the time most children enter first grade. For some children, however, these are continuing problems, suggestive of the need for more concerted, perhaps professional, assistance. Other problems seem to emerge in concert with the developmental stages and environmental demands associated with the middle childhood period. The child's entrance into the formal classroom situation and the formation of new peer and adult relationships present a host of novel academic and social expectations and demands. Oftentimes behavior patterns that did not present great difficulty to social agents during the preschool years now loom as problematic. Overactivity is one such example, but other problems emerge as well, such as school phobia, noncompliance, aggressiveness, and social withdrawal. The demands made by school and the development of relationships outside the immediate family and neighborhood provide the backdrop for the development and identification of behavioral problems that did not necessarily appear problematic during the preschool period.

Prevalence data suggest that behavior problems in childhood are more common than typically believed (Quay & Werry, 1979). To illustrate, Rubin and Balow (1978) report a longitudinal study from kindergarten through grade 6 in which teachers annually rated 1586 children who were normally distributed on measures of IQ, socioeconomic status, and school achievement. In any single year, from 23% to 31% of the children were judged by their teachers as manifesting behavior problems. Among children receiving three or more annual ratings, 59% were considered as having a problem by at least one teacher. Results indicate that behavior that at least one teacher is willing to classify as a problem is the norm rather than the exception for elementary school children. However, these problems represent transitional episodes for most children, as more adaptive characteristics are developed that represent a reasonable match with the instructional and interpersonal requirements of the social and educational environments. Rubin and Balow reported that only 7.5% of the children were consistently identified as exhibiting behavior problems.

In summary, many learning and behavior problems are of a temporary nature and disappear as children develop. A significant percentage of children, however, continue to present difficulties throughout the elementary school years. It should be remembered, nonetheless, that children with chronic and continuing learning and behavior difficulties are merely demonstrating different intensities, durations, and combinations of problems that are developmental characteristics of most children. These persisting difficulties do create problems both for children and their social and educational environments and render the teaching and learning process more difficult.

Individual differences in development and nature of problems

The types of learning and behavior problems acquired and the rate and consistency of development vary considerably among children. Some children have little difficulty acquiring some behavior characteristics—for example, the gross motor skills of walking, jumping, running—but nevertheless experience considerable difficulty in learning other types of behaviors such as verbal expression skills, visual perceptual skills, or the fine motor skills involved in cutting and writing.

Some children acquire rather complex and highly disruptive behavior characteristics and, as a result, have difficulty in relating to others; others are easy to get along with. Some are quite attentive to adult concern; others are relatively detached from social interaction. Some have no difficulty making sense out of visual stimulation, whereas others experience considerable difficulty with such. Some find that task completion or creative activities are highly reinforcing experiences and soon become quite independent in task initiation and completion. Others require more tangible and externally provided consequences for learning and performance. There may be rather variable behavior development even within a single behavior dimension such as perception or language. Auditory perception may be good; visual perception may be poor. Expressive language may be poor; receptive language may be good. These and related characteristics emphasize both the individuality as well as the wide range of differences among children with learning and behavior difficulties.

Cumulative effects of excessive failure experiences

Although various neurological, sensory, and other physical deficits or limitations may account for or contribute to many of the problematic learning and behavior characteristics of children, it is evident that inappropriate aspects of learning environments assume a significant role. Children with learning and behavior problems experience failure more frequently than do other children. Many do not acquire various skills as rapidly, nor do they reach the levels of performance or maturity expected by the home and school environments. As a result, these children usually receive limited positive consequences from the social environment. The reader will recall the Chapman *et al.* (1979) findings discussed earlier that children with learning difficulties received excessive negative feedback from the classroom teacher. Parents, siblings, peers, and teachers are not likely to provide frequent and spontaneous expressions of delight, satisfaction, approval, acceptance, or affection toward the child who fails to learn satisfactorily or who engages excessively in socially negative behaviors.

As further illustration, the child who whines, is sullen, and requires excessive prodding and unusual reinforcing consequences is the child who receives excessive negative feedback. Thus, unless the learning and social environments are well designed around the child's specific and unique combinations of learning and behavior characteristics, the child is most likely to receive an excessive amount of criticism, punishment, rejection, social isolation, and personal harshness.

These excessive failure experiences result in extremes of emotional reactions. The child is likely to become explosive, or fearful, or excessively shy and detached. Parents and teachers frequently are puzzled over the unpredictability of these emotional reactions and feel powerless to deal with the multitude of problems created. Not unusually, they react to the conflict quite personally and begin to behave in a defensive and negative manner themselves. Thus, a defeat cycle is initiated and maintained. The more the child fails, the more the child is punished. These aversive consequences in turn produce more inadequate learning and behavior, which produce more negative feedback.

To elaborate, the child with excessive failure experiences is likely to become quite cautious about entering into relationships or activities. After failure, or whenever required to do things that are unpleasant, it is not unusual for the child to display excessive negative emotionality, for example, to cry easily and frequently, to be fearful, or to be excessively defensive and prone to temper tantrums or other intense emotional outbursts. Excessive patterns of withdrawal, apathy, or active hesitancy over becoming involved with people or activities are often present because previous involvement has resulted so frequently in failure or has required an excessive investment of time and energy. The child learns to avoid the possibility of similar experiences. Those incentive conditions natural to the school setting that serve to initiate and maintain learning and performance, such as teacher approval or academic achievement, may have minimal or no reinforcing qualities for the child.

Accomplishments and task requirements that are rather simple for most children may be excessively difficult for children with learning and behavior problems. Children with attentional, motivational, cognitive, perceptual, language, or emotional difficulties may find that learning and performance requirements and instructional procedures are poorly designed for their individual characteristics. The parent or teacher, insensitive to or unaware of these characteristics, and more out of despair rather than deliberate intent, may at inappropriate times and in an excessive manner project the source of difficulty onto the child. The unsuccessful child will be prodded to "try harder" when there are inadequate incentives to insure such performance, to pay attention when the needed selective attention skills are lacking, to complete a task when high-strength competing behaviors are present, or to "decide to do your work" when the requisite skills are not under the child's self-control. These social pressures result in intensifying the child's negative and disruptive emotional reactions and in rendering the child even less able to learn and to relate satisfactorily.

Kagan, Rosman, Day, Albert, and Phillips (1964) describe this maladaptive cycle in specific reference to those children with an impulsive approach to cognitive tasks who fail excessively. Although not suggesting that all impulsive children are so influenced, these writers hypothesize, "The anxiety resulting from repeated failure, as a consequence of impulsive reporting, could lead to generalized expectations of failure and withdrawal of involvement from intellectual tasks [p. 13]." Epstein, Hallahan, and Kauffman (1975) and Messer (1970) provide partial support for this hypothesis. Staats (1975) emphasizes this in his description of "the downward spiral of cumulative–hierarchial learning." He notes that as a result of ineffective learning a child:

> will find himself in a less propitious social circumstance of reward for learning. Thus his attentional and working behaviors will be poor, and his learning will be at a less rapid rate than would be the case in better motivating conditions .... The less advanced the performance, the less the reward. The less the reward, the less the

maintenance of learning behaviors. Further, the social consequences of being a loser . . . can create conditions by which the child learns undesirable behaviors that are considered to be abnormal. These behaviors will frequently be such that they interfere with the further learning of the repertoires of skills demanded by society. When this occurs, the downward spiral of relative learning is accelerated [p. 285].

In a similar vein, Zigler (1973) speaks of the reduced flexibility and inefficient performance on tasks of cognitive functioning of children with developmental retardation as relating at least partially to the depressing influence of excessive failure experiences.

Koppitz (1971) and Cowen and Lorion (1974) highlight the increasing difficulty that children with chronic learning and behavior problems exhibit. In reporting a longitudinal study of children identified as learning disabled, Koppitz noted, "Only after they have failed repeatedly and had become quite frustrated and disturbed, were the more intelligent pupils finally sent to the LD class." She speculated, "It would have been far more efficient and effective, in the long run, to give these children extra help before the secondary problems developed [p. 183]." Cowen and Lorion's data indicate that younger children with fewer and less chronic failure experiences benefit more from specialized intervention efforts than do older children. Finally, Deshler (1978), in discussing adolescents characterized by chronic learning difficulties, suggests:

An adolescent's initial reactions to the demands of a classroom situation may be to withdraw by sitting in the back of the class and not participating. As the situation increased in stress, though, he may sleep in class, leave class while it is in session, and choose more and more often not to come to class at all. Finally, under severe stress, his behavior may become purposeless and entirely disorganized [p. 60].

Obviously, these difficulties did not suddenly appear in a typically developing adolescent. Rather, they represent the cumulative effect of literally thousands of negative learning experiences gained throughout childhood and extending into adolescence.

Summary

There is considerable support for the premise that children with learning and behavior difficulties acquire many inappropriate characteristics or fail to acquire desirable modes of behavior because the learning experiences provided by home and school have not been sufficiently sensitive to the highly individualized characteristics of each child. Children do learn in instructional environments in which they experience excessive failure, but too frequently they do not learn those academic, emotional, or social characteristics that were intended and that are deemed desirable. Such characteristics as patterns of noninvolvement, hyperactivity, emotional outbursts, aggressiveness, disinterest, distractibility, excessive daydreaming, low frustration tolerance, shyness, temper tantrums, antilearning attitudes, and unpredictable reactions to social approval are likely to develop. Academics become increasingly difficult due to the increased frequency and intensity of reactions that actively disrupt and interfere with the learning process. Children learn poor self-concept behaviors under conditions of excessive failure (Morena & Litrownik, 1974; Rosenthal, 1973). Many children learn to view themselves as inadequate and deficient; teachers and parents may come to view them as being unwilling and unable to accomplish anything, when in fact most are willing and able to learn and perform under more favorable instructional arrangements.

CLASSES OF EXCEPTIONAL LEARNING AND BEHAVIOR CHARACTERISTICS

Some learning and behavior problem areas reflect *behavior deficits:* the child is unable to engage in the behavior required or expected in various academic and/or social situations. Other problem areas reflect *excessive behavior characteristics:* The child engages in behaviors that are inappropriate in terms of the time, place, frequency, duration, or intensity of occurrence (Gardner, 1977; Ross, 1976).

The classes of exceptional learning and behavior characteristics described are quite arbitrarily defined in terms of the child's characteristics relative to various learning and performance expectations and/or instructional arrangements. The described behavior classes are viewed as exceptional as a discrepancy exists between what the instructional program expects the child to learn or do and the characteristics that the child demonstrates (Adelman, 1971a; Gardner, 1977; Lilly, 1979a). This approach to describing or "diagnosing" a child's difficulties differs dramatically from the category approach, which, as noted earlier, assigns the child to a single general class or diagnostic label or category.

In the following discussion of the various learning and behavior difficulties observed among children, a description of the more frequently occurring difficulties is followed by a brief summary of representative studies that illustrate behavioral intervention approaches to the particular difficulties described. For other difficulty areas, references are provided that describe behavioral intervention procedures associated with the problem areas.

BEHAVIOR DEFICITS

Children are viewed as having problems whenever they do not learn or behave as expected by the home and school environments or by themselves. These expectations may be based on a variety of chronological, mental age, social age, physical, legal, ethical, and other considerations. Illustrations of behavior deficit areas include academic skill deficits (Foxx & Jones, 1978; Lahey, 1976), social skill deficits (Barton & Osborne, 1978; Cooke & Appolloni, 1976; Walker, Greenwood, Hops, & Todd, 1979), self-control skill deficits (Bolstad & Johnson, 1972; Drabman, Spitalnik, & O'Leary, 1973; Rosenbaum & Drabman, 1979), perceptual skill deficits (Williams & Lahey, 1978), and language skill deficits (Burka & Jones, 1979; Knapczyk & Livingston, 1974). These and numerous other similar studies describe children who exhibit exceptional learning and behavior characteristics reflecting deficit behavior areas. In each, a discrepancy exists between what the child does and what the child or situation expects or requires. The child either lacks the necessary skills or, if present, they do not occur in a consistent or acceptable manner.

Learning difficulties and behavior deficits

Prior to discussion of various classes or degress of behavior deficits, it would be valuable to clarify the difference between learning difficulties and behavior deficits. A child may exhibit behavior deficits associated with or resulting from learning difficulties. Another child may demonstrate behavior deficits but have no learning difficulties. The term *learning difficulties* is a descriptive one denoting that a child so described consistently demonstrates problems in the acquisition, short- and long-term retention, and/or performance of various academic and related tasks under specific instructional conditions. Learning is defined as reliable changes in a child's behavior following exposure to a training, teaching, or educational experience. If a child consistently fails to exhibit the expected amount of behavior change—fails to learn after being exposed to structured and/or unstructured educational experiences—learning difficulties have been demonstrated. In this analysis, the expected amount of learning (behavior change) is based on a variety of child variables such as chronological age, mental age or other indices of cognitive characteristics, previous learning progress, level of skill development relative to specific learning tasks, and the conditions under which other types and levels of learning tasks were attained by a particular child. To restate, a child is described as demonstrating learning difficulties after reliable observation of a performance deficit. The critical factor in arriving at this conclusion is that a child does not acquire (learn), retain (remember), or transfer (generalize) expected behaviors after being exposed to a defined instructional program. This description does not imply an absolute learner characteristic. Under other instructional conditions (for example, braille reader, amplified auditory signals, frequent tangible reinforcers, color-highlighted visual cues), the child may learn more effectively.

This view of learning difficulties recognizes that children who have been highly restricted in their contact with teaching experiences may demonstrate specific and even generalized behavior (achievement or skill) deficits, but no learning difficulties. They may learn quite satisfactorily, employing their present learning characteristics, after being provided educational experiences designed to teach specific behavioral skills. Many children and adolescents from inner-city neighborhoods or isolated rural areas may exhibit behavioral deficits due to lack of exposure to experiences designed to teach the skills on which the middle class school curriculum and instructional method are based (Hall & Kaye, 1977). They should not be viewed as exhibiting generalized learning difficulties unless failure has been observed following exposure to an instructional program designed to attend to their specific learning characteristics (Begab, Haywood, & Garber, 1981; Feuerstein, 1970; Heber, 1978).

This distinction between behavior deficits and learning difficulties emphasizes the relative nature of both. A visually impaired child may experience considerable learning difficulties under the usual type of classroom instructional presentation but little, if any, difficulty in learning when provided a braille reader. A highly distractible child may have difficulty learning under the highly stimulating conditions of the regular classroom but may learn more effectively under a highly structured and stimulus-controlled environment (Cruickshank, 1975a; Gorton, 1972). The disruptive, poorly motivated 12-year-old with academic deficits may become an attentive, active learner under more suitable incentive conditions (Marholin & Steinman, 1977). Individualized instructional programming that accommodates the factors that underlie or contribute to learning difficulties and/or behavior deficits may thus serve to reduce or eliminate both.

Characteristics of behavior deficits

Depending on the behavior deficits present, a child may be described as exhibiting a general learning deficit, perceptual–motor deficits, language deficits, deficits in self-care behaviors, or a combination of these and other problems. Within any given behavioral area, a child's difficulty may represent one or a combination of the following:

1. *Absence or limited development of the desired behavior.* The child may never have engaged in the desired behavior, or has done so only infrequently and in an undependable manner, for example, never has labeled correctly the letters of the alphabet or never has demonstrated knowledge of multiplication facts. A child may occasionally spell some of his or her third-grade words correctly but most frequently misspells most of the required words.

2. *Inconsistent occurrence of desired behavior that is in the child's repertoire.* A child may know how to engage in specific behaviors such as reading, attending class, being polite, solving math problems requiring addition and subtraction skills, persisting at a difficult task, or cooperatively participating in group endeavors. Yet the child does not consistently engage in these behaviors in situations that require them.

3. *Behavior that occurs only under overly restricted cue and reinforcement conditions.* The adolescent is able to read third-grade-level materials but will do so only in a private remedial reading session. The child who refuses to speak in class may talk spontaneously and frequently at home with family members (Sanok & Ascione, 1979). Another child may demonstrate appropriate classroom behavior but only when the teacher is present (Marholin, Steinman, McInnis, & Head, 1975). Math assignment may be completed, but only when provided frequent token reinforcement that may be exchanged for desired tangible events. This same child seldom even attempts a math lesson just to please the teacher or for the satisfaction of task completion or achievement (Brooks & Snow, 1972).

4. *Behavior that is present but not in the correct form.* A child may be able to communicate with others even though he or she misarticulates many words and occasionally stutters.

Causes of learning difficulties and behavior deficits

1. Deficit behavior characteristics, as suggested, may be a result of a lack of opportunity to learn the desired behavior. Some children may be unable to cut with scissors, to blend sounds, or to read a story because they have never been exposed to a learning environment designed to facilitate development of these behaviors.

2. The child may have been provided inadequate or inappropriate learning experiences. The early developmental experiences and/or

the formal preschool or elementary school program did not result in normal school progress and general social adaptation. Children who grow up in poverty environments are generally at high risk for behavior deficits and associated learning difficulties due to the type and extensiveness of language, cognitive, and related stimulation experienced (Begab, Haywood, & Garber, 1981; Hall & Kaye, 1977; Heber, 1978). Other children may have been exposed to standard teaching methods and materials but because of various perceptual and attention difficulties were unable to learn efficiently (Cruickshank, 1975b; Ross, 1976).

3. Learning difficulties and related behavior deficits may reflect a variety of child characteristics that inhibit or compete with adequate learning. Such behavior characteristics as excessive anxiety, disruptive social behavior, hyperactivity, antilearning .attitudes, motivational characteristics different from those assumed by the instructional program, memory .difficulties, and selective attention problems all represent factors that contribute to a child's difficulty in learning and adapting to the standards of the classroom setting. Thus, exceptional characteristics are involved in producing, and at the same time are consequences of, other exceptional characteristics (Gardner, 1977, 1978).

4. Learning difficulties and related behavior deficits also may reflect neurological or other physical conditions that may restrict the learning or performance of desired behaviors. A child's motor behavior deficits may be related to cerebral palsy; speech production features such as articulation difficulties may reflect the effects of a cleft palate or a severe hearing loss. Various cognitive and language deficits may be related to central nervous system impairment. A child may have difficulty distinguishing colors due to color blindness. Care should be exercised, however, in assuming that the behavior deficits and learning difficulties are in fact totally, or even partially, a result of physical, sensory, or neurological limitations. Children with obvious neurological, sensory, or muscular impairment may well be able to acquire new behavior patterns and to engage in these under normal conditions if provided carefully designed learning experiences that reflect their unique learning and performance characteristics (Bijou, 1972). These characteristics would include such features as the present behavioral repertoires, their learning styles as reflected in the types, intensities, and mode of instructional presentation, as well as reinforcement variables.

CLASSES OF LEARNING AND BEHAVIOR DEFICITS

Cognitive and language behavior deficits

The most frequently occurring areas of difficulty in children with exceptional characteristics are those involving language and cognitive behavior deficits. Children labeled mentally retarded, emotionally disturbed, and learning disabled are all characterized by various language and cognitive difficulties. These include difficulties in both receptive and expressive speech and language areas as well as behavioral skills subsumed under the general areas of cognitive abilities and skills. Acquisitions, retention, retrieval (recall), and transfer (generalization) difficulties may be present (Hallahan & Kauffman, 1976; Kauffman, 1977; MacMillan, 1977).

Language difficulties. The child may demonstrate difficulties in understanding what is spoken or in language production. Problems of phonemic development related to sound discrimination and sequencing, syntax (the way a child goes about putting words and phrases together to produce sentences), morphology (word inflections), and semantics may be present. Language difficulties result from and also contribute to a variety of other exceptional characteristics. For example, a child with an auditory perceptual problem may well develop receptive and expressive language difficulties. Language difficulties may in turn contribute to underachievement in such academic areas as reading (Garcia & DeHaven, 1974; Sloane & MacAulay, 1968).

Memory difficulties. Most children learn and are able to retain their new learning and expand it into more complex behavioral patterns. Once behavior has been acquired, the teacher can depend on its being remembered.

In contrast, the child with exceptional learning characteristics frequently exhibits memory difficulties. The child seems to know something one day but forgets it the next (Ross, 1971; Turnure & Thurlow, 1973; Winschel & Lawrence, 1975).

Incidental or unstructured learning difficulties. Most children acquire many of their behavioral characteristics in the typical unstructured or unplanned experiences that represent the give and take of daily life. As children enter into more formal educational programs, many experiences are presented in a more structured fashion. Even in the school setting, a great percentage of what children learn is acquired incidentally to the formal teaching. This occurs as children attend to, become involved in, and find enjoyable many aspects of the environment that are in addition to the experiences presented in the organized and planned instructional program.

Many children with learning and behavior problems have difficulty learning in unstructured or noninstructional environments. It is not unusual for the educator to conclude, "He doesn't even know how to study," or "I have to teach many things to my children that most children just learn by growing up." These incidental learning difficulties frequently may reflect the result of other deficit behavior areas such as in curiosity and exploratory behavior, motivation, and the like (Hardman & Drew, 1975).

Deficits in imitation learning skills. Children acquire many of their behaviors through imitation learning. Children mimic the speech patterns, the motor activities, and the social interactions of parents, teachers, and peers. The more closely they imitate the behavior of others, the more frequent and enthusiastic the social attention received from these models. The social models to whom children are exposed thus significantly influence what they learn as well as the rate at which they acquire many skills (Bandura, 1977).

Many children with exceptional learning and behavior characteristics have poorly developed skills of imitation, a deficit that could be related to numerous factors. Early attempts at imitation by the young child may not be encouraged by the social environment. Selective attention skills may be poorly developed and in turn interfere with the child's perception of consistent behavior to imitate (Lovaas, 1977; Ross, 1976). In other cases, excessive emotional behaviors may disrupt the child's relationship with other people and provide less desired behavior to imitate. The child thus does not acquire many of the basic skills (acquired by the typical child through imitation) on which more complex skills are based (Cullinan, Kauffman, & LeFleur, 1975).

Difficulties in transfer of learning. Behaviors learned in one setting by most children readily generalize to another. The child learns a variety of language, academic, social, and sensorimotor skills in the instructional environment. These behaviors occur not only in those settings in which they were acquired initially but also in numerous other similar situations and at other times.

However, children with exceptional characteristics not unusually experience difficulty in generalization from the training setting to other settings. Behavior learned in one setting appears to be highly specific to aspects of that situation, and the child must be taught specifically to use the skill in new situations (Rincover & Koegel, 1975; Turkewitz &

O'Leary, 1975). This difficulty adds to the child's problems as excessive time is required to insure that behaviors in the child's repertoire will be used in numerous settings in which they would be adaptive. Marholin, Siegel, and Phillips (1976), in evaluating procedures for facilitating transfer, provide a number of useful suggestions for the educator.

Academic behavior deficits

Difficulties involving learning, retention, and generalization of academic behaviors also occur frequently among children with exceptional characteristics. The academic difficulties may be general to most or all academic subject areas or may be highly specific to certain subjects such as reading, spelling, writing, or mathematics.

Reading comprehension. Lahey, McNees, and Brown (1973), recognizing that many children with learning difficulties demonstrate reading comprehension problems even though oral reading may not be a problem area, developed a program to improve reading comprehension. Children attending sixth grade whose reading comprehension grade levels were 2 years below their oral reading grade level (based on the Spache Diagnostic Reading Scale) were provided social and tangible reinforcers following correct answers to comprehension questions. Under the new contingency, reading comprehension rose to grade level performance and remained there throughout the periods in which consistent reinforcement was provided.

Phonic skills. Lovitt and Hurlburt (1974) provided direct systematic instruction in phonic skills (for example, short vowels, consonant blends, sound blends, translocations, and digraphs–diphthongs) to a 10-year-old "dyslexic" boy and to four 9-year-old boys with chronic reading difficulties. The teacher provided verbal models, required the children to verbalize answers aloud, and provided feedback. These educators found that when phonic skills were defined and when systematic teaching procedures were followed, phonic skills could be taught in a brief period of time. It also was noted that oral reading improved as phonic skills developed.

Written composition. Brigham, Graubard, and Stans (1972) improved the composition skills of 13 boys who demonstrated a combination of academic failure and behavior problems. As a group, they were more than 2 years behind academically on standardized tests of achievement. Students were provided token reinforcement for demonstrating various aspects of written composition (1 point for each word used in their story,

2 points for each different word, and 3 points for each new word used). The writing output of all subjects was greatly improved. Both increased length and overall improvement in the quality of the compositions were noted.

Arithmetic. Lovitt and Curtiss (1968) found that having an 11-year-old boy verbalize an arithmetic problem prior to making a written response resulted in an increase in correct answer rate and a decrease in error rate. Van Houten, Hill, and Parsons (1975) and Fink and Carnine (1975) describe the facilitative effect of informational feedback combined with graphing and public posting of academic performance. Arithmetic and writing performance improved noticably under these contingency conditions. Smith, Lovitt, and Kidder (1972) emphasized the need for individual assessment in devising successful behaviorally based instructional programs for children who perform poorly on arithmetic tasks. After assessing the arithmetic error patterns involving subtraction problems of an 11-year-old girl with academic difficulties, it was decided that a mild punishment procedure would be useful in improving performance. After informing the child that each subtraction error would result in the loss of 1 minute of recess time, there was an immediate and dramatic improvement in performance. In contrast, analysis of the subtraction errors of a 10-year-old boy revealed a predictable pattern of errors. When provided a teaching aid that dealt directly with the faulty skills, performance increased to an acceptable level.

Sensorimotor and perceptual discrimination deficits

Many children exhibit various sensory and perceptual difficulties that assume central roles in various learning and behavior problems. The problems of some are directly related to various visual and auditory sensory limitations. Most, however, involve perceptual–discrimination difficulties associated with the concepts of *learning disabilities* and *perceptual handicaps.* Auditory, visual, kinesthetic, and tactile discrimination difficulties associated with sounds, numbers, forms, letters, words, spatial location, laterality, and directionality are frequently identified in children with learning difficulties. Other areas of difficulty include figure–ground discrimination, spatial and temporal orientation and sequencing, intergration of intersensory information, and obtaining closture of discriminations. In addition to mobility deficits associated with skeletal and muscular difficulties, children also exhibit difficulty with sensorimotor integration such as gross and fine eye–hand coordination, writing, and copying visual patterns (Lahey, 1976; Lahey, Delamater, Kupfer, & Hobbs, 1978).

Letter and number reversals. Stromer (1975) remediated various letter and number reversal difficulties in children from regular and special education classes by modeling correct and incorrect symbol formation, providing differential feedback following correct and incorrect symbol formation, providing praise for correct responses, charting correct responses, and imposing temporal delays between dictated letters and child responses. The reversal difficulties included reversal during letter naming (for example, saying *p* for *g*) and of two-digit numbers (for example, writing *31* for *13*), reversal of single-digit numbers (for example, *9* written with circle on right side of stem), written letter reversals on both sides of the "body midline" under dictation procedures, and letter reversals under naming, dictation, and copying exercises. All reversals were virtually eliminated in all cases, with follow-up observations indicating enduring effects. The reader will recall the earlier mentioned study by Cooper (1970), who reported similar results in his work with children provided various diagnostic labels.

Severe handwriting difficulties. Lahey *et al.* (1977) illustrated the use of various behavioral procedures in the remediation of severe perceptual motor disturbances in the handwriting of four boys diagnosed as "learning disabled." Each presented a high frequency of errors of orientation and sequence in copying work, often referred to as mirror writing or reversals. The perceptual–motor difficulties were of such pervasiveness and severity that teachers viewed their handwriting problem to be a major obstacle to classroom learning. During training sessions, the children were required to copy five words, five geometric figures, and their first name five times. Token reinforcement was provided for each correct response (containing no errors of orientation, sequence, or legibility), and corrective feedback was given following incorrect responses. Substantial improvement in the frequency of correct printing was obtained. Moreover, these changes generalized to other unreinforced handwriting responses.

These educators raise the questions of why these children had such severe perceptual motor problems after several years of schooling in view of the rather simple techniques that produced such rapid improvement. They suggested:

> The answer is that, contrary to our idealized view of teaching, teachers rarely provide any type of usable feedback to students. In our observations, we saw teachers only put marks and smiling faces on entire pages of written work, with very little explanation as to why the work was good or bad. It seems very likely that the problem of all these students could have been eliminated or prevented if adequate systematic consequences had been provided [p. 139].

Self-management skills deficits

Children with chronic learning and behavior difficulties typically show limitations in their self-management skills. The child may be excessively dependent on others to provide direction, initiative, controls, and incentives. Or the child may be impulsive and noncritical in academic and social behaviors. The implicit verbal skills involved in self-management (self-direction, self-control) are absent or of insufficient strength to compete with external stimulation or to insure a deliberate judgmental type of responsiveness. Meichenbaum (1977) noted that research with both impulsive and aggressive children suggests a deficiency in the children's ability to spontaneously use their language in planning and guiding their nonverbal behavior. Gardner (1977) and O'Leary and Dubey (1979) describe other approaches that have been used successfully with children with a range of learning and behavior difficulties.

Teaching self-management to impulsive children. In a somewhat classic study, Meichenbaum and Goodman (1971) taught self-instructional skills to children with such characteristics as marked hyperactivity, impulsivity, and distractibility. In their instructional program, a variety of motor and cognitive tasks were used in the following training experiences:

1. Initially the teacher acted as a model in performing a task while the child watched.
2. The child then performed the same task as the teacher provided verbal instructions.
3. Following this, the child was requested to repeat the task while verbalizing instructions aloud.
4. Next, the child completed the task while whispering the instructions.
5. Finally, while self-instructing covertly, the child performed the task.

The training program included a number of self-regulation components: initial questions about what was to be done and answers to the question in the form of planning and rehearsal, self-guidance through verbal cueing, and self-reinforcement. Thus, the children learned to evaluate the requirements of a task prior to beginning it, to cognitively rehearse solutions, to guide their behavior through self-instruction, and to reinforce themselves upon successful completion. Additionally, children were taught what to do after making an error. Following training, the children showed significant improvement in performance on a variety of tasks requiring cognitive self-direction and reflectivity.

Deficits in task-related prerequisite skills

Many children have difficulty with academic learning as a result of weak or absent skills that are prerequisite to or facilitative of effective learning, including attentional skills (focus and span), selective attention (attending to relevant aspects of learning tasks), a reflective cognitive style, persistence, concentration of attention, and the like.

Attention deficits. Effective learning of many skills requires that children focus attention on various aspects of the learning task. To learn to distinguish one word from another, children must focus attention on one and then on the other. They also must persist in attention behaviors and refrain from excessive attending, or otherwise responding, to other aspects of the present environment.

One of the most basic and major deficits of many children with developmental difficulties is in the area of attention behavior. Children labeled as mentally retarded, emotionally disturbed, brain-damaged, and perceptually handicapped have been described as having short attention spans and being distractible. In addition, the highly correlated behavior pattern of hyperactivity is frequently described (Hallahan & Cruickshank, 1976; Keogh, 1971; Ross & Ross, 1976). Children characterized as hyperactive are unable to engage in many activities in a concentrated fashion. They move from one aspect of the stimulus environment to another. Perseverence is limited. These children have difficulty in focusing on specific events long enough for these events to acquire any consistent influence on behavior. Hagen and Hale (1973), in studying children's development between the ages of 7 and 13, suggest that selective attention improves with age until early adolescence, by which time most have acquired the ability to use or not use selective attention depending upon the nature of the task. An implication of these findings is that children who demonstrate a delay in the development of selective attention will experience difficulties in learning. Evidence is beginning to accrue that implicates a developmental delay in selective attention in the academic difficulties of children with learning problems. Ross (1976) suggests that a child who does not possess age-appropriate skills in selective attention, who cannot inhibit responses to "extraneous stimuli," will demonstrate impulsivity, distractibility, and overactivity. The observation that many of these behaviors decrease significantly over time provides anecdotal support for the developmental lag hypothesis. Thus, learning disabled children progress through the same developmental sequence and eventually acquire the same level of selective attention ability, but at a slower rate (Hallahan, Kauffman, & Ball, 1973, 1974; Tarver, Hallahan, Cohen, & Kauffman, 1977; Tarver, Hallahan, Kauffman, & Ball, 1976). Wolf, Giles, and Hall (1968) and Novy, Burnett,

Powers, and Sulzer–Azaroff (1973) have demonstrated that attending to task could be influenced by behavioral procedures.

Limited persistence. Children with learning and behavior problems are not only less likely to become involved in and attend to learning tasks but also show a lack of persistence once a learning task is presented. Some children will typically persist for some time at an art project, leisure activity, or various academic endeavors, and will characteristically show enthusiasm and concentration; children with learning difficulties, however, all too frequently remain with a task or activity only for short periods. Sustained attention (attention span) is short. It is not unusual for these children to discard a task quickly when confronted with difficulty, to become frustrated easily, to be prone to excessive emotionality if required to remain at a task, and to lose interest. They may toss the materials aside or have a temper tantrum. They readily shift attention to other things in the environment.

Becoming involved and continuing involvement in given tasks have too frequently in the past resulted in failure for many children. These children have not been able to please themselves or others, and sufficient pleasant consequences have not been associated with persistence in the face of difficulty. Involvement in a difficult task is a cue to the child that failure is likely. Such recognition of difficulty creates an unpleasant emotional reaction, which the child may reduce or terminate by leaving the task (Staats, 1971).

Deficits in output skills

In addition to problems associated with initial learning, many children with exceptional characteristics also exhibit difficulties in output or performance skills. Their academic work typically is of poor quality, quantity is below expectations, and work output is erratic. A child, for example, may require 40% more time to complete an assignment than classmates (Brooks & Snow, 1972).

Interpersonal and social behavior deficits

Children with exceptional characteristics may exhibit difficulties involving sex-role behaviors. Some males exhibit excessively effeminate behaviors, and females may be characterized as excessively masculine. No value judgment is being suggested by the writer; such characteristics, however, do present difficulties for children as they reside in social and peer groups that usually respond to such sex-role behavior in a negative manner.

Children and youth also may display deficits in leisure and social interaction skills. Children may be excessively shy and thus described as loners due to the absence of a variety of leisure and social skills that would facilitate frequent and natural peer interactions and more general social interaction (Cartledge & Milburn, 1980; Hops, Walker, & Greenwood, 1980; Ross, Ross, & Evans, 1971; Walker *et al.*, 1979).

Emotional behavior deficits

Children and youth exhibit a variety of deficit emotional characteristics that contribute to learning and social interaction difficulties. These may include (*a*) deficits in the types of emotional behaviors expressed; (*b*) deficits in the intensity of emotional behaviors; and (*c*) deficits in the appropriateness of emotional behaviors. Children with learning and behavior difficulties not unusually have difficulty in expressing in a free, spontaneous, and realistic manner a variety of such emotions as described by the terms *glee, happy, affection, love, sad, guilt, shame, apprehension,* and *anger.* Other children may express both positive and negative emotional reactions but under inappropriate stimulus situations; for example, a child may laugh when a peer gets hurt, become highly jealous when others are praised, or be apathetic under glee-provoking conditions (Gardner, 1977; Kauffman, 1977; Ross, 1976).

Delay in level of motivational development

As implied earlier, a variety of factors (e.g., including cognitive limitations; restrictive sensory, physical, and neurological difficulties; attending, perceptual, motor, and activity level problems; and social and emotional characteristics) have been identified as contributing to the academic and social failures of children with learning and behavior difficulties. Although some combinations of these factors are involved in every case, an additional significant contributing factor is found in the unavailability and/or inadequate arrangements of appropriate incentive conditions associated with desired learning and behavior. If a child's motivational characteristics do not match those assumed by the instructional program, the acquisition and use of, for example, reading skills, will be hampered. If a child finds peer interaction or task achievement of little intrinsic value, failure in social and academic endeavors is likely to occur unless the instructional environment recognizes and programs for these learner characteristics. To anticipate the following discussion, children with learning and behavior difficulties typically demonstrate delays in development of their motivational features, and require more tangible, frequent, and immediately delivered reinforcing consequences than is typical of their peers who are progressing without excessive learning difficulty.

A child's motivational system is viewed in this discussion as comprising those varieties of events that have either reinforcing or aversive qualities. A child's motivational system is highly individualistic due to each child's unique learning history. Typically, as each child grows older, increasing numbers and types of events acquire positively reinforcing and/or aversive motivational qualities. Although some events do have primary, natural, or intrinsic positive or aversive qualities, most events and activities acquire these features through a process of learning. As a result, the characteristics of each child's motivational system depend upon the specific experiences of that child. A child with frequent and consistent difficulties of learning and behaving will have only limited experience in associating reinforcing events with neutral ones. Thus, the child will acquire fewer secondary reinforcers. Learning new behavior will be a more difficult undertaking as fewer reinforcing events are available to initiate, strengthen, and maintain these new behaviors.

Such events as completing a task, being successful, or even that of reaching a previously set behavior goal potentially may acquire positively reinforcing qualities. In fact, a child can gain increasing independence and self-responsibility only as events natural to various behaviors become secondary reinforcers. Task involvement, task completion, creating an art form, or any other type of accomplishment can become a reinforcing event (and thus self-maintaining) only after being associated on numerous occasions with other reinforcing consequences. However, for children with chronic learning and behavior difficulties, such accomplishments as initiating an academic task independently, completing a difficult project, or involvement in various artistic and social activities or relationships not infrequently hold only minimal, if any, reinforcement value due to their excessive failure experiences in these and related activities. In fact, it may well be that these and similar activities have actually acquired aversive qualities, with the result that the child will actively avoid approaching and/or becoming involved in such activities or experiences.

In this manner, differences in what becomes reinforcing or aversive to children, in what will initiate and sustain their behavior, in what they will strive to attain or to avoid—their motivational features—contribute to many of the observed differences in learning and behaving. Children who find different things rewarding and unpleasant will learn and perform quite differently in different settings. If a child has learned that academic achievement is reinforcing, situations in which the child can demonstrate achievement behavior will serve as cues for a variety of behaviors that potentially will result in satisfying academic achievement. In contrast, if a child has had frequent failure experiences in academic activities, such activities, and situations in which these occur, will become aversive. The child is likely to engage in a variety of inappropriate behaviors that interfere with academic achievement. This child will impress the educator as being uninterested, unmotivated, and as spending an excessive amount of time engaging in considerable nonproductive behavior.

Children with exceptional learning and behavior characteristics are at a distinct disadvantage in the regular classroom environment as typically structured since there are relatively few events in the setting that are highly reinforcing and too many that have aversive components. Typically, the incentives for a child to learn and perform satisfactorily in the academic instructional program consist of such events as grades and the approval of the teacher and other achieving students, as well as the rewarding aspects associated with task involvement, task completion, and achievement. However, as noted, many children with learning and behavior difficulties have not acquired a highly functional motivational system consistent with the kinds of incentives assumed by the instructional program. The learning-for-learning's sake philosophy that many educators hold is a laudable concept, but most typically is not a reality for children with difficulties. As a result of a developmental deficit in motivational characteristics, there is a mismatch between the types of motivational characteristics expected of the child and the actual motivational features of the child. Consequently, the child with a deficit motivational system will not learn as much as other children, even though in some instances he or she may have the requisite intellectual and language skills (Gardner, 1978; Hewett & Forness, 1974; MacMillan, 1973).

Staats (1971) has noted that in a setting in which there is a discrepancy between what motivates a child and what the instructional program assumes should be motivating, the child's attention and work behaviors will not be maintained, and poor learning will result. He emphasized that "as a further consequence of the poor learning, there will be even less reinforcement, this child's attention will deteriorate further, and the result will be a vicious cycle that will produce a downward spiral of cumulative learning [p. 303]." The reader will recognize that it serves no useful purpose to label a child as being poorly motivated, apathetic, or disinterested and to dismiss the child's lack of progress in the instructional program as being inevitable results of such features. As emphasized, such child characteristics are problems relative to the motivational tactics employed in the instructional program. These child characteristics are instructional problems just as surely as are such child characteristics as "difficulty in sound blending" or "confusing letters and words." Both the motivational and the perceptual discrimination difficulties must be approached in an individualized programmatic manner.

In light of these difficulties of motivational development, the teacher of children with learning and behavior difficulties (*a*) must insure a match between the motivational characteristics of the child and the variety of incentive conditions used in the instructional program; and (*b*) must pay careful attention to the process by which neutral and even aversive events and activities can become reinforcing. Activities and accomplishments that appear to be intrinsically motivating or reinforcing to other children cannot be depended upon for supporting learning and thus influencing prosocial behavior of the child with chronic learning and behavior problems. The motivating characteristics of these events must be developed through careful arrangement of the learning environment. The goals of an educational program for children with learning and behavior difficulties thus involve not only the development of new academic and social behaviors but also insurance that a range of naturally available events such as involvement in activities, accomplishments, and social interactions become highly reinforcing.

The following sections illustrate approaches used successfully by educators in various settings with children differing widely in the nature and severity of learning and behavior difficulties. Note that in most cases a contrived incentive system was required initially as a basis for developing sensitivity to the more natural consequence such as grades, teacher approval, task accomplishment, and anticipation of some delayed positive consequences.

Effects of contingent reinforcement. Walker, Hops, and Fiegenbaum (1976) evaluated the effects of a combined package of reinforcement conditions in influencing the classroom behaviors of 6–9-year-old children enrolled in grades 1, 2, or 3. Each child had been referred by the regular class teacher for special class placement due to high rates of disruptive classroom behavior, deficits in basic academic skills, and low rates of appropriate behavior in the regular classroom setting relative to their peers. Each had average or above scores on intelligence tests. In the special program, the children were provided token and social reinforcement for appropriate academic and social behavior. Such inappropriate behavior as talking back to the teacher, talking-out, out-of-seat, not attending, and disturbing others resulted in loss of earned tokens.

Under these contingency conditions, the children showed a substantial, immediate, and long-lasting improvement in appropriate behavior— from 38% appropriate behavior under usual classroom conditions to an average of 96% appropriate behavior under the new conditions. This study illustrated that appropriate behaviors were in the children's repertoires. For these children, however, disruptive behaviors were more likely to occur under the less influential incentive conditions present in the regular classroom setting.

Positive side effects of reinforcement. Ayllon and Roberts (1974) used positive reinforcement to increase reading achievement in five under-achieving and disruptive boys in a regular fifth-grade class. During a daily 15-minute workbook assignment period, which followed oral or group-reading activities, each boy was provided points for 80% or higher correct performance on worksheets. The points could be exchanged for a variety of backup reinforcers that included activities, privileges, and priorities.

Following initiation of the reinforcement procedure, reading performance increased from a mean accuracy level of approximately 45% to approximately 85%. Additionally, even though disruptive behavior was not dealt with directly, such behaviors as being out-of-seat without teacher permission, talking-out, and interfering with another student's studying were drastically reduced as each child became more involved in academic performance. Thus, the contingent positive reinforcement for academic achievement had produced study behaviors that successfully replaced disruptive behaviors.

Intended versus actual effects of teacher behavior. It is not unusual to find that types of social attentions intended by adults to be aversive (e.g., threats, disapprovals, reprimand) may, in fact, be positively reinforcing. Madsen, Becker, Thomas, Koser, and Plager (1968) demonstrated that the more frequently teachers instructed their children to sit down when away from their desks at inappropriate times, the more frequently they stood up. When provided praise for sitting and working, the frequency of standing up declined.

Thomas, Becker, and Armstrong (1968) found in a class of elementary students that frequent teacher disapproval for a variety of disruptive behaviors actually increased rather than decreased the frequency of such disruptions. Disapproval appeared to have reinforced, rather than discouraged, disruptive activities. After the disruptive behavior was ignored and appropriate behavior praised, the disruptions reduced significantly. Apparently, the secondary reinforcing aspects of the attention provided in these instances added more strength to the disruptive be-havior than was subtracted by the presumed unpleasant aspects of the reprimand. Thus, reprimands, ridicule, criticism, and other forms of social attentions used by the teacher in an effort to suppress behavior may, in fact, have a facilitative effect.

Providing reinforcement for groups of children. Medland and Stachnik (1972) successfully used a group reinforcement procedure in reducing the "virtually uncontrollable" disruptive behavior of 25 fifth graders. The class was divided into two teams of 14 members each and informed that the team or teams could receive extra free time if certain classroom rules were followed. These rules, concerned with out-of-seat, talking-out, and other disruptive behaviors, were presented to each group. Whenever one of the team members broke one of the rules there would be a mark against the team. A team or teams could win each day if they received 5 or fewer marks per day. A weekly bonus of extra activity time was also provided for the team receiving 20 or fewer marks for a week. Following introduction of the game, there was a 98% reduction in the disruptive behaviors.

Brooks and Snow (1972) describe an experience with a 10-year-old boy (Jim) who frequently left his class or group without permission and who engaged in frequent stealing. The classroom teacher explained to the class that Jim could earn points throughout the day for remaining with his group and for completing a specific part of his assigned academic work. On each occasion of accumulating 10 points, the entire class would be provided 15 minutes of free time. Additionally, for each occurrence of the designated inappropriate behavior on Jim's part, the entire class would lose 1 minute of the next free period. There was an immediate elimination of the inappropriate behavior and an increase in desired academic performance.

Fading contrived reinforcers. Jones and Kazdin (1975) illustrate the gradual removal of a contrived reinforcement procedure using tokens and the use of peer praise and activities naturally available to the classroom teacher to maintain desired classroom behavior. Four children out of a larger class were initially provided token reinforcement paired consistently with teacher praise for being attentive and remaining in their seats during a lesson period. These children had been selected due to bothersome levels of disruptive behaviors including not paying atten-tion to the lesson, excessively moving around in their chairs, and mov-ing their hands and feet repetitively. This individual token reinforce-ment procedure markedly reduced the designated inappropriate behavior. In an attempt to facilitate persistence of the behaviors under natural classroom conditions, these educators next extended the token program to include all children in the classroom. At the end of each day, students who received the maximum number of tokens possible were individually applauded by their peers. Each child individually came to the front of the class following announcement of perfect performance and received teacher praise and peer applause. This procedure was used to develop and/or increase the reinforcing value of achievement and social approval.

At the end of this intervention phase, the scheduled token, teacher, and peer reinforcement, and finally the group contingency were removed. Behavioral ratings of each of the four children were obtained during a follow-up period that extended for 12 weeks after the end of the formal program. These later ratings demonstrated a maintenance of the low levels of inappropriate behavior achieved during the initial token program.

As a final example, Chadwick and Day (1971) provided a token reinforcement program to improve academic skills of a group of seriously underachieving children. Points were awarded daily during a program for appropriate academic performance and personal and social classroom behaviors related to academic performance. Social reinforcement in the form of "warm praise and support" was paired consistently with the awarding of points. Backup reinforcers included a variety of tangible and activity events and were available at the end of the school day. The teacher extended her approval as the points were exchanged and encouraged continued academic performance. Under the token-paired-with-social-praise program, the children worked longer, faster, and more accurately. Furthermore, after termination of the point contingency, accuracy and efficiency of academic performance were maintained. The educators speculated that this maintenance effects was related to the increased reinforcement value of teacher-mediated social praise that had been paired consistently with the points and backup reinforcers. Additionally, it was suggested that the high performance level may have acquired some inherent reinforcement value and thus was self-maintaining due to the previous association with the token and teacher praise consequences.

Deficits in age-related personal and social responsibility behaviors

One outstanding feature of child and adolescent development is the progressive increase in skills of independence. Children acquire numerous skills that ensure that they will do things for and by themselves without excessive prompting and support from others. They depend increasingly less on others for assistance and direction. Children with chronic learning and behavior difficulties not infrequently develop patterns of dependency that persist for extended periods of time. They are unable to do much without the presence and assistance of others. An excessive amount of adult prompting, attention, and encouragement is required. These children cling to others and prefer to be physically close to adults or more independent peers. Thus, there is a wide array of deficit skills that result in continued failure in meeting the social and personal responsibility expectations of the child's environments (Gardner, 1978).

EXCESSIVE BEHAVIOR CHARACTERISTICS

Exceptional characteristics may also create problems of learning and of personal adaptation due to their excessive nature. Excessive behavior refers to behavior that actively interferes either with the performance of other desired behaviors or with the acquisition of new, appropriate modes of responding and is viewed as undesirable by others in the child's environment. Children who are too demanding, whose feelings are hurt too easily and too frequently, who talk too much or are too loud, who are overly active, who are too fearful of too many aspects of their instructional and academic environments, or who are too aggressive toward their peers provide illustrations of excessive behavior patterns.

In some instances, behavior is viewed as excessive if it occurs in situations in which it is inappropriate. Such excessive behavior patterns may not only disrupt the activities of other children and adults but also may interfere with the child's learning of new behaviors or engaging in other more appropriate behaviors. As an example, a child who is disruptive during language class may have appropriate skills of attending, and may attend for long periods of time during art class. The teacher knows from this observation that the child can sit still and participate in group activities under certain conditions. But under the conditions of the language class, the disruptive behavior is stronger than the desired behavior of attending and participation. Such excessive behavior patterns frequently interfere with the development of more appropriate characteristics. During the time a child is talking loudly, he or she cannot be listening to what the teacher is saying. As a result, the child misses the language lesson and does not learn the new concepts being presented.

Relative nature of excessiveness

It is important to recognize that most behavior is not excessive in any absolute sense. Although some behaviors are excessive regardless of where or when they occur, many behaviors may be excessive if they occur in one setting but may be appropriate for other situations. Additionally, some behavior may be quite adaptive and even characteristic of many children, but for a given child becomes inappropriate due to its extreme rate of occurrence. Asking for teacher assistance may be encouraged for all children when unusual difficulty is encountered. But seeking teacher assistance may be viewed as excessive and maladaptive when a child engages in this tactic on numerous occasions throughout the school day.

It may be true that specific behaviors become excessive because a child has numerous behavior deficits relative to the requirements of specific situations. The child may not have the required behavior (for example, reading skills) in his or her repertoire and therefore engages excessively in what he or she can do. A child may engage in temper tantrum behavior because of a deficit in the adaptive skills required in the situation. Similarly, a child may withdraw into stereotypic hand waving, become aggressive, begin to cry, or become hyperactive because the required or other more appropriate behaviors are not in the repertoire or, if present, are of low strength.

Some excessive behavior patterns may occur in a wide range of situations. (*He always talks too loudly. She is too aggressive in all her peer interactions.*) Other excessive patterns may be specific to situations or to types of situations. (*He only becomes hyperactive and distractible when required to interact verbally with adults. When working with peers, he is calm and is able to stick to his work.*)

Puzzling nature of excessive behavior

Excessively occurring behaviors frequently are puzzling to the educator due to the apparent self-defeating character of such behaviors. It is difficult to understand what the behavior accomplishes. In some instances, excessive behavior patterns appear to persist in the absence of any discernible positive consequences. These patterns become even more puzzling when they persist in the face of obvious punishment. (*I reprimand him every time it occurs, but it doesn't seem to do any good. He still persists in taking things from his peers. They isolate him and won't play with him for a while.*) There is a tendency for many teachers to view such behaviors as resulting from some internal psychic pathology or as reflecting some "deep-down disturbance."

Again, it may be that the child simply has no suitable alternative behaviors available. Even though the reinforcing consequences associated with the excessive behavior may be minimal, these consequences may be sufficient to maintain the excessive behavior patterns because the child has no alternative behaviors that produce more desirable consequences. The child must repeat perseveringly the behaviors that are available, even though these do not produce the most desired positive consequences.

In summary, the inappropriateness or excessiveness of a behavior is not an inherent or all-or-none characteristic of the child's behavior. Each behavior gains meaning only in relation to the requirements or expectations of specific situations.

CLASSES OF EXCESSIVE BEHAVIORS

Excessive disruptive interpersonal behavior

Such behavioral characteristics as verbal and physical aggression, threatening others, noncompliance, defiance, negativism, and other excessive behaviors involving direct social interaction that have a disrupting effect are frequent features of children with exceptional learning and behavior characteristics (Bash & Camp, 1980; Gardner, 1977; Kauffman, 1977; MacMillan, 1977).

Reducing disruptive behavior through rules, feedback, and reinforcement. Greenwood, Hops, Delquadri, and Guild (1974) evaluated the effects of rules, rules plus feedback, and rules plus feedback plus reinforcement (social praise and backup activity rewards) in reducing disruptive behavior in first-, second-, and third-grade children. Initially, the teacher in each class developed a set of explicit classroom rules, posted them on the bulletin board, and reviewed them with the class on a daily basis.

Next, the teacher provided immediate feedback to the class whenever everyone was following the rules. Additionally, at the end of daily reading and math periods, the teacher calculated and posted a percent score that indicated the proportion of time during the period when the entire class had followed the rules.

Finally, group activity rewards and social praise were provided whenever the class rules were followed for an agreed upon proportion of the periods. Individual children and the entire class were praised frequently for following rules during daily sessions. The rules produced no change in overall classroom behavior. After the addition of feedback, there was a small amount of improvement in two of the classrooms. Upon introduction of the entire package of rules, feedback, and reinforcement, substantial increases in appropriate behavior were obtained in all classrooms. This study demonstrated the necessity of providing reinforcement contingent upon desired behavior in children who demonstrated disruptive activities in the classroom setting.

Excessive disruptive socially inappropriate behavior

The defining characteristic of behaviors included in this class is that they violate legal requirements. This includes the variety of behaviors that result in children being labeled as *delinquent*, and include such activities as stealing, truancy, fire setting, and property damage or destruction (vandalism). Socially rejected sexual practices such as homosexuality, which imply strong rule violation, also fall in this class of excessive behavior characteristics (Phillips, Phillips, Fixen, & Wolf, 1971; Shapiro, 1979).

Excessive nonfunctional competing behaviors

Numerous behavior patterns occur that are nonfunctional in the sense that, in view of the excessive frequency of occurrence, they do not contribute to the personal, social, or physical adaptation or well-being of the child or adolescent. These include such behaviors as stereotyped responses, self-mutilation, compulsive rituals, excessive eating, excessive fantasies, excessive daydreaming, excessive masturbation, implusivity, antilearning attitudes, and bizzare speech (Azrin, Kaplan, & Foxx, 1973; Digate, Epstein, Cullinan, & Switzky 1978; Luiselli, Hellfern, Pemberton, & Reisman, 1977; Williams & Lahey, 1978).

Excessive emotional reactions

A common feature of most children with learning and behavior problems is that disruptive emotional reactions occur excessively and interfere with both desired learning and behavior in academic and social situations. The excessive disruptive emotionality may be created by a number of different events. Some reactions may result from the presentation of such external stimulation as feared objects or situations that require the child to engage in certain behaviors (Kanfer, Karoly, & Newman, 1975; Wish, Hasazi, & Jurgela, 1973). Reprimand or other cues of rejection may represent the source of the excessive emotional reaction. Other children react with excessive negative emotionality following the removal or threat of removal of certain persons or events. The "separation anxiety" reaction illustrates this (Patterson & Brodsky, 1966).

Various frustration conditions, including conflict, delay of expected reward, or thwarting of ongoing or anticipated activities, may produce excessive emotionality. The term *low frustration tolerance* describes the child's reactions. Finally, excessive emotional reactions may result from self-generated verbal behaviors. A child, by dwelling on certain though patterns, may cue and/or maintain a state of misery, depression, specific fears, and generalized anxiety.

Thus, a variety of commonly occurring experiences in the instructional environment are likely to result in excessive disruptive emotional reactions. These include the presentation of a new task that requires more attention and persistence than a child is accustomed to, a delay in meeting the child's demands, the least sign of failure or rejection, a change in the kind or amount of positive consequences from what is expected, or a minor confrontation with adult or peer. A child may have difficulty delaying gratification, waiting a turn, or accepting the fact that he or she cannot have everything wanted at that moment. The child may pout, scream, become angry, anxious, distractible, and hyperactive. The interruptions are frequently so intense that they disrupt effective learning and social interaction. These reactions interfere with attention to relevant aspects of a learning program, with efforts toward persistence and concentration, or with obtaining any pleasure out of completing a task. These behaviors render highly unlikely a variety of other adaptive behaviors.

Excessive motor behaviors

Excessive activity levels, including "hyperactivity" and distractibility, represent central characteristics of children who are labeled as learning disabled or perceptually handicapped. They also are frequent characteristics of children labeled as mentally retarded and emotionally disturbed. As noted earlier, such excessive behaviors frequently are present in the child who has attention and persistence difficulties. Other excessive motor behaviors include stereotypic movements and such speech features as stuttering and excessive vocal loudness.

As hyperactivity is one of the more common problematic behaviors of the middle childhood period, further elaboration is provided. Prevalence estimates range from 4% to 10%, placing many school-age children in jeopardy. *Jeopardy* is used advisedly, as overactivity in and of itself may not be deleterious to the child's development (Ross & Ross, 1976). What seems to be of particular relevance is the manner in which the child's behavior affects the social and nonsocial environment, and how the social environment in turn responds to the child's behavior. Simply looking at the child's behavior isolated from the antecedent and consequent events surrounding it does not provide sufficient data upon which to base intervention strategies. One must also assess the reciprocal relationship between the child's behavior and the physical and social environment. Such a view is espoused by Ross and Ross (1976) in their definition of hyperactivity: "The term hyperactive child refers to a child who consistently exhibits a high level of activity in situations in which it is clearly inappropriate, is unable to inhibit his activity on command, often appears capable of only one speed of response, and is often characterized by other physiological, learning, and behavioral symptoms and problems [p. 12]." Excessive motoric activity is thus not sufficient reason to identify a child as hyperactive. In fact, in infancy most children exhibit high levels of generalized motor activity. Furthermore, in many situations such as free-play or gym periods, high levels of activity are viewed as desirable for children of all ages. Excessive motor activity becomes of concern when it is disruptive to the social or nonsocial environment, or interferes with the child's learning and development. Typically in such cases concomitant problems of impulsivity, attention, concentration, and other behavioral deficits will also be evident.

Although hyperactivity is most commonly identified during the school years, it may be evident even in infancy. Not only may excessive motor activity by present, but the child may also have sleeping difficulties and cry more frequently and with a higher-pitched cry than normal infants (Wolff, 1969). During the preschool years, the hyperactive child may not be able to sustain interest in any activity, darting from one thing to another. Many of these children will not even maintain interest in television cartoons, which ostensibly would surely place them outside normal limits for preschool children! Hyperactive children attending a preschool program may not follow directions well, may be aggressive, and may be observed to flitter from one activity to another. Much of this behavior is tolerated by most preschool teachers. However, if these children enter the regular education sector with this same pattern of responses, they will almost assuredly be singled out. The demands of the school for compliance, concentration, attention, perseverence, and cooperation are considerable, and many hyperactive children simply do not measure up. Their aggressiveness may earn them the opprobrium of their peers and teacher; their inability to sustain attention and concentration and their impulsive responding may adversely affect their school work. Social and academic deficits are too often the unfortunate results.

At one time it was believed that children "outgrew" their hyperactivity, usually by the time they reached adolescence. Recent follow-up studies (Mendelson, Johnson, & Stewart, 1971; Weiss, Minde, & Werry, 1971), however, indicate that although the behavioral manifestations of overactivity may be reduced, these youngsters continue to experience difficulty even into adulthood. The social and academic deficits concomitant to hyperactivity during the formative years may account for much of the continued difficulty. Simply waiting for these children to "outgrow" their difficulties, or simply focusing one's intervention on the overactivity alone, will not provide children with the requisite assistance to overcome the adverse social and academic deficits. Clearly, one must not eliminate the behavioral excesses without concurrently attempting to remediate the behavioral deficits. For example, Weiss, Minde, and Werry (1971) followed a group of 64 hyperactive children over a 5-year period, assessing their academic and social functioning. Although hyperactivity had been the initial reason for referral and the children exhibited no demonstrable brain damage or severe emotional difficulties at intake, follow-up data indicated a number of subsequent difficulties. Eighty percent of the children had repeated one or more grades, 10% had been placed in special education classes, and another 5% had been expelled from school. Only 5% of the children were doing above-average school work. Although the overactivity seemed to subside for this group, problems in social adjustment, attention, and academic skills remained despite their normal intelligence.

Studies of the intelligence test performance of hyperactive youngsters are also reflective of difficulties that seem to accumulate over time. Data collected by Loney (1974) and Prinz and Loney (1974) indicated no difference in test performance between hyperactive children and controls in first and second grade, but significantly lower performance was noted for the hyperactive group in the fifth- and sixth-grade comparisons. These data may be reflective of a cumulative deficit in academic achievement that depresses the IQ score, and/or it may represent impaired performance during the testing situation due to a short attention span, impulsivity, and so forth. Whatever the causative factor(s), it seems likely that the lowered IQ scores noted for older hyperactive youngsters are indicative of performance or learning deficits and are not adequate measures of their intellectual ability. Unfortunately, the cumulative social and academic deficits begin to take a toll in the child's motivation and affective development as well, with antisocial behavior, poor self-concept, expectation of failure, and poor motivation reported as common sequelae. Such findings strongly suggest the need to identify and treat hyperactivity before the child's characteristics result in a host of secondary social, academic, affective, and motivational difficulties.

Reducing hyperactivity and increasing academic performance. Ayllon, Layman, and Kandel (1975) wondered if a positive reinforcement procedure could offer an alternative to drug treatment in controlling hyperactivity and at the same time be used to improve academic skills in math and reading. Three children, ages 8, 9, and 10, all average or above in general intellectual skills, all taking drugs for control of hyperactivity, all attending a self-contained learning disabilities class, and all making only minimal academic progress, were provided positive reinforcement for correct performance in math and reading. The children's hyperactivity and academic performance were measured during four different phases as follows:

Phase 1: On medication, usual classroom procedures
Phase 2: Off medication, usual classroom procedures
Phase 3: Off medication, reinforcement for correct math performance
Phase 4: Off medication, reinforcement for correct math and reading performance

The token reinforcement procedures used in Phases 3 and 4 consisted of check marks on an index card awarded by the teacher for correct math and reading responses during daily performance sessions. A variety of items and events were used as backup reinforcers.

Under the medication phase, math and reading performance averaged 12% correct, with hyperactivity occurring during about 20% of the class period. During the no-medication phase, hyperactivity occurred during about 85% of the class period and academic performance increased slightly. Introduction of the positive reinforcement contingency resulted in a dramatic increase in math and reading performance and a reduction in hyperactivity to the 20% level obtained under the medication condition.

This demonstration of the effectiveness of positive reinforcement for desired academic performance further emphasizes the usefulness of such procedures in managing other behavior (in this case, hyperactivity) that compete with successful academic performance. The excessive activity level not only was controlled by positive reinforcement as successfully as by a drug program, but also academic behavior improved dramatically when children were provided positive reinforcement. These findings have been replicated by Marholin *et al.* (1975) and Marholin and Steinman (1977).

Excessive avoidance of tasks and activities

Children who are successful in academic, social, and interpersonal endeavors frequently are curious about their environments, enter into new experiences with anticipation, and, even after failure, are challenged by competition and difficulty. It is felt by many that a child has a natural tendency to explore the environment and in this manner to learn about it. Some psychologists suggest that children are intrinsically motivated to be curious, spontaneous, and creative. Deci (1972) commented, "I am fascinated with a child's unflagging curiosity. He explores everything; for him objects exist to be touched, smelled, and tasted, and where possible, eaten. He learns, and learning excites and delights him [p. 57]."

In contrast, children with various learning and behavior difficulties exhibit much less exploratory behavior. In fact, much of the difficulties represent active avoidance instead of approach behaviors. Children with histories of excessive failure soon learn to avoid actively and to withdraw from new situations since they have little expectation that exploration or involvement will result in satisfying experiences. In familiar situations such as the reading assignment or athletic activities that previously resulted in excessive failure, the child actively and excessively avoids involvement. Muller and Madsen (1970), Sanok and Ascione (1979), and Word and Rozynko (1974) describe effective behavioral programs for remediation of such avoidance reactions.

Excessive avoidance of interpersonal interaction

Just as children and adolescents learn through excessive failure to avoid tasks and activities, they also learn to avoid social contact and interpersonal interaction. The child may actively be nonresponsive to attempts from others to get involved as such involvement previously has resulted in aversive experiences (Greenwood, Walker, & Hops, 1977; Ross *et al.*, 1971).

INTERRELATIONSHIPS OF EXCEPTIONAL CHARACTERISTICS

In any specific situation a child may experience difficulties due to closely related excessive and deficit characteristics. A child may be unable to meet the performance requirements in a reading class due to deficit reading skills. Another child may demonstrate similar academic deficiencies even though the required reading skills are in his or her repertoire; excessive disruptive behaviors occur and successfully compete with the desired reading performance. As another example, dependency may reflect deficits in skills of independence or may reflect excessive avoidance behavior based on high levels of negative emotionality evoked when an adult is not available to provide direction.

Removing or reducing the strength of excessive behavior patterns does not insure the spontaneous occurrence of desired behavior. Such intervention does, however, render it more likely under appropriate learning or performance conditions. In fact, in many instances excessive behavior patterns develop as a result of deficit areas. The child, for example, being unable to meet the learning and performance requirements of the classroom, develops a range of emotional and social disruptive behaviors that remove him or her, albeit temporarily, from these requirements. An instructional program should be designed both to reduce the deficit behavior areas and thus to reduce the usefulness of the excessive reactions (Lahey *et al.*, 1978).

It is useful to view learning and behavior problems as representative of either deficit or excessive difficulties because various rules of learning and related behavior management strategies are available for dealing with each class and various combinations of these (Gardner, 1978; Sulzer-Azaroff & Mayer, 1977). The general procedures used with deficit behavior patterns are concerned with developing, strengthening, maintaining, and generalizing new desired behavior patterns. If the problem area is one of excessive behavior, procedures relating to means of decreasing, restricting, or eliminating the behavior become pertinent. As noted, most learning and behavior problems of children represent both excessive and deficit components. A child may be unable (behavior deficit) to complete an academic task, and, at the same time, may display rather hyperactive and distractible (excessive) behaviors as the teacher is prompting the child to complete the task. Behavioral approaches are thus selected to teach successful task completion and to reduce or eliminate the distractible and hyperactive behaviors (Ayllon & Roberts, 1974; Ayllon *et al.*, 1975; Hamblin, Buckholdt, Ferritor, Kozloff, & Blackwell, 1971).

BEHAVIORAL ASSESSMENT

The primary purpose of behavioral assessment is to obtain information that will assist the classroom teacher in developing and implementing effective individualized learning programs for specific learning and behavior difficulties presented by specific children. Such child-specific assessment, as detailed by Gearheart and Willenberg (1980) and Meyen (1978), is consistent with the legal requirement of PL 94-142 that each handicapped child be provided an individualized educational program (IEP). Assessment data are used to specify precisely those deficit and excessive areas in which behavior change should occur and to determine the procedures that hold the best promise of resulting in such behavior change (Gardner, 1977; Lovitt, 1975; Marholin & Bijou, 1978).

The typical procedures selected for behavioral assessment of a child's difficluties may be described as "narrow-band" (specific child-related) rather than "broad-band" (group-related). Assessment data are needed that describe those child features and/or environmental conditions (*a*) assumed to contribute to or be responsible for the occurrence and maintenance of excessive problem behaviors; and (*b*) necessary for the development of new repertoires in behavior deficit areas. Although it may be of value to know how a child compares to other children (interindividual) on some dimensions (e.g., reading achievement, general cognitive skills), the most pertinent assessment data are those of an intra-individual nature. Without such, the most effective individualized program cannot be developed (Adelman, 1971a). Two children diagnosed as mentally retarded may obtain comparable mental age and intelligence quotients on norm-referenced intelligence tests but have quite different combinations of more specific learner characteristics pertinent to the development of individualized instructional programs. Thus, separate profiles of intra-individual differences would be needed by the educator in program development (Drew, Freston, & Logan 1972; Duffey & Fedner, 1978).

Assessment procedures that provide descriptions of what a child "does" in the various situations in which problems occur are used. A behavioral assessment of excessive behavior, for example, is usually initiated by an objective description of the problem behaviors. Labels such as *lazy, fidgety,* and *aggressive* are discarded in favor of a description of the problematic behaviors in observable and measurable terms. Thus, *lazy* may become a description of the number of math problems completed during math period; *fidgety* may become the number of times the child is out-of-seat per hour or the number of times the child drops pencils, books, or papers; and *aggressive* may become the number of times the child hits or pushes others. Recording is the next phase in the behavior assessment and consists of direct observations that result in a record of the frequency, duration, and percentage (or some other response feature) of the behavior prior to initiating treatment. During pretreatment or baseline, information also is obtained relative to possible external environmental conditions and various child characteristics that may be influencing the problem behaviors. Hypotheses are then developed as to which events may be most influential in initiating and maintaining the problem behaviors, and decisions are made about the specific instructional arrangements needed to assist the child in acquiring more appropriate behaviors.

To emphasize, direct observation of the child, whenever possible, is made in those environments and under those specific conditions in which the exceptional learning and behavior characteristics occur. Observation in situ is assumed to provide more functionally useful information than observation of the child as he or she responds to test materials or other stimulation in an office or playroom. This focus differs from more traditional psychodynamic, trait, and psychometric approaches to assessment of academic, ability, or personality characteristics. In these more traditional approaches, assessment procedures are selected that presumably identify what the child "has" or how he or she compares to others in some rank order. *Timothy has a psycholinguistic disability* and *Martha earned a perceptual score that is at the fifteenth percentile of children her own age* represent examples of such assessment results (O'Leary & Johnson, 1979; Salvia & Ysseldyke, 1978).

In making observations of a child's problem behaviors as they occur in specific situations, the assumption is made that the obtained data are *samples* of the behavior and its strength during periods and across situations in which observations are not made. Except in highly unusual instances, problem behaviors fluctuate over time periods and situations within a given day and across days. Some behavior problems may be situation-specific; others may occur in numerous different situations. The disruptive male student may be quite positive in his attitude concerning his studies on some days or in certain classes, but on most days or in other classes he may be quite negativistic. As a result, repeated observations (samples) should be made over time and across situations to insure representativeness (O'Leary & Johnson, 1979).

In contrast to the sample interpretation of assessment data, other approaches to assessment view test behavior as *signs* or indirect manifestations of some underlying personality, cognitive, or language construct, trait, or ability. The child's responses obtained during assessment, depending upon the specific theoretical orientation, are translated into signs of underlying motives, psychological traits, aptitudes, psycholinguistic or perceptual abilities, or the like. To assist the educator in interpretation of the test signs, many psychometric tests, including the newer diagnostic ones such as the Illinois Test of Psycholinguistic Abilities are *norm-referenced* (Gearheart & Willenberg, 1980; Kirk & Kirk, 1971; Salvia & Ysseldyke, 1978). A child's score on such tests is compared to some standard or group norm and provides some indication of where the child stands in respect to some hypothetical average. As noted by Drew *et al.* (1972), "Such information, viewed singularly, tells little concerning the actual skills a student possesses or the operations he can actually perform but, instead, focuses on relative abilities [p. 3]."

To emphasize, for children with exceptional characteristics, assessment data from norm-referenced tests frequently are used to describe the degree of deviancy, handicap, or disability of the child. In other instances, such assessment data are used as a basis for developing intervention programs designed to remediate the presumed internal disability. For example, assessment data obtained from the Illinois Test of Psycholinguistic Abilities may be used to select programs designed to influence the presumed internal psycholinguistic disabilities that the child's test performance suggested. Hammill and Larsen (1978) question the efficacy of such an approach to assessment and intervention, and should be consulted by the interested reader.

Behavioral assessment of academic difficulties makes use primarily of *criterion-referenced* measures in contrast to norm-referenced ones. These assessment procedures are designed to measure an individual child's performance relative to some specified behavioral objectives. The assessment information obtained represents a description of what the child actually does when presented a reading task (e.g., the child's word attack skills, speed of reading, use of context cues, or the specific types of errors made such as substitutions, reversals, or omissions). These criterion-referenced materials may consist of informal teacher-made tests or may be commercially prepared (Duffey & Fedner, 1978; Prager & Mann, 1973). Criterion-referenced measures indicate (*a*) what the child can do and which deficit skills need to be taught; and (*b*) what progress the child makes in relation to the instructional goal criteria. Answers to each of these questions provide direction to structuring, or restructuring, of the specific educational experiences provided the child. With this approach, as illustrated by Lovitt (1977) and Prager and Mann (1973), if a child experiences reading difficulties, the assessment procedure and the resulting educational program focus on letters and words and not on presumed laterality, psycholinguistic, or spatial orientation process difficulties. Thus, if a child were having difficulty learning a specific academic task, the teacher would break the task down into its constituent components, provide additional assistance at the sequential step not yet in the child's repertoire, and provide needed incentive to enhance active child participation in learning and integrating the new needed skill (Lovitt, 1977).

It is not being suggested that behavioral assessment should disregard norm-referenced information. Drew *et al.* (1972) and O'Leary and Johnson (1979) emphasize the need for comprehensive assessment of excessive and deficit problem areas and the possible value of both intra-individual and interindividual information. It may be valuable as an initial step in more specific individualized behavioral assessment to determine if the child's basic cognitive skills, as measured by norm-referenced intelligence tests, are commensurate with those assumed to be present by the instructional program in which a child may be placed. If a child is failing academic subjects, it may be important to know if the academic tasks are beyond the child's present skills of acquisition and retention. With such information, an administrative decision may be

Table 10.1
Assessment of Additional Educational Needs for an 8-Year-Old Child

Assessment questions	Assessment procedures	Program implications
Do general intellectual skills match the level and rate of classroom instruction?	Norm-referenced intelligence tests (e.g., Wechsler Intelligence Scale for Children; Slosson Intelligence Scale for Children and Adults)	Placement in more appropriate group instructional program
Is there a match between the child's more specific language, sensory, and perceptual skills and those required by the type, level, and rate of class instruction?	Norm-referenced and criterion-referenced assessment procedures (e.g., Goldman–Fristoe–Woodcock Test of Auditory Discrimination; Illinois Test of Psycholinguistic Abilities)	Match instructional methods, including type, level, and rate, to specific strengths and weaknesses of the child
Does the child have specific prerequisite academic skills?	Norm-referenced and criterion-referenced tests (e.g., Gates–Russell Spelling Diagnostic Test; teacher-constructed tests)	Match specific instructional program to skill level of student
Are the child's motivational characteristics consistent with those assumed by the instructional program?	Motivational analysis of instructional program and the child	Develop individual incentive system for the child
Does the child exhibit excessive behaviors that compete with academic learning and performance (e.g., disruptive behavior, excessive negative emotional arousal)?	Direct observation of child in instructional program	Develop specific program for reducing excessive behaviors

made that the child remain in the present class placement or be placed in another instructional program environment that represents a closer match with present cognitive skills. In either case, more specific assessment would be needed to design a specific program for the child.

Consistent with the individualized focus of behavioral assessment, each assessment question and assessment procedure has associated general and specific program implications. In illustration, consider an 8-year-old who is a candidate for additional educational services due to chronic failure in her academic program. The assessment questions, assessment procedure, and program implications shown in Table 10.1 may be evolved in planning for this child. In summary, information obtained through a variety of assessment procedures would be used in placement of a child in a specific educational program environment and in developing specific individualized instructional procedures to meet each of his or her program needs.

REMEDIATION AND PREVENTION OF PROBLEMS THROUGH INDIVIDUALIZED INSTRUCTIONAL MANAGEMENT

The child-centered nature of behavioral assessment and the individualized aspects of the behavioral intervention studies described emphasize the active role and responsibility assumed by the educator in providing suitable educational experiences for children with difficulties. The educator is actively involved in organizing, individualizing, and directing the following instructional components:

1. A description of a sequence of tasks to be taught and of desired behaviors that should occur as the child interacts with the academic and social aspects of the school environment, that is, the program behavioral objectives
2. Procedures for motivating the child to participate in the learning tasks and to engage in the desired behaviors
3. Procedures for getting and maintaining the child's attention to relevant aspects of the instructional environment and for insuring that interfering disruptive behaviors do not occur
4. Procedures for insuring that the child will engage in the task behavior to be acquired and in other desired behaviors in the child's repertoire
5. Procedures for providing positive consequences for appropriate (correct) responses and for correction of inappropriate (incorrect) responses

6. Procedures for insuring that the behaviors learned at one time will be maintained and also will generalize to other relevant conditions

Relative nature of exceptional characteristics

The implication of an individualized program approach is that for every exceptional learning and behavior characteristic presented by a child there is a corresponding exceptional instructional program characteristic. That is, for every child characteristic that impedes desired learning and behaving, there potentially is a counterpart instructional environment characteristic that is inappropriate or inadequate for that particular child characteristic at that particular time. Thus, the child's exceptional characteristics are relative to the requirements, expectations, and/or characteristics of the educational environment. To the extent that the instructional program is modified to match, and when possible to change, the child's exceptional characteristics, more effective learning and performance will ensue.

To report that a child has motivational deficits or has visual discrimination difficulties is to indicate that, relative to the motivation characteristics assumed or required by the present instructional environment, the child's motivational features are deficit and thus maladaptive; or relative to required visual discrimination skills, the child demonstrates visual discrimination difficulties. Under more individualized instructional arrangements, the child *may* learn and/or demonstrate visual discrimination skills in a highly active, motivated manner. Thus, these learning and/or performance difficulties are translated into inappropriate components of the instructional program.

With this reciprocal view, major programmatic focus and responsibility is placed on the inadequate components of the instructional program instead of on the exceptional characteristics of the child. The instructional environment must change initially to insure more appropriate learning and behaving.

A child's learning and behavior characteristics may include those of hyperactivity, impulsiveness, poor language skills, distractibility, and short attention span. At any specific time in the child's development, the educational program may adapt to these as new academic skills and social behaviors are being taught. At the same time, these exceptional learner characteristics may be, or may become, the primary focus of an instructional program. The individualized instructional objectives become those of teaching the child to become more deliberate, more controlled in motor activities, more attentive, and more persistent. These new child features will, in turn, influence the content and methodology of future instructional programs for that child. Thus, the learner's characteristics at any specific time may—or may not—be the learner's characteristics at another.

To further illustrate this program focus, two children may both score 2 years below grade placement on a standardized achievement test of reading. One child may be attentive, be persistent at a task, seek to please the teacher, and enjoy being successful. The second child may be overactive, distractible, minimally influenced by teacher praise, and easily upset when faced with difficult academic tasks. The instructional program required by these two children for effective learning of reading skills will obviously differ in numerous critical aspects. As each child changes as a result of more adequate programming, the programs continuously change to accommodate these new and more typical learning and behavior characteristics. With this focus, the developing child is not expected to fit a program; rather the instructional program is designed to fit the child.

In summary, the child's characteristics at any given time must form the basis for the specific instructional program provided. The task of the educator in the mainstream becomes that of (*a*) identifying the learning and behavior characteristics of the child that represent a mismatch with the regular or present instructional program and thus impede learning and appropriate performance or adaptation in that environment; and (*b*) rearranging the instructional environment to match the learning and performance features of the specific child. This obviously represents a challenge for the regular class educator in view of the increased heterogeneity of child needs associated with mainstreaming children with exceptional learning and behavior characteristics.

Integrated instructional program

The individualized educational program approach focuses on managing the instructional program to insure desirable academic *and* personal–social learning and performance. The principles and procedures of the behavioral approach are equally applicable to each. A child with behavior problems is also a child who is experiencing learning difficulties. A child, for example, who is disruptive in class, hyperactive, disinterested, and has poor peer relationships cannot be learning to capacity. In like manner, a child who is having learning difficulties is likely to develop various social, motivational, emotional, and self-concept difficulties.

The educator does not manage behavior problems with one program and learning or academic problems with another. Rather, an integrated instructional program is designed to deal with both at the same time. The teacher of a child with a low frustration tolerance, for example, may manage the explosive emotional outburst by setting realistic educational goals, providing adequate incentives for task involvement and accomplishment, and providing other instructional and personal support needed for academic success. By focusing on positive contingencies (positive consequences for task completion and temper control) rather than on negative ones (punishment for loss of temper or task failure), the teacher is likely to facilitate academic learning as well as self-control and self-esteem. Thus, by managing the total instructional environment, the teacher facilitates desired academic as well as social and emotional learning and behaving.

Prevention of problems

The individualized instructional appraoch assumes the realistic position that children with learning and behavior problems not only can avoid many unsatisfactory characteristics but also can acquire many contrasting desired patterns if provided appropriately designed and stimulating learning programs. Although there are obvious limitations to what any child can learn and do, the individualized approach insures that the child's potentials are not inadvertently overlooked by pessimistic concepts of deficits or limitations. Neurological, sensory, and physical characteristics may indeed restrict or limit what children may do or the manner in which they may learn or behave. A blind child will require an instructional program based on other-than-visual stimulation. A cerebral palsied child may require modification in the physical environment in order to facilitate independent mobility and self-care. A child with obvious and extensive central nervous system impairment may be restricted in the rate of learning and in the level of ultimate performance in conceptual–language skill areas. However, no decision can be made about what a child cannot learn or do until a highly individualized instructional program has been provided and evaluated.

This position emphasizes that children who fail to learn or behave as expected under certain conditions may well learn and behave differently under other conditions. This has been illustrated repeatedly in the intervention programs described. The sensitive educator will anticipate exceptional instructional program characteristics and ensure that these are modified prior to extreme or prolonged child failure. Such active and ongoing management and evaluation of the instructional program for children with exceptional learning and behavior characteristics represent ideal approaches to prevention.

REFERENCES

Abeson, A., Bolick, N., & Hass, J. A primer on due process: Education decisions for handicapped children. *Exceptional Children*, 1975, *42*, 68–75.

Abeson, A., & Zettel, J. The end of the quiet revolution: The Education of All Handicapped Children Act of 1975. *Exceptional Children*, 1977, *44*, 114–128.

Adelman, H. S. Remedial classroom instruction revised. *Journal of Special Education*, 1971, *5*, 311–322. (a)

Adelman, H. S. The not-so-specific learning disability population. *Exceptional Children*, 1971, *37*, 528–533. (b)

Algozzine, B., Mercer, C. D., & Countermine, T. The effects of labels and behavior on teacher expectations. *Exceptional Children*, 1977, *44*(2), 131–132.

Allport, G. W. *Patterns and growth in personality.* New York: Holt, 1961.

Ayllon, T., Layman, D., & Kandel, H. J. A behavioral–educational alternative to drug control of hyperactive children. *Journal of Applied Behavior Analysis*, 1975, *8*, 137–146.

Ayllon, T., & Roberts, M. D. Eliminating discipline problems by strengthening academic performance. *Journal of Applied Behavior Analysis*, 1974, *7*, 71–76.

Azrin, N. H., Kaplan, S. J., & Foxx, R. M. Autism reversal: Eliminating stereotyped self-stimulation of retarded individuals. *American Journal of Mental Deficiency*, 1973, *78*, 241–248.

Bandura, A. *Social learning theory.* Englewood Cliffs, N.J.: Prentice-Hall, 1977.

Bartel, N. R., & Guskin, S. L. A handicap as a social phenomenon. In W. M. Cruickshank (Ed.), *Psychology of exceptional children and youth.* Englewood Cliffs, N.J.: Prentice-Hall, 1971.

Barton, E. J., & Osborne, J. G. The development of classroom sharing by a teacher using positive practice. *Behavior Modification*, 1978, *2*, 231–250.

Bash, M. A., & Camp, B. W. Teacher training in the think aloud classroom program. In G. Cartledge & J. F. Milburn (Eds.), *Teaching social skills to children*, New York: Pergamon, 1980.

Begab, M. J., Haywood, H. C., & Garber, H. L. (Eds.). Psychosocial influences in retarded performance: Strategies for improving competence (Vol. 2). Baltimore: University Park Press, 1981.

Bijou, S. W. Behavior modification in teaching the retarded child. In C. E. Thoresen (Ed.), *Behavior modification in education: The seventy-second yearbook of the National Society for the Study of Education.* Chicago: Univ. of Chicago Press, 1972.

Bolstad, O. D., & Johnson, S. M. Self-regulation in the modification of disruptive classroom behavior. *Journal of Applied Behavior Analysis*, 1972, *5*, 443–454.

Brigham, T. A., Graubard, P. S., & Stans, A. Analysis of the effects of sequential reinforcement contingencies on aspects of composition. *Journal of Applied Behavior Analysis*, 1972, *5*, 421–429.

Brooks, R. B., & Snow, D. L. Two case illustrations of the use of behavior-modification techniques in the school setting. *Behavior Therapy*, 1972, *3*, 100–103.

Bruininks, R. H., & Rynders, J. E. Alternatives to special class placement for educable mentally retarded children. *Focus on Exceptional Children*, 1971, *3*, 1–12.

Bruininks, V. L. Actual and perceived peer status of learning-disabled students in mainstream programs. *Journal of Special Education*, 1978, *12*, 51–58.

Bryan, T. H. Social relationships and verbal interactions of learning disabled children. *Journal of Learning Disabilities*, 1978, *11*, 107–115.

Burka, A. A., & Jones, F. H. Procedures for increasing appropriate verbal participation in special elementary classrooms. *Behavior Modification*, 1979, *3*, 27–48.

Calhoun, G., & Elliott, R. N. Self-concept and academic achievement of educable retarded and emotionally disturbed pupils. *Exceptional Children*, 1977, *43*, 379–380.

Cartledge, G., & J. F. Milburn (Eds.). *Teaching social skills to children.* New York: Pergamon, 1980.

Chadwick, B. A., & Day, R. C. Systematic reinforcement: Academic performance of under-achieving students. *Journal of Applied Behavior Analysis*, 1971, *4*, 311–319.

Chapman, R. B., Larsen, S. C., & Parker, R. M. Interactions of first-grade teachers with learning disordered children. *Journal of Learning Disabilities*, 1979, *12*(4), 225–230.

Christoplos, F., & Renz, P. A critical examination of special education programs. *Journal of Special Education*, 1969, *3*, 371–379.

Cooke, T. P., & Appolloni, T. Developing positive social–emotional behaviors: A study of training and generalization effects. *Journal of Applied Behavior Analysis*, 1976, *9*, 65–78.

Cooper, J. O. *Eliminating letter and number reversal errors with modeling and reinforcement procedures.* Ann Arbor, Mich.: 1970. (University Microfilms No. 71-13, 390)

Cowen, E. L., & Lorion, R. P. Which kids are helped? *Journal of Special Education*, 1974, *8*, 187–192.

Cruickshank, W. M. The learning environment. In W. M. Cruickshank & D. P. Hallahan (Eds.), *Perceptual and learning disabilities in children* (Vol. 1). Syracuse: Syracuse Univ. Press, 1975. (a)

Cruickshank, W. M. The psychoeducational match. In W. M. Cruickshank & D. P. Hallahan (Eds.), *Perceptual and learning disabilities in children* (Vol. 1). Syracuse: Syracuse Univ. Press, 1975. (b)

Cullinan, D., Kauffman, J. M., & LeFleur, N. K. Modeling: Research with implications for special education. *Journal of Special Education*, 1975, *9*, 209–221.

Deci, E. L. Work—who does not like it and why. *Psychology Today*, 1972, *6*, 57–58.

Deshler, D. D. Psychoeducational aspects of learning-disabled adolescents. In L. Mann, L. Goodman, & S. L. Wiederholt (Eds.), *Teaching the learning-disabled adolescent.* Boston: Houghton-Mifflin, 1978.

Digate, G., Epstein, M. H., Cullinan, D., & Switzky, H. N. Modification of impulsivity: Implications for improved efficiency in learning for exceptional children. *Journal of Special Education*, 1978, *12*, 459–468.

Drabman, R. S., Spitalnik, R., & O'Leary, K. D. Teaching self-control to disruptive children. *Journal of Abnormal Psychology*, 1973, *82*, 10–16.

Drew, C. J., Freston, C. W., & Logan, D. R. Criteria and reference on evaluation. *Focus on Exceptional Children*, 1972, *4*, 1–10.

Duffey, J. B., & Fedner, M. L. Educational diagnosis with instructional use. *Exceptional Children*, 1978, *44*, 247–251.

Dunn, L. M. Special education for the mildly retarded: Is much of it justified? *Exceptional Children*, 1968, *35*, 5–22.

Dunn, L. M. (Ed.). *Exceptional children in the schools: Special education in transition* (2nd ed.). New York: Holt, 1973.

Epstein, M. H., Hallahan, D. P., & Kauffman, J. M. Implications of the reflectivity–impulsivity dimension for special education. *Journal of Special Education*, 1975, *9*, 11–25.

Feuerstein, R. A dynamic approach to the causation, prevention, and alleviation of retarded performance. In H. C. Haywood (Ed.), *Social–cultural aspects of mental retardation.* New York: Appleton, 1970.

Fink, W. T., & Carnine, D. W. Control of arithmetic errors using information feedback and graphing. *Journal of Applied Behavior Analysis*, 1975, *8*, 461.

Foster, G. G., & Salvia, J. Teacher response to label of learning-disabled as a function of demand characteristics. *Exceptional Children*, 1977, *43*, 533–534.

Foxx, R. M., & Jones, J. R. A remediation program for increasing the spelling achievement of elementary and junior high school students. *Behavior Modification*, 1978, *2*, 211–230.

Franks, D. J. Ethnic and social status characteristics of children in EMR and L.D. classes. *Exceptional Children*, 1971, *37*, 537–538.

Fuchs, D. Reading and perceptual–motor performance: Can we strengthen them simultaneously? *Journal of Special Education*, 1979, *13*, 265–273.

Gallagher, J. J. The special education contract for mildly handicapped children. *Exceptional Children*, 1972, *38*, 527–535.

Gampel, D. H., Gottlieb, J., & Harrison, R. H. Comparison of classroom behavior of special class EMR, integrated EMR, low IQ, and non-retarded children. *American Journal of Mental Deficiency*, 1974, *79*, 16–21.

Garcia, E., & DeHaven, E. D. Use of operant techniques in the establishment and generalization of language: A review and analysis. *American Journal of Mental Deficiency*, 1974, *79*, 169–178.

Gardner, W. I. *Behavior modification in mental retardation.* Chicago: Aldine-Atherton, 1971.

Gardner, W. I. *Learning and behavior characteristics of exceptional children and youth: A humanistic behavior analysis.* Boston: Allyn & Bacon, 1977.

Gardner, W. I. *Children with learning and behavior problems* (2nd ed.). Boston: Allyn & Bacon, 1978.

Gearheart, B. R., & Willenberg, E. P. *Application of pupil assessment information.* Denver: Lane, 1980.

Goldstein, A. P., Sprafkin, R. P., Gershaw, N. J., & Klein, P. Social skills training through structured learning. In G. Cartledge & J. F. Milburn (Eds.), *Teaching social skills to children*, New York: Pergamon, 1980.

Gorton, C. E. The effects of various classroom environments on performance of a mental task by mentally retarded and normal children. *Education and Training of the Mentally Retarded*, 1972, *7*, 32–38.

Gottlieb, J. Mainstreaming: Fulfilling the promise? *American Journal of Mental Deficiency*, 1981, *86*, 115–126.

Greenwood, C. R., Hops, H., Delquadri, J., & Guild, J. Group contingencies for group consequences in classroom management: A further analysis. *Journal of Applied Behavior Analysis*, 1974, *7*, 413–425.

Greenwood, C. R., Walker, H. M., & Hops, H. Issues in social interaction/withdrawal assessment. *Exceptional Children*, 1977, *43*, 490–499.

Hagen, J. W., & Hale, G. A. The development of attention in children. In A. D. Pick (Ed.), *Minnesota Symposium on Child Psychology* (Vol. 7). Minneapolis: Univ. of Minnesota Press, 1973.

Hall, V. C., & Kaye, D. B. Patterns of early cognitive development among boys in four subcultural groups. *Journal of Educational Psychology*, 1977, *69*, 66–87.

Hallahan, D. P., & Cruickshank, W. M. *Psychoeducational foundations of learning disabilities.* Englewood Cliffs, N.J.: Prentice-Hall, 1976.

Hallahan, D. P., & Kauffman, J. M. *Introduction to learning disabilities: A psycho-behavioral approach.* Englewood Cliffs, N.J.: Prentice-Hall, 1976.

Hallahan, D. P., Kauffman, J. M., & Ball, D. W. Selective attention and cognitive tempo of low achieving and high achieving sixth grade males. *Perceptual and Motor Skills*, 1973, *36*, 579–583.

Hallahan, D. P., Kauffman, J. M., & Ball, D. W. Developmental trends in recall of central and incidental auditory material. *Journal of Exceptional Child Psychology*, 1974, *17*, 409–421.

Hamblin, R. L., Buckholdt, D., Ferritor, D., Kozloff, M., & Blackwell, L. *The humanization processes: A social behavioral analysis of children's problems.* New York: Wiley, 1971.

Hammill, D. D., & Larsen, S. C. The effectiveness of psycholinguistic training: A reaffirmation of position. *Exceptional Children,* 1978, *44,* 402–417.

Hardman, M. L., & Drew, C. L. Incidental learning in the mentally retarded: A review. *Education and Training of the Mentally Retarded,* 1975, *10,* 3–9.

Hauser, C. Evaluating mainstream programs: Capitalizing on a victory. *Journal of Special Education,* 1979, *13,* 107–129.

Heber, R. Socio-cultural mental retardation: A longitudinal study. In D. Forgays (Ed.), *Primary prevention of psychopathology: Environmental influences* (Vol. 2). Hanover, New Hampshire: Univ. Press of New England, 1978.

Hewett, F. M., & Forness, S. R. *Education of exceptional learners.* Boston: Allyn & Bacon, 1974.

Hobbs, N. *The futures of children.* San Francisco: Jossey-Bass, 1975.

Hops, H., Walker, H. M., & Greenwood, C. R. PEERS: A program for remediating social withdrawal in school. In L. A. Hammerlynck (Ed.), *Behavioral systems for the developmentally disabled. School and family environments* (Vol. 2). New York: Brunner/Mazel, 1980.

Jones, R. L., Gottlieb, J., Guskin, S., & Yoshida, R. K. Evaluating mainstreaming programs: Models, caveats, considerations, and guidelines. *Exceptional Children,* 1978, *44,* 588–601.

Jones, R. T., & Kazdin, A. E. Programming response maintenance after withdrawing token reinforcement. *Behavior Therapy,* 1975, *6,* 153–164.

Kagan, J., Rosman, B., Day, D., Albert, J., & Phillips, W. Information processing in the child: Significance of analytic and reflective attitudes. *Psychological Monographs,* 1964, *78*(1, Whole No. 578).

Kanfer, F. H., Karoly, P., & Newman, A. Reduction of children's fear of the dark by competence-related and situational threat-related verbal cues. *Journal of Consulting and Clinical Psychology,* 1975, *43,* 251–258.

Kauffman, J. M. *Characteristics of children's behavior disorders.* Columbus, Ohio: Merrill, 1977.

Keogh, B. K. Hyperactivity and learning disorders: Review and speculation. *Exceptional Children,* 1971, *38,* 101–109.

Kirk, S. A., & Kirk, W. D. *Psycholinguistic learning disabilities: Diagnosis and remediation.* Chicago: Univ. of Illinois Press, 1971.

Kirp, D. L., Kuriloff, P. J., & Buss, W. G. Legal mandates and organizational change. In N. Hobbs (Ed.), *Issues in the classification of children* (Vol. 2). San Francisco: Jossey-Bass, 1975.

Knapczyk, D. R., & Livingston, G. The effects of prompting question-asking upon on-task behavior and reading comprehension. *Journal of Applied Behavior Analysis,* 1974, *7,* 115–121.

Koppitz, E. M. *Children with learning disabilities: A five year follow-up study.* New York: Grune & Stratton, 1971.

Lahey, B. B. Behavior modification with learning disabilities and related problems. In M. Hersen, R. Eisler, & P. Miller (Eds.), *Progress in behavior modification* (Vol. 3). New York: Academic Press, 1976.

Lahey, B. B., Busemeyer, M. K., O'Hara, C., & Beggs, V. E. Treatment of severe perceptual–motor disorders in children diagnosed as learning disabled. *Behavior Modification,* 1977, *1,* 123–140.

Lahey, B. B., Delamater, A., Kupfer, D. L., & Hobbs, S. A. Behavioral aspects of learning disabilities and hyperactivity. *Education and Urban Society,* 1978, *10,* 477–499.

Lahey, B. B., & Johnson, M. S. *Psychology and instruction.* Glenview, Ill.: Scott Foresman, 1977.

Lahey, B. B., McNees, M. P., & Brown, C. C. Modification of deficits in reading for comprehension. *Journal of Applied Behavior Analysis,* 1973, *6,* 475–480.

Lilly, M. S. Special education: A teapot in a tempest. *Exceptional Children,* 1970, *37,* 43–49.

Lilly, M. S. A merger of categories: Are we finally ready? *Journal of Learning Disabilities,* 1977, *10,* 115–121. (a)

Lilly, M. S. Evaluating individualized education programs. In S. Torres (Ed.), *A primer on individualized education programs for handicapped children.* Reston, Va.: Council for Exceptional Children, 1977. (b)

Lilly, M. S. Learning and behavior problems: Current trends. In M. S. Lilly (Ed.), *Children with exceptional needs: A survey of special education.* New York: Holt, 1979. (a)

Lilly, M. S. Special education: Emerging issues. In M. S. Lilly (Ed.), *Children with exceptional needs: A survey of special education.* New York: Holt, 1979. (b)

Loney, J. The intellectual functioning of hyperactive elementary school boys: A cross-sectional investigation. *American Journal of Orthopsychiatry,* 1974, *44,* 754–762.

Lovaas, O. I. *The autistic child: Language development through behavior modification.* New York: Irvington, 1977.

Lovitt, T. C. Applied behavior analysis and learning disabilities. Part 1: Characteristics of ABA, general recommendations and methodological limitations. *Journal of Learning Disabilities,* 1975, *8,* 432–443.

Lovitt, T. C. *In spite of my resistance...I've learned from children.* Columbus, Ohio: Merrill, 1977.

Lovitt, T. C., & Curtiss, K. A. Effects of manipulating an antecedent event on mathematics response rate. *Journal of Applied Behavior Analysis,* 1968, *1,* 329–333.

Lovitt, T., & Hurlburt, M. Using behavior analysis techniques to assess the relationship between phonics instruction and oral reading. *Journal of Special Education,* 1974, *8,* 57–72.

Luiselli, J. K., Helfern, C. S., Pemberton, B. W., & Reisman, J. The elimination of a child's in-class masturbation by overcorrection and reinforcement. *Journal of Behavior Therapy and Experimental Psychiatry,* 1977, *8,* 201–204.

MacMillan, D., Jones, R., & Aloia, C. The mentally retarded label: A theoretical analysis and review of the research. *American Journal of Mental Deficiency,* 1974, *79,* 241–261.

MacMillan, D. L. *Behavior modification in education.* New York: MacMillan, 1973.

MacMillan, D. L. *Mental retardation in school and society.* Boston: Little, Brown, 1977.

Madsen, C. H., Becker, W. C., Thomas, D. R., Koser, L., & Plager, E. An analysis of the reinforcing function of "sit down" commands. In R. K. Parker (Ed.), *Readings in educational psychology.* Boston: Allyn & Bacon, 1968.

Marholin, D., & Bijou, S. W. Behavioral assessment: Listen when the data speak. In D. Marholin (Ed.), *Child behavior therapy.* New York: Gardner Press, 1978.

Marholin, D., Siegel, L. J., & Phillips, D. Treatment and transfer: A search for empirical procedures. In M. Hersen, R. M. Eisler, & P. M. Miller (Eds.), *Progress in behavior modification* (Vol. 3). New York: Academic Press, 1976.

Marholin, D., & Steinman, W. M. Stimulus control in the classroom as a function of the behavior reinforced. *Journal of Applied Behavior Analysis,* 1977, *10,* 465–478.

Marholin, D., Steinman, W. M., McInnis, E. T., & Head, T. B. The effect of a teacher's presence on the classroom behavior of conduct problem children. *Journal of Abnormal Child Psychology,* 1975, *3,* 11–25.

Martin, E. W. Individualism and behaviorism as future trends in educating handicapped children. *Exceptional Children,* 1972, *38,* 517–525.

Medland, M. B., & Stachnik, T. J. Good-behavior game: A replication and systematic analysis. *Journal of Applied Behavior Analysis*, 1972, *5*, 45–51.

Meichenbaum, D. *Cognitive-behavior modification*. New York: Plenum, 1977.

Meichenbaum, D., & Goodman, J. Training impulsive children to talk to themselves. A means of developing self-control. *Journal of Abnormal Psychology*, 1971, *77*, 115–125.

Mendelson, W., Johnson, N., & Stewart, M. A. Hyperactive children as teenagers: A follow-up study. *Journal of Nervous and Mental Diseases*, 1971, *153*, 273–279.

Messer, S. Reflection–impulsivity: Stability and school failure. *Journal of Educational Psychology*, 1970, *61*, 487–490.

Meyen, E. L. *Exceptional children and youth: An introduction*. Denver: Love, 1978.

Meyerowitz, J. H. Peer groups and special classes. *Mental Retardation*, 1967, *5*(5), 23–26.

Morena, D. A., & Litrownik, A. J. Self-concept in educable mentally retarded and emotionally handicapped children. *Journal of Abnormal Child Psychology*, 1974, *2*, 281–292.

Muller, S. D., & Madsen, C. H. Group desensitization for anxious children with reading problems. *Psychology in the Schools*, 1970, *7*, 184–189.

Neisworth, J. T., & Greer, J. G. Functional similarities of learning disability and mild mental retardation. *Exceptional Children*, 1975, *42*, 17–24.

Norman, C. W. Data-based academic programming. In W. I. Gardner, *Learning and behavior characteristics of exceptional children and youth*. Boston: Allyn & Bacon, 1977.

Novy, P., Burnett, S., Powers, M., and Sulzer-Azaroff, B. Modifying attending-to-work behavior of a learning-disabled child. *Journal of Learning Disabilities*, 1973, *6*, 217–221.

O'Leary, K. D., & Johnson, S. B. Psychological assessment. In H. C. Quay & J. S. Werry (Eds.), *Psychopathological disorders of childhood* (2nd Ed.), New York: Wiley, 1979.

O'Leary, S., & Dubey, D. Applications of self-control procedures by children: A review. *Journal of Applied Behavior Analysis*, 1979, *12*, 449–465.

Patterson, G. R., & Brodsky, G. A behavior modification programme for a child with multiple problem behavior. *Journal of Child Psychology and Psychiatry*, 1966, *7*, 277–295.

Phillips, E. L., Phillips, E. A., Fixen, D. L., & Wolf, M. M. Achievement place: Modification of the behaviors of pre-delinquent boys within a token economy. *Journal of Applied Behavior Analysis*, 1971, *4*, 45–59.

Prager, B. B., & Mann, L. Criterion-referenced measurement: The world of gray versus black and white. *Journal of Learning Disabilities*, 1973, *6*, 18–30.

President's Committee on Mental Retardation. *The Six-hour retarded child*. Washington, D.C.: U.S. Government Printing Office, 1970.

Prinz, R., & Loney, J. Teacher-rated hyperactive elementary school girls: An exploratory developmental study. *Child Psychiatry and Human Development*, 1974, *4*, 246–257.

Quay, H. C., & Werry, J. S. (Eds.). *Psychopathological disorders of childhood* (2nd ed.). New York: Wiley, 1979.

Reschly, D. J., & Lamprecht, M. J. Expectancy effects of labels: Fact or artifact. *Exceptional Children*, 1979, *46*, 55–58.

Reynolds, M. C., & Balow, B. Categories and variables in special education. *Exceptional Children*, 1972, *38*, 357–366.

Rincover, A., & Koegel, R. L. Setting generality and stimulus control in autistic children. *Journal of Applied Behavior Analysis*, 1975, *8*, 235–246.

Rivers, L. W., Henderson, D. M., Jones, R. L., Lodner, J. A., & Williams, R. L. Mosaic of labels for black children. In N. Hobbs (Ed.), *Issues in the classification of children* (Vol. 1). San Francisco: Jossey-Bass, 1975.

Rosenbaum, M., & Drabman, R. Self-control training in the classroom: A review and critique. *Journal of Applied Behavior Analysis*, 1979, *12*, 467–485.

Rosenthal, J. H. Self-esteem in dyslexic children. *Academic Therapy*, 1973, *9*, 27–39.

Ross, A. O. *Psychological aspects of learning disabilities and reading disorders.* New York: McGraw-Hill, 1976.

Ross, D. Retention and transfer of mediation set in paired-associate learning of educable retarded children. *Journal of Educational Psychology,* 1971, *62,* 322–327.

Ross, D. M., & Ross, S. A. *Hyperactivity: Research, theory, and action.* New York: Wiley, 1976.

Ross, D. M., Ross, S. A., & Evans, T. A. The modification of extreme social withdrawal by modeling with guided participation. *Journal of Behavior Therapy and Experimental Psychiatry,* 1971, *2,* 273–279.

Rubin, R. A., & Balow, B. Prevalence of teacher identified behavior problems: A longitudinal study. *Exceptional Children,* 1978, *45,* 102–111.

Sabatino, D. A. Resource rooms: The renaissance in special education. *Journal of Special Education,* 1972, *6,* 335–347.

Salvia, J., & Ysseldyke, J. E. *Assessment in special and remedial education.* Boston: Houghton Mifflin, 1978.

Sanok, R. L., & Ascione, F. R. Behavioral interventions for childhood elective mutism: An evaluative review. *Child Behavior Therapy,* 1979, *1,* 49–68.

Shapiro, E. S. Restitution and positive practice overcorrection in reducing aggressive-disruptive behavior: A long-term follow up. *Journal of Behavior Therapy and Experimental Psychiatry,* 1979, *10,* 131–134.

Sloane, H. N., & MacAulay, B. D. (Eds.). *Operant procedures in remedial speech and language training.* Boston: Houghton Mifflin, 1968.

Smith, D. D., Lovitt, T. C., & Kidder, J. D. Using reinforcement contingencies and teaching aids to alter subtraction performance of children with learning disabilities. In G. Semb (Ed.), *Behavior analysis and education—1972.* Lawrence: Univ. of Kansas, 1972.

Staats, A. W. *Child learning, intelligence, and personality.* New York: Harper, 1971.

Staats, A. W. *Social behaviorism.* Homewood, Ill.: Dorsey Press, 1975.

Stromer, R. Modifying letter and number reversals in elementary school children. *Journal of Applied Behavior Analysis,* 1975, *8,* 211.

Stromer, R. Remediating academic deficiencies in learning disabled children. *Exceptional Children,* 1977, *43,* 432–440.

Sulzer-Azaroff, B., & Mayer, G. R. *Applying behavior analysis procedures with children and youth.* New York: Holt, 1977.

Tarver, S., Hallahan, D. P., Cohen, S. B., & Kauffman, J. M. The development of visual selective attention and verbal rehearsal in learning disabled boys. *Journal of Learning Disabilities,* 1977, *10,* 491–500.

Tarver, S., Hallahan, D. P., Kauffman, J. M., & Ball, D. W. Verbal rehearsal and selective attention in children with learning disabilities: A developmental lag. *Journal of Experimental Child Psychology,* 1976, *22,* 375–385.

Thomas, D. R., Becker, W. C., & Armstrong, M. Production and elimination of disruptive classroom behavior by systematically varying teacher's behavior. *Journal of Applied Behavior Analysis,* 1968, *1,* 35–45.

Turkewitz, H., O'Leary, K. D., & Ironsmith, M. Generalization and maintenance of appropriate behavior through self-control. *Journal of Consulting and Clinical Psychology,* 1975, *43,* 577–583.

Turnure, J. E., & Thurlow, M. L. Verbal elaboration and the promotion of transfer of training in educable mentally retarded children. *Journal of Experimental Child Psychology,* 1973, *15,* 134–148.

Van Houten, R., Hill, S., & Parsons, M. An analysis of a performance feedback system: The effects of timing and feedback, public posting, and praise upon academic performance and peer interaction. *Journal of Applied Behavior Analysis,* 1975, *8,* 449–457.

Walker, H. M., Greenwood, C. R., Hops, H., & Todd, N. M. Differential effects of reinforcing topographic components of social interaction. *Behavior Modification*, 1979, *3*, 291–321.

Walker, H. M., Hops, H., & Fiegenbaum, E. Deviant classroom behavior as a function of combinations of social and token reinforcement and cost contingency. *Behavior Therapy*, 1976, *7*, 76–88.

Wehman, P. Direct training of reading skills: A review. *Academic Therapy*, 1977, *12*, 463–470.

Weintraub, F. J., Abeson, A. R., & Braddock, D. L. *State law and education of handicapped children: Issues and recommendations*. Reston, Va: Council for Exceptional Children, 1975.

Weiss, G., Minde, K., Werry, J. S., Douglas, V., & Nemeth, E. Studies on the hyperactive child. VIII: Five-year follow-up. *Archives of General Psychiatry*, 1971, *24*, 409–414.

Williams, M., & Lahey, B. B. The functional independence of response latency and accuracy: Implications for the concept of conceptual tempo. *Journal of Abnormal Child Psychiatry*, 1978, *5*, 371–378.

Winschel, J. F., & Lawrence, E. A. Short-term memory: Curricular implications for the mentally retarded. *Journal of Special Education*, 1975, *9*, 395–408.

Wish, P. A., Hasazi, J. E., & Jurgela, A. R. Automated direct deconditioning of a childhood phobia. *Journal of Behavior Therapy and Experimental Psychiatry*, 1973, *4*, 279–283.

Wolf, M. M., Giles, D. K., & Hall, R. V. Experiments with token reinforcement in a remedial classroom. *Behavior Research and Therapy*, 1968, *6*, 51–64.

Wolff, P. H. The natural history of crying and other vocalizations in early infancy. In B. M. Ross (Ed.), *Determinants of infant behavior*. London: Methuen, 1969.

Word, P., & Rozynko, L. Behavior therapy of an eleven-year-old girl with reading problems. *Journal of Learning Disabilities*, 1974, *7*, 27–30.

Zigler, E. The retarded child as a whole person. In D. K. Routh (Ed.), *The experimental psychology of mental retardation*. Chicago: Aldine, 1973.

Index

EDUCATIONAL PSYCHOLOGY

continued from page ii

Jean Stockard, Patricia A. Schmuck, Ken Kempner, Peg Williams, Sakre K. Edson, and Mary Ann Smith. Sex Equity in Education

James R. Layton. The Psychology of Learning to Read

Thomas E. Jordan. Development in the Preschool Years: Birth to Age Five

Gary D. Phye and Daniel J. Reschly (eds.). School Psychology: Perspectives and Issues

Norman Steinaker and M. Robert Bell. The Experiential Taxonomy: A New Approach to Teaching and Learning

J. P. Das, John R. Kirby, and Ronald F. Jarman. Simultaneous and Successive Cognitive Processes

Herbert J. Klausmeier and Patricia S. Allen. Cognitive Development of Children and Youth: A Longitudinal Study

Victor M. Agruso, Jr. Learning in the Later Years: Principles of Educational Gerontology

Thomas R. Kratochwill (ed.). Single Subject Research: Strategies for Evaluating Change

Kay Pomerance Torshen. The Mastery Approach to Competency-Based Education

Harvey Lesser. Television and the Preschool Child: A Psychological Theory of Instruction and Curriculum Development

Donald J. Treffinger, J. Kent Davis, and Richard E. Ripple (eds.). Handbook on Teaching Educational Psychology

Harry L. Hom, Jr. and Paul A. Robinson (eds.). Psychological Processes in Early Education

J. Nina Lieberman. Playfulness: Its Relationship to Imagination and Creativity

Samuel Ball (ed.). Motivation in Education

Erness Bright Brody and Nathan Brody. Intelligence: Nature, Determinants, and Consequences

António Simões (ed.). The Bilingual Child: Research and Analysis of Existing Educational Themes

Gilbert R. Austin. Early Childhood Education: An International Perspective

Vernon L. Allen (ed.). Children as Teachers: Theory and Research on Tutoring

Joel R. Levin and Vernon L. Allen (eds.). Cognitive Learning in Children: Theories and Strategies

Donald E. P. Smith and others. A Technology of Reading and Writing (in four volumes).
> *Vol. 1. Learning to Read and Write: A Task Analysis (by Donald E. P. Smith)*
> *Vol. 2. Criterion-Referenced Tests for Reading and Writing (by Judith M. Smith, Donald E. P. Smith, and James R. Brink)*
> *Vol. 3. The Adaptive Classroom (by Donald E. P. Smith)*
> *Vol. 4. Designing Instructional Tasks (by Judith M. Smith)*

Phillip S. Strain, Thomas P. Cooke, and Tony Apolloni. Teaching Exceptional Children: Assessing and Modifying Social Behavior